ROYAL HISTORICAL SOCIETY
GUIDES AND HANDBOOKS

No. 13

HANDBOOK OF MEDIEVAL EXCHANGE

ROYAL HISTORICAL SOCIETY
GUIDES AND HANDBOOKS

MAIN SERIES

1. *Guide to English commercial statistics 1696–1782.* By G. N. Clark and Barbara M. Franks. 1938.
2. *Handbook of British chronology.* Edited by F. M. Powicke, Charles Johnson and W. J. Harte. 1939. 2nd edition, edited by F. M. Powicke and E. B. Fryde, 1961.
3. *Medieval libraries of Great Britain. A list of surviving books.* Edited by N. R. Ker. 1941. 2nd edition, 1964.
4. *Handbook of dates for students of English history.* Edited by C. R. Cheney. 1945. Reprinted, 1982.
5. *Guide to the national and provincial directories of England and Wales, excluding London, published before 1856.* By Jane E. Norton. 1950.
6. *Handbook of oriental history.* Edited by C. H. Philips. 1951.
7. *Texts and Calendars. An analytical guide to serial publications.* By E. L. C. Mullins. 1958. Reprinted (with corrections), 1978.
8. *Anglo-Saxon Charters. An annotated list and bibliography.* By P. H. Sawyer. 1968.
9. *A Centenary Guide to the publications of the Royal Historical Society 1868–1968 and of the former Camden Society 1838–1897.* By Alexander Taylor Milne. 1968.
10. *Guide to the local administrative units of England.* Volume I. *Southern England.* By Frederic A. Youngs, Jr. 1979. 2nd edition, 1981.
11. *Guide to bishops' registers of England and Wales. A survey from the middle ages to the abolition of episcopacy in 1646.* By David M. Smith. 1981.
12. *Texts and Calendars II. An analytical guide to serial publications, 1957–1982.* By E. L. C. Mullins. 1983.

SUPPLEMENTARY SERIES

1. *A Guide to the papers of British Cabinet Ministers, 1900–1951.* Compiled by Cameron Hazlehurst and Christine Woodland. 1974.
2. *A Guide to the reports of the U.S. Strategic Bombing Survey.* I *Europe.* II *The Pacific.* Edited by Gordon Daniels. 1981.

HANDBOOK OF MEDIEVAL EXCHANGE

BY

PETER SPUFFORD

WITH THE ASSISTANCE OF WENDY WILKINSON AND SARAH TOLLEY

LONDON

OFFICES OF THE ROYAL HISTORICAL SOCIETY

UNIVERSITY COLLEGE LONDON, GOWER STREET

LONDON WC1E 6BT

1986

First published 1986

Distributed for the Royal Historical Society
by Boydell & Brewer Ltd
PO Box 9 Woodbridge Suffolk IP12 3DF
and Wolfeboro New Hampshire 03894-2069

British Library Cataloguing in Publication Data

Spufford, Peter
Handbook of medieval exchange.—(Royal Historical Society guides and handbooks; no. 13)
1. Foreign exchange—History 2. Money—Europe—History
I. Title. II. Wilkinson, Wendy III. Tolley, Sarah
IV. Royal Historical Society V. Series
332.4′5 HG3942

ISBN 0–86193–105–X

Printed in Great Britain by St Edmundsbury Press,
Bury St Edmunds, Suffolk

CONTENTS

TABLES, GRAPHS AND MAPS

PREFACE

In 1960 when the late Professor Sir Michael Postan asked me to contribute the section on currency and coinage to the first edition of the third volume of the *Cambridge Economic History of Europe*, he suggested that I incorporate two lists in it. One was to be of the principal coins in use in medieval Europe, the other of the principal rates at which the main currencies of Europe were exchangeable with each other. The first I could do, the second I could not, since the basic work had simply never been done. A considerable number of people told me over the following years how useful such a list would be. The theme has constantly been reiterated. For instance, in 1962, when he was summing up at the conference on *Finances et Compatibilité Urbaines du XIIIe au XVIe siècle*, Professor Dhondt regretted that it was impossible to make direct comparisons between different cities since their accounts were kept in different currencies. He expressed the wish that it would one day be possible to 'réduire toutes les valeurs monétaires à unité standard.' Yet again, when Professor Rolf Sprandel was preparing *Das Eisengewerbe im Mittelalter*[1] he wished to be able to compare the prices of iron in different parts of Europe. No reference work existed to enable him to do so. As a consequence he had to expend a great deal of labour in making his own conversion of values into a common currency.

I therefore eventually set out in 1973 to bring together as complete a dossier as possible of all the knowable rates of exchange in medieval Europe. No such compilation covering the whole of western Europe had ever been made before.

Such a project would not have been possible without the generous support of the Social Sciences Research Council of Great Britain, now the Economic and Social Research Council, which paid for Miss Wilkinson to assist me for twenty-one months in 1975–7.

Miss Wilkinson divided her time between the Keele University Library, the Cambridge University Library, the Library of the Institute of Historical Research and the British Library (Reference Division), formerly the British Museum Library. Of these four, the Cambridge University Library was by far the most useful for our purposes and we would like to thank its library staff.

With the limited time and resources available to us it was not possible to use other libraries in this country, or to look abroad for volumes and series not held, or only incompletely held, by these four libraries.

The new 'Potthast', the *Repertorium Fontium Historiae Medii Aevi*, I, Series Collectionum[2] provided the starting point for the systematic coverage of likely printed sources for rates of exchange between currencies. The

[1] Stuttgart, 1968.
[2] Rome, 1962.

scanning of series was augmented by searching a large number of individual volumes, many of which were referred to in the first edition of Philip Grierson's *Bibliographie numismatique*.[3]

Of the sources available to us in printed form, the most useful was the material drawn from the Vatican Archives by Göller, items numbered (215) and (216) in the list of sources, Hoberg (251) and (252), Kirsch (268), Mohler (347) and above all Schäfer (439), (440) and (441).[4] For a very limited period, between 1384 and 1411, the material drawn from the Datini Archives by the late Raymond de Roover was even more useful. His material for the Bruges and Barcelona branches of Datini's businesses was published in *The Bruges Money Market around 1400* (138). The exchange rate material for the London and Paris branches was also abstracted by Professor de Roover, but he unfortunately died before it was ready for publication.

The only important compilation made before we began this work was that made for Italy by Carlo Cipolla (111). In our search for italian material we have mainly limited ourselves to volumes published since 1948, the date of Professor Cipolla's compilation, and have unashamedly based our italian sections on his fundamental work.

Professor Sprandel's then recent work on payment systems in the Baltic (462), was particularly useful in gathering up the sparse material available for this area.

With Miss Wilkinson's assistance I was able to assemble 9,000 or so rates of exchange by 1977. These appeared as the first fruits of the project as Peter Spufford and Wendy Wilkinson, *Interim Listing of the Exchange Rates of Medieval Europe*,[5] henceforth *Interim Listing*. This, the final report to the S.S.R.C. from that first stage of the project, was a 400-page typescript volume, including introduction, bibliographies of sources used and of sources consulted without success, indexes of currencies and places of exchange, as well as the exchange rates themselves. In other words, it was this *Handbook* in embryo.

Some two hundred copies of this listing were duplicated and distributed for comment to economic and social historians not only in the British Isles, but also in north America, eastern and western Europe, and indeed throughout the world. We would like to express our gratitude to the Keele University Library for putting its reproduction services at our disposal to make copies of the *Interim Listing* available for circulation. I asked the recipients to send me additions and corrections and ideas for the improvement of the *Interim Listing*.

In addition to many of the sources which are listed in this *Handbook* and which provided much of the material for it, Miss Wilkinson also searched the books and series which were named at the end of the *Interim Listing*, although they provided no material for it. In a work of this magnitude,

[3] Brussels, 1966. The second, much enlarged, edition did not appear until 1979.

[4] A bibliography of general works on exchange, combined with the list of sources used for compiling the tables, will be found below, pp. 323–50. For a description of the reference system used in this *Handbook* see p. l–lvii.

[5] Keele, 1977.

involving the scanning of many thousands of volumes, we could not guarantee that no directly usable items were overlooked in them. Our helpful correspondents did not point out any such omissions, so that we may now feel the more secure in the thoroughness of our search.

Between 1977 and 1983 I attempted to follow up some of the loose ends left out from the first stage of the project.

We had no intention of undertaking archival research at the initial stage. We wished first to map out from printed sources the general outline of our knowledge, and our lack of knowledge, of exchange rates. The limited number of direct references to documentary sources in the *Interim Listing* were those noted down by myself over a number of years in the course of other research, together with some unpublished rates between the florin and *moneta piccola* in Florence between 1425 and 1455 sent to us by Professor Aldo De Maddalena (130).

In 1978 the Social Science Research Council paid for me to make a brief exploratory visit to Italian archives. I visited archives in Florence, Siena, Rome, Venice and Prato.

In the archives in Florence I was warmly welcomed and greatly assisted by Professor Guido Pampaloni. I found that the organization of the *libri di ricordanze* of florentine merchants makes it possible to pick out exchange material very quickly. Entries for bills given and bills received were separated out, not only from other business, but also from each other. Although easy to use, not very many such registers survive. I selected material from the Strozzi business in Florence, the Strozzi business in Naples and the Manelli business in Avignon as suitable for microfilming. I had hoped to be able to add a minimum of 2,000 quotations (for various years between 1428 and 1489) to the corpus of material for the *Handbook* and maybe a great many more. Unfortunately the microfilm sent turned out to be almost unreadable. There are, therefore, sadly, very few entries from this source in the *Handbook* (519).[6] A further visit will ultimately have to be made, and, if satisfactory microfilms cannot be made, the registers will need to be worked on *in situ*.

The rich notarial archive in Siena turned out to be totally unrewarding because Sienese notaries ceased to notarize exchange transactions at a very early date. No *libri di ricordanze* were included amongst the papers deposited in the Archivio di Stato in Siena from the Tolomei, Bonsignori or Piccolomini, all notable commercial and banking families, nor amongst the bankruptcy papers of the Mercanzia.

In the Vatican Archives I worked through the manuscript inventory of the Fondo Camerale. Since the Görresgesellschaft have a plan to publish the receipts and expenditures of the Avignon popes up to 1378, I looked at material after that date, and *outside* the 'Datini' period, 1391–1411. From 1418 onwards to 1531 there is a vast series of *Introitus et Exitus* of the *Camera Apostolica* here, and a handful of volumes of this series have also escaped to the Archivio di Stato in Rome. Before 1391 there are sixteen volumes of *Manuale receptorum et expensarum* of the *Camera Apostolica* going back to

[6] I am grateful to Dr. Rosalind Brown for her efforts to assist me in deciphering the microfilm.

1378. There is also a single volume of *Introitus et Exitus* from before the Avignon period. I noted down the call numbers of some 140 volumes before 1499, ranging in size from 50 folios to 274 folios, mostly in the 180–220 folio range. This makes a total of over 50,000 pages. A spot check suggested that they are magnificent for evidence of what was circulating in many different parts of Europe throughout the period, and give the total values put by the *campsores* of the *camera* on a vast number of mixed batches of currency. However they only very intermittently give specific exchange rates for individual currencies. There seems to be only a sprinkling of such references in each volume. They were not worth microfilming *in toto* since they are too extensive. The amount of work spent on a detailed search of these volumes would produce a very low return for the time invested.

In the Archivio di Stato in Venice I was fortunate enough to be able to meet Professor Mueller. He assured me that there should be nothing available in these archives that he had not already covered himself, or was about to cover in his then current year working in the archives. Because so many prominent commercial families of later medieval Venice still survive to this day most of the relevant papers are in private hands, and relatively few in the Archivio di Stato. In their *libri di ricordanze* Venetian merchants, unlike Florentines, did not sort out their exchange business from their other exchange business, which makes their books much more laborious to use. Professor Mueller has since generously given me access to many of his notes and a selection of his material is reproduced in the venetian section of the *Handbook* pp. 80–92. The full material will appear in the two volumes of *Money and Banking in Medieval–Renaissance Venice* which he is writing with Professor F. C. Lane. The first volume is due to appear in 1985 from the Johns Hopkins University Press.

The problem with the Datini archives in Prato is that there is too much material spread over a relatively short period of years. The much used and much admired work of de Roover on the Bruges money market was based on the 2,383 business letters from Bruges in these archives. Bruges was, however, far from being one of the most important places with which Datini dealt. Twelve other cities produced more business letters in this collection of papers. The largest quantity were written from Florence. There are nearly 34,000 in all. I discovered that half a dozen scholars are working on this abundant material at present. They hope eventually to produce editions of the letters from some of the cities represented. Understandably, they are mostly concentrating on the less prolific groups of correspondence. Professor Mueller has, however, been working on the venetian correspondence, the sixth largest group. He has very generously allowed me access to his notes. The Venice–Florence exchange table for these years (pp. 87–91) is based on his work in Prato. No other work is yet approaching completion, but in the long run, from the work of these scholars, our knowledge of exchange in London, Paris, Milan and Majorca will be extended quite considerably. It was very obvious that more of the problems within the period 1391–1411 could be resolved here. A lifetime could easily be spent on this material before all its resources were properly exhausted. However a relatively short time in the archives would enable some major gaps to be filled in outline. I therefore concluded that a month's return visit to Prato to work in the Datini archives on letters from his correspondents in Bologna, Avignon, Genoa, and Perugia could be very useful.

The visit to the italian archives removed the lurking suspicion and fear that there might be a large quantity of material in Italy which was easily accessible and would vitiate any definitive listing based almost entirely on printed sources. Instead the correctness of the first impulse to work primarily from such printed material was strongly confirmed. The only unpublished sources that were found which were of easy and immediate use were the limited number of *libri di ricordanze* in the florentine archives and the single similar volume in Milan.

My visit to Italy made it clear that, with the exception of certain selected sources in the Datini archives in Prato, hardly any archival work would be cost effective. This confirmed my original supposition, that if the work was to remain on a european scale, it would have to continue to draw on printed sources and the archival discoveries of a multitude of other historians.

A short visit to New York in March 1981 to look at part of the papers of the late Raymond de Roover produced more material than the visits to italian archives. Not only had he himself worked for many years on the problems of exchange, but the part of his papers which I saw incorporated a large amount of material earlier accumulated from merchants' notebooks by Allan Evans, the editor of Pegolotti, for the purpose of elucidating the mechanisms of medieval exchange. These papers were deposited by Dr. Florence Edler de Roover with the American Numismatic Society, through the Medieval Academy of America. I should like to thank Dr. Edler de Roover and the American Numismatic Society for permission to consult these papers and Dr. Alan Stahl for his helpfulness while I was at the American Numismatic Society. In this *Handbook* I have used many of the internal florentine rates abstracted by Professor de Roover from the Medici Account Books now in the Harvard Business School Library (142). I hope at a later date to be able to complete Allan Evans's original plan and produce a useful publication based on the texts that he had gathered from archives throughout Europe.

On the same visit I was able to have very fruitful discussions with Professor Elizabeth Brown, Professor de Roover's successor at Brooklyn College, and with Professor Martha Howell and a group of people at the University of Rutgers experienced in the application of computer listing to medieval material. In the course of these discussions Professor Howell volunteered to take over the future collection of material. The material that appears in the *Handbook* is already in a machine-readable form, and Professor Howell is using this as the core of a data-bank that can be expanded to a scale much larger than could ever be conventionally published. I trust that she will eventually achieve my initial ambition of bringing together all the knowable rates of exchange for the whole of medieval Europe. All enquiries, and additional information, should be sent to her at the Department of History, Rutgers University, New Brunswick, New Jersey 08903, United States of America.

In a work of this magnitude errors are bound to exist as well as omissions, although I am pleased to be able to say how very few actual errors were discovered by the users of the *Interim Listing*. However, I should be very pleased if those who do discover errors in this *Handbook* would communicate them to Professor Howell.

When the *Interim Listing* was being compiled, no one else was working in the field, nor had anyone done so since the death of Professor de Roover. There are now a number of different projects under way in various countries. I know that these projects have been greatly encouraged by the success of the *Interim Listing*.

In 1983 the Economic and Social Research Council once again assisted me. It unfortunately felt able to appoint Mrs. Sarah Tolley as my research assistant for only four months, to help me assimilate all the material provided by academics corresponding with me, who had used the *Interim Listing* and with immense generosity flooded me with additional material which they had themselves found. It is a very great pity that the Economic and Social Research Council was unable to appoint Mrs. Tolley for longer. In the circumstances, we cannot call this as definitive a work as would have been possible in better circumstances. We can only apologize to those correspondents whose references have not been used, and assure them of our gratitude, our sorrow, and the long term prospect that these references will be incorporated by Professor Howell in her data-bank.

The Nuffield Foundation was able to provide me with some of the financial assistance that the Economic and Social Research Council were unable to afford me. They have generously paid for visits abroad, to meet with scholars and to work in the Datini papers in Prato. I was able to meet Professor Blockmans of Rotterdam, Professor van Cauwenberghe, Dr. Bernard and Dr. Aerts in Brussels, Professor van der Wee in Leuven, Professor van Uytven of Antwerp, Professor Berghaus and Dr. Ilisch in Münster, Professor Mueller in Venice, and Professor Irsigler and Dr. Metz in Trier, all of whom have provided both material and encouragement for the enterprise. I thank them all, and the Nuffield Foundation for making the visit possible. The material from Prato will be available in Professor Howell's data-bank.

In addition to the material which appears in this *Handbook* I have also accumulated a certain amount of other material. The unused material falls into two main categories.

Firstly, I have details of transactions involving a currency on the one hand and marks of silver or ounces of gold on the other. Before the introduction of gold currencies, many long distance transactions were, of course, carried out with the aid of bars of a mark weight of silver of guaranteed fineness, or less commonly with the aid of gold by the ounce. There was a slight resurgence of the use of silver by the mark during the currency famines of the late fourteenth century and the fifteenth. It is my intention to publish these at a later date as a supplementary publication. Had more finances been available at the last stage it might have been possible for them to have appeared as an appendix to this *Handbook*.

Secondly, I have details of cross-exchanges between major currencies, both of which have adequate primary series of exchanges with the florentine florin. At an early stage I deliberately decided not to collect this material systematically as it would have been totally impossible to do so in the time provided by the available funding, and would have ultimately resulted in the *Handbook* being an unpublishably large work of several volumes. The small amount of haphazardly collected cross-exchanges between major currencies has been transferred to Professor Martha Howell of Rutgers.

Mrs. Tolley was able to help me to cope with the overwhelmingly generous flood of additional material sent over the intervening years by the recipients of the *Interim Listing*, many of whom sent useful suggestions for its amplification along with exchange rates from their own work. This whole enterprise has provided an amazing and heart-warming example of international co-operation. I have been overwhelmed by the generosity of so many scholars, from so many countries, and by the magnitude of their response. I have been sent microfilm and vast amounts of xerox of original medieval documents in practically every west european language, which contained exchange rates and which needed to be read and abstracted. Above all, I have been sent hundreds of references to obscure publications from all over Europe purporting to contain printed rates of exchange. Furthermore, a considerable number of correspondents said that they would send references, or more such references, at a later date, but had not yet done so when Mrs. Tolley began to work on the project. I wrote individually to all the 200 recipients and an astonishingly large number of them were able to provide even more references than they had done already, guiding me particularly to very recent publications.

Over so long a period of time and in a work of such wide international collaboration I have incurred an enormous number of debts of gratitude. I would firstly like to thank for their generosity in providing me with exchange rates, in some cases in very large numbers, that they themselves have abstracted from archives all over Europe and have not yet published, Professor Meurice Arnould, Emeritus of the Free University of Brussels, for material from the departmental archives of the Nord at Lille; Professor Peter Berghaus of the Landesmuseum of Westphalia and the University of Münster, for material from various westphalian archives; Professor Rosalind Berlow of New York, for material from the departmental archives of the Côte d'Or at Dijon; Professor Thomas Bisson of the University of California, Berkeley, for material from the archives of the Crown of Aragon; Professor Thomas Blomquist of Northern Illinois University for material from the capitular archives of Lucca; Professor Elizabeth Brown of the City University of New York, for material from various french departmental archives; Dr. Raymond Cazelles, formerly in charge of the Musée Condé at Chantilly for material from the national archives in Paris; Dr. Wendy Childs of the University of Leeds; Dr. John Day of Paris for further material from the archives of the Crown of Aragon; Professor Aldo De Maddalena of the Bocconi University of Milan for material from the Sanminiato, Guasconi, Pazzi archive in his institute; Dr. Clare Dickstein-Bernard of Brussels for material from the city archives of Brussels; Professor Giuseppe Felloni of the University of Genoa for material from the state archives at Genoa; M. Joseph Ghyssens of Brussels for material from the city archives of Louvain; Professor Franz Irsigler of the University of Trier for material from rhineland archives; Dr. Anthony Luttrell of Bath for material from the archives of the Hospitallers; M. Denis Menjot of the University of Nice for material from the municipal archives of Nice; Professor John Munro of the University of Toronto for material from the city archives of Malines; Dr. Michael Prestwich of the University of Durham for material from various english record offices; Professor Rolf Sprandel of the University of Würzburg for material from Würzburg; and Dr. Malcolm Vale of St. John's College, Oxford. There was sadly no opportunity of taking up the generous offer of Professor Nicolai Rubinstein of Westfield College, London, of working through his notes of material in florentine archives.

I would also like to thank Professor Frederic Lane, Emeritus of Johns Hopkins University and Professor Reinhold Mueller of the University of Venice for their great generosity in allowing me to abstract large numbers of rates of exchange in advance of publication from their forthcoming volumes on *Money and Banking in Medieval–Renaissance Venice*; Dr. Alan Stahl of the American Numismatic Society for allowing me to abstract rates of exchange from his monograph on the venetian *tornesello* ahead of its publication, Dr. Peter King of the University of St. Andrews for sending me extracts in advance from his forthcoming volume on *The Finances of the Cistercian Order in the Fourteenth Century* and Mr. William Scott of Edinburgh for allowing me to see his article on 'Sterling and the usual money of Scotland' before its publication.

I would also like to thank Drs. Bacharach, Misbach and Rechenbach, and M. Kessedjian for permission to cite information from their unpublished theses. I have not been able to trace Dr. Lievre, whose thesis, submitted in Dijon in 1927, I have quoted without permission. I trust that after this length of time this does not cause distress.

I have been continually astonished by the liberality with which so many scholars have sent me copies of their own publications, many of which have been of the greatest value in this compilation. For their gifts not only of offprints, but also of complete volumes I would like to thank Professor Gian Luigi Basini of the University of Parma; Dr. Mario Bernocchi of Prato; Professor Wim Blockmans of the University of Rotterdam; Professor W. M. Bowsky of the University of California, Davis; Professor Carlo Cipolla of the University of California, Berkeley, and the Scuola Normale at Pisa; Dr. John Day of Paris; Dr. Clare Dickstein-Bernard of Brussels; Dr. Françoise Dumas, chief librarian of the Institut de France; Professor Giuseppe Felloni of Genoa; Professor Philip Grierson of Gonville and Caius College, Cambridge; Dr. Stefan Kazimir of the Slovak Academy in Bratislava; Dr. Colin Martin of Berne; Professor John McCusker of the University of Maryland; Professor Michel Mollat of Paris; Professor Emmanuella Nohejlová-Prátova of Prague; and Dr. Jorgen Steen Jensen of the National Museum in Copenhagen. I would also like to thank Professor Charles de la Roncière of the University of Aix-en-Provence for making available to me a copy of his doctorat d'état.

For their gifts of offprints I would like to thank Dr. David Abulafia of Gonville and Caius College, Cambridge; Dr. Erik Aerts of the Archives Générales of Belgium; Miss Marion Archibald of the British Museum; Professor Maurice Arnould, Emeritus of the Free University of Brussels; Professor Thomas Bisson of the University of California, Berkeley; Dr. Giorgetta Bonfiglio Dosio of the archives of the Veneto; Professor Elizabeth Brown of the City University of New York; Professor Guy Cabourdin of the University of Nancy; Professor Pierre Capra of the University of Bordeaux; the late Dr. Karel Castelin of Prague; Professor Eddy van Cauwenberghe of Brussels; Dr. Christopher Challis of the University of Leeds; Professor Pierre Cockshaw of the Free University of Brussels and the Royal Library of Belgium; the late Professor Michael Dolley; Professor David Farmer of the University of Saskatchewan; Dr. Hubert Frere of Liège; Professor Jean Gautier-Dalché of the University of Nice; M. Joseph Ghyssens of Brussels; Dr. Octavio Gil Farres of Madrid; Mr. John Gilbert of Cheltenham; Dr. Jarmila Hásková of the National Museum in Prague; Dr. Gert and Dr. Vera Hatz of the Museum for the History of Hamburg; Dr. Wolfgang Hess of the University of Munich; Professor James Holt of Fitzwilliam College, Cambridge; Dr. Peter Ilisch of the Landesmuseum of Westphalia; Professor Franz Irsigler of the University of Trier; Dr. Michael Jones of the University of Nottingham; Dr. Philip Jones of Brasenose College, Oxford; Professor Ryszard Kiernowski of the Polish Academy; Dr. Peter King of the University of St. Andrews; Professor Frederic Lane, Emeritus of Johns Hopkins University; Professor Mavis Mate of the University of Oregon; Dr. Rainer Metz of the University of Trier; Dr. Nicholas Morard of the cantonal archives of Fribourg; Professor John Munro of the University of Toronto; Dr. Michael Prestwich of the University of Durham; Professor Walter Prevenier of the University of Ghent; Professor Maurice Rey of the University of Besançon; Professor Louise Robbert of the University of Missouri, St. Louis; Professor Gigliola Rondinini of the University of Milan; Mr. Mark Steel of Solihull; Dr. Gerald Stefke of the University of Hamburg; Professor Wolfgang von Stromer of the Free University of Berlin; Professor Raymond van Uytven of the University of Antwerp; Professor Hermann van der Wee of the University of Leuven; Professor Harald Witthöft of the University of Siegen; Professor Zbigniew Zabinski of the University of Cracow; and Dr. Léon Zylbergeld of the city archives in Brussels.

I would like to thank a number of people for going to great lengths to provide me with photocopies of articles and sections of books which were not available in England, as well as for copies of their own work and further useful references. Professor Peter Berghaus of the Landesmuseum of Westphalia and the University of Münster provided me with otherwise unobtainable german material; Professor H. Enno van Gelder of the University of Leiden, formerly of the royal coin cabinet in the Hague, provided me with otherwise unobtainable dutch material; Professor Antoni Maczak of the University of Warsaw provided me with otherwise unobtainable polish material; and Dr. Angus Mackay of the University of Edinburgh allowed me to use his own copies of offprints of spanish articles I would not otherwise have found. Dr.

Françoise Dumas, chief librarian of the Institut de France and Dr. Stanislawa Kubiak of the University of Cracow have provided me with abstracts from a wide range of printed french and polish documents unavailable to me in England. They have all gone to a very great deal of trouble on my behalf.

Most of the people I have already thanked also sent me references to printed material, but the following did so as well: Dr. Christopher Allmand of the University of Liverpool; Professor Michel Balard of the University of Rheims; Professor Guy Bois of the University of Besançon; Dr. Cecil Clough of the University of Liverpool; Professor Charles-Emmanuel Dufourcq of the University of Paris; Professor Léopold Genicot of the Catholic University of Louvain; Professor Alberto Grohmann of the University of Perugia; Professor Bernard Guillemain of the University of Bordeaux; Professor John Larner of the University of Glasgow; Professor J. P. Leguay of the Centre Universitaire of Savoy; Dr. V. Pfaff of Mannheim; Dr. Alan Ryder of the University of Bristol; Dr. Marie-Rose Desmed-Thielmans of the Archives Générales of Belgium and the Free University of Brussels; and Professor Pierre Toubert of the University of Paris. I should like to thank them all for their helpful suggestions, but have to confess that, unfortunately, not all the references that they gave me could be tracked down in this country, particularly in the limited time available. Professor Henri Dubois of the University of Paris provided me with introductions to a large number of french historians. This proved most useful and I am very grateful to him for this.

Amongst so many who have helped me it is invidious to thank a few individuals for their particular encouragement, I should nevertheless like to do so, without, I hope, giving offence to those I do not name. First of all I was much inspired by the late Professor Raymond de Roover and the late Professor Sir Michael Postan. I can no longer thank them directly, but would nevertheless like to express my gratitude for the warmth of their encouragement at the earliest stages of the project. I should like to thank Professor de Roover's widow, Dr. Florence Edler de Roover of Florence, and Professors Julius Kirshner of Chicago and Richard Goldthwaite of Johns Hopkins, who have been handling Professor Roover's papers, for continuing the encouragement that he gave me at the beginning. I have also been much heartened by those who are currently making major regional studies of monetary history, by Professor Eddy van Cauwemberghe who is running a major project on the monetary history of the southern Netherlands, and by Professor Franz Irsigler and Dr. Metz who are running an even larger project at Trier on the monetary history of the Rhineland and associated areas. Professors Spooner and McCusker who have been working on exchange rates in later periods have also given me their moral support.

For the warmth of their friendship over many years and of their continuing interest in the project I should like specially to thank Peter Berghaus in Münster; Tom Bisson in Berkeley; Wim Blockmans in Rotterdam; Carlo Cipolla in Pisa; Pierre Cockshaw in Brussels; John Day in Paris; Aldo De Maddalena in Milan; Françoise Dumas in Paris; Martha Howell in New Brunswick; Frederick Lane in Baltimore; Antoni Maczak in Warsaw; Reinhold Mueller in Venice; John Munro in Toronto; Hermann van der Wee in Leuven; the members of the History Department at Keele; and here in Cambridge, Charles Wilson, Jim Holt and Philip Grierson.

It is a pleasure above all to thank my two research assistants without whom this work could never have been accomplished. Both Miss Wilkinson and Mrs. Tolley, formerly Miss Hanbury-Tenison, brought an extraordinary energy and determination to this work, as well as broad enough linguistic capacities to cope with books and articles in the whole range of most european languages. Whereas Miss Wilkinson, who carried the major share of the burden of compilation, had to enter each individual entry laboriously onto separate file cards ready for us to sort together by hand, Mrs. Tolley has had her share of the work speeded up by the Cambridge University computer. I would therefore like to thank Dr. John Dawson of the Cambridge University Literary and Linguistic Computing Centre for his benign oversight of the computing aspects of this production, and his assistants, the Ven. S. K. Yeshe-Zangmo, who fed the whole of the *Interim Listing* into the computer ready for Mrs. Tolley, and has given us unfailingly helpful advice from day to day, and Mrs. Monique Johnson who has fed in much of the additional material that Mrs. Tolley lacked time to handle. A great deal of exacting typing has gone into this project and I should like to thank Mrs. Clare Baggott, Mrs. Carolyn Busfield and Mr. Richard Chesser for many hours of tedious labour.

Finally I should like to thank the Royal Historical Society for taking the volume into their series of handbooks, and its successive literary directors, who with Dr. Richard Barber of Boydell and Brewer have so patiently and helpfully assisted me to bring the volume to publication. It would, of course, never have come anywhere near publication without the continuous and insistent support of my wife, Dr. Margaret Spufford, who, despite so much historical work of her own, has found a great deal of time and energy to keep my work going as well.

The *Interim Listing* was concluded on the most appropriate day for a work based on the florentine florin, the feast day of St. John the Baptist, 1977. The introduction to this *Handbook* was completed in 1984 on the quindene of St. Eligius, patron saint of goldsmiths.

Peter Spufford
Queens' College
Cambridge

FOR PHILIP GRIERSON

INTRODUCTION

CURRENCY

The period covered by the *Handbook* runs from the earliest available twelfth-century material up to the late fifteenth century. This finishing date is designed to tie in with the work that Professor F. C. Spooner of the University of Durham has in progress. He is preparing a compilation of exchanges for the whole of Europe from the late fifteenth century onwards.

In the twelfth century the currency of Europe consisted of silver *penny* coinages: *deniers* in France; *denari* in Italy; *dineros* in Spain; *dinheros* in Portugal; *penningen* in the Low Countries; *pfennige* in Germany; *denars* in Hungary; and so on, described universally in Latin as *denarii*. In the thirteenth and fourteenth centuries multi-denominational coinages were introduced into most parts of Europe. In the first half of the thirteenth century italian cities north of Rome introduced new, larger, silver coins known on account of their greater size as *grossi* (big ones) by contrast with the pre-existing *denarii*, which were soon called *piccoli* (little ones). Although they were all of approximately the same size as each other, containing about two grams of fine silver, the early *grossi* were initially worth between four and twenty-six of the *piccoli*, depending on how little silver the local *denaro* contained. In the second half of the thirteenth century, larger silver coins were also introduced in Rome and southern Italy, in France (*gros*) and the Low Countries (*groten*), and in the fourteenth century in the Empire (*groschen*) and England (*groats*). Many of these later *gros*, for example the *gros tournois* in France, were twice as large as the early Italian *grossi*. As well as the generic name, *grossi*, many of these larger pieces also acquired local soubriquets. The *grosso* of Venice, for example, was also known as a *matapan*, that of Florence as a *fiorino*, and that of Naples and Provence as a *gigliato* or *julhat*.

In the middle of the thirteenth century gold coins began to be issued regularly outside muslim-influenced Spain and Sicily. The earliest were the florentine *fiorino d'oro* or florin, worth 240 florentine *denari* or 20 florentine *grossi* and the genoese *genovino*, worth 96 genoese *denari*. Both began to be issued in 1252. These were coinages made of gold imported from Africa. In the second half of the thirteenth century the use of gold coins in Europe spread only slowly outside northern Italy. The opening up of gold mines in Europe itself in the first half of the fourteenth century, principally at Kremnica in the kingdom of Hungary, caused the use of gold coins in Europe to spread much more rapidly. By the middle of the fourteenth century gold coinages were established in France, the Low Countries, England and the Rhineland, as well as Hungary, and the gold currency of Italy and Spain had become much more abundant.[1] Meanwhile the old, smaller penny coinages continued to be

[1] See my *Money and its Use in Medieval Europe* (Cambridge, 1986) for further details of both the new larger silver coinages and the gold coinages of the thirteenth and fourteenth centuries.

struck alongside the new, larger, silver coinages and the even newer gold coinages. These penny coinages were already of varying weights and finenesses by the beginning of the thirteenth century. Some, like the english pennies and the cologne *pfennigs* were still of good silver; others, like the venetian or lucca *denari* were not only much smaller, but heavily debased. The process of differentiation continued over the next three hundred years. By 1500, english pennies, although somewhat reduced in size, continued to be minted in fine silver. Most other small *denari* or *deniers* were struck in 'billon', which was silver so debased that the actual silver content was generally under a twelfth, and in extreme cases as little as a ninety-sixth, part of the whole. Billon coins always contained much more alloy, generally copper, than silver. As a consequence of their colour they were generically known as *monnaie noire* or black money.

Some of the new, larger, silver coinages issued from the thirteenth century onwards were still being minted of fine silver in 1500. Many others, particularly in the fourteenth century, had their silver content reduced, or were replaced by new coins of a lower silver content. Their silver content was not generally reduced below half, so that they retained a 'silver' appearance. They were consequently generically known as white money, in contrast to the black money. In France, for example, good silver *gros tournois* were replaced by 1400 as the standard large silver coins by *blancs*, which were minted half of silver and half of alloy. In the Rhineland, good silver *groschen* had similarly been replaced by half silver *weisspfennigs*.

In the late middle ages most european countries were using a multi-denominational currency, effectively minted in three different metals, billon, silver, and gold. More than one denomination was frequently minted in each metal. In France, for example, black, billon, two *denier* pieces or *doubles tournois* were minted as well as black *deniers tournois*, and in Florence, black, four *denaro* pieces, *quattrini* as well as *denari piccoli*. In silver, white *soldini* were minted in Venice as well as *grossi*, and in England, silver half *groats* as well as silver *groats*. In gold as well, halves of standard denominations were frequently minted. So sometimes were quarters or doubles. The currency of most countries in Europe after 1200 was thus generally not only abundant, but also increasingly complex.

MONEY OF ACCOUNT

In most parts of late medieval Europe, and in many places up to the eighteenth or even the nineteenth century, a dichotomy existed in the functions of money. On the one hand, money of account was the *measure of value*, whilst on the other, the actual coin was the *medium of exchange* and the *store of wealth*.

Money of account derived its name from its function. As a measure of value it was used almost exclusively for accounting purposes. Most financial transactions were first determined and expressed in money of account, although payments were naturally made subsequently in coin, or surprisingly often in other goods. Coin itself was valued as a commodity in terms of money of account, and, like any other commodity, its value frequently varied. This variation of the value of coin in terms of money of account has been the cause of much confusion of thought about the nature of money of account. This confusion has resulted in the expression of a differing concept of money of account by practically every writer on medieval money.

With the decline of the *denier* at different rates, in different places, in the eleventh and twelfth centuries a standard of reference was needed for the wide variety of *deniers* that might be circulating in any region in addition to the indigenous coinage. Such a need was particularly felt in such regions as Champagne because of the international trading fairs there. With the introduction in the thirteenth century of the fine silver *grosso* and the gold *florin* in addition to the often base *denaro*, a common denominator became necessary to express the varying values of gold, silver and billon coins. Money of account supplied both these needs.

Although the need for money of account was not felt until the eleventh and, more seriously, the twelfth and thirteenth centuries, the form taken by money of account dated from a much earlier period. As early as the eighth century and probably even in the seventh, the system of pounds and shillings had been in use. With regional modifications, the relationship of twelve *deniers* or pennies to the *sou* or shilling (also *schilling*, *skilling*, *soldo*, or *sueldo*, in Latin *solidus*), and of twenty shillings to the *livre* or pound (also *pfund*, *pond*, or *lira*, in Latin *libra*), had gradually become established throughout western Europe. This was basically a system of counting coins, rather than a system of money. A shilling meant a dozen coins, and a pound meant a score of dozens. Marc Bloch maintained that before the thirteenth century the *sou* and the *livre* were no more than *unités numériques*.

When using the *Handbook* it should be borne in mind that although most of the rates were quoted in *soldi* or shillings, they are based on *denari* or pennies, so that a value for the florin of 66s. 3d. could equally be expressed as 795 *denari*, or as 3 li. 6s. 3d.

This system of pounds, shillings and pence was not, however, universal. Variants on it are noted in the relevant places in the *Handbook*. In Bavaria, and places like Austria which were settled from Bavaria, the *schilling* meant thirty coins and the *pfund* or *talent* meant eight sets of thirty coins. In England the mark, which was there a weight two-thirds of the size of the pound, had been transformed into a unit of account, two-thirds of the pound sterling and was frequently used alongside it as 13s. 4d. or 160 pence. By derivation from England, the mark was also used in the southern Netherlands as a unit of 160 deniers. At Cologne and at Lübeck marks were quite independently transformed into units of account, of 12 and 16 schillings respectively, and pounds were not used there. See Map 1 p. xxii for systems of reckoning.

In some cases the development of money of account was facilitated by a transitional stage in which the new coins of the thirteenth century neatly represented the old multiples of *deniers*. The *grossi* of Florence and Rome, the earliest *gros tournois* and the earliest Prague *groschen* were all originally intended to be *soldi*, *sous* or *schillings*, containing twelve times as much silver as their respective *deniers*, but they soon ceased to fulfil this function.

SYSTEMS OF RECKONING

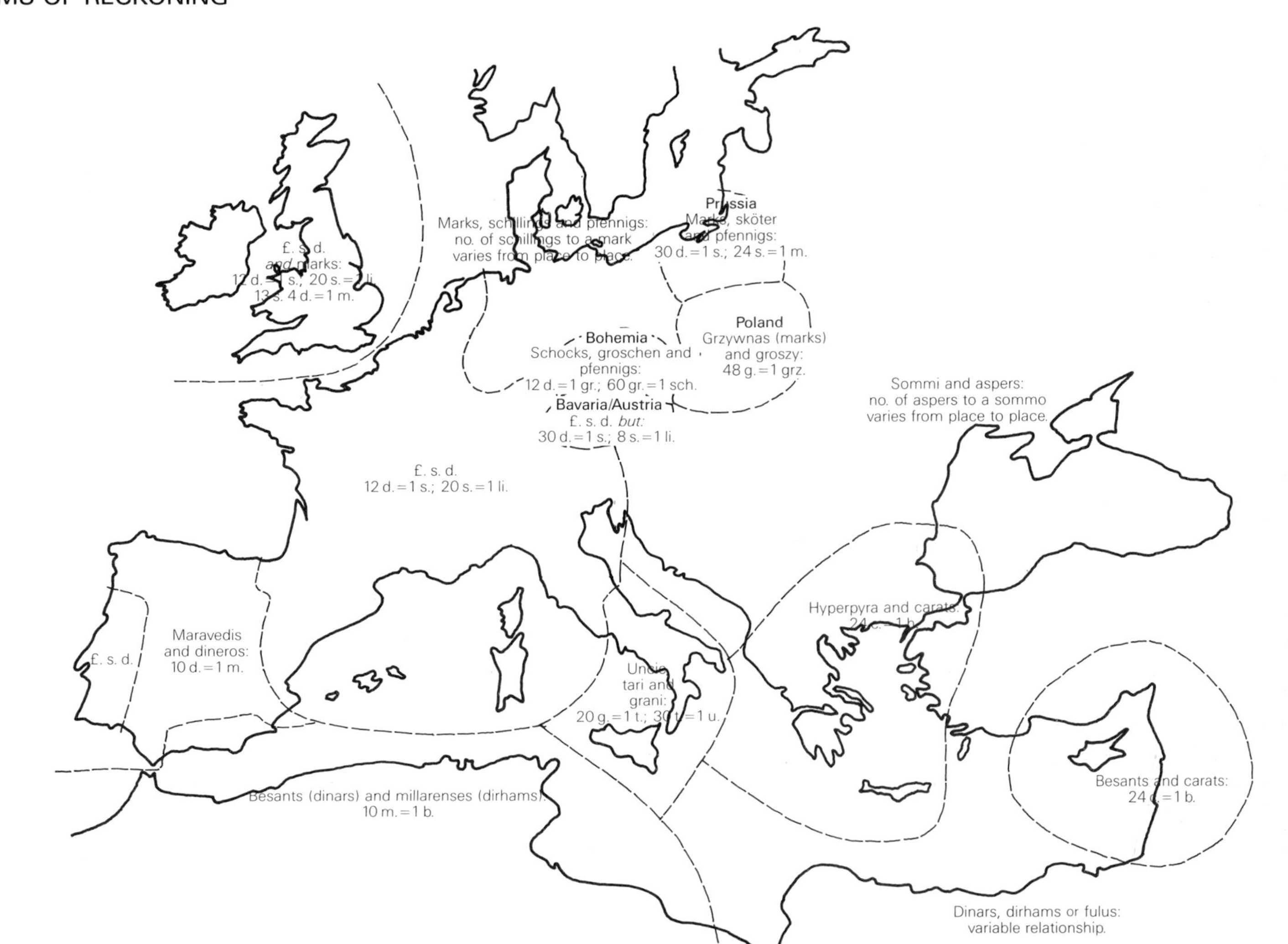

£. s. d.
and marks:
12 d. = 1 s.; 20 s. = 1 li.
13 s. 4 d. = 1 m.
Marks, schillings and pfennigs:
no. of schillings to a mark
varies from place to place.
Prussia
Marks, sköter
and pfennigs:
30 d. = 1 s.; 24 s. = 1 m.
Poland
Grzywnas (marks)
and groszy:
48 g. = 1 grz.
Bohemia
Schocks, groschen and
pfennigs:
12 d. = 1 gr.; 60 gr. = 1 sch.
Bavaria/Austria
£. s. d. *but:*
30 d. = 1 s.; 8 s. = 1 li.
Sommi and aspers:
no. of aspers to a sommo
varies from place to place.
£. s. d.
12 d. = 1 s.; 20 s. = 1 li.
Maravedis
and dineros:
10 d. = 1 m.
£. s. d.
Uncie
tari and
grani:
20 g. = 1 t.; 30 t. = 1 u.
Hyperpyra and carats:
24 c. = 1 h.
Besants and carats:
24 c. = 1 b.
Besants (dinars) and millarenses (dirhams):
10 m. = 1 b.
Dinars, dirhams or fulus:
variable relationship.

Similarly the florentine florin and the french *chaise a l'écu* were originally intended to represent the florentine *lira* and the french *livre tournois*, but both were soon raised in value. The english *noble* was only kept at a fixed value, half of the mark sterling or one third of the pound sterling, by altering the weight of gold that it contained from time to time.

The habit of counting coins in dozens and scores of dozens was so ingrained that when a new coin did not coincide neatly with a multiple of the pre-existing coins, a new system of pounds, shillings and pence was automatically constructed on the basis of the new coin. In Venice, after the creation of the *grosso* or *matapan*, two concurrent systems of money of account came into use. One was based on the old little *denaro* (*piccolo*), the other on the new great *denaro* (*grosso*). There was no firm relationship between the two systems of accounting, for whereas the billon *denaro* of the *lira*, *soldo* and *denaro piccolo* system sank further and further in quality, eventually becoming undisguised copper in the late fifteenth century, the good silver *denaro* of the *li.s.d. grosso* system very largely conserved its fineness and weight.

Two concurrent, and divergent, systems of money of account similarly came into existence in Florence, with the creation of the silver *fiorino* or *grosso*, and in France, with the creation of the *gros tournois*. In France the system of account based on the larger coin expired when the relevant *grosso* or *gros* ceased to circulate, several decades after it ceased to be issued. In Castille by contrast, although the *maravedi* had only an ephemeral life as a large silver coin, it survived for over two centuries as a unit of account, with the meaning of ten small castillian *dineros*.

In other places the newer *gros* ousted the older *deniers* so completely that methods of accounting based on the *denier* either ceased, or continued to be used only on the basis of a notional relationship between the defunct *denier* and the surviving *gros*.

This occurred in Flanders early in the fourteenth century when the new *groot penning* supplanted both the Flemish version of the french *denier parisis* and the flemish version of the english *sterling*. The new *groot* was held to be worth three of the old flemish *sterlings* and twelve of the old flemish *deniers parisis*. The flemish systems of account based on their *groot*, their *sterling* and their *parisis* were thereafter fossilized in this relationship. All three moneys of account were thus in reality tied to the *groot*. A similar transition to reckoning in the new great coins took place not only in neighbouring Brabant, which also had its *groot*, but in other places as far away as Naples and Bohemia, where accounting came to be carried out in terms of *grossi gigliati* and *prague groschen* respectively. Initially the prague *groschen* were struck at 60 to the local mark weight of silver, so that the mark was a convenient multiple of these *groschen*. Even when they ceased to be minted at 60 to the mark, they continued to be reckoned for convenience in multiples of 60, each called a *sexagena* or *schock*. In neighbouring Meissen *groschen* were also counted in sixties. Reckoning in *schocks*, or sixties, occasionally spread to other denominations, and was reinforced in the mid-fifteenth century when a *schock* of the meissen *groschen* was temporarily worth an imperial gold *gulden*.

Not only were new systems of money of account constructed using the larger silver pieces as *denari* or *soldi*, but others were built up using the new gold pieces as *lire*. The florentine gold florin, the french *franc* and the electoral *rheingulden* all became pounds of account. Unfortunately for simplicity of comprehension, all three coins became in time detached from their namesakes as pounds of account.

In Florence, the gold florin (*fiorino*) began as the *lira* in the system of money based on the *denaro piccolo*, whilst the *grosso* was still the *soldo*. The *grosso* was also, confusingly, called a *fiorino*. I shall distinguish it from its gold namesake as the 'silver florin'. The gold florin thus began as equal to 20 silver florins or *soldi affiorino*. As the *denaro piccolo* and the silver florin evolved differently, the gold florin came to have different values in silver florins and in *piccoli*. This evolution came to an end in 1279 when the silver florin ceased to be struck. By that time the gold florin had become worth 29 silver florins (29 *soldi affiorino*). Silver florins remained in circulation until they were withdrawn in 1296. Accounting in *lira*, *soldi* and *denari affiorino* did not, however, vanish with the silver florin, like most other systems based on large silver coins. Instead, it continued into the fourteenth century, because it had effectively become based on the gold florin, rather than the silver florin, at the fossilized rate of 29 *soldi* to the gold florin.

The french case was much simpler. The gold *franc* was first issued at the value of a *livre tournois*, it then increased in value in money *tournois* as the silver coinage was debased, but the word *franc* remained as an alternative term for the *livre tournois*, not only when gold *francs* of a different, higher, value were actually in circulation, but for long after gold *francs* had ceased to circulate.

In the Netherlands the electoral florins or *gulden* from the Rhineland were commercially current in the 1440s at 40 flemish *groten*. In the 1450s they were officially current at that rate. Consequently, by the 1460s they had become equated in men's minds with the pound of 40 *groten*. The principal silver coin in circulation in the Netherlands, the burgundian *stuiver* or *patard*, formed a natural shilling for it, being valued at two *groten*. The *gulden* as an accounting unit remained into the sixteenth century as the name of the pound of 40 *groten*, even though the gold *rheingulden* had officially become worth 42 flemish *groten* as early as 1467. By 1488, it was worth 90 flemish *groten*. This was indeed a strange fossilized system, yet it continued to attach itself to monetary reality by its fixed relationship to the flemish *groot*.

Similar fossilized systems existed elsewhere. In France the system of *livre*, *sou* and *denier parisis*, based on the *denier parisis* until it ceased to be struck in 1365, continued in use for at least another century and a half. It kept in contact with reality by the fossilization of the thirteenth- and fourteenth-century relationship of 4:5 with the *denier tournois*, i.e. 16 *sous parisis* always equalled one *livre tournois*.

In Flanders the flemish system of *livre*, *sou* and *denier parisis* was similarly kept in contact with reality, through the equivalence of the flemish *sou parisis* to the flemish *groot*. After 1433 there was no distinct brabançon coinage, yet the brabançon money of account continued to be used. It was also kept in

CURRENCIES OF LATE MEDIEVAL EUROPE

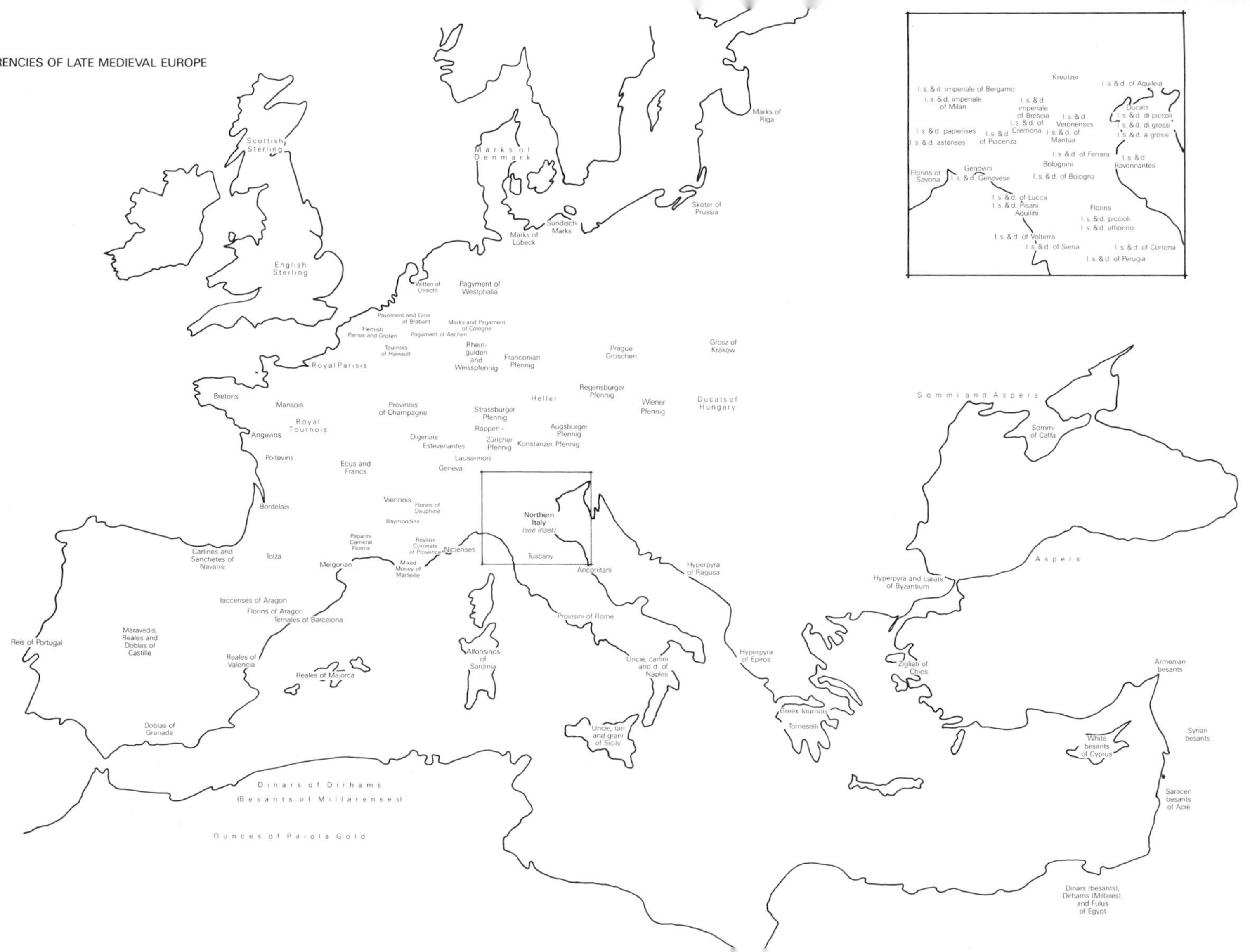

Scottish Sterling
English Sterling
Marks of Denmark
Marks of Riga
Sköter of Prussia
Sundisch Marks
Marks of Lübeck
Witten of Utrecht
Pagyment of Westphalia
Payement and Gros of Brabant
Flemish Parisis and Groten
Marks and Pagament of Cologne
Pagament of Aachen
Tournois of Hainault
Rhein-gulden and Weisspfennig
Franconian Pfennig
Prague Groschen
Grosz of Krakow
Royal Parisis
Regensburger Pfennig
Heller
Wiener Pfennig
Ducats of Hungary
Bretons
Mansois
Royal Tournois
Provinois of Champagne
Strassburger Pfennig
Rappen - Züricher Pfennig
Augsburger Pfennig
Konstanzer Pfennig
Angevins
Digenais
Estevenantes
Lausannois
Poitevins
Ecus and Francs
Geneva
Viennois
Florins of Dauphiné
Raymondins
Bordelais
Northern Italy (see inset)
Tuscany
Paparini Cameral Florins
Royaux Coronats of Provence
Niciensis
Mixed Money of Marseille
Carlines and Sanchetes of Navarre
Tolza
Melgorian
Anconitani
Hyperpyra of Ragusa
Iaccenses of Aragon
Florins of Aragon
Ternales of Barcelona
Provisini of Rome
Maravedis, Reales and Doblas of Castille
Reis of Portugal
Reales of Valencia
Alfonsinos of Sardinia
Uncie, carlini and d. of Naples
Hyperpyra of Epiros
Reales of Majorca
Uncie, tari and grani of Sicily
Greek tournois
Torneselli
Doblas of Granada
Dinars of Dirhams
(Besants of Millarenses)
Ounces of Paiola Gold
Sommi and Aspers
Sommi of Caffa
Aspers
Hyperpyra and carats of Byzantium
Zigliati of Chios
Armenian besants
Syrian besants
White besants of Cyprus
Saracen besants of Acre
Dinars (besants), Dirhams (Millares), and Fulus of Egypt

Kreutzer
l. s. & d. of Aquileia
l. s. & d. imperiale of Bergamo
l. s. & d. imperiale of Milan
l. s. & d. imperiale of Brescia
l. s. & d. of Cremona
l. s. & d. Veronenses
Ducats
l. s. & d. di piccoli
l. s. & d. di grossi
l. s. & d. a grossi
l. s. & d. papienses
l. s. & d. astenses
l. s. & d. of Piacenza
l. s. & d. of Mantua
l. s. & d. of Ferrara
Bolognini
l. s. & d. Ravennantes
Florins of Savona
Genovini
l. s. & d. Genovese
l. s. & d. of Bologna
l. s. & d. of Lucca
l. s. & d. Pisani
Aquilini
Florins
l. s. & d. piccioli
l. s. & d. affiorino
l. s. & d. of Volterra
l. s. & d. of Siena
l. s. & d. of Cortona
l. s. & d. of Perugia

touch with reality by the fossilization of its relationship with the flemish money of account, as it had existed in 1433. Three brabançon *groten* had then equalled two flemish *groten*. Thereafter brabançon money of account was based on the flemish *groot*.

The misnomer 'imaginary money' has often been applied to late medieval money of account, perhaps because the real coin on which the money of account was actually based was not always evident on first inspection, as in the cases above. To untangle the maze of moneys of account which were created in the last three centuries of the Middle Ages is beyond the scope of this introduction. Brief details of many of them are given at the heads of appropriate tables. It may, however, be taken as axiomatic that on closer inspection an historical explanation may be found for the existence of each money of account, and that such an historical explanation will indicate to which real coin the system continued to be attached. See Map 2 p. xxv.

The real coins involved at the base of these accounting systems may mostly be looked up in either F. von Schrötter *Wörterbuch der Münzkunde* (447) which is arranged alphabetically, or in the third volume of A. Engel and R. Serrure, *Traité de numismatique du moyen âge*, Paris, 1905, reprinted 1964, which is arranged geographically by issuers. This is, however, outdated in many particulars and it is in many ways now preferable to refer first to the magnificently illustrated single volume by Philip Grierson, *Monnaies du moyen âge*, Fribourg, 1976, and to follow up the references given there, or else to my *Money and its Use in Medieval Europe*.

MONEY CHANGERS—BANCHE DEL GIRO

Before the introduction of gold florins in the thirteenth century the primary role of the money changer was to effect exchanges between small local *denari* on the one hand, and cast ingots of silver, or pounds of unminted gold dust on the other. The latter were only used by merchants and other travellers, and for large local payments. For payments between different localities, local *denari* were obviously useless. Unminted silver, provided its fineness was known, was also more convenient for large local payments than minted silver, which would have to be counted out, or weighed, in the form of thousands, or even tens of thousands, of separate coins. Unminted silver bars generally conformed to a limited number of accepted standards of fineness each used over wide areas of Europe.[2]

There is some evidence to suggest that these bars or ingots of silver were also frequently of a standard weight, the mark, even though the mark weight itself, of course, varied from place to place. In the spring of 1204, Wolfger Bishop of Passau set out for Rome. His chamberlain brought with them a supply of silver bars to exchange along the route into local currency to pay for the needs of the bishop's party. The weights of the bars exchanged were generally, though not always, in round numbers of marks. He changed three

[2] For a longer discussion of the use of silver in bar form see my *Money and Its Use*.

marks at Tarvis, crossing the Alps into Italy, a single mark at Padua, four marks at Ferrara, then two more marks there, and yet another two before they moved on to Bologna where he exchanged an odd weight of silver into bolognese *denari*. Across the Apennines in Florence, he exchanged a round five marks, but an odd weight in Siena. In Rome itself, on all the five occasions when he exchanged bars for currency, complete numbers of marks were involved, first eleven marks, then another eleven, then sixteen, then three and finally another three before they started the return journey.[3] In other words, in eleven transactions out of thirteen the chamberlain was offering silver bars which weighed a complete number of marks, which strongly suggests that most of the bars that he was carrying weighed a mark or an exact multiple.

The use of uncoined gold dust for payments was limited to regions bordering on the Mediterranean. It was normally measured by the ounce.

Such exchange transactions, between unminted silver or gold and local currencies were only gradually replaced by exchanges between gold coins and local currencies, and continued in some parts of Europe until the fourteenth century. As a consequence rates for marks of silver, and ounces of gold in various local currencies survive in an appreciable number. We have not collected them systematically and they therefore do not appear in the *Handbook*. However we have made a haphazard accumulation and I hope that, at some future date, I may be able to produce a supplementary listing of exchange rates between local currencies and marks of silver, and where appropriate, ounces of gold.

As well as exchanges between mark bars of silver and local currencies, money changers must also commonly have made exchanges with the coinage of adjacent principalities, although there is surprisingly little direct evidence that they did so. At the end of the twelfth century more or less fixed relationships frequently existed between the coinages of adjacent principalities. In western France, for example, the *deniers* of Le Mans were taken as double those of Anjou or Tours; in southern France the *deniers* of Le Puy was taken as half those of neighbouring Clermont; in the Rhineland the *pfennigs* of Cologne were taken as double those of neighbouring Aachen; in Tuscany, the *denari* of the principal cities were all equivalent to one another. A number of these rates appear in the listings.

By the time that gold coins replaced marks of silver and ounces of gold in the transactions of money changers, some of them had already taken considerable steps towards becoming local bankers. Within certain of the leading commercial cities some money changers extended their activities from manual money-changing to taking deposits, and then to transferring sums from one account to another on the instructions of the depositors. At the same time many money changers, even in these few cities, continued only to exchange money. Elsewhere the activities of all money changers remained limited to simple exchange.

[3] W. Jesse, *Quellenbuch zur Münz- und Geldgeschichte des Mittelalters* (Halle, 1924), document 370, p. 251.

In Genoa, the most precocious centre for such local banking facilities, the notarial register of Guglielmo Cassinese (1190–2) indicates that local payments could then not only be made by transfer between accounts with the same bank, but also between accounts in different banks in the city.[4] This was possible because the bankers maintained accounts in each other's banks. In this way inter-locking banking systems came into existence. The largest of these was at Florence, where there were reputedly as many as eighty banks by the early fourteenth century.

By the fourteenth century it had become customary amongst merchants within a limited number of cities to make payments as far as possible by assignment on their bank accounts (*per ditta di banco*). Such assignment was initially normally made by oral instruction by the account holder in person at the bank. By 1321, it was apparent that some venetian bankers were reluctant to pay out cash, instead of making transfers between accounts, for in that year the Great Council had to legislate that bankers were to be compelled to pay out cash within three days if asked to do so.[5] By allowing overdrafts and thus letting their cash reserves fall below, and often well below, the total of their deposits, such local deposit-bankers were not only facilitating payments, but also effectively increasing the money supply.

In Venice, to which so much unminted silver came in the course of the thirteenth century, it had become normal practice by the fourteenth century for merchants to be paid for the bullion that they brought to the city by crediting them with its value in a bank account. Its importers could then immediately pay for their purchases of spices and other merchandise by assignment on their bank accounts.[6]

As well as these current accounts, on which no interest was paid, these money-changer bankers also ran deposit accounts on which interest accumulated. These were suitable for sums of money which were not required for several years, the dowries of orphan girls, for example, and could therefore be invested by the banker in long-term enterprises. Some venetian bankers invested directly in trading voyages. A complete round trip from Venice to the Levant, back to Venice, onwards to Flanders, and back to Venice again, took two years. To make an investment in such a voyage the banker had to be certain that his depositors would not call for their money suddenly.

Such transfer banking developed in other cities much more slowly than in Genoa. In Venice, for example, the earliest direct evidence of a money changer running bank accounts is as late as 1274. Even then it is not clear if

[4] Raymond de Roover, 'New interpretations of the history of banking', *Journal of World History*, ii (1954), reprinted in his selected studies *Business, Banking, and Economic Thought in Late Medieval and Early Modern Europe* (Chicago, 1974), pp. 213–19.

[5] Reinhold C. Mueller, *The Procuratori di San Marco and the Venetian Credit Market* (Ph.D., Johns Hopkins, 1969, printed Arno Press, New York, 1977), p. 188. Another habit, of which the bankers' account holders complained in Barcelona and Genoa as well as Venice, was to send them to other banks to look for cash. R. C. Mueller, 'The role of bank money in Venice 1300–1500', *Studi Veneziani*, n.s., iii (1979), p. 75.

[6] Mueller, 'Bank money', pp. 61–7.

they were current or deposit accounts. Indirect evidence, however, suggests that such banking activities had by then already been going on for several years.[7] Outside Italy the earliest evidence is a little later still. The Privilege of Barcelona in 1284 implies that current account banking, with credit transfer between accounts, already existed there at that date, and the register of the treasure of Aragon for 1302–4 shows that it then also existed at Valencia and Lerida.[8] The evidence for money changers acting as local bankers in Bruges also begins around 1300.[9] Later evidence suggests that they were also acting in this way in the course of the fourteenth century in Liège, Frankfurt, Strasbourg, Constantinople, and perhaps London.[10]

Bank accounts were quite clearly part of the money supply by the early fourteenth century and legislation was introduced to protect those who used them. In Venice a guarantee of 3,000 lire was required in 1270 before a money changer banker was allowed to set up in business.[11] In Barcelona, from 1300, book entries by credit transfer legally ranked equally with original deposits among the liabilities of bankers. Those who failed were forbidden ever to keep a bank again, and were to be detained on bread and water until all their account holders were satisfied in full. In 1321 the legislation there was greatly increased in severity. Bankers who failed and did not settle up in full within a year were to be beheaded and their property sold for the satisfaction of their account holders. This was actually enforced. Francesch Castello was beheaded in front of his bank in 1360.[12]

In the course of the fourteenth century, written instructions, or cheques, supplemented and eventually supplanted oral instructions. The earliest surviving florentine cheque so far discovered was drawn on the Castellani bank by two patrician Tornaquinci in November 1368 to pay a draper, Sengnia Ciapi, for black cloth for a family funeral. Within a hundred years cheques were in use there by very modest men for modest purposes. In 1477, a florentine haberdasher wrote a cheque to pay for the emptying of a cess pit.[13]

Nevertheless, even at the end of the fifteenth century, most transactions inside the city, as in the country, were met by payment in coin. Only in a

[7] Mueller, *Procuratori*, pp. 163–4.

[8] A. P. Usher, *The Early History of Deposit Banking in Mediterranean Europe*, i (Cambridge, Mass., 1934), pp. 239, 256–7.

[9] R. de Roover, *Money, Banking and Credit in Medieval Bruges* (Cambridge, Mass., 1948), pp. 171ff.

[10] R. de Roover, *L'Evolution de la lettre de change (XIVe–XVIIIe siècles)* (Paris, 1953), pp. 24ff.

[11] In 1318 this was increased to 5,000 lire to compensate for the decline of the lira. Mueller, 'Bank money', p. 73.

[12] Usher, *Deposit Banking*, pp. 239–42.

[13] Two pisan cheques of 1374 are illustrated as document 155 in Federigo Melis, *Documenti per la Storia Economica* (Florence, 1972). See his sections on banking, pp. 75–104, 463–96 and also his *Note di storia della banca pisana nel Trecento* (Pisa, 1955). On the use of cheques in fourteenth- and fifteenth-century Florence see Marco Spallanzani, 'A note on florentine banking in the Renaissance: orders of payment and cheques', *Journal of European Economic History*, vii (1978), 145–65. Similar written orders to pay came into use in Genoa and Barcelona, but venetian banks continued to insist on the presence of the payer, or of an agent with a notarized power of attorney, to give oral instructions. Mueller, 'Bank money', 47–96.

limited number of cities was there a sufficiently developed system of *banche del giro* or *banche di scritte* for payment to be made frequently and easily by transfer in the books of the bank, and even in these cities banking facilities were only ever available to a relatively restrained number of people. Around 1500, perhaps 4,000 out of a total adult male population of 30,000 in Venice had current bank accounts. That is to say that nearly 90% did not have such accounts, and, of those who did, a high proportion, precisely a half, were noble.[14] This emphasizes that, even in Venice, by far the most commercially sophisticated city in Europe in 1500, the vast majority of transactions, although not the largest ones, were still carried out with actual metallic coin. In less advanced cities, the use of coin was even more dominant. It was not until the seventeenth century that anything except coined money made a really significant contribution to the internal money supply outside a few favoured cities. Even then this was only true in England and Holland, which were by that time the most advanced countries commercially. Right up to the nineteenth century the role of coined money was in many places dominant, and everywhere important. It is virtually only in the twentieth century that coin has been relegated to the role of small change in the money supply. These later developments took place in societies which were increasingly urban and industrialized. Medieval Europe was predominantly rural and overwhelmingly agricultural. In such a society the money supply was the supply of metallic coin, with only insignificant exceptions. In most places the role of the money changer did not develop further, but continued to be strictly limited to the exchanging of currency in one metal for that in another.

INTERNATIONAL BANKING

International banking was developing at the same time as local banking. The great growth in the scale of international trade in the thirteenth century led, amongst other things, to the first appearance of international banking. However, the appearance of international banking in its turn contributed to the transformation of the way in which international trade was carried on. The use of various instruments of payment, out of which the bill of exchange was gradually perfected, depended on frequent contacts and mutual confidence between merchants.

No longer did every prospective purchaser or returning vendor need to carry with him large and stealable quantities of precious metals, whether in coin, or in marks of silver, or ounces of gold, depending on the trading area. Instead a manager could send and receive remittances from his factors and agents by bills of exchange without moving around Europe himself. This transformation of the methods of trade, which enabled a merchant to manage

[14] F. C. Lane, 'Venetian bankers 1496–1533', *Journal of Political Economy*, xlv (1937), 187–206, reprinted in his *Venice and History* (Baltimore, 1966). Robert S. Lopez, 'Une histoire à trois niveaux: la circulation monétaire', *Mélanges en l'honneur de Fernand Braudel*, ii (1973), 335–41 extrapolating from de Roover's work, suggested that in Bruges around 1400, only 1 in 40 of the total population, perhaps 1 in 10 of the adult males, had bank accounts.

an international business without leaving his own home city, was so radical that de Roover christened it 'the commercial revolution of the thirteenth century'. The bill of exchange seems to have evolved into its definitive form by the end of the thirteenth century. Its evolution had begun over a hundred years earlier with the notarized *instrumentum ex causa cambii*. The surviving genoese notarial registers include some such instruments from the late twelfth century, mostly involving transactions between Genoa and the Champagne fairs. In the thirteenth century, the Champagne fairs were not only the principal bullion market of Europe but also the principal money market as well, and the forcing house for the development of the bill of exchange. By the first half of the fourteenth century it had become normal to make commercial payments by bill of exchange between a wide range of cities in western Europe.

The normal commercial bill of exchange involved four parties. First there was the deliverer or remitter who wished to remit money to a distant place. He paid his money to a taker or drawer, who drew up a bill on that place, which he gave to the remitter. The remitter sent his bill to the payee, who presented it to the payer, who was, of course, a correspondent, or agent of the drawer. The latter normally accepted the bill, and as acceptor became bound to pay the bill on maturity. A bill became due for payment after a customary period known as *usance*. Custom varied. Between some places it was a fixed time after the original drawing up of a bill. Between others it was a fixed time after the acceptor had sight of the bill.[15] If, however, the payer refused to pay, the payee had a notarized statement of protest drawn up declaring why the payer refused to pay. The protest was then sent back to the deliverer, who had legal redress against the drawer of the bill.[16] Until the sixteenth century, when their connotation changed, protests were relatively rare, and the whole system of international banking relied on the confident expectation that bills would normally be accepted by the payers named in them. When the payer had paid the payee, he would enter it up against the account of the drawer. This would frequently be balanced out over a period of time with other commercial or banking transactions. If the account remained unbalanced, a further bill needed to be drawn in the opposite direction to settle the balance. Sometimes such bills were drawn at once and a rechange operation followed immediately on the first exchange transaction. Although medieval bills were not discounted, as far as we can ascertain at present, they became negotiable in the last decades of the fourteenth century. However examples of such change of beneficiary are rare before the late sixteenth century. In the two earliest known examples, dating from 1386 and 1394, the change of beneficiary was written out on a separate piece of paper which was then pinned to the bill. However by 1410 'endorsement' had developed, the

[15] See below pp. 315–21 for details of usance between the principal banking places of the mid-fifteenth century, and the time that bill-carrying couriers were expected to take on the road between some of them. See diagram p. xxxii.

[16] Details of a considerable number of such protests, sent back by their agents and correspondents, remain among the Medici papers in Florence, and were published by Dr. Giulia Camerani Marri in *I Documenti Commerciali del Fondo Diplomatico Mediceo* (Florence, 1951).

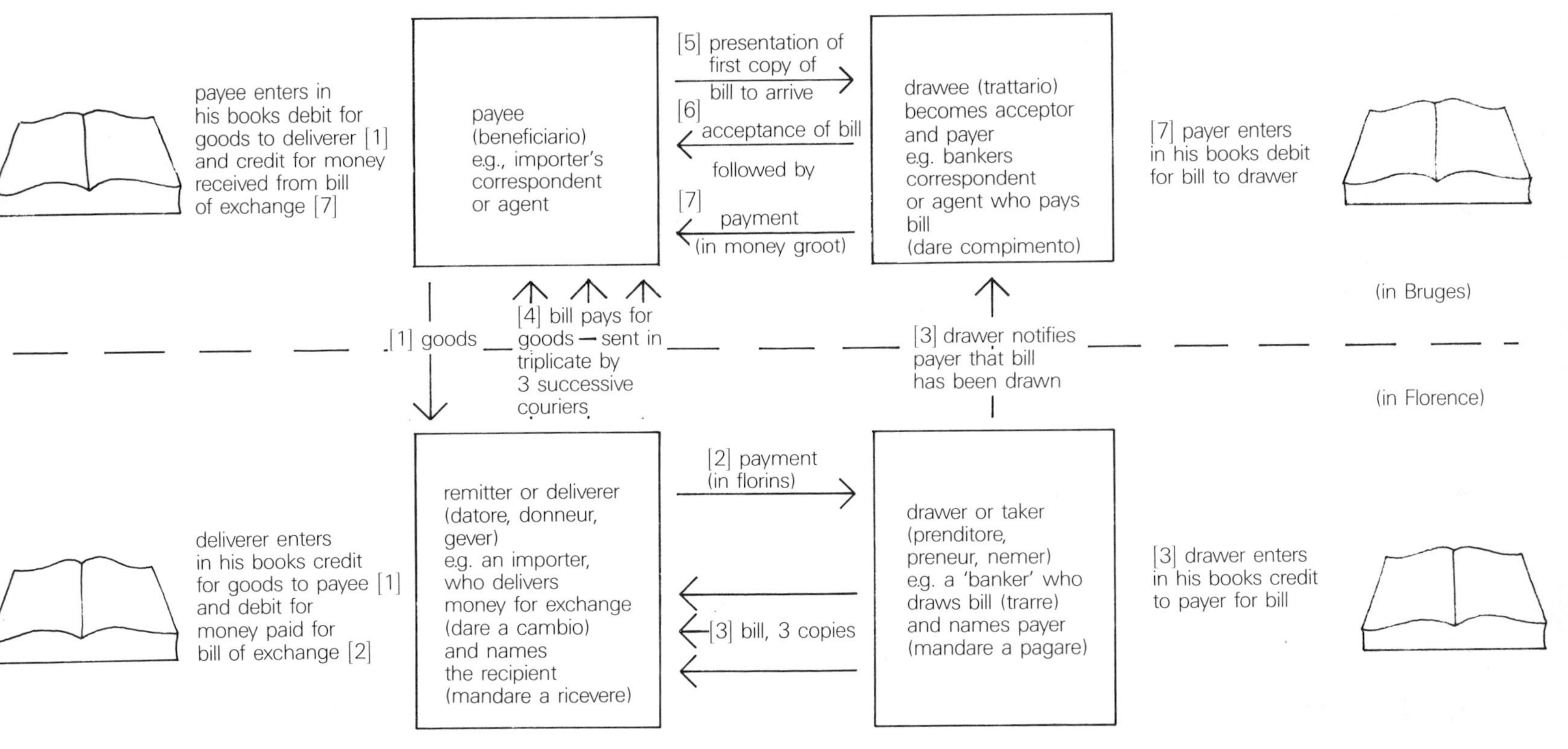

The parties to a normal bill of exchange, e.g., one to enable an importer in Florence to pay his correspondent in Bruges

The steps in the operation described on p.xxxi are numbered here in the order in which they took place.
The same numbers are used to indicate the point at which the various parties made entries in their books.

practice of writing the change of payee on the back of the bill itself.[17]

The medieval merchant-banking network was focused on the great trading cities of north Italy, particularly of Tuscany. Inside Italy bills of exchange could be acquired very easily, for practically every city of importance was a banking place. In the fifteenth century bills could normally be obtained easily in Bologna, Ferrara, Florence, Genoa, Lucca, Milan, Naples, Palermo, Perugia, Pisa, Siena, Venice and 'in Apulia' presumably at Barletta. They were also sometimes obtainable at Aquileia, Camerino, Cremona, Fano, Gaeta, Padua, Pesaro, Piacenza and Viterbo. Outside Italy fully fledged banking places were much more spread out however. The only places at which bills of exchange could certainly be purchased over long periods of time were Avignon in the Rhône valley, Montpellier in southern France, Barcelona, Valencia and Seville in the Iberian peninsular, London in England, Bruges in the Netherlands, and Paris in northern France, until it ceased to be a banking place when it stopped being a royal residence. Only the last three were outside mediterranean Europe. Bills could also always be found at the papal curia, not only at its permanent homes in Rome and Avignon, but also at temporary residences of the pope, such as Florence, Constance or Basle. Bills of exchange could also usually be purchased during the greater international fairs. Bills could therefore be purchased at an early date at the Champagne fair towns, and later at Geneva, and then at Lyons and Medina del Campo. At a great many other cities they could sometimes be found, for example in Lisbon, or Palma de Majorca or in those cities of south Germany which were to become of such importance from the fifteenth century.[18] At the beginning of the century a small number of south german merchant-bankers were already beginning to emulate the italian multi-branched companies. Some of them, based on Nuremberg and Prague, had branches at Krakow and Buda, as well as at Bruges, Milan and Venice.[19]

Even between these cities, although the majority of transactions could be carried out by bill of exchange, any eventual imbalance had ultimately to be settled up in gold or silver. When an imbalance between two banking places became too great, the rate of exchange rose (or fell) to such an extent that it passed one of the specie points. In other words, it temporarily became cheaper, in one direction, to transport bullion with all its attendant costs and risks, than to buy a bill of exchange. The net quantity of silver or gold transported from Bruges to London, or Paris to Florence, did not diminish as a result of the development of bills of exchange, but the amount of business that it represented was increased out of all proportion. The bill of exchange

[17] Raymond de Roover, 'Le marché monétaire au moyen âge et au début des temps modernes' *Revue Historique*, xciv (1970), 33–4, henceforth 'Le marché monétaire'; Henri Lapeyre, 'Une lettre de change endossée en 1430', *Annales Economies Sociétés Civilisations*, xiii (1958), 260–4; Federigo Melis, 'Una girata cambiaria del 1410 nell'archivio datini di prato', *Economia e Storia*, V (1958), 412–21.

[18] De Roover, *La lettre de change*, 'Le marché monétaire', 9–16; Allan Evans, manuscript notes at the American Numismatic Society, New York. Most, but far from all, the exchange rates in the *Handbook* fall within the geographical area outlined above. See maps below pp. 314, 352 and 366.

[19] Wolfgang von Stromer, *Oberdeutsche Hochfinanz 1350–1450* (1970).

enormously multiplied the supply of money available for international transactions between these cities.

Although bills of exchange were developed by merchants for merchants, they very quickly came to be used by non-merchants as well. Successive popes were the most considerable non-commercial users of bills of exchange. Papal collectors in England and the Low Countries, northern France, the spanish kingdoms and Italy normally used bills of exchange to transmit the money they had collected to the apostolic camera at Avignon in the first half of the fourteenth century.[20] Bishops travelling to the curia no longer needed to ensure that their chamberlains were loaded down with an adequate quantity of mark bars of silver. The cameral merchants to whom prelates and papal collectors frequently entrusted the transport of the money due to the 'apostolic camera' were most commonly the leading banking houses of the day. They already had a multitude of branches in many parts of christendom, and were managing the commercial flow of money around Europe. They were naturally accustomed to moving sums of money in the same direction with great regularity. Firms such as the Bonsignori of Siena, the Bardi, the Peruzzi and the Accaiuoli of Florence, the Malabayla of Asti, and the Alberti, and the Medici of Florence handled this business in turn. Prelates sent the 'common services' and other sums that they owed at their own expense. However papal collectors did so at the expense of the *camera*. The cameral accounts therefore give a clear picture of how the system worked in practice.

The papal collectors gathered a great deal of the money involved in small sums, in silver, and even in black money. They had to take what they had collected to a local money changer and exchange it for gold, since, at this point, they were moving from the circuit of silver to the circuit of gold. For example, in March 1386, Pons de Cros, the papal collector at Le Puy in France, paid 8 *livres* to change 400 *livres tournois* of silver into gold. This represented the exchange of nearly 10,000 *blancs*, or of even more coins if it was in smaller denominations, presumably from a great iron-bound chest in which it had been accumulated, into 400 gold *francs*, which one may equally presume were in a small leather bag. The rates paid by papal collectors suggest that the usual charge for such a service was 4d. or 5d. in the pound, although they were occasionally charged as little as 3d. in the pound or as much as 8d. This was, of course, the opposite operation from the service performed by money changers for manufacturers who sold their goods, cloth for example, on the international market for gold, but needed to pay their employees in silver.

The papal collectors then had the choice of carrying the gold to the camera themselves, sending someone whom they trusted with it, or else purchasing a bill of exchange. Because 'banking places' were so widely dispersed outside Italy, papal collectors had frequently to travel some distance to purchase bills of exchange. The papal collector at Toledo, for example, had to go to Seville, over 300 kilometres away. In March 1386, Pons de Cros was fortunate enough

[20] Yves Renouard, *Les Relations des papes d'Avignon et des compagnies commerciales et bancaires de 1316 à 1378* (Bibliothèque des écoles françaises d'Athènes et de Rome, cli, 1941).

to find someone in Le Puy itself from whom he could purchase a bill of exchange with the 400 gold *francs* that he had obtained from the money changer. He usually had to take the risks of carrying the gold himself, but on this occasion he was able to carry a bill to Avignon instead. He was also fortunate in that this service only cost him 5 *francs*, just over 1% of the sum involved. Bills of exchange rarely cost as little as this. Up to 5% of the sum transferred was commonly charged. Over long distances it could be higher. For example, at Seville, in June 1393, the papal sub-collector Miguel Rodriguez purchased a bill of exchange from the genoese Francesco di Gentile with 400 gold *doblas*, payable at Avignon by Frederigo Imperiale within fifteen days of being presented to him. On this occasion the sub-collector was not going to Avignon himself, nor had he a messenger to send, so that di Gentile himself transmitted the bill of exchange to Imperiale, who, just under six weeks later, paid the sum of 480 cameral florins into the papal treasury in gold. In Seville, however, 400 *doblas* were worth 533 cameral florins. Rodriguez had in effect paid 53 florins, 10% of the sum remitted, for the service provided.[21] All these were straightforward bills of exchange. They were used quite simply to remit sums of money from one place to another. A service was provided and charged for. How di Gentile and Imperiale carried out the business between them was no concern of Rodriguez. Patently they were in regular correspondence with each other, had accounts with each other, and could draw bills on each other as well as send goods to each other. From time to time, they would naturally have to settle up, but if possible they would do so by buying a bill from a third party, drawn on a fourth party, who wanted money transmitted in the opposite direction. However, there were basic imbalances between certain places. In the last resort, gold or silver had actually to be carried from place to place. Gold, for example, was commonly carried from Seville to Genoa. Before this stage was reached, a very great deal of business had passed in each direction. The combination of a great body of bills of exchange with occasional remittances in precious metals, primarily gold in the fourteenth and fifteenth centuries, represented an enormous commercial advance on the older pattern of carrying a vast bulk of silver in bars on practically every occasion. The overall contribution of the papacy to this business was slight, although for the limited number of firms who acted as papal bankers it was of considerable importance. However, owing to the preservation of papal records it is the papal business that is most clearly visible to us, yet the papacy were only using a system set up for commercial purposes.

Noblemen, whether on pilgrimage or representing their princes on embassies could also avail themselves of bills of exchange. There were, however, limits. Certain international political payments, such as wages to keep whole armies in the field for protracted periods, subsidies for expensive allies, or royal ransoms and dowries, could easily prove too large for the normal commercial system to handle, and so had to be transmitted largely, or wholly, in silver, or

[21] Jean Favier, *Les Finances pontificales à l'époque du grande schisme d'occident 1378–1409* (Bibliothèque des écoles françaises d'Athènes et de Rome, ccxi, 1966), pp. 451–79.

gold.[22] Nevertheless, a very large proportion of normal payments was made by bill of exchange by the early fourteenth century between the cities in which the medieval merchant banking network then operated.

However, outside this range of banking places, even ordinary international payments had still to be made primarily in bullion. Where there was a large and continuous imbalance of trade, as there was between the mining centres of Europe and the commercially advanced areas, a bill of exchange system had little chance of developing and bills were very rarely to be purchased. In the fourteenth century, papal collectors in Poland normally had to take bullion to Bruges or Venice before they could make use of the west european banking system by acquiring bills of exchange to remit to the curia.[23] Until the fifteenth century even the most prominent trading cities of northern Germany, such as Lübeck, basically remained outside this network of exchanges.

Between christian Europe, muslim north Africa, and the Levant, the use of bills was little developed, although the scale of trade was very large, and the division of labour between manager, carrier and factor developed early. This was so because there were not only chronic imbalances of trade here, but also decided differences in the values given to gold and to silver in the three areas concerned. Since Europe was a silver producer, silver was less valued in Europe than Africa, and gold less valued in Africa than Europe. When this disproportion in value was sufficiently great to overcome the risks and costs of the voyage across the western Mediterranean it occasionally became worthwhile to take european silver to muslim north Africa (the Maghreb) in order to purchase african gold. Much more frequently it was common sense to carry additional silver southwards and gold northwards along with other more ordinary merchandise.[24] The balances both between christian Europe and the Levant, and between the Maghreb and the Levant were strongly in favour of the Levant, and were consequently settled by sending enormous quantities of european silver and african gold.[25] The near east itself had a generally

[22] For example when John XXII needed to pay 60,000 florins to the papal army in Lombardy in the summer of 1328 he had to send it in coin. It is an excellent example of the risks involved in carrying coin, for despite a guard of 150 cavalry, the convoy was ambushed and over half the money lost on the way. Giovanni Villani, *Cronica*, bk. x, ch. 91.

[23] Pope Benedict XII was unable to persuade the Bardi to set up a branch in Krakow. Armando Sapori, 'Gli Italiani in Polonia fino a tutto il quattrocento', *Studi di Storia Economica*, iii (Florence, 1967), 149–76.

[24] Andrew M. Watson, 'Back to gold—and silver', *Economic History Review*, 2nd ser., xx (1967), 1–34, and R. S. Lopez, 'Back to gold, 1252', *ibid.*, 2nd ser., ix (1956), 219–40.

[25] As a consequence of this chronic imbalance between the Maghreb and the Levant, payments from one to the other were normally made in coin, although a number of banking instruments had already evolved within the central countries of the muslim world. The *suftajda* there was the equivalent of the european bill of exchange, and the *ṡakk* of the cheque. Although the *suftajda* and the *ṡakk* evolved some two centuries before their western counterparts, there is no convincing evidence that they had any direct influence on european developments, apart from the possible derivation of the word 'cheque' from *ṡakk*. Indirect influence is probable, but too nebulous to pin down, for considerable numbers of eleventh- and twelfth-century italian merchants must have become aware of the banking instruments used by the muslim merchants with whom they traded in the cities of the eastern Mediterranean. Eliyahu Ashtor, 'Banking instruments between the muslim east and the christian west', *Journal of European Economic History*, i (1972), 553–73.

unfavourable balance with the middle and far east, so that much african gold and european silver continued further into Asia.[26] Such circumstances were the very antithesis of the more balanced trading conditions in which the bill of exchange evolved. Bills between european cities and those in the Maghreb or the Levant, or even Byzantium were therefore relatively rare. Nevertheless in the early fifteenth century bills could sometimes be obtained at or for Constantinople or Pera, for Alexandria, for Caffa in the Crimea, for Famagusta in Cyprus, and for Rhodes and Chios.

International banking and local banking soon came to be combined, where that was possible. Thus bills of exchange could be bought by debiting a bank account and their proceeds credited to a bank account. Raymond de Roover has described how this was done in Bruges and Barcelona; Reinhold Mueller in Venice, and Jacques Heers in Genoa. Heers gives a late but vivid example of how important this combination of the two forms of banking became. Between 1456 and 1459 an account book of the Piccamiglio records the receipt of payments from abroad by bills of exchange totalling 159,710 genoese lire. Of these only 11,753 lire worth of bills were paid to them in cash. All the rest, over 92.5% of them, were met by crediting their accounts in local giro banks.[27]

TRANSFER OR CREDIT

All normal bills of exchange involved a transfer element, since their function was to transmit money from one place to another. They normally also involved an exchange operation, unless the two places concerned were using the same currency, like Pisa and Florence. However, one of the principal problems presented by bills of exchange is that of how much there was a credit element in such bills, over and above the exchange and transfer elements. The late Raymond de Roover, whose expertise on medieval exchange was unrivalled in his lifetime, was by far the most eloquent protagonist of the view that every bill of exchange involved a credit element. He quite rightly pointed out that every deliverer was deprived of the use of his money until his agent, the payee, received payment in another place at a later time. From this he assumed that the deliverer always demanded an interest payment from the drawer to compensate for the inability to use the money himself in the meanwhile. I would agree that on certain occasions the credit element was indeed vital to the bill, as for example when a merchant who wished to purchase goods for transmission to another place went to a 'banker' and effectively asked him to invest in his enterprise. In return he would offer a bill of exchange drawn on his agent in the place to which the goods were destined, which ordered his agent to pay the banker's agent a sum which passed on some of the profit of the enterprise to the 'banker'. In such cases

[26] E. Ashtor, *Les métaux précieux et la balance des payements du proche-orient à la basse époque* (Paris, 1971).

[27] Mueller, 'Bank money', pp. 57–9; Jacques Heers, *Gênes au XVe siècle* (abridged edn., Paris, 1971), p. 90.

the 'banker' was clearly investing in an enterprise and depriving himself of the use of money which he might have used directly in trade himself. A well-known hypothetical narrative ostensibly presented by the merchants of Antwerp to the doctors of Paris in 1530 eloquently describes the procedure:

> The diligence and vigilance of merchants has brought them to such great subtlety and art that they have found a way to make of money a merchandise like cloth, silk, spices, pearls, or wool, wherein there is profit and loss, risk and venture. This business is very profitable to traders, some of whom would often be unable to send their goods abroad, to dispatch their cargoes, or to meet their commitments from day to day, were it not for this new found commerce of money, by which a man who has money gains and another who has none and who takes it from him gains likewise, since he is in a stronger position to carry on his business than if he had no such remedy.

When the time came to baptize this business of the merchants they called it 'exchange', *because it bears some resemblance to real exchange* (my italics). The manner of dealing is as follows:

> Certain merchants are rich and powerful (though some more than others, for even those who have little deal in this way) and keep their money in cash and will not lay it out on merchandise unless it be for some good and plainly profitable stroke of business which according to the common opinion and judgement of merchants is bound to succeed. They believe that their profit will be neither so great nor so certain if they deal in merchandise as it is in this other business which they call 'exchange', and therefore they keep their money in coin in their strong-boxes, and earn their bread with it. And they do so as follows:
>
> There comes the time of the 'fair', as the merchants say, which is held at certain times of the year such as Christmas, Easter, June, and September, according to the places where the merchants are. In these fairs they pay one another what they owe, and sell their merchandise, and dispatch their cargoes to other parts. Now it so happens that at the time of the fair the merchants sometimes find themselves with a great deal of money, and sometimes with less, and then there are great rises and falls; and according to whether money is plentiful or scarce among merchants so do those who have money give it at more or less interest to those who are in need of it. This price, be it cheap or dear, is fixed by the merchants themselves according to the need which they know others feel for their money and according to the scarcity or abundance of money which they see prevails at a particular fair. This price which they set upon money they call the 'market-rate' (?*precio de la bolsa*) since no one claims for himself the power of fixing the rate but it is attributed to the community of the *bourse*, which is the place where the merchants meet.
>
> So much being understood, let us take the case of Anthony, a merchant who owes a thousand ducats at the current fair of mid-Lent, and who has not got the money. Anthony goes to a broker (the person who acts as go-between among the merchants) and says to him:
>
> 'I need a thousand ducats. Let someone give them to me in cash, and I will repay them at the May fair at Medina del Campo in Spain.'
>
> The broker replies: 'Very well, I will undertake to procure the money.' And he goes to one of the merchants who announces that he keeps his money in cash to earn his living with it and says:

'Will you give me a thousand ducats, to be repaid at the May fair in Spain in six weeks' time?'

Ferdinand replies: 'What is the market-rate?' which means 'how many *plaques* must I give here to receive a ducat in Spain?'

The broker answers: 'Sir, you must give 36 *plaques*[28] here and you will receive a ducat there, which is worth 37½ *plaques*. This is the current market-rate, which is sometimes higher, sometimes lower.'

If Ferdinand is satisfied with the rate, he asks who requires the money. The broker replies: 'Anthony, whom you well know.' If Ferdinand thinks that Anthony is a solid, honest man who will repay the money he answers: 'Very well, I am satisfied, and will give him one thousand ducats at the rate of 36 *plaques* to the ducat.' Anthony gives him a letter or a bill requesting Anthony's factor or partner in Spain to pay Ferdinand's factor or partner there 1,000 ducats for the May fair at the rate of 37½ *plaques* to the ducat.

This transfer of money, so much more being paid afterwards at the fair on each coin, is what is known as 'exchange'.

It should be noted that Ferdinand, who gives the money to Anthony on the understanding that he shall repay it with the agreed increment to his partner or servant at the May fair at Medina del Campo in Spain, intends that the said partner or servant shall in his turn give the money to some other person who is similarly in need of it, so that at the June fair Ferdinand here in Antwerp may recover his thousand ducats together with whatever increment he may have gained on the two occasions when he and his servant have given them—the first time, Ferdinand here in Flanders, and the second, his servant at Medina del Campo.

But it sometimes (though rarely) happens that when the money is sent back from Medina money is very plentiful among the merchants, and no one will take it except at a market-rate, which is so low that when Ferdinand recovers his money in Antwerp he has been without it for three or four months and has gained nothing. Indeed, he may even have lost. For although he sent the money to Spain with the intention of gaining the same increment on the rechange back to Antwerp, it may happen that money is so abundant in the place to which it was sent that he loses on the return transaction, and this loss may be greater than the profit on the first occasion.

It is a contract which is most necessary to the Christian republic, in that it supplies the diverse countries with merchandise. For the merchants often keep their fortunes laid out in such a manner that they could not dispatch new cargoes, send goods to countries where great need and shortage might be felt, meet their daily commitments or maintain their credit, were it not for this instrument of exchange.

Both he who gives and he who takes in exchange have every intention of making use of each other, and both understand the business equally, and freely agree upon the rate, and both are gainers and thereby serve the republic.[29]

In this long narrative the credit element is as clearly evident as the transfer and exchange elements. Professor de Roover provided numerous illustrations

[28] *Plaques*, *patards* or *stuivers*, coins of two *gros* or *groten* current in the Netherlands.

[29] Extract translated by Marjorie E. H. Grice-Hutchinson in *The School of Salamanca: readings in Spanish monetary theory 1544–1605* (Oxford, 1952) from text printed in full by J. A. Goris, *Etudes sur les colonies marchandes méridionales à Anvers de 1488 à 1567* (1925), pp. 510–45.

of occasions of this type. He maintained that, as in the hypothetical case made out at Antwerp in 1530, the interest rate was represented by the difference between the exchange rates in the two places. From the reports sent by Datini's correspondents in Bruges and Barcelona he was able to draw a graph of the rates quoted in the two places for exchanges between them and demonstrate the continuing difference in the rates in the two places. I reproduce his graph below (Graph 1, p. xli). The figures on which it is based are not included in the *Handbook*, although a representative selection of the rates of exchange both from Barcelona to Florence and from Bruges to Florence do appear (see pp. 139–44 and 215–17). At almost any time between 1395 and 1405, a bill drawn at these rates either from Bruges on Barcelona, or from Barcelona on Bruges, and then rechanged by the payee, would have brought a profit for the deliverer. An exchange and rechange which began in May 1404 would, for example, have brought the deliverer a profit of just over 5% in something under four months.[30] Professor de Roover believed that the size of the profit, as well as being a function of the length of time for which the money was tied up, naturally fluctuated, like other interest rates, with the availability of investment funds. Hence the merchant notebooks regularly contain notes of when there was *larghezza* or *stretteza* in the key places.

This is indeed the de Roover orthodoxy, backed with an immense amount of information. Unfortunately not all rates for bills will fit the pattern. If an apparently similar graph is drawn from the Borromei papers, it shows, on the contrary, that between 1436 and 1439, a bill drawn either from Venice on London, or from Venice on Bruges, and then rechanged by the payee, would almost always have brought a loss to the deliverer (Graph 2, p. xlii).[31] This is quite patently unbelievable. The Borromei bills do not fit the de Roover pattern. Quite patently they cannot be investment bills. If they are regarded as straightforward transfers of funds, they become much more comprehensible. Deliverers who actually needed their money in another place were paying for its transfer. In November 1439 the two rates were under 6% apart, which would imply a charge of just under 3% to a deliverer wishing to have his money transferred either from London or from Venice. There would be no rechange, since the deliverer actually required the money sent to remain in the payee's hands. There were many such occasions when a deliverer mainly wished to transfer funds to another place, and was prepared to pay for the transfer. He did not lose the use of the money, because he had no use for it where it then was. His advantage was to have the use of the money in another place as rapidly and as cheaply as possible.

There were thus two quite different types of occasion when bills of exchange were used. On the second type of occasion the transfer element was of primary importance. A merchant, papal collector or travelling nobleman

[30] *Bruges Money Market c.1400* (Brussels, 1968), pp. 24–5, 35. *Usance* was 30 days from sight, and the courier between Bruges and Barcelona normally took 19 or 20 days according to Uzzano's notebook.

[31] G. Biscaro, 'Il banco Borromei e compagno di Londra 1436–1439', *Archivio Storico Lombardo*, 4th ser., xix (1913), 37–126. This combines the graphs on pp. 202 and 203. The *par* value provided by the gold content of the ducat and the noble has also been added.

Ecu of 22 groten in sueldos of Barcelona in Bruges and in Barcelona 1395-1404

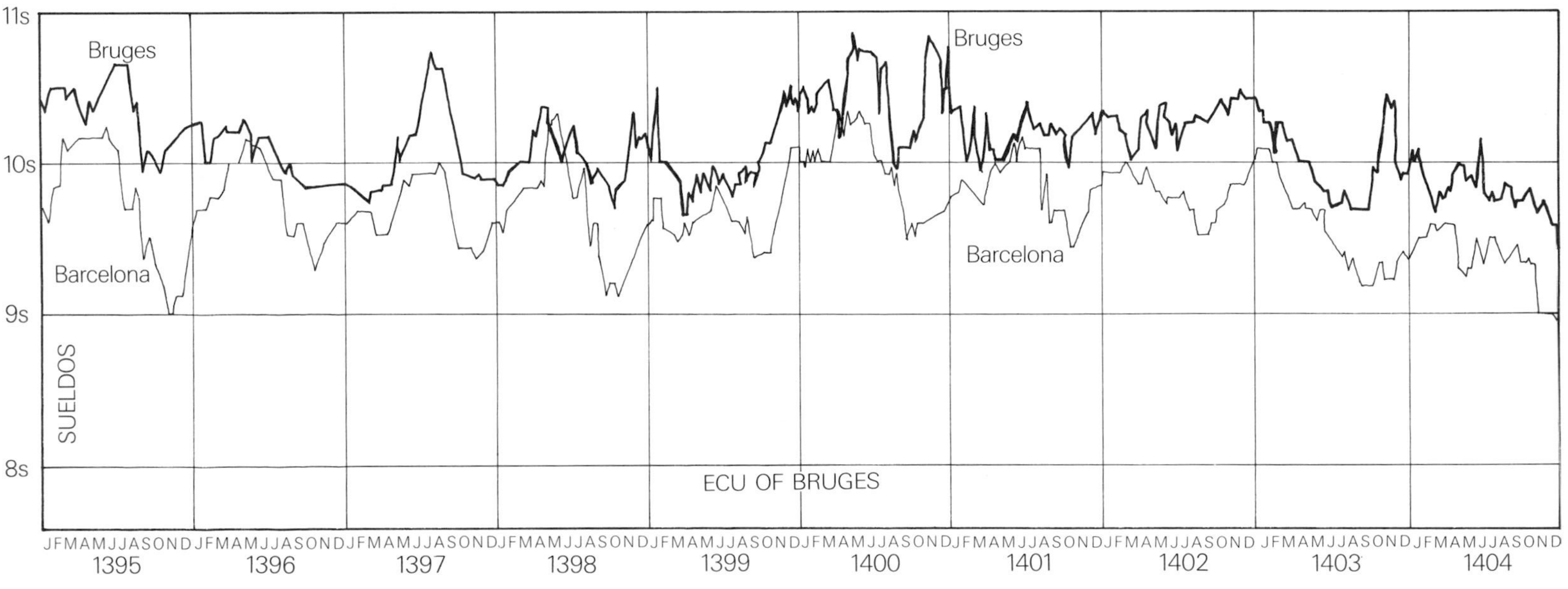

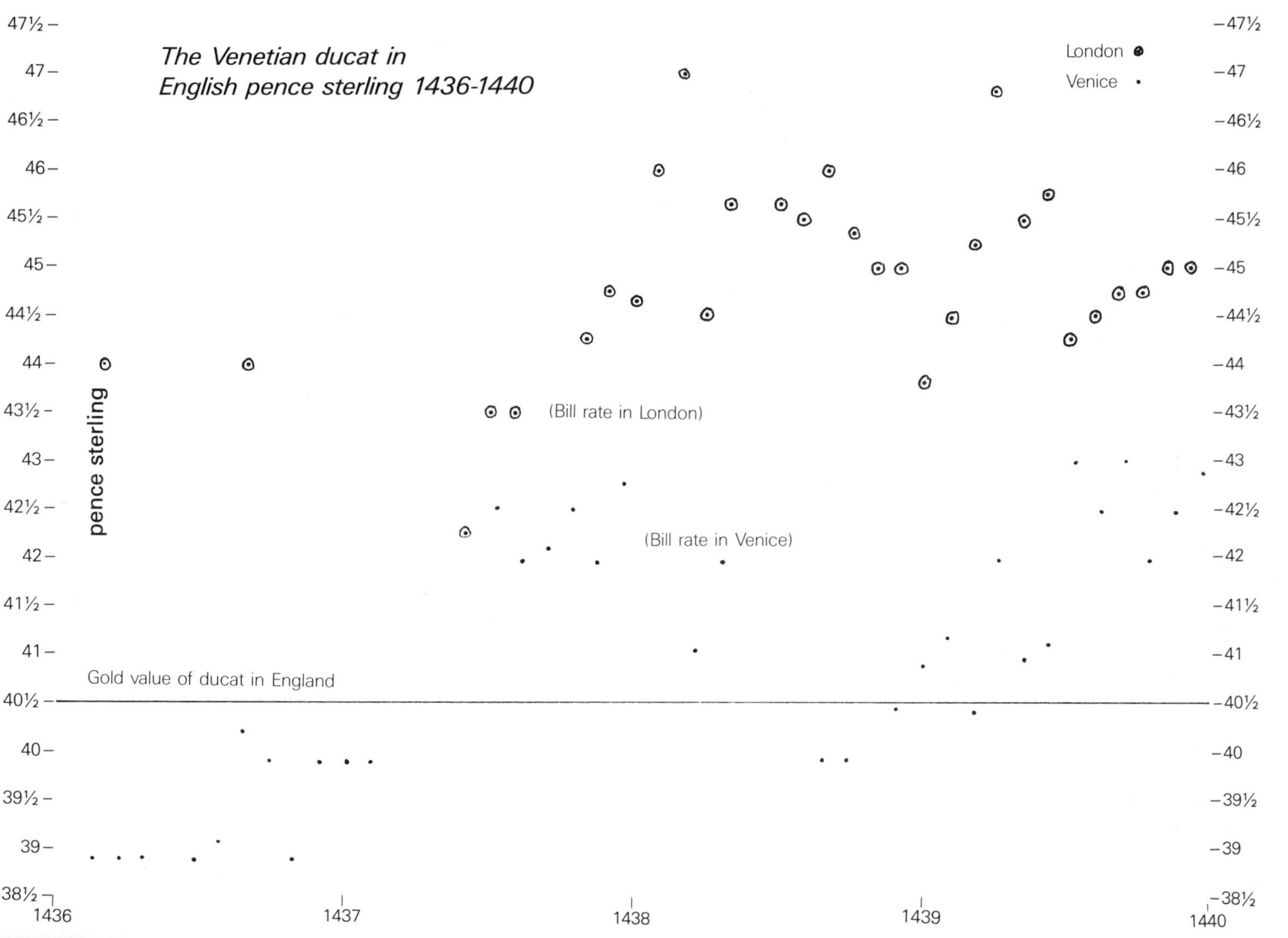

The Venetian ducat in
English pence sterling 1436-1440
London
Venice
pence sterling
(Bill rate in London)
(Bill rate in Venice)
Gold value of ducat in England
47½
47
46½
46
45½
45
44½
44
43½
43
42½
42
41½
41
40½
40
39½
39
38½
1436
1437
1438
1439
1440

simply wished to transfer funds from one place to another and the bill of exchange was the means of doing so. He delivered his money to a 'banker' who drew a bill instructing his own agent in the relevant place to pay the deliverer's agent, or even the deliverer himself, the equivalent sum. The 'banker' performed a service and explicitly charged for it. De Roover failed to see that the second type of occasion could exist as well as the first. Numerous examples show that it did.

One of the earliest transfer transactions, for which evidence survives, took place in 1161. On this occasion Domenico Centocori delivered 40 *perpers* in Constantinople to Stefanno Mozzorbo, to be repaid by Mozzorbo's agent, Fantinum da Mulinum, at 'Armiro' in Negroponte *michi vel meum missum*. The notarized instrument survives, and the receipt, which shows that this turned out to be a three party transaction not a four party one, for Centocori travelled to 'Armiro' and was himself paid by da Mulinum. He avoided the risk of carrying gold.[32]

It was this evolving system of transfers that Giraldus Cambrensis used as early as 1203 when he arranged for money to be sent to him at Troyes from England.[33]

It was for the purpose of transferring money, received from the sales of finished cloth, back to Florence at the beginning of the fourteenth century that the Del Bene agent in Naples regularly bought bills of exchange with the proceeds. The Del Bene themselves similarly bought bills in Florence to transfer money to their agent in Champagne to enable him to purchase fresh supplies of unfinished french and flemish cloth.[34]

Throughout the later middle ages papal collectors were always faced with the problem of whether it was cheaper to arrange to travel, or to send their servants to travel, with what they had collected, or to purchase bills of exchange which obviated both the necessity, and the risk, of travelling with large sums of money. For them the transfer function of the bill was paramount. Papal collectors commonly paid up to 5% of the sum involved for its transfer at the end of the fourteenth century.[35]

It would seem then that there were two sets of rates for bills of exchange, one for what the Antwerp narrative called *real exchange*, for those who wished to transfer funds, and the other for 'exchange', for those who wished to invest funds.

Each type of source naturally provides evidence of only the rates of exchange that were relevant to its author. Papal collectors only wrote down what it actually cost them to transfer money. On the other hand de Roover's Datini evidence was very largely drawn not from the bills themselves, but from the rates reported by correspondents. Since these correspondents were on the inside of the merchant-banking network it would have been natural for them to quote the investment rate, since the object of the information was to

[32] E. Ashtor, in *Journal of European Economic History*, i (1972), 571.
[33] George B. Parks, *The English Traveller to Italy*, i (Rome, 1954), 209ff.
[34] A. Sapori, *Una compagnia di Calimala ai primi del Trecento* (Florence, 1932).
[35] J. Favier, *Les Finances pontificales*, pp. 451–79.

inform the recipients whether or not a profitable rechange could be made and so to encourage, or to discourage, them from investing money in bills of exchanges. The Borromei information, on the contrary, is drawn from actual bills, and would seem therefore to represent simple transfers of funds without any credit element.

One can hypothesize a little about the sort of credit structures that would make one sort of bill more common for different purposes at different times and in different places. In England around 1300, for example, credit in the wool trade was primarily credit from buyer to seller; in 1450, it was primarily from seller to buyer. The buyer paid only one third of the purchase price at once. In 1300 an italian merchant buying wool in England needed to raise investment funds before he could purchase english wool. He could do this by selling a bill of exchange to an investor at the investment rate. In 1450 an english merchant selling wool in the Netherlands would want to buy a bill of exchange at the transfer rate with the proceeds of his sales, so that his money could be transferred back to England to pay in arrears for the wool he had just sold.

As well as the investment bill which de Roover took to be normal, he also concentrated on a special sort of investment bill. He pointed out that bills of exchange were also used by those who did not wish to transmit money from one place to another at all. Such a person would sell a bill of exchange to an investor, drawn on a third party in another place, without any intention of sending his goods there or dispatching any cargo thither. When the payer was presented with the bill, he would meet it with another bill, drawn on the original seller of the first bill, who would have to meet it by repaying the investor the investment with accrued charges. These might be the normal charges for the double exchange, based on the difference in the investment rates for bills between the two places, in which case there was a slight risk for the investor, or the charges might be specified in advance, in which case the investor was certain of his profit. This sort of 'dry' exchange in which no money was transferred was a thinly disguised loan especially if the rates were fixed. The disguise became even thinner if the third party was another branch of the same bank, or did not even exist. The pre-adjusted rates make yet a third group of rates to add to straightforward transfer rates and investment rates.

Such non-transferring bills of exchange, used purely as credit instruments, may have developed by the mid-thirteenth century. Sivéry has recently suggested that an associate of the Bonsignori obtained 11½% from such a bill in 1252.[36] By the early fourteenth century, they certainly existed and were frowned upon. In 1301 the venetian government clamped down on such bills, and only permitted bills of exchange if the money involved was actually to be used in the place to which the bill was to be sent. The consuls of the merchants were instructed not to register any except licit exchanges.[37] It is not

[36] Gérard Sivéry, 'Mouvements de capitaux et taux d'interêt en occident au XIIIe siècle', *Annales E.S.C.*, xxxviii (1983), 143.

[37] Mueller, *Procuratori*, p. 367.

entirely clear why they should have been regarded in this way, or indeed why such subterfuge should have been necessary in an environment where money could be borrowed, and interest paid on it, quite overtly both for commercial and civic purposes.

De Roover read widely in the scholastic writings of the fifteenth and sixteenth centuries, many of which disapproved of loans as usurious. Another strand of scholastic writing, going back at least to the late thirteenth century relied on the doctrine of *lucrum cessans* to justify commercial loans. *Lucrum cessans* was the profit that the lender might have made, if he had traded with his money himself, instead of lending it to another to do so. In 1271 Hostiensis wrote 'If some merchant, who is accustomed to pursue trade, and the commerce of the fairs and there profit much, has . . . lent [me] money with which he would have done business, I remain obliged from this to his *interesse*.'[38]

A quite specific example of loans being available overtly and separated from exchange is provided by the sienese Vincenti firm in 1260. They needed money to invest in their export business. They obviously had the option of borrowing in Siena. They quoted two interest rates for loans in Siena, one between merchants and one for non-merchants, i.e. for consumption loans. They regarded even the rate for loans between merchants as too high. It was high because investment funds were very short in Siena on account of the heavy taxation for the war with Florence. They then considered whether they would do better to borrow in London or at one of the Champagne fairs, and concluded that, for the time being, it was cheapest to borrow in Champagne. They therefore instructed their agent in Provins to borrow money to be ready to pay bills that they had drawn on him. These bills were not themselves instruments of credit: they were merely the means of transferring overtly borrowed money.[39]

Some people even continued to regard all investment in bills of exchange, not merely in dry exchange, with suspicion. In March 1390 Domenico di Cambio wrote to Francesco Datini 'I would rather earn 12% with merchandise than 18% on exchange dealings.'[40] Others regarded it as a perfectly ordinary form of investment. The florentine nobleman, Buonocorso Pitti, by turns adventurer, cloth manufacturer and politician, who invested at one time or another in saffron, horses, wine, wool and land, in 1391 also invested 5,000 florins, the proceeds of wool sales and successful gambling for high stakes, with Luigi and Gherardo Canigiani, and accepted bills of exchange in return. He made no comment in his private notebook on the morality of what he was doing, but merely congratulated himself 'this money greatly improved the credit enjoyed by the Canigiani.'[41] Nevertheless the whole problem of how licit it was to deal in exchange remained open for some tender consciences. It was this problem which exercised the writer of the long narrative supposedly

[38] J. T. Noonan, *The Scholastic Analysis of Usury* (Cambridge, Mass., 1957).

[39] *Lettere Volgari del secolo XIII scritte da Senese*, ed. C. Paoli and E. Piccolomini (Siena, 1871), p. 16.

[40] Iris Origo, *The World of San Bernardino* (1963), p. 88.

[41] *Two Memoirs of Renaissance Florence*, ed. Gene Brucker (New York, 1967), p. 47.

presented by the merchants of Antwerp to the doctors of Paris in 1530. Consciences may in fact have been growing tenderer at this time. The picture drawn there is not of dry exchange, but of investment in moving goods from place to place. It is not clear how common dry exchange, *cambio con la ricorsa* as it was then known, was in the sixteenth century outside the pages of scholastic writings. W. Brulez, for example, found no single case of such exchange and re-exchange in the della Faille papers.[42] However, this may have been because by the middle of the sixteenth century the notarized protest was becoming increasingly used as a cumbersome substitute for dry exchange. Another sixteenth-century way of getting round objections to exchange as a risky way of taking interest, was to make the interest element more overt. In other words, the investor delivered a round sum, of let us say 300 ducats, but the drawer wrote out a bill asking the payer to pay the foreign currency equivalent of a slightly higher sum, let us say 304½ ducats. A surprisingly large number of surviving sixteenth-century bills from Spain are for such sums. Such bills could then proceed as if only performing transfer and exchange functions.[43]

Although for long aware of the pitfalls of dry exchange as written up by de Roover, I have only recently become aware that the two types of occasion for sending other bills of exchange, which I have called here, transfer bills and investment bills, led to two different sets of rates, vaguely analogous to those existing today as 'Bank buys' and 'Bank sells'. I did not realize the difference early enough to distinguish them in this *Handbook*. All are simply labelled as 'Bills', as opposed to rates for manual exchange, official rates, rates used in accounts and so forth. I cannot yet see how the investment rate and the transfer rate relate to one another. The merchants notebooks stress that *larghezza* and *stretezza* were brought about by real trading situations and hence real transfers of funds, which would suggest that the investment rate was dependent upon the transfer rate, but I leave this as an open question.

As the long Antwerp narrative suggested, exchange rates were not negotiated individually, but fixed at regular and frequent intervals by 'the community of the *bourse*, which is the place where the merchants meet'. It was so called in Antwerp by analogy with Bruges, its predecessor as the principal banking place of north-western Europe. At Bruges in the fifteenth century the international merchant-banking community had met regularly and frequently in the *Place de la bourse*, so called from the Beurze family, probably in the loggia of the florentine consular house there. In Barcelona they met in the *Llotja de cambis*, the loggia of the money changers, in London somewhere in Lombard Street, and in Paris somewhere in the *Buffeterie*, later called *rue des*

[42] W. Brulez, *De Firma della Faille en de internationale handel van vlaamse firmas in de 16e eeuw* (Brussels, 1959), pp. 194–7, quoted by Eric Aerts, 'Prof. R. de Roover and medieval banking history', *Revue de la Banque* (Brussels, 1980), pp. 265–6, who concluded that de Roover had been too much influenced by reading the treatises of scholastics and their arguments about morality.

[43] F. H. abed al-Hussein, *Trade and Business Community in Old Castille. Medine del Campo 1500–1575* (Ph.D. thesis, University of East Anglia, 1982), pp. 82, 93, relying on his own researches and those of Lapeyre.

Lombards, possibly in the cloister of St. Merri.[44] The rates fixed by the merchant community in each of these places were then available in written form, *listini*, which brokers had ready to hand for their clients.

Exchange brokers, whose function is so clearly described in the Antwerp narrative, are attested as early as the beginning of the fourteenth century, and are no more than a specialized case of the general use of brokers for bringing buyer and seller together. Brokerage charges (*senseraggio*), according to Pegolotti's notebook, were moderate. In Bruges two *groten* per hundred reals of 24 groats was normally paid, less than one per mille. In Constantinople and Pera two *carats* per hundred *perpers* were paid, effectively the same scale of charges as in Bruges.[45] In Pisa however, only two *soldi* were due per hundred florins, according to an ordinance of 1323, at a time when the florin was worth just over sixty *soldi*, in other words ⅓ per mille. This brokerage fee was paid both by the deliverer and the taker. The broker's fee for manual exchange, between silver money and florins was even smaller, only one *soldo* per hundred florins. In sixteenth-century Valladolid, there were fifteen exchange brokers, all licensed by the city, and in Medina del Campo there were twenty six.[46] It is not now clear how widespread or how early such a system of licensing was for exchange brokers.

Raymond de Roover presumed that the *listini* of the brokers lay behind the rates reported by Datini's correspondents. He was able to use these reports to reconstruct the way in which the money market changed, and in doing so revealed the speed of that change. For 8 January 1399, de Roover collected from the Datini papers no fewer than four separate reports of the rates fixed that day in Bruges. The evolution of the rates can thus be traced over a very few hours. The rate for bills to London was at 26 pence sterling to the *écu* or *schild* of 24 flemish *gros* or *groten* all through the day. Other rates, however, changed very slightly during the day. For example the first correspondent reported the rate for bills to Barcelona as 10 *sueldos* of Barcelona per *écu* or *schild* of 22 flemish *gros* or *groten*. The second reported the same rate, but the third reported 10s. to 10s. ½d., and the fourth 10s. ½d. to 10s. 1d. In the same way the first correspondent reported the rate for bills to Paris as 34 *groten* and 2 *miten* per gold *franc*, the second and third correspondents reported 34 *groten* and 3 *miten* per *franc*, and the fourth 34 *groten* and 4 *miten*.[47] In other words, exchange to Paris was gradually growing dearer during the day, whilst that to Barcelona was gradually growing cheaper.

If change on the money market was as rapid as that, we do well to be suspicious of the pretended accuracy of any attempts at statistical analysis of

[44] Raymond de Roover, *opera cit.*, and for Paris, 'Le Marché monétaire à Paris du règne de Philippe le Bel au début du XVe siècle', *Académie des Inscriptions et Belles Lettres, Comptes Rendus* (1968), pp. 553–4.

[45] F. B. Pegolotti, *La Pratica della Mercatura*, ed. Allan Evans (Cambridge, Mass., 1936), p. 45.

[46] Al-Hussein, *Medina del Campo*, p. 92.

[47] Raymond de Roover, 'Renseignements complémentaires sur le marché monétaire à Bruges au XIVe et au XVe siècle', *Handelingen van het Genootschap 'Société d'Emulation' te Brugge*, cix (1972), p. 69.

the money market. Only for the period of the Datini papers can anything approaching a safe statistical analysis be attempted. Raymond de Roover, in conjunction with Hyman Sardy, made such an analysis from the reported figures from Bruges and Barcelona. Frederic Lane and Reinhold Mueller have abstracted the comparable reports from Venice, which will appear in the second volume of their *Money and Banking in Medieval–Renaissance Venice*. Otherwise no close enough international series are available. For the evolution of local exchange an analysis of the rates registered daily in Florence by the *proveditori degli cambiatori* would be possible. They survive from 1389 to 1432.[48] Such analysis as de Roover and Sardy did confirmed that there were indeed seasonal changes in international rates, just as merchants noted down in their notebooks. These were geared to patterns of trade which followed a regular calendar, such as annual cycles of fairs, or the arrival or departure of galley fleets. However, they also reveal that such regular seasonal patterns of change were frequently cut across by uncalendarable political events or natural calamities.

Lane and Mueller's rates for investment bills from Venice to Pisa between 1384 and 1392, according to the Datini correspondents, show that rates were generally low between March and May, that they were rising in June, high in July and August, suddenly dropping at the beginning of September, and low again from September to December, with a slight rise in January and February. At this time high meant 104 florins at Pisa for 100 ducats in Venice, and low meant 101 florins at Pisa for 100 ducats in Venice.[49] In the summer months of stringency, *strettezza*, when investment funds were hard to find, lenders could thus command much higher interest rates, than at other times of the year, particularly the months of abundance *larghezza* in the autumn when investment funds were easy to find. Half a century later Uzzanno in his notebook recorded:

> Vinegia ae caro di denari da Maggio a di 8.di Settembre per l'andata delle galee, che partono di Luglio, e d'Agosto, e di Settembre, il perchè comincia a migliorare, perchè ogn'uno si comincia a mettere in punto, e più vi rimettono volontieri, e questa carestia viene per gli assai contanti portano le galee, perchè molte mercatantie vi si vendono al tempo delle galee che bisogno si paghino in quel tempo annovi a essere molti bisogni, e molti danari escono di banchi contanti, il perchè v'è sempre caro de' contanti da un per cento più che l'usato.
>
> Il perchè l'argiento vi ritocca, e quelle d'Alessandria portano oro, e simile le nave di Soria portano oro, il perchè ogni contanti v' à buona condizione in questi tempi; stannosi poi insino a Gennajo, e al Gennajo vi si ricominciano a sentire perchè vi si fà più di mercatantia, e partonsi le navi di Catalogna, che portano contanti, e argiento assai, e vi è richiesta di denari di Catalogna: alquanto

[48] The rates printed below (pp. 7–23, 34–9) were abstracted by me for the *Interim Listing* directly from the Archivio di Stato in Florence, Miscellanea Repubblica, Box 33. The complete series has since been published by Mario Bernocchi, as the fourth volume of his *Le Monete della Repubblica Fiorentina* (Florence, 1978). The quantity of surviving material may be judged by the fact that that is a larger volume than this.

[49] Lane and Mueller, *op. cit.* vol. i. These rates are not reprinted in this *Handbook*.

cominciasi ariscaldare a mezzo Dicembre per li termini del Natale, e dura tutto Gennajo, tanto si partino tutti navili di Soria.[50]

As with other merchant notebooks, this need not have been up to date information, but it suggests that the pattern evidenced by the Datini correspondents continued for some time. It was moreover a pattern that was evident at the time, and explicable in terms of a calendar of sailings.

All commercial rates of exchange, however much they might vary seasonally, or from day to day, or even from hour to hour, were ultimately based on a *par* value. The *par* value was determined by the precious metal content of the two coinages on which the moneys of account to be exchanged were based. If all moneys of account had been either silver based or gold based this would have been relatively easy to calculate. Unfortunately, they were not all silver based or all gold based and the intrinsic values of the precious metals involved were also free to vary in relation to each other with the preferences of the market. *Par* values were thus frequently neither easily calculable nor static. Local exchange naturally always involved two metals. However exchange between two places need not do so. The *par* value was of course most evident when the same currency was used in both places. In these cases, quotations of rates of exchange were frequently actually quoted as a percentage above or below *par*. Gradual fluctuations in *par* values were continually brought about by change in the market's preferences between silver and gold and the consequent changes in the ratio of the values set on them. Sudden changes in *par* values on the other hand were usually brought about by government decisions to change the precious metal content of coins. Exchange rates normally reacted as soon as such changes were known.

Par values then provided a central rate about which actual exchange values fluctuated. There were also outside limits to such fluctuations, beyond which it was foolish to buy a bill of exchange to transfer money. When the actual rates quoted for bills reached these limits, it had become not only cheaper to send specie instead of a bill to the required destination to be reminted into local currency there, but worth the risks involved to do so. John Munro attempted to determine what these limits, or specie points, were between England and the Netherlands from 1385 to 1476.[51] To do so he deliberately did not compare, as had hitherto been usual, either the relative prices at which the mints bought silver and gold, or alternatively, the relative values of coin minted from similar weights of silver and gold. Instead he made a series of cross-calculations between the mint-prices for a mark of gold and the value of coin minted from a mark of silver; and between the mint-prices for a mark of silver and the value of coin minted from a mark of gold. He argued persuasively that these ratios were the vital ones in determining whether at any time merchants chose to bring gold or silver to be minted in either country and if so which.

[50] Published in G. F. Pagnini della Ventura, *Della Decima e delle altre gravezze*, iv (Lisbon–Lucca, 1766), 156–7.

[51] *Wool, Cloth and Gold. The Struggle for Bullion in Anglo-Burgundian Trade 1340–1478* (Brussels–Toronto, 1973).

Historians are already well served for general comment on the mechanism of exchange by the works of the late Raymond de Roover, *L'Evolution de la lettre de change*, item numbered (134) in the list of sources, his introduction to *The Bruges Money Market circa 1400* (138), and the relevant sections of *The Rise and Decline of the Medici Bank 1397–1494* (137) and *Money, Credit and Banking in Medieval Bruges*, and by a large number of pertinent articles in both French and English. Many of his English papers were posthumously collected by Julius Kirschner and published as *Business, Banking and Economic Thought*, Chicago, 1974. His french papers have not yet been collected. For a commentary on one country there is Carlo Cipolla's masterly introduction to *I movimenti dei cambi in Italia* (111). Tommaso Zerbi (513) and Antonia Borlandi (56) have shown what can be done for the cities of Milan and Bologna. Although José Gentil da Silva's *Banque et crédit en italie au XVIIe siècle* (two volumes, Paris, 1969) refers to a later period, there is also much to be learnt from it, as from John McCusker's *Money and Exchange in Europe and America 1600–1775* (New York, 1978).

DIFFERENT SORTS OF EXCHANGE

In this *Handbook* rates of exchange for various different sorts of transactions have been listed together, although the nature of the transaction has been indicated by a code-letter. However in very many cases it has only been possible to guess at the nature of the transactions involved.

'A' The simplest form of exchange was that used in making up accounts, when a merchant, or government official, translated a sum in one currency into another for his own convenience. Whether or not any actual exchange of currencies took place was not the immediate concern of the man preparing his accounts. The letter 'A' has been used to indicate such evaluations in *Accounts*. Such evaluations need not be the market rate for the day, for conservatism and convenience conspired to keep rates unchanged at round figures. On the other hand accounts in the same place at the same time might use different rates for different purposes (see pp. 4–7). The letter 'A' has also been used to cover the occasions in which a stipulated payment could be made either in one currency or in another. In these circumstances the documents implicitly, if not explicitly, give an equivalence between the two currencies.

'M' The simplest and most common form of actual exchange of currencies was straightforward manual exchange of one currency for another. This was most commonly the exchange of the gold coinage of a particular locality for the 'silver' or 'billon' coinage of the same place. The letter 'M' has been used to indicate such *Manual* exchanges. Money changers had to make a livelihood, however. They therefore either made a charge for their services, or else ran two slightly different rates: one for those who wished to exchange gold for 'silver'; and the other for those who wished to exchange 'silver' for gold. In addition, such money changers would also exchange the silver coinages of neighbouring territories and gold coins from a considerable distance, into local currencies.

'O' In most places the activities of such money changers were constrained by government regulations which usually required them to bring to the mint all the foreign coins that they acquired, except for those specifically exempted, and permitted to be put back into circulation. Government regulations often then went on to specify official exchange rates not only between the gold and silver currencies that they had themselves issued but also for such foreign currencies as they permitted to circulate. They frequently added the rates at which the mint would take in such forbidden foreign currencies as they thought the money changers might meet, and withdrew from circulation. The letter 'O' has been used to indicate such *Official* rates. These official rates of exchange usually bore some relationship to market rates when they were first promulgated. However, with daily fluctuations in the market rates, the official rates frequently came to be quite out of touch with the commercial rates in a surprisingly short time. Such fixed official rates could take no account of seasonal changes in money supply, of fluctuations in the gold:silver ratio, or the market's relative preference for gold or silver.

'L' The really considerable fortunes built up in many places by some money changers did not, however, derive from their direct function as exchangers of money, but from their use of their substantial sums of ready cash to make loans to their customers. This could be done in the guise of an exchange contract. The money changer disbursed a sum in one currency, let us say in 'gold'. Instead of at once receiving an equivalent sum in another currency, let us say in 'silver', he allowed the customer to delay completing the exchange operation for a specified period of time. The exchange rate quoted on such an occasion was obviously not the daily market rate, but included an interest element. The letter 'L' has been used on the few occasions on which such *Loans* could be detected under the guise of manual exchange. They were forbidden in Venice in 1317.[52]

'B' As well as manual exchanges on the spot, there was also long-distance exchange between places, as well as between currencies. Manual exchange involved only two parties, but long-distance exchange involved more. A letter of credit for a businessman, a pilgrim, or an envoy travelling to another place involved three parties, whilst the normal commercial bill of exchange involved four parties (see above, pp. xxxi–xxxiii). The letter 'B' has been used to indicate rates for *Bills of Exchange* and similar instruments, like the *Instrumentum ex causa cambii* or the *Cambium Maritimum*.

The value of exchange rates derived from bills of exchange is further

[52] The transaction had to be completed within eight days. In 1359 a changer was fined for allowing a customer a month to complete the transaction. Mueller, *Procurati*, pp. 316–17.

complicated by the various ways in which medieval businessmen used bills of exchange. Bills of exchange were of course developed, and went on being used, primarily for the transfer of money from one place to another, but they could also function as a cloak for loans, by the system of exchange and re-exchange. The price of bills could also be affected by those who played the exchanges in the hope of making a profit from alterations in the exchange rates which had been foreseen and on which they speculated. Most of our knowledge of the rates for such exchanges comes from commercial correspondence in which factors and branch managers quoted the going rates in their reports to head office, or in letters to other branches and correspondents. In the major banking centres such rates of exchange were fixed daily by the bankers meeting together. Very few of the bills of exchange actually survive, but we know of the contents of other bills from entries in a limited number of account books, and from notarized protests when the payer refused to pay.

The rates for exchange between two places were not of course the same in both of them, the difference being related to the overall balance of payments between them. For example, between London and Venice there was very little difference because of the near equilibrium in the balance of payments between them.

Where the names of two places are given for bills of exchange, the first is that of the place from which the money was sent, and the second is that of the place to which it was transferred. When only a single place-name is given it is generally that of the place of origin of the transfer.

'C' Where the nature of the original rate was not clear when this *Handbook* was compiled, a vague 'C' is used to indicate some sort of *Commercial* rate as opposed to an official one.

'H' Most rates have been found in printed sources, quoted directly by historians in a form which makes the original source recognizable. However, some rates quoted by historians, have been so transformed by them for their own purposes, that it has not always been clear what was the original rate. An attempt has been made to recalculate back to the original rates, but an 'H' has been used to indicate that such rates are derived from modern *Historians*.

Quite often, exchange arrangements quoted the rate of exchange as well as the sums involved. Where only the actual sums were given, they have been reduced to a rate in the form most commonly given in other documents. For example, 91 li. 4s. imperiale for 57 florins, appears as 1 florin to 32 *soldi* imperiale.

For certain very limited periods and for certain particular exchanges, there is a very great deal of material available in almost daily series. It was not thought proper, in a *Handbook* which attempts to cover over three centuries, to include daily quotations. In these cases a quotation for only one business day of each month has normally been selected.

When such frequent quotations survive it is possible to discern the seasonal cycles of *larghezza* and *strettezza* of easy money and tight money, as noted by medieval merchants in their manuals or notebooks. Half a dozen notebooks, those named after da Canal, Pegolotti, Datini, Ricci, Uzzanno and Chiarini, have been used extensively for preparing the short notices which precede each section of the *Handbook*. They are also of enormous value in understanding how the medieval money market actually worked.

Although all these different sorts of exchange have been put together in this *Handbook*, the differences between them should not be forgotten. We believe, however that for most purposes historians will only want to look up a generally applicable rate of exchange for a particular date and composite tables seemed to us to provide the quickest means for them to do so. We realize that we are doing a disservice to those who need greater precision, but believe that such historians will be prepared to disaggregate the information for constructing their own tables and graphs.

As an indication of the way they might be sorted out, a number of graphs have been inserted which can give an approximate idea of some of the more prolific series. For example the ducat to sterling rates for bills of exchange, as given by the Borromei papers, give rise to two graphs, one for rates from Venice to London, and the other for rates from London to Venice (see pp. 202 and 203, and above p. xlii).

LAYOUT OF THE HANDBOOK

For transactions inside any one 'country', accounting naturally took place in one of the local moneys of account, and payment unless made by assignment on a bank, was made in coins available on the spot, in gold, silver or billon according to the scale of the transaction. For transactions across 'national' boundaries, however, this was not adequate. The different moneys had to be reduced to a common denominator. Since the people most frequently concerned in such inter-'national' transactions were papal officials and italian merchants, it was natural that it should be italian money that was used as the common denominator, and it was most frequently the florentine florin that was so used. The florentine florin was the gold coin *par excellence* of Tuscany, and it was tuscan merchants, above all others, who provided the multi-branched commercial and banking network, within which so many of these transactions took place. Papal treasurers and even papal collectors only rarely used cameral merchants from outside a charmed circle of Florentines, Lucchese and Sienese for the transmission of funds across Europe, whether from collectors in fourteenth-century England to the papal curia at Avignon, or onwards from Avignon to paymasters in Perugia for papal troops in central Italy. The amount due from a new archbishop of York was thus fixed in florins, although of course paid over to the transmitting bankers in sterling. In noting the cost of transmitting english wool to Porto Pisano for cloth manufacture in Tuscany, Pegolotti expressed the various sums actually to be paid out along the way in the relevant local moneys of account, but then summarized the costs by conversion into florentine florins.

The material has therefore been laid out around the florentine gold florin.

The coinage of the florentine republic, and in particular the florin, has recently been made the object of a detailed study by Mario Bernocchi (31). Detailed information on the minute transformations in weight and fineness of the standard coin over two and a half centuries can be found there.

For historians wishing to make comparisons between prices, wages, rents or taxes in two or more different currencies the natural procedure is therefore to follow the medieval example and convert them into florentine florins. The *Handbook* is laid out to make such conversion as simple as possible. If the currencies involved were important ones it is only necessary to look at the primary lists in which the values of the florentine florin are given in the major currencies of Europe. These are arranged in date order. In the case of less important currencies it may be necessary to make a double calculation, first converting the given sums of money from a minor currency to a major one, and then converting that into florentine florins.

The gold genovino, sometimes called the genoese florin was also used as a common denominator for inter-'national' transactions. Its issue began in 1252, the same year as the florentine florin. The two coins were almost identical in weight and fineness.

The venetian gold ducat was also used in this way. It was not issued until 1284, and was initially marginally heavier than the then contemporary florentine and genoese florins. In modern, metric, terms it weighed 3.56 grams against 3.54 grams. In transactions between western Europe and the outside world, the genovino and particularly the ducat were more important than the florentine florin. However, inside western Europe the florentine florin was clearly of more importance until the fifteenth century, when the ducat achieved such a position of predominance that 'ducat' came to replace 'florin' as the generic name for gold coins of the same size and fineness.

Apart from these, the aragonese gold florin had a certain vogue for transactions between the spanish kingdoms, whilst the gold florin or gulden of the rhineland electors was similarly much used for transactions between german states, and the hungarian florin (or ducat) for transactions in central Europe. However, outside their own regions none of these could bear comparison with the florentine florin and its genoese and venetian counterparts.

When separate rates for both ducats and for florins have survived in adequate numbers, the primary series of exchange rates to the florin has been followed up with a parallel listing of exchange rates to the venetian ducat and the hungarian ducat. When separate rates have not survived in adequate numbers they have been listed together, but distinguished, when possible, by the letters F (florin), G (genovino), V (venetian ducat), and H (hungarian ducat).

The arrangement of this listing therefore, begins in Florence, with local exchange between the gold florin and the already existing currencies of Florence, the *piccolo* or small *denaro*, and the *grosso* or silver *fiorino*.[53]

[53] For convenience, a table of currencies is to be found immediately after this introduction in the order in which they appear in the *Handbook* with an accompanying map. There is also an alphabetical index of currencies, with a further map, at the end of the volume.

Local exchange within the florentine state is followed in the *Handbook* by exchange with the currencies of other tuscan states including Lucca, Pisa and Siena. Each of these was itself the home of a number of major banking houses with multiple branches throughout Europe that reckoned in florentine florins for their international transactions.

After Tuscany the *Handbook* follows a geographical order from south to north. It starts with the currencies of Sicily and then Naples, then those of Rome and central Italy, and next those of northern Italy. The order of material in the *Handbook* then crosses the Alps westwards to the Rhône valley, where transactions to and from the papal curia, when at Avignon, were of major importance, and from there proceeds to the spanish kingdoms. After these it moves northwards again through France to England and the Low Countries and virtually ends with german currencies. Apart from Bohemia, there is not enough surviving material for the scandinavian or slavonic parts of Europe to give their currencies more than the briefest entries. This reflects the commercial conditions in late medieval Europe.

A small number of exchange rates between western Europe and Byzantium, the Maghreb and the Levant will be found under Genoa, and rather more at the end of the volume.

In view of the sparseness of the material in some parts, the *Handbook* has been framed in terms of currencies, rather than in terms of places of exchange. For example, all exchanges between florins and money *tournois* are listed together whether they took place at Paris or elsewhere in France, at the curia or even in Piedmont or England. The place to which every item refers has however been given, and an index has been provided at the end, together with a map.

In order to extend the usefulness of the *Handbook*, many of the primary series of exchange rates between florins and major and minor local currencies have been followed by one or more secondary series giving what is known of the rates between major and minor local currencies in the same general area. For example, the primary series of exchange rates between the florin and money *tournois* has been followed by secondary exchange rates between money *tournois* and the moneys of Anjou, Agen, Artois, Bordeaux, Brittany, Clermont, Maine, Metz and Poitou. Direct rates of exchange between florins and many of these less important currencies could not be found, and have probably not survived. Indeed, exchanges between florins and these currencies may well have taken place very rarely, or not at all.

The secondary series has been used for three other purposes as well as for exchanges between major and minor currencies in the same general area.

Firstly, it has been used for giving the values of the principal gold coins of the area. Castillian gold *doblas*, for example, are listed after *maravedis* and *reals*, so that the historian who is dealing with sums expressed in *doblas* rather than in *maravedis* may also be able to use the *Handbook*.

Secondly, the secondary series has also been used for a number of non-local transactions, which went outside the part of Europe in which exchanges involving florins usually took place. The area in which florins were quoted very roughly coincided with the network of exchange places operated by the tuscan bankers. For example direct exchange between florentine florins and the money of Lübeck was relatively uncommon, since Lübeck was not an italian banking place. However, exchange between florentine florins and flemish money was common since Bruges was an italian banking place. At the same time Bruges was frequented by hanseatic merchants so that exchanges took place between flemish money and the money of Lübeck. A number of exchanges with Lübeck have therefore been put among the secondary series under flemish money.

Thirdly, the secondary series has been used for transactions which took place before the introduction of the florin. The most important secondary series of this sort will be found under money *provinois*, the money of the Champagne fairs. The source of many of these entries is to be found in the notarial registers of Genoa. Many of these are derived from the series *Notai liguri del secolo XII* (106, 233–4, 274) and the work of Mme Doehaerd (154), Mme de Sturler (297) and Misbach (344). Other, as yet unpublished, notarial records, should yield some further material for this early period. However a great many items in these registers are profoundly disappointing for this purpose, since they merely state that an exchange had taken, or should take, place without in any way specifying the rate involved.

In the later middle ages exchange rates were described as either 'certain' or 'uncertain'. They were 'certain' when the home currency was quoted in fixed units, and the foreign currency treated as variable. They were 'uncertain' when the foreign currency was quoted in fixed units, for example florins or ducats, and the home currency treated as variable.[54] This distinction has been followed in the layout of the *Handbook*. Apart from the primary series of rates between florins or ducats and variable amounts of other currencies, all other rates have been placed, as far as possible, under the currency for which the quotations were 'certain'. Cross references have, of course, been added for 'uncertain' rates, to the place where they were 'certain'.

In order that users of the *Handbook* may know whether any exchange rate quoted is reliable or not, I have given a reference for each of them that can be followed up. Following up my references is particularly necessary when two or three very different rates are given for a relatively short space of time. Such differences may reflect radical changes in actual conditions, but they may equally reflect modern scholars' inability to read medieval figures aright, or their carelessness in transcription or proof-reading. This *Handbook* cannot be any more reliable than the work of the hundreds of different scholars on which it is based. An easily usable means of getting back to my sources is therefore vital to users of this *Handbook*. For convenience, and for the sake of space, I have given a reference number to every source that I have used, whether printed, by private communication, or from manuscripts. The final column of every entry gives such a reference number in brackets, together with volume, page, folio or item numbers as relevant. The reference numbers themselves can easily be looked up in the bibliography and list of sources,

[54] For a fuller discussion of 'certain' and 'uncertain' quotations see de Roover, 'Marché monétaire', pp. 16–19.

below pp. 323–50. Each number is there given as full a bibliographical entry as possible. The entries are arranged alphabetically by the personal names of authors, editors, or providers of information. The items derived by me directly from manuscripts appear at the end of the list.

USES OF THE HANDBOOK

The comparison of the finances of different cities and of the prices of iron in different countries are only two of the many uses to which it will be possible to put this *Handbook*. It can be used as much for the comparison of royal finances as of civic finances. It can be used as much for the comparison of the prices of cloth, or of grain, as of iron. It can therefore be used to elucidate profits on commodities transported from one region to another. It can equally be used for the comparison of wages or of rents.

A detailed example of its use can be provided by a consideration of the information that it gives on the extent of debasement in the later middle ages. Since international exchange rates were always ultimately based on the precious metal content of currency, they can be used in the long term as measures of the deterioration or improvement of various currencies, at least as perceived by the merchant community. Throughout the fourteenth and fifteenth centuries the florentine florin remained essentially the same in weight and fineness.[55] It is, therefore, an effective yardstick against which to measure the deviations in other currencies.

When the debasements or strengthenings of a currency were very large, the exchange rates, as with modern devaluations, altered radically within weeks or even days. Nevertheless some general indications of the variety of experience in different countries may be gathered. The experience of Castille, where the *maravedi* in 1500 only retained one sixty-fifth of its 1300 value, against the florentine florin, was patently very different from the experience of its neighbour Aragon, where the money of Jacca was still worth over half of its value for two hundred years earlier. On p. lx, the long term change of a dozen currencies are tabulated, in order from that of Castille, the least stable, to those of Aragon and England, the most stable. Where, as in France, the post-war strengthening of a currency attempted to counteract the war-time debasements, the cumulative effect is barely apparent in the table, but where, as in Castille, the post-war strengthening of the *maravedi* was negligible, the cumulative effect was enormous. The graph on p. 00, is designed to show both the long term trends and the short term debasements and strengthenings of the twelve currencies. This detailed example shows one particular way in which the material collected in this *Handbook* can be used.

[55] When first struck in 1252 new florins were supposed to weigh 3.54 grams. In the course of the fourteenth and fifteenth centuries they never dropped lower than 3.33 grams. This was less than 6% below the original weight, and they were generally struck within 2% of it. In 1500 they were being issued at 3.53 grams. M. Bernocchi, *Le Monete della Repubblica Fiorentina*, iii (Florence, 1976).

Professor Warren Van Egmond of the centre for the study of medieval mathematics at the University of Siena used the *Interim Listing* for checking the verisimilitude of the examples cited in late medieval italian 'merchant arithmetics' or *abbaci* from the late thirteenth century onwards, when they dealt with problems involving the exchange of currencies. Unfortunately his results were highly variable. Sometimes the authors of his manuscripts gave realistic rates in the problems they posed, and sometimes utterly unrealistic ones. There was, however, a complete lack of consistency in their choice. He even found realistic and unrealistic rates for the same exchange on the same folio. As a consequence Professor Van Egmond could not use the *Listing*, as he had hoped, as a means of dating his manuscripts. His examples do, however, offer an insight into the complexity of the commercial arithmetic at the disposal of late medieval merchants and bankers, and the nature of the choices that might be involved before a bill of exchange was drawn. For example, a merchant arithmetic of 1328 poses the problem:

> Io sono a Monpeslieri e voglio fare uno cambio a Parigi ed o fiorini ed agnelli e reali d'oro. Siche lo firino vale a Monpeslieri soldi 12 denari 8 tor. e l'agnello vale soldi 14 denari 8 tor. e l' reale vale soldi 15 denari 2 tor. e a Parigi vale el fiorino soldi 10 di parigini e l'angenello vale soldi 11 denari 4 di parigini e 'l reale vale soldi 11 denari 8 parigini. Or voglio mandare a Parigi e tornare ad Monpeslieri libre 1000 tor.

Other correspondents have remarked that they have already used the figures in the *Interim Listing* to convert incomes, duties, revenues, etc. to a meaningful common denominator. I trust that in future not only economic history textbooks, but also political history textbooks will be able to make such comparisons on the basis of figures in the *Handbook*. It should be therefore a tool of very wide use for a whole range of historians.

NOTE TO TABLE I AND GRAPH 3

It will be realized that all the currencies involved in these tables were based on silver coins, and that exchange rates between these currencies and gold florins therefore incorporate the different relative values placed on gold and silver in each place and at each date. However both Table I and Graph 3 have, for simplicity, been constructed without taking changing gold:silver rates into account. Gold:silver ratios were certainly not constant throughout Europe in the fourteenth and fifteenth centuries. Graph 4, on p. lxii, illustrates how some gold:silver ratios changed in the first half of the fourteenth century, and Table II, on p. lxiii, indicates how the venetian gold:silver ratio changed over the next 150 years. The overall effect of the changes in the ratios between the two metals is that Table I and Graph 3 slightly underestimate the degree of debasement in the fourteenth century and slightly overestimate it in the fifteenth century. The small extent of this underestimation and over-estimation can be illustrated from the sterling currency of England. New English pennies struck in 1300 should have contained 1.44 grams of sterling silver, those struck in 1400 should have contained 1.17 grams, and those struck in 1500, 0.78 grams. Therefore the actual decline in the silver content of the penny should have raised the exchange rate between sterling and the florin by a factor of 1.2 in the fourteenth century, of 1.5 in the fifteenth century, and by 1.8 over the two centuries combined. However, the decline of the value of gold in terms of silver in the fourteenth century meant that the exchange rate actually rose only by a factor of 1.1, whilst the increase in the value of gold in the fifteenth century made no significant difference to the exchange rate. Over the two centuries together, the exchange rate actually rose by 1.7.

TABLE I: CHANGES IN TWELVE MAJOR CURRENCIES 1300–1500

	florin in	*c. 1300*	*c. 1400*		*c. 1500*		*1300–1500*
Castille	maravedis & dineros (1 maravedi = 10 dineros)	5m. 8d.	66m.	(× 11.4)	375m.	(× 5.7)	(× 65)
Cologne	schillinge & pfennige (1 schilling = 12 pfennige)	6s. 8pf.	42s.	(× 6.3)	112s.	(× 2.7)	(× 16.8)
Flanders	groten & miten (1 groot = 24 miten)	13gr. 3m. fl.	33gr. 12m. fl.	(× 2.6)	80gr. fl.	(× 2.4)	(× 6.1)
Austria	pfennige (1 schilling = 30 pfennige)	2s.6$^2/_3$pf.	5s.	(× 2.3)	11s.	(× 2.2)	(× 5)
France	sous & deniers tournois (1 sou = 12 deniers)	10s. tourn.	22s. tourn.	(× 2.2)	38s. 9d. tourn.	(× 1.8)	(× 3.9)
Hanse	schillinge & pfennige of Lübeck (1 schilling = 12 pfennige)	8s. lub.	10s. 6d. lub.	(× 1.3)	31s. lub.	(× 2.9)	(× 3.9)
Rome	soldi & denari provisini (1 soldo = 12 denari)	34s. prov.	73s. prov.	(× 2.1)	130s. prov.	(× 1.8)	(× 3.8)
Florence	soldi & denari piccoli (1 soldo = 12 denari)	46s. 6d. pic.	77s. 11d. pic.	(× 1.7)	140s. pic.	(× 1.8)	(× 3)
Bohemia	prague groschen	12gr.	20gr.	(× 1.7)	30gr.	(× 1.5)	(× 2.5)
Venice	soldi & denari piccoli (1 soldo = 12 denari)	64s. pic.	93s. pic.	(× 1.5)	124s. pic.	(× 1.3)	(× 1.9)
Aragon	sueldos & dineros of Jacca (1 sueldo = 12 dineros)	11s. 6d. jac.	15s. 1d. jac.*	(× 1.3)			(× 1.9)
			10s. 4d. jac. (Aragonese fl.)		16s. jac.	(× 1.5)	
England	shillings and pence sterling (1 shilling = 12 pence)	2s. 8d. sterl.	3s. sterl.	(× 1.1)	4s. 7d. sterl.	(× 1.5)	(× 1.7)

* Value calculated from other rates.

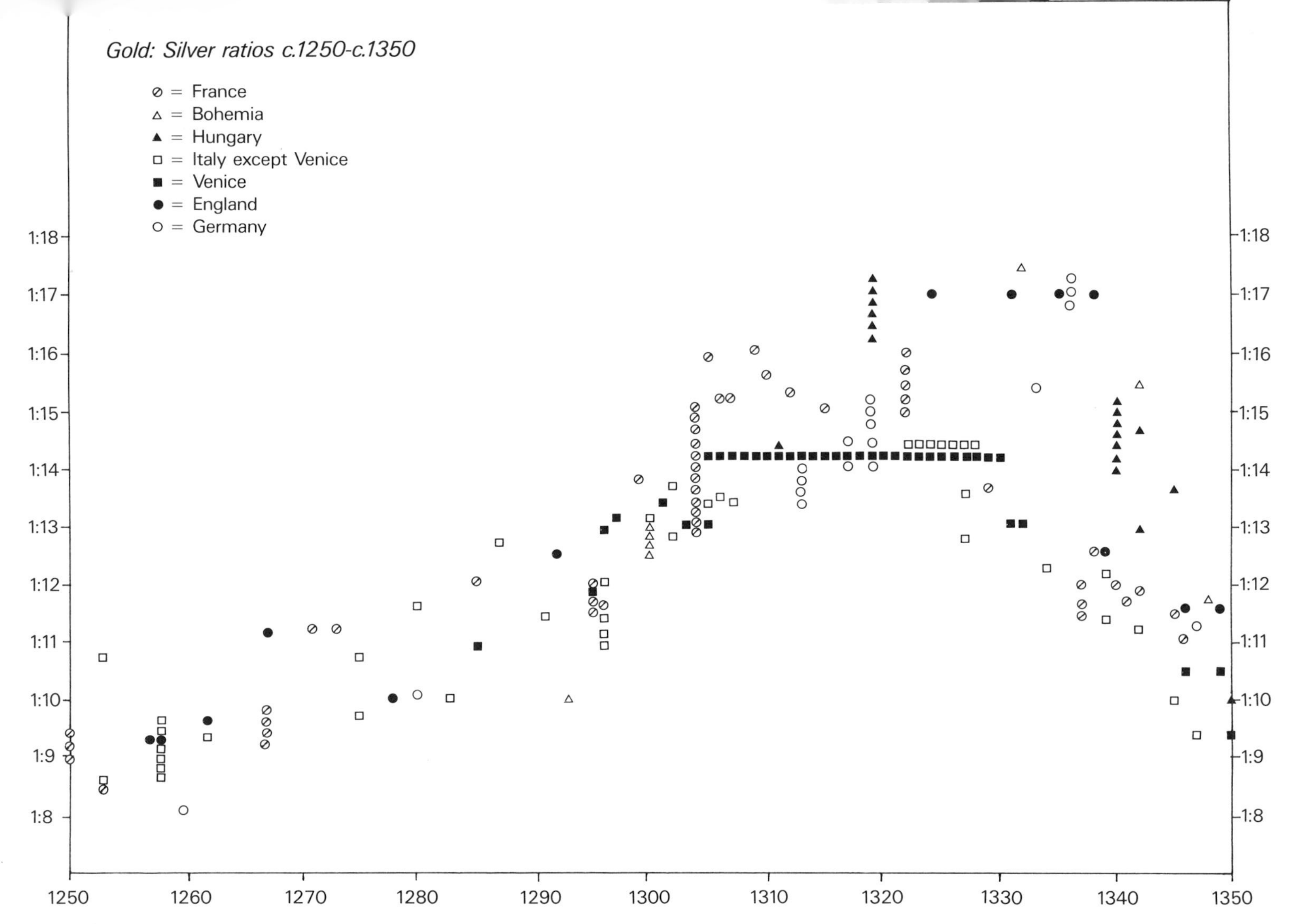
Gold: Silver ratios c.1250-c.1350
= France
= Bohemia
= Hungary
= Italy except Venice
= Venice
= England
= Germany
1:18
1:17
1:16
1:15
1:14
1:13
1:12
1:11
1:10
1:9
1:8
1250
1260
1270
1280
1290
1300
1310
1320
1330
1340
1350

TABLE II: VENETIAN GOLD:SILVER RATIOS *c.* 1330–*c.* 1500

1305–30	1:14.2
1331–2	1:13.1
1346	1:10.5
1349	1:10.5
1350	1:9.4
1353–7	1:9.6
1358	1:10.5
1369	1:10.2
1374	1:9.9
1379	1:10.2
1380	1:11.4
1382	1:10.7
1398	1:11
1399	1:11.3
1408	1:11.2
1417	1:12.5
1429	1:10.6
1449–52	1:11.4
1455–60	1:12
1463–4	1:11.9
1509	1:10.7

SECTIONS OF HANDBOOK

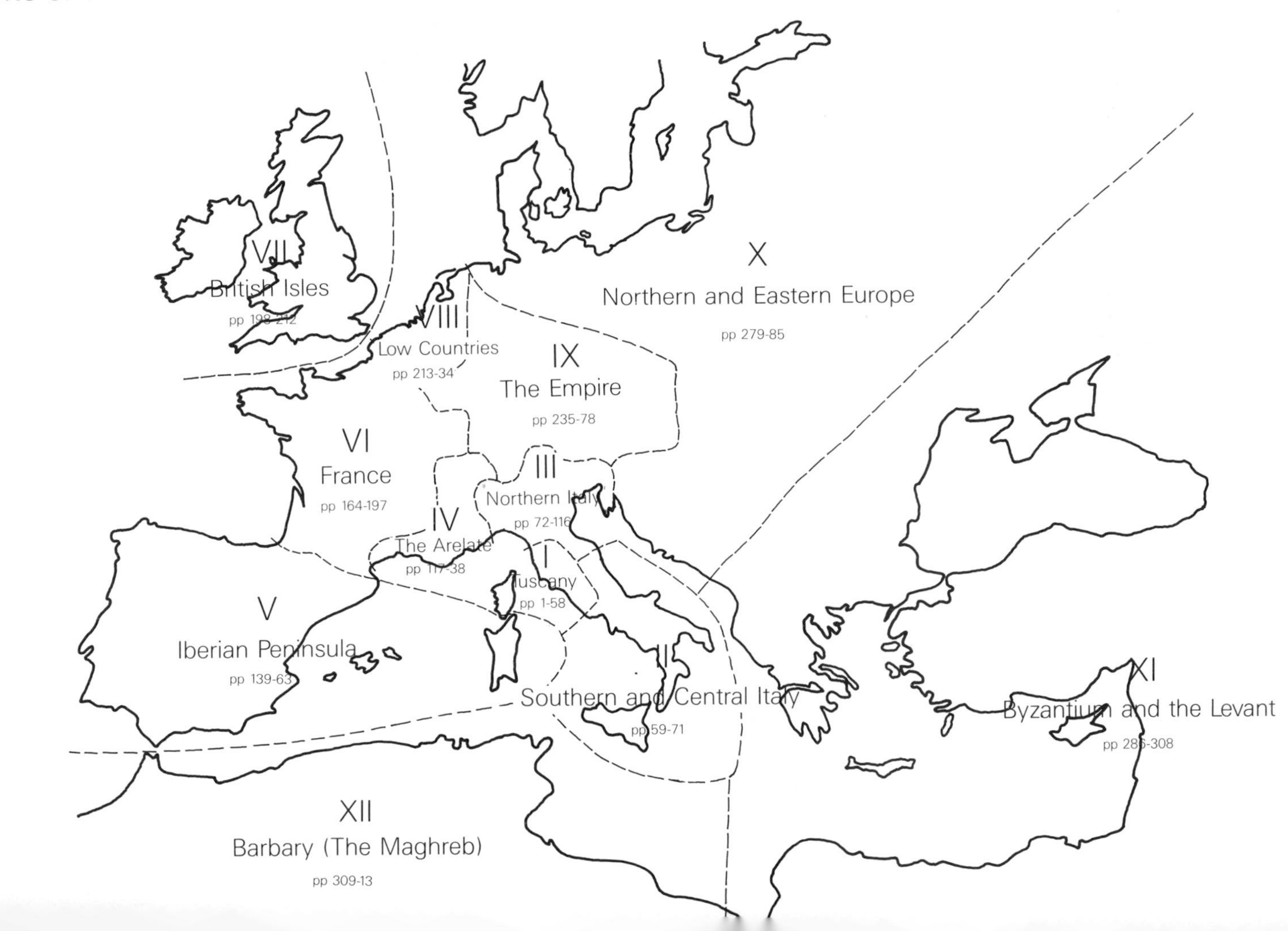
VII
British Isles
pp 198-212
VIII
Low Countries
pp 213-34
X
Northern and Eastern Europe
pp 279-85
IX
The Empire
pp 235-78
VI
France
pp 164-197
III
Northern Italy
pp 72-116
IV
The Arelate
pp 117-38
I
Tuscany
pp 1-58
V
Iberian Peninsula
pp 139-63
II
Southern and Central Italy
pp 59-71
XI
Byzantium and the Levant
pp 286-308
XII
Barbary (The Maghreb)
pp 309-13

ORDER OF LISTINGS

ORDER OF LISTINGS

ORDER OF LISTINGS

ORDER OF LISTINGS

ORDER OF LISTINGS

ORDER OF LISTINGS

ORDER OF LISTINGS

ORDER OF LISTINGS

ORDER OF LISTINGS

ORDER OF LISTINGS

ORDER OF LISTINGS

ORDER OF LISTINGS

ORDER OF LISTINGS

ORDER OF LISTINGS

ORDER OF LISTINGS

ORDER OF LISTINGS

ORDER OF LISTINGS

ORDER OF LISTINGS

ORDER OF LISTINGS

ORDER OF LISTINGS

ORDER OF LISTINGS

ORDER OF LISTINGS

ORDER OF LISTINGS

ABBREVIATIONS

In Date column:
All dates are in the form: year.month.day, including dates in the muslim era on pp.300-6. I have tried to ensure, as far as I could, that christian dates are in new style years.
After the date, the currency which was exchanged is indicated, if it was not as in the heading. Abbreviations used here:

B = Bohemian ducat
D = ducat, type not specified
F = Florentine florin
G = Genoese florin or genovino
H = Hungarian ducat
V = Venetian florin

In Rate column:
Most rates have been expressed in the form li. s. d.:

li.= pfund, pound, etc as well as lira, livre, etc.
s. = schilling, shilling, sol, soldo, sou, etc.
d. = penny, pfennig, etc as well as denaro, etc.
pf. = pfennig (not normally used)
picc. = in piccoli (to distinguish from grossi)

Other denominations:

gr. = groot, groschen; gr.Fl. = money groot of Flanders
hyp. = hyperpyron
k. = grosz of Krakow
kr. = kreutzer
m. = maravedi (in a Spanish context)
m. = mijt, mite (in an English or Flemish context)
mk. = mark
ö = öre
pl. = plakken
rhguld.= rheingulden
st. = stuiver
wpf. = weisspfennig

In Type column:
The types of exchange, explained in detail above, pp. l-lii, are:

A = used in accounting
B = used in bills of exchange
C = used in a commercial context, i.e. not official
H = used by a modern historian, type not clear
L = a loan element involved
M = manual exchange
O = an official rate
? = type of exchange not clear
? with O or C = 'perhaps official' or 'perhaps commercial'
H with A,N, C, M or O = type of exchange clear, but so presented by the historian that the rate only approximate
MC = rate for manual and other commercial exchange
ML = manual exchange involving a loan element
OM = official rate actually used for manual exchange

On pp. 4-7 only: R = used in accounting for rents received
W = used in accounting for wages paid
AW = rate used for wages and in other accounts
WR = used in accounting for wages and rents
LWR= used in accounting for loans, wages and rents

On pp. 110-12 only: CM = used in cambium maritimum
R = used in re-exchange

SECTION I
TUSCANY

FLORENCE

In Florence itself a considerable number of different methods of accounting were used, based not only on the billon denari piccioli, but also on good silver grossi, and on the gold florin. This Handbook therefore begins with the relationships between some of these different moneys within Florence itself.

After the rates for Florentine gold florins in Florentine soldi and denari piccioli, rates will be found for other florins in Florentine soldi and denari piccioli

See below p.25 for the fiorino di suggello
See below p.26 for the fiorino largo
See below p.28 for the fiorino largo di grossi
See below p.32 for the fiorino largo d'oro in oro

After these will be found rates for florins in money other than Florentine soldi and denari piccioli

See below p.34 for florins in soldi and denari affiorino
See below p.34 for florins in grossi guelfi
See below p.34 for florins in soldi and denari piccioli when payment to be made in silver grossi

The Florentine florin in Florentine soldi and denari

The basis for this accounting system was the Florentine denaro picciolo. (As well as the standard abbreviations used throughout the Handbook, the following additional abbreviations will be found in this table

R = Rents
W = Wages both refer to accounting conversion rates).

In 1252 the Florentine florin weighed 3.54 grams.

Date	Rate	Place	Type	Reference
1252-1258	20 s.	Florence	C	(111) p.81
1252	20 s.	Florence	O	(258) p.85
1271	30 s.	Florence	M	(507) p.78
1272-1277	30 s.	Florence	C	(111) p.81
1274	29 s. 2 d.	Florence	M	(31) III p.78
1275-1278	33 s.	Curia	B	(439) p.897
1276	30 s.	Florence	M	(31) III p.78
1277	33 s. 5 d.	Florence	M	(31) III p.78
1278	35 s. 4 d.	Florence	M	(31) III p.78
1279.07	33 s.	Florence	M	(31) III p.78
1279	34 s. 10 d.	Florence	C	(96) p.297
1280	34 s.	Florence	M	(31) III p.78
1280	33 s.	Florence	C	(111) p.81
1281	33 s.	Florence	C	(96) p.245
1281	35 s. 6 d.	Florence	C	(111) p.81
1282	33 s. 4 d.	Florence	M	(31) III p.78
1282	32 s.	Florence	C	(111) p.81
1283	37 s. 6 d.	Florence	M	(31) III p.78
1283	33 s.	Florence	C	(111) p.81
1284	36 s.	Florence	M	(31) III p.78
1284	40 s.	Curia	B	(439) p.897
1285	37 s.	Florence	M	(31) III p.78
1286	36 s.	Florence	M	(31) III p.78
1286	35 s.	Florence	C	(111) p.81
1286.10.04	36 s.	Florence	A	(92) App.I
1286.11	36 s. 2 d.	Florence	A	(92) App.I
1287.02.21	36 s. 4 d.	Florence	A	(92) App.I
1287.03.17	36 s. 1 d.	Florence	A	(92) App.I
1287.06.31	36 s. 7 d.	Florence	A	(92) App.I
1287.12.04	36 s. 7 d.	Florence	A	(92) App.I
1287	37 s. 7 d.	Florence	A	(92) p.13
1288	38 s. 3 d.	Florence	A	(92) p.13
1288	36 s. 8 d.	Florence	A	(92) p.13
1288.07	36 s. 8 d.	Florence	M	(31) III p.78
1288	40 s.	Curia	B	(439) p.898
1288.08.11	38 s. 3 d.	Florence	A	(92) App.I
1288.08.15	36 s. 8 d.	Florence	A	(92) App.I

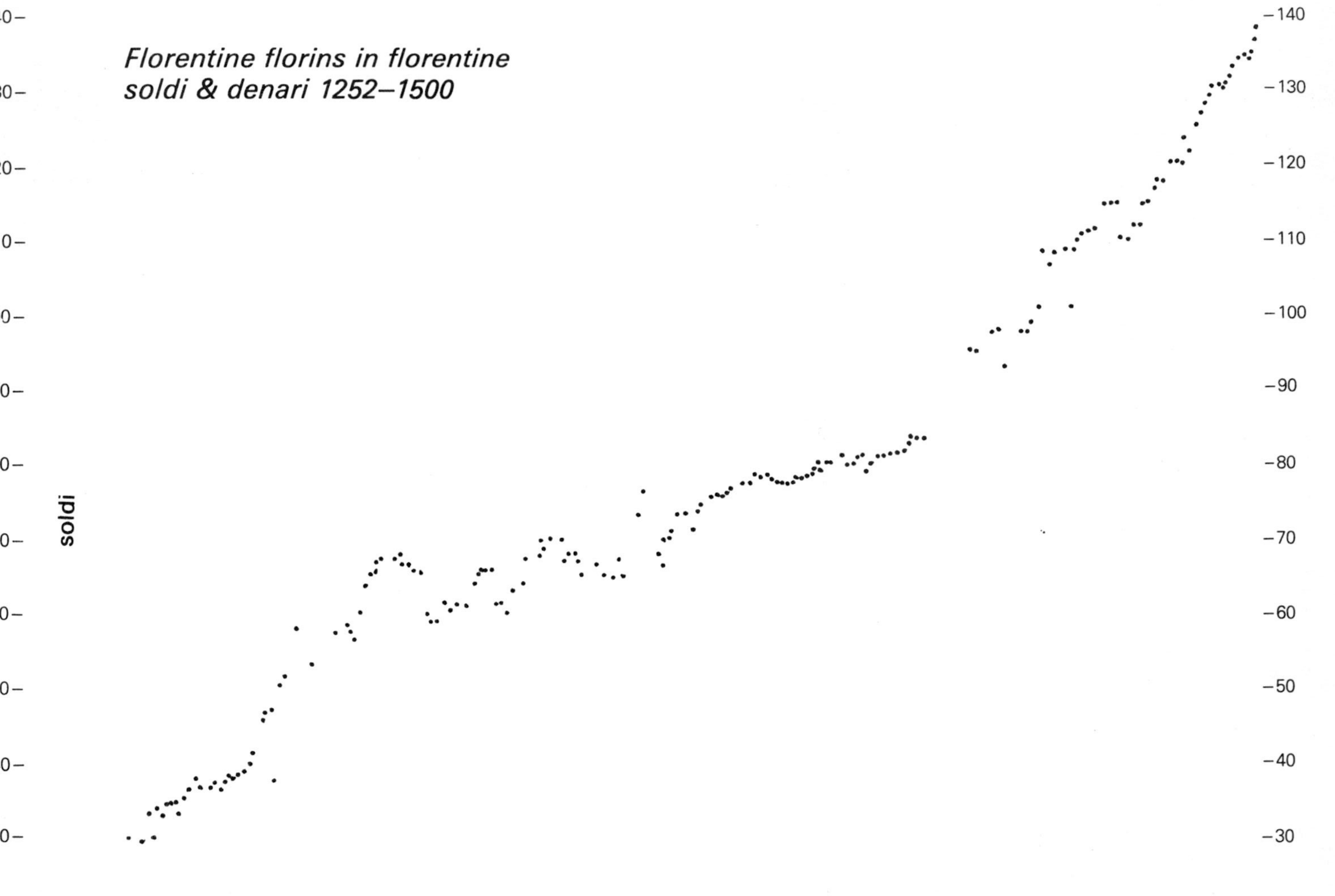
Florentine florins in florentine
soldi & denari 1252–1500
soldi
140
130
120
110
100
90
80
70
60
50
40
30
20
1252
1260
1270
1280
1290
1300
1310
1320
1330
1340
1350
1360
1370
1380
1390
1400
1410
1420
1430
1440
1450
1460
1470
1480
1490
1500

THE FLORENTINE FLORIN IN FLORENTINE SOLDI AND DENARI

Date	Rate	Place	Type	Reference
1289	36 s. 10 d.	Florence	M	(31) III p.78
1289.02.16	36 s. 10 d.	Florence	A	(92) App.I
1289.03.05	37 s.	Florence	A	(92) App.I
1289.09.05	37 s. 10 d.	Florence	A	(92) App.I
1290	36 s.	Florence	M	(31) III p.78
1290	40 s.	Curia	B	(439) p.898
1291	37 s. 8 d.	Florence	C	(111) p.81
1292	38 s. 9 d.	Florence	M	(31) III p.78
1292	38 s. 2 d.	Florence	C	(111) p.81
1292	42 s.	Curia	B	(439) p.898
1293	38 s.	Florence	M	(31) III p.78
1293	37 s. 9 d.	Florence	C	(111) p.81

In 1294 the Florentine florin weighed 3.46 grams.

Date	Rate	Place	Type	Reference
1294	38 s. 8 d.	Florence	M	(31) III p.78
1295	39 s. 3 d.	Florence	M	(31) III p.78
1296.06	40 s. 6 d.	Florence	M	(31) III p.78
1296.12	42 s. 6 d.	Florence	M	(31) III p.78
1296	40 s.	Florence	C	(111) p.81
1297.01.01	42 s.	Florence	C	(118) III p.61
1298	48 s. 6 d.	Curia	B	(439) p.898
1298	45 s. 11 d.	Florence	C	(111) p.81
1299	46 s. 2 d.	Florence	M	(31) III p.78
1300	46 s. 6 d.	Florence	C	(111) p.81
1301	37 s. 6 d.	Florence	M	(31) III p.78
1301	50 s.	Curia	B	(439) p.898
1301	37 s. 6 d.	Florence	C	(111) p.81
1302	52 s.	Curia	B	(439) p.899
1302	51 s.	Florence	C	(111) p.81
1303	52 s.	Florence	C	(111) p.82
1305	58 s. 8 d.	Florence	C	(111) p.82
1308	53 s. 6 d.	Curia	B	(439) p.899
1308	53 s. 6 d.	Florence	C	(111) p.82
1313	57 s. 6 d.	Florence	C	(111) p.82
1315	58 s.	Florence	C	(111) p.82
1316.04.08	56 s. 6 d.	Florence	C	(427) p.382
1316.05.06	57 s.	Florence	C	(427) p.382
1316.10.23	56 s.	Florence	C	(427) p.382
1316.11.20	56 s. 6 d.	Florence	C	(427) p.382
1317	56 s. 6 d.	Florence	C	(111) p.82
1317.12.01	63 s.	Siena	M	(288) p.60
1317.12.15	63 s. 6 d.	Siena	M	(288) p.60
1317.12.31	64 s.	Siena	M	(288) p.60
1318.01.04	68 s. 6 d.	Florence	C	(427) p.382
1318.05.01	68 s.	Florence	C	(427) p.382
1318.11.11	61 s. 3 d.	Florence	C	(427) p.382
1319	66 s.	Curia	B	(439) p.900
1319.01.25	62 s. 6 d.	Florence	C	(427) p.382
1319.04.20	64 s. 4 d.	Florence	C	(427) p.382
1319.06.23	63 s. 6 d.	Florence	C	(427) p.382
1320	65 s.	Florence	C	(111) p.82
1321	65 s. 6 d.	Florence	C	(427) p.382
1322	66 s.	Florence	C	(111) p.82
1322	66 s. 8 d.	Florence	C	(427) p.382
1323	66 s. 6 d.	Florence	C	(111) p.82
1323	67 s.	Florence	C	(427) p.382
1323.04-05	66 s. 6 d.	Florence	C	(427) p.382
1323.05.16	66 s. 6 d.	Florence	C	(427) p.382
1323.11.12	66 s. 2 d.	Florence	C	(427) p.382

In 1324 the Florentine florin weighed 3.52 grams.

Date	Rate	Place	Type	Reference
1324-1325	66 s. 9 d.	Florence	C	(111) p.82
1324	66 s.	Florence	C	(427) p.382
1324	66 s. 6 d.	Curia	B	(439) p.901
1324.11.18	66 s. 9 d.	Florence	C	(427) p.382
1325	66 s. 8 d.	Florence	C	(427) p.382
1325.05	67 s.	Florence	L	(289) IV p.503
1325.05.15	66 s. 9 d.	Florence	C	(427) p.382
1326	66 s.	Florence	C	(427) p.382
1326	67 s.	Florence	C	(111) p.82

THE FLORENTINE FLORIN IN FLORENTINE SOLDI AND DENARI

Date	Rate	Place	Type	Reference
1326.04	67 s.	Florence	R	(289) IV p.504
1327-1328	65 s.	Florence	C	(427) p.382
1327-1329	66 s.	Florence	C	(111) p.82
1328	65 s. 4 d.	Florence	C	(427) p.382
1328.09	65 s. 3 d.	Florence	M	(289) IV p.520
1329-1330	65 s.	Florence	M	(31) III p.79
1329	65 s.	Florence	C	(427) p.382
1329	66 s.	Florence	C	(427) p.382
1329.06	60 s.	Florence	L	(289) IV p.507
1329.08	60 s.	Florence	L	(289) IV p.507
1330	63 s. 4 d.	Florence	C	(427) p.382
1330	65 s.	Florence	C	(111) p.83
1330.03-02	65 s.	Florence	C	(427) p.382
1331-1332	60 s.	Florence	C	(111) p.83
1331	60 s.	Curia	B	(439) p.901
1331	64 s.	Florence	C	(427) p.382

From 1332 the basis for this accounting system was normally the quattrino (4d. piece), the smallest coin commonly minted for the rest of the fourteenth and fifteenth centuries.

Date	Rate	Place	Type	Reference
1332	60 s.	Florence	C	(427) p.382
1332.02	62 s. 6 d.	Florence	R	(289) IV p.510
1332.05	60 s.	Florence	R	(289) IV p.510
1332.08	57 s. 6 d.	Florence	R	(289) IV p.510
1332.09	56 s. 7 d.	Florence	R	(289) IV p.510
1332.10	60 s.	Florence	R	(289) IV p.510
1332.11	61 s. 1 d.	Florence	R	(289) IV p.510
1332.12	60 s. 6 d.	Florence	R	(289) IV p.510
1333	59 s.	Florence	C	(111) p.83
1333	59 s. 9 d.	Florence	C	(427) p.382
1334	59 s. 6 d.	Florence	C	(427) p.382
1334.01	59 s.	Florence	R	(289) IV p.512
1334.11	59 s. 10 d.	Florence	R	(289) IV p.512
1334.12	59 s. 10 d.	Florence	R	(289) IV p.512
1335	62 s.	Curia	B	(439) p.902
1335	50 s. 8 d.	Florence	C	(111) p.83
1335.05	59 s.	Florence	R	(289) IV p.513
1335.07	59 s.	Florence	R	(289) IV p.513
1335.09	56 s. 6 d.	Florence	R	(289) IV p.513
1335.10	60 s.	Florence	R	(289) IV p.513
1335.11	60 s. 3 d.	Florence	R	(289) IV p.513
1335.12	60 s. 8 d.	Florence	R	(289) IV p.513
1336	61 s.	Florence	C	(111) p.83
1336.01	61 s.	Florence	R	(289) IV p.514
1336.04	61 s.	Florence	R	(289) IV p.514
1336.07	61 s.	Florence	R	(289) IV p.514
1336.12	62 s. 4 d.	Florence	R	(289) IV p.514
1337-1339	62 s.	Florence	C	(111) p.83
1337.02.13	65 s.	Florence	C	(427) p.382
1337.02.13	62 s.	Florence	C	(427) p.382
1338.02	62 s. 7 d.	Florence	R	(289) IV p.516
1338	62 s.	Florence	C	(427) p.382
1338.03	62 s. 6 d.	Florence	R	(289) IV p.516
1338.04	62 s. 2 d.	Florence	R	(289) IV p.516
1338.05	62 s. 6 d.	Florence	R	(289) IV p.516
1338.06	62 s. 6 d.	Florence	R	(289) IV p.516
1338.07	61 s. 7 d.	Florence	R	(289) IV p.516
1338.08	62 s.	Florence	R	(289) IV p.516
1338.09	61 s. 11 d.	Florence	R	(289) IV p.516
1338.10	62 s.	Florence	R	(289) IV p.516
1338.11	62 s.	Florence	R	(289) IV p.516
1339	62 s.	Florence	C	(427) p.382
1339.01	62 s. 6 d.	Florence	R	(289) IV p.517
1341	64 s.	Florence	C	(111) p.83
1341.04	64 s.	Florence	R	(289) IV p.519
1342	65 s. 8 d.	Florence	C	(111) p.83
1342.01	64 s. 10 d.	Florence	L	(289) IV p.520
1342.04	65 s. 8 d.	Florence	LWR	(289) IV p.520
1342.06	65 s. 4 d.	Florence	L	(289) IV p.520
1342.07	65 s. 6 d.	Florence	L	(289) IV p.520
1342.08	65 s. 3 d.	Florence	L	(289) IV p.520

THE FLORENTINE FLORIN IN FLORENTINE SOLDI AND DENARI

Date	Rate	Place	Type	Reference
1342.09	65 s. 4 d.	Florence	L	(289) IV p.520
1342.10	65 s.	Florence	L	(289) IV p.520
1342.10	65 s. 4 d.	Florence	LA	(289) IV p.520
1342.11	65 s. 8 d.	Florence	LA	(289) IV p.520
1342.12	65 s. 10 d.	Florence	A	(289) IV p.520
1343-1344	65 s. 6 d.	Florence	C	(111) p.83
1343.01	66 s. 1 d.	Florence	L	(289) IV p.521
1343.02	66 s.	Florence	L	(289) IV p.521
1343.03	66 s. 1 d.	Florence	W	(289) IV p.521
1343.04	66 s.	Florence	R	(289) IV p.521
1343.08	64 s. 9 d.	Florence	L	(289) IV p.521
1343.08	64 s. 8 d.	Florence	A	(289) IV p.521
1343.09	63 s. 6 d.	Florence	L	(289) IV p.521
1343.09	64 s. 6 d.	Florence	A	(289) IV p.521
1343.10	65 s. 6 d.	Florence	A	(289) IV p.521
1343.11	65 s. 8 d.	Florence	A	(289) IV p.521
1343.12	66 s.	Florence	R	(289) IV p.521
1343.12	67 s. 7 d.	Florence	A	(289) IV p.521
1344.4.22	65 s. 2 d.	Florence	C	(438) p.95
1344	65 s.	Curia	B	(439) p.902
1344	66 s.	Florence	M	(31) III p.79
1344.01	65 s. 9 d.	Florence	A	(289) IV p.522
1344.02	65 s. 8 d.	Florence	A	(289) IV p.522
1344.02	65 s. 6 d.	Florence	W	(289) IV p.522
1344.03	65 s. 2 d.	Florence	AW	(289) IV p.522
1344.04	65 s. 2 d.	Florence	A	(289) IV p.522
1344.04	66 s.	Florence	W	(289) IV p.522
1344.05	65 s. 4 d.	Florence	A	(289) IV p.522
1344.06	65 s. 4 d.	Florence	A	(289) IV p.522
1344.07	68 s.	Florence	A	(289) IV p.522
1344.08	64 s. 8 d.	Florence	A	(289) IV p.522
1344.09	65 s. 5 d.	Florence	A	(289) IV p.522
1344.10	65 s. 3 d.	Florence	A	(289) IV p.522
1344.10	65 s. 6 d.	Florence	W	(289) IV p.522
1344.11	65 s. 6 d.	Florence	A	(289) IV p.522
1344.12	65 s. 2 d.	Florence	A	(289) IV p.522
1344.12	66 s.	Florence	C	(427) p.382
1345	62 s. 8 d.	Florence	M	(31) III p.79
1345	62 s.	Florence	C	(111) p.83
1345.01	65 s. 6 d.	Florence	A	(289) IV p.523
1345.02	65 s. 4 d.	Florence	A	(289) IV p.523
1345.02	65 s. 6 d.	Florence	W	(289) IV p.523
1345.09	62 s. 1 d.	Florence	A	(289) IV p.523
1345.10	62 s. 2 d.	Florence	A	(289) IV p.523
1345.11	63 s. 4 d.	Florence	A	(289) IV p.523
1345.12	63 s. 7 d.	Florence	A	(289) IV p.523
1346	62 s.	Florence	C	(111) p.84
1346.01	63 s. 7 d.	Florence	A	(289) IV p.523
1346.02	62 s. 11 d.	Florence	A	(289) IV p.523
1346.03	62 s. 1 d.	Florence	A	(289) IV p.523
1346.04	62 s. 9 d.	Florence	A	(289) IV p.523
1346.05	62 s. 8 d.	Florence	A	(289) IV p.523
1346.06	62 s. 3 d.	Florence	A	(289) IV p.523
1346.12	62 s.	Florence	C	(427) p.382
1347	60 s.	Florence	C	(111) p.84
1347	62 s. 2 d.	Florence	M	(31) III p.79
1347.01	62 s. 4 d.	Florence	W	(289) IV p.525
1347.02	62 s.	Florence	R	(289) IV p.525
1347.02	62 s. 6 d.	Florence	L	(289) IV p.525
1347.03	68 s. 8 d.	Florence	R	(289) IV p.525
1347.03	62 s. 6 d.	Florence	L	(289) IV p.525
1347.04	62 s.	Florence	RL	(289) IV p.525
1347.05	62 s.	Florence	RWL	(289) IV p.525
1347.05	61 s. 3 d.	Florence	A	(289) IV p.525
1347.06	60 s. 3 d.	Florence	A	(289) IV p.525
1347.07.02	61 s.	Florence	C	(427) p.382
1347.08	61 s. 3 d.	Florence	R	(289) IV p.525
1347.08	60 s. 5 d.	Florence	L	(289) IV p.525
1347.08	61 s. 8 d.	Florence	A	(289) IV p.525
1347.09	62 s.	Florence	W	(289) IV p.525
1347.09	61 s. 5 d.	Florence	A	(289) IV p.525
1347.10	62 s. 6 d.	Florence	R	(289) IV p.525

THE FLORENTINE FLORIN IN FLORENTINE SOLDI AND DENARI

Date	Rate	Place	Type	Reference
1347.10	62 s. 5 d.	Florence	L	(289) IV p.525
1347.10	62 s. 5 d.	Florence	A	(289) IV p.525
1347.11	62 s. 6 d.	Florence	R	(289) IV p.525
1347.11	61 s. 9 d.	Florence	A	(289) IV p.525
1347.12	62 s. 9 d.	Florence	R	(289) IV p.525
1347.12	62 s. 1 d.	Florence	A	(289) IV p.525
1348	63 s.	Florence	C	(111) p.84
1348.01	62 s. 8 d.	Florence	A	(289) IV p.526
1348.01	62 s. 6 d.	Florence	W	(289) IV p.526
1348.01	62 s. 11 d.	Florence	R	(289) IV p.526
1348.01	63 s.	Florence	L	(289) IV p.526
1348.02	62 s. 8 d.	Florence	A	(289) IV p.526
1348.04	62 s. 8 d.	Florence	L	(289) IV p.526
1348.05	63 s. 1 d.	Florence	A	(289) IV p.526
1348.05	61 s. 4 d.	Florence	W	(289) IV p.526
1348.05	63 s.	Florence	L	(289) IV p.526
1348.06	63 s. 2 d.	Florence	A	(289) IV p.526
1348.07	60 s. 2 d.	Florence	W	(289) IV p.526
1348.07	60 s. 2 d.	Florence	L	(289) IV p.526
1348.08	61 s. 7 d.	Florence	W	(289) IV p.526
1348.08	61 s. 8 d.	Florence	L	(289) IV p.526
1348.09	61 s. 9 d.	Florence	W	(289) IV p.526
1348.09	62 s. 6 d.	Florence	L	(289) IV p.526
1348.10.13	63 s.	Florence	C	(427) p.382
1348.11	63 s. 9 d.	Florence	A	(289) IV p.526
1348.12	63 s. 11 d.	Florence	A	(289) IV p.526
1349.08	63 s. 10 d.	Florence	A	(289) IV p.527
1349.11	62 s. 6 d.	Florence	A	(289) IV p.527
1350.08	64 s.	Florence	A	(289) IV p.528
1350.09	64 s. 4 d.	Florence	A	(289) IV p.528
1350.10	64 s. 3 d.	Florence	A	(289) IV p.528

In the second half of the fourteenth century the Florentine florin weighed 3.34 or 3.33 grams.

Date	Rate	Place	Type	Reference
1351	64 s.	Florence	M	(31) III p.79
1351	68 s. 9 d.	Florence	C	(111) p.84
1351.10	65 s. 6 d.	Florence	R	(289) IV p.529
1351.10	66 s.	Florence	R	(289) IV p.529
1352.05.10	67 s. 9 d.	Florence	C	(438) p.105
1352.12	67 s. 4 d.	Florence	W	(289) IV p.530
1352-1353	68 s.	Florence	C	(111) p.84
1353.02	68 s.	Florence	W	(289) IV p.531
1353.05-06	68 s.	Florence	C	(438) p.111
1353.05-06	67 s. 9 d.	Florence	C	(438) p.113
1353.06	69 s.	Florence	W	(289) IV p.531
1353.10	68 s. 6 d.	Florence	W	(289) IV p.531
1354	70 s.	Florence	M	(31) III p.79
1354	69 s. 10 d.	Florence	C	(111) p.84
1354.12.05	69 s. 10 d.	Florence	C	(427) p.382
1355	69 s.	Florence	C	(111) p.84
1355.11.28	71 s.	Florence	C	(427) p.382
1356-1358	70 s.	Florence	M	(31) III p.79
1356.01	69 s.	Florence	R	(289) IV p.534
1356.03	69 s. 4 d.	Florence	R	(289) IV p.534
1356.04	69 s.	Florence	W	(289) IV p.534
1356.05	68 s. 6 d.	Florence	R	(289) IV p.534
1357.01	68 s. 4 d.	Florence	R	(289) IV p.535
1358	67 s. 10 d.	Florence	C	(438) p.138
1358	70 s.	Florence	C	(111) p.84
1358.05	68 s.	Florence	R	(289) IV p.536
1358.07	66 s. 11 d.	Florence	C	(438) p.144
1358.09	67 s.	Florence	R	(289) IV p.536
1358.11	67 s. 3 d.	Florence	M	(289) IV p.536
1358.11.03	70 s.	Florence	C	(427) p.382
1359	67 s. 3 d.	Florence	M	(31) III p.79
1360	68 s.	Florence	M	(31) III p.79
1361	68 s.	Florence	C	(111) p.84
1361.10	68 s.	Florence	R	(289) IV p.539
1362	67 s. 2 d.	Florence	M	(31) III p.79
1362.08	65 s. 4 d.	Florence	R	(289) IV p.540
1362.11	66 s.	Florence	R	(289) IV p.540

THE FLORENTINE FLORIN IN FLORENTINE SOLDI AND DENARI

Date	Rate	Place	Type	Reference
1363	65 s. 10 d.	Florence	M	(31) III p.79
1363.01	66 s. 9 d.	Florence	A	(289) IV p541
1363.02	66 s. 8 d.	Florence	A	(289) IV p541
1363.10	65 s.	Florence	R	(289) IV p541
1363.11	65 s.	Florence	R	(289) IV p541
1364.05	65 s. 6 d.	Florence	A	(289) IV p541
1364.06	65 s. 5 d.	Florence	A	(289) IV p541
1364.06	67 s.	Florence	W	(289) IV p541
1364.07	65 s. 8 d.	Florence	A	(289) IV p541
1364.08	65 s. 8 d.	Florence	A	(289) IV p541
1364.10	66 s. 10 d.	Florence	R	(289) IV p541
1364.11	66 s.	Florence	R	(289) IV p541
1364.11	66 s. 3 d.	Florence	A	(289) IV p541
1365	66 s. 4 d.	Florence	M	(31) III p.79
1365.01	66 s. 2 d.	Florence	A	(289) IV p.543
1365.02	66 s. 9 d.	Florence	A	(289) IV p.543
1365.03	66 s. 5 d.	Florence	A	(289) IV p.543
1365.04	66 s. 9 d.	Florence	A	(289) IV p.543
1365.06	66 s. 2 d.	Florence	A	(289) IV p.543
1365.08	66 s. 3 d.	Florence	A	(289) IV p.543
1365.10	66 s. 9 d.	Florence	W	(289) IV p.543
1365.10	66 s. 7 d.	Florence	A	(289) IV p.543
1365.11	67 s. 3 d.	Florence	W	(289) IV p.543
1365.11	66 s. 10 d.	Florence	A	(289) IV p.543
1365.11	66 s.	Florence	W	(289) IV p.543
1365.12	68 s.	Florence	W	(289) IV p.543
1365.12	66 s. 9 d.	Florence	A	(289) IV p.543
1366.01	67 s. 1 d.	Florence	A	(289) IV p.544
1366.02	67 s. 5 d.	Florence	A	(289) IV p.544
1366.03	68 s.	Florence	W	(289) IV p.544
1366.07	68 s.	Florence	R	(289) IV p.544
1366.10	67 s.	Florence	W	(289) IV p.544
1367.01	67 s.	Florence	W	(289) IV p.545
1367.02	67 s. 2 d.	Florence	W	(289) IV p.545
1367.04	67 s.	Florence	W	(289) IV p.545
1368.06	66 s.	Florence	W	(289) IV p.546
1368.07	67 s.	Florence	W	(289) IV p.546
1368.08	66 s.	Florence	R	(289) IV p.546
1368.10	66 s. 6 d.	Florence	A	(460) p.148
1368.10	66 s.	Florence	WR	(289) IV p.546
1368.11	66 s.	Florence	W	(289) IV p.546
1368-1369	65 s. 8 d.	Florence	M	(31) III p.79
1369.03	65 s. 6 d.	Florence	R	(289) IV p.527
1370	65 s. 6 d.	Florence	M	(31) III p.79
1370	68 s. 3 d.	Florence	C	(111) p.84
1370.11	66 s. 6 d.	Florence	W	(289) IV p.548
1371	65 s. 2 d.	Florence	M	(31) III p.79
1374	73 s. 4 d.	Florence	M	(31) III p.79
1375	76 s. 8 d.	Florence	M	(31) III p.79
1375.10	70 s.	Florence	W	(289) IV p.553
1378	68 s.	Florence	C	(111) p.84
1379-1380	70 s.	Florence	C	(111) p.84
1379.05	76 s.	Florence	W	(289) IV p.557
1381	72 s.	Florence	M	(31) III p.79
1381	72 s. 6 d.	Florence	C	(111) p.84
1382	73 s.	Florence	M	(31) III p.79
1383	74 s.	Florence	M	(31) III p.79
1384	73 s. 4 d.	Florence	M	(31) III p.79
1385	72 s. 4 d.	Florence	M	(31) III p.79
1386	74 s.	Florence	M	(31) III p.79
1386	73 s. 4 d.	Florence	C	(111) p.84
1387	74 s. 6 d.	Florence	M	(31) III p.79

From 1389 to 1432 the rates are mainly taken from those noted down by the proveditori degli cambiatori (520). They noted down two rates each day when the exchange was carried on. The column in which the lower rates were entered was headed 'dassene' (one gives for it) and that in which the higher rates were entered, 'vale'. These rates were presumably those for the exchange of gold to silver and of silver to gold. I have abstracted the rates for the first working day of each month. Mario Bernocchi has recently published the full series (31) IV.

THE FLORENTINE FLORIN IN FLORENTINE SOLDI AND DENARI

Date	Rate	Place	Type	Reference
1389.01.04	75 s. 2 2/3 d.	Florence	M	(520)
1389.01.04	75 s. 4 5/6 d.	Florence	M	(520)
1389.02.01	75 s.	Florence	M	(520)
1389.02.01	75 s. 2 d.	Florence	M	(520)
1389.03.01	74 s. 6 d.	Florence	M	(520)
1389.03.01	74 s. 8 d.	Florence	M	(520)
1389.04.01	74 s. 8 3/5 d.	Florence	M	(520)
1389.04.01	74 s. 10 3/5 d.	Florence	M	(520)
1389.05.04	74 s. 8 d.	Florence	M	(520)
1389.05.04	74 s. 10 1/2 d.	Florence	M	(520)
1389.06.01	74 s. 4 d.	Florence	M	(520)
1389.06.01	74 s. 6 d.	Florence	M	(520)
1389.07.01	73 s. 10 d.	Florence	M	(520)
1389.07.01	74 s. 1/5 d.	Florence	M	(520)
1389.08.02	73 s. 9 d.	Florence	M	(520)
1389.08.02	73 s. 11 3/4 d.	Florence	M	(520)
1389.09.01	73 s. 6 3/5 d.	Florence	M	(520)
1389.09.01	73 s. 8 3/5 d.	Florence	M	(520)
1389.10.01	73 s. 11 d.	Florence	M	(520)
1389.10.01	75 s. 1 d.	Florence	M	(520)
1389.11.03	73 s. 8 d.	Florence	M	(520)
1389.11.03	73 s. 10 d.	Florence	M	(520)
1389.12.01	74 s. 2 d.	Florence	M	(520)
1389.12.01	74 s. 4 d.	Florence	M	(520)
1390.01.03	75 s. 4 d.	Florence	M	(520)
1390.01.03	75 s. 6 d.	Florence	M	(520)
1390.02.01	75 s. 3 d.	Florence	M	(520)
1390.02.01	75 s. 5 d.	Florence	M	(520)
1390.03.01	74 s. 10 d.	Florence	M	(520)
1390.03.01	75 s.	Florence	M	(520)
1390.04.02	74 s. 10 d.	Florence	M	(520)
1390.04.02	74 s. 11 3/5 d.	Florence	M	(520)
1390.05.02	75 s. 6 4/5 d.	Florence	M	(520)
1390.05.02	75 s. 8 4/5 d.	Florence	M	(520)
1390.06.01	76 s. 4 d.	Florence	M	(520)
1390.06.01	76 s. 6 d.	Florence	M	(520)
1390.07.01	76 s. 1 d.	Florence	M	(520)
1390.07.01	76 s. 3 3/5 d.	Florence	M	(520)
1390.08.02	74 s. 8 d.	Florence	M	(520)
1390.08.02	74 s. 10 2/5 d.	Florence	M	(520)
1390.09.01	74 s. 7 d.	Florence	M	(520)
1390.09.01	74 s. 9 2/5 d.	Florence	M	(520)
1390.10.01	75 s. 10 d.	Florence	M	(520)
1390.10.01	76 s. 1 d.	Florence	M	(520)
1390.11.03	75 s. 2 d.	Florence	M	(520)
1390.11.03	75 s. 4 d.	Florence	M	(520)
1390.12.01	75 s. 4 d.	Florence	M	(520)
1390.12.01	75 s. 6 d.	Florence	M	(520)
1391.01.02	76 s.	Florence	M	(520)
1391.01.02	76 s. 2 d.	Florence	M	(520)
1391.02.01	75 s. 9 d.	Florence	M	(520)
1391.02.01	75 s. 10 3/5 d.	Florence	M	(520)

In 1390 the Florentine florin weighed 3.52 grams.

Date	Rate	Place	Type	Reference
1391.03.01	75 s. 8 d.	Florence	M	(520)
1391.03.01	75 s. 10 d.	Florence	M	(520)
1391.04.01	75 s. 3 d.	Florence	M	(520)
1391.04.01	75 s. 5 3/5 d.	Florence	M	(520)
1391.05.02	75 s.	Florence	M	(520)
1391.05.02	75 s. 2 4/5 d.	Florence	M	(520)
1391.06.01	75 s. 1 d.	Florence	M	(520)
1391.06.01	75 s. 3 d.	Florence	M	(520)
1391.07.01	73 s. 11 d.	Florence	M	(520)
1391.07.01	74 s. 1 1/5 d.	Florence	M	(520)
1391.08.02	74 s. 5 d.	Florence	M	(520)
1391.08.02	74 s. 6 4/5 d.	Florence	M	(520)
1391.09.01	73 s. 4 d.	Florence	M	(520)
1391.09.01	73 s. 6 d.	Florence	M	(520)
1391.10.02	75 s.	Florence	M	(520)
1391.10.02	75 s. 1 3/5 d.	Florence	M	(520)
1391.11.03	73 s. 11 d.	Florence	M	(520)

THE FLORENTINE FLORIN IN FLORENTINE SOLDI AND DENARI

Date	Rate	Place	Type	Reference
1391.11.03	74 s. 1 d.	Florence	M	(520)
1391.12.01	74 s. 1 3/5 d.	Florence	M	(520)
1391.12.01	74 s. 3 3/5 d.	Florence	M	(520)
1392.01.02	75 s. 2 d.	Florence	M	(520)
1392.01.02	75 s. 4 4/5 d.	Florence	M	(520)
1392.02.01	75 s. 1 d.	Florence	M	(520)
1392.02.01	75 s. 1 4/5 d.	Florence	M	(520)
1392.03.01	74 s. 9 d.	Florence	M	(520)
1392.03.01	74 s. 10 4/5 d.	Florence	M	(520)
1392.04.01	75 s.	Florence	M	(520)
1392.04.01	75 s. 2 2/5 d.	Florence	M	(520)
1392.05.02	75 s.	Florence	M	(520)
1392.05.02	75 s. 2 d.	Florence	M	(520)
1392.06.01	75 s.	Florence	M	(520)
1392.06.01	75 s. 2 3/5 d.	Florence	M	(520)
1392.07.01	74 s. 8 d.	Florence	M	(520)
1392.07.01	74 s. 10 4/5 d.	Florence	M	(520)
1392.08.02	75 s. 2 d.	Florence	M	(520)
1392.08.02	75 s.	Florence	M	(520)
1392.09.02	74 s. 11 d.	Florence	M	(520)
1392.09.02	75 s. 1 d.	Florence	M	(520)
1392.10.01	75 s. 6 d.	Florence	M	(520)
1392.10.01	75 s. 8 4/5 d.	Florence	M	(520)
1392.11.04	75 s. 8 d.	Florence	M	(520)
1392.11.04	75 s. 9 3/5 d.	Florence	M	(520)
1392.12.02	76 s. 3 d.	Florence	M	(520)
1392.12.02	76 s. 5 d.	Florence	M	(520)
1393.01.02	76 s. 10 d.	Florence	M	(520)
1393.01.02	77 s.	Florence	M	(520)
1393.02.01	75 s. 3 d.	Florence	M	(520)
1393.02.01	75 s. 5 d.	Florence	M	(520)
1393.03.01	76 s. 4 d.	Florence	M	(520)
1393.03.01	76 s. 6 d.	Florence	M	(520)
1393.04.01	75 s. 2 d.	Florence	M	(520)
1393.04.01	75 s. 4 d.	Florence	M	(520)
1393.05.05	76 s. 1 d.	Florence	M	(520)
1393.05.05	76 s. 3 d.	Florence	M	(520)
1393.06.02	75 s. 8 d.	Florence	M	(520)
1393.06.02	75 s. 10 d.	Florence	M	(520)
1393.07.01	75 s.	Florence	M	(520)
1393.07.01	75 s. 2 3/5 d.	Florence	M	(520)
1393.08.04	75 s.	Florence	M	(520)
1393.08.04	75 s. 2 d.	Florence	M	(520)
1393.09.01	74 s. 6 d.	Florence	M	(520)
1393.09.01	74 s. 8 1/5 d.	Florence	M	(520)
1393.10.01	75 s. 9 d.	Florence	M	(520)
1393.10.01	75 s. 11 1/5 d.	Florence	M	(520)
1393.11.04	75 s. 10 3/5 d.	Florence	M	(520)
1393.11.04	76 s. 3/5 d.	Florence	M	(520)
1393.12.01	76 s. 1 d.	Florence	M	(520)
1393.12.01	76 s. 3 d.	Florence	M	(520)
1394.01.02	76 s. 10 d.	Florence	M	(520)
1394.01.02	77 s. 4/5 d.	Florence	M	(520)
1394.02.03	76 s. 7 1/5 d.	Florence	M	(31) IV p.34
1394.02.03	76 s. 9 1/5 d.	Florence	M	(31) IV p.34
1394.03.04	76 s. 7 3/5 d.	Florence	M	(31) IV p.35
1394.03.04	76 s. 9 4/5 d.	Florence	M	(31) IV p.35
1394.04.01	76 s. 8 3/5 d.	Florence	M	(31) IV p.35
1394.04.01	76 s. 10 4/5 d.	Florence	M	(31) IV p.35
1394.05.02	76 s. 8 1/5 d.	Florence	M	(31) IV p.36
1394.05.02	76 s. 10 2/5 d.	Florence	M	(31) IV p.36
1394.06.01	76 s. 7 3/5 d.	Florence	M	(31) IV p.36
1394.06.01	76 s. 10 1/5 d.	Florence	M	(31) IV p.36
1394.07.01	76 s. 6 3/5 d.	Florence	M	(31) IV p.37
1394.07.01	76 s. 8 3/5 d.	Florence	M	(31) IV p.37
1394.08.03	76 s. 2 1/5 d.	Florence	M	(31) IV p.37
1394.08.03	76 s. 4 2/5 d.	Florence	M	(31) IV p.37
1394.09.01	75 s. 7 4/5 d.	Florence	M	(31) IV p.38
1394.09.01	75 s. 9 4/5 d.	Florence	M	(31) IV p.38
1394.10.01	76 s. 9 4/5 d.	Florence	M	(31) IV p.38
1394.10.01	77 s. 1/5 d.	Florence	M	(31) IV p.38
1394.11.03	76 s. 8 2/5 d.	Florence	M	(31) IV p.39

THE FLORENTINE FLORIN IN FLORENTINE SOLDI AND DENARI

Date	Rate	Place	Type	Reference
1394.11.03	76 s. 10 1/5 d.	Florence	M	(31) IV p.39
1394.12.01	76 s. 9 2/5 d.	Florence	M	(31) IV p.39
1394.12.01	76 s. 11 2/5 d.	Florence	M	(31) IV p.39
1395.01.02	77 s. 6 3/5 d.	Florence	M	(520)
1395.01.02	77 s. 9 2/5 d.	Florence	M	(520)
1395.02.01	77 s. 3/5 d.	Florence	M	(31) IV p.40
1395.02.01	77 s. 2 4/5 d.	Florence	M	(31) IV p.40
1395.03.01	77 s. 2 d.	Florence	M	(31) IV p.41
1395.03.01	77 s. 4 d.	Florence	M	(31) IV p.41
1395.04.01	76 s. 7 1/5 d.	Florence	M	(31) IV p.41
1395.04.01	76 s. 9 3/5 d.	Florence	M	(31) IV p.42
1395.05.04	77 s. 2 1/5 d.	Florence	M	(31) IV p.42
1395.05.04	77 s. 4 1/5 d.	Florence	M	(31) IV p.42
1395.06.02	76 s. 5 1/5 d.	Florence	M	(31) IV p.42
1395.06.02	76 s. 7 3/5 d.	Florence	M	(31) IV p.42
1395.07.01	76 s. 1 2/5 d.	Florence	M	(31) IV p.43
1395.07.01	76 s. 4 1/5 d.	Florence	M	(31) IV p.43
1395.08.02	76 s. 4 3/5 d.	Florence	M	(31) IV p.43
1395.08.02	76 s. 6 2/5 d.	Florence	M	(31) IV p.43
1395.09.01	76 s. 1 d.	Florence	M	(31) IV p.44
1395.09.01	76 s. 3 1/5 d.	Florence	M	(31) IV p.44
1395.10.01	76 s. 10 4/5 d.	Florence	M	(31) IV p.44
1395.10.01	77 s. 1 3/5 d.	Florence	M	(31) IV p.44
1395.11.03	75 s. 11 2/5 d.	Florence	M	(31) IV p.45
1395.11.03	76 s. 1 3/5 d.	Florence	M	(31) IV p.45
1395.12.01	76 s. 7 4/5 d.	Florence	M	(31) IV p.45
1395.12.01	76 s. 10 1/5 d.	Florence	M	(31) IV p.45
1396.01.02	77 s. 3/5 d.	Florence	M	(520)
1396.01.02	77 s. 3 3/5 d.	Florence	M	(520)
1396.02.01	76 s. 10 2/5 d.	Florence	M	(31) IV p.46
1396.02.01	77 s. 2/5 d.	Florence	M	(31) IV p.46
1396.03.01	76 s. 3 2/5 d.	Florence	M	(31) IV p.47
1396.03.01	76 s. 6 1/5 d.	Florence	M	(31) IV p.47
1396.04.01	76 s. 9 2/5 d.	Florence	M	(31) IV p.47
1396.04.01	76 s. 11 1/5 d.	Florence	M	(31) IV p.47
1396.05.02	76 s. 11 3/5 d.	Florence	M	(31) IV p.48
1396.05.02	77 s. 2 d.	Florence	M	(31) IV p.48
1396.06.02	76 s. 8 d.	Florence	M	(31) IV p.48
1396.06.02	76 s. 10 d.	Florence	M	(31) IV p.48
1396.07.01	76 s. 3 2/5 d.	Florence	M	(31) IV p.49
1396.07.01	76 s. 6 d.	Florence	M	(31) IV p.49
1396.08.02	76 s. 3 d.	Florence	M	(31) IV p.49
1396.08.02	76 s. 5 d.	Florence	M	(31) IV p.49
1396.09.01	76 s. 1 2/5 d.	Florence	M	(31) IV p.50
1396.09.01	76 s. 4 d.	Florence	M	(31) IV p.50
1396.10.02	76 s. 11 2/5 d.	Florence	M	(31) IV p.50
1396.10.02	77 s. 2 d.	Florence	M	(31) IV p.50
1396.11.03	76 s. 6 3/5 d.	Florence	M	(31) IV p.51
1396.11.03	76 s. 9 d.	Florence	M	(31) IV p.51
1396.12.01	76 s. 9 4/5 d.	Florence	M	(31) IV p.51
1396.12.01	77 s. 1/5 d.	Florence	M	(31) IV p.51
1397.01.02	77 s. 3 1/5 d.	Florence	M	(520)
1397.01.02	77 s. 9 4/5 d.	Florence	M	(520)
1397.02.01	77 s. 2 1/5 d.	Florence	M	(31) IV p.52
1397.02.01	77 s. 5 d.	Florence	M	(31) IV p.52
1397.03.03	76 s. 9 3/5 d.	Florence	M	(31) IV p.53
1397.03.03	77 s.	Florence	M	(31) IV p.53
1397.04.02	76 s. 11 3/5 d.	Florence	M	(31) IV p.53
1397.04.02	77 s. 1 4/5 d.	Florence	M	(31) IV p.53
1397.05.02	77 s. 3 2/5 d.	Florence	M	(31) IV p.54
1397.05.02	77 s. 6 d.	Florence	M	(31) IV p.54
1397.06.01	77 s. 7 2/5 d.	Florence	M	(31) IV p.54
1397.06.01	77 s. 10 d.	Florence	M	(31) IV p.54
1397.07.02	77 s. 8 4/5 d.	Florence	M	(31) IV p.55
1397.07.02	77 s. 11 1/5 d.	Florence	M	(31) IV p.55
1397.08.02	77 s. 7 d.	Florence	M	(31) IV p.55
1397.08.02	77 s. 9 3/5 d.	Florence	M	(31) IV p.55
1397.09.01	77 s. 1 3/5 d.	Florence	M	(31) IV p.56
1397.09.01	77 s. 4 d.	Florence	M	(31) IV p.56
1397.10.01	77 s. 8 d.	Florence	M	(31) IV p.56
1397.10.01	77 s. 10 4/5 d.	Florence	M	(31) IV p.56
1397.11.03	77 s. 5 2/5 d.	Florence	M	(31) IV p.57

THE FLORENTINE FLORIN IN FLORENTINE SOLDI AND DENARI

Date	Rate	Place	Type	Reference
1397.11.03	77 s. 8 d.	Florence	M	(31) IV p.57
1397.12.01	77 s. 6 4/5 d.	Florence	M	(31) IV p.57
1397.12.01	77 s. 9 1/5 d.	Florence	M	(31) IV p.57
1398.01.02	78 s. 2 2/5 d.	Florence	M	(520)
1398.01.02	78 s. 5 4/5 d.	Florence	M	(520)
1398.02.01	77 s. 8 1/5 d.	Florence	M	(31) IV p.58
1398.02.01	77 s. 10 3/5 d.	Florence	M	(31) IV p.58
1398.03.01	77 s. 4 4/5 d.	Florence	M	(31) IV p.59
1398.03.01	77 s. 7 1/5 d.	Florence	M	(31) IV p.59
1398.04.01	76 s. 4 1/5 d.	Florence	M	(31) IV p.59
1398.04.01	76 s. 6 3/5 d.	Florence	M	(31) IV p.59
1398.05.02	77 s. 1 d.	Florence	M	(31) IV p.60
1398.05.02	77 s. 4 d.	Florence	M	(31) IV p.60
1398.06.01	76 s. 9 1/5 d.	Florence	M	(31) IV p.60
1398.06.01	76 s. 11 4/5 d.	Florence	M	(31) IV p.60
1398.07.01	76 s. 4/5 d.	Florence	M	(31) IV p.61
1398.07.01	76 s. 3 3/5 d.	Florence	M	(31) IV p.61
1398.08.02	76 s. 3 1/5 d.	Florence	M	(31) IV p.61
1398.08.02	76 s. 6 d.	Florence	M	(31) IV p.61
1398.09.02	76 s. 3 2/5 d.	Florence	M	(31) IV p.62
1398.09.02	76 s. 6 d.	Florence	M	(31) IV p.62
1398.10.01	77 s. 9 d.	Florence	M	(31) IV p.62
1398.10.01	77 s. 11 2/5 d.	Florence	M	(31) IV p.62
1398.11.04	76 s. 10 2/5 d.	Florence	M	(31) IV p.63
1398.11.04	77 s. 2/5 d.	Florence	M	(31) IV p.63
1398.12.02	77 s. 2 3/5 d.	Florence	M	(31) IV p.63
1398.12.02	77 s. 5 4/5 d.	Florence	M	(31) IV p.63
1399.01.02	77 s. 8 3/5 d.	Florence	M	(520)
1399.01.02	77 s. 11 1/5 d.	Florence	M	(520)
1399.02.01	76 s. 11 3/5 d.	Florence	M	(31) IV p.64
1399.02.01	77 s. 1 4/5 d.	Florence	M	(31) IV p.64
1399.03.01	77 s. 2 1/5 d.	Florence	M	(31) IV p.65
1399.03.01	77 s. 4 2/5 d.	Florence	M	(31) IV p.65
1399.04.03	76 s. 9 3/5 d.	Florence	M	(31) IV p.65
1399.04.03	77 s.	Florence	M	(31) IV p.65
1399.05.02	77 s. 1 d.	Florence	M	(31) IV p.66
1399.05.02	77 s. 6 d.	Florence	M	(31) IV p.66
1399.06.02	76 s. 11 4/5 d.	Florence	M	(31) IV p.66
1399.06.02	77 s. 1 4/5 d.	Florence	M	(31) IV p.66
1399.07.01	76 s. 3 3/5 d.	Florence	M	(31) IV p.67
1399.07.01	76 s. 5 3/5 d.	Florence	M	(31) IV p.67
1399.08.02	76 s. 7 d.	Florence	M	(31) IV p.67
1399.08.02	76 s. 9 d.	Florence	M	(31) IV p.67
1399.09.09	75 s. 9 3/5 d.	Florence	M	(31) IV p.68
1399.09.09	75 s. 11 3/5 d.	Florence	M	(31) IV p.68
1399.10.01	77 s. 2/5 d.	Florence	M	(31) IV p.68
1399.10.01	77 s. 2 2/5 d.	Florence	M	(31) IV p.68
1399.11.04	76 s. 10 1/5 d.	Florence	M	(31) IV p.69
1399.11.04	77 s. 1 d.	Florence	M	(31) IV p.69
1399.12.01	77 s. 3 4/5 d.	Florence	M	(31) IV p.69
1399.12.01	77 s. 5 4/5 d.	Florence	M	(31) IV p.69
1400.01.02	77 s. 11 3/5 d.	Florence	M	(520)
1400.01.02	78 s. 1 4/5 d.	Florence	M	(520)
1400.02.04	77 s. 4 1/5 d.	Florence	M	(520)
1400.02.04	77 s. 6 2/5 d.	Florence	M	(520)
1400.03.03	77 s. 4 1/5 d.	Florence	M	(520)
1400.03.03	77 s. 6 1/5 d.	Florence	M	(520)
1400.04.01	76 s. 3 3/5 d.	Florence	M	(520)
1400.04.01	76 s. 6 d.	Florence	M	(520)
1400.05.04	76 s. 6 3/5 d.	Florence	M	(520)
1400.05.04	76 s. 9 d.	Florence	M	(520)
1400.06.01	76 s. 5 1/5 d.	Florence	M	(520)
1400.06.01	76 s. 7 1/5 d.	Florence	M	(520)
1400.07.01	76 s. 1 d.	Florence	M	(520)
1400.07.01	76 s. 3 d.	Florence	M	(520)
1400.07.19-08.29	76 s. 1 d.	Florence	M	(520)
1400.08.30	76 s. 2 d.	Florence	M	(520)
1400.09.01-07	76 s. 7 d.	Florence	M	(520)
1400.09.20	76 s. 6 d.	Florence	M	(520)
1400.09.20	76 s. 8 d.	Florence	M	(520)
1400.10.01	77 s.	Florence	M	(520)
1400.10.01	77 s. 4 d.	Florence	M	(520)

Date	Rate	Place	Type	Reference
1400.11.03	76 s. 6 d.	Florence	M	(520)
1400.11.03	76 s. 7 4/5 d.	Florence	M	(520)
1400.12.01	76 s. 9 d.	Florence	M	(520)
1400.12.01	76 s. 11 d.	Florence	M	(520)
1401.01.03	77 s. 1 2/5 d.	Florence	M	(520)
1401.01.03	77 s. 4 d.	Florence	M	(520)
1401.02.04	76 s. 7 3/5 d.	Florence	M	(31) IV p.76
1401.02.04	76 s. 10 d.	Florence	M	(31) IV p.76
1401.03.01	76 s. 6 d.	Florence	M	(31) IV p.77
1401.03.01	76 s. 8 d.	Florence	M	(31) IV p.77
1401.04.02	76 s. 3 1/5 d.	Florence	M	(31) IV p.77
1401.04.02	76 s. 5 d.	Florence	M	(31) IV p.77
1401.05.02	76 s. 4 3/5 d.	Florence	M	(31) IV p.78
1401.05.02	76 s. 7 4/5 d.	Florence	M	(31) IV p.78
1401.06.01	76 s.	Florence	M	(31) IV p.78
1401.06.01	76 s. 2 2/5 d.	Florence	M	(31) IV p.78
1401.07.01	75 s. 5 1/5 d.	Florence	M	(31) IV p.79
1401.07.01	75 s. 7 1/5 d.	Florence	M	(31) IV p.79
1401.08.02	74 s. 9 3/5 d.	Florence	M	(31) IV p.79
1401.08.02	74 s. 11 4/5 d.	Florence	M	(31) IV p.79
1401.09.01	75 s. 2 3/5 d.	Florence	M	(31) IV p.80
1401.09.01	75 s. 4 2/5 d.	Florence	M	(31) IV p.80
1401.10.01	75 s. 7 3/5 d.	Florence	M	(31) IV p.80
1401.10.01	75 s. 10 d.	Florence	M	(31) IV p.80
1401.11.01	75 s. 9 d.	Florence	M	(31) IV p.81
1401.11.01	75 s. 11 d.	Florence	M	(31) IV p.81
1401.12.01	76 s. 4 d.	Florence	M	(31) IV p.81
1401.12.01	76 s. 6 d.	Florence	M	(31) IV p.81
1402.01.02	76 s. 10 d.	Florence	M	(520)
1402.01.02	77 s. 2/5 d.	Florence	M	(520)
1402.02.01	76 s.	Florence	M	(31) IV p.82
1402.02.01	76 s. 2 1/5 d.	Florence	M	(31) IV p.82
1402.03.01	76 s.	Florence	M	(31) IV p.83
1402.03.01	76 s. 2 d.	Florence	M	(31) IV p.83
1402.04.01	76 s. 4/5 d.	Florence	M	(31) IV p.83
1402.04.01	76 s. 2 4/5 d.	Florence	M	(31) IV p.83
1402.05.02	76 s. 4 1/5 d.	Florence	M	(31) IV p.84
1402.05.02	76 s. 6 d.	Florence	M	(31) IV p.84

28 May 1402 new florins ordered to weigh only 3.33 grams. Only a very few seem to have been struck and florins were very soon again being minted at the accustomed weight of 3.54 grams (223) pp.422-5.

Date	Rate	Place	Type	Reference
1402.06.01	76 s. 1 1/5 d.	Florence	M	(31) IV p.84
1402.06.01	76 s. 3 2/5 d.	Florence	M	(31) IV p.84
1402.07.01	75 s. 11 1/5 d.	Florence	M	(31) IV p.85
1402.07.01	76 s. 1 1/5 d.	Florence	M	(31) IV p.85
1402.08.02	75 s. 6 2/5 d.	Florence	M	(31) IV p.85
1402.08.02	75 s. 8 1/5 d.	Florence	M	(31) IV p.85
1402.09.01	76 s. 5 d.	Florence	M	(31) IV p.86
1402.09.01	76 s. 7 1/5 d.	Florence	M	(31) IV p.86
1402.10.02	76 s. 10 2/5 d.	Florence	M	(31) IV p.86
1402.10.02	77 s. 1/5 d.	Florence	M	(31) IV p.86
1402.11.03	76 s. 7 d.	Florence	M	(31) IV p.87
1402.11.03	76 s. 9 d.	Florence	M	(31) IV p.87
1402.12.01	76 s. 8 2/5 d.	Florence	M	(520)
1402.12.01	76 s. 10 4/5 d.	Florence	M	(520)
1403.01.02	77 s. 2 2/5 d.	Florence	M	(520)
1403.01.02	77 s. 4 3/5 d.	Florence	M	(520)
1403.02.01	77 s. 1 4/5 d.	Florence	M	(31) IV p.93
1403.02.01	77 s. 3 4/5 d.	Florence	M	(31) IV p.93
1403.03.01	76 s. 10 d.	Florence	M	(31) IV p.94
1403.03.01	77 s. 1/5 d.	Florence	M	(31) IV p.94
1403.04.02	76 s. 9 2/5 d.	Florence	M	(31) IV p.94
1403.04.02	76 s. 11 2/5 d.	Florence	M	(31) IV p.94
1403.05.02	76 s. 10 d.	Florence	M	(31) IV p.95
1403.05.02	77 s.	Florence	M	(31) IV p.95
1403.06.01	76 s. 9 3/5 d.	Florence	M	(31) IV p.95
1403.06.01	76 s. 11 4/5 d.	Florence	M	(31) IV p.95
1403.07.02	76 s. 2/5 d.	Florence	M	(31) IV p.96
1403.07.02	76 s. 2 2/5 d.	Florence	M	(31) IV p.96
1403.08.02	76 s. 8 1/5 d.	Florence	M	(31) IV p.96

THE FLORENTINE FLORIN IN FLORENTINE SOLDI AND DENARI

Date	Rate	Place	Type	Reference
1403.08.02	76 s. 10 1/5 d.	Florence	M	(31) IV p.96
1403.09.01	76 s. 9 3/5 d.	Florence	M	(31) IV p.97
1403.09.01	76 s. 11 4/5 d.	Florence	M	(31) IV p.97
1403.10.01	77 s.	Florence	M	(31) IV p.97
1403.10.01	77 s. 2 1/5 d.	Florence	M	(31) IV p.97
1403.11.03	76 s. 7 1/5 d.	Florence	M	(31) IV p.98
1403.11.03	76 s. 9 2/5 d.	Florence	M	(31) IV p.98
1403.12.01	76 s. 8 2/5 d.	Florence	M	(520)
1403.12.01	76 s. 10 2/5 d.	Florence	M	(520)
1404.01.02	77 s.	Florence	M	(520)
1404.01.02	77 s. 2 1/5 d.	Florence	M	(520)
1404.02.01	76 s. 2 4/5 d.	Florence	M	(31) IV p.99
1404.02.01	76 s. 4 3/5 d.	Florence	M	(31) IV p.99
1404.03.01	75 s. 10 1/5 d.	Florence	M	(31) IV p.100
1404.03.01	76 s. 1 1/5 d.	Florence	M	(31) IV p.100
1404.04.03	75 s. 9 d.	Florence	M	(31) IV p.100
1404.04.03	75 s. 11 4/5 d.	Florence	M	(31) IV p.100
1404.05.02	75 s. 10 4/5 d.	Florence	M	(31) IV p.101
1404.05.02	76 s. 1 2/5 d.	Florence	M	(31) IV p.101
1404.06.02	76 s. 1 d.	Florence	M	(31) IV p.101
1404.06.02	76 s. 3 2/5 d.	Florence	M	(31) IV p.101
1404.07.01	76 s. 2 2/5 d.	Florence	M	(31) IV p.102
1404.07.01	76 s. 4 4/5 d.	Florence	M	(31) IV p.102
1404.08.02	76 s. 1 1/5 d.	Florence	M	(31) IV p.102
1404.08.02	76 s. 3 4/5 d.	Florence	M	(31) IV p.102
1404.09.01	75 s. 8 4/5 d.	Florence	M	(31) IV p.103
1404.09.01	75 s. 11 d.	Florence	M	(31) IV p.103
1404.10.01	76 s. 10 d.	Florence	M	(31) IV p.103
1404.10.01	76 s. 11 4/5 d.	Florence	M	(31) IV p.103
1404.11.04	76 s. 7 d.	Florence	M	(31) IV p.104
1404.11.04	76 s. 9 2/5 d.	Florence	M	(31) IV p.104
1404.12.02	76 s. 10./45 d.	Florence	M	(31) IV p.105
1404.12.02	77 s. 2 2/5 d.	Florence	M	(31) IV p.105
1405.01.02	77 s. 3 2/5 d.	Florence	M	(520)
1405.01.02	77 s. 6 2/5 d.	Florence	M	(520)
1405.02.04	76 s. 9 d.	Florence	M	(31) IV p.105
1405.02.04	76 s. 11 d.	Florence	M	(31) IV p.105
1405.03.04	76 s. 10 1/5 d.	Florence	M	(31) IV p.106
1405.03.04	77 s. 1/5 d.	Florence	M	(31) IV p.106
1405.04.01	76 s. 3 2/5 d.	Florence	M	(31) IV p.106
1405.04.01	76 s. 5 4/5 d.	Florence	M	(31) IV p.106
1405.05.02	76 s. 7 3/5 d.	Florence	M	(31) IV p.107
1405.05.02	76 s. 10 d.	Florence	M	(31) IV p.107
1405.06.01	75 s. 11 1/5 d.	Florence	M	(31) IV p.107
1405.06.01	76 s. 2 1/5 d.	Florence	M	(31) IV p.107
1405.07.01	76 s. 1 2/5 d.	Florence	M	(31) IV p.108
1405.07.01	76 s. 3 1/5 d.	Florence	M	(31) IV p.108
1405.08.03	75 s. 10 2/5 d.	Florence	M	(31) IV p.108
1405.08.03	76 s. 3/5 d.	Florence	M	(31) IV p.108
1405.09.01	76 s. 11 2/5 d.	Florence	M	(31) IV p.109
1405.09.01	77 s. 1 4/5 d.	Florence	M	(31) IV p.109
1405.10.01	77 s. 5 1/5 d.	Florence	M	(31) IV p.109
1405.10.01	77 s. 7 3/5 d.	Florence	M	(31) IV p.109
1405.11.03	77 s. 3 1/5 d.	Florence	M	(31) IV p.110
1405.11.03	77 s. 6 d.	Florence	M	(31) IV p.110
1405.12.01	77 s. 7 4/5 d.	Florence	M	(31) IV p.110
1405.12.01	77 s. 9 4/5 d.	Florence	M	(31) IV p.110
1406.01.02	77 s. 10 2/5 d.	Florence	M	(520)
1406.01.02	78 s. 1 d.	Florence	M	(520)
1406.02.01	77 s. 3 3/5 d.	Florence	M	(31) IV p.111
1406.02.01	77 s. 6 1/5 d.	Florence	M	(31) IV p.111
1406.03.01	77 s. 2/5 d.	Florence	M	(31) IV p.112
1406.03.01	77 s. 2 3/5 d.	Florence	M	(31) IV p.112
1406.04.01	76 s. 4 4/5 d.	Florence	M	(31) IV p.112
1406.04.01	76 s. 7 d.	Florence	M	(31) IV p.112
1406.05.04	76 s. 7 1/5 d.	Florence	M	(31) IV p.113
1406.05.04	76 s. 9 2/5 d.	Florence	M	(31) IV p.113
1406.06.02	76 s. 7 1/5 d.	Florence	M	(31) IV p.113
1406.06.02	76 s. 9 3/5 d.	Florence	M	(31) IV p.113
1406.07.01	76 s.	Florence	M	(31) IV p.114
1406.07.01	76 s. 3 d.	Florence	M	(31) IV p.114
1406.08.02	76 s. 11 1/5 d.	Florence	M	(31) IV p.114

THE FLORENTINE FLORIN IN FLORENTINE SOLDI AND DENARI

Date	Rate	Place	Type	Reference
1406.08.02	77 s. 1 3/5 d.	Florence	M	(31) IV p.114
1406.09.01	78 s.	Florence	M	(31) IV p.115
1406.09.01	78 s. 1 1/5 d.	Florence	M	(31) IV p.115
1406.10.01	78 s. 3 4/5 d.	Florence	M	(31) IV p.115
1406.10.01	78 s. 5 4/5 d.	Florence	M	(31) IV p.115
1406.11.03	77 s. 7 1/5 d.	Florence	M	(31) IV p.116
1406.11.03	77 s. 9 d.	Florence	M	(31) IV p.116
1406.12.01	78 s. 1 2/5 d.	Florence	M	(31) IV p.116
1406.12.01	78 s. 3 4/5 d.	Florence	M	(31) IV p.116
1407.01.03	78 s. 1 1/2 d.	Florence	M	(520)
1407.01.03	78 s. 3 4/5 d.	Florence	M	(520)
1407.02.01	77 s. 4 d.	Florence	M	(31) IV p.117
1407.02.01	77 s. 6 d.	Florence	M	(31) IV p.117
1407.03.01	78 s. 1 2/5 d.	Florence	M	(31) IV p.118
1407.03.01	78 s. 4 d.	Florence	M	(31) IV p.118
1407.04.01	77 s. 11 4/5 d.	Florence	M	(31) IV p.118
1407.04.01	78 s. 2 d.	Florence	M	(31) IV p.118
1407.05.02	78 s. 1 2/5 d.	Florence	M	(31) IV p.119
1407.05.02	78 s. 3 1/5 d.	Florence	M	(31) IV p.119
1407.06.01	77 s. 1 1/5 d.	Florence	M	(31) IV p.119
1407.06.01	77 s. 3 d.	Florence	M	(31) IV p.119
1407.07.01	77 s. 5 2/5 d.	Florence	M	(31) IV p.120
1407.07.01	77 s. 7 1/5 d.	Florence	M	(31) IV p.120
1407.08.02	77 s. 3 2/5 d.	Florence	M	(31) IV p.120
1407.08.02	77 s. 5 4/5 d.	Florence	M	(31) IV p.120
1407.09.01	77 s. 5 4/5 d.	Florence	M	(31) IV p.121
1407.09.01	77 s. 8 d.	Florence	M	(31) IV p.121
1407.10.01	77 s. 6 4/5 d.	Florence	M	(31) IV p.121
1407.10.01	77 s. 8 4/5 d.	Florence	M	(31) IV p.121
1407.11.03	76 s. 11 3/5 d.	Florence	M	(31) IV p.122
1407.11.03	77 s. 1 3/5 d.	Florence	M	(31) IV p.122
1407.12.01	77 s. 1 4/5 d.	Florence	M	(31) IV p.122
1407.12.01	77 s. 3 4/5 d.	Florence	M	(31) IV p.122
1408.01.02	77 s. 7 1/5 d.	Florence	M	(520)
1408.01.02	77 s. 10 d.	Florence	M	(520)
1408.02.01	77 s. 4 4/5 d.	Florence	M	(31) IV p.123
1408.02.01	77 s. 7 2/5 d.	Florence	M	(31) IV p.123
1408.03.01	77 s. 6 4/5 d.	Florence	M	(31) IV p.124
1408.03.01	77 s. 9 1/5 d.	Florence	M	(31) IV p.124
1408.04.02	77 s. 2 3/5 d.	Florence	M	(31) IV p.124
1408.04.02	77 s. 4 2/5 d.	Florence	M	(31) IV p.124
1408.05.02	77 s. 6 d.	Florence	M	(31) IV p.125
1408.05.02	77 s. 8 d.	Florence	M	(31) IV p.125
1408.06.01	77 s. 1 2/5 d.	Florence	M	(31) IV p.125
1408.06.01	77 s. 3 3/5 d.	Florence	M	(31) IV p.125
1408.07.02	76 s. 10 1/5 d.	Florence	M	(31) IV p.126
1408.07.02	77 s. 1 1/5 d.	Florence	M	(31) IV p.126
1408.08.02	77 s. 4 2/5 d.	Florence	M	(31) IV p.126
1408.08.02	77 s. 6 d.	Florence	M	(31) IV p.126
1408.09.01	77 s. 6 2/5 d.	Florence	M	(31) IV p.127
1408.09.01	77 s. 9 2/5 d.	Florence	M	(31) IV p.127
1408.10.01	77 s. 8 1/5 d.	Florence	M	(31) IV p.127
1408.10.01	77 s. 10 1/5 d.	Florence	M	(31) IV p.127
1408.11.03	77 s. 4 2/5 d.	Florence	M	(31) IV p.128
1408.11.03	77 s. 7 3/5 d.	Florence	M	(31) IV p.128
1408.12.01	77 s. 9 1/5 d.	Florence	M	(31) IV p.128
1408.12.01	78 s. 1/5 d.	Florence	M	(31) IV p.128
1409.01.02	78 s.	Florence	M	(520)
1409.01.02	78 s. 3 1/5 d.	Florence	M	(520)
1409.02.01	77 s. 9 d.	Florence	M	(31) IV p.129
1409.02.01	77 s. 11 4/5 d.	Florence	M	(31) IV p.129
1409.03.01	78 s. 3/5 d.	Florence	M	(31) IV p.130
1409.03.01	78 s. 2 1/5 d.	Florence	M	(31) IV p.130
1409.04.01	77 s. 8 2/5 d.	Florence	M	(31) IV p.130
1409.04.01	77 s. 10 4/5 d.	Florence	M	(31) IV p.130
1409.05.02	77 s. 7 1/5 d.	Florence	M	(31) IV p.131
1409.05.02	77 s. 9 1/5 d.	Florence	M	(31) IV p.131
1409.06.01	77 s. 9 1/5 d.	Florence	M	(31) IV p.131
1409.06.01	77 s. 11 4/5 d.	Florence	M	(31) IV p.131
1409.07.01	77 s. 6 3/5 d.	Florence	M	(31) IV p.132
1409.07.01	77 s. 8 4/5 d.	Florence	M	(31) IV p.132
1409.08.02	77 s. 10 2/5 d.	Florence	M	(31) IV p.132

THE FLORENTINE FLORIN IN FLORENTINE SOLDI AND DENARI

Date	Rate	Place	Type	Reference
1409.08.02	78 s. 1 d.	Florence	M	(31) IV p.132
1409.09.02	78 s. 4 2/5 d.	Florence	M	(31) IV p.133
1409.09.02	78 s. 6 2/5 d.	Florence	M	(31) IV p.133
1409.10.01	78 s. 8 3/5 d.	Florence	M	(31) IV p.133
1409.10.01	78 s. 10 3/5 d.	Florence	M	(31) IV p.133
1409.11.04	78 s. 11 d.	Florence	M	(31) IV p.134
1409.11.04	79 s. 1 2/5 d.	Florence	M	(31) IV p.134
1409.12.02	79 s. 4 2/5 d.	Florence	M	(31) IV p.134
1409.12.02	79 s. 6 3/5 d.	Florence	M	(31) IV p.134
1410.01.02	80 s. 4 d.	Florence	M	(520)
1410.01.02	80 s. 6 2/5 d.	Florence	M	(520)
1410.02.01	80 s. 2/5 d.	Florence	M	(520)
1410.02.01	80 s. 2 3/5 d.	Florence	M	(520)
1410.03.01	80 s. 3 2/5 d.	Florence	M	(520)
1410.03.01	80 s. 5 2/5 d.	Florence	M	(520)
1410.04.01	79 s. 2 3/4 d.	Florence	M	(520)
1410.04.01	79 s. 4 1/5 d.	Florence	M	(520)
1410.05.02	79 s. 1 d.	Florence	M	(520)
1410.05.02	79 s. 3 1/5 d.	Florence	M	(520)
1410.06.02	78 s. 11 d.	Florence	M	(520)
1410.06.02	79 s. 2/5 d.	Florence	M	(520)
1410.07.01	78 s. 4 d.	Florence	M	(520)
1410.07.01	78 s. 6 d.	Florence	M	(520)
1410.08.02	78 s. 11 d.	Florence	M	(520)
1410.08.02	79 s. 1 2/5 d.	Florence	M	(520)
1410.09.01	79 s. 4 d.	Florence	M	(520)
1410.09.01	79 s. 6 1/5 d.	Florence	M	(520)
1410.10.01	80 s. 2 3/5 d.	Florence	M	(520)
1410.10.01	80 s. 5 d.	Florence	M	(520)
1410.11.04	80 s.	Florence	M	(520)
1410.11.04	80 s. 2 d.	Florence	M	(520)
1410.12.01	80 s. 2 d.	Florence	M	(520)
1410.12.01	80 s. 4 2/5 d.	Florence	M	(520)
1411.01.02	80 s. 2 4/5 d.	Florence	M	(520)
1411.01.02	80 s. 4 4/5 d.	Florence	M	(520)
1411.02.04	79 s. 9 d.	Florence	M	(520)
1411.02.04	79 s. 10 4/5 d.	Florence	M	(520)
1411.03.02	79 s. 8 d.	Florence	M	(520)
1411.03.02	79 s. 11 d.	Florence	M	(520)
1411.04.01	79 s. 8 4/5 d.	Florence	M	(520)
1411.04.01	79 s. 10 3/5 d.	Florence	M	(520)
1411.05.02	79 s. 7 3/5 d.	Florence	M	(520)
1411.05.02	79 s. 9 4/5 d.	Florence	M	(520)
1411.06.03	79 s. 9 1/5 d.	Florence	M	(520)
1411.06.03	79 s. 11 1/5 d.	Florence	M	(520)
1411.07.01	79 s. 3 3/5 d.	Florence	M	(520)
1411.07.01	79 s. 6 d.	Florence	M	(520)
1411.08.03	79 s. 7 1/5 d.	Florence	M	(520)
1411.08.03	79 s. 9 3/5 d.	Florence	M	(520)
1411.09.01	79 s.	Florence	M	(520)
1411.09.01	79 s. 2 3/5 d.	Florence	M	(520)
1411.10.01	80 s.	Florence	M	(520)
1411.10.01	80 s. 2 1/5 d.	Florence	M	(520)
1411.11.03	80 s. 4/5 d.	Florence	M	(520)
1411.11.03	80 s. 3 d.	Florence	M	(520)
1411.12.01	80 s. 4 4/5 d.	Florence	M	(520)
1411.12.01	80 s. 6 3/5 d.	Florence	M	(520)
1412.01.02	80 s. 11 d.	Florence	M	(520)
1412.01.02	81 s. 1 1/5 d.	Florence	M	(520)
1412.02.01	80 s. 8 3/5 d.	Florence	M	(31) IV p.147
1412.02.01	80 s. 10 3/5 d.	Florence	M	(31) IV p.147
1412.03.01	80 s. 6 3/5 d.	Florence	M	(31) IV p.148
1412.03.01	80 s. 8 4/5 d.	Florence	M	(31) IV p.148
1412.04.02	79 s. 10 4/5 d.	Florence	M	(31) IV p.148
1412.04.02	80 s. 1 2/5 d.	Florence	M	(31) IV p.148
1412.05.02	79 s. 1 2/5 d.	Florence	M	(31) IV p.149
1412.05.02	79 s. 3 3/5 d.	Florence	M	(31) IV p.149
1412.06.01	79 s. 3 3/5 d.	Florence	M	(31) IV p.149
1412.06.01	79 s. 5 4/5 d.	Florence	M	(31) IV p.149
1412.07.01	79 s. 10 d.	Florence	M	(31) IV p.150
1412.07.01	80 s.	Florence	M	(31) IV p.150
1412.08.02	80 s. 1/5 d.	Florence	M	(31) IV p.150

THE FLORENTINE FLORIN IN FLORENTINE SOLDI AND DENARI

Date	Rate	Place	Type	Reference
1412.08.02	80 s. 2 2/5 d.	Florence	M	(31) IV p.150
1412.09.01	80 s. 1 3/5 d.	Florence	M	(31) IV p.151
1412.09.01	80 s. 3 3/5 d.	Florence	M	(31) IV p.151
1412.10.01	80 s. 4 2/5 d.	Florence	M	(31) IV p.151
1412.10.01	80 s. 6 4/5 d.	Florence	M	(31) IV p.151
1412.11.03	80 s. 6 2/5 d.	Florence	M	(31) IV p.152
1412.11.03	80 s. 8 2/5 d.	Florence	M	(31) IV p.152
1412.12.01	80 s. 9 4/5 d.	Florence	M	(31) IV p.152
1412.12.01	81 s.	Florence	M	(31) IV p.152
1413.01.02	80 s. 11 d.	Florence	M	(520)
1413.01.02	81 s. 1 3/5 d.	Florence	M	(520)
1413.02.01	80 s. 4 d.	Florence	M	(31) IV p.153
1413.02.01	80 s. 6 d.	Florence	M	(31) IV p.153
1413.03.01	80 s. 6 2/5 d.	Florence	M	(31) IV p.154
1413.03.01	80 s. 8 2/5 d.	Florence	M	(31) IV p.154
1413.04.01	79 s. 9 4/5 d.	Florence	M	(31) IV p.154
1413.04.01	79 s. 11 3/5 d.	Florence	M	(31) IV p.154
1413.05.02	79 s.	Florence	M	(31) IV p.155
1413.05.02	79 s. 2 d.	Florence	M	(31) IV p.155
1413.06.02	79 s. 7 1/5 d.	Florence	M	(31) IV p.155
1413.06.02	79 s. 9 2/5 d.	Florence	M	(31) IV p.155
1413.07.01	80 s. 3 4/5 d.	Florence	M	(31) IV p.156
1413.07.01	80 s. 5 4/5 d.	Florence	M	(31) IV p.156
1413.08.02	79 s. 9 d.	Florence	M	(31) IV p.156
1413.08.02	79 s. 11 d.	Florence	M	(31) IV p.156
1413.09.01	80 s. 3 d.	Florence	M	(31) IV p.157
1413.09.01	80 s. 5 d.	Florence	M	(31) IV p.157
1413.10.02	80 s. 3 4/5 d.	Florence	M	(31) IV p.157
1413.10.02	80 s. 6 d.	Florence	M	(31) IV p.157
1413.10.03	80 s.	Florence	A	(142)
1413.11.03	80 s. 2 d.	Florence	M	(31) IV p.158
1413.11.03	80 s. 4 d.	Florence	M	(31) IV p.158
1413.12.01	80 s. 4 4/5 d.	Florence	M	(31) IV p.158
1413.12.01	80 s. 8 1/5 d.	Florence	M	(31) IV p.158
1414.01.02	80 s. 9 1/5 d.	Florence	M	(520)
1414.01.02	80 s. 11 1/5 d.	Florence	M	(520)
1414.02.01	80 s. 9 2/5 d.	Florence	M	(31) IV p.159
1414.02.01	80 s. 11 1/5 d.	Florence	M	(31) IV p.159
1414.03.01	80 s. 9 2/5 d.	Florence	M	(31) IV p.160
1414.03.01	80 s. 11 4/5 d.	Florence	M	(31) IV p.160
1414.04.02	80 s. 9 4/5 d.	Florence	M	(31) IV p.160
1414.04.02	80 s. 11 4/5 d.	Florence	M	(31) IV p.160
1414.05.02	80 s. 11 2/5 d.	Florence	M	(31) IV p.161
1414.05.02	81 s. 1 3/5 d.	Florence	M	(31) IV p.161
1414.06.01	80 s. 10 d.	Florence	M	(31) IV p.161
1414.06.01	81 s. 2/5 d.	Florence	M	(31) IV p.161
1414.07.02	80 s. 5 1/5 d.	Florence	M	(31) IV p.162
1414.07.02	80 s. 7 2/5 d.	Florence	M	(31) IV p.162
1414.08.02	80 s. 5 d.	Florence	M	(31) IV p.162
1414.08.02	80 s. 7 d.	Florence	M	(31) IV p.162
1414.09.01	79 s. 8 3/5 d.	Florence	M	(31) IV p.163
1414.09.01	79 s. 10 3/5 d.	Florence	M	(31) IV p.163
1414.10.01	79 s. 6 1/5 d.	Florence	M	(31) IV p.163
1414.10.01	79 s. 8 1/5 d.	Florence	M	(31) IV p.163
1414.11.03	80 s. 3 4/5 d.	Florence	M	(31) IV p.164
1414.11.03	80 s. 5 d.	Florence	M	(31) IV p.164
1414.11.29	80 s.	Florence	A	(142)
1414.12.01	80 s. 9 d.	Florence	M	(31) IV p.164
1414.12.01	80 s. 11 d.	Florence	M	(31) IV p.164
1415.01.02	81 s. 2 1/5 d.	Florence	M	(520)
1415.01.02	81 s. 4 d.	Florence	M	(520)
1415.02.01	81 s. 3/5 d.	Florence	M	(31) IV p.165
1415.02.01	81 s. 3 d.	Florence	M	(31) IV p.165
1415.03.01	80 s. 11 2/5 d.	Florence	M	(31) IV p.166
1415.03.01	81 s. 1 4/5 d.	Florence	M	(31) IV p.166
1415.04.04	80 s. 9 1/5 d.	Florence	M	(31) IV p.166
1415.04.04	80 s. 11 1/5 d.	Florence	M	(31) IV p.166
1415.05.02	80 s. 7 4/5 d.	Florence	M	(31) IV p.167
1415.05.02	80 s. 9 4/5 d.	Florence	M	(31) IV p.167
1415.06.01	79 s. 8 d.	Florence	M	(31) IV p.167
1415.06.01	79 s. 10 d.	Florence	M	(31) IV p.167
1415.07.01	80 s. 4/5 d.	Florence	M	(31) IV p.168

Date	Rate	Place	Type	Reference
1415.07.01	80 s. 3 d.	Florence	M	(31) IV p.168
1415.08.02	80 s. 1 d.	Florence	M	(31) IV p.168
1415.08.02	80 s. 3 d.	Florence	M	(31) IV p.168
1415.09.02	80 s. 2 1/5 d.	Florence	M	(31) IV p.169
1415.09.02	80 s. 4 2/5 d.	Florence	M	(31) IV p.169
1415.10.01	80 s. 2 1/5 d.	Florence	M	(31) IV p.169
1415.10.01	80 s. 4 2/5 d.	Florence	M	(31) IV p.169
1415.11.04	79 s. 10 d.	Florence	M	(31) IV p.170
1415.11.04	80 s.	Florence	M	(31) IV p.170
1415.12.02	79 s. 8 1/5 d.	Florence	M	(31) IV p.170
1415.12.02	79 s. 10 1/5 d.	Florence	M	(31) IV p.170
1416.01.02	80 s. 10 d.	Florence	M	(520)
1416.01.02	81 s. 1 d.	Florence	M	(520)
1416.02.01	80 s. 6 2/5 d.	Florence	M	(31) IV p.171
1416.02.01	80 s. 8 4/5 d.	Florence	M	(31) IV p.171
1416.03.04	80 s. 5 d.	Florence	M	(31) IV p.172
1416.03.04	80 s. 7 d.	Florence	M	(31) IV p.172
1416.04.01	80 s. 7 4/5 d.	Florence	M	(31) IV p.172
1416.04.01	80 s. 9 4/5 d.	Florence	M	(31) IV p.172
1416.05.02	80 s. 1 d.	Florence	M	(31) IV p.173
1416.05.02	80 s. 3 2/5 d.	Florence	M	(31) IV p.173
1416.06.01	80 s. 2/5 d.	Florence	M	(31) IV p.173
1416.06.01	80 s. 2 2/5 d.	Florence	M	(31) IV p.173
1416.07.01	79 s. 10 2/5 d.	Florence	M	(31) IV p.174
1416.07.01	80 s. 2/5 d.	Florence	M	(31) IV p.174
1416.08.03	78 s. 3 1/5 d.	Florence	M	(31) IV p.174
1416.08.03	78 s. 5 3/5 d.	Florence	M	(31) IV p.174
1416.09.01	78 s. 4 3/5 d.	Florence	M	(31) IV p.175
1416.09.01	78 s. 6 4/5 d.	Florence	M	(31) IV p.175
1416.09.13	80 s.	Florence	A	(142)
1416.10.01	79 s. 2 d.	Florence	M	(31) IV p.175
1416.10.01	79 s. 4 2/5 d.	Florence	M	(31) IV p.175
1416.11.03	79 s. 10 1/5 d.	Florence	M	(31) IV p.176
1416.11.03	80 s. 1/5 d.	Florence	M	(31) IV p.176
1416.12.01	80 s. 7 1/5 d.	Florence	M	(31) IV p.176
1416.12.01	80 s. 9 2/5 d.	Florence	M	(31) IV p.176
1417.01.02	80 s. 10 d.	Florence	M	(520)
1417.01.02	81 s. 1 2/5 d.	Florence	M	(520)
1417.02.01	80 s. 8 2/5 d.	Florence	M	(31) IV p.177
1417.02.01	80 s. 10 2/5 d.	Florence	M	(31) IV p.177
1417.03.01	80 s. 9 2/5 d.	Florence	M	(31) IV p.178
1417.03.01	80 s. 11 3/5 d.	Florence	M	(31) IV p.178
1417.04.01	80 s. 4 3/5 d.	Florence	M	(31) IV p.178
1417.04.01	80 s. 6 3/5 d.	Florence	M	(31) IV p.178
1417.05.04	80 s. 6 3/5 d.	Florence	M	(31) IV p.179
1417.05.04	80 s. 7 3/5 d.	Florence	M	(31) IV p.179
1417.06.02	79 s. 8 d.	Florence	M	(31) IV p.179
1417.06.02	79 s. 10 3/5 d.	Florence	M	(31) IV p.179
1417.07.01	80 s. 3 2/5 d.	Florence	M	(31) IV p.180
1417.07.01	80 s. 5 2/5 d.	Florence	M	(31) IV p.180
1417.07.20	80 s.	Florence	A	(142)
1417.08.02	79 s. 5 3/5 d.	Florence	M	(31) IV p.180
1417.08.02	79 s. 7 4/5 d.	Florence	M	(31) IV p.180
1417.09.01	79 s. 9 d.	Florence	M	(31) IV p.181
1417.09.01	80 s.	Florence	M	(31) IV p.181
1417.10.01	80 s. 7 1/5 d.	Florence	M	(31) IV p.181
1417.10.01	80 s. 9 2/5 d.	Florence	M	(31) IV p.181
1417.11.03	80 s. 7 d.	Florence	M	(31) IV p.182
1417.11.03	80 s. 8 3/5 d.	Florence	M	(31) IV p.182
1417.12.01	80 s. 10 d.	Florence	M	(31) IV p.182
1417.12.01	81 s.	Florence	M	(31) IV p.182
1418.01.03	81 s. 3/5 d.	Florence	M	(520)
1418.01.03	81 s. 3 d.	Florence	M	(520)
1418.01.11	80 s.	Florence	A	(142)
1418.02.01	81 s. 2 d.	Florence	M	(520)
1418.02.01	81 s. 4 3/5 d.	Florence	M	(520)
1418.03.01	82 s. 1 1/5 d.	Florence	M	(31) IV p.189
1418.03.01	82 s. 4 d.	Florence	M	(31) IV p.189
1418.03.26	81 s.	Florence	A	(142)
1418.04.01	82 s.	Florence	M	(31) IV p.189
1418.04.01	82 s. 1 4/5 d.	Florence	M	(31) IV p.189
1418.05.02	82 s. 9 3/5 d.	Florence	M	(31) IV p.190

Date	Rate	Place	Type	Reference
1418.05.02	82 s. 1/5 d.	Florence	M	(31) IV p.190
1418.06.01	80 s. 9 2/5 d.	Florence	M	(31) IV p.190
1418.06.01	81 s.	Florence	M	(31) IV p.190
1418.07.01	80 s. 6 3/5 d.	Florence	M	(31) IV p.191
1418.07.01	80 s. 9 3/5 d.	Florence	M	(31) IV p.191
1418.08.02	80 s. 8 3/5 d.	Florence	M	(31) IV p.191
1418.08.02	80 s. 11 3/5 d.	Florence	M	(31) IV p.191
1418.09.01	80 s. 7 1/5 d.	Florence	M	(31) IV p.192
1418.09.01	80 s. 9 1/5 d.	Florence	M	(31) IV p.192
1418.10.01	80 s. 6 4/5 d.	Florence	M	(31) IV p.192
1418.10.01	80 s. 9 3/5 d.	Florence	M	(31) IV p.192
1418.10.15	81 s. 4 d.	Florence	M	(142)
1418.10.29	80 s. 6 d.	Florence	M	(142)
1418.10.31	81 s. 6 d.	Florence	M	(142)
1418.11.03	81 s. 2 d.	Florence	M	(31) IV p.193
1418.11.03	81 s. 4 1/5 d.	Florence	M	(31) IV p.193
1418.11.08	80 s. 8 d.	Florence	M	(142)
1418.12.01	81 s. 3 d.	Florence	M	(31) IV p.193
1418.12.01	81 s. 6 d.	Florence	M	(31) IV p.193
1419.01.02	81 s. 7 d.	Florence	M	(520)
1419.01.02	81 s. 10 d.	Florence	M	(520)
1419.02.01	81 s. 1 d.	Florence	M	(31) IV p.194
1419.02.01	81 s. 4 1/5 d.	Florence	M	(31) IV p.194
1419.02.25	79 s. 6 d.	Florence	M	(142)
1419.03.01	79 s. 6 d.	Florence	M	(31) IV p.195
1419.03.01	79 s. 9 2/5 d.	Florence	M	(31) IV p.195
1419.03.04	79 s. 4 d.	Florence	M	(142)
1419.03.18	79 s. 6 d.	Florence	M	(142)
1419.04.01	80 s. 5 d.	Florence	M	(31) IV p.195
1419.04.01	80 s. 7 d.	Florence	M	(31) IV p.195
1419.04.15	79 s. 10 d.	Florence	M	(142)
1419.05.02	79 s. 10 d.	Florence	M	(31) IV p.196
1419.05.02	80 s. 3/5 d.	Florence	M	(31) IV p.196
1419.05.20	79 s. 4 d.	Florence	M	(142)
1419.06.01	78 s. 10 d.	Florence	M	(31) IV p.196
1419.06.01	79 s. 1 d.	Florence	M	(31) IV p.196
1419.06.17	78 s.	Florence	M	(142)
1419.07.01	78 s. 8 d.	Florence	M	(31) IV p.197
1419.07.01	78 s. 10 4/5 d.	Florence	M	(31) IV p.197
1419.08.02	78 s. 8 d.	Florence	M	(31) IV p.197
1419.08.02	78 s. 10 4/5 d.	Florence	M	(31) IV p.197
1419.09.01	77 s. 6 d.	Florence	M	(31) IV p.198
1419.09.01	77 s. 8 2/5 d.	Florence	M	(31) IV p.198
1419.09.16	79 s. 6 d.	Florence	M	(142)
1419.10.02	77 s. 10 d.	Florence	M	(31) IV p.198
1419.10.02	78 s.	Florence	M	(31) IV p.198
1419.10.14	79 s. 3 d.	Florence	M	(142)
1419.11.03	78 s. 8 d.	Florence	M	(31) IV p.199
1419.11.03	78 s. 10 3/5 d.	Florence	M	(31) IV p.199
1419.11.14	79 s. 10 d.	Florence	M	(142)
1419.11.16	80 s.	Florence	M	(142)
1419.12.01	79 s. 6 d.	Florence	M	(31) IV p.199
1419.12.01	79 s. 8 4/5 d.	Florence	M	(31) IV p.199
1419.12.05	79 s.	Florence	M	(142)
1420.01.02	79 s. 10 d.	Florence	M	(520)
1420.01.02	80 s. 1 d.	Florence	M	(520)
1420.01.09	79 s. 6 d.	Florence	M	(142)
1420.01.12	78 s. 10 d.	Florence	M	(142)
1420.01.27	79 s. 4 d.	Florence	M	(142)
1420.02.01	79 s. 6 d.	Florence	M	(520)
1420.02.01	79 s. 9 d.	Florence	M	(520)
1420.02.03	79 s.	Florence	M	(142)
1420.02.10	79 s. 6 d.	Florence	M	(142)
1420.02.20	79 s. 6 d.	Florence	M	(142)
1420.03.01	79 s. 10 d.	Florence	M	(520)
1420.03.01	80 s. 2/5 d.	Florence	M	(520)
1420.03.08	79 s. 8 d.	Florence	M	(142)
1420.03.11	79 s. 6 d.	Florence	M	(142)
1420.04.01	79 s. 7 d.	Florence	M	(520)
1420.04.01	79 s. 10 d.	Florence	M	(520)
1420.05.02	79 s. 10 d.	Florence	M	(520)
1420.05.02	80 s. 4/5 d.	Florence	M	(520)

THE FLORENTINE FLORIN IN FLORENTINE SOLDI AND DENARI

Date	Rate	Place	Type	Reference
1420.05.02	80 s.	Florence	M	(142)
1420.06.01	79 s. 4 d.	Florence	M	(520)
1420.06.01	79 s. 6 3/5 d.	Florence	M	(520)
1420.06.22	79 s. 8 d.	Florence	M	(142)
1420.07.01	79 s. 1 d.	Florence	M	(520)
1420.07.08	79 s.	Florence	M	(142)
1420.07.01	79 s. 3 1/5 d.	Florence	M	(520)
1420.08.02	78 s. 11 d.	Florence	M	(520)
1420.08.02	79 s. 2 d.	Florence	M	(520)
1420.09.02	79 s. 7 d.	Florence	M	(520)
1420.09.02	79 s. 10 d.	Florence	M	(520)
1420.10.01	79 s. 9 d.	Florence	M	(520)
1420.10.01	80 s. 1/5 d.	Florence	M	(520)
1420.10.05	79 s. 6 d.	Florence	M	(142)
1420.10.19	79 s. 4 d.	Florence	M	(142)
1420.11.04	79 s. 5 d.	Florence	M	(520)
1420.11.04	79 s. 8 d.	Florence	M	(520)
1420.11.13	79 s. 10 d.	Florence	M	(142)
1420.12.02	80 s. 3 d.	Florence	M	(520)
1420.12.02	80 s. 6 d.	Florence	M	(520)
1420.12.31	80 s.	Florence	M	(142)

In 1421 the Florentine florin weighed 3.54 grams.

Date	Rate	Place	Type	Reference
1421.01.02	80 s. 7 d.	Florence	M	(520)
1421.01.02	80 s. 9 3/5 d.	Florence	M	(520)
1421.01.20	80 s. 5 d.	Florence	M	(142)
1421.02.01	80 s. 5 d.	Florence	M	(31) IV p.206
1421.02.01	80 s. 8 d.	Florence	M	(31) IV p.206
1421.03.01	80 s. 6 d.	Florence	M	(31) IV p.207
1421.03.01	80 s. 9 1/5 d.	Florence	M	(31) IV p.207
1421.04.01	80 s. 2 d.	Florence	M	(31) IV p.207
1421.04.01	80 s. 5 1/5 d.	Florence	M	(31) IV p.207
1421.05.02	80 s. 3 d.	Florence	M	(31) IV p.208
1421.05.02	80 s. 5 3/5 d.	Florence	M	(31) IV p.208
1421.05.20	79 s. 8 d.	Florence	M	(142)
1421.06.02	80 s. 3 d.	Florence	M	(31) IV p.208
1421.06.02	80 s. 6 d.	Florence	M	(31) IV p.208
1421.07.01	80 s. 2 d.	Florence	M	(31) IV p.209
1421.07.01	80 s. 4 1/5 d.	Florence	M	(31) IV p.209
1421.07.10	79 s. 9 1/2 d.	Florence	M	(142)
1421.07.31	79 s. 11 d.	Florence	M	(142)
1421.08.02	80 s. 3 d.	Florence	M	(31) IV p.209
1421.08.02	80 s. 5 2/5 d.	Florence	M	(31) IV p.209
1421.09.01	80 s. 3 d.	Florence	M	(31) IV p.210
1421.09.01	80 s. 5 d.	Florence	M	(31) IV p.210
1421.09.27	80 s. 4 d.	Florence	M	(142)
1421.10.01	80 s. 7 d.	Florence	M	(31) IV p.210
1421.10.01	80 s. 10 d.	Florence	M	(31) IV p.210
1421.10.24	79 s. 3 d.	Florence	M	(142)
1421.11.04	80 s. 8 d.	Florence	M	(31) IV p.211
1421.11.04	80 s. 11 d.	Florence	M	(31) IV p.211
1421.12.01	81 s.	Florence	M	(31) IV p.211
1421.12.01	81 s. 2 2/5 d.	Florence	M	(31) IV p.211
1421.12.10	81 s.	Florence	M	(142)
1422.01.02	81 s. 5 d.	Florence	M	(520)
1422.01.02	81 s. 7 1/5 d.	Florence	M	(520)
1422.02.04	80 s. 10 d.	Florence	M	(31) IV p.212
1422.02.04	81 s. 2 d.	Florence	M	(31) IV p.212
1422.02.17	80 s. 8 d.	Florence	M	(142)
1422.03.02	80 s. 10 d.	Florence	M	(31) IV p.213
1422.03.02	81 s. 1 d.	Florence	M	(31) IV p.213
1422.04.01	80 s. 8 d.	Florence	M	(31) IV p.213
1422.04.01	80 s. 11 d.	Florence	M	(31) IV p.213
1422.05.02	80 s. 6 d.	Florence	M	(31) IV p.214
1422.05.02	80 s. 9 2/5 d.	Florence	M	(31) IV p.214

In 1422 the Florentine florin weighed 3.55 grams. The weight change was introduced in May 1422, increasing the weight of the new florin by 1/240 of its weight. The reason for this was to make the florin more nearly equivalent to the Venetian ducat so that it could be used in the Levant alongside the ducat, and thus assist Florentine merchants using the galleys newly established at Porto Pisano to break into the lucrative trade with Egypt. Officials drew attention to the change by increasing the the module of the coin. The 'fiorino largo', struck from 1422 onwards, had a diameter of 21.5 mm instead of the 19.5 mm of the 'fiorino stretto'. (223) pp.427-30. A separate table for fiorini larghi is printed below (pp.26-33)

Date	Rate	Place	Type	Reference
1422.06.03	79 s. 6 d.	Florence	M	(31) IV p.214
1422.06.03	79 s. 8 2/5 d.	Florence	M	(31) IV p.214
1422.07.01	79 s. 3 d.	Florence	M	(31) IV p.215
1422.07.01	79 s. 5 3/5 d.	Florence	M	(31) IV p.215
1422.07.08	78 s. 10 d.	Florence	M	(142)
1422.08.03	79 s. 5 d.	Florence	M	(31) IV p.215
1422.08.03	79 s. 7 1/5 d.	Florence	M	(31) IV p.215
1422.09.01	79 s. 3 d.	Florence	M	(31) IV p.216
1422.09.01	79 s. 5 2/5 d.	Florence	M	(31) IV p.216
1422.10.01	79 s. 8 d.	Florence	M	(31) IV p.216
1422.10.01	79 s. 11 2/5 d.	Florence	M	(31) IV p.216
1422.11.03	80 s.	Florence	M	(31) IV p.217
1422.11.03	80 s. 3 1/5 d.	Florence	M	(31) IV p.217
1422.12.01	80 s. 10 d.	Florence	M	(31) IV p.217
1422.12.01	81 s. 4/5 d.	Florence	M	(31) IV p.217
1423.01.02	81 s.	Florence	M	(520)
1423.01.02	81 s. 2 7/10 d.	Florence	M	(520)
1423.02.01	80 s. 10 d.	Florence	M	(31) IV p.218
1423.02.01	81 s. 1 d.	Florence	M	(31) IV p.218
1423.03.01	80 s. 5 d.	Florence	M	(31) IV p.219
1423.03.01	80 s. 7 3/5 d.	Florence	M	(31) IV p.219
1423.04.03	79 s. 10 d.	Florence	M	(31) IV p.219
1423.04.03	80 s. 1 d.	Florence	M	(31) IV p.219
1423.04.11	79 s. 6 d.	Florence	M	(142)
1423.05.04	80 s. 1 d.	Florence	M	(31) IV p.220
1423.05.04	80 s. 4 d.	Florence	M	(31) IV p.220
1423.06.01	79 s. 5 d.	Florence	M	(31) IV p.220
1423.06.01	79 s. 8 d.	Florence	M	(31) IV p.220
1423.07.01	79 s. 9 d.	Florence	M	(31) IV p.221
1423.07.01	79 s. 11 3/5 d.	Florence	M	(31) IV p.221
1423.08.02	80 s. 3 d.	Florence	M	(31) IV p.221
1423.08.02	80 s. 5 3/5 d.	Florence	M	(31) IV p.221
1423.09.01	80 s. 8 d.	Florence	M	(31) IV p.222
1423.09.01	80 s. 10 1/5 d.	Florence	M	(31) IV p.222
1423.10.01	80 s. 9 d.	Florence	M	(31) IV p.222
1423.10.01	81 s.	Florence	M	(31) IV p.222
1423.11.03	80 s. 8 d.	Florence	M	(31) IV p.223
1423.11.03	80 s. 11 d.	Florence	M	(31) IV p.223
1423.11.20	81 s.	Florence	M	(142)
1423.12.01	81 s. 1 d.	Florence	M	(31) IV p.223
1423.12.01	81 s. 5 3/5 d.	Florence	M	(31) IV p.223
1423.12.09	80 s. 10 d.	Florence	M	(142)
1424.01.03	81 s.	Florence	M	(520)
1424.01.03	81 s. 3 1/5 d.	Florence	M	(520)
1424.02.01	81 s.	Florence	M	(31) IV p.224
1424.02.01	81 s. 4 1/5 d.	Florence	M	(31) IV p.224
1424.03.01	81 s.	Florence	M	(31) IV p.224
1424.03.01	81 s. 3 d.	Florence	M	(31) IV p.225
1424.04.01	81 s.	Florence	M	(31) IV p.225
1424.04.01	81 s. 4 2/5 d.	Florence	M	(31) IV p.225
1424.05.02	81 s.	Florence	M	(31) IV p.226
1424.05.02	81 s. 4 d.	Florence	M	(31) IV p.226
1424.06.02	80 s. 8 d.	Florence	M	(31) IV p.226
1424.06.02	81 s.	Florence	M	(31) IV p.226
1424.07.01	80 s. 10 d.	Florence	M	(31) IV p.227
1424.07.01	81 s. 1 d.	Florence	M	(31) IV p.227
1424.08.02	80 s. 5 d.	Florence	M	(31) IV p.227
1424.08.02	80 s. 8 d.	Florence	M	(31) IV p.227
1424.09.01	80 s. 3 d.	Florence	M	(31) IV p.228
1424.09.01	80 s. 6 4/5 d.	Florence	M	(31) IV p.228
1424.10.02	80 s.	Florence	M	(31) IV p.228
1424.10.02	80 s. 2 1/5 d.	Florence	M	(31) IV p.228
1424.11.03	80 s. 6 d.	Florence	M	(31) IV p.229
1424.11.03	80 s. 9 2/5 d.	Florence	M	(31) IV p.229
1424.12.01	81 s. 4 d.	Florence	M	(31) IV p.229
1424.12.01	81 s. 7 d.	Florence	M	(31) IV p.229
1425.01.02	81 s. 1 d.	Florence	M	(520)

THE FLORENTINE FLORIN IN FLORENTINE SOLDI AND DENARI

Date	Rate	Place	Type	Reference
1425.01.02	81 s. 4 d.	Florence	M	(520)
1425.02.01	81 s. 2 d.	Florence	M	(31) IV p.230
1425.02.01	81 s. 5 d.	Florence	M	(31) IV p.230
1425.03.01	80 s. 11 3/5 d.	Florence	M	(31) IV p.231
1425.03.01	81 s. 4 2/5 d.	Florence	M	(31) IV p.231
1425.04.02	80 s. 6 d.	Florence	M	(31) IV p.231
1425.04.02	80 s. 9 2/5 d.	Florence	M	(31) IV p.231
1425.05.02	81 s. 1 d.	Florence	M	(31) IV p.232
1425.05.02	81 s. 4 d.	Florence	M	(31) IV p.232
1425.06.01	80 s. 1 d.	Florence	M	(31) IV p.232
1425.06.01	80 s. 4 3/5 d.	Florence	M	(31) IV p.232
1425.07.02	79 s. 6 d.	Florence	M	(31) IV p.233
1425.07.02	79 s. 9 3/5 d.	Florence	M	(31) IV p.233
1425.08.02	80 s. 6 d.	Florence	M	(31) IV p.233
1425.08.02	80 s. 8 d.	Florence	M	(31) IV p.233
1425.09.01	79 s. 8 d.	Florence	M	(31) IV p.234
1425.09.01	79 s. 11 d.	Florence	M	(31) IV p.234
1425.10.01	80 s. 6 d.	Florence	M	(31) IV p.234
1425.10.01	80 s. 8 1/5 d.	Florence	M	(31) IV p.234
1425.11.03	79 s. 10 d.	Florence	M	(31) IV p.235
1425.11.03	81 s. 1 4/5 d.	Florence	M	(31) IV p.235
1425.12.01	80 s. 7 d.	Florence	M	(31) IV p.235
1425.12.01	80 s. 9 4/5 d.	Florence	M	(31) IV p.235
1426.01.02	80 s. 11 d.	Florence	M	(520)
1426.01.02	81 s. 2 d.	Florence	M	(520)
1426.02.01	81 s. 3 d.	Florence	M	(31) IV p.236
1426.02.01	81 s. 6 d.	Florence	M	(31) IV p.236
1426.03.01	81 s. 4 d.	Florence	M	(31) IV p.237
1426.03.01	81 s. 6 3/5 d.	Florence	M	(31) IV p.237
1426.04.04	80 s. 10 4/5 d.	Florence	M	(31) IV p.237
1426.04.04	81 s. 1 d.	Florence	M	(31) IV p.237
1426.05.02	81 s. 2 1/5 d.	Florence	M	(31) IV p.238
1426.05.02	81 s. 4 3/5 d.	Florence	M	(31) IV p.238
1426.06.01	81 s. 6 4/5 d.	Florence	M	(31) IV p.238
1426.06.01	81 s. 9 1/5 d.	Florence	M	(31) IV p.238
1426.07.01	81 s. 4 2/5 d.	Florence	M	(31) IV p.239
1426.07.01	81 s. 6 4/5 d.	Florence	M	(31) IV p.239
1426.08.02	81 s. 10 2/5 d.	Florence	M	(31) IV p.239
1426.08.02	82 s. 1 d.	Florence	M	(31) IV p.239
1426.09.02	81 s. 11 3/5 d.	Florence	M	(31) IV p.240
1426.09.02	82 s. 2 3/5 d.	Florence	M	(31) IV p.240
1426.10.01	82 s. 2/5 d.	Florence	M	(31) IV p.240
1426.10.01	82 s. 3 1/5 d.	Florence	M	(31) IV p.240
1426.11.04	81 s. 5 2/5 d.	Florence	M	(31) IV p.241
1426.11.04	81 s. 8 1/5 d.	Florence	M	(31) IV p.241
1426.12.02	82 s. 4/5 d.	Florence	M	(31) IV p.241
1426.12.02	82 s. 3 3/5 d.	Florence	M	(31) IV p.241
1427.01.02	82 s. 5 3/5 d.	Florence	M	(520)
1427.01.02	82 s. 8 2/5 d.	Florence	M	(520)
1427.01.21	83 s.	Florence	M	(142)
1427.02.04	82 s. 9 4/5 d.	Florence	M	(31) IV p.242
1427.02.04	83 s. 3/5 d.	Florence	M	(31) IV p.242
1427.03.01	82 s. 6 3/5 d.	Florence	M	(31) IV p.243
1427.03.01	82 s. 9 d.	Florence	M	(31) IV p.243
1427.04.01	82 s. 2 2/5 d.	Florence	M	(31) IV p.243
1427.04.01	82 s. 5 d.	Florence	M	(31) IV p.243
1427.04.20	82 s.	Florence	M	(142)
1427.04	82 s. 6 d.	Florence	M	(142)
1427.05.02	82 s. 6 2/5 d.	Florence	M	(31) IV p.244
1427.05.02	82 s. 9 1/5 d.	Florence	M	(31) IV p.244
1427.06.02	82 s. 2 4/5 d.	Florence	M	(31) IV p.244
1427.06.02	82 s. 6 1/5 d.	Florence	M	(31) IV p.244
1427.07.01	81 s. 8 4/5 d.	Florence	M	(31) IV p.245
1427.07.01	81 s. 11 d.	Florence	M	(31) IV p.245
1427.08.02	82 s. 4/5 d.	Florence	M	(31) IV p.245
1427.08.02	82 s. 4 d.	Florence	M	(31) IV p.245
1427.09.01	82 s. 2 3/5 d.	Florence	M	(31) IV p.246
1427.09.01	82 s. 5 2/5 d.	Florence	M	(31) IV p.246
1427.10.01	82 s. 4 2/5 d.	Florence	M	(31) IV p.246
1427.10.01	82 s. 7 d.	Florence	M	(31) IV p.246
1427.10.04	82 s. 6 d.	Florence	M	(142)
1427.11.04	82 s. 6 2/5 d.	Florence	M	(31) IV p.247

THE FLORENTINE FLORIN IN FLORENTINE SOLDI AND DENARI

Date	Rate	Place	Type	Reference
1427.11.04	82 s. 9 3/5 d.	Florence	M	(31) IV p.247
1427.12.01	83 s. 4 d.	Florence	M	(31) IV p.247
1427.12.01	83 s. 6 3/5 d.	Florence	M	(31) IV p.247
1427.12.22	83 s. 8 d.	Florence	M	(142)
1428.01.02	83 s. 8 1/5 d.	Florence	M	(520)
1428.01.02	83 s. 11 d.	Florence	M	(520)
1428.02.03	82 s. 10 3/5 d.	Florence	M	(31) IV p.248
1428.02.03	83 s. 2 d.	Florence	M	(31) IV p.248
1428.02.28	83 s.	Florence	M	(142)
1428.03.01	83 s. 5 1/5 d.	Florence	M	(31) IV p.249
1428.03.01	83 s. 8 4/5 d.	Florence	M	(31) IV p.249
1428.04.03	82 s. 3 3/5 d.	Florence	M	(31) IV p.249
1428.04.03	82 s. 6 4/5 d.	Florence	M	(31) IV p.249
1428.04.04	82 s.	Florence	M	(142)
1428.05.04	82 s. 5 3/5 d.	Florence	M	(31) IV p.250
1428.05.04	82 s. 9 d.	Florence	M	(31) IV p.250
1428.05.15	82 s. 6 d.	Florence	M	(142)
1428.06.01	82 s. 8 4/5 d.	Florence	M	(31) IV p.250
1428.06.01	83 s.	Florence	M	(31) IV p.250
1428.06	82 s. 4 d.	Florence	M	(142)
1428.07.01	82 s. 2/5 d.	Florence	M	(31) IV p.251
1428.07.01	82 s. 3 4/5 d.	Florence	M	(31) IV p.251
1428.07.17	81 s. 9 d.	Florence	M	(142)
1428.08.02	82 s. 4 2/5 d.	Florence	M	(31) IV p.251
1428.08.02	82 s. 7 d.	Florence	M	(31) IV p.251
1428.09.01	82 s. 4 3/5 d.	Florence	M	(31) IV p.252
1428.09.01	82 s. 7 4/5 d.	Florence	M	(31) IV p.252
1428.10.01	83 s.	Florence	M	(31) IV p.252
1428.10.01	83 s. 3 d.	Florence	M	(31) IV p.252
1428.10.27	82 s. 6 d.	Florence	M	(142)
1428.11.03	82 s. 10 1/5 d.	Florence	M	(31) IV p.253
1428.11.03	83 s. 1 4/5 d.	Florence	M	(31) IV p.253
1428.11.27	83 s. 4 d.	Florence	M	(142)
1428.12.01	83 s. 5 2/5 d.	Florence	M	(31) IV p.253
1428.12.01	83 s. 8 3/5 d.	Florence	M	(31) IV p.253
1428.12.18	83 s. 6 d.	Florence	M	(142)
1428.12.24	83 s.	Florence	M	(142)
1429.01.03	83 s. 2 d.	Florence	M	(520)
1429.01.03	83 s. 5 d.	Florence	M	(520)
1429.02.01	83 s. 1 1/5 d.	Florence	M	(31) IV p.254
1429.02.01	83 s. 3 4/5 d.	Florence	M	(31) IV p.254
1429.03.01	83 s. 3/5 d.	Florence	M	(31) IV p.255
1429.03.01	83 s. 3 3/5 d.	Florence	M	(31) IV p.255
1429.04.01	82 s. 10 1/5 d.	Florence	M	(31) IV p.255
1429.04.01	83 s. 1 2/5 d.	Florence	M	(31) IV p.255
1429.05.02	82 s. 6 4/5 d.	Florence	M	(31) IV p.256
1429.05.02	82 s. 10 d.	Florence	M	(31) IV p.256
1429.06.01	82 s. 5 d.	Florence	M	(31) IV p.256
1429.06.01	82 s. 8 d.	Florence	M	(31) IV p.256
1429.07.01	82 s. 3 d.	Florence	M	(31) IV p.257
1429.07.01	82 s. 6 2/5 d.	Florence	M	(31) IV p.257
1429.07.04	82 s. 6 d.	Florence	M	(142)
1429.07.30	82 s. 4 d.	Florence	M	(142)
1429.08.02	82 s. 6 d.	Florence	M	(31) IV p.257
1429.08.02	82 s. 9 1/5 d.	Florence	M	(31) IV p.257
1429.09.01	82 s. 6 4/5 d.	Florence	M	(31) IV p.258
1429.09.01	82 s. 10 d.	Florence	M	(31) IV p.258
1429.09.03	82 s. 6 d.	Florence	M	(142)
1429.10.01	82 s. 8 4/5 d.	Florence	M	(31) IV p.258
1429.10.01	83 s.	Florence	M	(31) IV p.258
1429.10.26	82 s. 6 d.	Florence	M	(142)
1429.11.03	82 s. 6 1/5 d.	Florence	M	(31) IV p.259
1429.11.03	82 s. 9 4/5 d.	Florence	M	(31) IV p.259
1429.12.01	83 s. 4 1/5 d.	Florence	M	(31) IV p.259
1429.12.01	83 s. 5 2/5 d.	Florence	M	(31) IV p.259
1429.12.20	83 s. 1 d.	Florence	M	(142)
1430.01.02	83 s. 2 3/5 d.	Florence	M	(520)
1430.01.02	83 s. 5 4/5 d.	Florence	M	(520)
1430.01.09	83 s.	Florence	M	(142)
1430.01.14	83 s. 4 d.	Florence	M	(142)
1430.02.04	83 s. 5 4/5 d.	Florence	M	(520)
1430.02.04	83 s. 8 1/5 d.	Florence	M	(520)

Date	Rate	Place	Type	Reference
1430.03.01	83 s. 2 1/5 d.	Florence	M	(520)
1430.03.01	83 s. 5 d.	Florence	M	(520)
1430.03.15	83 s. 4 d.	Florence	M	(142)
1430.04.01	82 s. 5 1/5 d. (sic)	Florence	M	(520)
1430.04.01	83 s. 3 3/5 d.	Florence	M	(520)
1430.04	83 s.	Florence	M	(142)
1430.05.02	82 s. 10 3/5 d.	Florence	M	(520)
1430.05.02	83 s. 1 2/5 d.	Florence	M	(520)
1430.06.01	82 s. 7 1/5 d.	Florence	M	(520)
1430.06.01	82 s. 10 4/5 d.	Florence	M	(520)
1430.06.22	81 s. 8 d.	Florence	M	(142)
1430.07.01	81 s. 8 3/5 d.	Florence	M	(520)
1430.07.01	82 s. 1/5 d.	Florence	M	(520)
1430.08.02	82 s. 3 2/5 d.	Florence	M	(520)
1430.08.02	82 s. 7 d.	Florence	M	(520)
1430.09.01	82 s.	Florence	M	(520)
1430.09.01	82 s. 3 d.	Florence	M	(520)
1430.09.	82 s. 6 d.	Florence	M	(142)
1430.10.02	82 s. 1 1/5 d.	Florence	M	(520)
1430,10,02	82 s. 4 2/5 d.	Florence	M	(520)
1430.11.03	82 s. 6 2/5 d.	Florence	M	(520)
1430.11.03	82 s. 9 3/5 d.	Florence	M	(520)
1430.12.01	82 s. 9 4/5 d.	Florence	M	(520)
1430.12.01	83 s. 1 4/5 d.	Florence	M	(520)
1431.01.02	82 s. 11 3/5 d.	Florence	M	(520)
1431.01.02	83 s. 3 1/5 d.	Florence	M	(520)
1431.02.01	82 s. 10 2/5 d.	Florence	M	(520)
1431.02.01	83 s. 1 3/5 d.	Florence	M	(520)
1431.03.01	82 s. 10 2/5 d.	Florence	M	(520)
1431.03.01	83 s. 1 3/5 d.	Florence	M	(520)
1431.04.05	82 s. 6 d.	Florence	M	(520)
1431.04.05	82 s. 9 1/5 d.	Florence	M	(520)
1431.05.02	80 s. 11 1/5 d.	Florence	M	(520)
1431.05.02	81 s. 2 2/5 d.	Florence	M	(520)
1431.06.01	80 s. 11 2/5 d.	Florence	M	(520)
1431.06.01	81 s. 2 4/5 d.	Florence	M	(520)
1431.07.02	81 s. 10 4/5 d.	Florence	M	(520)
1431.07.02	82 s. 2 d.	Florence	M	(520)
1431.08.02	82 s. 11 d.	Florence	M	(520)
1431.08.02	83 s. 1/5 d.	Florence	M	(520)
1431.08.05	83 s.	Florence	M	(142)
1431.09.01	83 s. 5 1/5 d.	Florence	M	(520)
1431.09.01	83 s. 8 d.	Florence	M	(520)
1431.10.01	82 s. 4 4/5 d.	Florence	M	(520)
1431.10.01	82 s. 8 d.	Florence	M	(520)
1431.11.03	82 s. 5 4/5 d.	Florence	M	(520)
1431.11.03	82 s. 9 2/5 d.	Florence	M	(520)
1431.12.01	83 s. 5 4/5 d.	Florence	M	(520)
1431.12.01	83 s. 9 2/5 d.	Florence	M	(520)
1431.12.24	83 s. 8 d.	Florence	M	(142)
1432.01.02	83 s. 6 1/5 d.	Florence	M	(520)
1432.01.02	83 s. 10 1/5 d.	Florence	M	(520)
1432.02.01	83 s. 10 d.	Florence	M	(31) IV p.272

The 1422 weight standard for the florin was given up in the 1430s, probably in 1432 or 1433, and new florins were again supposed to weigh 3.54 grams.

Date	Rate	Place	Type	Reference
1432	79 s. 9 d.	Florence	M	(520)
1440.02.07	82 s.	Florence	M	(142)
1440.07.16	82 s.	Florence	M	(142)
1440.10.08	83 s.	Florence	M	(142)

In 1442 the Florentine florin weighed 3.54 grams.

Date	Rate	Place	Type	Reference
1444	82 s. 6 d.	Florence	M	(31) III p.87
1445.08	82 s.	Florence	M	(142)
1447.03	77 s. 7 d.	Florence	M	(31) III p.87
1447	86 s.	Florence	M	(142)
1448-1478	82 s.	Florence	M	(142)
1449.07.02	82 s.	Florence	M	(142)
1449.10.22	84 s. 11 d.	Florence	M	(142)
1450.02	82 s.	Florence	M	(31) III p.87

THE FLORENTINE FLORIN IN FLORENTINE SOLDI AND DENARI

Date	Rate	Place	Type	Reference
1451 from 05	82 s.	Florence	M	(142)
1451.07.18	80 s.	Florence	M	(142)
1455.08.03	82 s.	Florence	M	(142)
1457.10.03	82 s.	Florence	M	(142)
1458.09.24	82 s.	Florence	M	(142)
1459.06.11	82 s.	Florence	M	(142)
1459.09.05	82 s.	Florence	M	(142)
1460.02.04	86 s.	Florence	M	(142)
1460.02.21	82 s.	Florence	M	(142)
1460.05.22	82 s.	Florence	M	(142)
1460.08.06	88 s.	Florence	M	(142)
1460.09.01	88 s.	Florence	M	(142)
1460.10.13	83 s.	Florence	M	(142)
1460.10.15	88 s.	Florence	M	(142)
1460.11.05	88 s.	Florence	M	(142)
1461.01.31	88 s.	Florence	M	(142)
1461.02.10	88 s.	Florence	M	(142)

In 1460 the Florentine florin weighed 3.52 grams.

Date	Rate	Place	Type	Reference
1461.04.10	88 s.	Florence	M	(142)
1461.09.11	89 s.	Florence	M	(142)
1461.10.30	89 s.	Florence	M	(142)
1461.11.03	88 s.	Florence	M	(142)
1462.01.05	91 s.	Florence	M	(142)
1462.03.05	91 s.	Florence	M	(142)
1462.04.23	90 s.	Florence	M	(142)
1462.05.14	88 s. 7 d.	Florence	M	(142)
1462.07.16	82 s.	Florence	M	(142)
1462.09.20	91 s.	Florence	M	(142)
1463.01.04	92 s.	Florence	M	(142)
1463.01.24	90 s.	Florence	M	(142)
1463.01.31	90 s.	Florence	M	(142)
1463.01.31	91 s.	Florence	M	(142)
1463.01.31	92 s.	Florence	M	(142)
1463.03.15	92 s. 3 d.	Florence	M	(142)
1463.04.08	90 s.	Florence	M	(142)
1463.10.12	91 s.	Florence	M	(142)
1463.12.24	91 s.	Florence	M	(142)
1464.01.11	91 s.	Florence	M	(142)
1464.04.30	92 s.	Florence	M	(142)
1464.11.20	93 s.	Florence	M	(142)
1464.12.22	100 s.	Florence	M	(142)
1465.07.06	82 s.	Florence	M	(142)
1466.05	82 s.	Florence	M	(142)
1466.06.16	82 s.	Florence	M	(142)
1466.10.09	82 s.	Florence	M	(142)
1467.05.06	90 s.	Florence	M	(142)
1467.05.13	91 s.	Florence	M	(142)
1467.05.28	87 s.	Florence	M	(142)
1467.06.30	91 s.	Florence	M	(142)
1467.07.02	91 s.	Florence	M	(142)
1467.08.12	89 s. 6 d.	Florence	M	(142)
1468.01.05	90 s.	Florence	M	(142)
1468.01.09	91 s.	Florence	M	(142)
1468.01.15	90 s.	Florence	M	(142)
1468.05.09	82 s.	Florence	M	(142)
1468.06.01	82 s.	Florence	M	(142)
1469.01.13	92 s.	Florence	M	(142)
1469.01.31	91 s. 6 d.	Florence	M	(142)
1469.04.17	89 s.	Florence	M	(142)
1469.06.16	92 s.	Florence	M	(142)
1469.07.17	90 s.	Florence	M	(142)
1469.07.30	92 s.	Florence	M	(142)
1469.09.02	89 s.	Florence	M	(142)
1469.09.27	94 s. 2 d.	Florence	M	(142)
1470.11.13	88 s. 4 d.	Florence	M	(142)
1471.06.11	82 s.	Florence	M	(142)
1471.07	83 s.	Florence	M	(142)
1471.10.31	89 s.	Florence	M	(142)
1471.11.02	86 s.	Florence	M	(142)
1472.01.27	82 s.	Florence	M	(142)

THE FLORENTINE FLORIN IN FLORENTINE SOLDI AND DENARI

Date	Rate	Place	Type	Reference
1472.03.09	90 s.	Florence	M	(142)
1472.04.08	90 s.	Florence	M	(142)
1472.07.03	90 s.	Florence	M	(142)
1473.07.31	89 s.	Florence	M	(142)
1472.08.08	89 s.	Florence	M	(142)
1472.11.28	90 s.	Florence	M	(142)
1472.12.09	90 s.	Florence	M	(142)
1472.12.12	92 s.	Florence	M	(142)
1473.04.24	90 s.	Florence	M	(142)
1473.05.26	82 s.	Florence	M	(142)
1473.07.07	90 s.	Florence	M	(142)
1473.10.02	90 s.	Florence	M	(142)
1474.01.19	90 s.	Florence	M	(142)
1474.04.25	82 s.	Florence	M	(142)
1474.06	82 s.	Florence	M	(142)
1474.07.23	90 s.	Florence	M	(142)
1476.05.29	90 s.	Florence	M	(142)
1477.08.09	82 s.	Florence	M	(142)
1478.07.19	82 s.	Florence	M	(142)

In 1479 the Florentine florin weighed 3.53 grams.

Date	Rate	Place	Type	Reference
1480.06.03	90 s.	Florence	M	(142)
1480-1504	82 s.	Florence	A	(142)
1481.05.04	82 s.	Florence	M	(142)
1481.11	85 s. 4 d.	Florence	M	(142)
1482.08	82 s.	Florence	M	(142)
1483.04	82 s.	Florence	M	(142)
1484.02.11	89 s.	Florence	M	(142)
1484.04.06	89 s.	Florence	M	(142)
1484.06	82 s.	Florence	M	(142)
1485.05.24	82 s.	Florence	M	(142)
1488.06.04	82 s.	Florence	M	(142)
1489.07.15	82 s.	Florence	M	(142)
1490.06.22	82 s.	Florence	M	(142)
1492.06.02	82 s.	Florence	M	(142)
1492.11.10	90 s.	Florence	M	(142)
1495.01.26	92 s.	Florence	M	(142)
1498 from 08	82 s.	Florence	M	(142)
1499.06.23	82 s.	Florence	M	(142)

In 1510 the Florentine florin weighed 3.51 grams.

Fiorini di suggello

Fiorini di suggello were initially florins which had been passed as within the required tolerances by one of the assayers in the assay office of the Florentine mint and sealed up by him in a leather bag. For a long period these 'sealed florins' were those with which bills of exchange were supposed to be paid. The system of sealing florins was first regulated in 1294, and was probably then of quite recent origin. In the course of the fourteenth and fifteenth centuries the standards applied by the assayers changed no less than six times, so that there was considerable variation between bags sealed at different dates with different coloured seals. Bernocchi (31) III, pp.274-300 has attempted to express and explain the confusion, and has, furthermore, suggested that the fiorino di suggello became a unit of account apart from the florins sealed in bags, which was not necessarily always even linked to gold. The system was abolished in 1471, but seems to have been falling out of use ever since the introduction of the fiorini larghi in 1422. The following quotations have been abstracted by courtesy of Professor Aldo De Maddalena from a much larger body of material, the Libro di Giovanni del mas[ro] Antonio da Saminiato mccccxxv-mccccIxxxxiii, at the Bocconi University at Milan. I have used some of the rates starting in January 1432 when the notebooks of the proveditori degli cambiatori come to an end. Where there is more than one quotation for a month I have taken the last one.

he fiorino di suggello in Florentine soldi and denari

ate	Rate	Place	Type	Reference
432.01.15	82 s.	Empoli	C	(130)
432.02.21	87 s. 4 d.	Empoli	C	(130)
432.03.24	82 s. 9 d.	Empoli	C	(130)

THE FIORINO DI SUGGELLO IN FLORENTINE SOLDI AND DENARI

Date	Rate	Place	Type	Reference
1432.04.05	80 s. 2 d.	Empoli	H	(130)
1432.05.12	81 s.	Empoli	C	(130)
1432.06.13	82 s. 3 d.	Empoli	H	(130)
1432.07.24	81 s.	Empoli	C	(130)
1432.08.06	80 s.	Empoli	C	(130)
1432.09.27	82 s.	Empoli	C	(130)
1432.10.30	82 s.	Empoli	C	(130)
1432.11.19	80 s. 2 d.	Empoli	C	(130)
1432.12.24	82 s. 6 d.	Empoli	H	(130)
1433.01.29	82 s. 6 d.	Empoli	C	(130)
1433.02.11	80 s. 9 d.	Empoli	H	(130)
1433.03.28	80 s. 9 d.	Empoli	C	(130)
1433.04.30	82 s. 7 d.	Empoli	C	(130)
1433.05.09	81 s. 9 d.	Empoli	H	(130)
1433.06.01	83 s. 11 d.	Empoli	H	(130)
1433.09.02	84 s.	Empoli	H	(130)
1433.10.03	84 s.	Empoli	C	(130)
1434.01.01	80 s.	Empoli	H	(130)
1434.02.10	83 s.	Empoli	C	(130)
1434.04.10	82 s. 4 d.	Empoli	C	(130)
1434.07.27	82 s. 4 d.	Empoli	C	(130)
1434.08.09	83 s.	Empoli	C	(130)
1434.09.07	81 s. 10 d.	Empoli	C	(130)
1434.11.15	80 s.	Empoli	H	(130)
1435.03.06	82 s. 10 d.	Empoli	C	(130)
1435.06.13	84 s. 2 d.	Empoli	H	(130)
1435.10.05	83 s.	Empoli	C	(130)
1435.11.23	94 s.	Empoli	C	(130)
1436.01.19	83 s. 5 d.	Empoli	C	(130)
1436.06.14	83 s. 5 d.	Empoli	C	(130)
1436.07.09	84 s.	Empoli	C	(130)
1436.08.04	84 s.	Empoli	C	(130)
1437.07.23	82 s. 6 d.	Empoli	H	(130)
1437.10.25	82 s. 6 d.	Empoli	H	(130)
1437.11.19	82 s. 6 d.	Empoli	H	(130)
1437.12.19	82 s. 6 d.	Empoli	H	(130)
1438.01.28	82 s. 6 d.	Empoli	H	(130)
1438.02.13	82 s. 6 d.	Empoli	H	(130)
1438.08.29	85 s.	Empoli	C	(130)
1439.10.25	85 s.	Empoli	C	(130)
1439.11.04	85 s.	Empoli	C	(130)
1440.10.30	85 s.	Empoli	C	(130)
1440.11.07	85 s.	Empoli	C	(130)
1441.01.03	85 s. 6 d.	Empoli	C	(130)
1441.04.20	87 s. 4 d.	Empoli	C	(130)
1441.09.08	92 s.	Empoli	C	(130)
1444.01.09	86 s.	Empoli	C	(130)
1444.10.31	88 s. 1 d.	Empoli	H	(130)
1445.01.09	81 s. 4 d.	Empoli	H	(130)
1447.07.06	86 s. 8 d.	Empoli	H	(130)
1448	85 s.	Florence	O	(31) III p.294
1448.03.10	85 s. 6 d.	Empoli	C	(130)
1450.05.19	84 s.	Empoli	C	(130)
1454.06.15	84 s. 4 d.	Empoli	H	(130)
1454.08.26	93 s. 4 d.	Empoli	H	(130)
1454.09.13	85 s.	Empoli	C	(130)
1454.10.21	86 s. 6 d.	Empoli	H	(130)
1455.08.22	85 s. 4 d.	Empoli	C	(130)
1461	86 s. 8 d.	Florence	O	(31) III p.294
1464	88 s. 4 d.	Florence	O	(31) III p.294

The fiorino largo in Florentine soldi and denari

In 1432 when the weight of the florin was reduced from that of the ducat to the traditional florin weight of 3.54 grams a distinctive value began to be put on the ducat-sized florins, the fiorini larghi, particularly those sealed in bags. These sealed bags of fiorini larghi could also contain Venetian ducats. As actual fiorini larghi diminished in number, the fiorino largo gradually became a unit of account, by 1464 reckoned at 20% above the actual gold florin.

THE FIORINO LARGO IN FLORENTINE SOLDI AND DENARI

Date	Rate	Place	Type	Reference
1441	95 s.	Florence	M	(520)
1443	95 s.	Florence	M	(507) p.87
1445-1446	97 s.	Florence	C	(111) p.84
1447.06	92 s.	Florence	M	(31) III p.87
1448	93 s. 6 d.	Florence	M	(31) III p.87
1448-1452	96 s.	Florence	C	(111) p.84
1449.07.11	96 s.	Florence	M	(142)
1449.08.13	96 s.	Florence	M	(142)
1449.08.21	96 s.	Florence	M	(142)
1449.10.14	96 s.	Florence	M	(142)
1449.11.02	96 s.	Florence	M	(142)
1451.05.25	96 s.	Florence	M	(142)
1451.12.18	96 s.	Florence	M	(142)
1451-1452	96 s.	Florence	M	(31) III p.87
1453	99 s.	Florence	C	(111) p.84
1453.04.07	99 s.	Florence	M	(142)
1453.04.16	99 s.	Florence	M	(142)
1453.05.09	99 s.	Florence	M	(142)
1454	101 s. 10 d.	Florence	C	(111) p.84
1455	108 s.	Florence	M	(31) III p.87
1456.07.02	106 s.	Florence	M	(31) III p.87
1456.07.02	106 s.	Florence	M	(31) III p.87
1456.07.30	107 s.	Florence	M	(31) III p.87
1456.09	108 s.	Florence	M	(31) III p.87
1457.09.24	108 s.	Florence	M	(142)
1457.10.18	108 s.	Florence	M	(142)
1457-1460	108 s.	Florence	C	(111) p.85
1458.06.19	108 s.	Florence	M	(142)
1458.10.27	108 s.	Florence	M	(142)
1459.09.07	108 s.	Florence	M	(142)
1460.06.07	108 s.	Florence	M	(142)
1460.10.28	108 s.	Florence	M	(142)
1461	101 s. 10 d.	Florence	M	(31) III p.87
1462	108 s.	Florence	M	(31) III p.87
1462	109 s.	Florence	C	(111) p.85
1463	110 s.	Florence	C	(111) p.85
1463.02.12	110 s.	Florence	M	(142)
1463.06.16	109 s.	Florence	M	(142)
1463.10.29	110 s.	Florence	M	(142)
1464-1466	112 s.	Florence	C	(111) p.85
1464	106 s.	Florence	M	(31) III p.87
1464.01.13	110 s.	Florence	M	(142)
1464.02.01	110 s.	Florence	M	(142)
1464.03.07	110 s.	Florence	M	(142)
1464.04.19	110 s.	Florence	M	(142)

Hitherto the fiorino largo, as an accounting unit, had been linked to gold, but, with the end of the silver famine, the fiorino largo could be expressed in May 1464 both in terms of gold and in terms of the new silver grossi. This was only satisfactory so long as the relative values of gold and silver remained fixed.

Date	Rate	Place	Type	Reference
1464.09.04	112 s.	Florence	M	(142)
1464.10.	112 s.	Florence	M	(142)
1464.11.15	112 s.	Florence	M	(142)
1465.01.20	112 s.	Florence	M	(142)
1465.04.04	112 s.	Florence	M	(142)
1465.07.06	112 s.	Florence	M	(142)
1466.02.24	112 s.	Florence	M	(142)
1466.10.16	112 s.	Florence	M	(142)
1467-1470	114 s.	Florence	C	(111) p.85
1467.02.14	112 s.	Florence	M	(142)
1467.02.26	113 s.	Florence	M	(142)
1467.03.07	114 s.	Florence	M	(142)
1467.08.05	114 s.	Florence	M	(142)
1467.09.09	114 s.	Florence	M	(142)
1467.09.10	113 s.	Florence	M	(142)
1468.07.15	114 s.	Florence	M	(142)
1468.08.12	114 s.	Florence	M	(142)
1468.10.20	114 s.	Florence	M	(142)
1468.11.05	114 s.	Florence	M	(142)
1469.01.04	114 s.	Florence	M	(142)
1469.03.04	114 s.	Florence	M	(142)

THE FIORINO LARGO IN FLORENTINE SOLDI AND DENARI

Date	Rate	Place	Type	Reference
1469.09.19	114 s.	Florence	M	(142)
1469.12.02	114 s.	Florence	M	(142)
1470.05	114 s.	Florence	M	(142)
1470.11.17	110 s.	Florence	M	(142)
1470.11.29	104 s.	Florence	M	(142)
1471-1473	110 s.	Florence	C	(111) p.85
1471.01.28	109 s.	Florence	M	(142)
1471.02.21	109 s.	Florence	M	(142)
1471.06.23	110 s.	Florence	M	(142)
1471.07.02	110 s.	Florence	M	(142)
1471.07.13	112 s.	Florence	M	(142)

When the relative values of gold and silver changed, in 1471, a distinction had to be made between the fiorino largo as an accounting unit expressed in silver, the 'fiorino largo di grossi', and as an accounting unit expressed in gold, the 'fiorino largo d'oro in oro'. I believe the following rates to be for the former, the fiorino largo di grossi.

Date	Rate	Place	Type	Reference
1471.10.22	111 s.	Florence	O	(282)
1471.10.24	110 s.	Florence	M	(142)
1471.11.26	110 s.	Florence	M	(142)
1472.02.01	110 s.	Florence	M	(142)
1472.04.21	110 s.	Florence	M	(142)
1472.05.16	110 s.	Florence	M	(142)
1472.10.18	110 s.	Florence	M	(142)
1473.06.08	110 s.	Florence	M	(142)
1473.09.28	110 s.	Florence	M	(142)
1473.10.25	110 s.	Florence	M	(142)
1473.11.24	110 s.	Florence	M	(142)
1473.12.11	110 s.	Florence	M	(142)
1474-1475	112 s.	Florence	C	(111) p.85
1474.02.08	110 s.	Florence	M	(142)
1474.02.10	110 s.	Florence	M	(142)
1474.02.11	111 s.	Florence	M	(142)
1474.02.14	110 s.	Florence	M	(142)
1474.03.12	109 s.	Florence	M	(142)
1474.03.18	110 s.	Florence	M	(142)
1474.04.22	110 s.	Florence	M	(142)
1474.05.23	110 s.	Florence	M	(142)
1474.06.17	110 s.	Florence	M	(142)
1474.06.28	111 s.	Florence	M	(142)
1474.07.08	110 s.	Florence	M	(142)
1474.07.08	112 s.	Florence	M	(142)
1474.07.23	112 s.	Florence	M	(142)
1474.08.20	110 s.	Florence	M	(142)
1474.08.31	112 s.	Florence	M	(142)
1474.09.26	110 s.	Florence	M	(142)
1474.10.07	112 s.	Florence	M	(142)
1474.10.20	110 s.	Florence	M	(142)
1474.10.26	112 s.	Florence	M	(142)
1474.11.05	110 s.	Florence	M	(142)
1474.11.14	112 s.	Florence	M	(142)
1474.12.15	110 s.	Florence	M	(142)
1475.01.09	110 s.	Florence	M	(142)
1475.02.05	112 s.	Florence	M	(142)
1475.02.11	110 s.	Florence	M	(142)
1475.02.25	112 s.	Florence	M	(142)
1475.03.04	110 s.	Florence	M	(142)
1475.04.10	110 s.	Florence	M	(142)
1475.04.12	112 s.	Florence	M	(142)
1475.05.08	112 s.	Florence	M	(142)
1475.05.20	110 s.	Florence	M	(142)
1475.05.27	112 s.	Florence	M	(142)
1475.06.03	113 s.	Florence	M	(142)
1475.06.10	110 s.	Florence	M	(142)
1475.06.21	112 s.	Florence	M	(142)
1475.07.01	110 s.	Florence	M	(142)
1475.07.01	112 s.	Florence	M	(142)
1475.07.06	111 s.	Florence	M	(142)
1475.07.06	113 s.	Florence	M	(142)
1475.07.21	110 s.	Florence	M	(142)
1475.07.27	112 s.	Florence	M	(142)

Date	Rate	Place	Type	Reference
1475.07.29	111 s.	Florence	M	(142)
1475.08.12	113 s.	Florence	M	(142)
1475.08.16	112 s.	Florence	M	(142)
1475.10.17	110 s.	Florence	M	(142)
1475.10.17	112 s.	Florence	M	(142)
1475.10.27	113 s.	Florence	M	(142)
1475.11.23	113 s.	Florence	M	(142)
1475.12.23	110 s.	Florence	M	(142)
1475.12.23	112 s.	Florence	M	(142)
1476-1477	114 s.	Florence	C	(111) p.85
1476.01.05	111 s. 6 d.	Florence	M	(142)
1476.01.05	112 s.	Florence	M	(142)
1476.02.22	114 s.	Florence	M	(142)
1476.02.24	112 s.	Florence	M	(142)
1476.04.08	112 s.	Florence	M	(142)
1476.05.16	112 s.	Florence	M	(142)
1476.05.17	114 s.	Florence	M	(142)
1476.05.24	112 s.	Florence	M	(142)
1476.05.29	114 s.	Florence	M	(142)
1476.06.01	112 s.	Florence	M	(142)
1476.06.01	114 s.	Florence	M	(142)
1476.06.05	113 s.	Florence	M	(142)
1476.06.15	111 s.	Florence	M	(142)
1476.06.18	114 s.	Florence	M	(142)
1476.07.09	112 s.	Florence	M	(142)
1476.10.09	112 s.	Florence	M	(142)
1476.10.10	114 s.	Florence	M	(142)
1476.10.19	112 s.	Florence	M	(142)
1476.10.23	114 s.	Florence	M	(142)
1476.11.07	114 s.	Florence	M	(142)
1476.11.28	112 s.	Florence	M	(142)
1476.12.17	114 s.	Florence	M	(142)
1476.12.23	112 s.	Florence	M	(142)
1476.12.23	114 s.	Florence	M	(142)
1477.01.16	114 s.	Florence	M	(142)
1477.01.28	112 s.	Florence	M	(142)
1477.01.28	114 s.	Florence	M	(142)
1477.02.08	114 s.	Florence	M	(142)
1477.02.14	113 s.	Florence	M	(142)
1477.02.22	112 s.	Florence	M	(142)
1477.02.22	114 s.	Florence	M	(142)
1477.03.10	114 s.	Florence	M	(142)
1477.04.23	114 s.	Florence	M	(142)
1477.05.17	112 s.	Florence	M	(142)
1477.05.21	114 s.	Florence	M	(142)
1477.06.01	114 s.	Florence	M	(142)
1477.07.23	114 s.	Florence	M	(142)
1477.08.07	114 s.	Florence	M	(142)
1477.09.16	114 s.	Florence	M	(142)
1477.10.17	114 s.	Florence	M	(142)
1477.11.04	114 s.	Florence	M	(142)
1477.11.22	112 s.	Florence	M	(142)
1477.11.26	114 s.	Florence	M	(142)
1477.11.27	112 s.	Florence	M	(142)
1477.11.29	112 s.	Florence	M	(142)
1477.11.29	114 s.	Florence	M	(142)
1477.12.05	114 s.	Florence	M	(142)
1478	115 s.	Florence	C	(111) p.85
1478.01.05	113 s.	Florence	M	(142)
1478.01.13	114 s.	Florence	M	(142)
1478.02.06	113 s.	Florence	M	(142)
1478.02.14	112 s.	Florence	M	(142)
1478.02.14	115 s.	Florence	M	(142)
1478.03.03	114 s.	Florence	M	(142)
1478.03.10	115 s.	Florence	M	(142)
1478.03.14	112 s.	Florence	M	(142)
1478.03.26	114 s.	Florence	M	(142)
1478.03.31	115 s.	Florence	M	(142)
1478.03.31	116 s.	Florence	M	(142)
1478.04.15	114 s.	Florence	M	(142)
1478.04.15	115 s.	Florence	M	(142)
1478.04.22	113 s. 6 d.	Florence	M	(142)

THE FIORINO LARGO IN FLORENTINE SOLDI AND DENARI

Date	Rate	Place	Type	Reference
1478.04.28	115 s.	Florence	M	(142)
1478.06.09	113 s.	Florence	M	(142)
1478.06.19	114 s.	Florence	M	(142)
1478.07.11	115 s.	Florence	M	(142)
1478.07.31	113 s. 4 d.	Florence	M	(142)
1478.08.06	114 s.	Florence	M	(142)
1478.09.09	113 s. 4 d.	Florence	M	(142)
1478.09.30	114 s.	Florence	M	(142)
1478.10.17	113 s.	Florence	M	(142)
1478.10.21	115 s.	Florence	M	(142)
1478.11.10	115 s.	Florence	M	(142)
1479	116 s.	Florence	C	(111) p.85
1479.01.08	115 s.	Florence	M	(142)
1479.02.05	115 s.	Florence	M	(142)
1479.03.03	113 s.	Florence	M	(142)
1479.03.06	114 s.	Florence	M	(142)
1479.03.20	115 s.	Florence	M	(142)
1479.03.23	116 s.	Florence	M	(142)
1479.04.02	116 s.	Florence	M	(142)
1479.04.17	113 s. 2 d.	Florence	M	(142)
1479.05.15	116 s.	Florence	M	(142)
1479.05.21	113 s. 2 d.	Florence	M	(142)
1479.06.07	114 s.	Florence	M	(142)
1479.06.08	113 s. 9 d.	Florence	M	(142)
1479.07.03	116 s.	Florence	M	(142)
1479.07.05	113 s. 9 d.	Florence	M	(142)
1479.08.13	117 s.	Florence	M	(142)
1479.09.25	114 s.	Florence	M	(142)
1479.10.11	116 s.	Florence	M	(142)
1479.12.24	114 s.	Florence	M	(142)
1480	117 s.	Florence	C	(111) p.85
1480.02.24	117 s.	Florence	M	(142)
1480.03.23	118 s.	Florence	M	(142)
1480.07.17	117 s.	Florence	M	(142)
1480.08.11	117 s.	Florence	M	(142)
1480.08.17	112 s. 2 d.	Florence	M	(142)
1480.09.12	117 s.	Florence	M	(142)
1480 from 10	117 s.	Florence	M	(142)
1481.02.28	112 s. 7 d.	Florence	M	(142)
1481.03.27	111 s.	Florence	M	(142)
1481.04.13	115 s.	Florence	M	(142)
1481.04.26	112 s. 8 d.	Florence	M	(142)
1482.02.05	115 s.	Florence	M	(142)
1482.07.02	112 s.	Florence	M	(142)
1482.08.09	112 s.	Florence	M	(142)
1482.10.02	112 s.	Florence	M	(142)
1482.12.11	112 s.	Florence	M	(142)
1483.01.21	112 s.	Florence	M	(142)
1483.03.12	113 s.	Florence	M	(142)
1483.03.24	112 s. 8 d.	Florence	M	(142)
1483.03.29	113 s.	Florence	M	(142)
1483.04.15	112 s.	Florence	M	(142)
1483.04.15	112 s. 8 d.	Florence	M	(142)
1483.04.24	113 s.	Florence	M	(142)
1483.05.30	113 s.	Florence	M	(142)
1483.06.26	113 s.	Florence	M	(142)
1483.08.08	113 s.	Florence	M	(142)
1484	115 s.	Florence	M	(31) III p.88
1484.01.10	114 s.	Florence	M	(142)
1484.02.24	115 s.	Florence	M	(142)
1484.03.19	115 s.	Florence	M	(142)
1484.04.03	115 s.	Florence	M	(142)
1484.06.05	115 s.	Florence	M	(142)
1484.09.23	109 s.	Florence	M	(142)
1484.09.23	115 s. 4 d. di quattrini	Florence	M	(142)
1484.10.19	115 s. 4 d.	Florence	M	(142)
1484.12.04	115 s. 8 d.	Florence	M	(142)
1485.01.05	115 s. 4 d.	Florence	M	(142)
1485.05.24	115 s. 8 d.	Florence	M	(142)
1485.07.30	115 s. 10 d.	Florence	M	(142)
1486.09.05	116 s.	Florence	M	(142)

THE FIORINO LARGO IN FLORENTINE SOLDI AND DENARI

Date	Rate	Place	Type	Reference
1490.07.24	116 s. 6 d.	Florence	M	(142)
1490.08.26	116 s. & d.	Florence	M	(142)
1490.09.11	116 s. 6 d.	Florence	M	(142)
1490.10.14	116 s. 6 d.	Florence	M	(142)
1490.11.06	116 s. 6 d.	Florence	M	(142)
1491.02.28	117 s.	Florence	M	(142)
1491.03.03	116 s. 6 d.	Florence	M	(142)
1491.05.16	116 s. 6 d.	Florence	M	(142)
1491.05.21	111 s. 4 d. moneta nuova	Florence	M	(142)
1491.06.16	116 s. 6 d.	Florence	M	(142)
1491.06.21	117 s.	Florence	M	(142)
1491.07.09	111 s. 4 d. moneta nuova	Florence	M	(142)
1491.07.14	116 s. 6 d.	Florence	M	(142)
1491.08.09	116 s. 6 d.	Florence	M	(142)
1491.08.25	117 s.	Florence	M	(142)
1491.09.09	116 s. 6 d.	Florence	M	(142)
1491.10.22	113 s. 2 d. moneta nuova	Florence	M	(142)
1491.10.31	116 s. 6 d.	Florence	M	(142)
1491.11.08	117 s.	Florence	M	(142)
1491.12.12	116 s. 6 d.	Florence	M	(142)
1492.01.14	116 s. 6 d.	Florence	M	(142)
1492.02.15	116 s. 4 d.	Florence	M	(142)
1492.03.10	118 s.	Florence	M	(142)
1492.04.12	116 s. 6 d.	Florence	M	(142)
1492.06.07	118 s.	Florence	M	(142)
1492.07.14	116 s. 6 d.	Florence	M	(142)
1492.08.16	116 s. 6 d.	Florence	M	(142)
1492.09.20	118 s.	Florence	M	(142)
1492.10.05	116 s. 6 d.	Florence	M	(142)
1492.11.21	116 s. 6 d.	Florence	M	(142)
1493.02.06	116 s. 6 d.	Florence	M	(142)
1493.03.29	118 s.	Florence	M	(142)
1493.03.29	116 s. 6 d.	Florence	M	(142)
1493.07.16	93 s. 4 d. moneta nuova	Florence	M	(142)
1493.08.09	118 s.	Florence	M	(142)
1493.08.23	116 s. 6 d.	Florence	M	(142)
1493.09.02	116 s. 6 d.	Florence	M	(142)
1493.10.17	116 s. 6 d.	Florence	M	(142)
1493.11.18	116 s. 6 d.	Florence	M	(142)
1493.12.05	116 s. 6 d.	Florence	M	(142)
1494.01.14	116 s. 6 d.	Florence	M	(142)
1494.02.13	116 s. 6 d.	Florence	M	(142)
1494.04.17	116 s. 6 d.	Florence	M	(142)
1494.05.05	111 s.	Florence	M	(142)
1494.05.06	116 s. 6 d.	Florence	M	(142)
1494.06.21	116 s. 6 d.	Florence	M	(142)
1494.07.16	116 s. 6 d.	Florence	M	(142)
1494.09.19	116 s. 6 d.	Florence	M	(142)
1494.10.07	116 s. 6 d.	Florence	M	(142)
1495.06.10	120 s.	Florence	M	(142)
1495.08.03	120 s.	Florence	M	(142)
1495.09.24	120 s.	Florence	M	(142)
1495.10.06	120 s.	Florence	M	(142)
1495.11.10	120 s.	Florence	M	(142)
1495.12.11	120 s.	Florence	M	(142)
1496.01.21	120 s.	Florence	M	(142)
1496.02.09	120 s.	Florence	M	(142)
1496.02.15	116 s. 6 d.	Florence	M	(142)
1496.06	120 s.	Florence	M	(142)
1496.08.04	120 s.	Florence	M	(142)
1496.10.01	120 s.	Florence	M	(142)
1497.03.23	120 s.	Florence	M	(142)
1497.09.26	120 s.	Florence	M	(142)

The fiorino largo d'oro in oro in Florentine soldi and denari

See above pp.20, 26, 27 and 28 for the evolution of the fiorino largo as an accounting unit. After 1471 the fiorino largo d'oro in oro remained persistently above that of the fiorini largo di grossi. For fuller details of this accounting unit see Bernocchi (31) III, pp.295-300.

Date	Rate	Place	Type	Reference
1481.02.16	120 s.	Florence	M	(142)
1481.03.27	120 s.	Florence	M	(142)
1481.04.26	118 s.	Florence	M	(142)
1481.08.11	120 s.	Florence	M	(142)
1481.09.01	120 s.	Florence	M	(142)
1481.11.07	118 s.	Florence	M	(142)
1481-1483	120 s.	Florence	C	(111) p.85
1482.03.04	118 s.	Florence	M	(142)
1482.03.19	120 s.	Florence	M	(142)
1482.04.01	118 s.	Florence	M	(142)
1482.05.09	120 s.	Florence	M	(142)
1482.05.23	118 s.	Florence	M	(142)
1482.05.30	120 s.	Florence	M	(142)
1482.06.10	120 s.	Florence	M	(142)
1482.06.19	118 s.	Florence	M	(142)
1482.09.26	120 s.	Florence	M	(142)
1482.09.29	119 s.	Florence	M	(142)
1482.10.17	120 s.	Florence	M	(142)
1482.11.09	120 s.	Florence	M	(142)
1482.12.24	120 s.	Florence	M	(142)
1483.01.28	120 s.	Florence	M	(142)
1483.02.22	120 s.	Florence	M	(142)
1483.03.01	121 s.	Florence	M	(142)
1483.03.04	120 s.	Florence	M	(142)
1483.04.21	120 s.	Florence	M	(142)
1483.05.05	120 s.	Florence	M	(142)
1483.06.05	120 s.	Florence	M	(142)
1483.07.18	120 s.	Florence	M	(142)
1483.08.19	120 s.	Florence	M	(142)
1483.09.03	121 s.	Florence	M	(142)
1483.10.08	120 s.	Florence	M	(142)
1483.11.06	120 s.	Florence	M	(142)
1484.01.07	120 s.	Florence	M	(142)
1484.03.12	120 s.	Florence	M	(142)
1484.03.16	120 s.	Florence	M	(142)
1484.04.24	120 s.	Florence	M	(142)
1484.05.29	123 s.	Florence	M	(142)
1484.06.18	123 s.	Florence	M	(142)
1484.07.01	120 s.	Florence	M	(142)
1484.07.17	123 s.	Florence	M	(142)
1484.08.03	123 s.	Florence	M	(142)
1484.09.20	123 s.	Florence	M	(142)
1484.10.20	123 s.	Florence	M	(142)
1484.10.23	120 s.	Florence	M	(142)
1484.11.13	123 s.	Florence	M	(142)
1484.11.17	120 s.	Florence	M	(142)
1484.12.29	123 s.	Florence	M	(142)
1484-1485	123 s.	Florence	C	(111) p.85
1485	122 s. 4 d.	Florence	C	(360) p.40
1485.01.19	120 s.	Florence	M	(142)
1485.02.03	123 s.	Florence	M	(142)
1485.03.10	123 s.	Florence	M	(142)
1485.04.08	123 s.	Florence	M	(142)
1485.05.31	123 s.	Florence	M	(142)
1485.07.02	123 s.	Florence	M	(142)
1485.09.07	124 s.	Florence	M	(142)
1485.10.07	123 s.	Florence	M	(142)
1485.11.03	123 s.	Florence	M	(142)
1485.11.18	122 s.	Florence	M	(142)
1486	125 s.	Florence	C	(111) p.85
1486.01.11	124 s.	Florence	M	(142)
1486.02.01	123 s.	Florence	M	(142)
1486.03	124 s.	Florence	M	(142)
1486.03.21	123 s.	Florence	M	(142)
1486.04.23	124 s.	Florence	M	(142)

THE FIORINO LARGO D'ORO IN ORO IN FLORENTINE SOLDI AND DENARI

Date	Rate	Place	Type	Reference
1486.05.31	126 s.	Florence	M	(142)
1486.06.09	124 s.	Florence	M	(142)
1486.07.07	124 s.	Florence	M	(142)
1486.09.02	124 s.	Florence	M	(142)
1486.11.01	125 s.	Florence	M	(142)
1487	126 s.	Florence	C	(111) p.85
1488	127 s.	Florence	C	(111) p.85
1488.09.27	126 s.	Florence	M	(142)
1488.10.06	126 s.	Florence	M	(142)
1488.11.21	126 s.	Florence	M	(142)
1489	129 s.	Florence	C	(111) p.85
1489.08.11	127 s.	Florence	M	(142)
1489.11.23	128 s.	Florence	M	(142)
1489.12.31	129 s.	Florence	M	(142)
1490-1492	130 s.	Florence	C	(111) p.86
1490.01.09	129 s.	Florence	M	(142)
1490.03.17	129 s.	Florence	M	(142)
1490.04.01	129 s.	Florence	M	(142)
1490.05.09	130 s.	Florence	M	(142)
1490.06.18	130 s.	Florence	M	(142)
1490.07.17	130 s.	Florence	M	(142)
1490.08.15	130 s.	Florence	M	(142)
1490.09.18	130 s.	Florence	M	(142)
1490.09.28	129 s.	Florence	M	(142)
1490.10.17	130 s.	Florence	M	(142)
1490.11.30	130 s.	Florence	M	(142)
1491.01.07	130 s.	Florence	M	(142)
1491.03.07	130 s.	Florence	M	(142)
1491.06.06	130 s.	Florence	M	(142)
1491.07.31	130 s.	Florence	M	(142)
1491.09.09	130 s.	Florence	M	(142)
1491.10.06	130 s.	Florence	M	(142)
1491.11.12	130 s.	Florence	M	(142)
1491.12.07	130 s.	Florence	M	(142)
1492.01.04	130 s.	Florence	M	(142)
1492.03.31	130 s.	Florence	M	(142)
1492.04.14	130 s.	Florence	M	(142)
1492.07.11	130 s.	Florence	M	(142)
1492.09.06	130 s.	Florence	M	(142)
1492.12.19	130 s.	Florence	M	(142)
1493	131 s.	Florence	C	(111) p.86
1493.01.28	130 s.	Florence	M	(142)
1493.03.01	130 s.	Florence	M	(142)
1493.04.06	130 s.	Florence	M	(142)
1493.07.16	130 s.	Florence	M	(142)
1493.12.05	131 s.	Florence	M	(142)
1494	132 s.	Florence	C	(111) p.86
1494.05.16	130 s.	Florence	M	(142)
1494.07.11	131 s.	Florence	M	(142)
1494.08.09	131 s.	Florence	M	(142)
1494.09.06	131 s.	Florence	M	(142)
1494.09.22	132 s.	Florence	M	(142)
1494.10.03	132 s.	Florence	M	(142)
1495	133 s.	Florence	C	(111) p.86
1495.03.21	132 s.	Florence	M	(142)
1495.05.11	133 s.	Florence	M	(142)
1496-1497	134 s.	Florence	C	(111) p.86
1498	135 s.	Florence	C	(111) p.86
1498.08.27	135 s.	Florence	M	(142)
1498.10.02	135 s.	Florence	M	(142)
1498.10.14	136 s.	Florence	M	(142)
1499	137 s.	Florence	M	(31) III p.88
1499.01.07	136 s.	Florence	M	(142)
1499.10.13	136 s.	Florence	M	(142)
1499	138 s.	Florence	C	(111) p.86
1500	140 s.	Florence	C	(111) p.86

Affiorino

The gold florin, when first issued, was equal to 20 silver florins, (fiorini), the original Florentine silver grossi, struck from the 1230s onwards at a value of 12 denari, a soldo of piccioli. A soldo affiorino was thus a fiorino grosso. As the denaro picciolo and the grosso evolved differently, the gold florin came to have a different value, 'affiorino', in grossi from its value in piccioli. This evolution came to an end in 1279 when the silver fiorino ceased to be struck. By that time the gold florin had become worth 29 silver florins. Silver florins remained in circulation until 1296, but accounting in lire, soldi and denari affiorino continued well into the fifteenth century. After the disappearance of the silver florin, this money of account was tied to the gold florin at the fossilized rate of 29 soldi to the gold florin. In other words any sums expressed affiorino after 1279, may be immediately converted into gold florins at the rate of 29 soldi to the florin.

The Florentine florin in Florentine soldi and denari affiorino

Date	Rate	Place	Type	Reference
1252	20 s.	Florence	M	(31) III p.78
1260	25 s.	Florence	M	(31) III p.78
1272.10.20	26 s. 5 d.	Champagne/Florence	C	(444) I p.16
1273-1276	27 s. 1/2 d.	Florence	M	(31) III p.78
1273	26 s. 1/2 d.	Florence	C	(444) I p.19
1274.01-1275	27 s. 1/2 d.	Florence	C	(444) I p.25
1274.08	27 s. 2 2/3 d.	Florence	C	(444) I p.24
1277	27 s. 5 1/2 d.	Florence	M	(31) III p.78
1278	29 s. 3 1/2 d.	Florence	M	(31) III p.78
1279-1296	29 s.	Florence	M	(31) III p.78

For other references to money affiorino see below p.39

Grossi guelfi

The silver fiorino was replaced by a new grosso known as the guelfo. It was issued from 1277 to 1297 and again from 1314 onwards. Although the guelfo was never valued at a soldo of piccioli, the habit of accounting as if the grosso was a soldo was transferred from the silver fiorino to the guelfo. Thus the valuation of the gold florin at 18 soldi, meant at 18 grossi guelfi. The guelfo when first issued was in fact valued at 20 denari piccioli, by 1297 it was valued at 28 denari piccioli, when re-issued in 1314, at 30 denari piccioli, in 1318 at 32 denari etc.

The Florentine florin in Florentine grossi guelfi

Date	Rate	Place	Type	Reference
1296-1298	18 s.	Curia	B	(439) p.898
1320	12 s.	Curia	B	(439) p.900
1320	13 s.	Curia	B	(439) p.900
1327-1328	13 s. 6 d.	Curia	B	(439) p.901
1333-1334	12 s.	Curia	B	(439) p.901
1333-1334	13 s.	Curia	B	(439) p.901

The Florentine grosso guelfo in soldi and denari provisini of Rome

Date	Rate	Place	Type	Reference
1285	1 s. 6 d.	Rome	C	(401) p.306

The Florentine florin in Florentine soldi and denari, when payment made in grossi d'argento

From 1418 to 1432 the proveditori degli cambiatori noted down not only the rates of exchange between florins and piccioli when quattrini (4d.) were involved, but also when grossi were involved. They noted down two rates each day when exchange was carried on. These rates are presumably one for the exchange of florins to grossi, and the other for the exchange of grossi to florins. At this period the grosso was a coin worth 5s. 6d. of piccioli. It will be noted from the slight difference in rates that the money-changer preferred handling grossi to quattrini. I have again abstracted the rates for the first working day of each month.

THE FLORIN IN FLORENTINE SOLDI AND DENARI (IN GROSSI)

Date	Rate	Place	Type	Reference
1418.02.01	80 s. 11 1/5 d.	Florence	M	(520)
1418.02.01	81 s. 2 1/5 d.	Florence	M	(520)
1418.03.01	81 s. 9 2/5 d.	Florence	M	(31) IV p.277
1418.03.01	82 s. 2/5 d.	Florence	M	(31) IV p.277
1418.04.01	81 s. 7 d.	Florence	M	(31) IV p.277
1418.04.01	81 s. 9 3/5 d.	Florence	M	(31) IV p.277
1418.05.02	81 s. 5 2/5 d.	Florence	M	(31) IV p.278
1418.05.02	81 s. 8 d.	Florence	M	(31) IV p.278
1418.06.01	80 s. 6 4/5 d.	Florence	M	(31) IV p.278
1418.06.01	80 s. 9 1/5 d.	Florence	M	(31) IV p.278
1418.07.01	80 s. 3 2/5 d.	Florence	M	(31) IV p.279
1418.07.01	80 s. 5 3/5 d.	Florence	M	(31) IV p.279
1418.08.02	80 s. 5 d.	Florence	M	(31) IV p.279
1418.08.02	80 s. 7 3/5 d.	Florence	M	(31) IV p.279
1418.09.01	80 s. 2 3/5 d.	Florence	M	(31) IV p.280
1418.09.01	80 s. 4 4/5 d.	Florence	M	(31) IV p.280
1418.10.01	80 s. 4 1/5 d.	Florence	M	(31) IV p.280
1418.10.01	80 s. 7 1/5 d.	Florence	M	(31) IV p.280
1418.11.03	80 s. 11 d.	Florence	M	(31) IV p.281
1418.11.03	81 s. 1 4/5 d.	Florence	M	(31) IV p.281
1418.12.01	81 s. 1 d.	Florence	M	(31) IV p.281
1418.12.01	81 s. 3 2/5 d.	Florence	M	(31) IV p.281
1419.01.02	81 s. 2 d.	Florence	M	(520)
1419.01.02	81 s. 4 3/5 d.	Florence	M	(520)
1419.02.01	80 s. 10 d.	Florence	M	(31) IV p.282
1419.02.01	81 s. 1 1/5 d.	Florence	M	(31) IV p.282
1419.03.01	79 s. 6 d.	Florence	M	(31) IV p.283
1419.03.01	79 s. 9 d.	Florence	M	(31) IV p.283
1419.04.01	80 s.	Florence	M	(31) IV p.283
1419.04.01	80 s. 1 4/5 d.	Florence	M	(31) IV p.283
1419.05.02	79 s. 5 d.	Florence	M	(31) IV p.284
1419.05.02	79 s. 7 d.	Florence	M	(31) IV p.284
1419.06.01	78 s. 8 d.	Florence	M	(31) IV p.284
1419.06.01	78 s. 10 1/5 d.	Florence	M	(31) IV p.284
1419.07.01	78 s. 5 d.	Florence	M	(31) IV p.285
1419.07.01	78 s. 7 4/5 d.	Florence	M	(31) IV p.285
1419.08.02	78 s. 3 d.	Florence	M	(31) IV p.285
1419.08.02	78 s. 5 2/5 d.	Florence	M	(31) IV p.285
1419.09.01	77 s. 4 d.	Florence	M	(31) IV p.286
1419.09.01	77 s. 6 2/5 d.	Florence	M	(31) IV p.286
1419.10.02	77 s. 7 d.	Florence	M	(31) IV p.286
1419.10.02	77 s. 9 1/5 d.	Florence	M	(31) IV p.286
1419.11.03	78 s. 2 d.	Florence	M	(31) IV p.287
1419.11.03	77 s. 4 4/5 d.	Florence	M	(31) IV p.287
1419.12.01	79 s.	Florence	M	(31) IV p.287
1419.12.01	79 s. 2 2/5 d.	Florence	M	(31) IV p.287
1420.01.02	79 s. 6 d.	Florence	M	(520)
1420.01.02	79 s. 9 d.	Florence	M	(520)
1420.02.01	79 s.	Florence	M	(520)
1420.02.01	79 s. 2 4/5 d.	Florence	M	(520)
1420.03.01	79 s. 6 d.	Florence	M	(520)
1420.03.01	79 s. 8 4/5 d.	Florence	M	(520)
1420.04.01	79 s. 4 d.	Florence	M	(520)
1420.04.01	79 s. 6 3/5 d.	Florence	M	(520)
1420.05.02	79 s. 6 d.	Florence	M	(520)
1420.05.02	79 s. 9 1/5 d.	Florence	M	(520)
1420.06.01	79 s. 1 d.	Florence	M	(520)
1420.06.01	79 s. 3 4/5 d.	Florence	M	(520)
1420.07.01	78 s. 10 d.	Florence	M	(520)
1420.07.01	79 s. 3/5 d.	Florence	M	(520)
1420.08.02	78 s. 9 d.	Florence	M	(520)
1420.08.02	79 s.	Florence	M	(520)
1420.09.02	79 s. 3 d.	Florence	M	(520)
1420.09.02	79 s. 6 d.	Florence	M	(520)
1420.10.01	79 s. 7 d.	Florence	M	(520)
1420.10.01	79 s. 10 2/5 d.	Florence	M	(520)
1420.11.04	79 s. 3 d.	Florence	M	(520)
1420.11.04	79 s. 6 d.	Florence	M	(520)
1420.12.02	79 s. 10 d.	Florence	M	(520)
1420.12.02	80 s. 1 d.	Florence	M	(520)
1421.01.02	80 s.	Florence	M	(520)
1421.01.02	80 s. 3 3/5 d.	Florence	M	(520)

THE FLORIN IN FLORENTINE SOLDI AND DENARI (IN GROSSI)

Date	Rate	Place	Type	Reference
1421.02.01	80 s. 1 d.	Florence	M	(31) IV p.294
1421.02.01	80 s. 4 d.	Florence	M	(31) IV p.294
1421.03.01	80 s. 3 d.	Florence	M	(31) IV p.295
1421.03.01	80 s. 6 2/5 d.	Florence	M	(31) IV p.295
1421.04.01	80 s.	Florence	M	(31) IV p.295
1421.04.01	80 s. 2 3/5 d.	Florence	M	(31) IV p.295
1421.05.02	80 s.	Florence	M	(31) IV p.296
1421.05.02	80 s. 2 d.	Florence	M	(31) IV p.296
1421.06.02	80 s.	Florence	M	(31) IV p.296
1421.06.02	80 s. 2 d.	Florence	M	(31) IV p.296
1421.07.01	80 s. 1 d.	Florence	M	(31) IV p.297
1421.07.01	80 s. 3 1/5 d.	Florence	M	(31) IV p.297
1421.08.02	80 s. 1 d.	Florence	M	(31) IV p.297
1421.08.02	80 s. 3 d.	Florence	M	(31) IV p.297
1421.09.01	80 s. 1 d.	Florence	M	(31) IV p.298
1421.09.01	80 s. 3 d.	Florence	M	(31) IV p.298
1421.10.01	80 s. 5 d.	Florence	M	(31) IV p.298
1421.10.01	80 s. 8 d.	Florence	M	(31) IV p.298
1421.11.04	80 s. 6 d.	Florence	M	(31) IV p.299
1421.11.04	80 s. 9 d.	Florence	M	(31) IV p.299
1421.12.01	80 s. 8 d.	Florence	M	(31) IV p.299
1421.12.01	80 s. 11 d.	Florence	M	(31) IV p.299
1422.01.02	80 s. 11 d.	Florence	M	(520)
1422.01.02	81 s. 1 1/5 d.	Florence	M	(520)
1422.02.04	80 s. 8 d.	Florence	M	(31) IV p.300
1422.02.04	80 s. 10 1/5 d.	Florence	M	(31) IV p.300
1422.03.02	80 s. 7 d.	Florence	M	(31) IV p.301
1422.03.02	80 s. 9 d.	Florence	M	(31) IV p.301
1422.04.01	80 s. 5 d.	Florence	M	(31) IV p.301
1422.04.01	80 s. 7 d.	Florence	M	(31) IV p.301
1422.05.02	80 s. 4 d.	Florence	M	(31) IV p.302
1422.05.02	80 s. 7 d.	Florence	M	(31) IV p.302
1422.06.03	79 s. 2 d.	Florence	M	(31) IV p.302
1422.06.03	79 s. 4 2/5 d.	Florence	M	(31) IV p.302
1422.07.01	78 s. 11 d.	Florence	M	(31) IV p.303
1422.07.01	79 s. 1 3/5 d.	Florence	M	(31) IV p.303
1422.08.03	79 s.	Florence	M	(31) IV p.303
1422.08.03	79 s. 3 d.	Florence	M	(31) IV p.303
1422.09.01	78 s. 10 d.	Florence	M	(31) IV p.304
1422.09.01	79 s. 1 d.	Florence	M	(31) IV p.304
1422.10.01	79 s. 5 d.	Florence	M	(31) IV p.304
1422.10.01	79 s. 7 d.	Florence	M	(31) IV p.304
1422.11.03	79 s. 10 d.	Florence	M	(31) IV p.305
1422.11.03	80 s. 2/5 d.	Florence	M	(31) IV p.305
1422.12.01	80 s. 5 d.	Florence	M	(31) IV p.305
1422.12.01	80 s. 7 1/5 d.	Florence	M	(31) IV p.305
1423.01.02	80 s. 6 d.	Florence	M	(520)
1423.01.02	80 s. 10 7/10 d.	Florence	M	(520)
1423.02.01	80 s. 2 d.	Florence	M	(31) IV p.306
1423.02.01	80 s. 6 4/5 d.	Florence	M	(31) IV p.306
1423.03.01	79 s. 10 d.	Florence	M	(31) IV p.307
1423.03.01	80 s. 3/5 d.	Florence	M	(31) IV p.307
1423.04.03	79 s. 7 d.	Florence	M	(31) IV p.307
1423.04.03	79 s. 9 d.	Florence	M	(31) IV p.307
1423.05.04	79 s. 8 d.	Florence	M	(31) IV p.308
1423.05.04	79 s. 11 1/5 d.	Florence	M	(31) IV p.308
1423.06.01	79 s. 3 d.	Florence	M	(31) IV p.308
1423.06.01	75 s. 5 d.	Florence	M	(31) IV p.308
1423.07.01	79 s. 4 d.	Florence	M	(31) IV p.309
1423.07.01	79 s. 6 3/5 d.	Florence	M	(31) IV p.309
1423.08.02	80 s.	Florence	M	(31) IV p.309
1423.08.02	80 s. 2 2/5 d.	Florence	M	(31) IV p.309
1423.09.01	80 s. 2 d.	Florence	M	(31) IV p.310
1423.09.01	80 s. 4 3/5 d.	Florence	M	(31) IV p.310
1423.10.01	80 s. 3 d.	Florence	M	(31) IV p.310
1423.10.01	80 s. 4 3/5 d.	Florence	M	(31) IV p.310
1423.11.03	80 s. 4 d.	Florence	M	(31) IV p.311
1423.11.03	80 s. 6 3/5 d.	Florence	M	(31) IV p.311
1423.12.01	81 s.	Florence	M	(31) IV p.311
1423.12.01	81 s. 2 d.	Florence	M	(31) IV p.311
1424.01.03	80 s. 8 d.	Florence	M	(520)
1424.01.03	80 s. 11 d.	Florence	M	(520)

THE FLORIN IN FLORENTINE SOLDI AND DENARI (IN GROSSI)

Date	Rate	Place	Type	Reference
1424.02.01	80 s. 9 d.	Florence	M	(31) IV p.312
1424.02.01	81 s.	Florence	M	(31) IV p.312
1424.03.01	81 s. 6 d.	Florence	M	(31) IV p.313
1424.03.01	80 s. 9 d.	Florence	M	(31) IV p.313
1424.04.01	80 s. 2 d.	Florence	M	(31) IV p.313
1424.04.01	80 s. 10 d.	Florence	M	(31) IV p.313
1424.05.02	80 s. 9 d.	Florence	M	(31) IV p.314
1424.05.02	81 s.	Florence	M	(31) IV p.314
1424.06.02	80 s. 5 d.	Florence	M	(31) IV p.314
1424.06.02	80 s. 8 d.	Florence	M	(31) IV p.314
1424.07.01	80 s. 5 d.	Florence	M	(31) IV p.315
1424.07.01	80 s. 8 d.	Florence	M	(31) IV p.315
1424.08.02	80 s.	Florence	M	(31) IV p.315
1424.08.02	80 s. 2 d.	Florence	M	(31) IV p.315
1424.09.01	79 s. 10 d.	Florence	M	(31) IV p.316
1424.09.01	80 s. 1 4/5 d.	Florence	M	(31) IV p.316
1424.10.03	79 s. 9 d.	Florence	M	(31) IV p.316
1424.10.03	80 s.	Florence	M	(31) IV p.316
1424.11.03	80 s. 2 d.	Florence	M	(31) IV p.317
1424.11.03	80 s. 4 2/5 d.	Florence	M	(31) IV p.317
1424.12.01	80 s. 8 d.	Florence	M	(31) IV p.317
1424.12.01	80 s. 11 d.	Florence	M	(31) IV p.317
1425.01.02	80 s. 7 d.	Florence	M	(520)
1425.01.02	80 s. 9 d.	Florence	M	(520)
1425.02.01	80 s. 6 d.	Florence	M	(31) IV p.318
1425.02.01	80 s. 8 1/5 d.	Florence	M	(31) IV p.318
1425.03.01	80 s. 3 3/5 d.	Florence	M	(31) IV p.319
1425.03.01	80 s. 5 4/5 d.	Florence	M	(31) IV p.319
1425.04.02	80 s. 2 d.	Florence	M	(31) IV p.319
1425.04.02	80 s. 4 3/5 d.	Florence	M	(31) IV p.319
1425.05.02	79 s. 11 d.	Florence	M	(31) IV p.320
1425.05.02	80 s. 2/5 d.	Florence	M	(31) IV p.320
1425.06.01	79 s. 8 d.	Florence	M	(31) IV p.320
1425.06.01	79 s. 10 d.	Florence	M	(31) IV p.320
1425.07.02	79 s. 3 d.	Florence	M	(31) IV p.321
1425.07.02	79 s. 6 d.	Florence	M	(31) IV p.321
1425.08.02	79 s. 9 d.	Florence	M	(31) IV p.321
1425.08.02	79 s. 11 d.	Florence	M	(31) IV p.321
1425.09.03	79 s. 7 d.	Florence	M	(31) IV p.322
1425.09.03	79 s. 9 3/5 d.	Florence	M	(31) IV p.322
1425.10.01	80 s. 2 d.	Florence	M	(31) IV p.322
1425.10.01	80 s. 4 d.	Florence	M	(31) IV p.322
1425.11.03	80 s. 8 d.	Florence	M	(31) IV p.323
1425.11.03	80 s. 10 2/5 d.	Florence	M	(31) IV p.323
1425.12.01	80 s.	Florence	M	(31) IV p.323
1425.12.01	80 s. 3 2/5 d.	Florence	M	(31) IV p.323
1426.01.02	80 s. 4 d.	Florence	M	(520)
1426.01.02	80 s. 6 2/5 d.	Florence	M	(520)
1426.02.01	81 s. 1 d.	Florence	M	(31) IV p.324
1426.02.01	81 s. 3 d.	Florence	M	(31) IV p.324
1426.03.01	80 s. 10 d.	Florence	M	(31) IV p.325
1426.03.01	81 s.	Florence	M	(31) IV p.325
1426.04.04	80 s. 6 2/5 d.	Florence	M	(31) IV p.325
1426.04.04	80 s. 8 2/5 d.	Florence	M	(31) IV p.325
1426.05.04	80 s. 10 3/5 d.	Florence	M	(31) IV p.326
1426.05.04	81 s. 1 d.	Florence	M	(31) IV p.326
1426.06.03	81 s. 3 1/5 d.	Florence	M	(31) IV p.326
1426.06.03	81 s. 5 3/5 d.	Florence	M	(31) IV p.326
1426.07.01	81 s. 3/5 d.	Florence	M	(31) IV p.327
1426.07.01	81 s. 2 4/5 d.	Florence	M	(31) IV p.327
1426.08.02	81 s. 5 1/5 d.	Florence	M	(31) IV p.327
1426.08.02	81 s. 8 d.	Florence	M	(31) IV p.327
1426.09.02	81 s. 4 d.	Florence	M	(31) IV p.328
1426.09.02	81 s. 6 4/5 d.	Florence	M	(31) IV p.328
1426.10.01	81 s. 10 d.	Florence	M	(31) IV p.328
1426.10.01	82 s. 3/5 d.	Florence	M	(31) IV p.328
1426.11.04	81 s. 1 4/5 d.	Florence	M	(31) IV p.329
1426.11.04	81 s. 4 3/5 d.	Florence	M	(31) IV p.329
1426.12.01	81 s. 8 d.	Florence	M	(31) IV p.329
1426.12.01	81 s. 10 3/5 d.	Florence	M	(31) IV p.329
1427.01.02	82 s. 1/5 d.	Florence	M	(520)
1427.01.02	82 s. 3 d.	Florence	M	(520)

THE FLORIN IN FLORENTINE SOLDI AND DENARI (IN GROSSI)

Date	Rate	Place	Type	Reference
1427.02.01	82 s. 3 2/5 d.	Florence	M	(31) IV p.330
1427.02.01	82 s. 6 d.	Florence	M	(31) IV p.330
1427.03.01	82 s. 2 3/5 d.	Florence	M	(31) IV p.331
1427.03.01	82 s. 5 1/5 d.	Florence	M	(31) IV p.331
1427.04.01	81 s. 6 2/5 d.	Florence	M	(31) IV p.331
1427.04.01	81 s. 9 d.	Florence	M	(31) IV p.331
1427.05.02	82 s. 1 4/5 d.	Florence	M	(31) IV p.332
1427.05.02	82 s. 4 3/5 d.	Florence	M	(31) IV p.332
1427.06.02	81 s. 11 3/5 d.	Florence	M	(31) IV p.332
1427.06.02	82 s. 3 d.	Florence	M	(31) IV p.332
1427.07.01	81 s. 5 2/5 d.	Florence	M	(31) IV p.333
1427.07.01	81 s. 7 3/5 d.	Florence	M	(31) IV p.333
1427.08.02	81 s. 8 4/5 d.	Florence	M	(31) IV p.333
1427.08.02	82 s.	Florence	M	(31) IV p.333
1427.09.01	81 s. 10 2/5 d.	Florence	M	(31) IV p.334
1427.09.01	82 s. 1 d.	Florence	M	(31) IV p.334
1427.10.01	82 s. 4/5 d.	Florence	M	(31) IV p.334
1427.10.01	82 s. 3 2/5 d.	Florence	M	(31) IV p.334
1427.11.04	82 s. 2 3/5 d.	Florence	M	(31) IV p.335
1427.11.04	82 s. 5 4/5 d.	Florence	M	(31) IV p.335
1427.12.01	82 s. 8 d.	Florence	M	(31) IV p.335
1427.12.01	82 s. 10 3/5 d.	Florence	M	(31) IV p.335
1428.01.02	82 s. 9 2/5 d.	Florence	M	(520)
1428.01.02	83 s.	Florence	M	(520)
1428.02.03	82 s. 6 d.	Florence	M	(31) IV p.336
1428.02.03	82 s. 9 d.	Florence	M	(31) IV p.336
1428.03.01	83 s. 1/5 d.	Florence	M	(31) IV p.337
1428.03.01	83 s. 3 4/5 d.	Florence	M	(31) IV p.337
1428.04.03	81 s. 11 1/5 d.	Florence	M	(31) IV p.337
1428.04.03	82 s. 2 2/5 d.	Florence	M	(31) IV p.337
1428.05.04	81 s. 11 3/5 d.	Florence	M	(31) IV p.338
1428.05.04	82 s. 2 4/5 d.	Florence	M	(31) IV p.338
1428.06.01	82 s. 6 1/5 d.	Florence	M	(31) IV p.338
1428.06.01	82 s. 9 2/5 d.	Florence	M	(31) IV p.338
1428.07.01	81 s. 6 4/5 d.	Florence	M	(31) IV p.339
1428.07.01	81 s. 10 d.	Florence	M	(31) IV p.339
1428.08.02	82 s. 1 3/5 d.	Florence	M	(31) IV p.339
1428.08.02	82 s. 4 2/5 d.	Florence	M	(31) IV p.339
1428.09.01	82 s. 3 3/5 d.	Florence	M	(31) IV p.340
1428.09.01	82 s. 6 d.	Florence	M	(31) IV p.340
1428.10.01	82 s. 6 d.	Florence	M	(31) IV p.340
1428.10.01	82 s. 9 1/5 d.	Florence	M	(31) IV p.340
1428.11.03	82 s. 5 d.	Florence	M	(31) IV p.341
1428.11.03	82 s. 8 d.	Florence	M	(31) IV p.341
1428.12.01	83 s. 1 1/5 d.	Florence	M	(31) IV p.341
1428.12.01	83 s. 4 4/5 d.	Florence	M	(31) IV p.341
1429.01.03	82 s. 10 1/5 d.	Florence	M	(520)
1429.01.03	83 s. 1 2/5 d.	Florence	M	(520)
1429.02.01	82 s. 10 d.	Florence	M	(31) IV p.342
1429.02.01	83 s. 3/5 d.	Florence	M	(31) IV p.342
1429.03.01	82 s. 9 2/5 d.	Florence	M	(31) IV p.343
1429.03.01	83 s. 4/5 d.	Florence	M	(31) IV p.343
1429.04.01	82 s. 5 1/5 d.	Florence	M	(31) IV p.343
1429.04.01	82 s. 8 2/5 d.	Florence	M	(31) IV p.343
1429.05.02	82 s. 2 3/5 d.	Florence	M	(31) IV p.344
1429.05.02	82 s. 6 d.	Florence	M	(31) IV p.344
1429.06.01	82 s. 3 d.	Florence	M	(31) IV p.344
1429.06.01	82 s. 6 d.	Florence	M	(31) IV p.344
1429.07.01	81 s. 11 4/5 d.	Florence	M	(31) IV p.345
1429.07.01	82 s. 4 d.	Florence	M	(31) IV p.345
1429.08.02	82 s. 4 d.	Florence	M	(31) IV p.345
1429.08.02	82 s. 7 1/5 d.	Florence	M	(31) IV p.345
1429.09.01	82 s. 3 4/5 d.	Florence	M	(31) IV p.346
1429.09.01	82 s. 6 4/5 d.	Florence	M	(31) IV p.346
1429.10.01	82 s. 5 d.	Florence	M	(31) IV p.346
1429.10.01	82 s. 7 1/5 d.	Florence	M	(31) IV p.346
1429.11.03	82 s. 4 2/5 d.	Florence	M	(31) IV p.347
1429.11.03	82 s. 7 d.	Florence	M	(31) IV p.347
1429.12.01	83 s. 1 1/5 d.	Florence	M	(31) IV p.347
1429.12.01	83 s. 3 3/5 d.	Florence	M	(31) IV p.347
1430.01.02	83 s. 11 3/5 d.(sic)	Florence	M	(520)

THE FLORIN IN FLORENTINE SOLDI AND DENARI (IN GROSSI)

Date	Rate	Place	Type	Reference
1430.01.02	83 s. 3 1/5 d.	Florence	M	(520)
1430.02.04	83 s. 2 2/5 d.	Florence	M	(520)
1430.02.04	83 s. 5 1/5 d.	Florence	M	(520)
1430.03.01	82 s. 10 d.	Florence	M	(520)
1430.03.01	83 s. 4/5 d.	Florence	M	(520)
1430.04.01	82 s. 8 4/5 d.	Florence	M	(520)
1430.04.01	82 s. 11 3/5 d.	Florence	M	(520)
1430.05.02	82 s. 7 3/5 d.	Florence	M	(520)
1430.05.02	82 s. 10 1/5 d.	Florence	M	(520)
1430.06.01	82 s. 5 d.	Florence	M	(520)
1430.06.01	82 s. 8 1/5 d.	Florence	M	(520)
1430.07.01	81 s. 4 d.	Florence	M	(520)
1430.07.01	81 s. 8 1/5 d.	Florence	M	(520)
1430.08.02	81 s. 5 3/5 d.	Florence	M	(520)
1430.08.02	81 s. 9 3/5 d.	Florence	M	(520)
1430.09.01	81 s. 10 d.	Florence	M	(520)
1430.09.01	82 s. 1 d.	Florence	M	(520)
1430.10.02	81 s. 7 3/5 d.	Florence	M	(520)
1430.10.02	81 s. 10 4/5 d.	Florence	M	(520)
1430.11.03	82 s. 4 1/5 d.	Florence	M	(520)
1430.11.03	82 s. 7 2/5 d.	Florence	M	(520)
1430.12.01	82 s. 6 d.	Florence	M	(520)
1430.12.01	82 s. 10 d.	Florence	M	(520)
1431.01.02	82 s. 9 d.	Florence	M	(520)
1431.01.02	83 s. 2/5 d.	Florence	M	(520)
1431.02.01	82 s. 7 d.	Florence	M	(520)
1431.02.01	82 s. 9 4/5 d.	Florence	M	(520)
1431.03.01	82 s. 6 4/5 d.	Florence	M	(520)
1431.03.01	82 s. 10 d.	Florence	M	(520)
1431.04.05	82 s. 2 2/5 d.	Florence	M	(520)
1431.04.05	82 s. 9 2/5 d.	Florence	M	(520)
1431.08.02	82 s. 9 4/5 d.	Florence	M	(520)
1431.08.02	83 s. 4/5 d.	Florence	M	(520)
1431.09.01	83 s. 3 1/5 d.	Florence	M	(520)
1431.09.01	83 s. 6 d.	Florence	M	(520)
1431.10.01	82 s. 2 2/5 d.	Florence	M	(520)
1431.10.01	82 s. 5 3/5 d.	Florence	M	(520)
1431.11.03	82 s. 5 d.	Florence	M	(520)
1431.11.03	82 s. 8 2/5 d.	Florence	M	(520)
1431.12.01	83 s. 4 2/5 d.	Florence	M	(520)
1431.12.01	83 s. 8 d.	Florence	M	(520)
1432.01.02	83 s. 3 2/5 d.	Florence	M	(520)
1432.01.02	83 s. 7 2/5 d.	Florence	M	(520)
1432.02.01	83 s. 3 3/5 d.	Florence	M	(520)

By 1484 the grosso was valued at 6s. 8d. of piccioli

1484	111 s.	Florence	C	(360) p.40

For the lira di grossi in lire, soldi and denari affiorino see under VENICE p.87
For the cameral florin in soldi and denari affiorino see under AVIGNON p.126
For the livre tournois in soldi and denari affiorino see under FRANCE p.179
For the gros tournois in denari of Florence see under FRANCE p.187
For the white besant in soldi and denari affiorino see under CYPRUS p.299
For the dirham in soldi of Florence see under EGYPT p.302

LUCCA

The coinage of Lucca was the oldest in Tuscany, minted continuously since the Lombard period. By the late thirteenth century it had been surpassed in importance by the coinages of Pisa, Siena and Florence. When the Florentine florin was introduced the coinages of the Tuscan cities were identical in value, so that in 1252 the Florentine florin was also worth a lira in Lucca.

The Florentine florin in soldi and denari of Lucca

Date	Rate	Place	Type	Reference
in old money				
1290	20 s.	Curia	B?	(439) p.898
1291.08.13	20 s.	Viterbo	B?	(179) p.87
1291	20 s.	Curia	B?	(439) p.97
1325-1326	20 s.	Curia	B?	(439) p.901
1334	20 s.	Curia	B?	(439) p.901
in new money				
1287	38 s. 6 d.	Genoa	B	(187A) f.1068
1291	38 s. 6 d.	Genoa	B	(187A) f.1069
1291	44 s.	Curia	B	(439) p.97
1291.01.16	44 s.	Pistoia	B	(179) p.60
1292	38 s. 6 d.	Genoa	B	(187A) f.1051
1292	38 s. 6 d.	Lucca	O	(325) p.55

The lira of Lucca in soldi and denari of Verona

Date	Rate	Place	Type	Reference
1165	60 s.	Curia	O?	(385) p.102

The lira of Lucca in soldi and denari of Pavia

Date	Rate	Place	Type	Reference
1160	6 s. 8 d.	Spoleto	?	(83) p.49
1164	10 s. old money	Rome	?	(83) p.22
1164	35 s. 10 d. new money	Genoa	?	(83) p.22

The lira of Lucca in soldi and denari of Genoa

Date	Rate	Place	Type	Reference
1164	23 s. 4 d.	Genoa	?	(104)

See also the lira of Genoa in soldi and denari of Lucca under GENOA p.106

For the lira of Bologna in soldi and denari of Lucca see under BOLOGNA p.80
For the lira di grossi of Venice in soldi and denari of Lucca see under VENICE p.86
For the lira imperiale of Milan in soldi and denari of Lucca see under MILAN p.102
For the gold morabetino in soldi and denari of Lucca see under CASTILE p.156
For the livre of Provins in soldi and denari of Lucca see under CHAMPAGNE FAIRS p.165
For the gros tournois in denari of Lucca see under FRANCE p.187
For the pound sterling in soldi and denari of Lucca see under ENGLAND p.208

PISA

In 1252 the money of Pisa also shared a common value with that of Florence, so that the Florentine florin similarly began here at a value of one lira. However, Florentine and Pissan money diverged in value within a generation, and were never quite interchangeable again.

The Florentine florin in soldi and denari of Pisa

Date	Rate	Place	Type	Reference
1252	20 s.	Pisa	O	(111) p.79
1254	20 s.	Curia	?	(439) p.896
1260	24 s. 6 d.	Pisa	C	(111) p.79
1268	24 s. 6 d.	Curia	B	(439) p.896
1276.06.17	34 s. 6 d.	Pisa	C	(94) p.147

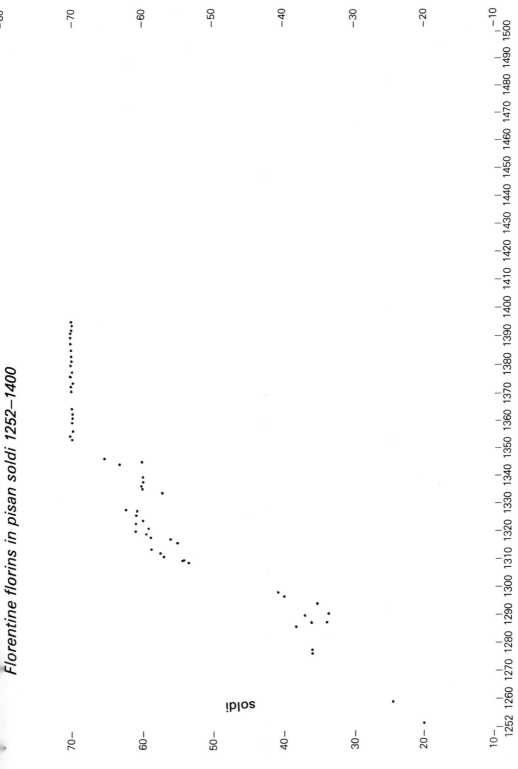

Florentine florins in pisan soldi 1252–1400

THE FLORENTINE FLORIN IN SOLDI AND DENARI OF PISA

Date	Rate	Place	Type	Reference
1277.05.27	27 s. 10 d.	Genoa	L	(381) p.348
1277-1278	36 s.	Pisa	C	(111) p.79
1278.06.19	36 s. 10 d.	Pisa	H	(248) p.196
1278.11.13	36 s. 6 d.	Pisa	C	(94) p.147
1279.01.09	36 s. 10 d.	Pisa	MC	(94) p.147
1283.04.05	34 s. 4 d.	Pisa	MC	(94) p.147
1283.05.16	34 s. 4 d.	Pisa	H	(248) p.196
1285.11.21	34 s.	Pisa	O	(94) p.417
1286	38 s. 6 d.	Curia	B	(439) p.896
1286.03.28	34 s.	Pisa	H	(248) p.196
1286.08.08	36 s. 10 d.	Pisa	MC	(94) p.147
1286.09.16	36 s. 10 d.	Pisa	MC	(94) p.147
1287	38 s. 4 d.	Pisa	C	(111) p.79
1287.01.14	36 s. 10 d.	Pisa	MC	(94) p.147
1287.09.13	38 s. 4 d.	Pisa	H	(248) p.196
1287.10.20	36 s. 10 d.	Pisa	MC	(94) p.147
1288	34 s. 6 d.	Pisa	C	(111) p.79
1288.01.03	36 s. 10 d.	Pisa	MC	(94) p.147
1288.05.03	36 s. 10 d.	Pisa	MC	(94) p.147
1289	36 s. 4 d.	Pisa	C	(111) p.79
1289.01.17	36 s. 10 d.	Pisa	H	(248) p.196
1289.01.27	36 s. 10 d.	Pisa	MC	(94) p.147
1289.02.11	36 s. 10 d.	Pisa	MC	(94) p.147
1290	36 s. 6 d.	Curia	B	(439) p.898
1290.04	36 s. 10 d.	Pisa	MC	(94) p.147
1291.02.10	37 s. 6 d.	Lucca	B	(179) p.68
1291.02.25	37 s. 6 d.	Florence	B	(179) p.67
1291	37 s. 6 d.	Pisa	C	(111) p.79
1291.04.01	36 s. 10 d.	Pisa	MC	(94) p.147
1291.04.30	36 s. 10 d.	Pisa	H	(248) p.196
1291.06.23	36 s. 10 d.	Pisa	H	(248) p.196
1291.08.11	36 s. 10 d.	Pisa	MC	(94) p.147
1291.09.07	34 s. 6 d.	Pisa	MC	(94) p.147
1291.10.02	34 s. 6 d.	Pisa	MC	(94) p.147
1291.12.07	36 s. 10 d.	Pisa	MC	(94) p.148
1292.01.02	36 s. 6 d.	Pisa	H	(248) p.196
1292.01.06	36 s. 10 d.	Pisa	MC	(94) p.148
1292.01.23	36 s. 10 d.	Pisa	H	(248) p.196
1292.02.07	34 s. 5 d.	Pisa	H	(248) p.196
1292.02.16	36 s. 10 d.	Pisa	H	(248) p.196
1292.02.23	36 s. 10 d.	Pisa	H	(248) p.196
1292.10.10	36 s. 10 d.	Pisa	MC	(94) p.148
1292-1294	37 s. 6 d.	Curia	B	(439) p.898
1292	34 s. 2 d.	Pisa	C	(111) p.79
1293.04	36 s. 10 d.	Pisa	MC	(94) p.148
1293.09.03	38 s. 4 d.	Pisa	H	(248) p.196
1293.12.15-16	38 s. 4 d.	Pisa	MC	(94) p.148
1294.07.06	38 s. 9 d.	Pisa	MC	(94) p.148
1294.07.27	38 s. 8 d.	Pisa	MC	(94) p.148
1295	34 s. 6 d.	Pisa	C	(111) p.79
1295.03.16	34 s. 6 d.	Pisa	H	(248) p.196
1295.12.03	34 s. 6 d.	Pisa	H	(248) p.196
1296	34 s. 6 d.	Curia	B	(439) p.898
1296.07.23	40 s.	Pisa	MC	(94) p.148
1296-1297	40 s. 2 d.	Pisa	H	(248) p.196
1297	42 s.	Rome	B	(439) p.109
1297	40 s.	Pisa	B	(179) p.49
1297	42 s.	Pisa	C	(111) p.79
1297.05.20	41 s.	Pisa	MC	(94) p.148
1927.06.01	40 s.	Pisa	MC	(94) p.148
1297.08.14	42 s. 8 d.	Pisa	MC	(94) p.148
1297.12.19	43 s. 3 d.	Pisa	MC	(94) p.148
1298-1299	42 s.	Curia	B	(439) p.898
1298	41 s.	Pisa	C	(111) p.79
1299.08.02	46 s. 4 d.	Pisa	MC	(94) p.148
1302.09.13	41 s.	Pisa	MC	(94) p.148
1302.12.07	50 s. 3 d.	Pisa	MC	(94) p.148
1304.09.26	53 s. 6 d.	Pisa	O	(94) p.148
1305.12.03	52 s. 6 d.	Pisa	MC	(94) p.148
1306.01.21	53 s. 10 d.	Pisa	MC	(94) p.148
1306.05.24	53 s. 11 d.	Pisa	MC	(94) p.148
1306.06.23	54 s. 6 d.	Pisa	MC	(94) p.149

THE FLORENTINE FLORIN IN SOLDI AND DENARI OF PISA

Date	Rate	Place	Type	Reference
1308.01.03	53 s. 8 d.	Pisa	MC	(94) p.149
1308.02.22	53 s. 8 d.	Pisa	MC	(94) p.149
1308.06.28	54 s.	Pisa	MC	(94) p.149
1309.07.31	53 s. 6 d.	Pisa	O	(94) p.149
1310.06.31	53 s. 6 d.	Pisa	C	(60) p.97
1310.07.20	54 s.	Pisa	O	(94) p.149
1311	54 s.	Pisa	C	(111) p.79
1312	54 s.	Curia	B	(439) p.899
1312	57 s.	Curia	B	(439) p.899
1312.05.26	57 s.	Pisa	MC	(94) p.149
1312.09.06	58 s.	Pisa	MC	(94) p.149
1313.06.23	57 s.	Pisa	C	(60) p.109
1314	58 s. 6 d.	Pisa	C	(111) p.79
1314.05.04	58 s. 6 d.	Pisa	O	(94) p.149
1314.06.10	58 s. 6 d.	Pisa	O	(94) p.149
1315	59 s.	Pisa	C	(111) p.79
1315	58 s. 6 d.	Curia	B	(439) p.900
1316	58 s.	Curia	B	(439) p.900
1316	50 s.	Pisa	C	(111) p.79
1316.11	50 s. 9 d.	Pisa	O	(94) p.149
1316.12.14	56 s.	Pisa	O	(94) p.149
1316-1318	55 s. 9 d.	Curia	B	(439) p.900
1317	55 s. 9 d.	Pisa	C	(111) p.79
1317.08.25	56 s.	Pisa	O	(94) p.149
1318	56 s.	Pisa	C	(111) p.79
1318.11.21	56 s. 10 d.	Pisa	MC	(94) p.149
1319	58 s. 9 d.	Pisa	B	(417) p.48
1319	58 s. 9 d.	Pisa	C	(111) p.79
1319.03.23	58 s. 9 d.	Pisa	O	(94) p.149
1319.12.02	58 s.	Pisa	MC	(94) p.149
1320	59 s.	Pisa	C	(111) p.79
1320.09.22	59 s.	Pisa	MC	(94) p.149
1320.10.03	58 s. 9 d.	Pisa	MC	(94) p.149
1321-1324	61 s. 8 d.	Pisa	C	(111) p.79
1321	61 s. 8 d.	Curia	B	(439) p.900
1321.02.02	59 s. 4 d.	Pisa	MC	(94) p.149
1321.03.14	59 s. 3 d.	Pisa	MC	(94) p.149
1322	59 s. 4 d.	Pisa	B	(417) p.48
1322	61 s. 8 d.	Curia	B	(439) p.900
1322.02.23	59 s.	Pisa	MC	(94) p.149
1322.03.02	59 s. 4 d.	Pisa	O	(94) p.149
1322.04.05	59 s. 4 d.	Pisa	O	(94) p.149
1322.10.13	60 s.	Pisa	O	(94) p.150
1322.12.28	60 s.	Pisa	MC	(94) p.150
1323.03.09	60 s.	Pisa	MC	(94) p.150
1323.07.02	60 s.	Pisa	MC	(94) p.150
1324.01.01	60 s.	Pisa	MC	(94) p.150
1324.01.07	61 s. 8 d.	Pisa	MC	(94) p.150
1324.07.31	60 s. 3 d.	Pisa	MC	(94) p.150
1324.09.27	61 s. 8 d.	Pisa	MC	(94) p.150
1324.11.03	60 s.	Pisa	MC	(94) p.150
1324	61 s. 8 d.	Curia	B	(439) p.901
1325	60 s.	Pisa	C	(111) p.80
1325	60 s.	Avignon	B	(439) p.109
1325.05.15	61 s.	Pisa	MC	(94) p.150
1326	60 s.	Curia	B	(439) p.901
1326.01.01	63 s. 3 d.	Pisa	MC	(94) p.150
1326.01.28	63 s. 9 d.	Pisa	MC	(94) p.150
1326.05.20	60 s. 10 d.	Pisa	MC	(94) p.150
1326.10.23	60 s. 10 d.	Pisa	MC	(94) p.150
1327-1328	61 s.	Pisa	C	(111) p.80
1327	61 s.	Pisa	B	(417) p.48
1327.01.01	61 s.	Pisa	MC	(94) p.150
1327.06.13	61 s.	Pisa	MC	(94) p.150
1327.08.06	61 s. 2 d.	Pisa	MC	(94) p.150
1327.11.02	61 s.	Pisa	O	(94) p.150
1328	61 s.	Avignon	B	(270) p.109
1328.03.01	61 s. 4 d.	Pisa	MC	(94) p.150
1328.02.04	61 s. 8 d.	Pisa	MC	(94) p.150
1328.05.16	62 s.	Pisa	MC	(94) p.150
1328.06.04	61 s.	Pisa	MC	(94) p.150
1328.06.06	62 s.	Pisa	MC	(94) p.150

THE FLORENTINE FLORIN IN SOLDI AND DENARI OF PISA

Date	Rate	Place	Type	Reference
1328.06.18	62 s. 2 d.	Pisa	MC	(94) p.150
1328.06.21	62 s.	Pisa	O	(94) p.150
1328.09.02	62 s. 2 d.	Pisa	MC	(94) p.150
1329	62 s. 2 d.	Pisa	B	(417) p.48
1329	62 s.	Avignon	B	(439) p.109
1329	62 s.	Pisa	C	(111) p.80
1329.01.28	62 s. 2 d.	Pisa	MC	(94) p.150
1329.05.08	61 s. 6 d.	Pisa	M	(94) p.151
1329.06.28	62 s. 2 d.	Pisa	M	(94) p.151
1329.07.05	62 s. 2 d.	Pisa	O	(94) p.151
1329.08.03	62 s. 2 d.	Pisa	M	(94) p.151
1329.09.23	62 s. 4 d.	Pisa	M	(94) p.151
1329.11.03	62 s. 3 d.	Pisa	M	(94) p.151
1329.12.22	62 s.	Pisa	M	(94) p.151
1330.01.18	62 s. 6 d.	Pisa	O	(94) p.151
1330.04.21	61 s. 9 d.	Pisa	M	(94) p.151
1330.04.28	61 s. 8 d.	Pisa	M	(94) p.151
1339.05.09	62 s. 6 d.	Pisa	O	(94) p.151
1330.07.04	62 s. 6 d.	Pisa	M	(94) p.151
1330.08.03	60 s.	Pisa	M	(94) p.151
1330.08.11	61 s.	Pisa	M	(94) p.151
1330.10.15	60 s.	Pisa	M	(94) p.151
1330.10.27	61 s. 8 d.	Pisa	M	(94) p.151
1330.12.04 & 20	60 s.	Pisa	M	(94) p.151
1331.01.04	60 s. 5 d.	Pisa	M	(94) p.151
1331.11.11	58 s.	Pisa	M	(94) p.151
1332.04.01	58 s.	Pisa	O	(94) p.151
1333.04.01	54 s.	Pisa	M	(94) p.151
1335	57 s. 6 d.	Pisa	B	(417) p.48
1335	57 s. 6 d.	Pisa	C	(111) p.80
1335.10.23	57 s. 6 d.	Pisa	M	(94) p.151
1335.11.29	57 s. 6 d.	Pisa	MO	(94) p.151
1336.07.23	58 s. 6 d.	Pisa	M	(94) p.151
1336-40	60 s.	Pisa	C	(111) p.80
1337.01.31	58 s.	Pisa	M	(94) p.151
1337.02.18	58 s. 6 d.	Pisa	M	(94) p.151
1337.04.05	58 s. 6 d.	Pisa	M	(94) p.151
1337.05.16 & 28	58 s. 8 d.	Pisa	M	(94) p.151
1337.06.09	59 s.	Pisa	M	(94) p.151
1337.10.31	59 s.	Pisa	MC	(94) p.152
1338.01.23	59 s.	Pisa	MC	(94) p.152
1338.01.28	59 s. 6 d.	Pisa	MC	(94) p.152
1338.03.06	59 s. 6 d.	Pisa	MC	(94) p.152
1338.04.06	59 s. 8 d.	Pisa	MC	(94) p.152
1338.05.07	60 s.	Pisa	MC	(94) p.152
1338.07.02	60 s.	Pisa	MC	(94) p.152
1338.11.26	61 s.	Pisa	MC	(94) p.152
1338.12.13	60 s.	Pisa	MC	(94) p.152
1339.01.01	60 s.	Pisa	MC	(94) p.152
1339.01.13	62 s.	Pisa	MC	(94) p.152
1339.02.25	60 s.	Pisa	MC	(94) p.152
1340	60 s.	Pisa	B	(417) p.48
1340.01.03	60 s.	Pisa	MC	(94) p.152
1340.09.01	60 s.	Pisa	O	(94) p.152
1340.09.10	61 s.	Pisa	MC	(94) p.152
1341.01.12	60 s.	Pisa	MC	(94) p.152
1342.01.01	60 s.	Pisa	MC	(94) p.152
1342.03.23	61 s.	Pisa	MC	(94) p.152
1342.11.30	61 s.	Pisa	MC	(94) p.152
1343.01.01	61 s.	Pisa	MC	(94) p.152
1343.03.20	61 s. 3 d.	Pisa	O	(94) p.152
1343.05.23	61 s.	Pisa	MC	(94) p.152
1343.08.07	61 s. 6 d.	Pisa	MC	(94) p.152
1343.09.26	62 s.	Pisa	MC	(94) p.152
1343.10.01	61 s. 6 d.	Pisa	MC	(94) p.153
1343.10.05	62 s.	Pisa	MC	(94) p.153
1343.11.05	61 s. 6 d.	Pisa	MC	(94) p.153
1343.11.25	61 s. 10 d.	Pisa	MC	(94) p.153
1343.12.06	61 s. 6 d.	Pisa	MC	(94) p.153
1343.12	62 s.	Pisa	MC	(94) p.153
1344.01.01	62 s.	Pisa	MC	(94) p.153
1344.03.15	62 s. 6 d.	Pisa	MC	(94) p.153

THE FLORENTINE FLORIN IN SOLDI AND DENARI OF PISA

Date	Rate	Place	Type	Reference
1344.03.18	62 s.	Pisa	MC	(94) p.153
1344.06.01	61 s. 6 d.	Pisa	MC	(94) p.153
1344.06.16	61 s.	Pisa	MC	(94) p.153
1344.08.19	63 s. 1 1/2 d.	Pisa	MC	(94) p.153
1344.08.25	61 s. 6 d.	Pisa	MC	(94) p.153
1344.08.28	63 s.	Pisa	MC	(94) p.153
1344.09.06	64 s.	Pisa	MC	(94) p.153
1344.09.15	61 s.	Pisa	MC	(94) p.153
1344.09.26	63 s.	Pisa	MC	(94) p.153
1344.12.17	63 s. 4 d.	Pisa	MC	(94) p.153
1344.12.18	63 s. 3 d.	Pisa	MC	(94) p.153
1344.12.21	63 s. 4 d.	Pisa	MC	(94) p.153
1344.12.22	63 s.	Pisa	MC	(94) p.153
1345	63 s. 6 d.	Pisa	B	(417) p.48
1345	63 s. 6 d.	Pisa	C	(111) p.80
1345.01	63 s.	Pisa	MC	(94) p.153
1345.01.23	63 s. 6 d.	Pisa	MC	(94) p.153
1345.01.27	63 s. 4 d.	Pisa	MC	(94) p.153
1345.02.24	63 s. 6 d.	Pisa	MC	(94) p.153
1345.03.01	63 s.	Pisa	MC	(94) p.153
1345.05.01	63 s. 6 d.	Pisa	MC	(94) p.154
1345.05.01	63 s. 6 d.	Pisa	O	(94) p.154
1345.05.20	64 s. 4 d.	Pisa	MC	(94) p.154
1345.06.06	64 s.	Pisa	MC	(94) p.154
1345.06.18	63 s. 6 d.	Pisa	MC	(94) p.154
1345.07.21	62 s.	Pisa	MC	(94) p.154
1345.08.26	64 s.	Pisa	MC	(94) p.154
1345.08.30	62 s.	Pisa	MC	(94) p.154
1345.10.24	63 s.	Pisa	MC	(94) p.154
1345.11.06-12.01	62 s.	Pisa	O	(94) p.154
1345.12.06	62 s. 6 d.	Pisa	MC	(94) p.154
1345.12.19	63 s. 6 d.	Pisa	MC	(94) p.154
1345.12.20	62 s.	Pisa	MC	(94) p.154
1346	60 s.	Pisa	C	(111) p.80
1346.01.28	64 s.	Pisa	MC	(94) p.154
1346.02.02	63 s.	Pisa	MC	(94) p.154
1346.03.23	63 s. 6 d.	Pisa	MC	(94) p.154
1346.04.10	64 s.	Pisa	MC	(94) p.154
1346.04.19	63 s. 6 d.	Pisa	MC	(94) p.154
1346.04.26	64 s.	Pisa	MC	(94) p.154
1346.05.18	63 s. 6 d.	Pisa	MC	(94) p.154
1346.06.11	64 s.	Pisa	MC	(94) p.154
1346.07.09	63 s. 6 d.	Pisa	MC	(94) p.154
1347.01.02	64 s.	Pisa	MC	(94) p.155
1347.01.29	63 s. 6 d.	Pisa	MC	(94) p.155
1347.02.26	64 s.	Pisa	MC	(94) p.155
1347.12.05	64 s.	Pisa	MC	(94) p.155
1348	64 s.	Pisa	B	(417) p.48
1348	64 s.	Pisa	C	(111) p.80
1348.01.16	64 s. 6 d.	Pisa	O	(94) p.155
1348.02.09 & 28	64 s.	Pisa	MC	(94) p.155
1348.12.05	64 s.	Pisa	MC	(94) p.155
1349.04.07	64 s.	Pisa	MC	(94) p.155
1349.11.05	64 s.	Pisa	MC	(94) p.155
1350.01.01	64 s.	Pisa	MC	(94) p.155
1350.10.29	64 s.	Pisa	MC	(94) p.155
1351.01.02	64 s.	Pisa	MC	(94) p.155
1351.12.11	68 s.	Pisa	MC	(94) p.155
1352.01.15	69 s.	Pisa	MC	(94) p.155
1352.07.15	70 s.	Pisa	MC	(94) p.155
1353.02.11	70 s.	Pisa	MC	(94) p.155
1353.06.04	71 s.	Pisa	MC	(94) p.155
1353.10.01	72 s.	Pisa	MC	(94) p.155
1353.12.21	70 s.	Pisa	MC	(94) p.155
1354	70 s.	Pisa	B	(417) p.48
1354.01.09	70 s.	Pisa	MC	(94) p.155
1354.05.20	73 s.	Pisa	MC	(94) p.155
1354.06.27	72 s.	Pisa	MC	(94) p.155
1354.07.28	71 s.	Pisa	MC	(94) p.155
1354.08.28	73 s.	Pisa	MC	(94) p.155
1354.09.23	73 s.	Pisa	MC	(94) p.155
1354.10.28	73 s.	Pisa	MC	(94) p.155

THE FLORENTINE FLORIN IN SOLDI AND DENARI OF PISA

Date	Rate	Place	Type	Reference
1354.12.23	73 s.	Pisa	MC	(94) p.155
1354-1395	70 s.	Pisa	B	(319) p.68
1354-1365	70 s.	Pisa	C	(111) p.80
1355.02.18	73 s.	Pisa	MC	(94) p.155
1355.09.12	73 s.	Pisa	M	(94) p.155
1355.12.02	72 s.	Pisa	MC	(94) p.156
1355.12.13	70 s.	Pisa	MC	(94) p.156
1356.01.01	72 s.	Pisa	MC	(94) p.156
1356.02.20	70 s.	Pisa	MC	(94) p.156
1357	70 s.	Pisa	MC	(94) p.156
1358	70 s.	Pisa	MC	(94) p.156
1359	70 s.	Pisa	MC	(94) p.156
1360	70 s.	Pisa	MC	(94) p.156
1361.11.07	70 s.	Pisa	MC	(94) p.156
1361.11.16	71 s. 8 d.	Pisa	MC	(94) p.156
1361.12.22	70 s.	Pisa	MC	(94) p.156
1362	70 s.	Pisa	MC	(94) p.156
1363	70 s.	Pisa	MC	(94) p.156
1366	70 s.	Pisa	MC	(94) p.156
1367	70 s.	Pisa	MC	(94) p.156
1367	77 s.	Pisa	C	(111) p.80
1368	70 s.	Pisa	MC	(94) p.157
1369	70 s.	Pisa	MC	(94) p.157
1370.02.24	70 s.	Pisa	O	(94) p.157
1371.12.15	70 s.	Pisa	O	(94) p.157
1371-1396	70 s.	Pisa	C	(111) p.80
1372.01.02	70 s.	Pisa	MC	(94) p.157
1372.02.28	71 s.	Pisa	MC	(94) p.157
1372.03.10	70 s.	Pisa	MC	(94) p.157
1373.01.04	70 s.	Pisa	MC	(94) p.157
1373.05.24	71 s. 6 d.	Pisa	MC	(94) p.157
1373.06.02	71 s.	Pisa	MC	(94) p.157
1373.06	70 s.	Pisa	MC	(94) p.157
1373.08.13	71 s.	Pisa	MC	(94) p.157
1373.09.13	71 s.	Pisa	MC	(94) p.157
1373.09.15	70 s.	Pisa	MC	(94) p.157
1373.10.19	71 s.	Pisa	MC	(94) p.157
1373.11.06	71 s.	Pisa	MC	(94) p.157
1374.04.26	71 s.	Pisa	MC	(94) p.157
1374.05.24	71 s. 6 d.	Pisa	MC	(94) p.157
1374.05.31	71 s. 4 d.	Pisa	MC	(94) p.157
1374.06.13	72 s.	Pisa	MC	(94) p.157
1375.07.28	76 s. 6 d.	Pisa	MC	(94) p.158
1376.02.18	70 s.	Pisa	MC	(94) p.158
1376.03.21	75 s.	Pisa	MC	(94) p.158
1376.05.26	70 s.	Pisa	MC	(94) p.158
1377-1404	70 s.	Pisa	MC	(94) p.158
1403.07.13	71 s.	Piombino	C	(243) p.202
1419.01.27	86 s.	Pisa	MC	(94) p.158
1419.02.08	85 s.	Pisa	MC	(94) p.158
1419.11.28	84 s.	Pisa	MC	(94) p.158
1424.10.02	80 s. 3 d.	Pisa	MC	(94) p.158
1424.10.05	80 s. 4 d.	Pisa	MC	(94) p.158
1424.11.16	81 s. 2 d.	Pisa	MC	(94) p.158
1424.12.09	81 s. 3 d.	Pisa	MC	(94) p.158
1425.01.24	81 s. 2 d.	Pisa	MC	(94) p.158
1429	82 s.	Pisa	MC	(94) p.158

The fiorino largo in soldi and denari of Pisa

Date	Rate	Place	Type	Reference
1424	85 s. 3 d.	Pisa	M	(94) p.160
1425	85 s. 3 d.	Pisa	M	(94) p.160
1426	85 s. 3 d.	Pisa	M	(94) p.160
1427	88 s.	Pisa	M	(94) p.160
1428	88 s.	Pisa	M	(94) p.160
1429	90 s.	Pisa	M	(94) p.160
1430.02.21	90 s.	Pisa	M	(94) p.160
1430.10.27	88 s.	Pisa	M	(94) p.160
1431	90 s.	Pisa	M	(94) p.160

THE FIORINO LARGO IN SOLDI AND DENARI OF PISA

Date	Rate	Place	Type	Reference
1432	90 s.	Pisa	M	(94) p.160
1434.01.30	92 s.	Pisa	M	(94) p.160
1434.08.11	91 s.	Pisa	M	(94) p.160
1435.03.25	91 s.	Pisa	M	(94) p.160
1435.04.08	92 s.	Pisa	M	(94) p.160
1438.01.10	92 s.	Pisa	M	(94) p.160
1438.04.19	94 s.	Pisa	M	(94) p.160
1438.05.31	90 s.	Pisa	M	(94) p.160
1438.12.01	94 s.	Pisa	M	(94) p.160
1439	94 s.	Pisa	M	(94) p.160
1441	95 s.	Pisa	M	(94) p.160
1442	95 s.	Pisa	M	(94) p.160
1443.15.07	85 s. 8 d.	Pisa	M	(94) p.160
1443.09.17	94 s.	Pisa	M	(94) p.161
1443	94 s. 8 d.	Pisa	O	(94) p.161
1444	95 s.	Pisa	M	(94) p.161
1445.05.16	96 s.	Pisa	M	(94) p.161
1445.09.13	97 s.	Pisa	M	(94) p.161
1445.12.06	96 s.	Pisa	M	(94) p.161
1446	96 s.	Pisa	M	(94) p.161
1447	95 s.	Pisa	M	(94) p.161
1450	95 s.	Pisa	M	(94) p.161
1451	95 s.	Pisa	M	(94) p.161
1453.04.28	98 s. 6 d.	Pisa	M	(94) p.161
1453.05.02	98 s.	Pisa	M	(94) p.161
1453.07.02	99 s.	Pisa	M	(94) p.161
1454.02.15	99 s.	Pisa	M	(94) p.161
1454.04.03	100 s.	Pisa	M	(94) p.161
1454.05.14	99 s.	Pisa	M	(94) p.161
1454.08.03	102 s.	Pisa	M	(94) p.161
1455.01.15	102 s.	Pisa	M	(94) p.161
1455.05.17	103 s.	Pisa	M	(94) p.161
1455.10.25	104 s.	Pisa	M	(94) p.161
1456.01.03	104 s.	Pisa	M	(94) p.162
1456.04.10	105 s.	Pisa	M	(94) p.162
1456.05.23	106 s.	Pisa	M	(94) p.162
1456.08.14	107 s.	Pisa	M	(94) p.162
1456.10.30	104 s.	Pisa	M	(94) p.162
1456.12.03	105 s.	Pisa	M	(94) p.162
1457.01.08	105 s.	Pisa	M	(94) p.162
1457.04.14	106 s.	Pisa	M	(94) p.162
1458.01.07	107 s.	Pisa	M	(94) p.162
1458.02.04	105 s.	Pisa	M	(94) p.162
1458.03.11	106 s.	Pisa	M	(94) p.162
1460	107 s.	Pisa	M	(94) p.162
1461	107 s.	Pisa	M	(94) p.162
1462.01.16	107 s.	Pisa	M	(94) p.163
1462.02.12	108 s.	Pisa	M	(94) p.163
1462.03.30	108 s.	Pisa	M	(94) p.163
1462.04.01	107 s.	Pisa	M	(94) p.163
1463.01.03	107 s.	Pisa	M	(94) p.163
1463.04.16	108 s.	Pisa	M	(94) p.163
1464.01.03	108 s.	Pisa	M	(94) p.163
1464.12.01	108 s.	Pisa	M	(94) p.163
1464.12.24	110 s.	Pisa	M	(94) p.163
1465	110 s.	Pisa	M	(94) p.163
1466.01.13	110 s.	Pisa	M	(94) p.163
1466.10.31	111 s.	Pisa	M	(94) p.163
1466.11.21	110 s.	Pisa	M	(94) p.163
1466.12.10	111 s.	Pisa	M	(94) p.163
1466.12.17	110 s.	Pisa	M	(94) p.163
1467.01.07	111 s.	Pisa	M	(94) p.163
1467.04.11	112 s.	Pisa	M	(94) p.164
1467.11.18	111 s.	Pisa	M	(94) p.164
1467.12.04	112 s.	Pisa	M	(94) p.164
1467.12.11	111 s.	Pisa	M	(94) p.164
1468.01.04	111 s.	Pisa	M	(94) p.164
1468.02.04	112 s.	Pisa	M	(94) p.164
1469	112 s.	Pisa	M	(94) p.164
1470.02.18	112 s.	Pisa	M	(94) p.164
1470.09.30	110 s.	Pisa	M	(94) p.164
1471.03.01	109 s.	Pisa	M	(94) p.164

THE FIORINO LARGO IN SOLDI AND DENARI OF PISA

Date	Rate	Place	Type	Reference
1471.03.04	110 s.	Pisa	M	(94) p.164
1471.11.30	109 s.	Pisa	M	(94) p.164
1472	110 s.	Pisa	M	(94) p.164
1473	110 s.	Pisa	M	(94) p.164
1474.01.04	110 s.	Pisa	M	(94) p.164
1474.06.22	111 s.	Pisa	M	(94) p.164
1475.01.03	112 s.	Pisa	M	(94) p.164
1475.02.08	111 s.	Pisa	M	(94) p.164
1477	113 s.	Pisa	M	(94) p.165
1478.02.16	113 s.	Pisa	M	(94) p.165
1478.04.21	114 s.	Pisa	M	(94) p.165
1479.01.16	114 s.	Pisa	M	(94) p.165
1479.04.18	115 s.	Pisa	M	(94) p.165
1480	118 s.	Pisa	M	(94) p.165
1481	119 s.	Pisa	M	(94) p.165
1482.01.31	118 s.	Pisa	M	(94) p.165
1482.07.20	119 s.	Pisa	M	(94) p.165
1483	119 s.	Pisa	M	(94) p.165
1486	123 s.	Pisa	M	(94) p.165
1487	124 s.	Pisa	M	(94) p.165
1488	125 s.	Pisa	M	(94) p.165
1489	125 s.	Pisa	M	(94) p.165
1492	130 s.	Pisa	M	(94) p.165
1496.04.20	132 s.	Pisa	M	(94) p.165
1496.11.09	133 s.	Pisa	M	(94) p.165

For the uncia of Sicily in soldi and denari of Pisa see under SICILY pp.59 and 66
For the uncia of Naples in soldi and denari of Pisa see under NAPLES p.64
For the lira of Bologna in soldi and denari of Pisa see under BOLOGNA p.80
For the lira imperiale in soldi and denari of Pisa see under MILAN p.102
For the lira of Genoa in soldi and denari of Pisa see under GENOA p.106
For the livre of royaux coronats in soldi and denari of Pisa see under PROVENCE p.119
For the livre of mixed money of Marseille in soldi and denari of Pisa see under MARSEILLE p.120
For the gold morabetino in soldi and denari of Pisa see under CASTILE p.156
For the livre of Provins in soldi and denari of Pisa see under CHAMPAGNE FAIRS p.165
For the livre tournois in soldi and denari of Pisa see under FRANCE p.182
For the gros tournois in denari of Pisa see under FRANCE p.187

Aquilini

The aquilino was the late-thirteenth-century grosso of Pisa, and was so called from the imperial eagle on the reverse. Pisan grossi, struck from the 1230s onwards, initially had a value of 12 denari (a soldo of piccioli). For a short time the soldo of Pisa was the grosso. As the denaro picciolo and the grosso evolved differently, the grosso came to be worth a great deal more than a soldo of piccioli. However, for accounting purposes it sometimes continued to be used as a soldo, like successive grossi in Florence (the silver fiorino, and the guelfo). In other words the valuation of the florin at 15 soldi and 6 denari aquilini meant that the florin was actually exchangeable for fifteen and a half silver aquilini. The lira aquilini was thus a unit of 20 grossi aquilini.

The grosso aquilino in denari of Pisa

Date	Rate	Place	Type	Reference
1263.09.03	24 d.	Pisa	H	(248) p.197
1272.08.31	26 d.	Pisa	H	(295) p.197
1279.04.22	33 d.	Pisa	H	(248) p.197
1283.02.01	29 d.	Pisa	H	(248) p.197
1283.08.01	31 d.	Pisa	H	(248) p.197
1290.04.15	31 d.	Pisa	H	(248) p.197
1290.10.26	29 d.	Pisa	H	(248) p.197
1292.10.17	31 d.	Pisa	H	(248) p.197
1294.05.13	33 d.	Pisa	H	(248) p.197
1296-1297	33 d.	Pisa	H	(248) p.197

The new grosso aquilino in denari of Pisa

Date	Rate	Place	Type	Reference
1297.07.29	24 d.	Pisa	H	(248) p.197
1298.01.31	24 d.	Pisa	H	(248) p.197
1298.07.25	24 d.	Pisa	H	(248) p.197
1301	24 d.	Pisa	H	(248) p.197
1302	24 d.	Pisa	H	(248) p.197
1305	24 d.	Pisa	H	(248) p.197

The lira aquilina (i.e. 20 aquilini) in soldi and denari of Pisa

Date	Rate	Place	Type	Reference
1299.02	55 s.	Cagliari	A	(70) p.279
1299.03	53 s. 4 d.	Cagliari	A	(70) p.279
1300.06	52 s. 6 d.	Cagliari	A	(70) p.279
1300.12	32 s. (?)	Cagliari	A	(70) p.279
1301.06?	51 s. 4 d.	Cagliari	A	(70) p.279
1301.10	55 s.	Cagliari	A	(70) p.279
1303.01?	54 s. 2 d.	Cagliari	A	(70) p.279
1303.12	52 s. 6 d.	Cagliari	A	(70) p.279
1304.01	53 s. 4 d.	Cagliari	A	(70) p.279
1304.03	63 s. 4d. (?)	Cagliari	A	(70) p.279
1304?	53 s. 4 d.	Cagliari	A	(70) p.279
1305	53 s. 4 d.	Cagliari	A	(70) p.279
1305	53 s. 6 d.	Cagliari	A	(70) p.279
1307	54 s. 2 d.	Cagliari	A	(70) p.279
1307	53 s. 4 d.	Cagliari	A	(70) p.279
1318.06	52 s. 11 d.	Sassari	A	(70) p.280

The Florentine florin in soldi and denari aquilini

Date	Rate	Place	Type	Reference
1278	15 s. 6 d.	Curia	C	(439) p.897
1284-1286	15 s.	Curia	C	(439) p.897
1288	15 s.	Curia	C	(439) p.898
1290	15 s.	Curia	C	(439) p.898
1298.09.09	15 s. 6 d.	Pisa	C	(60) p.48
1316.12.15	22 s. 6 d.	Pisa	C	(319) I p.141

VOLTERRA

The Florentine florin in soldi and denari of Volterra

Date	Rate	Place	Type	Reference
1266.11.15	29 s.	Naples	O	(180) p.32

For the lira of Siena in soldi and denari of Volterra see under SIENA p.57

SIENA

In 1252 the money of Siena also shared a common value with that of Florence, so that the Florentine florin similarly began here at a value of one lire. However, Florentine and Sienese money diverged in value within a generation and were never quite interchangeable again.

The Florentine florin in soldi and denari of Siena

Date	Rate	Place	Type	Reference
1270	32 s. 6 d.	Siena	C	(118) IV p.321
1277.02.07	38 s. 6 d.	Siena	C	(10) p.9
1277-1282	35 s. 6 d.	Siena	C	(10) p.248
1278.01	38 s. 2 d.	Siena	C	(10) p.76
1278.03.01	37 s. 9 d.	Siena	C	(10) p.84
1278.03.23	38 s. 6 d.	Siena	C	(10) p.31
1278.04.25	38 s. 7 d.	Pisa	C	(10) p.23
1278	38 s. 6 d.	Siena	C	(10) p.32
1279.01.02	34 s. 7 d.	Siena	C	(10) p.145
1279.01.29	34 s. 10 d.	Siena	C	(10) p.148
1279.01.29-02.05	35 s. 3 d.	Siena	C	(10) p.150
1279.02.05-29	34 s. 10 d.	Siena	C	(10) p.151
1279.09	33 s. 11 d.	Siena	C	(10) p.127
1279.10	34 s. 6 d.	Siena	C	(10) p.136
1279.12.11	35 s. 1 d.	Siena	C	(10) p.142
1279.12	35 s.	Siena	C	(10) p.141
1279.12	35 s. 1 d.	Siena	C	(10) p.142
1280.04.15	35 s.	Siena	C	(10) p.159
1280.10.21-28	35 s. 2 d.	Siena	C	(10) p.193
1280.11.25-12.02	35 s. 5 d.	Siena	C	(10) p.200
1280.12.05	35 s. 6 d.	Siena	C	(10) p.203
1280.12.09-16	35 s. 7 d.	Siena	C	(10) p.203
1280.12.30-1281.01.06	35 s. 6 d.	Siena	C	(10) p.208
1281.02.03-12	35 s. 7 d.	Siena	C	(10) p.215
1281.08.11-18	35 s. 3 d.	Siena	C	(10) p.243
1281.12.22	35 s. 8 d.	Siena	C	(10) p.248
1282.01	35 s. 9 d.	Siena	C	(10) p.249
1292	42 s.	Curia	B	(439) p.898
1296	42 s.	Curia	B	(439) p.898
1296	20 s. old money	Curia	B	(439) p.898
1302.01.20	50 s.	Siena	C	(111) p.156
1302.02.27	49 s. 10 d.	Siena	C	(111) p.156
1302.03.31	50 s.	Siena	C	(111) p.156
1302.04.30	50 s. 2 d.	Siena	C	(111) p.156
1302.05.26	50 s. 3 d.	Siena	C	(111) p.156
1302.06.25	50 s. 4 d.	Siena	C	(111) p.156
1302.07.30	49 s. 8 d.	Siena	C	(111) p.157
1302.08.27-11.26	49 s. 10 d.	Siena	C	(111) p.157
1302.12.28	50 s. 3 d.	Siena	C	(111) p.157
1306.01.21	52 s. 10 d.	Siena	C	(111) p.157
1306.02.28	53 s. 8 d.	Siena	C	(111) p.157
1306.03.10	53 s. 4 d.	Siena	C	(111) p.157
1306.04.19	53 s. 6 d.	Siena	C	(111) p.157
1306.05.27	53 s. 4 d.	Siena	C	(111) p.157
1306.06.30	53 s. 8 d.	Siena	C	(111) p.157
1307.01.31	53 s. 6 d.	Siena	C	(111) p.157
1307.02.27	53 s. 5 d.	Siena	C	(111) p.157
1307.03.09-04.19	53 s. 6 d.	Siena	C	(111) p.157
1307.05.25	53 s. 7 d.	Siena	C	(111) p.157
1307.06.30	53 s. 4 d.	Siena	C	(111) p.157
1307.07.31	53 s. 6 d.	Siena	C	(111) p.157
1307.08.26	53 s. 7 d.	Siena	C	(111) p.158
1307.09.30-11.24	53 s. 8 d.	Siena	C	(111) p.158
1307.12.30-1309	53 s. 10 d.	Siena	C	(111) p.158
1310.01-08	53 s. 6 d.	Siena	C	(111) p.160
1310.09.05	53 s. 8 d.	Siena	C	(111) p.160
1310.11.28	53 s. 10 d.	Siena	C	(111) p.160
1310.12.31	54 s. 2 d.	Siena	C	(111) p.160
1311.01-04	54 s. 3 d.	Siena	C	(111) p.160
1311.05-06	53 s. 4 d.	Siena	C	(111) p.161
1313.02	53 s. 4 d.	Siena	C	(111) p.161
1314.07-08	58 s. 2 d.	Siena	C	(111) p.161
1314.09-10	58 s.	Siena	C	(111) p.161
1314.11.27	58 s. 8 d.	Siena	C	(111) p.161
1314.12.31	58 s. 10 d.	Siena	C	(111) p.161
1315.02.27	58 s. 1 d.	Siena	C	(111) p.161
1315.03.29	57 s. 10 d.	Siena	C	(111) p.161
1315.04.28	58 s. 4 d.	Siena	C	(111) p.161
1315.05.23	58 s.	Siena	C	(111) p.161
1315.06.30	57 s.	Siena	C	(111) p.161

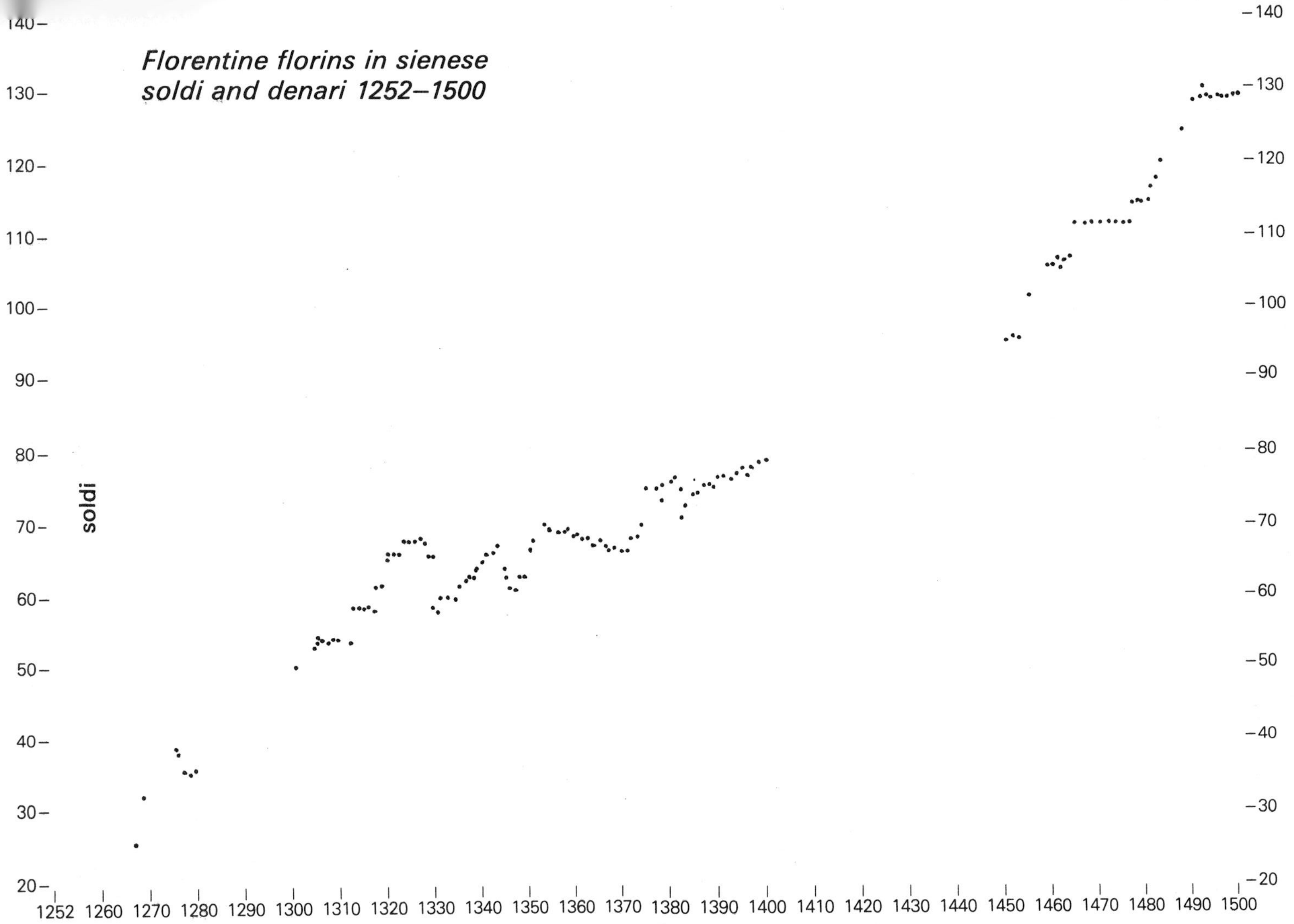

Florentine florins in sienese soldi and denari 1252–1500

soldi

140 130 120 110 100 90 80 70 60 50 40 30 20

1252 1260 1270 1280 1290 1300 1310 1320 1330 1340 1350 1360 1370 1380 1390 1400 1410 1420 1430 1440 1450 1460 1470 1480 1490 1500

THE FLORENTINE FLORIN IN SOLDI AND DENARI OF SIENA

Date	Rate	Place	Type	Reference
1315.07-1316.09	58 s.	Siena	C	(111) p.162
1316.09.30	57 s. 9 d.	Siena	C	(111) p.162
1316.10-1319.01	58 s.	Siena	C	(111) p.163
1319.02	58 s. 10 d.	Siena	O	(64) p.226
1319.02.27-03.26	61 s.	Siena	C	(111) p.163
1319.04.19	62 s.	Siena	C	(111) p.163
1319.05.14	62 s. 6 d.	Siena	C	(111) p.164
1319.06.05	62 s. 8 d.	Siena	C	(111) p.164
1319.07.31	62 s.	Siena	C	(111) p.164
1319.08-1321.01	63 s. 6 d.	Siena	C	(111) p.164
1321.02.28	63 s. 8 d.	Siena	C	(111) p.164
1321.03.30	64 s.	Siena	C	(111) p.164
1321.04.28	64 s. 2 d.	Siena	C	(111) p.164
1321.05.18	63 s. 4 d.	Siena	C	(111) p.164
1321.06.30	66 s.	Siena	C	(111) p.164
1321.07.20-08.20	64 s.	Siena	C	(111) p.164
1321.10-11	65 s.	Siena	C	(111) p.165
1321.12.31	66 s.	Siena	C	(111) p.165
1322.01-03	66 s. 8 d.	Siena	C	(111) p.165
1322.04.30	65 s. 4 d.	Siena	C	(111) p.165
1322.05.28	66 s. 8 d.	Siena	C	(111) p.165
1322.06.30	66 s.	Siena	C	(111) p.165
1322.07.26	66 s. 2 d.	Siena	C	(111) p.165
1322.08.20	66 s.	Siena	C	(111) p.165
1322.10.26	66 s. 5 d.	Siena	C	(111) p.165
1322.12.31	66 s. 6 d.	Siena	C	(111) p.165
1323.01-02	66 s.	Siena	C	(111) p.165
1323.03-12	67 s.	Siena	C	(111) p.165
1324.01.14	66 s. 8 d.	Siena	C	(111) p.165
1324.02.09	65 s. 7 d.	Siena	C	(111) p.165
1324.03-05	66 s. 8 d.	Siena	C	(111) p.165
1324.06.30	66 s.	Siena	C	(111) p.165
1325.01-02	68 s.	Siena	C	(111) p.166
1325.03.23	68 s. 6 d.	Siena	C	(111) p.166
1325.04-05	67 s.	Siena	C	(111) p.166
1325.06.30	66 s.	Siena	C	(111) p.166
1326.07-09	66 s. 8 d.	Siena	C	(111) p.166
1326.10.27	66 s. 9 d.	Siena	C	(111) p.166
1326.11-12	67 s. 4 d.	Siena	C	(111) p.166
1327.01-04	67 s. 8 d.	Siena	C	(111) p.166
1327.05.29	66 s. 10 d.	Siena	C	(111) p.166
1327.06.18	66 s. 8 d.	Siena	C	(111) p.166
1327.07.27	65 s. 4 d.	Siena	C	(111) p.166
1327.08.31	67 s.	Siena	C	(111) p.166
1327.09.05	65 s. 3 d.	Siena	C	(111) p.166
1327.10-12	67 s.	Siena	C	(111) p.166
1328.01-03	67 s. 4 d.	Siena	C	(111) p.166
1328.04.30	67 s. 6 d.	Siena	C	(111) p.167
1328.06-12	67 s.	Siena	C	(111) p.167
1329.01.31	67 s. 1 d.	Siena	C	(111) p.168
1329.02.28	66 s. 10 d.	Siena	C	(111) p.169
1329.03-04	67 s.	Siena	C	(111) p.169
1329.05.31	65 s. 8 d.	Siena	C	(111) p.169
1329.06.30	65 s. 6 d.	Siena	C	(111) p.169
1329.07.31	66 s. 7 d.	Siena	C	(111) p.169
1329.08.31	66 s. 4 d.	Siena	C	(111) p.170
1329.09-10	66 s. 6 d.	Siena	C	(111) p.170
1329.11.29	67 s.	Siena	C	(111) p.170
1329.12.30	66 s. 9 d.	Siena	C	(111) p.170
1330.01-02	67 s.	Siena	C	(111) p.171
1330.03.31	66 s. 8 d.	Siena	C	(111) p.171
1330.04-05	66 s. 10 d.	Siena	C	(111) p.172
1330.07-08	66 s. 4 d.	Siena	C	(111) p.172
1330.09-10	66 s. 6 d.	Siena	C	(111) p.172
1330.11.29	66 s. 8 d.	Siena	C	(111) p.173
1330.12.29	66 s.	Siena	C	(111) p.173
1331.01-02	66 s. 8 d.	Siena	C	(111) p.173
1331.03.31	66 s.	Siena	C	(111) p.174
1331.04.30	65 s. 6 d.	Siena	C	(111) p.174
1331.05.31	63 s.	Siena	C	(111) p.174
1331.06.28	64 s.	Siena	C	(111) p.175
1331.07.31	63 s.	Siena	C	(111) p.175

THE FLORENTINE FLORIN IN SOLDI AND DENARI OF SIENA

Date	Rate	Place	Type	Reference
1331.08.31	64 s.	Siena	C	(111) p.175
1331.09.27	65 s.	Siena	C	(111) p.175
1331.10-11	62 s. 10 d.	Siena	C	(111) p.176
1331.12.31	62 s. 6 d.	Siena	C	(111) p.176
1332.01.31	63 s. 4 d.	Siena	C	(111) p.176
1332.02-03	61 s. 6 d.	Siena	C	(111) p.177
1332.04.30	61 s. 4 d.	Siena	C	(111) p.177
1332.05.30	59 s. 6 d.	Siena	C	(111) p.177
1332.06.30	59 s.	Siena	C	(111) p.177
1332.07.31	59 s. 7 d.	Siena	C	(111) p.178
1332.07-09	58 s.	Siena	C	(111) p.178
1332.10.31	60 s.	Siena	C	(111) p.178
1332.11.28	60 s. 8 d.	Siena	C	(111) p.179
1332.12.30	56 s.	Siena	C	(111) p.179
1333.01.30	59 s.	Siena	C	(111) p.179
1333.03	60 s.	Siena	C	(111) p.180
1333.04.30	60 s. 6 d.	Siena	C	(111) p.180
1333.05-06	60 s.	Siena	C	(111) p.181
1333.08.27	60 s. 6 d.	Siena	C	(111) p.181
1333.09.30	60 s.	Siena	C	(111) p.181
1333.10-11	61 s.	Siena	C	(111) p.182
1333.12.31	60 s.	Siena	C	(111) p.182
1334.01.31	60 s. 6 d.	Siena	C	(111) p.182
1334.02.28	60 s. 4 d.	Siena	C	(111) p.182
1334.03.30	59 s. 8 d.	Siena	C	(111) p.183
1334.04-07	59 s. 10 d.	Siena	C	(111) p.183
1334.09.30	59 s. 8 d.	Siena	C	(111) p.183
1334.10.31	60 s. 3 d.	Siena	C	(111) p.184
1334.11.29	60 s. 5 d.	Siena	C	(111) p.184
1334.12.31	60 s. 8 d.	Siena	C	(111) p.184
1335.01.31	61 s.	Siena	C	(111) p.184
1335.02.28	60 s. 11 d.	Siena	C	(111) p.185
1335.03-06	60 s. 10 d.	Siena	C	(111) p.185
1335.05.31	60 s. 4 d.	Siena	C	(111) p.185
1335.06.30	60 s. 2 d.	Siena	C	(111) p.186
1335.08.29	60 s. 3 d.	Siena	C	(111) p.186
1335.09.18	60 s. 1 d.	Siena	C	(111) p.186
1335.10.03	60 s. 8 d.	Siena	C	(111) p.186
1335.11.29	60 s.	Siena	C	(111) p.186
1335.12.30	61 s.	Siena	C	(111) p.186
1336.01.31	61 s. 8 d.	Siena	C	(111) p.186
1336.02.29	61 s. 9 d.	Siena	C	(111) p.186
1336.03.30	62 s.	Siena	C	(111) p.187
1336.04.30	62 s. 2 d.	Siena	C	(111) p.187
1336.05.31	61 s. 4 d.	Siena	C	(111) p.187
1336.06.28	61 s. 7 d.	Siena	C	(111) p.187
1336.07.27	62 s. 3 d.	Siena	C	(111) p.188
1336.08-09	62 s.	Siena	C	(111) p.188
1336.10.31	62 s. 4 d.	Siena	C	(111) p.188
1336.11.30	62 s. 10 d.	Siena	C	(111) p.188
1336.12.30	63 s.	Siena	C	(111) p.189
1337-1339	59 s.	Siena	O	(64) p.226
1337.07.31	62 s. 10 d.	Siena	C	(111) p.189
1337.08.31	63 s. 3 d.	Siena	C	(111) p.189
1337.09.30	62 s. 4 d.	Siena	C	(111) p.190
1337.10.30	63 s. 6 d.	Siena	C	(111) p.190
1337.11.29	63 s. 8 d.	Siena	C	(111) p.190
1337.12.31	63 s. 3 d.	Siena	C	(111) p.190
1338.01-02	63 s. 6 d.	Siena	C	(111) p.191
1338.03.31	63 s. 2 d.	Siena	C	(111) p.191
1338.04.30	63 s. 8 d.	Siena	C	(111) p.191
1338.05.30	63 s. 1 d.	Siena	C	(111) p.192
1338.06.30	63 s.	Siena	C	(111) p.192
1338.07.31	62 s.	Siena	C	(111) p.192
1338.08.31	62 s. 11 d.	Siena	C	(111) p.192
1338.09.30	63 s.	Siena	C	(111) p.193
1338.10.31	62 s. 11 d.	Siena	C	(111) p.193
1338.11.29	63 s. 3 d.	Siena	C	(111) p.193
1338.12.31	63 s. 6 d.	Siena	C	(111) p.194
1339.01.30	63 s. 9 d.	Siena	C	(111) p.194
1339.02.27	63 s. 6 d.	Siena	C	(111) p.194
1339.03-04	63 s. 2 d.	Siena	C	(111) p.194

THE FLORENTINE FLORIN IN SOLDI AND DENARI OF SIENA

Date	Rate	Place	Type	Reference
1339.06-07	63 s. 1 d.	Siena	C	(111) p.195
1339.07.28	63 s.	Siena	C	(111) p.195
1339.08.31	63 s. 1 d.	Siena	C	(111) p.195
1339.09.30	62 s. 6 d.	Siena	C	(111) p.196
1339.10.30	63 s. 2 d.	Siena	C	(111) p.196
1339.11-12	63 s. 6 d.	Siena	C	(111) p.196
1340.01.31	64 s.	Siena	C	(111) p.197
1340.02-03	63 s. 8 d.	Siena	C	(111) p.197
1340.04-05	63 s. 10 d.	Siena	C	(111) p.197
1340.06.30	63 s. 9 d.	Siena	C	(111) p.197
1341.07.31	65 s.	Siena	C	(111) p.198
1341.08.31	64 s. 10 d.	Siena	C	(111) p.198
1341.09.28	65 s.	Siena	C	(111) p.198
1341.10.31	65 s. 6 d.	Siena	C	(111) p.198
1341.11.29	66 s.	Siena	C	(111) p.199
1341.12.31	66 s. 6 d.	Siena	C	(111) p.199
1342.01.31	65 s. 10 d.	Siena	C	(111) p.199
1342.02-03	66 s.	Siena	C	(111) p.200
1342.04.30	66 s. 6 d.	Siena	C	(111) p.200
1342.05.31	65 s. 10 d.	Siena	C	(111) p.200
1342.06.30	66 s.	Siena	C	(111) p.201
1343.01.31	66 s. 5 d.	Siena	C	(111) p.201
1343.02.28	66 s. 6 d.	Siena	C	(111) p.201
1343.03-04	66 s. 7 d.	Siena	C	(111) p.202
1343.05.31	65 s. 9 d.	Siena	C	(111) p.202
1343.06.30	66 s. 2 d.	Siena	C	(111) p.202
1343.07.26	66 s. 4 d.	Siena	C	(111) p.202
1343.08.29	66 s.	Siena	C	(111) p.202
1343.09.30	65 s.	Siena	C	(111) p.202
1343.10.31	66 s.	Siena	C	(111) p.203
1343.11.27	66 s. 2 d.	Siena	C	(111) p.203
1343.12.31	66 s. 4 d.	Siena	C	(111) p.203
1344.01-02	66 s. 9 d.	Siena	C	(111) p.203
1344.03-04	66 s. 2 d.	Siena	C	(111) p.204
1344.05.31	65 s.	Siena	C	(111) p.204
1344.06.30	65 s. 10 d.	Siena	C	(111) p.204
1344.07.30	66 s.	Siena	C	(111) p.205
1344.08.31	65 s. 9 d.	Siena	C	(111) p.205
1344.09.30	65 s. 6 d.	Siena	C	(111) p.205
1344.10.30	65 s. 9 d.	Siena	C	(111) p.206
1344.11.30	66 s. 3 d.	Siena	C	(111) p.206
1344.12.31	66 s.	Siena	C	(111) p.206
1345.01.31	66 s. 2 d.	Siena	C	(111) p.206
1345.02.28	65 s. 11 d.	Siena	C	(111) p.207
1345.03.31	65 s. 7 d.	Siena	C	(111) p.207
1345.04.30	65 s. 9 d.	Siena	C	(111) p.207
1345.05.31	65 s. 2 d.	Siena	C	(111) p.207
1345.06.30	63 s. 7 d.	Siena	C	(111) p.208
1345.07.30	62 s. 5 d.	Siena	C	(111) p.208
1345.08.31	63 s. 2 d.	Siena	C	(111) p.208
1345.09.30	62 s. 7 d.	Siena	C	(111) p.208
1345.10.31	63 s. 2 d.	Siena	C	(111) p.209
1345.11.30	64 s.	Siena	C	(111) p.209
1345.12.31	63 s. 10 d.	Siena	C	(111) p.209
1346.01.31	64 s.	Siena	C	(111) p.210
1346.02-03	62 s. 10 d.	Siena	C	(111) p.210
1346.04.29	63 s. 6 d.	Siena	C	(111) p.210
1346.05.31	62 s. 10 d.	Siena	C	(111) p.211
1346.06.30	62 s.	Siena	C	(111) p.211
1347.07.31	62 s. 2 d.	Siena	C	(111) p.211
1347.08.31	63 s.	Siena	C	(111) p.211
1347.09.30	62 s. 5 d.	Siena	C	(111) p.211
1347.10-1348.03	63 s.	Siena	C	(111) p.213
1348.04.30	62 s. 8 d.	Siena	C	(111) p.213
1348.05.31	62 s. 9 d.	Siena	C	(111) p.124
1348.06.30	61 s.	Siena	C	(111) p.214
1349.01-1350.06	63 s.	Siena	C	(111) p.219
1351.07.30	66 s. 3 d.	Siena	C	(111) p.219
1351.07-09	66 s. 6 d.	Siena	C	(111) p.220
1351.09.29	67 s.	Siena	C	(111) p.220
1351.10.31	66 s.	Siena	C	(111) p.220
1351.12.31	67 s. 3 d.	Siena	C	(111) p.221

THE FLORENTINE FLORIN IN SOLDI AND DENARI OF SIENA

Date	Rate	Place	Type	Reference
1352.01.31	67 s. 6 d.	Siena	C	(111) p.221
1352.02.28	68 s. 1 d.	Siena	C	(111) p.221
1352.03.31	68 s. 2 d.	Siena	C	(111) p.221
1352.04.30	68 s.	Siena	C	(111) p.221
1352.05.31	68 s. 6 d.	Siena	C	(111) p.222
1352.06.30	68 s. 8 d.	Siena	C	(111) p.222
1352.07.03	68 s. 7 d.	Siena	C	(111) p.222
1352.09-10	69 s. 2 d.	Siena	C	(111) p.222
1352.11.29	69 s. 6 d.	Siena	C	(111) p.222
1352.12.31	69 s. 5 d.	Siena	C	(111) p.223
1354.01.31	70 s. 11 d.	Siena	C	(111) p.223
1354.02.28	71 s.	Siena	C	(111) p.223
1354.03-04	70 s. 10 d.	Siena	C	(111) p.224
1354.05.31	70 s. 9 d.	Siena	C	(111) p.224
1354.06.30	70 s. 8 d.	Siena	C	(111) p.224
1354.07-08	70 s. 10 d.	Siena	C	(111) p.224
1354.09.30	70 s.	Siena	C	(111) p.225
1354.10.30	70 s. 5 d.	Siena	C	(111) p.225
1354.11.29	70 s. 10 d.	Siena	C	(111) p.225
1354.12.16	70 s. 8 d.	Siena	C	(111) p.225
1355.07.29	71 s.	Siena	C	(111) p.225
1355.08.27	70 s. 7 d.	Siena	C	(111) p.226
1355.09.30	70 s. 6 d.	Siena	C	(111) p.226
1355.10-11	70 s. 8 d.	Siena	C	(111) p.226
1355.12.31	69 s. 10 d.	Siena	C	(111) p.226
1357.01-07	69 s.	Siena	C	(111) p.228
1357.08.31	68 s. 10 d.	Siena	C	(111) p.228
1357.09-10	69 s.	Siena	C	(111) p.228
1357.10.31	69 s. 1 d.	Siena	C	(111) p.229
1357.11-12	69 s.	Siena	C	(111) p.229
1358.01.31	69 s. 3 d.	Siena	C	(111) p.229
1358.02.28	69 s. 4 d.	Siena	C	(111) p.230
1358.03.28	69 s. 4 d.	Siena	C	(111) p.230
1358.04-05	69 s. 6 d.	Siena	C	(111) p.230
1359.01-02	69 s.	Siena	C	(111) p.230
1359.03.27	69 s. 1 d.	Siena	C	(111) p.230
1359.04.30	68 s. 10 d.	Siena	C	(111) p.230
1359.05.28	69 s.	Siena	C	(111) p.230
1359.06.29	68 s. 4 d.	Siena	C	(111) p.230
1360.02.29	69 s.	Siena	C	(111) p.230
1360.03.31	68 s. 9 d.	Siena	C	(111) p.231
1360.04-05	68 s. 4 d.	Siena	C	(111) p.231
1360.06.30	68 s.	Siena	C	(111) p.231
1361.07.31	68 s. 5 d.	Siena	C	(111) p.232
1361.08.31	68 s. 4 d.	Siena	C	(111) p.232
1361.09.30	68 s.	Siena	C	(111) p.232
1361.10.31	68 s. 4 d.	Siena	C	(111) p.232
1361.11-12	68 s. 6 d.	Siena	C	(111) p.233
1362.01	67 s.	Siena	C	(111) p.233
1362.03	68 s.	Siena	C	(111) p.233
1362.05-06	67 s.	Siena	C	(111) p.233
1362.07.30	67 s. 5 d.	Siena	C	(111) p.233
1362.08.31	67 s.	Siena	C	(111) p.233
1362.09.30	67 s. 1 d.	Siena	C	(111) p.233
1362.10.31	66 s. 11 d.	Siena	C	(111) p.234
1362.11-12	67 s. 6 d.	Siena	C	(111) p.234
1363.01-02	67 s. 9 d.	Siena	C	(111) p.234
1363.03.31	67 s. 10 d.	Siena	C	(111) p.235
1363.04.29	67 s. 8 d.	Siena	C	(111) p.235
1363.05.31	67 s. 6 d.	Siena	C	(111) p.235
1363.06.30	66 s. 2 d.	Siena	C	(111) p.236
1364.12.01	67 s.	Siena	C	(111) p.236
1365-1366.02	68 s.	Siena	C	(111) p.236
1366.03-1369.01	67 s.	Siena	C	(111) p.236
1369.06-1370.01	68 s.	Siena	C	(111) p.236
1370.04-05	66 s. 6 d.	Siena	C	(111) p.236
1370.07	67 s.	Siena	C	(111) p.236
1370.09-10	66 s. 6 d.	Siena	C	(111) p.236
1371	67 s.	Siena	C	(111) p.236
1371.04	66 s. 8 d.	Siena	C	(111) p.236
1371.06-10	66 s.	Siena	C	(111) p.236
1371.12	68 s.	Siena	C	(111) p.236

THE FLORENTINE FLORIN IN SOLDI AND DENARI OF SIENA

Date	Rate	Place	Type	Reference
1372.01	66 s. 6 d.	Siena	C	(111) p.236
1372.05	68 s.	Siena	C	(111) p.236
1372.07	73 s.	Siena	C	(111) p.236
1372.08	70 s.	Siena	C	(111) p.236
1373.01-03	69 s. 6 d.	Siena	C	(111) p.236
1373.05	67 s. 6 d.	Siena	C	(111) p.236
1373.06-12	69 s. 6 d.	Siena	C	(111) p.236
1374.01-06	70 s.	Siena	C	(111) p.236
1374.07-12	73 s.	Siena	C	(111) p.236
1375.05	72 s.	Siena	C	(111) p.236
1375.07	74 s.	Siena	C	(111) p.236
1375.08-12	76 s.	Siena	C	(111) p.236
1377.01-03	76 s.	Siena	C	(111) p.237
1377.04-06	75 s.	Siena	C	(111) p.237
1377.07	74 s.	Siena	C	(111) p.237
1377.08-12	73 s.	Siena	C	(111) p.237
1378	73 s.	Siena	C	(111) p.237
1379	75 s.	Siena	C	(111) p.237
1380	75 s.	Siena	C	(111) p.237
1381.01	77 s.	Siena	C	(111) p.237
1381.02-12	74 s.	Siena	C	(111) p.237
1382.01	70 s.	Siena	C	(111) p.237
1382.02-12	72 s.	Siena	C	(111) p.237
1383.02	75 s.	Siena	C	(111) p.237
1383.08-12	74 s.	Siena	C	(111) p.237
1384.01-06	72 s.	Siena	C	(111) p.238
1384.07-12	74 s.	Siena	C	(111) p.238
1385	74 s.	Siena	C	(111) p.238
1386.01-03	75 s.	Siena	C	(111) p.238
1386.04-07	74 s. 8 d.	Siena	C	(111) p.238
1386.08	75 s.	Siena	C	(111) p.238
1386.09-10	74 s. 8 d.	Siena	C	(111) p.238
1386.11	75 s.	Siena	C	(111) p.238
1386.12	74 s. 8 d.	Siena	C	(111) p.238
1387-1388	75 s.	Siena	C	(111) p.238
1389.01-03	75 s. 2 d.	Siena	C	(111) p.238
1389.04-12	75 s.	Siena	C	(111) p.238
1390.01-10	76 s.	Siena	C	(111) p.238
1390.11-12	76 s. 1 d.	Siena	C	(111) p.238
1391.01	76 s. 6 d.	Siena	C	(111) p.238
1391.02	76 s. 5 d.	Siena	C	(111) p.238
1391.03	76 s. 9 d.	Siena	C	(111) p.238
1381.04	76 s.	Siena	C	(111) p.238
1391.05	76 s. 6 d.	Siena	C	(111) p.238
1391.06	76 s.	Siena	C	(111) p.238
1391.06	77 s.	Siena	C	(111) p.238
1391.07	77 s.	Siena	C	(111) p.238
1391.08-12	74 s. 8 d.	Siena	C	(111) p.238
1392-1392.07	74 s. 8 d.	Siena	C	(111) p.238
1393.07-12	77 s.	Siena	C	(111) p.238
1394-1396.06	77 s.	Siena	C	(111) p.238
1396.07	77 s. 10 d.	Siena	C	(111) p.238
1396.11-1397.02	78 s.	Siena	C	(111) p.238
1397.03-04	76 s. 6 d.	Siena	C	(111) p.238
1397.05	75 s.	Siena	C	(111) p.238
1397.06	77 s.	Siena	C	(111) p.238
1397.08	73 s.	Siena	C	(111) p.238
1397.11	74 s. 10 d.	Siena	C	(111) p.238
1397.12-1398.02	76 s.	Siena	C	(111) p.238
1398.03	76 s. 8 d.	Siena	C	(111) p.238
1398.06-1399.04	77 s.	Siena	C	(111) p.238
1399.05-1400.06	78 s.	Siena	C	(111) p.238
1451-1453	95 s.	Siena	C	(111) p.87
1455	102 s.	Siena	C	(111) p.87
1459-1460	105 s.	Siena	C	(111) p.87
1461	106 s.	Siena	C	(111) p.87
1462	105 s.	Siena	C	(111) p.87
1463	106 s.	Siena	C	(111) p.87
1464	106 s. 8 d.	Siena	C	(111) p.87
1465-1476	112 s.	Siena	C	(111) p.87
1477-1480	114 s.	Siena	C	(111) p.88
1481	116 s.	Siena	C	(111) p.88

THE FLORENTINE FLORIN IN SOLDI AND DENARI OF SIENA

Date	Rate	Place	Type	Reference
1482	118 s.	Siena	C	(111) p.88
1483	120 s.	Siena	C	(111) p.88
1487	124 s.	Siena	C	(111) p.88
1490-1491	128 s.	Siena	C	(111) p.88
1492-1493	130 s.	Siena	C	(111) p.88
1494-1499	128 s. 8 d.	Siena	C	(111) p.88

The lira of Siena in soldi and denari of Volterra

Date	Rate	Place	Type	Reference
1221.10.29	24 s. 10 d.	Siena	B	(111) p.93

The lira of Siena in soldi and denari of Ravenna

Date	Rate	Place	Type	Reference
1223.04.20	20 s. 11 1/2 d.	Siena	L	(40) p.196

For the lira of Genoa in soldi and denari of Siena see under GENOA p.107
For the livre of Provins in soldi and denari of Siena see under CHAMPAGNE FAIRS p.165
For the gros tournois in denari of Siena see under FRANCE p.187

CORTONA

The Florentine florin in soldi and denari of Cortona

Date	Rate	Place	Type	Reference
1278.03.01	48 s.	Viterbo	C	(108) V p.339
1291.08.26	45 s.	Orvieto	B	(179) p.55
1320	76 s. 6 d.	Curia	B	(439) p.900
1321	78 s.	Curia	B	(439) p.900
1321	80 s.	Curia	B	(439) p.900
1322	79 s.	Curia	B	(439) p.900
1322	80 s.	Curia	B	(439) p.900
1323	80 s.	Curia	B	(439) p.900
1324	80 s.	Curia	B	(439) p.901
1325	80 s. 8 d.	Curia	B	(439) p.901
1326-1328	81 s.	Curia	B	(439) p.901
1326-1328	82 s.	Curia	B	(439) p.901
1329-1331	85 s.	Curia	B	(439) p.901
1329-1331	85 s. 6 d.	Curia	B	(439) p.901
1332	78 s.	Curia	B	(439) p.901
1348.07-08	79 s.	Orvieto	O	(90) p.202
1348.09	76 s.	Orvieto	O	(90) p.202
1349.01	80 s.	Orvieto	O	(90) p.202
1361.01	87 s.	Orvieto	O	(90) p.202

For the lira of paparini in soldi and denari of Cortona see under ROME p.70
For the Venetian grosso in denari of Cortona see under VENICE p.86
For the gros tournois in denari of Cortona see under FRANCE p.188

PERUGIA

Perugia was granted mint rights in 1259, with the specification that their silver coin was to be minted according to the money of Siena.

The Florentine florin in lire, soldi and denari of Perugia

Date	Rate	Place	Type	Reference
1272	1 li. 6 s.	Perugia	A	(390) p.115
1276	2 li. 3 s.	Perugia	A	(390) p.115
1277	2 li. 4 s. 3 d.	Perugia	A	(390) p.115
1279	2 li. 3 s. 8 d.	Perugia	A	(390) p.115
1281	2 li. 5 s. 2 d.	Perugia	A	(390) p.115
1282	2 li. 4 s. 11 d.	Perugia	A	(390) p.115
1285	2 li. 5 s. 11 d.	Perugia	A	(390) p.115
1286	2 li. 5 s. 1 d.	Perugia	A	(390) p.115
1293	2 li. 5 s. 8 d.	Perugia	A	(390) p.115
1306	3 li. 5 s.	Perugia	A	(390) p.115
1311	3 li. 4 s.	Perugia	A	(390) p.115
1316	3 li. 12 s.	Perugia	A	(390) p.115
1320	3 li. 18 s.	Perugia	A	(390) p.115
1326	4 li. 1 s.	Perugia	A	(390) p.115
1332	4 li. 6 s. 6 d.	Perugia	A	(390) p.115
1333	4 li.	Perugia	A	(390) p.115
1334	4 li. 6 s. 6 d.	Perugia	A	(390) p.115
1335	3 li. 18 s.	Perugia	A	(390) p.115
1336	4 li. 2 d.	Perugia	A	(390) p.115
1337	3 li. 18 s.	Perugia	A	(390) p.115
1338	3 li. 18 s.	Perugia	A	(390) p.115
1339	3 li. 18 s.	Perugia	A	(390) p.115
1340	4 li. 1d.	Perugia	A	(390) p.115
1341	4 li. 2 s.	Perugia	A	(390) p.115
1344	4 li. 4 s. 3 d.	Perugia	A	(390) p.115
1345	4 li. 3 s. 6 d.	Perugia	A	(390) p.115
1346	4 li. 4 s.	Perugia	A	(390) p.115
1347	4 li. 3 s. 2 d.	Perugia	A	(390) p.115
1351	4 li. 2 s. 5 d.	Perugia	A	(390) p.115
1352	4 li. 2 s. 10 d.	Perugia	A	(390) p.116
1353	4 li. 4 s. 8 d.	Perugia	A	(390) p.116
1354	4 li. 7 s. 9 d.	Perugia	A	(390) p.116
1355	4 li. 7 s.	Perugia	A	(390) p.116
1356	4 li. 7 s. 7 d.	Perugia	A	(390) p.116
1358	4 li. 7 s.	Perugia	A	(390) p.116
1359	4 li. 7 s.	Perugia	A	(390) p.116
1364	4 li. 4 s. 4 d.	Perugia	A	(390) p.116
1365	4 li. 4 s. 3 d.	Perugia	A	(390) p.116
1366	4 li. 4 s. 10 d.	Perugia	A	(390) p.116
1367	4 li. 4 s.	Perugia	A	(390) p.116
1368	4 li. 4 s.	Perugia	A	(390) p.116
1369	4 li. 2 s. 9 d.	Perugia	A	(390) p.116
1370	4 li. 3 d.	Perugia	A	(390) p.116
1371	4 li. 2 s. 10 d.	Perugia	A	(390) p.116
1372	4 li. 3 s.	Perugia	A	(390) p.116
1376	4 li. 6 s. 10 d.	Perugia	A	(390) p.116
1377	4 li. 7 s.	Perugia	A	(390) p.116
1383	4 li. 8 s.	Perugia	A	(390) p.116
1384	4 li. 8 s.	Perugia	A	(390) p.116
1385	4 li. 10 s.	Perugia	A	(390) p.116
1391	4 li. 8 s. 4 d.	Perugia	A	(390) p.116
1392	4 li. 10 s.	Perugia	A	(390) p.116
1399	4 li. 2 s. 6 d.	Perugia	A	(390) p.116
1400	4 li. 10 s. 8 d.	Perugia	A	(390) p.116

SECTION II
SOUTHERN AND CENTRAL ITALY

SICILY AND SOUTHERN ITALY UNTIL 1282

Sicily and southern Italy were accustomed to the use of gold, coined and uncoined, under Muslim, Norman, Hohenstaufen and early Angevin rule. Gold was commonly weighed by the ounce. See below p.312. Reckoning was therefore carried out in terms of the uncia (oncia) of gold which was divided into 30 tari or tareni, each of which was divided into 20 grani (grains). Gold tari coins were struck by the Muslim and Norman rulers and Frederick II in 1231 added to these a gold augustale. Each augustale was reckoned as a quarter of an ounce or 7.1/2 tari. Charles of Anjou continued the issue of 7.1/2 tari pieces, with a reale from 1266 and 1278 and a saluto or carlino d'oro from 1278.

The Florentine florin in tari and grani
20 grani = 1 tareno

Date	Rate	Place	Type	Reference
1266.11.15	6t.	Naples	O	(180) p.32
1268	6t.	Naples	O	(33) p.160
1268	6t.	Sicily	B	(179) p.17
1269	6t.	Naples	O	(33) p.158
1271-1287	6t.	Naples	C	(111) p.95
1277-1278	5t. 15g.	Naples	C	(188) XVIII p.247
1277-1284	6t.	Naples	C	(126) p.497

After 1282 see below pp.63 and 65

The uncia of Sicily (30 tari) in soldi of Pisa

Date	Rate	Place	Type	Reference
1203.08.27	100s.	Pisa	H	(295) p.197
1253.03.22	120s.	Pisa	H	(295) p.197
1263	110s.	Pisa	H	(295) p.197
1268	120s.	Pisa	H	(295) p.197
1269.06.05	125s.	Pisa	H	(295) p.197
1271.04.24	160s.	Pisa	H	(295) p.197

After 1282 see below pp.64 and 66

The uncia of Sicily (30 tari) in soldi of Venice

Date	Rate	Place	Type	Reference
1228	193 s.	Venice	?	(412) p.66

The uncia of Sicily (30 tari) in soldi and denari of Genoa

Some of these ounces may be ounces of tari weighed in Genoa by the Genoese ounce rather than Sicilian units of weight and account

Date	Rate	Place	Type	Reference
1158	38 s. 6 d.	Genoa	?	(93) p.113
1160.03.18	33 s. 6 d.	Sicily	?	(93) p.124
1160.03.26	33 s.	Sicily	?	(93) p.124
1160.04.24	35 s.	Sicily	?	(93) p.124
1162.09.18	35 s. 10 d.	Genoa	M	(2) p.248
1182	45 s.	Sicily	A	(187A) f.1027
1182	38 s.	Genoa	C?	(344) p.213
1182	45 s. 9 d.	Genoa	C?	(344) p.213
1182	40 s. 2 d.	Genoa	C?	(344) p.213
1182	42 s.	Genoa	C?	(344) p.213
1184	41 s.	Sicily-Genoa	B	(187A) f.1027
1186	42 s. 9 d.	Genoa	C?	(344) p.213
1186	42 s.	Genoa	C?	(344) p.213
1186	44 s.	Genoa	C?	(344) p.213
1186	38 s.	Genoa	C?	(344) p.213

THE UNCIA OF SICILY IN SOLDI AND DENARI OF GENOA

Date	Rate	Place	Type	Reference
1190	44 s. 6 d.	Sicily	A	(187A) f.1027
1191	35 s.	Genoa	A	(187A) f.1025
1191.01	42 s. 7 d.	Naples	C	(233) no.22
1191.01	58 s.	Naples	C	(233) no.25
1191.01.27	40 s.	Naples/Sicily	B	(233) no.151
1191.03.27	24 s.	Messina	C	(233) no.362
1191	42 s.	Sicily	?	(93) p.126
1191.08.25	42 s.	Genoa	C	(2) p.268
1191.09.25	42 s.	Constantinople	L	(2) no.1134
1191.09.27	35 s.	Messina/Palermo	C	(2) p.195
1191.09.27	35 s.	Sicily	B	(233) no.1145
1191.09.27	40 s.	Messina/Palermo	C	(2) p.195
1192	39 s.	Genoa	A	(187A) f.1025
1192.03.07	36 s.	Palermo/Messina	B	(233) no.1701
1192.03.07	39 s.	Messina	C	(2) p.198
1192.03.07	50 s.	Genoa	C	(2) p.198
1200	26 s. 8 d.	Genoa	C?	(344) p.213
1203	46 s. 3 d.	Genoa	A	(187A) f.1025
1203	43 s.	Genoa	A	(187A) f.1025
1203	40 s.	Genoa	A	(187A) f.1026
1203	35 s.	Genoa	A	(187A) f.1027
1203.14.02	34 s.	Sicily	B	(274) no.102
1203.09	26 s.	Alexandria	C	(234) no.528
1203.09.13	40 s.	Messina	B	(4199 no.544
1203.09.16	46 s.	Sicily	C	(234) no.560
1203.09.18	42 s.	Sicily	L	(4199 no.594
1203.09.19	42 s.	Messina	L	(234) no.626
1203.09.20	42 s.	Messina	L	(234) no.654
1203.09.23	42 s.	Messina	L	(234) no.731
1203.09.23	44 s.	Messina	L	(234) no.769
1203.09.24	42 s.	Messina	L	(234) no.87444
1205	40 s.	Genoa	A	(187A) f.1026
1205.05.06	60 s.	Sicily	L	(234) no.1029
1205.05.06	49 s. 1 d.	Sicily	C	(234) no.1032
1205.05.08	51 s. 9 d.	Outremer	C	(234) no.1087
1205.05.09	42 s.	Messina	L	(234) no.1103
1205.05.13	41 s.	Sicily	L	(234) no.1166
1205.05.24	40 s.	Messina	L	(234) no.1239
1205.05.28	48 s. 5 d.	Outremer	C	(234) no.1313
1205.06.02	40 s.	Genoa	C	(234) no.1410
1206	40 s.	Genoa	A	(187A) f.1026
1206.03.11	40 s.	Messina	L	(234) no.1600
1206.03.22	40 s.	Messina	L	(234) no.1712
1206.03.30	40 s.	Messina	L	(234) no.1793
1206.04.27	40 s.	Messina	L	(234) no.1970
1207	40 s. 2 d.	Genoa	C?	(344) p.214
1210.06.23	54 s. 6 d.	Genoa	?	(274) I p.268
1210	39 s.	Genoa	A	(187A) f.1027
1210	40 s. 5 d.	Genoa	C?	(344) p.214
1210	44 s.	Genoa	C?	(344) p.214
1210	33 s.	Genoa	C?	(344) p.214
1210	40 s.	Genoa	C?	(344) p.214
1213	40 s. 7 d.	Genoa	C?	(344) p.214
1213	46 s. 10 d.	Genoa	A	(187A) f.1026
1213	45 s.	Genoa	L	(187A) f.1028
1213	35 s.	Genoa	C?	(344) p.214
1213	48 s. 7 d.	Genoa	C?	(344) p.214
1213.10.29	45 s.	Genoa	C	(381) p.345
1214	40 s. 2 d.	Genoa	C?	(344) p.214
1214	50 s.	Genoa	C?	(344) p.214
1214	42 s.	Genoa	C?	(344) p.214
1215	43 s. 2 d.	Genoa	C?	(344) p.214
1215	52 s.	Genoa	C?	(344) p.214
1216	42 s.	Genoa	A	(187A) f.1028
1216	44 s.	Messina-Genoa	B	(187A) f.1027
1216	40 s.	Genoa	A	(187A) f.1027
1216	70 s.	Genoa	A	(187A) f.1035
1216	40 s.	Genoa	C?	(344) p.215
1216	46 s. 7 d.	Genoa	C?	(344) p.215
1216	43 s. 2 d.	Genoa	C?	(344) p.215
1216	42 s. 5 d.	Genoa	C?	(344) p.215
1216.08.13	40 s.	Genoa	?	(274) II p.69

THE UNCIA OF SICILY IN SOLDI AND DENARI OF GENOA

Date	Rate	Place	Type	Reference
1216.11.13	43 s.	Genoa	?	(274) II p.85
1225.04.25	43 s. 2 d.	Genoa	L	(381) p.346
1226	44 s.	Genoa	C?	(344) p.215
1227	50 s.	Genoa	A	(187A) f.1027
1227.06.18	50 s.	Genoa	L	(381) p.346
1233	43 s. 1 d.	Genoa	A	(187A) f.1033
1233	52 s. 7 d.	Genoa	A	(187A) f.1033
1233	52 s. 7 d.	Genoa	C?	(344) p.215
1236	52 s.	Genoa	C?	(344) p.215
1239	50 s.	Genoa	C?	(344) p.215
1239	50 s.	Genoa	A	(187A) f.1029
1239.08.16	50 s.	Genoa	L	(381) p.346
1241.01.07	50 s.	Genoa	M	(381) p.347
1245	38 s. 3 d.	Genoa	C?	(344) p.215
1251	51 s. 5 d.	Genoa	A	(187A) f.1029
1251	56 s.	Genoa	A	(187A) f.1029
1252	54 s.	Genoa	A	(187A) f.1029
1252	65 s.	Genoa	A	(187A) f.1030
1252	54 s.	Genoa	C?	(344) p.215
1252	45 s.	Genoa	C	(344) p.215
1253	56 s. 6 d.	Genoa	A	(187A) f.1030
1253	54 s.	Genoa	A	(187A) f.1030
1253	50 s.	Genoa	E	(187A) f.1030
1253	52 s. 9 d.	Genoa	A	(187A) f.1030
1253	55 s.	Genoa	A	(187A) f.1030
1253	53 s. 4 d.	Genoa	A	(187A) f.1030
1253	54 s.	Genoa	A	(187A) f.1031
1253	50 s.	Genoa	C?	(344) p.215
1253	52 s.	Genoa	C?	(344) p.215
1253	54 s.	Genoa	C?	(344) p.215
1253	64 s.	Genoa	C?	(344) p.215
1253	45 s.	Genoa	C?	(344) p.215
1253.03.22	53 s. 10 d.	Genoa	L	(381) p.347
1253.11.13	53 s.	France	?	(432) p.300
1253.11.18	53 s.	Genoa	M	(381) p.347
1253.12.02	54 s. 7 d.	Genoa	L	(381) p.347
1253.12.06	54 s.	Genoa	L	(381) p.347
1253.12.21	55 s.	Genoa	L	(381) p.347
1254.10.10	48 s.	Genoa	?	(154) II p.971
1261	61 s.	Genoa	A	(187A) f.1031
1262	78 s.	Genoa	A	(187A) f.1035
1263	60 s.	Genoa	A	(187A) f.1035
1264	60 s.	Genoa	B	(187A) f.1032
1264	60 s.	Genoa	A	(187A) f.1032
1264	62 s. 2 d.	Genoa	A	(187A) f.1035
1264.09.27	60 s.	Genoa-Palermo	B	(381) p.348
1265	60 s.	Genoa	A	(187A) f.1035
1265.11.08	70 s.	Agrigento-Genoa	B	(381) p.348
1268	59 s. 11 d.	Genoa	A	(187A) f.1033
1269	82 s.	Genoa	A	(187A) f.1035

After 1282 see below pp.64 and 66

The uncia of Sicily (30 tari) in sous and deniers royaux coronats of Provence

Date	Rate	Place	Type	Reference
1158.10.24	38 s.	Palermo	C	(105) app.8
1160.04.24	35 s.	Sicily	B	(105) no.641
1162.01.06	37 s. 4 d.	Salerno	C	(105) no.935
1162.09.18	35 s.	Genoa	M	(105) no.970
1200.02.15	55 s.	Messina-Marseille	B	(45) no.1
1230	48 s.	Marseille	?	(43) p.229
1235.04.19	48 s.	Marseille	C	(45) no.61
1248.03.23	45 s. 5 d.	Marseille	C	(45) no.160
1248	49 s. 8 d.	Marseille-Acre	C	(45) no.503

The uncia of Sicily (30 tari) in mixed money of Marseille

Date	Rate	Place	Type	Reference
1248.03.16	58 s. 10 d.	Marseille-Messina	B	(45) no.17
1248.03.18	65 s.	Marseille	C	(45) no.67
1248.03.18	70 s.	Marseille	C	(45) no.48
1248.03.18	67 s. 10 d.	Marseille	C	(45) no.82
1248.03.30	68 s.	Marseille-Sicily	C	(45) no.314
1248.03.30	70 s.	Marseille-Sicily	B	(45) no.321
1248.03.30	70 s.	Marseille	C	(45) no.324
1248.04.01	70 s.	Marseille	C	(45) no.339
1248.04.09	65 s.	Marseille-Naples or Gaeta?	B	(45) no.418
1248.04.14	60 s.	Marseille-Acre	C	(45) no.502
1248.05.08	60 s.	Marseille	C	(45) no.702

The uncia of Sicily (30 tari) in sous and deniers parisis of France

Date	Rate	Place	Type	Reference
1277-1284	40 s.	Naples	C	(126) p.497

The uncia of Sicily (30 tari) in sous and deniers tournois of France

Date	Rate	Place	Type	Reference
1248.07.17	48 s.	Marseille	B	(45) no.888
1268	42 s. 1 d.	Sicily	?	(179) p.16
1272-1273	50 s.	Sicily	?	(188) X p.191
1274-1280	51 s. 3 d.	Rome	?	(439) p.76
1275	50 s.	Provence	?	(43) p.263
1277-1284	50 s.	Naples	?	(126) p.497

The uncia of Sicily (30 tari) in soldi of Chiarenza

Date	Rate	Place	Type	Reference
1277-1284	50 s.	Naples	?	(126) p.497

SICILY AND SOUTHERN ITALY AFTER 1282

After the Sicilian Vespers of 1282, the Regno, the mainland kingdom of Sicily based on Naples, remained under Angevin rule, whilst Trinacria, the island kingdom of Sicily reverted to the Hohenstaufen rule in the person of Constance and her husband Peter III of Aragon. The currency of the two kingdoms gradually diverged, so two separate series are given here.

NAPLES AFTER 1282

Under Charles II (d. 1309) coined gold ceased to be struck, but by this time the tari had become equivalent to two silver carlini. The first silver carlino, or saluto d'argento was struck in 1278, but the type that was to continue throughout the fourteenth and fifteenth centuries was that introduced in 1303, known from the lilies on its reverse as the gigliato, (or, in Provence where it was introduced in 1330, as the iulhat). Reckoning was either still carried out in terms of uncie, tari and grani, or directly in silver carlini. However, even when a sum was expressed nominally in gold, in uncie, tari and grani, it represented a reality in silver, reckoning the uncia at 60 silver carlini and the tari at 2 silver carlini. By the time Pegolotti compiled his notebook he could even write of tari d'argento (177) p.182. When Pegolotti was making his notes:- 1 grano = 6 denari piccioli, i.e. 1 carlino = 60 denari piccioli. In the following tables all the rates have been expressed in carlini and denari, although some of the earlier rates were originally expressed in tari and grani.

The Florentine florin in silver carlini and denari of Naples
One carlino = 60 denari piccioli

Date	Rate	Place	Type	Reference
Before 1282 see above p.59				
1280-1286	circa 12 c.	Curia	B	(439) p.897
1280-1286	circa 13 c.	Curia	B	(439) p.897
1284	12 c.	Naples	B	(443) p.301
1287	12 c.	Rome	B	(439) p.76
1291	12 c.	Naples	H	(461) p.374
1295.10.08	12 c.	Benevento	B	(226) CLIV p.20
1296-1298	circa 13 c.	Curia	B	(439) p.898
1297	circa 13 c.	Naples	C	(111) p.95
1298-1300	13 c. 30 d.	Naples	C	(111) p.95
1302-1303	12 c.	Curia	B	(439) p.899
1302-1303	13 c.	Curia	B	(439) p.899
1309-1312	13 c.	Curia	B	(439) p.899
1309-1312	13 c. 30 d.	Curia	B	(439) p.899
1309-1315	12 c.	Naples	C	(111) p.95
1311-1312	13 c.	Curia	B	(439) p.899
1311-1312	13 c. 30 d.	Curia	B	(439) p.899
1318	13 c.	Curia	B	(439) p.900
1319	13 c. 48 d.	Curia	B	(439) p.900
1320	14 c. 20 d.	Naples	C	(111) p.96
1320	14 c. 20 d.	Curia	B	(439) p.900
1321	14 c. 20 d.	Curia	B	(439) p.900
1322-1326	14 c. 30 d.	Naples	C	(111) p.96
1322	13 c. 24 d.	Avignon	B	(439) p.77
1322	13 c. 30 d.	Curia	B	(439) p.900
1322	14 c.	Curia	B	(439) p.900
1322	14 c. 30 d.	Curia	B	(439) p.77
1323-1324	14 c. 30 d.	Curia	B	(439) p.900
1324-1326	14 c. 30 d.	Curia	B	(439) p.96
1325	15 c. 50 d.	Curia	B	(439) p.901
1326-1327	14 c. 40 d.	Curia	B	(439) p.901
1326-1327	16 c.	Curia	B	(439) p.901
1327	13 c. 30 d.	Naples	C	(111) p.96
1329	13 c. 20 d.	Naples	C	(111) p.96
1329	14 c.	Curia	B	(439) p.901
1330	circa 13 c. 30 d.	Curia	B	(439) p.901
1333-1334	12 c.	Curia	B	(439) p.901
1333-1334	13 c. 30 d.	Curia	B	(439) p.901
1333	13 c.	Naples	C	(111) p.96
1334-1342	14 c.	Barcelona	C	(321) pp.448 and 466
1334-1342	14 c. 12 d.	Barcelona	C	(321) p.466
1335-1340	12 c.	Naples	C	(438) p.207
1336-1337	12 c.	Curia	B	(439) p.902
1336-1337	12 c. 30 d.	Curia	B	(439) p.902
1336	12 c.	Naples	C	(111) p.96
1342	11 c.	Naples	C	(111) p.96
1344	11 c. 24 d.	Naples	C	(111) p.96
1349-1350	12 c.	Naples	C	(111) p.96
1349-1351	12 c.	Curia	B	(439) p.902
1349-1351	13 c.	Curia	B	(439) p.902
1359	11 c.	Naples	C	(111) p.96
1364	10 c.	Naples	C	(111) p.96
1368	9 c. 48 d.	Naples	C	(111) p.97
1371	10 c.	Naples	C	(111) p.97
1381	9 c. 36 d.	Naples	C	(111) p.97
1382.03.28	9 c. 48 d.	Gaeta	M	(121) p.654
1382.03.30-04.02	9 c. 48 d.	Naples	M	(121) p.654
1382.04.05	9 c. 18 d.	San Lucido	M	(121) p.654
1382.04.06	9 c. 30 d.	Tropea	M	(121) p.654
1382.04.08	9 c. 30 d.	Reggio	M	(121) p.654
1382.10.29	8 c. 21 d.	Otranto	M	(121) p.654
1382.11.03	9 c.	La Castella	M	(121) p.654
1382.11.05	10 c.	Reggio	M	(121) p.654
1382.11.17	10 c.	Gaeta	M	(121) p.654
1404-1469	10 c.	Naples	C	(111) p.97

During this long period when the florin was fixed at 10 carlini gigliati, or 5 tari of carlini gigliati, Alfonso I (1435-58) began the issue of a gold ducat of similar weight and fineness. At the end of the fifteenth century a ducat of 10 carlini was sometimes used as a unit of account, based on the silver carlino, distinct from the actual gold ducat which increased in value in terms of carlini.

The gold ducat of Naples in carlini and denari of Naples
One carlino = 60 denari piccioli

Date	Rate	Place	Type	Reference
1470.11.28	10 c.	Naples	B	(488) p.32
1472.07.08	10 c.	Naples	C	(499) I p.397
1478-1479	9 c. 45 d.	Rome	B	(488) p.266
1479.10.13	11 c. 30 d.	Naples	H	(180) p.34
1491	11 c.	Naples	C	(360) p.57
1491	11 c. 30 d.	Naples	C	(360) p.57
1491-1493	11 c. 30 d.	Naples	C	(111) p.97
1494	12 c. 30 d.	Naples	C	(111) p.97
1497	12 c.	Naples	C	(111) p.97

The uncia of Naples (60 carlini) in soldi and denari of Pisa

Date	Rate	Place	Type	Reference
Before 1282 see above p.59				
1283.09.24	170 s.	Pisa	H	(295) p.197
1283.11.03	150 s.	Pisa	H	(295) p.197
1299	210 s.	Pisa	H	(295) p.197
1299	205 s.	Pisa	H	(295) p.197
1299	206 s. 6 d.	Pisa	H	(295) p.197
1299	205 s.	Pisa	H	(295) p.197
1304.01.26	205 s.	Pisa	H	(295) p.197
1308	205 s.	Pisa	H	(295) p.197
1308	200 s.	Pisa	H	(295) p.197

The carlino of Naples in soldi and denari provisini of Rome

Date	Rate	Place	Type	Reference
1285	2 s. 7 d.	Rome	C	(401) p.306

The uncia of Naples (60 Carlini) in soldi and denari of Genoa

Date	Rate	Place	Type	Reference
Before 1282 see above pp.59-61				
1292	70 s.	Genoa	A	(187A) f.1035
1292	69 s.	Genoa	A	(187A) f.1035
1294	70 s.	Genoa	A	(187A) f.1032
1298.09.04	75 s.	Genoa	B	(154) IV p.863

The ducat of 10 carlini of Naples in sueldos and dineros of Barcelona

Date	Rate	Place	Type	Reference
1457.03.19	15 s. 6 d.	Naples	M	(293) p.169
1457.04.06	15 s. 5 d.	Naples	M	(293) p.169
1458.06.05	15 s. 6 d.	Naples	M	(293) p.169
1458.06.14	15 s.	Naples-Barcelona	B	(293) p.173
1458.07.31	15 s.	Naples	M	(293) p.169
1458.09	15 s.	Naples	M	(293) p.169
1460.07.28	13 s. 10 d.	Naples	M	(293) p.169
1462.05.29	14 s. 6 d.	Naples	M	(293) p.169
1479.10.25	18 s. 7 d.	Naples	M	(293) p.169

The uncia of Naples (60 carlini) in sous parisis of France

Date	Rate	Place	Type	Reference
Before 1282 see above p.62				
1292.07.22	72 s.	Paris	C	(118) III p.44

SICILY AFTER 1282

After 1282 the Sicilians went on reckoning in uncia, tari and grani at the rate of
1 uncia = 30 tari
1 tareno = 20 grani
However, as in Naples, reckoning ceased to be based on gold and instead came to be based on silver. king Peter III or Aragon replaced the Angevin silver carlino by his own piereale or raonesi d'argento. They were initially of the same weight and fineness, and were consequently sometimes known as Sicilian carlini. A tari was reckoned as 2 raonesi d'argento or piereale. Pegolotti noted that, except in Messina, the uncia was reckoned as 60 raonesi, whilst in Messina, the uncia was reckoned as 60 raonesi less 4 grani. He also noted that the grano was then worth 1s 6d of piccioli i.e. 1 piereale was worth 15s. of piccioli (177) p.107.

The Florentine florin in tari and grani of Sicily
20 grani = 1 tari

Date	Rate	Place	Type	Reference
Before 1282 see above p.59				
1288	5 t.	Sicily	C	(512) p.81
1289	5 t.	Sicily	C	(512) p.81
1298.11.2	5 t.	Sicily	C	(512) p.17
1315	9 t.	Sicily	C	(111) p.98

Pegolotti (177) p.115 included among his notes a ready reckoner for converting from florins expressed in tari and grani, into uncie expressed in lire, soldi and denari a fiorino. The, presumably likely, values that he included for the florin, range from 7 tari to 8 tari 1 grano.

Date	Rate	Place	Type	Reference
1332.11.01	8 t.	Palermo	O	(318) p.181n
1332.11.01	8 t. 2 g.	Palermo	O	(318) p.181n
The lower of these two rates was the official rate for bankers, the higher for private transactions.				
1343	7 t. 2 g.	Genoa	C	(187B) f.763
1344.03.15	5 t. 15 g.	Curia	B	(347) p.345
1367.07.10	6 t.	Sicily	B	(309) II p.54
1368-1373	6 t.	Sicily	B	(226) CXII p.143
1382.04.07-08	6 t. 2 1/2 g.	Messina	M	(121) p.654
1382.11.05-12	6 t. 1 1/2 g.	Messina	M	(121) p.654
1388.08.17	6 t. 3 g.	Sicily	B	(24) p.360
1403	6 t.	Sicily	C	(111) p.98
1409	5 t. 10 g.	Palermo	B	(187B) fo 763
1422.07.17	6 t. 10 g.	Palermo	B	(81) p.38
1430-1451	7 t.	Sicily	C	(111) p.98
1458-1460	8 t.	Sicily	C	(111) p.98
1479	11 t.	Sicily	C	(111) p.98
1486	12 t. 5 g.	Sicily	C	(111) p.98

The Venetian ducat in tari and grani of Sicily
20 grani = 1 tareno

Date	Rate	Place	Type	Reference
1310	6 t. 15 g.	Sicily	H	(180) p.32
1336	6 t.	Sicily	H	(180) p.32
1344	5 t. 9 g.	Sicily	H	(180) p.32
1434.07.27	7 t.	Venice	B	(488) p.132
1434.11.10	6 t. 15 g.	Venice	B	(488) p.132

The uncia of Sicily (30 tari) in soldi of Pisa

Date	Rate	Place	Type	Reference
Before 1282 see above p.59				
1288	70 s.	Sicily	C	(512) p.81
1289	70 s.	Sicily	C	(512) p.81
1299.01.15	205 s.	Sicily	C	(512) p.34
1299.03.25	210 s.	Pisa	C	(512) p.81

The uncia of Sicily (30 tari) in soldi and denari of Genoa

Date	Rate	Place	Type	Reference
Before 1282 see above pp.59-61				
1287	72 s.	Sicily	C	(512) p.LXXXI
1288	70 s.	Sicily	C	(512) p.81
1289	71 s.	Sicily	C	(512) p.81
1298.09.24	70 s.	Sicily	C	(512) p.12
1299.01.15	75 s.	Sicily	C	(512) p.34

The uncia of Sicily (30 tari) in sueldos of Barcelona

Date	Rate	Place	Type	Reference
1287	60 s.	Sicily	C	(512) p.81
1483	50 s.	Barcelona	O	(489) p.28
1483	50 s.	Valencia	O	(489) p.28
1483	50 s.	Jaca	O	(489) p.28

The uncia of Sicily (30 tari) in ducats of Aragon

Date	Rate	Place	Type	Reference
1483	2 1/2 d.	Barcelona	O	(489) p.28
1483	2 1/2 d.	Valencia	O	(489) p.28
1483	2 1/2 d.	Jaca	O	(489) p.28

The uncia of Sicily (30 tari) in sueldos and dineros reales of Majorca

Date	Rate	Place	Type	Reference
1309.01.20	60 s.	Sicily	C	(512) p.136

For the gold dinar in tari and grani of Sicily see under EGYPT p.306

Florins of Sicily

Reckoning in fifteenth century Sicily was sometimes carried out in florins rather than uncie. This florin was a unit of 6 tari. In terms of actual coin it was represented by 12 silver piereale.

The florin of Sicily (6 tari) in sueldos and dineros of Barcelona

Date	Rate	Place	Type	Reference
1432.11.26	14 s. 8 d.	Naples/Barcelona	B	(488) p.34
1432.11.27	18 s.	Naples/Barcelona	B	(488) p.34
1475-1476	14 s.	Palermo	B	(488) p.265
1478.04.02	13 s. 8 d.	Barcelona	B	(488) p.39
1478.04.10	11 s. 7 d.	Barcelona	B	(488) p.39

The florin of Sicily (6 tari) in sueldos and dineros of Valencia

Date	Rate	Place	Type	Reference
1478.03.31	11 s. 8 d.	Saragossa	O?M	(488) p.39

The florin of Sicily (6 tari) in sueldos and dineros iaccenses of Aragon

Date	Rate	Place	Type	Reference
1474-1475	10 s. 6 d.	Saragossa	B	(488) p.265
1474-1475	11 s. 6 d.	Palermo	B	(488) p.265
1474-1475	11 s.	Palermo	B	(488) p.265
1475-1476	11 s.	Palermo	B	(488) p.265
1476-1477	10 s. 1 1/2 d.	Valencia	B	(488) p.265
1476-1477	10 s. 6 d.	Saragossa	B	(488) p.265
1476-1477	12 s.	Saragossa	B	(488) p.265
1477-1478	10 s.	Bilbao	B	(488) p.266
1483-1484	11 s.	Palermo?	B	(488) p.266

ROME AND THE PATRIMONY OF ST PETER

Provisini of Rome

From the 980s onwards (for two centuries) there was no indigenous coinage in Rome. Instead, the denari of Pavia and of Lucca in turn provided the circulating medium of central Italy, until the 1150s when deniers provinois, minted at the fair-town of Provins for the counts of Champagne, began to flood in from France. By the 1170s these deniers, known in central Italy as denari provisini, had become the dominant currency of the area. When the senate of Rome, by arrangement with the pope, began to mint denari, it was in imitation of these deniers of Champagne. The earliest senatorial provisini, struck before 1184, probably as early as 1176-7, were identical in weight and fineness with their French prototypes. However, their metal content was gradually reduced, so that by the 1190s 18 new senatorial provisini were reckoned as equal to 12 old French provisini. In 1208 Innocent III fixed an official rate of exchange of 16 senatorial provisini for 12 French provisini, but by this time the number of original French deniers provinois in circulation was very small. Senatorial provisini, however, remained the standard money of Rome for the remainder of the middle ages and accounting was carried on in terms of lire, soldi and denari provisini. When, in the fifteenth century, the actual denaro provisino became so small and so debased as to be unusable, even for small change, the quattrino (4d. piece) became the link coin by which the money of account was attached to the currency.

The Florentine florin in soldi and denari provisini of Rome

Date	Rate	Place	Type	Reference
1259-1281	20 s.	Curia	C	(111) p.90
1274-1280	19 s. 6 d.	Rome	B	(226) CXXVIII, 26
1274	16 s.	Rome	B	(439) p.III
1277-1278	20 s.	Curia	B	(439) p.897
1280	circa 20 s.	Curia	B	(439) p.897
1283	20 s. 9 d.	Curia	C	(111) p.91
1285	25 s.	Curia	C	(111) p.91
1285	24 s. 9 1/2 d.	Curia	B	(439) p.III
1286	circa 26 s.	Curia	B	(439) p.897
1290-1292	26 s.	Curia	B	(439) p.898
1291	25 s.	Rome	B	(439) p.III
1291	35 s.	Curia	C	(111) p.91
1293-1297	27 s.	Curia	C	(111) p.91
1293-1297	29 s.	Curia	C	(111) p.91
1296-1299	26 s.	Curia	B	(439) p.898
1296-1299	26 s. 6 d.	Curia	B	(439) p.898
1296-1299	27 s. 6 d.	Curia	B	(439) p.898
1296-1299	29 s.	Curia	B	(439) p.898
1297	29 s. 8 d.	Rome	B	(439) p.50
1297	30 s. 6 d.	Piedmont	A	(110) p.488
1299	31 s.	Curia	C	(111) p.91
1299	33 s.	Curia	C	(111) p.91
1300	34 s.	Curia	B	(439) p.898
1302	34 s.	Curia	C	(111) p.92
1302-1303	34 s.	Curia	B	(439) p.899

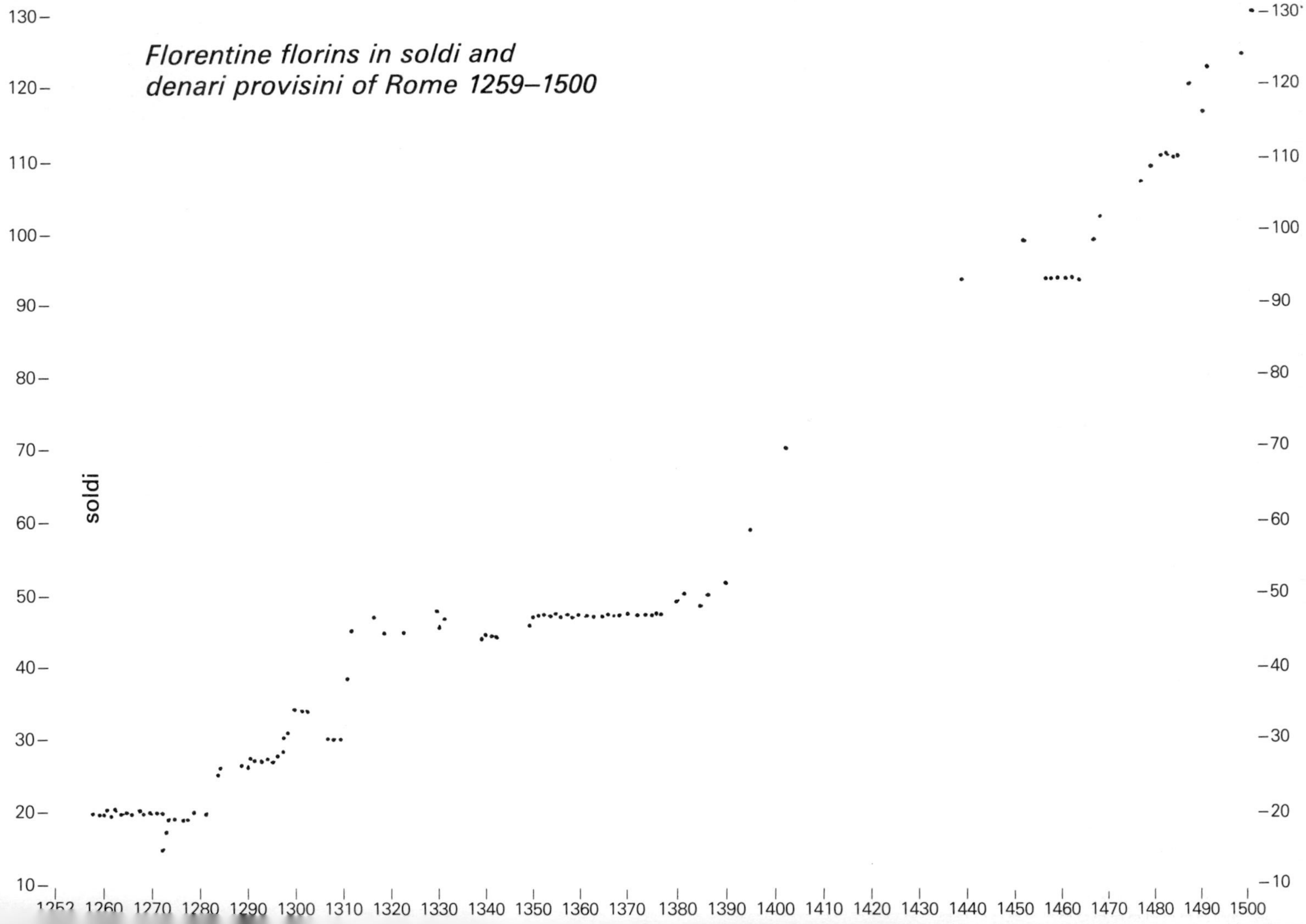

Florentine florins in soldi and denari provisini of Rome 1259–1500

THE FLORENTINE FLORIN IN SOLDI AND DENARI PROVISINI OF ROME

Date	Rate	Place	Type	Reference
1307	30 s.	Curia	B	(439) p.899
1309	30 s.	Curia	B	(439) p.899
1309	37 s.	Curia	C	(111) p.92
1310	30 s.	Curia	B	(439) p.899
1312	38 s.	Curia	B	(439) p.899
1313-1319	45 s.	Rome	B	(226) CXXVIII, 26
1317	47 s. 6 d.	Curia	C	(111) p.92
1323	42 s.	Curia	B	(439) p.900
1323	45 s.	Curia	B	(439) p.900
1323	47 s.	Curia	C	(111) p.92
1330-1331	48 s.	Curia	B	(439) p.901
1331-1333	45 s. 16(sic) d.	Rome	B	(226) CXXVIII, 26
1331	46 s. 6 d.	Curia	C	(111) p.92
1332	47 s.	Curia	C	(111) p.92
1339-1340	44 s.	Curia	B	(439) p.902
1339-1342	44 s.	Curia	C	(111) p.92
1349	46 s.	Curia	C	(111) p.92
1350-1379	47 s.	Curia	C	(111) p.93
1351-9	47 s.	Viterbo	A	(479) II p.383
1367.05.09	47 s.	Curia	B	(441) p.225
1377	47 s.	Avignon	B	(268) p.222
1377	48 s. 6 d.	Avignon	B	(268) p.222
1380	49 s.	Curia	C	(111) p.93
1381	50 s.	Curia	C	(111) p.93
1385	49 s.	Curia	C	(111) p.93
1386	50 s.	Curia	C	(111) p.93
1390	52 s. 6 d.	Curia	C	(111) p.93
1390	55 s.	Curia	C	(111) p.93
1395	58 s.	Curia	C	(111) p.93
1403	67 s. 9 d.	Curia	C	(111) p.93
1403	73 s.	Curia	C	(111) p.93
1439	93 s. 4 d.	Curia	C	(111) p.94
1452	98 s. 8 d.	Curia	C	(111) p.94
1456-1463	93 s. 4 d.	Curia	C	(111) p.94
1466	98 s. 8 d.	Curia	C	(111) p.94
1468-1475	102 s. 8 d.	Curia	C	(111) p.94
1476	106 s. 8 d.	Curia	C	(111) p.94
1478	109 s. 4 d.	Curia	C	(111) p.94
1480-1484	110 s. 8 d.	Curia	C	(111) p.94
1486	120 s.	Curia	C	(111) p.94
1489	116 s. 8 d.	Curia	C	(111) p.94
1490-1492	122 s. 8 d.	Curia	C	(111) p.94
1497	124 s. 8 d.	Curia	C	(111) p.94
1499-1501	130 s.	Curia	C	(111) p.94

The lira of Roman provisini in bolognini grossi

Date	Rate	Place	Type	Reference
1285	26 2/3 grossi	Rome	?	(401) p.306
1291.09.01	28 grossi	Orvieto	A	(179) p.63

For the carlino of Naples in soldi and denari provisini of Rome see under NAPLES p.64
For the Venetian grosso in denari provisini of Rome see under VENICE p.86
For the kreutzer in denari provisini of Rome see under TYROL p.94
For the lira of Pavia (papienses) in soldi and denari provisini of Rome see under PAVIA p.104
For the livre of Provins in soldi and denari provisini of Rome see under CHAMPAGNE FAIRS p.165
For the gros tournois in soldi and denari provisini of Rome see under FRANCE p.188
For the pound sterling in soldi and denari provisini of Rome see under ENGLAND p.208
For the besant in soldi and denari provisini of Rome see under BESANT p.294

Grossi of Rome

The romanino or grosso of Rome, introduced by the Senator Brancaleone d'Andolo, probably in 1253, began at the value of a roman soldo, 12 denari provisini. When it was first issued it was the largest silver coin in circulation in Europe, with a weight of 3.31 grams. Its value in provisini naturally increased as the silver content of the latter diminished, and by 1285, it was worth 29 provisini, (401) p.306: and, in 1296, 47 denari piccioli in Florence (31) p.161

The Florentine florin in grossi of Rome

Date	Rate	Place	Type	Reference
1290-1292	10 grossi	Curia	B	(439) p.898
1292	10 grossi	Curia	B	(439) p.898
1292	11 grossi	Curia	B	(439) p.898
1302	12 1/2 grossi	Curia	B	(439) p.899
1315	circa 12 1/2 grossi	Curia	B	(439) p.900

Paparini

The mint of Rome itself was controlled by the Senate, but the popes from Nicholas IV onwards minted denari papales (papalini or paparini) for the patrimony of St Peter from a mint at Viterbo.

The Florentine florin in soldi and denari paparini

Date	Rate	Place	Type	Reference
1297	35 s. 8 d.	Piedmont	A	(110) p.488
1305-1306	43 s. 4 d.	Curia	B	(439) p.899
1308	40 s.	Curia	B	(439) p.899
1308-1309	40 s.	Curia	A	(101) p.XVIII
1317	47 s.	Curia	B	(439) p.900
1324-1325	42 s. 6 d.	Curia	B	(439) p.901
1331	57 s.	Curia	B	(439) p.901
1332-1334	52 s.	Curia	B	(439) p.901
1335-1336	52 s.	Curia	B	(439) p.902
1337	54 s.	Curia	B	(439) p.902
1338	50 s.	Curia	B	(439) p.902
1341	54 s.	Curia	B	(439) p.902
1351-9	58 s.	Viterbo	A	(479) II p.383

The lira of paparini in soldi and denari of Cortona

Date	Rate	Place	Type	Reference
1351-9	30 s.	Viterbo	A	(479) II p.383

Papal bolognini

In the fifteenth century the popes also struck coins in imitation of those of Bologna (see below p.72). These derivative bolognini themselves became the basis of a money of account. The value of papal bolognini eventually diverged greatly from that of Bolognese bolognini. I trust that the following are all in terms of papal bolognini.

The Florentine florin in Papal soldi and denari bolognini

Date	Rate	Place	Type	Reference
1439	70 s.	Curia	C	(111) p.94
1452	74 s.	Curia	C	(111) p.94
1456-1463	70 s.	Curia	C	(111) p.94
1458	48 s.	Rome	M	(508) p.2
1466.01.13	68 s.	Viterbo	C	(108) V p.359
1466	74 s.	Curia	C	(111) p.94
1468-1475	77 s.	Curia	C	(111) p.94
1476	80 s.	Curia	C	(111) p.94
1478	82 s.	Curia	C	(111) p.94

THE FLORENTINE FLORIN IN PAPAL SOLDI AND DENARI BOLOGNINI

Date	Rate	Place	Type	Reference
1480	83 s.	Curia	C	(111) p.94
1484	82 s.	Curia	C	(111) p.94
1486	90 s.	Curia	C	(111) p.94
1489	87 s. 6 d.	Curia	C	(111) p.94
1490-1492	92 s.	Curia	C	(111) p.94
1497	93 s. 6 d.	Curia	C	(111) p.94
1499-1501	97 s. 6 d.	Curia	C	(111) p.94

The Venetian ducat in Papal soldi and denari bolognini

Date	Rate	Place	Type	Reference
1426	(?)55 s. 6 d.	Rome	C	(317) 1885, p.49
1458	(?)36 s.	Rome	M	(508) p.2
1458	48 s.	Rome	M	(508) p.2
1460	50 s.	Viterbo	C	(108) V p.82
1466.01.13	70 s.	Viterbo	C	(108) V p.359

For papal moneys of Avignon and the Comtat Venaissin see below pp.121-8

ANCONA

It is astonishing that no more quotations are available for the money of Ancona, for the grosso of Ancona (anconitani or agonitani) circulated widely in the northern part of the 'papal state' and were much imitated in the fifteenth century, in Ravenna, for example, and in Ascoli, Camerino and even Bologna.

The Florentine florin in soldi and denari of Ancona

Date	Rate	Place	Type	Reference
1329	43 s. 6 d.	Curia	B	(439) p.901
1348	42 s.	Genoa	C	(187B) f.763

The Florentine florin in grossi of Ancona

Date	Rate	Place	Type	Reference
1322	20 grossi	Curia	B	(439) p.900
1328	20 grossi	Curia	B	(439) p.901
1334	20 grossi	Curia	B	(439) p.901

SECTION III
NORTHERN ITALY

RAVENNA

Although the Emperor Henry IV authorised the archbishops of Ravenna to strike denari as early as 1063, minting of ravennantes does not seem to have begun there until the thirteenth century.

The Florentine florin in soldi and denari of Ravenna

Date	Rate	Place	Type	Reference
1278	28 s.	Ravenna	B	(439) p.112
1280	circa 27 s.	Curia	B	(439) p.897
1286	25 s. 8 d.	Ravenna	B	(439) p.112
1290-1292	26 s. 6 d.	Rome	B	(439) p.112
1290	26 s.	Curia	B	(439) p.898
1290	26 s. 6 d.	Curia	B	(439) p.898
1290	26 s. 7 d.	Rome	B	(439) p.112
1291.03.23	26 s. 10 d.	Pesaro	B	(179) p.89
1291.04.29	26 s. 6 d.	Ravenna	B	(179) p.97
1291.05.15	26 s. 10 d.	Orte	B	(179) p.94
1291	26 s. 10 d.	Rome	B	(439) p.122
1292	27 s. 6 d.	Ravenna	B	(439) p.112
1292	27 s.	Curia	B	(439) p.898
1298-1299	31 s.	Curia	B	(439) p.898
1298-1299	35 s. 8 d.	Curia	B	(439) p.898
1298	36 s.	Rome	B	(439) p.112
1299	32 s. 6 d.	Ravenna	B	(309) II p.14
1309	36 s.	Rome	B	(439) p.112
1324	45 s.	Avignon	B	(439) p.112
1327	49 s. 6 d.	Avignon	B	(439) p.112
1329	44 s.	Avignon	B	(439) p.112
1332	44 s. 6 d.	Curia	B	(439) p.901
1348	46 s.	Avignon	B	(439) p.112
1354	60 s.	Avignon	B	(439) p.112
1357	circa 55 s.	Avignon	B	(439) p.112
1360	46 s. 8 d.	Avignon	B	(439) p.112

The Venetian ducat in soldi and denari of Ravenna

Date	Rate	Place	Type	Reference
1357	60 s.	Avignon	B	(439) p.112

For the lira of Siena in soldi and denari of Ravenna see under SIENA p.57
For the Venetian grosso in denari of Ravenna see under VENICE p.86
For the besant in soldi and denari of Ravenna see under BESANT p.294

BOLOGNA

The city of Bologna was nominally within the patrimony of St Peter, but was effectively an autonomous state of its own. It acquired the right to strike money from the Emperor Henry VI in 1191, and its denari, and later grossi, were among the principal currencies of central and northern Italy. In the fifteenth century the coinage of Bologna had such a vogue that derivative bolognini were struck, notably by the popes, but also at a number of other cities: Milan, Ferrara, Mantua, Perugia and Lucca for example.

The Florentine florin in soldi and denari of Bologna

Date	Rate	Place	Type	Reference
1264	24 s.	Curia	B	(439) p.896
1266-1267	27 s. 6 d.	Curia	B	(439) p.896
1267	27 s. 6 d.	Curia	B	(439) p.79
1267	27 s. 5 d.	Bologna	B	(439) p.74
1280-1282	31 s. 6 d.	Curia	B	(439) p.897
1280-1282	33 s.	Curia	B	(439) p.897
1284	30 s. 2 d.	Curia	B	(439) p.897
1285	30 s. 1 d.	Bologna	B	(111) p.74
1286	31 s.	Curia	B	(439) p.897
1286	30 s. 7 d.	Bologna	B	(111) p.74
1288-1291	30 s. 6 d.	Bologna	B	(111) p.74
1288	30 s. 6 d.	Curia	B	(439) p.898
1290	30 s.	Curia	B	(439) p.898
1291.09.01	35 s.	Orvieto	B	(179) p.63
1291-1292	30 s. 6 d.	Curia	B	(439) p.898
1291	30 s. 6 d.	Bologna	B	(179) p.98
1292-1294	30 s.	Bologna	C	(111) p.74
1296	30 s.	Curia	B	(439) p.898
1297	33 s. 6 d.	Bologna	C	(111) p.74
1298	40 s.	Curia	B	(439) p.898
1305	40 s.	Curia	B	(439) p.899
1305	41 s.	Bologna	C	(111) p.74
1312	40 s.	Curia	B	(439) p.79
1313	44 s. 4 d.	Curia	B	(439) p.79
1313	44 s. 4 d.	Bologna	C	(111) p.74
1316	40 s. 2 d.	Curia	B	(439) p.79
1319-1322	40 s.	Bologna	C	(111) p.74
1323	42 s. 6 d.	Curia	B	(439) p.79
1323	46 s. 6 d.	Bologna	C	(111) p.74
1326.04	40 s.	Curia	B	(439) p.79
1326.05	38 s. 6 d.	Curia	B	(439) p.79
1328	40 s. 10 d.	Curia	B	(439) p.79
1330	41 s.	Curia	B	(439) p.901
1330	40 s. 6 d.	Bologna	C	(111) p.74
1330	44 s.	Curia	B	(439) p.901
1331	40 s.	Bologna	C	(111) p.74
1331	42 s.	Bologna	C	(111) p.74
1332	44 s.	Bologna	C	(111) p.74
1333	36 s.	Curia	B	(439) p.901
1333	33 s.	Curia	B	(439) p.901
1334	40 s.	Curia	B	(439) p.901
1336-1339	36 s.	Curia	B	(439) p.79
1336	36 s.	Curia	B	(439) p.902
1336	41 s.	Curia	B	(439) p.79
1337	39 s.	Curia	B	(439) p.902
1337	35 s.	Bologna	C	(111) p.74
1338-1339	36 s.	Bologna	C	(111) p.74
1338	36 s.	Curia	B	(439) p.902
1338	39 s.	Curia	B	(439) p.902
1348	31 s. 8 d.	Bologna	C	(111) p.74
1349-1362	32 s.	Bologna	C	(111) p.75
1350-1352	34 s.	Curia	B	(439) p.79
1350-1352	32 s.	Curia	B	(439) p.79
1350.04	27 s.	Curia	B	(439) p.79
1350.07	28 s.	Curia	B	(439) p.79
1352	32 s.	Bologna	B	(439) p.79
1359	33 s.	Bologna	B	(56) p.418

Throughout the years 1360-4 the official value of the Florentine florin in bologna was 32 soldi of bolognini. The following figures indicate for how much of this period the market value exceeded the official values. They are mostly taken from a much fuller series, published with graphs and commentary by Antonia Borlandi (56).

Date	Rate	Place	Type	Reference
1360.04.01	33 s. 1 d.	Bologna	C	(479) II p.418
1360.04.15	32 s. 10 d.	Bologna	C	(479) II p.418
1360.04.30	33 s.	Bologna	C	(56) p.455
1360.05.30	32 s. 3 d.	Bologna	C	(479) II p.418
1360.05.31	32 s. 3 d.	Bologna	C	(56) p.455
1360.06.01	32 s.	Bologna	C	(479) II p.418
1360.06.16	31 s.	Bologna	C	(479) II p.418

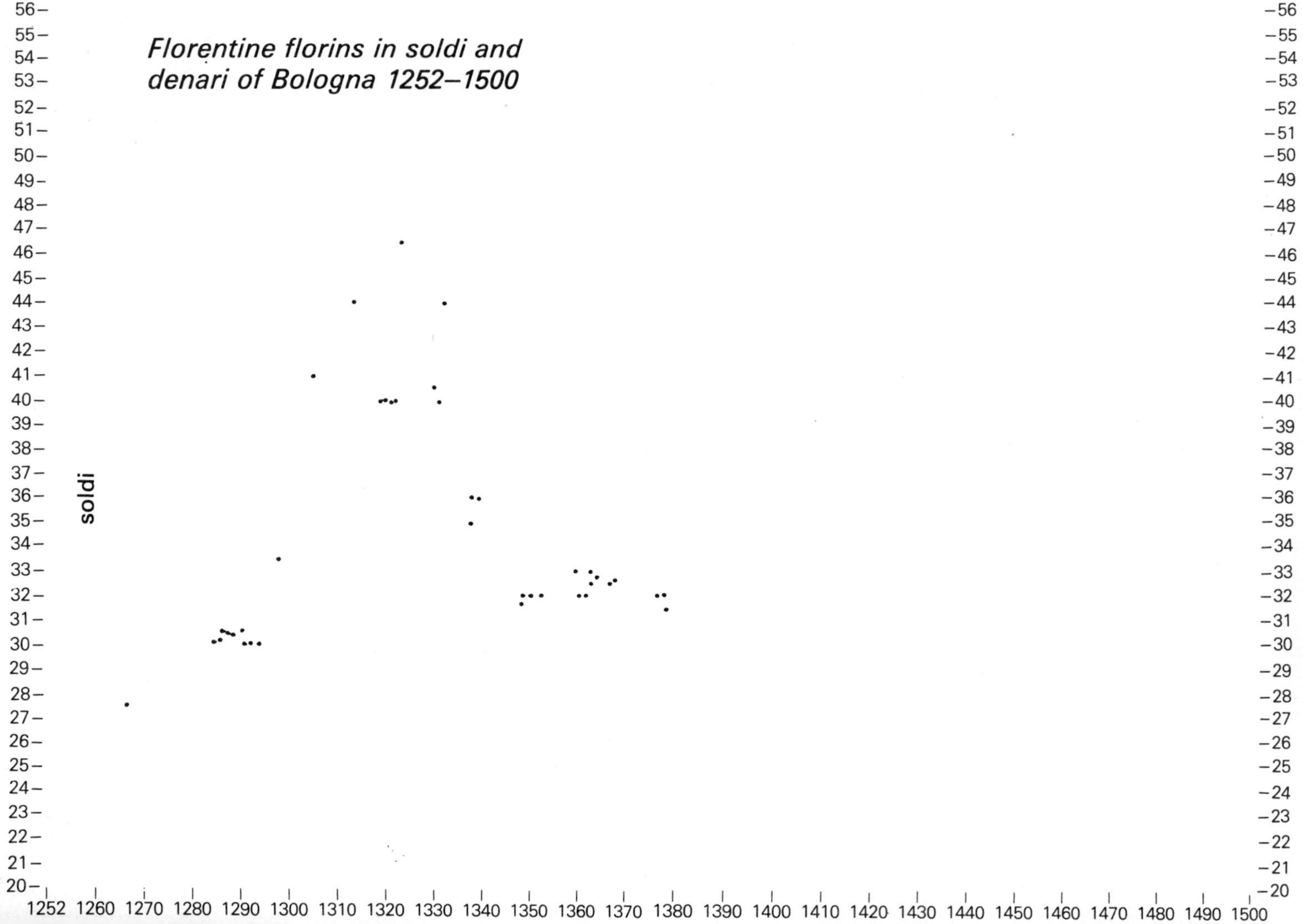

Florentine florins in soldi and denari of Bologna 1252–1500

soldi

56 55 54 53 52 51 50 49 48 47 46 45 44 43 42 41 40 39 38 37 36 35 34 33 32 31 30 29 28 27 26 25 24 23 22 21 20

1252 1260 1270 1280 1290 1300 1310 1320 1330 1340 1350 1360 1370 1380 1390 1400 1410 1420 1430 1440 1450 1460 1470 1480 1490 1500

THE FLORENTINE FLORIN IN SOLDI AND DENARI OF BOLOGNA

Date	Rate	Place	Type	Reference
1360.06.30	31 s.	Bologna	C	(56) p.456
1360.07.31	31 s. 3 d.	Bologna	C	(56) p.456
1360.08.01	31 s. 3 d.	Bologna	C	(479) II p.418
1360.08.31	30 s. 9 d.	Bologna	C	(56) p.457
1360.09.10	30 s.	Bologna	C	(479) II p.418
1360.09.16	29 s.	Bologna	C	(479) II p.418
1360.09.30	30 s. 4 d.	Bologna	C	(56) p.457
1360.10.31	31 s. 10 1/2 d.	Bologna	C	(56) p.458
1360.11.30	32 s.	Bologna	C	(56) p.458
1360.12.01	32 s. 5 d.	Bologna	C	(479) II p.418
1360.12.31	32 s. 4 d.	Bologna	C	(56) p.459
1361.01.01	32 s. 3 d.	Bologna	C	(479) II p.418
1361.01.31	32 s. 5 d.	Bologna	C	(56) p.459
1361.02.28	32 s. 7 d.	Bologna	C	(56) p.459
1361.03.31	32 s. 8 d.	Bologna	C	(56) p.460
1361.04.01	32 s. 8 d.	Bologna	C	(479) II p.418
1361.04.30	33 s. 2 d.	Bologna	C	(56) p.460
1361.05.01	33 s. 1 d.	Bologna	C	(479) II p.418
1361.05.31	32 s. 9 d.	Bologna	C	(56) p.461
1361.07.01	31 s. 5 d.	Bologna	C	(479) II p.418
1361.06.30-07.31	32 s.	Bologna	C	(56) p.462
1361.08.31	32 s. 4 d.	Bologna	C	(56) p.462
1361.09.30	32 s. 9 d.	Bologna	C	(56) p.463
1361.10.01	32 s. 11 d.	Bologna	C	(479) II p.418
1361.10.31	33 s. 2 1/2 d.	Bologna	C	(56) p.463
1361.11.30	33 s. 2 1/2 d.	Bologna	C	(56) p.464
1361.12.01	33 s. 2 d.	Bologna	C	(479) II p.418
1361.12.31-1362.01.31	33 s. 7 d.	Bologna	C	(56) p.465
1362.02.28	33 s. 6 d.	Bologna	C	(56) p.465
1362.03.31	33 s. 6 1/2 d.	Bologna	C	(56) p.466
1362.04.30	33 s. 5 d.	Bologna	C	(56) p.466
1362.05.31-06.30	33 s.	Bologna	C	(56) p.467
1362.07.31	33 s. 3 d.	Bologna	C	(56) p.467
1362.08.31	33 s.	Bologna	C	(56) p.468
1362.09.30	33 s. 1 1/2 d.	Bologna	C	(56) p.468
1362.10.31	32 s. 11 d.	Bologna	C	(56) p.469
1362.11.30	33 s. 1 d.	Bologna	C	(56) p.469
1362.12.31	33 s.	Bologna	C	(56) p.470
1363.01.31-02.28	33 s. 1 d.	Bologna	C	(56) p.470
1363.03.31-04.30	33 s.	Bologna	C	(56) p.471
1363.05.31	32 s. 9 d.	Bologna	C	(56) p.472
1363.06.30	32 s. 4 d.	Bologna	C	(56) p.472
1363.07.31	32 s. 6 d.	Bologna	C	(56) p.472
1363.08.31	32 s. 8 d.	Bologna	C	(56) p.473
1363.09.30	32 s. 7 1/2 d.	Bologna	C	(56) p.474
1363.10.31	32 s. 9 d.	Bologna	C	(56) p.474
1363.11.30	32 s. 5 d.	Bologna	C	(56) p.475
1364.01.02	32 s. 4 d.	Bologna	C	(479) II p.418
1364.01.31	31 s. 10 d. (sic)	Bologna	C	(56) p.476
1364.02.01	32 s. 10 d.	Bologna	C	(479) II p.418
1364.02.29	32 s. 11 d.	Bologna	C	(56) p.476
1364.04.01	32 s. 8 d.	Bologna	C	(479) II p.418
1364.04.30	32 s. 10 d.	Bologna	C	(56) p.477
1364.05.31	32 s. 10 d.	Bologna	C	(56) p.477
1367.05.31	32 s. 6 d.	Curia	B	(441) p.224
1368-1381	31 s. 6 d.	Bologna	C	(111) p.75
1368	32 s. 8 d.	Bologna	C	(56) p.407
1369.06.22	33 s.	Curia	B	(28) p.675
1376.06.16	32 s.	Bologna	B	(438) p.29
1376.10.14	31 s. 6 d.	Bologna	B	(438) p.30
1377.06.17	32 s.	Bologna	B	(438) p.33
1378.03.16	31 s. 6 d.	Bologna	B	(438) p.38
1378.04.24	31 s. 6 d.	Bologna	B	(438) p.40
1392.10.04	36 s.	Pistoia	B	(24) p.330
1435	33 s. 3 d.	Rome	B	(309) p.25
1436.08.01-1437.01	41 s. 6 d.	Perugia	O	(500) p.79
1439	41 s. 24 d. (sic)	Perugia	O	(500) p.79
1457	40 s.	Perugia	O	(367) p.219
1458	35 s.	Bologna	M	(508) p.2
1465	36 s.	Perugia	O	(367) p.293
1473	40 s.	Perugia	O	(367) p.362
1474	40 s.	Perugia	O	(367) p.383

The florin of Savona in soldi and denari of Bologna

The Florin of Savona, first issued in 1350, and identical in weight and fineness with the Florentine florin, was officially accepted in Bologna from 1361 to 1364 on a par with the Florentine florin, at 32 soldi bolognini. The following quotations, extracted from the fuller series published by Antonia Borlandi (56) indicate how much less the market valued the Savona florin.

Date	Rate	Place	Type	Reference
1361.02.20	31 s. 4 d.	Bologna	C	(56) p.459
1361.03.01	31 s. 4 1/2 d.	Bologna	M	(479) II p.418
1361.03.31	31 s. 5 d.	Bologna	C	(56) p. 460
1361.04.01	31 s. 5 d.	Bologna	M	(479) II p.418
1361.04.30	31 s. 6 d.	Bologna	C	(56) p. 460
1361.05.31	31 s. 1 d.	Bologna	C	(56) p. 461
1361.06.30-07.31	30 s. 7 d.	Bologna	C	(56) p.462
1361.08.31	30 s. 5 d.	Bologna	C	(56) p.462
1361.09.30	31 s.	Bologna	C	(56) p.463
1361.10.01	31 s. 1 d.	Bologna	M	(479) II p.418
1361.10.31-11.30	31 s. 5 d.	Bologna	C	(56) p.464
1361.12.31	31 s. 11 d.	Bologna	C	(56) p.464
1362.01.01	31 s. 11 1/2 d.	Bologna	M	(479) II p.418
1362.01.31	32 s.	Bologna	C	(56) p.465
1362.02.28	31 s. 11 1/2 d.	Bologna	C	(56) p.465
1362.03.31	31 s. 11 d.	Bologna	C	(56) p.466
1362.04.30	31 s. 9 1/2 d.	Bologna	C	(56) p.466
1362.05.31	31 s. 8 d.	Bologna	C	(56) p.466
1362.06.30	31 s. 6 d.	Bologna	C	(56) p.467
1362.07.31	31 s. 8 d.	Bologna	C	(56) p.467
1362.08.31	31 s. 8 1/2 d.	Bologna	C	(56) p.468
1362.09.30	31 s. 7 d.	Bologna	C	(56) p.468
1362.10.31	31 s. 4 1/2 d.	Bologna	C	(56) p.469
1362.11.01	31 s. 5 d.	Bologna	M	(479) II p.418
1362.11.30	31 s. 5 d.	Bologna	C	(56) p.469
1362.12.01	31 s. 5 1/2 d.	Bologna	M	(479) II p.418
1362.12.31	31 s. 5 1/2 d.	Bologna	C	(56) p.470
1363.01.31	31 s. 2 1/2 d.	Bologna	C	(56) p.470
1363.02.28	31 s. 4 1/2 d.	Bologna	C	(56) p.470
1363.03.31	31 s.	Bologna	C	(56) p.471
1363.05.31	30 s. 8 1/4 d.	Bologna	C	(56) p.472
1363.06.30	31 s. 6 d.	Bologna	C	(56) p.472
1363.07.31	31 s. 1 1/2 d.	Bologna	C	(56) p.473
1363.08.31	30 s. 9 d.	Bologna	C	(56) p.473
1363.09.30	30 s. 1 d.	Bologna	C	(56) p.474
1363.10.31	29 s. 10 d.	Bologna	C	(56) p.474
1364.01.03	30 s.	Bologna	C	(479) II p.418
1364.01.31	30 s. 5 1/2 d.	Bologna	C	(56) p.476
1364.02.29	30 s. 8 d.	Bologna	C	(56) p.476
1364.04.30	30 s. 6 d.	Bologna	C	(56) p.477
1364.05.31	29 s. 10 d.	Bologna	C	(56) p.477
1364.06.30	29 s. 2 d.	Bologna	C	(56) p.478
1374	31 s. 6 d.	Bologna	C	(56) p.407

The Venetian ducat in soldi and denari of Bologna

From 1360-1364 the official rate for the Venetian Ducat was 34 soldi bolognini. For fuller details of the relationship between the official rate and market rate see Antonia Borlandi (56).

Date	Rate	Place	Type	Reference
1360.04.01	33 s. 8 d.	Bologna	C	(479) II p.418
1360.04.05	33 s. 6 d.	Bologna	C	(479) II p.418
1360.04.10	33 s. 7 1/2 d.	Bologna	C	(479) II p.418
1360.04.30	33 s. 9 1/2 d.	Bologna	C	(56) p.455
1360.05.01	33 s. 8 1/2 d.	Bologna	C	(479) II p.418
1360.05.15	33 s. 5 1/2 d.	Bologna	C	(479) II p.418
1360.05.31	33 s. 5 d.	Bologna	C	(56) p.455
1360.06.01	33 s. 4 d.	Bologna	C	(479) II p.418
1360.06.15	33 s.	Bologna	C	(479) II p.418
1360.06.20	32 s. 6 d.	Bologna	C	(479) II p.418

THE VENETIAN DUCAT IN SOLDI AND DENARI OF BOLOGNA

Date	Rate	Place	Type	Reference
1360.06.30	32 s. 7 d.	Bologna	C	(56) p.456
1360.07.01	32 s. 8 1/2 d.	Bologna	C	(479) II p.418
1360.07.31	32 s. 7 d.	Bologna	C	(56) p.456
1360.08.01	32 s. 6 1/4 d.	Bologna	C	(479) II p.418
1360.08.31	32 s. 7 d.	Bologna	C	(56) p.457
1360.09.01	31 s. 10 d.	Bologna	C	(479) II p.418
1360.09.16	30 s. 10 d.	Bologna	C	(479) II p.418
1360.09.30	31 s. 7 d.	Bologna	C	(56) p.457
1360.10.01	31 s. 8 d.	Bologna	C	(479) II p.418
1360.10.10	33 s. 10 d.	Bologna	C	(479) II p.418
1360.10.31	32 s. 11 d.	Bologna	C	(56) p.458
1360.11.01	32 s. 10 1/2 d.	Bologna	C	(479) II p.418
1360.11.30	33 s. 3 d.	Bologna	C	(56) p.458
1360.12.01	33 s. 5 d.	Bologna	C	(479) II p.418
1360.12.31	33 s. 5 1/2 d.	Bologna	C	(56) p.459
1361.01.02	33 s. 2 1/2 d.	Bologna	C	(479) II p.418
1361.01.20	33 s. 7 1/2 d.	Bologna	C	(479) II p.418
1361.01.31	33 s. 7 1/4 d.	Bologna	C	(56) p.459
1361.02.01	33 s. 6 1/2 d.	Bologna	C	(479) II p.418
1361.02.10	33 s. 3 d.	Bologna	C	(479) II p.418
1361.02.28	33 s. 6 1/2 d.	Bologna	C	(56) p.459
1361.03.01	33 s. 6 d.	Bologna	C	(479) II p.418
1361.03.15	33 s. 4 d.	Bologna	C	(479) II p.418
1361.03.25	33 s. 4 3/4 d.	Bologna	C	(479) II p.418
1361.03.31	33 s. 4 3/4 d.	Bologna	C	(56) p.460
1361.04.01	33 s. 5 1/2 d.	Bologna	C	(479) II p.418
1361.04.30	33 s. 6 d.	Bologna	C	(56) p.460
1361.05.01	33 s. 6 d.	Bologna	C	(479) II p.418
1361.05.31	33 s. 1 1/2 d.	Bologna	C	(56) p.461
1361.06.01	33 s. 2 d.	Bologna	C	(479) II p.418
1361.06.30	32 s. 7 d.	Bologna	C	(56) p.461
1361.07.31	32 s. 6 d.	Bologna	C	(56) p.462
1361.08.31	32 s. 7 1/2 d.	Bologna	C	(56) p.462
1361.09.30	33 s. 1 d.	Bologna	C	(56) p.463
1361.10.01	33 s. 2 d.	Bologna	C	(479) II p.418
1361.10.31	33 s. 6 1/2 d.	Bologna	C	(56) p.463
1361.11.30	33 s. 7 d.	Bologna	C	(56) p.464
1361.12.01	33 s. 8 d.	Bologna	C	(479) II p.418
1361.12.25	34 s. 4 d.	Bologna	C	(479) II p.418
1361.12.31	34 s. 4 d.	Bologna	C	(56) p.464
1362.01.31	34 s.	Bologna	C	(56) p.465
1362.02.28	34 s. 1/2 d.	Bologna	C	(56) p.465
1362.03.31	33 s. 11 d.	Bologna	C	(56) p.466
1362.04.30	33 s. 10 d.	Bologna	C	(56) p.466
1362.05.31	33 s. 6 1/2 d.	Bologna	C	(56) p.466
1362.06.30	33 s. 6 d.	Bologna	C	(56) p.467
1362.07.31	33 s. 8 1/2 d.	Bologna	C	(56) p.467
1362.08.31	33 s. 9 d.	Bologna	C	(56) p.468
1362.09.30	33 s. 7 1/2 d.	Bologna	C	(56) p.468
1362.10.31	33 s. 6 d.	Bologna	C	(56) p.469
1362.11.30	33 s. 6 1/2 d.	Bologna	C	(56) p.469
1362.12.31	33 s. 7 1/2 d.	Bologna	C	(56) p.470
1363.01.31	33 s. 7 d.	Bologna	C	(56) p.470
1363.02.28	33 s. 11 d.	Bologna	C	(56) p.470
1363.03.31	33 s. 9 d.	Bologna	C	(56) p.471
1363.04.30	33 s. 7 d.	Bologna	C	(56) p.471
1363.05.31	33 s. 1/4 d.	Bologna	C	(56) p.472
1363.06.30	33 s. 1 d.	Bologna	C	(56) p.472
1363.07.31	33 s. 2 d.	Bologna	C	(56) p.473
1363.08.31	33 s. 3 d.	Bologna	C	(56) p.473
1363.09.30	33 s. 1 d.	Bologna	C	(56) p.474
1363.10.31	33 s. 6 d.	Bologna	C	(56) p.474
1363.12.31	33 s. 5 d.	Bologna	C	(56) p.475
1364.01.02	33 s. 5 1/2 d.	Bologna	C	(479) II p.418
1364.01.31	33 s. 10 1/2 d.	Bologna	C	(56) p.476
1364.04.01	32 s. 8 d.	Bologna	C	(479) II p.418
1364.04.30	33 s. 7 d.	Bologna	C	(56) p.477
1364.05.31	33 s. 2 d.	Bologna	C	(56) p.477
1364.06.30	33 s. 1 d.	Bologna	C	(56) p.478
1375	34 s.	Piedmont	A	(110) p.500

The florin of Bologna (bolognino d'oro) in soldi and denari of Bologna

In 1380 the city of Bologna began the issue of its own gold coin, the bolognino d'oro, at a weight of 3.55 grams. It was thus similar in weight and fineness to the Venetian ducat, and hence very slightly heavier than the Florentine florin.

Date	Rate	Place	Type	Reference
1382-1383	32 s.	Bologna	C	(111) p.76
1384-1387	35 s.	Bologna	C	(111) p.77
1388	35 s. 4 d.	Bologna	C	(111) p.77
1389	36 s.	Bologna	C	(111) p.77
1390-1393	37 s.	Bologna	C	(111) p.77
1394	37 s. 1 d.	Bologna	C	(111) p.77
1395	36 s. 6 d.	Bologna	C	(111) p.77
1398	37 s.	Bologna	C	(111) p.77
1399	35 s.	Bologna	C	(111) p.77
1400	36 s.	Bologna	C	(111) p.77
1401-1407	37 s.	Bologna	C	(111) p.77
1408	35 s.	Bologna	C	(111) p.77
1409-1410	37 s.	Bologna	C	(111) p.77
1411	38 s.	Bologna	C	(111) p.77
1412	39 s.	Bologna	C	(111) p.77
1413	40 s.	Bologna	C	(111) p.77
1414	39 s. 5 1/2 d.	Bologna	C	(111) p.77
1415	39 s.	Bologna	C	(111) p.77
1416	40 s.	Bologna	C	(111) p.77
1417	39 s.	Bologna	C	(111) p.77
1418-1419	37 s.	Bologna	C	(111) p.77
1420-1421	39 s.	Bologna	C	(111) p.77
1422-1423	38 s.	Bologna	C	(111) p.77
1422-1423	40 s.	Bologna	C	(111) p.77
1425-1427	40 s.	Bologna	C	(111) p.77
1428	41 s. 6 d.	Bologna	C	(111) p.77
1429	43 s.	Bologna	C	(111) p.77
1430	43 s. 6 d.	Bologna	C	(111) p.77
1431	42 s. 6 d.	Bologna	C	(111) p.77
1432	43 s. 6 d.	Bologna	C	(111) p.77
1433-1434	44 s.	Bologna	C	(111) p.77
1436	44 s. 5 d.	Bologna	C	(111) p.77
1437	43 s.	Bologna	C	(111) p.77
1438	45 s.	Bologna	C	(111) p.77
1439-1440	44 s.	Bologna	C	(111) p.77
1441	48 s.	Bologna	C	(111) p.77
1446	46 s.	Bologna	C	(111) p.77
1449	48 s. 6 d.	Bologna	C	(111) p.77
1450	49 s.	Bologna	C	(111) p.77
1451	49 s.	Bologna	C	(111) p.78
1452	49 s. 6 d.	Bologna	C	(111) p.78
1453-1454	50 s.	Bologna	C	(111) p.78
1455	53 s.	Bologna	C	(111) p.78
1456	57 s.	Bologna	C	(111) p.78
1458	56 s.	Bologna	C	(111) p.78
1459	57 s. 6 d.	Bologna	C	(111) p.78
1460-1463	56 s.	Bologna	C	(111) p.78
1464	55 s.	Bologna	C	(111) p.78
1465-1466	56 s.	Bologna	C	(111) p.78
1467-1471	57 s.	Bologna	C	(111) p.78
1475	56 s.	Bologna	C	(111) p.78
1478	59 s. 10 d.	Bologna	C	(111) p.78
1479	58 s. 6 d.	Bologna	C	(111) p.78
1483	58 s.	Bologna	C	(111) p.78
1485	60 s.	Bologna	C	(111) p.78
1487-1490	62 s.	Bologna	C	(111) p.78
1494-1495	64 s.	Bologna	C	(111) p.78
1500	70 s.	Bologna	C	(111) p.78

Bolognini d'oro in soldi and denari of Bologna 1382–1500

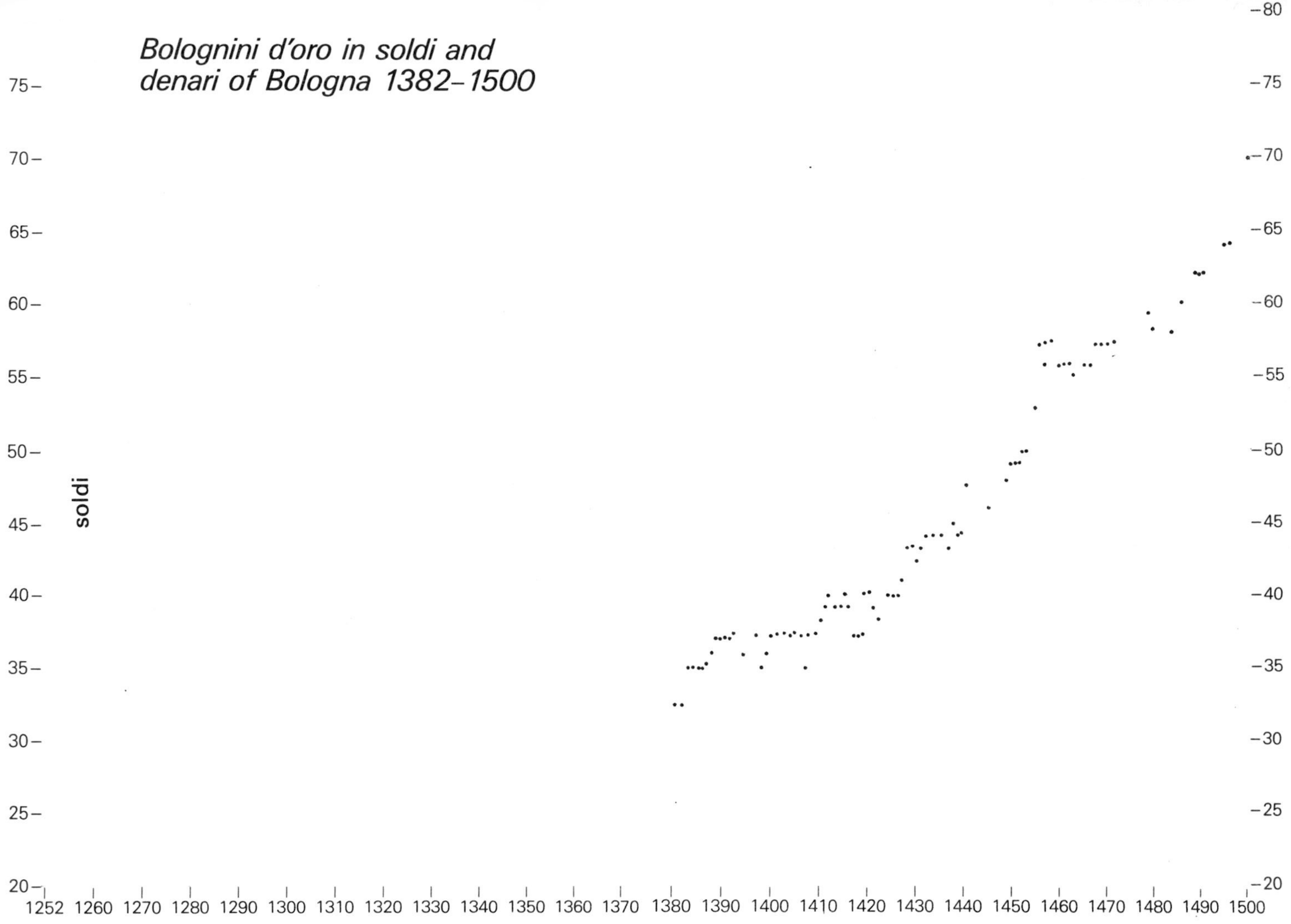

The lira of Bologna in soldi and denari of Lucca

Date	Rate	Place	Type	Reference
1243.01.22	16 s.	Lucca	A	(48)

The lira of Bologna in soldi and denari of Pisa

Date	Rate	Place	Type	Reference
1211	54 s. 6 d.	Florence	HB	(444) I p.10
1220	16 s. 3 1/2 d.	Florence	M	(31) III p.130

For the lira of provisini of Rome in bolognini grossi see under ROME p.69
For the lira imperiale in soldi and denari of Bologna see under MILAN p.102
For the lira of Genoa in soldi and denari of Bologna see under GENOA p.107

FERRARA

The only references to the money of Ferrara that I have found appear under MILAN p.102

VENICE

The accounting systems in use at various times in late medieval Venice were at least as complex and diverse as those in late medieval Florence. For most of the twelfth century, the Venetians used Veronese money for internal accounting purposes, although denari had for some time been intermittently struck in Venice in the name of an Emperor 'Henry'. (For the money of Verona see p.93)

However, from Vitale Michiel II (doge 1156-72) onwards distinctively Venetian denari were struck in the name of the ruling Doge, and from the 1180s, accounting was carried out in terms of Venetian money. After the introduction of grossi these denari were known as piccoli. The Venetian section therefore begins with the rates for the Florentine florin and the Venetian ducat in soldi and denari piccoli of Venice. After these will be found a great diversity of rates relating to the grosso, first 'di grossi', and then 'a grossi'.

See below p.85 for the lira di grossi and the lira di piccoli and for internal rates between the grosso and the piccolo
See below pp.85-6 for rates for the Florentine florin and the Venetian ducat in grossi
See below p.86 for external rates for the grosso and the lira di grossi in other currencies in the thirteenth century
See below p.87 for the lira di grossi in lire, soldi and denari affiorino of Florence
See below p.91 for the lira di grossi a oro
See below p.92 for the lira a grossi and for rates for the ducat in soldi and denari a grossi

The Florentine florin in soldi and denari piccoli of Venice

Date	Rate	Place	Type	Reference
1275-1276	52 s.	Venice	A	(284) I
1277-1279	53 s. 4 d.	Venice	A	(284) I
1280	49 s.	Venice	A	(284) I
1280	53 s. 4 d.	Venice	A	(284) I
1281-1286	40 s. 1 d.	Hungary	B	(404) I p.9

The Venetian ducat

In 1284 the Venetians began striking their own gold coin, the ducato d'oro. At 3.56 grams it was very slightly heavier than the Florentine and Genoese florins. For internal purposes the ducat at once supplanted the florin.

The Venetian ducat in soldi and denari piccoli of Venice

Date	Rate	Place	Type	Reference
1284.10.31	48 s.	Venice	O	(111) p.69
1284-1286	50 s. 8 d.	Venice	A	(284) I
1284-1286	53 s. 4 d.	Venice	A	(284) I
1285	49 s.	Venice	O	(284) I
1288-1289	circa 52 s.	Venice	A	(284) I
1290	49 s. 4 d.	Venice	A	(284) I
1290	53 s. 4 d.	Venice	A	(284) I
1291	49 s. 4 d.	Venice	A	(284) I
1292-1298	53 s. 4 d.	Venice	A	(284) I
1300-1302	64 s.	Venice	A	(284) I
1305	64 s.	Venice	A	(284) I
1309	64 s.	Venice	A	(284) I
1310	64 s.	Venice	C	(111) p.69
1314.10.30	65 s. 10 d.	Venice	A	(284) I
1317	67 s. 2 d.	Venice	A	(284) I
1319	64 s.	Venice	A	(284) I
1320	64 s.	Venice	A	(284) I
1320	66 s.	Venice	C	(111) p.69
1322	64 s.	Venice	A	(284) I
1323	64 s.	Venice	A	(284) I
1324	64 s.	Venice	A	(284) I
1326	64 s.	Venice	A	(284) I
1328.09.12-1351	64 s.	Venice	O	(111) p.69
1329	66 s. 1 d.	Venice	A	(284) I
1329.09.09	68 s.	Venice	A	(284) I
1330	67 s. 11 d.	Venice	A	(284) I
1331	70 s.	Venice	C	(345) p.60
1331.09.17	70 s.	Venice	A	(284) I
1333	64 s.	Venice	A	(284) I
1335	64 s.	Venice	A	(284) I
1337.09.11	65 s. 2 d.	Venice	A	(284) I
1338.06.26	66 s. 8 d.	Venice	A	(284) I
1338.11.28	66 s. 6 d.	Venice	A	(284) I
1339.01.09	66 s. 6 d.	Venice	A	(284) I
1340.11.01	64 s.	Venice	A	(284) I
1341	68 s.	Venice	A	(284) I
1342.07.24	64 s.	Venice	A	(284) I
1345.01.29	66 s. 8 d.	Venice	A	(284) I
1345	circa 70 s.	Venice	C	(345) p.60
1349-50	64 s.	Venice	C	(345) p.60
1351	63 s.	Venice	A	(284) I
1352-1353	66 s.	Venice	C	(111) p.69
1353.02.18	64 s. 6 d.	Venice	A	(284) I
1354	71 s.	Venice	A	(284) I
1356	66 s.	Venice	A	(284) I
1356	68 s.	Venice	C	(111) p.69
1357-1360	70 s.	Venice	C	(111) p.69
1357.01.27	69 s. 8 1/2 d.	Venice	A	(284) I
1358.08.17	70 s.	Venice	A	(284) I
1359	68 s.	Venice	A	(284) I
1359.08.17	71 s. 8 d.	Venice	A	(284) I
1360.06.27	72 s.	Venice	A	(284) I
1361	70 s.	Venice	A	(284) I
1361.06.17	73 s.	Venice	A	(284) I
1362.04.29	72 s.	Venice	A	(284) I
1362.05	74 s.	Venice	A	(284) I
1363.05.06	74 s.	Venice	A	(284) I
1364.06.22	74 s.	Venice	A	(284) I
1365.08.23	74 s.	Venice	A	(284) I
1366.06.20	74 s.	Venice	A	(284) I
1367.04.12	74 s.	Venice	A	(284) I
1368.07.01	74 s.	Venice	A	(284) I
1369.02.10	74 s.	Venice	A	(284) I
1370.02.12	72 s.	Venice	A	(284) I

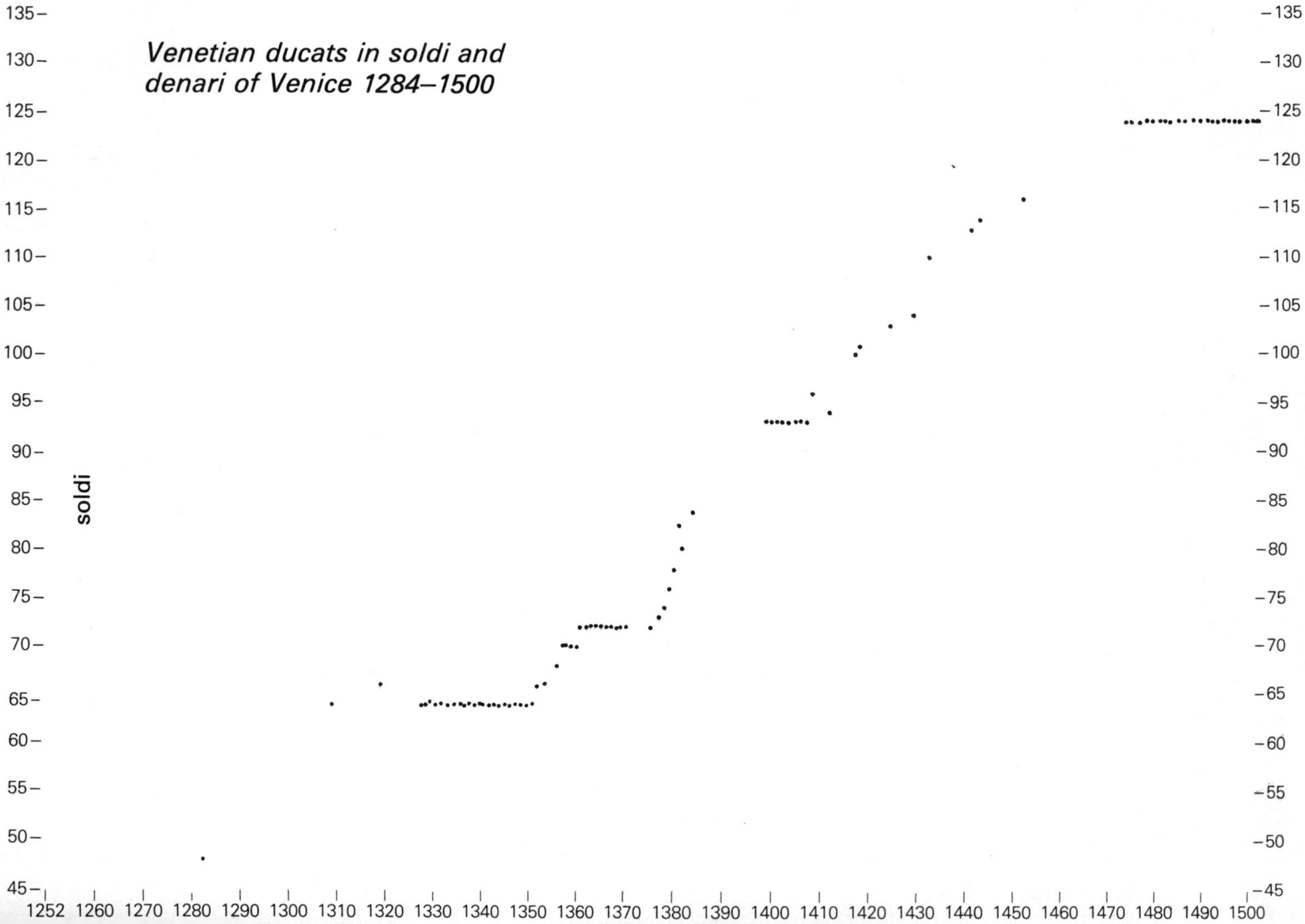

Venetian ducats in soldi and denari of Venice 1284–1500

THE VENETIAN DUCAT IN SOLDI AND DENARI PICCOLI OF VENICE

Date	Rate	Place	Type	Reference
1370.05.31	70 s.	Venice	A	(284) I
1371.02.24	70 s.	Venice	A	(284) I
1371.11.14	71 s.	Venice	A	(284) I
1373.02.04	72 s. 4 d.	Venice	A	(284) I
1373.08.09	70 s. 4 d.	Venice	A	(284) I
1374.02.17	72 s.	Venice	A	(284) I
1374.05.30	73 s.	Venice	A	(284) I
1374.09.13	71 s.	Venice	A	(284) I
1375	72 s.	Piedmont	A	(110) p.500
1375.02.16	73 s.	Venice	A	(284) I
1375.06.16	73 s. 4 d.	Venice	A	(284) I
1376.03.15	73 s. 3 d.	Venice	A	(284) I
1376.08.13	73 s. 6 d.	Venice	A	(284) I
1377	73 s.	Venice	C	(111) p.69
1377.05.02	74 s.	Venice	A	(284) I
1378	74 s.	Venice	C	(111) p.69
1378.10.27	76 s.	Venice	A	(284) I
1379	76 s.	Venice	C	(111) p.69
1379.02.18	76 s.	Venice	A	(284) I
1379.07.09	77 s.	Venice	O	(284) I
1380	78 s.	Venice	C	(111) p.69
1380.03.03	81 s.	Venice	A	(284) I
1380.07.17	83 s. 6 d.	Ferrara	B	(358) p.58 n.2
1380.09.28	85 s.	Venice	A	(284) I
1380	86 s.	Venice	C	(111) p.69
1381.05.09	85 s.	Venice	A	(284) I
1381	82 s. 6 d.	Venice	C	(111) p.70
1382	80 s.	Venice	C	(111) p.69
1383.02.21	80 s.	Venice	A	(284) I
1384.04.13	80 s.	Venice	A	(284) I
1385.03.04	81 s.	Venice	A	(284) I
1385.04.12	80 s.	Venice	A	(284) I
1386.10.05	80 s.	Venice	A	(284) I
1387.01.15	80 s.	Venice	A	(284) I
1388.09.24	81 s.	Venice	A	(284) I
1389.06.19	82 s.	Venice	A	(284) I
1390.06.14	80 s.	Venice	A	(284) I
1390.08.12	84 s.	Venice	A	(284) I
1391.03.02	84 s.	Venice	A	(284) I
1391.08.11	82 s.	Venice	A	(284) I
1392.02.23	82 s.	Venice	A	(284) I
1392.06.01	83 s.	Venice	A	(284) I
1393.05.08	81 s.	Venice	A	(284) I
1393.10.21	84 s.	Venice	A	(284) I
1394.10.30	82 s.	Venice	A	(284) I
1395.02.25	81 s.	Venice	A	(284) I
1395.10.19	82 s.	Venice	A	(284) I
1396.05.17	84 s.	Venice	A	(284) I
1397.07.26	88 s.	Venice	A	(284) I
1397.09.01	89 s.	Venice	A	(284) I
1398.03.04	90 s.	Venice	A	(284) I
1399.04.04	90 s.	Venice	A	(284) I
1399.08.07	89 s.	Venice	A	(284) I
1400.01	89 s. 6 d.	Venice	A	(284) I
1400.02.12	85 s.	Venice	A	(284) I
1400.05.29	87 s.	Venice	A	(284) I
1400.07.10	90 s.	Venice	A	(284) I
1401.01.29	90 s.	Venice	A	(284) I
1401.04.18	91 s.	Venice	A	(284) I
1401.10.31	92 s.	Venice	A	(284) I
1402.05.27	92 s.	Venice	A	(284) I
1402.10.01	93 s.	Venice	A	(284) I
1403.04.11	94 s.	Venice	A	(284) I
1404.05.24	91 s.	Venice	A	(284) I
1405.01.02	92 s.	Venice	A	(284) I
1407.05.10	93 s.	Venice	A	(284) I
1407.10.31	95 s.	Venice	A	(284) I
1408	96 s.	Venice	C	(111) p.69
1408.06	95 s.	Venice	A	(284) I
1409.05.01	94 s. 6 d.	Venice	A	(284) I
1410.06.10	94 s.	Venice	A	(284) I
1411.10.29	100 s.	Venice	A	(284) I

THE VENETIAN DUCAT IN SOLDI AND DENARI PICCOLI OF VENICE

Date	Rate	Place	Type	Reference
1412	94 s. 8 d.	Venice	C	(111) p.69
1413	100 s.	Venice	C	(273) I
1414.11.10	100 s.	Venice	C	(273) I
1415.01.29	100 s.	Venice	A	(284) I
1417	100 s.	Venice	C	(111) p.69
1418	101 s.	Venice	C	(111) p.69
1418.02.22	100 s.	Venice	A	(284) I
1418.03.09	104 s.	Venice	A	(284) I
1421.04.30	103 s.	Venice	A	(284) I
1421.08.22	103 s.	Venice	A	(284) I
1422	104 s.	Venice	A	(284) I
1422.03.07	108 s. old money	Venice	A	(284) I
1422.03.26	100 s.	Venice	A	(284) I
1423.01.14	104 s.	Venice	A	(284) I
1423.09.15	104 s.	Venice	A	(284) I
1424	103 s.	Venice	C	(111) p.69
1424.02.15	100 s.	Venice	A	(284) I
1424.09.27	103 s.	Venice	A	(284) I
1425.08.31	104 s. 2 d.	Venice	A	(284) I
1426.06.28	103 s.	Venice	A	(284) I
1427.02.08	104 s.	Venice	A	(284) I
1427.07.13	105 s.	Venice	A	(284) I
1428.01.20	104 s.	Venice	A	(284) I
1428.03.11	103 s.	Venice	A	(284) I
1428.08.08	100 s.	Venice	O	(284) I
1428.08.18	104 s.	Venice	A	(284) I
1429	104 s.	Venice	C	(111) p.69
1429.08.01	104 s. 3 d.	Venice	A	(284) I
1429.08.23	104 s.	Venice	A	(284) I
1430.09.22	106 s.	Venice	A	(284) I
1431.02.13	106 s.	Venice	A	(284) I
1431.11.06	105 s.	Venice	A	(284) I
1432.08.16	107 s.	Venice	A	(284) I
1432.10.25	107 s. 6 d.	Venice	A	(284) I
1432.12.29	108 s.	Venice	A	(284) I
1433	110 s.	Venice	C	(111) p.69
1433.02.12	108 s.	Venice	A	(284) I
1433.05.17	100 s.	Venice	O	(284) I
1434.08.12	110 s.	Venice	A	(284) I
1435.07.20	110 s. 5 d.	Venice	A	(284) I
1436.03.15	111 s. 2 1/2 d.	Venice	A	(284) I
1437.09.15	111 s.	Venice	A	(284) I
1437.10.17	110 s.	Venice	A	(284) I
1437.10.30	111 s.	Venice	A	(284) I
1438	110 s.	Venice	A	(284) I
1439.07.21	113 s.	Venice	A	(284) I
1440.04.22	114 s.	Venice	A	(284) I
1441	113 s.	Venice	C	(111) p.69
1441.09.07	114 s.	Venice	A	(284) I
1442.02.15	113 s. 8 1/2 d.	Venice	A	(284) I
1442.11.21	114 s.	Venice	A	(284) I
1443	114 s.	Venice	C	(111) p.69
1443.03.22	113 s. 6 d.	Venice	A	(284) I
1443.05.09	114 s.	Venice	A	(284) I
1444.01.23	114 s.	Venice	A	(284) I
1445.06.28	114 s.	Venice	A	(284) I
1446-1451	114 s.	Venice	A	(284) I
1452	116 s.	Venice	C	(111) p.69
1452.01.07	114 s.	Venice	A	(284) I
1453	114 s.	Venice	H	(359) p.281
1453.01.22	114 s.	Venice	A	(284) I
1453.10.09	118 s.	Venice	A	(284) I
1454.01.02	120 s.	Venice	A	(284) I
1454.12.04	122 s.	Venice	A	(284) I
1455.01.15	123 s.	Venice	A	(284) I
1455.03.26	123 s.	Venice	A	(284) I
1455.04.14-1472.05	124 s.	Venice	A	(284) I
1472.05-.06	116 s.	Venice	A	(284) I
1472.05-.06	118 s.	Venice	A	(284) I
1472.05-.06	120 s.	Venice	A	(284) I
1472.05-.06	122 s.	Venice	A	(284) I
1472.06-1500	124 s.	Venice	O	(111) pp.70-71

As well as giving values for the ducat in soldi and denari piccoli in Venice, Professors Lane and Mueller, (284) I, will also give values for the ducat in soldi and denari piccoli elsewhere in Venetian territory — in Treviso, Udine, Padua and Verona on the Italian mainland and at Zara on the Adriatic coast. These values were sometimes significantly different from those given above for Venice itself.

The lira di grossi and the lira di piccoli

In 1201 Venice was the first state to strike grossi, initially known as ducati (since Venice was a duchy), but later as matapans. After the creation of the grosso, two concurrent systems of money of account came into use, the one based on the old little denaro (piccolo), the other on the new great denaro (grosso). In both systems the soldo meant a dozen denari, and the lira a score of dozens. There was no firm relationship between the two systems of accounting, for whereas the base denaro of the lira, soldo and denaro piccolo system sank further and further in quality, the denaro of the li. s. d. grosso system very largely conserved its fineness and weight. It is not clear what was the initial relationship between the two systems, but it seems probably that the grosso was originally intended to equal two soldi (twenty-four) piccoli. If this was the original value, it very soon changed, for during the first half of the thirteen century a tolerably stable relationship existed of 26 piccoli to one grosso. In 1267 the grosso still equalled only 27 piccoli, but from then on the relationship frequently changed and is listed below.

The Venetian grosso in denari piccoli of Venice

Date	Rate	Place	Type	Reference
1201	24 d.	Venice		
This was probably the intended initial value of the grosso.				
1202-1254	26 d.	Venice	C	(284) I
1254	26 1/9 d.	Venice	O	(345) p.47
1259.03.19	26 2/3 d.	Venice	C	(356) II p.374
1265	27 d.	Venice	C	(412) p.49
1267	26 d.	Venice	C	(412) p.49
1268-1280	28 d.	Venice	C	(284) I
1269	28 d.	Venice	O	(345) p.47
1269	28 d.	Venice	C	(412) p.49
1274	28 d.	Venice	C	(412) p.49
1274	28 d.	Venice	O	(284) I
1275	30 d.	Venice	C	(412) p.49
1276	27 d.	Venice	C	(412) p.49
1280-1331	32 d.	Venice	C	(284) I
1282	32 d.	Venice	C	(313)
1282	32 d.	Venice	O	(345) p.47
1290	32 d.	Venice	C	(412) p.49
1291	32 d.	Venice	C	(412) p.49
1298	32 d.	Venice	C	(412) p.49
1307.03.23	28 d.	Venice	C	(298) I p.72
1307	30 d.	Venice	C	(284) I
1308.10.26	32 d.	Venice	C	(298) I p.90
1321	32 d.	Venice	O	(345) p.57
1331-1332	36 d.	Venice	C	(284) I
1341.03.08	32 d.	Venice	O	(32) p.43
1344	41 d.	Venice	C	(284) I
1352	41 d.	Venice	C	(284) I
by1370	44-48 d.	Venice	C	(284) I
1379(-1468)	48 d. or 4 soldini	Venice	O	(284) I

The Florentine florin in grossi of Venice

Date	Rate	Place	Type	Reference
1277	20 grossi	Curia	B	(439) p.897
1280	18 1/2 grossi	Curia	B	(439) p.897
1280	20 grossi	Curia	B	(439) p.897
1290-1294	20 grossi	Curia	B	(439) p.898
1291	18 1/2 grossi	Venice	B	(179) p.98
1296	20 grossi	Curia	B	(439) p.898
1300	24 grossi	Curia	B	(439) p.898
1305	24 grossi	Curia	B	(439) p.899
1308-1309	24 grossi	Curia	B	(439) p.899

THE FLORENTINE FLORIN IN GROSSI OF VENICE

Date	Rate	Place	Type	Reference
1308-1309	24 grossi	Curia	A	(229) p.XVIII
1319-1320	24 grossi	Curia	B	(439) p.900
1319-1320	26 grossi	Curia	B	(439) p.900
1321-1323	24 grossi	Curia	B	(439) p.900
1326.02.18	24 1/4 grossi	Pisa-Venice	B	(298) III p.18
1326	24 grossi	Curia	B	(439) p.901
1326	25 grossi	Curia	B	(439) p.901
1333-1335	24 grossi	Castello Venezia	B	(226) XCVI p.383
1339.03.20	24 grossi 11 1/2 picc.	Venice	C	(334) p.388
1344.05	18 grossi	Jerusalem	A	(11) App.C
1346 Spring	18 grossi	Jerusalem	A	(11) App.C

The Venetian ducat in grossi of Venice

Date	Rate	Place	Type	Reference
1284-1285	18 grossi	Venice	O	(345) p.53
1284-1286	19 grossi	Venice	A	(284) I
1284-1286	20 grossi	Venice	A	(284) I
1285.05.03	18 1/3 grossi	Venice	O	(284) I
1290	18 1/2 grossi	Venice	A	(284) I
1292-1298	20 grossi	Venice	A	(284) I
13th c. end	18-20 grossi	Venice	H	(180) p.32
1305-1310	18 1/2 grossi	Venice	O	(345) p.53
1305-1310	24 grossi	Venice	C	(345) p.53
1305-1325	24 grossi	Venice	C	(409) p.61
1314 b	28 grossi	Venice	C	(345) p.53
1328	24 grossi	Venice	O	(345) p.54
1328	20 grossi	Venice	C	(409) p.61
1328	22 grossi	Venice	C	(409) p.61
1362.01.02	18 grossi novi	Venice	O	(101) no.140
1384.10.09	18 grossi	Jerusalem	A	(11) App.C
1458.05.08	28 grossi novi	Venice	A	(11) App.C
1458.06.08	24-26 grossi	Levant	A	(11) App.C

The Venetian grosso in other currencies

A small number of thirteenth century rates also survive between the Venetian grosso or the lira di grossi and other currencies.

The Venetian lira (di grossi?) in lire and soldi of Lucca

Date	Rate	Place	Type	Reference
1230.11.27	12 li. 10 s.	Lucca	A	(48)

The Venetian grosso in denari of Cortona

Date	Rate	Place	Type	Reference
1278.03.01	30 d.	Viterbo	C	(108) V p.339

The Venetian grosso in denari provisini of Rome

Date	Rate	Place	Type	Reference
1285	16 d.	Rome	C	(401) p.306

The Venetian grosso in denari of Ravenna

Date	Rate	Place	Type	Reference
1290	17 d.	Rome	B	(439) p.112

The Venetian grosso in denari of Verona

Date	Rate	Place	Type	Reference
1294.02.26	28 d.	Padua	C	(118) IV p.325

The Venetian lira di grossi in shillings and pence sterling of England

Date	Rate	Place	Type	Reference
1217.11.15-1218.02.06	30 s.	London	M	(392) p.20

The lira di grossi in Florentine lire, soldi and denari affiorino

This can be translated into Florentine florins in lire, soldi and denari di grossi on the basis of 29 soldi affiorino to each florin. This information is derived from the Datini archive at Prato and will appear with a detailed commentary in the second volume of Lane and Mueller's Money and Banking in Medieval - Renaissance Venice (284). I am much indebted to Professor Mueller for permission to include it here. I have again used only the first rate given in each month when more than one rate was quoted.

Date	Rate	Place	Type	Reference
1383.11.07	14 li. 18 s. 8 d.	Venice-Florence	B	(284) II
1384.01.07	14 li. 19 s. 2 d.	Venice-Florence	B	(284) II
1384.02.13	14 li. 19 s. 6 d.	Venice-Florence	B	(284) II
1384.03.26	14 li. 19 s.	Venice-Florence	B	(284) II
1384.04.15	14 li. 19 s. 6 d.	Venice-Florence	B	(284) II
1384.05.02	14 li. 19 s.	Venice-Florence	B	(284) II
1384.06.07	14 li. 17 s.	Venice-Florence	B	(284) II
1384.07.07	14 li. 19 s. 2 d.	Venice-Florence	B	(284) II
1384.08.05	15 li.	Venice-Florence	B	(284) II
1384.09.15	14 li. 19 s. 8 d.	Venice-Florence	B	(284) II
1384.10.04	14 li. 18 s.	Venice-Florence	B	(284) II
1384.11.02	14 li. 18 s.	Venice-Florence	B	(284) II
1384.12.03	14 li. 15 s.	Venice-Florence	B	(284) II
1385.01.06	14 li. 18 s. 2 d.	Venice-Florence	B	(284) II
1385.02.10	14 li. 17 s. 9 d.	Venice-Florence	B	(284) II
1385.03.02	15 li. 1 s. 6 d.	Venice-Florence	B	(284) II
1385.04.08	15 li. 2 s. 9 d.	Venice-Florence	B	(284) II
1385.05.04	15 li. 5 s.	Venice-Florence	B	(284) II
1385.06.02	15 li. 3 s. 6 d.	Venice-Florence	B	(284) II
1385.07.06	15 li. 4 s. 3 d.	Venice-Florence	B	(284) II
1385.08.01	15 li. 6 s. 10 d.	Venice-Florence	B	(284) II
1385.09.16	14 li. 18 s.	Venice-Florence	B	(284) II
1385.10.05	14 li. 18 s. 8 d.	Venice-Florence	B	(284) II
1385.11.04	15 li. 4 s. 9 d.	Venice-Florence	B	(284) II
1385.12.07	15 li. 6 s. 3 d.	Venice-Florence	B	(284) II
1386.01.05	15 li. 5 s. 6 d.	Venice-Florence	B	(284) II
1386.02.06	14 li. 19 s. 4 d.	Venice-Florence	B	(284) II
1386.03.02	15 li. 3 d.	Venice-Florence	B	(284) II
1386.04.05	15 li. 4 d.	Venice-Florence	B	(284) II
1386.05.15	15 li. 1 s.	Venice-Florence	B	(284) II
1386.06.07	15 li. 3 s.	Venice-Florence	B	(284) II
1386.07.03	15 li. 6 s.	Venice-Florence	B	(284) II
1386.08.04	15 li. 7 s.	Venice-Florence	B	(284) II
1386.09.01	15 li. 3 s. 4 d.	Venice-Florence	B	(284) II
1386.10.06	15 li. 1 s. 10 d.	Venice-Florence	B	(284) II
1386.11.06	15 li. 4 s. 2 d.	Venice-Florence	B	(284) II
1386.12.04	15 li. 5 s. 3 d.	Venice-Florence	B	(284) II
1387.01.10	15 li. 1 s. 8 d.	Venice-Florence	B	(284) II
1387.02.05	14 li. 15 s. 4 d.	Venice-Florence	B	(284) II
1387.03.07	14 li. 14 s. 4 d.	Venice-Florence	B	(284) II
1387.04.04	14 li. 12 s. 2 d.	Venice-Florence	B	(284) II
1387.05.02	14 li. 13 s. 8 d.	Venice-Florence	B	(284) II
1387.06.04	14 li. 13 s.	Venice-Florence	B	(284) II
1387.07.04	15 li. 1 s. 6 d.	Venice-Florence	B	(284) II
1387.08.03	15 li. 9 d.	Venice-Florence	B	(284) II
1387.09.04	14 li. 13 s.	Venice-Florence	B	(284) II
1387.10.03	14 li. 15 s. 6 d.	Venice-Florence	B	(284) II
1387.11.05	14 li. 14 s. 6 d.	Venice-Florence	B	(284) II
1387.12.03	14 li. 15 s. 10 d.	Venice-Florence	B	(284) II

THE LIRA DI GROSSI IN FLORENTINE LIRE, SOLDI AND DENARI AFFIORINO

Date	Rate	Place	Type	Reference
1388.01.08	14 li. 16 s. 7 d.	Venice-Florence	B	(284) II
1388.02.08	14 li. 17 s. 4 d.	Venice-Florence	B	(284) II
1388.03.07	14 li. 16 s. 5 d.	Venice-Florence	B	(284) II
1388.04.04	14 li. 18 s. 6 d.	Venice-Florence	B	(284) II
1388.05.02	14 li. 18 s.	Venice-Florence	B	(284) II
1388.06.04	15 li. 6 d.	Venice-Florence	B	(284) II
1388.07.16	15 li. 5 s. 8 d.	Venice-Florence	B	(284) II
1388.08.01	15 li. 5 s. 6 d.	Venice-Florence	B	(284) II
1388.09.03	14 li. 15 s. 10 d.	Venice-Florence	B	(284) II
1388.10.07	14 li. 15 s. 4 d.	Venice-Florence	B	(284) II
1388.11.13	15 li. 10 d.	Venice-Florence	B	(284) II
1388.12.03	15 li.	Venice-Florence	B	(284) II
1389.01.05	15 li. 4 s.	Venice-Florence	B	(284) II
1389.02.03	14 li. 19 s. 8 d.	Venice-Florence	B	(284) II
1389.03.05	15 li. 1 s.	Venice-Florence	B	(284) II
1389.04.01	14 li. 19 s. 6 d.	Venice-Florence	B	(284) II
1389.05.06	14 li. 19 s. 2 d.	Venice-Florence	B	(284) II
1389.06.12	15 li. 3 s. 6 d.	Venice-Florence	B	(284) II
1389.07.03	15 li. 7 s. 2 d.	Venice-Florence	B	(284) II
1389.09.10	15 li. 6 s. 6 d.	Venice-Florence	B	(284) II
1389.10.12	15 li. 8 s. 6 d.	Venice-Florence	B	(284) II
1389.11.20	15 li. 10 s.	Venice-Florence	B	(284) II
1389.12.04	15 li. 7 s. 2 d.	Venice-Florence	B	(284) II
1390.01.04	15 li. 2 s. 10 d.	Venice-Florence	B	(284) II
1390.03.05	15 li. 6 s. 9 d.	Venice-Florence	B	(284) II
1390.05.07	15 li. 6 s. 8 d.	Venice-Florence	B	(284) II
1390.06.02	14 li. 18 s. 6 d.	Venice-Florence	B	(284) II
1390.08.09	15 li. 13 s. 6 d.	Venice-Florence	B	(284) II
1390.12.29	15 li. 14 s.	Venice-Florence	B	(284) II
1391.01.14	15 li. 8 s.	Venice-Florence	B	(284) II
1391.02.01	15 li. 9 s. 9 d.	Venice-Florence	B	(284) II
1391.03.01	15 li. 9 s. 10 d.	Venice-Florence	B	(284) II
1391.04.05	15 li. 8 s.	Venice-Florence	B	(284) II
1391.05.12	15 li. 5 s. 4 d.	Venice-Florence	B	(284) II
1391.06.07	15 li. 8 s.	Venice-Florence	B	(284) II
1391.07.05	15 li. 12 s.	Venice-Florence	B	(284) II
1391.08.02	15 li. 10 s.	Venice-Florence	B	(284) II
1391.09.13	15 li. 7 s. 10 d.	Venice-Florence	B	(284) II
1391.10.19	15 li. 4 s. 3 d.	Venice-Florence	B	(284) II
1391.11.04	15 li. 3 s. 6 d.	Venice-Florence	B	(284) II
1391.12.02	15 li. 5 s. 3 d.	Venice-Florence	B	(284) II
1392.01.18	15 li. 6 s.	Venice-Florence	B	(284) II
1392.02.10	15 li. 6 s.	Venice-Florence	B	(284) II
1392.03.02	15 li. 2 s. 6 d.	Venice-Florence	B	(284) II
1392.06.01	15 li. 6 s.	Venice-Florence	B	(284) II
1392.07.02	15 li. 12 s. 3 d.	Venice-Florence	B	(284) II
1392.08.01	15 li. 11 s.	Venice-Florence	B	(284) II
1392.09.11	15 li. 6 s.	Venice-Florence	B	(284) II
1392.10.09	15 li. 2 s. 6 d.	Venice-Florence	B	(284) II
1392.11.12	15 li. 2 s. 3 d.	Venice-Florence	B	(284) II
1392.12.05	15 li. 4 s.	Venice-Florence	B	(284) II
1393.01.16	15 li. 4 s. 2 d.	Venice-Florence	B	(284) II
1393.02.12	15 li. 5 s.	Venice-Florence	B	(284) II
1393.03.01	15 li. 8 s. 4 d.	Venice-Florence	B	(284) II
1393.04.05	15 li. 8 s.	Venice-Florence	B	(284) II
1393.05.08	15 li. 10 s.	Venice-Florence	B	(284) II
1393.06.29	15 li. 10 s. 2 d.	Venice-Florence	B	(284) II
1393.07.05	15 li. 11 s. 6 d.	Venice-Florence	B	(284) II
1393.08.08	15 li. 13 s.	Venice-Florence	B	(284) II
1393.09.25	15 li. 6 s. 2 d.	Venice-Florence	B	(284) II
1393.10.01	15 li. 7 s.	Venice-Florence	B	(284) II
1393.11.08	15 li. 7 s. 4 d.	Venice-Florence	B	(284) II
1393.12.04	15 li. 6 s. 10 d.	Venice-Florence	B	(284) II
1394.01.15	15 li. 9 s.	Venice-Florence	B	(284) II
1394.02.06	15 li. 8 s. 2 d.	Venice-Florence	B	(284) II
1394.03.05	15 li. 9 s.	Venice-Florence	B	(284) II
1394.04.02	15 li. 11 s.	Venice-Florence	B	(284) II
1394.05.05	15 li. 8 s. 9 d.	Venice-Florence	B	(284) II
1394.06.03	15 li. 9 s.	Venice-Florence	B	(284) II
1394.07.04	15 li. 10 s. 9 d.	Venice-Florence	B	(284) II
1394.08.04	15 li. 11 s.	Venice-Florence	B	(284) II
1394.09.04	15 li. 4 s.	Venice-Florence	B	(284) II

THE LIRA DI GROSSI IN FLORENTINE LIRE, SOLDI AND DENARI AFFIORINO

Date	Rate	Place	Type	Reference
1394.10.01	15 li. 4 s.	Venice-Florence	B	(284) II
1394.11.04	15 li. 4 s. 10 d.	Venice-Florence	B	(284) II
1394.12.03	15 li. 11 s. 2 d.	Venice-Florence	B	(284) II
1395.01.05	15 li. 9 s. 9 d.	Venice-Florence	B	(284) II
1395.02.06	15 li. 6 s. 6 d.	Venice-Florence	B	(284) II
1395.03.04	15 li. 5 s. 10 d.	Venice-Florence	B	(284) II
1395.04.03	15 li. 5 s.	Venice-Florence	B	(284) II
1395.05.06	15 li. 5 s. 6 d.	Venice-Florence	B	(284) II
1395.06.05	15 li. 8 s.	Venice-Florence	B	(284) II
1395.07.03	15 li. 12 s.	Venice-Florence	B	(284) II
1395.08.05	15 li. 13 s. 8 d.	Venice-Florence	B	(284) II
1395.09.01	15 li. 7 s. 10 d.	Venice-Florence	B	(284) II
1395.10.05	15 li. 2 s. 9 d.	Venice-Florence	B	(284) II
1395.11.04	15 li. 6 s. 2 d.	Venice-Florence	B	(284) II
1395.12.01	15 li. 7 s. 6 d.	Venice-Florence	B	(284) II
1396.01.05	15 li. 6 s.	Venice-Florence	B	(284) II
1396.02.05	15 li. 4 s.	Venice-Florence	B	(284) II
1396.03.04	15 li. 2 s. 6 d.	Venice-Florence	B	(284) II
1396.04.01	15 li. 10 d.	Venice-Florence	B	(284) II
1396.05.02	15 li. 2 s.	Venice-Florence	B	(284) II
1396.06.03	15 li. 5 s. 9 d.	Venice-Florence	B	(284) II
1396.07.04	15 li. 8 s. 10 d.	Venice-Florence	B	(284) II
1396.08.04	15 li. 4 s. 2 d.	Venice-Florence	B	(284) II
1396.09.02	14 li. 18 s. 8 d.	Venice-Florence	B	(284) II
1396.10.03	15 li. 5 s. 3 d.	Venice-Florence	B	(284) II
1396.11.12	15 li. 9 s. 3 d.	Venice-Florence	B	(284) II
1396.12.02	15 li. 6 s. 6 d.	Venice-Florence	B	(284) II
1397.01.05	15 li. 9 s. 4 d.	Venice-Florence	B	(284) II
1397.02.03	15 li. 5 s. 10 d.	Venice-Florence	B	(284) II
1397.03.10	15 li. 6 s. 6 d.	Venice-Florence	B	(284) II
1397.04.05	15 li. 3 s.	Venice-Florence	B	(284) II
1397.05.05	15 li.	Venice-Florence	B	(284) II
1397.06.05	14 li. 17 s. 10 d.	Venice-Florence	B	(284) II
1397.07.07	15 li. 5 s.	Venice-Florence	B	(284) II
1397.08.04	15 li. 8 s.	Venice-Florence	B	(284) II
1397.09.01	15 li. 4 s. 2 d.	Venice-Florence	B	(284) II
1397.10.06	15 li. 9 s. 6 d.	Venice-Florence	B	(284) II
1397.11.03	15 li. 6 s. 6 d.	Venice-Florence	B	(284) II
1397.12.01	15 li. 5 s. 9 d.	Venice-Florence	B	(284) II
1398.01.03	15 li. 4 s. 6 d.	Venice-Florence	B	(284) II
1398.02.01	15 li. 6 s. 4 d.	Venice-Florence	B	(284) II
1398.03.05	15 li. 7 s. 4 d.	Venice-Florence	B	(284) II
1398.04.03	15 li. 8 s. 6 d.	Venice-Florence	B	(284) II
1398.05.04	15 li. 8 s. 10 d.	Venice-Florence	B	(284) II
1398.06.08	15 li. 7 s. 9 d.	Venice-Florence	B	(284) II
1398.07.06	15 li. 8 s. 9 d.	Venice-Florence	B	(284) II
1398.08.02	15 li. 13 s.	Venice-Florence	B	(284) II
1398.09.27	15 li. 6 s. 10 d.	Venice-Florence	B	(284) II
1398.10.03	15 li. 8 s.	Venice-Florence	B	(284) II
1398.11.05	15 li. 13 s. 4 d.	Venice-Florence	B	(284) II
1398.12.10	15 li. 13 s.	Venice-Florence	B	(284) II
1399.01.02	15 li. 11 s. 6 d.	Venice-Florence	B	(284) II
1399.02.05	15 li. 11 s. 9 d.	Venice-Florence	B	(284) II
1399.03.04	15 li. 8 s. 6 d.	Venice-Florence	B	(284) II
1399.04.05	15 li. 6 s.	Venice-Florence	B	(284) II
1399.05.06	15 li. 6 s.	Venice-Florence	B	(284) II
1399.06.06	15 li. 9 s. 11 d.	Venice-Florence	B	(284) II
1399.07.05	15 li. 12 s. 8 d.	Venice-Florence	B	(284) II
1399.08.05	15 li. 14 s. 2 d.	Venice-Florence	B	(284) II
1399.09.03	15 li. 9 s. 5 d.	Venice-Florence	B	(284) II
1399.10.01	15 li. 8 s. 10 d.	Venice-Florence	B	(284) II
1399.11.05	15 li. 4 s. 8 d.	Venice-Florence	B	(284) II
1399.12.04	15 li. 7 s. 10 d.	Venice-Florence	B	(284) II
1400.01.05	15 li. 12 s. 4 d.	Venice-Florence	B	(284) II
1400.02.05	15 li. 6 s. 8 d.	Venice-Florence	B	(284) II
1400.03.06	15 li. 7 s.	Venice-Florence	B	(284) II
1400.04.09	15 li. 7 s.	Venice-Florence	B	(284) II
1400.05.06	15 li. 8 s. 3 d.	Venice-Florence	B	(284) II
1400.06.05	15 li. 7 s. 4 d.	Venice-Florence	B	(284) II
1400.07.03	15 li. 8 s. 10 d.	Venice-Florence	B	(284) II
1400.08.12	15 li. 14 s.	Venice-Florence	B	(284) II
1400.09.04	15 li. 3 s. 6 d.	Venice-Florence	B	(284) II

THE LIRA DI GROSSI IN FLORENTINE LIRE, SOLDI AND DENARI AFFIORINO

Date	Rate	Place	Type	Reference
1400.10.02	15 li. 4 s.	Venice-Florence	B	(284) II
1400.11.13	15 li. 1 s. 8 d.	Venice-Florence	B	(284) II
1400.12.06	15 li. 3 s.	Venice-Florence	B	(284) II
1401.01.01	15 li. 4 s.	Venice-Florence	B	(284) II
1401.02.03	15 li. 2 s. 10 d.	Venice-Florence	B	(284) II
1401.03.03	15 li. 2 s. 3 d.	Venice-Florence	B	(284) II
1401.04.02	15 li. 2 s. 9 d.	Venice-Florence	B	(284) II
1401.05.06	15 li. 4 s. 8 d.	Venice-Florence	B	(284) II
1401.06.04	15 li. 10 s. 10 d.	Venice-Florence	B	(284) II
1401.07.02	15 li. 10 s.	Venice-Florence	B	(284) II
1401.08.05	15 li. 9 s.	Venice-Florence	B	(284) II
1401.09.03	15 li. 7 s. 6 d.	Venice-Florence	B	(284) II
1401.10.01	15 li. 11 s. 8 d.	Venice-Florence	B	(284) II
1401.11.05	15 li. 10 s. 6 d.	Venice-Florence	B	(284) II
1401.12.03	15 li. 6 s. 4 d.	Venice-Florence	B	(284) II
1402.01.07	15 li. 7 s. 6 d.	Venice-Florence	B	(284) II
1402.02.04	15 li. 8 s. 4 d.	Venice-Florence	B	(284) II
1402.03.06	15 li. 10 s. 10 d.	Venice-Florence	B	(284) II
1402.04.01	15 li. 13 s. 4 d.	Venice-Florence	B	(284) II
1402.05.06	15 li. 9 s.	Venice-Florence	B	(284) II
1402.06.03	15 li. 9 s.	Venice-Florence	B	(284) II
1402.07.08	15 li. 9 s.	Venice-Florence	B	(284) II
1402.08.05	15 li. 10 s. 6 d.	Venice-Florence	B	(284) II
1402.09.02	15 li. 3 s.	Venice-Florence	B	(284) II
1402.10.07	15 li. 6 s. 6 d.	Venice-Florence	B	(284) II
1402.11.04	15 li. 11 s. 8 d.	Venice-Florence	B	(284) II
1402.12.02	15 li. 14 s.	Venice-Florence	B	(284) II
1403.01.05	15 li. 17 s. 10 d.	Venice-Florence	B	(284) II
1403.02.03	15 li. 11 s. 8 d.	Venice-Florence	B	(284) II
1403.03.03	15 li. 11 s.	Venice-Florence	B	(284) II
1403.04.07	15 li. 9 s.	Venice-Florence	B	(284) II
1403.05.05	15 li. 12 s. 8 d.	Venice-Florence	B	(284) II
1403.06.02	15 li. 13 s.	Venice-Florence	B	(284) II
1403.07.07	15 li. 18 s. 6 d.	Venice-Florence	B	(284) II
1403.08.04	15 li. 11 s. 6 d.	Venice-Florence	B	(284) II
1403.09.01	15 li. 8 s. 6 d.	Venice-Florence	B	(284) II
1403.10.06	15 li. 7 s. 10 d.	Venice-Florence	B	(284) II
1403.11.03	15 li. 10 s. 10 d.	Venice-Florence	B	(284) II
1403.12.01	15 li. 12 s. 8 d.	Venice-Florence	B	(284) II
1404.01.05	15 li. 14 s.	Venice-Florence	B	(284) II
1404.02.04	15 li. 11 s. 6 d.	Venice-Florence	B	(284) II
1404.03.01	15 li. 10 s.	Venice-Florence	B	(284) II
1404.04.05	15 li. 14 s.	Venice-Florence	B	(284) II
1404.05.03	15 li. 13 s. 10 d.	Venice-Florence	B	(284) II
1404.06.07	15 li. 7 s. 8 d.	Venice-Florence	B	(284) II
1404.07.05	15 li. 12 s. 10 d.	Venice-Florence	B	(284) II
1404.08.02	15 li. 10 s. 8 d.	Venice-Florence	B	(284) II
1404.09.06	15 li. 9 s.	Venice-Florence	B	(284) II
1404.10.04	15 li. 13 s. 8 d.	Venice-Florence	B	(284) II
1404.11.08	15 li. 4 s. 6 d.	Venice-Florence	B	(284) II
1404.12.12	15 li. 5 s. 10 d.	Venice-Florence	B	(284) II
1405.01.05	15 li. 3 s. 4 d.	Venice-Florence	B	(284) II
1405.02.08	15 li. 4 s. 6 d.	Venice-Florence	B	(284) II
1405.03.14	15 li. 3 s. 2 d.	Venice-Florence	B	(284) II
1405.04.04	15 li. 3 s.	Venice-Florence	B	(284) II
1405.05.02	15 li. 3 s.	Venice-Florence	B	(284) II
1405.06.06	15 li. 2 s. 10 d.	Venice-Florence	B	(284) II
1405.07.04	15 li. 6 s.	Venice-Florence	B	(284) II
1405.08.08	15 li. 14 s.	Venice-Florence	B	(284) II
1405.09.19	15 li. 8 s.	Venice-Florence	B	(284) II
1405.10.10	15 li. 15 s.	Venice-Florence	B	(284) II
1405.11.07	15 li. 10 s.	Venice-Florence	B	(284) II
1405.12.01	15 li. 8 s. 6 d.	Venice-Florence	B	(284) II
1406.01.02	15 li. 7 s.	Venice-Florence	B	(284) II
1406.02.18	15 li. 7 s. 4 d.	Venice-Florence	B	(284) II
1406.03.05	15 li. 5 s.	Venice-Florence	B	(284) II
1406.04.04	15 li. 3 s. 4 d.	Venice-Florence	B	(284) II
1406.05.04	15 li. 6 s. 2 d.	Venice-Florence	B	(284) II
1406.06.26	15 li. 9 s. 6 d.	Venice-Florence	B	(284) II
1406.07.11	15 li. 13 s. 4 d.	Venice-Florence	B	(284) II
1406.08.07	15 li. 10 s.	Venice-Florence	B	(284) II
1406.09.13	15 li. 5 s. 6 d.	Venice-Florence	B	(284) II

THE LIRA DI GROSSI IN FLORENTINE LIRE, SOLDI AND DENARI AFFIORINO

Date	Rate	Place	Type	Reference
1406.10.02	15 li. 7 s.	Venice-Florence	B	(284) II
1406.11.06	15 li. 8 s. 6 d.	Venice-Florence	B	(284) II
1406.12.07	15 li. 13 s. 2 d.	Venice-Florence	B	(284) II
1407.01.03	15 li. 12 s.	Venice-Florence	B	(284) II
1407.02.06	15 li. 6 s. 4 d.	Venice-Florence	B	(284) II
1407.03.05	15 li. 8 s.	Venice-Florence	B	(284) II
1407.04.02	15 li. 11 s. 4 d.	Venice-Florence	B	(284) II
1407.05.07	15 li. 12 s. 6 d.	Venice-Florence	B	(284) II
1407.06.07	15 li. 13 s. 2 d.	Venice-Florence	B	(284) II
1407.07.02	15 li. 15 s. 8 d.	Venice-Florence	B	(284) II
1407.08.06	15 li. 13 s. 2 d.	Venice-Florence	B	(284) II
1407.09.10	15 li. 6 s. 8 d.	Venice-Florence	B	(284) II
1407.10.02	15 li. 7 s.	Venice-Florence	B	(284) II
1407.11.12	15 li. 12 s. 3 d.	Venice-Florence	B	(284) II
1407.12.03	15 li. 12 s. 6 d.	Venice-Florence	B	(284) II
1408.01.08	15 li. 11 s.	Venice-Florence	B	(284) II
1408.02.08	15 li. 8 s. 3 d.	Venice-Florence	B	(284) II
1408.03.08	15 li. 8 s. 6 d.	Venice-Florence	B	(284) II
1408.05.18	15 li. 10 s.	Venice-Florence	B	(284) II
1408.06.02	15 li. 13 s.	Venice-Florence	B	(284) II
1408.07.14	15 li. 13 s. 8 d.	Venice-Florence	B	(284) II
1408.08.18	15 li. 12 s. 2 d.	Venice-Florence	B	(284) II
1408.09.01	15 li. 9 s. 8 d.	Venice-Florence	B	(284) II
1408.10.03	15 li. 12 s. 6 d.	Venice-Florence	B	(284) II
1408.11.18	15 li. 12 s. 4 d.	Venice-Florence	B	(284) II
1408.12.15	15 li. 18 s. 2 d.	Venice-Florence	B	(284) II
1409.01.18	15 li. 8 s. 2 d.	Venice-Florence	B	(284) II
1409.02.02	15 li. 7 s. 3 d.	Venice-Florence	B	(284) II
1409.03.02	15 li. 10 s.	Venice-Florence	B	(284) II
1409.04.13	15 li. 8 s. 9 d.	Venice-Florence	B	(284) II
1409.05.04	15 li. 3 s.	Venice-Florence	B	(284) II
1409.06.02	15 li. 6 s.	Venice-Florence	B	(284) II
1409.07.20	15 li. 13 s. 4 d.	Venice-Florence	B	(284) II
1409.08.03	15 li. 12 s.	Venice-Florence	B	(284) II
1409.09.13	15 li. 2 d.	Venice-Florence	B	(284) II
1409.10.05	14 li. 18 s.	Venice-Florence	B	(284) II
1409.11.16	14 li. 17 s. 8 d.	Venice-Florence	B	(284) II
1409.12.23	15 li. 6 s.	Venice-Florence	B	(284) II
1410.01.18	15 li. 7 s. 6 d.	Venice-Florence	B	(284) II
1410.02.01	15 li. 7 s.	Venice-Florence	B	(284) II
1410.03.01	15 li. 7 s.	Venice-Florence	B	(284) II
1410.04.05	15 li. 8 s. 6 d.	Venice-Florence	B	(284) II
1410.05.03	15 li. 8 s. 6 d.	Venice-Florence	B	(284) II
1410.06.14	15 li. 12 s. 4 d.	Venice-Florence	B	(284) II
1410.07.17	15 li. 12 s. 6 d.	Venice-Florence	B	(284) II
1410.08.09	15 li. 11 s. 10 d.	Venice-Florence	B	(284) II
1410.10.04	15 li. 5 s.	Venice-Florence	B	(284) II
1411.01.01	15 li. 13 s.	Venice-Florence	B	(284) II
1411.02.06	15 li. 7 s. 6 d.	Venice-Florence	B	(284) II

Lire di grossi a oro

For a generation at the beginning of the fourteenth century the ducat had remained at 24 grossi; 2 soldi di grossi (177) p.140. This also became a fossilized relationship for the lire di grossi was a convenient 10 ducats. The fall in the value of the ducat in the 1330s led to a splitting of the lira di grossi. In some accounts a distinction was made very soon after 1332 between lire di grossi 'in monete' and lire di grossi 'a oro'. The lira di grossi in monete was based on the soldino and other silver coins such as the piccolo and the mezzanino. The lira di grossi a oro was based on the ducat. When this split widened in the 1360s, it became important whether the salaries, prices and debts of various kinds that had been recorded in lira di grossi were considered as 'in monete' or 'a oro'. After the 1360s the distinction became necessary and the lira di grossi a oro came to be most widely used. Unlike the lira di grossi a monete, which was based on the same silver coins as the lira di piccoli (before 1379 primarily the soldino), the grosso of the lira di grossi a oro was tied to the gold ducat, not to silver. Its value compared to the silver grosso coin depended on the exchange rate established in the market place between gold ducats and the silver coins. This was expressed in 'soldi di piccoli'. If the ducat was valued at less than 96 soldi di piccoli, the grosso a oro was worth less than the new silver grosso coin; if the ducat was valued at more than 96 soldi di piccoli, the grosso a oro was worth more than the grosso coin. The grosso in monete on the other hand was always worth exactly two-thirds of the new grosso coin (345) pp.60-2.

Lire a grossi

Long after the actual relationship between grossi and piccoli changed, the extraordinary rate of 26.1/9 piccoli to the grosso remained enshrined in the accounting system. As well as reckoning in lire, soldi and denari di piccoli, and in lire, soldi and denari di grossi, Venetians also kept accounts in lire, soldi and denari di piccoli a grossi, or more simply lire, soldi and denari a grossi. In the 'a grossi' system, the denaro was no longer the actual denaro piccoli, but a fraction of the grosso, worked out at the rate of 26.1/9 denari to the actual grosso. The relationship is clarified by a number of merchant notebooks, the earliest of which was the Zibaldone da Canal (474) probably compiled in the second decade of the fourteenth century. By the time that the da Canal notebook was compiled the actual relationship between the grosso and the piccolo had for some time been such that 20 soldi (a lira) di grossi were equal to 32 lire di piccoli. The compiler also noted down the traditional relationship between money di grossi and money a grossi in the form: 20 soldi di grossi = 26 li. 2s. 2d. a grossi. However, this relationship was in the process of simplification at the time when this notebook was being compiled, for its author noted that as well as the old lire di grossi complida at 26 li. 2s. 2d. a grossi, men were also beginning to reckon in lire di grossi manca which was rounded off to 26 lire a grossi. It was the rounded off rate of 26 denari a grossi to the actual grosso that was noted by Pegolotti in his notebook (177) p.140.

Altogether, between 1280 and 1331 there were four moneys of account in use in Venice:

1 lira di piccoli = 240 piccoli = 7.1/2 grossi coins
1 lira a grossi = 1 li. 4 s. 6 d. piccoli = 9.1/5 grossi coins
1 lira di grossi manca = 26 lire a grossi = 239 grossi coins
1 lira di grossi complida = 32 lire di piccoli = 240 grossi coins (345) p.51

The Venetian ducat in soldi and denari a grossi

Date	Rate	Place	Type	Reference
1284.09	39 s.	Venice	O	(313) pp.265-6
1285.05.30	40 s.	Venice	O	(101) no.40
1296.07.14	39 s. 6 d.	Venice	O	(101) no.65
1338.03.08	39 s. 6 d.	Venice	O	(101) no.93
1338.03.08	39 s.	Venice	O	(101) no.93
1342.10.02	39 s.	Venice	O	(101) no.95
1391.03.27	52 s.	Venice	C	(243) p.201

For the uncia of Sicily in soldi and denari of Venice see under SICILY p.59
For the lira of Verona in soldi and denari of Venice see under VERONA p.93
For the lira imperiale in soldi and denari of Venice see under MILAN p.103
For the lira of Genoa in soldi and denari of Venice see under GENOA p.107
For the gros tournois in soldi and denari of Venice see under FRANCE p.188
For the hyperpyron in soldi and denari of Venice see under BYZANTIUM p.286
For the hyperpyron in grossi and denari of Venice see under BYZANTIUM p.287
For Venetian colonies in Greece see below pp.291-2
For the besant in soldi and denari of Venice see under BESANT p.294
For the besant of Armenia in soldi a grossi see under ARMENIA p.295
For the besant of Acre in soldi and denari of Venice see under ACRE p.297
For the saracen besant in soldi and denari a grossi see under CYPRUS p.299
For the dirham in grossi of Venice see under EGYPT p.302
For the besant of Alexandria in soldi of Venice see under EGYPT p.306

AQUILEIA

The Venetian ducat in lire, soldi and denari of Aquileia

Date	Rate	Place	Type	Reference
1283	3 li.	Aquileia	C	(511) II p.291
1351	3 li. 4 s.	Aquileia	C	(511) II p.291
1353	3 li. 6 s.	Aquileia	C	(511) II p.291
1356	3 li. 8 s.	Aquileia	C	(511) II p.291
1359	3 li. 10 s.	Aquileia	C	(511) II p.291
1365	3 li. 12 s.	Aquileia	C	(511) II p.292
1370	3 li. 14 s.	Aquileia	C	(511) II p.292
1377	3 li. 16 s.	Aquileia	C	(511) II p.292
1378	3 li. 18 s.	Aquileia	C	(511) II p.292
1379	4 li.	Aquileia	C	(511) II p.292
1382	4 li. 2 s.	Aquileia	C	(511) II p.292
1399-1407	4 li. 4 s.	Aquileia	C	(511) II p.292
1412	4 li. 13 s.	Aquileia	C	(511) II p.292
1417	4 li. 14 s. 8 d.	Aquileia	C	(511) II p.292
1418	5 li.	Aquileia	C	(511) II p.292
1429	5 li. 1 s.	Aquileia	C	(511) II p.292
1441	5 li. 4 s.	Aquileia	C	(511) II p.292
1443	5 li. 13 s.	Aquileia	C	(511) II p.292
1453-1508	6 li. 4 s.	Aquileia	C	(511) II p.292

VERONA

The mint at Verona was one of the four old-established mints of Italy and the denarii Veronenses had at one time a wide circulation, not only in north Italy, but also through the Alps where they were known as Berner or Perner pfennige and were used for accounting. Suhle in (447) p.72, suggests that at the beginning of the thirteenth century the area in which the money of Verona was used for accounts stretched northwards so far that it joined the area which used the money of Regensburg. The earliest groschen of the Tyrol were deliberately introduced as pieces of twenty veronenses and were hence known as Zwanziger. However, from the later twelfth century the denari of Verona began to be supplanted in north-east Italy by the denari of Venice. After the area in which Veronese money was used had contracted, the relationship between the lira of account used in Verona (and Vicenza) and the Venetian lira di piccoli became fossilized, so that, in the fourteenth and fifteenth centuries,

4 li. picc. of Venice = 3 li. of Verona
(1 li. picc. of Venice = 15s. of Verona;
1 li. of Verona = 1 li. 6s. 8d. picc. of Venice) (284) I

Rates between Veronese money and other north Italian money will be found not only under Venice, but also under Milan (imperiale), Pavia, Genoa and Lucca. Across the Alps in south Germany, rates are listed under Regensburger pfennige. There is even a single rate listed as far away as Castile (morabetinos). There are more twelfth century rates for the hyperpyron of Constantinople in money of Verona than in money of Venice since the Venetians were at this time still using Veronese currency extensively.

For the lira of Lucca in soldi and denari of Verona see under LUCCA p.40
For the Venetian grosso in denari of Verona see under VENICE p.87
For the lira imperiale in soldi and denari of Verona see under MILAN p.103
For the lira of Pavia (papienses) in soldi and denari of Verona see under PAVIA p.104
For the lira of Genoa in soldi and denari of Verona see under GENOA p.107
For the gold morabetino in soldi and denari of Verona see under CASTILE p.157
For the pfennig of Regensburg in denari of Verona see under REGENSBURG p.266
For the hyperpyron in soldi and denari of Verona see under BYZANTIUM p.286

THE TYROL

About 1258 the first grosso tirolino was struck at Merano at the value of a soldo of Verona. It does not seen to have been a great success, and about 1271 count Meinhard II produced a slightly heavier grosso at the value of twenty denari of Verona the same value as the grosso of Verona itself. For a century pieces of this sort were issued in prolific quantities by the counts of the Tyrol from the produce of their silver mines. They had a great success and were widely imitated both in north Italy, by such rulers as the bishops of Trento, and in what are today Switzerland, Austria and South Germany. They circulated extensively and became the standard coin for this whole south German region. These grossi tirolini were known by various names; as aquilini, from their obverse type of an eagle displayed; as kreutzer, from their reverse type of a double cross, or as etschkreutzer from the valley of the Adige or Etsch in which they originated.

The Venetian ducat in kreutzer

Date	Rate	Place	Type	Reference
1303	33 kr.	Trentino	C	(111) p.68
1316	30 kr.	Trentino	C	(111) p.68
1339	45 3/4 kr.	Trentino	C	(111) p.68
1356-1386	36 kr.	Trentino	C	(111) p.68
1392	38 kr.	Trentino	C	(111) p.68
1411	36 kr.	Trentino	C	(111) p.68
1419	40 kr.	Trentino	C	(111) p.68
1420	44 kr.	Trentino	C	(111) p.68
1421	39 kr.	Trentino	C	(111) p.68
1426-1432	48 kr.	Trentino	C	(111) p.68
1433	54 kr.	Trentino	C	(111) p.68
1434-1435	55 kr.	Trentino	C	(111) p.68
1436	48 kr.	Trentino	C	(111) p.68
1440-1442	58 kr.	Trentino	C	(111) p.68
1443-1447	60 kr.	Trentino	C	(111) p.68
1450	68 kr.	Trentino	C	(111) p.68
1450	49 kr.	Trentino	C	(111) p.68
1451	49 kr.	Trentino	C	(111) p.68
1454-1463	60 kr.	Trentino	C	(111) p.68
1464-1467	72 kr.	Trentino	C	(111) p.68
1468	70 kr.	Trentino	C	(111) p.68
1470-1473	72 kr.	Trentino	C	(111) p.68
1475	78 kr.	Trentino	C	(111) p.68
1476-1478	80 kr.	Trentino	C	(111) p.68
1479-1480	78 kr.	Trentino	C	(111) p.68
1482-1483	79 1/5 kr.	Trentino	C	(111) p.68
1484	78 kr.	Trentino	C	(111) p.68
1487	82 kr.	Trentino	C	(111) p.68
1495-1500	80 kr.	Trentino	C	(111) p.68

The kreutzer in denari provisini of Rome

Date	Rate	Place	Type	Reference
1285	20 d.	Rome	C	(401) p.306

MANTUA

The Florentine florin in soldi and denari of Mantua

Date	Rate	Place	Type	Reference
1341	78 s.	Mantua	B	(439) p.99
1342	80 s.	Mantua	B	(439) p.99
1343	73 s.	Milan	B	(439) p.99
1350	72 s.	Avignon	B	(439) p.99
1400	80 s.	Rome	B	(439) p.99

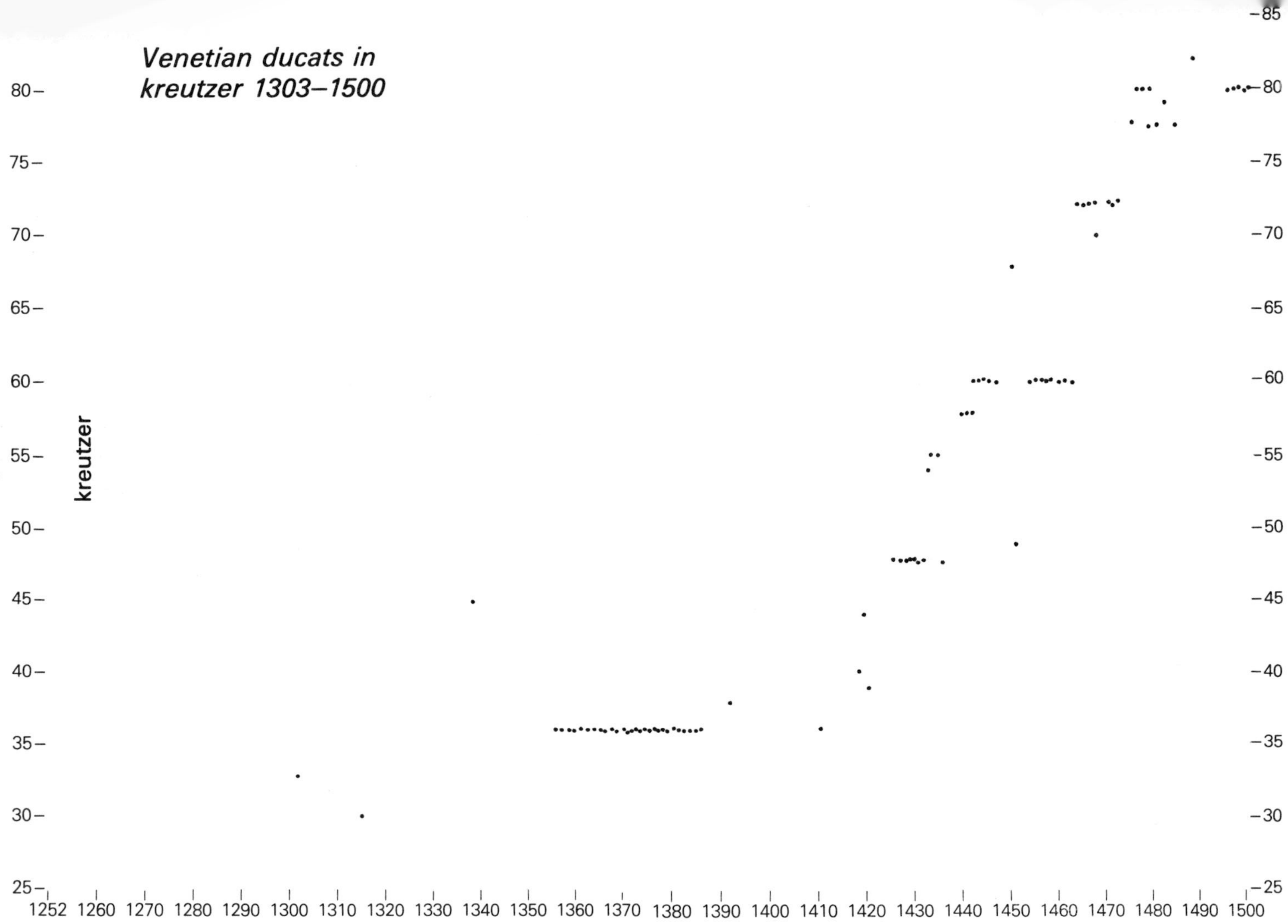

Venetian ducats in kreutzer 1303–1500

MANTUA

For the lira of imperiali in soldi and denari of Mantua see under MILAN p.103

CREMONA

The only references to the money of Cremona that I have found appear below under MILAN p.103

PIACENZA

The only reference to the money of Piacenza that I have found appears below under GENOA p.107

BRESCIA

For the use of imperial money in general see under MILAN below

The lira imperiale of Brescia in soldi imperiali of Bergamo

Date	Rate	Place	Type	Reference
1307	25 s.	Bergamo	C	(111) p.52

For the lira imperiale in soldi of Brescia see under MILAN p.103

BERGAMO

For the use of imperial money in general see under MILAN below

The Venetian ducat in soldi and denari imperiali of Bergamo

Date	Rate	Place	Type	Reference
1449 until 06.07	32 s.	Bergamo	O	(298) X p.32
1449 from 06.07	40 s.	Bergamo	O	(298) X p.32

For the lira imperiale of Brescia in soldi imperiale of Bergamo see under BRESCIA above

MILAN

Between 1155 and 1161 the Emperor Frederick I in an attempt to improve the rapidly deteriorating currency of Lombardy, attempted to close the existing mints of Pavia and Milan and strike a new imperial coinage at the imperial stronghold of Noceto. The new denari imperiali contained double the amount of silver in the existing denari pavesi and milanesi and were to be worth two of them. The Milanese copied the new imperial denari almost at once and the mint at Noceto had only an ephemeral existence. In consequence denari imperiali soon came to be thought of as primarily the money of Milan. Their circulation spread rapidly. In 1175 a chronicler at Parma was able to write: 'imperiales mediolaneses currebant per totam Italiam'.

Some other towns also struck denari imperiali, e.g. Brescia and Bergamo, but they remained principally the money of Milan.

The lira imperiale in money of Milan

Date	Rate	Place	Type	Reference
1160	40 s. mediolanus novus	Milan	H	(241) p.605
1162	20 s.	Milan	H	(241) p.605
1170.06.30	20 s.	Milan	O	(241) p.595
1179.06.05	40 s. mediolanus novus	Milan	O	(241) p.598
1186.09.23	40 s. mediolanus novus	Milan	O	(241) p.598

The Florentine florin in soldi and denari imperiali of Milan

Date	Rate	Place	Type	Reference
1252	10 s.	Milan	C	(111) p.52
1278	13 s. 4 d.	Bergamo	C	(111) p.52
1279	15 s. 7 d.	Bergamo	C	(111) p.52
1280-1284	12 s.	Curia	B	(439) p.897
1280	15 s. 6 d.	Bergamo	C	(111) p.52
1281	15 s. 4 d.	Bergamo	C	(111) p.53
1285	15 s. 6 d.	Bergamo	C	(111) p.53
1286-1288	15 s. 4 d.	Bergamo	C	(111) p.53
1287	15 s. 2 d.	Genoa	B	(187A) f.1051
1289	12 s.	Brescia	C	(111) p.53
1292	15 s.	Bergamo	C	(111) p.54
1293	18 s.	Bergamo	C	(111) p.54
1295	15 s. 4 d.	Bergamo	C	(111) p.54
1296	15 s. 8 d.	Bergamo	C	(111) p.54
1296	16 s. 6 d.	Curia	B	(439) p.898
1297	15 s.	Bergamo	C	(111) p.54
1297	16 s. 8 d.	Cremona	C	(111) p.54
1298	16 s. 8 d.	Bergamo	C	(111) p.54
1299	17 s. 10 d.	Bergamo	C	(111) p.54
1300	17 s. 3 d.	Bergamo	C	(111) p.54
1301	19 s.	Bergamo	C	(111) p.55
1302	18 s.	Bergamo	C	(111) p.55
1303	24 s.	Bergamo	C	(111) p.55
1304	25 s.	Bergamo	C	(111) p.55
1305	24 s. 2 d.	Bergamo	C	(111) p.55
1306	25 s.	Bergamo	C	(111) p.55
1306	21 s.	Brescia	C	(111) p.55
1308	28 s. 6 d.	Bergamo	C	(111) p.55
.309	27 s. 5 d.	Bergamo	C	(111) p.55
.310	26 s. 9 d.	Bergamo	C	(111) p.55
310	28 s.	Piedmont	A	(110) p.491
310	22 s. 6 d.	Brescia	C	(111) p.55
311.10.04	19 s. 6 d.	Milan	O	(365) p.94
311.11.07	19 s. 4 d.	Italy	C	(258) p.152
311-1312	28 s. 2 d.	Curia	B	(439) p.98
311	26 s. 5 d.	Bergamo	C	(111) p.55
311	28 s.	Milan	C	(111) p.55
312	30 s.	Bergamo	C	(111) p.55
315	30 s.	Milan	C	(111) p.55
316	26 s.	Milan	C	(111) p.55
317	29 s. 10 d.	Milan	C	(461) p.374
317	30 s. 3 1/2 d.	Milan	C	(461) p.375
317	30 s. 6 d.	Bergamo	C	(111) p.55
319	30 s. 3 d.	Parma	C	(111) p.55
321	31 s. 6 d.	Curia	B	(439) p.900
321	31 s. 3 d.	Milan	C	(111) p.55
322	30 s.	Bergamo	C	(111) p.55
325	31 s.	Bergamo	C	(111) p.55
326	32 s. 4 d.	Parma	C	(111) p.55
330-1334	32 s.	Piacenza	C	(111) p.55
333	32 s.	Bergamo	C	(111) p.55
333	32 s. 6 d.	Milan	C	(111) p.55
337	30 s.	Bergamo	C	(111) p.56

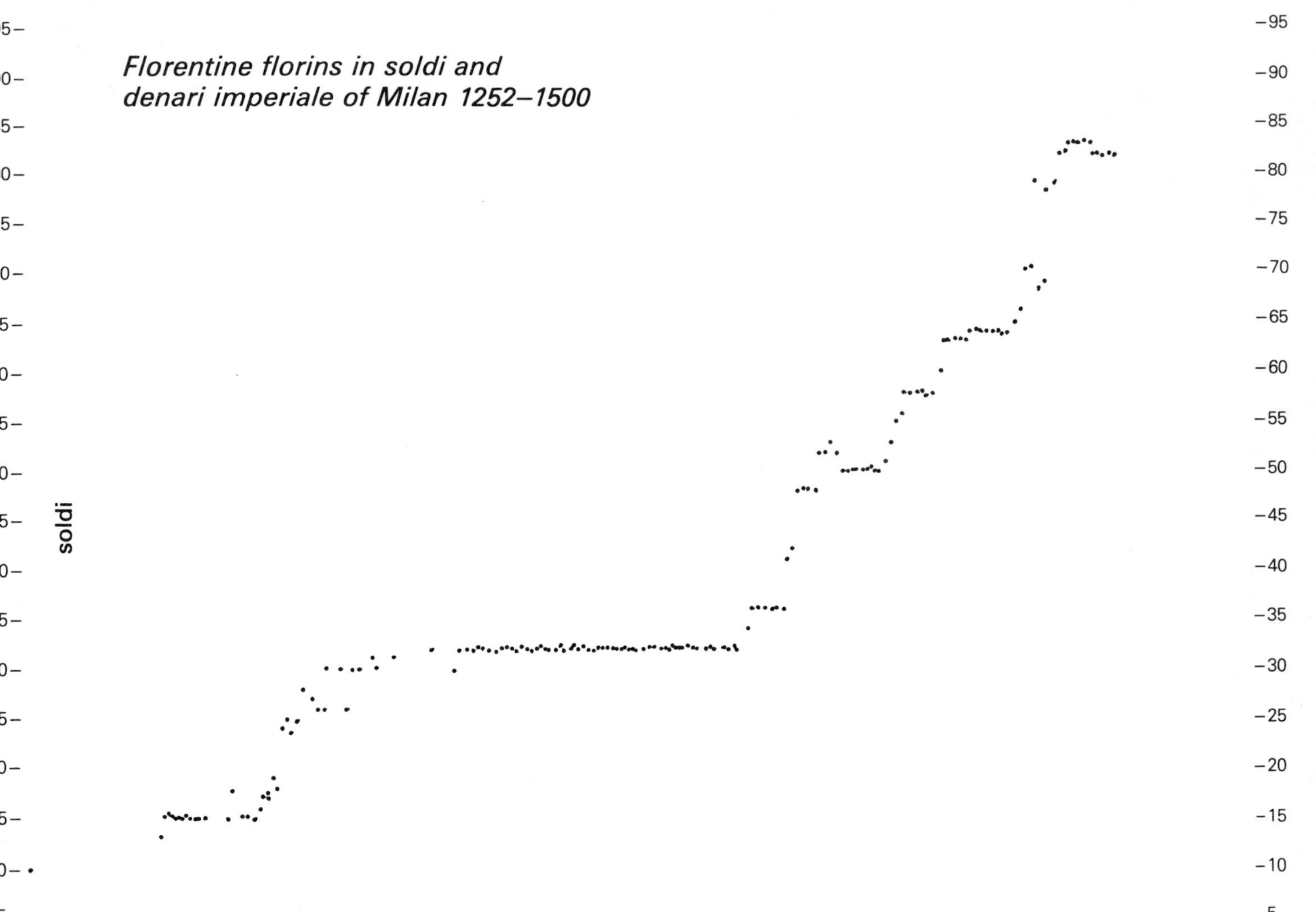

Florentine florins in soldi and
denari imperiale of Milan 1252–1500
soldi
95
90
85
80
75
70
65
60
55
50
45
40
35
30
25
20
15
10
5
1350
1360
1370
1380
1390
1400
1410
1420
1430
1440
1450
1460
1470
1480
1490
1500

THE FLORENTINE FLORIN IN SOLDI AND DENARI IMPERIALI OF MILAN

Date	Rate	Place	Type	Reference
1337	31 s. 6 d.	Piacenza	C	(111) p.56
1338	37 s.	Piedmont	A	(110) p.496
1339-1340	32 s. 6 d.	Bergamo	C	(111) p.56
1339	32 s. 8 d.	Milan	C	(111) p.56
1340-1395	32 s.	Milan	C	(458)
1341	32 s. 3 d.	Bergamo	C	(111) p.56
1341	32 s. 6 d.	Piacenza	C	(111) p.56
1343	32 s. 6 d.	Genoa	C	(187B) f.762
1345.12.02	32 s. 10 d.	Curia	B	(347) p.517
1346-1357	32 s.	Bergamo	C	(111) p.56
1356.11.16	32 s.	Milan	C	(514) p.45
1356.11.24-1357.03.13	32 s.	Milan	C	(514) p.25
1357.03.14	29 s. 4 d.	Milan	C	(514) p.45
1357.07.03	32 s.	Milan	C	(514) p.33
1360-1399	32 s.	Milan	C	(111) p.56
1363	37 s. 6 d.	Parma	C	(111) p.56
1364-1385	32 s.	Parma	C	(111) p.56
1364	32 s.	Bergamo	C	(111) p.56
1365	33 s.	Piacenza	C	(111) p.56
1367-1389	32 s.	Bergamo	C	(111) p.56
1368-1375	32 s.	Brescia	C	(111) p.56
1387	32 s.	Cremona	C	(111) p.56
1390.12.25	32 s.	Milan	C	(514) p.26
1391.02.15	42 s. 8 d.	Milan	C	(514) p.59
1394	47 s. 10 d.	Milan	C	(514) p.39
1397	34 s.	Lombardy	C	(111) p.57
1398-1404	36 s.	Lombardy	C	(111) p.57
1399	32 s.	Pavia	C	(111) p.56
1404.07-08	38 s. 6 d.	Milan	C	(458)
1404.07-08	39 s. 3 d.	Milan	C	(458)
1405.06	39 s. 6 d.	Milan	C	(458)
1405.06	39 s. 8 d.	Milan	C	(458)
1405	41 s.	Lombardy	C	(111) p.57
1406	42 s.	Lombardy	C	(111) p.57
1407.09	44 s. 6 d.	Milan	C	(458)
1407.09	48 s. 9 d.	Milan	C	(458)
1407	48 s. 6 d.	Lombardy	C	(111) p.57
1408-1410	48 s.	Lombardy	C	(111) p.57
1410.03-07	52 s.	Milan	C	(458)
1410.10-11	47 s.	Milan	C	(458)
1411	48 s. 6 d.	Lombardy	C	(111) p.57
1412-1413	52 s.	Lombardy	C	(111) p.57
1413	52 s.	Milan	C	(458)
1414	53 s.	Lombardy	C	(111) p.57
1415	52 s.	Lombardy	C	(111) p.57
1416-1424	50 s.	Lombardy	C	(111) p.57
1423	53 s.	Milan	C	(458)
1423	53 s. 6 d.	Milan	C	(458)
1425	51 s.	Lombardy	C	(111) p.57
1426	56 s.	Milan	C	(458)
1426	57 s. 6 d.	Milan	C	(458)
1426	52 s.	Lombardy	C	(111) p.57
1427	55 s.	Lombardy	C	(111) p.57
1428	56 s.	Lombardy	C	(111) p.57
1429	58 s.	Lombardy	C	(111) p.57
1430-1435	59 s.	Lombardy	C	(111) p.57
1436	61 s.	Milan	C	(458)
1436	61 s. 6 d.	Milan	C	(458)
1436	60 s.	Lombardy	C	(111) p.57
1437-1441	63 s. 6 d.	Lombardy	C	(111) p.57
1440	51 s. 2 d.	Brescia	C	(461) p.377
1442-1450	64 s.	Lombardy	C	(111) p.57
1450	65 s.	Milan	C	(461) p.377
1451	65 s.	Lombardy	C	(111) p.57
1452	66 s.	Lombardy	C	(111) p.57
1453-1454	70 s.	Lombardy	C	(111) p.57
1454.09.06	60 s. 3 d.	Florence	B	(81) p.77
455	79 s.	Lombardy	C	(111) p.57
456	68 s.	Lombardy	C	(111) p.57
457	69 s.	Lombardy	C	(650 p.57
458	78 s.	Lombardy	C	(111) p.57
459	79 s.	Lombardy	C	(111) p.57

THE FLORENTINE FLORIN IN SOLDI AND DENARI IMPERIALI OF MILAN

Date	Rate	Place	Type	Reference
1460-1461	82 s.	Lombardy	C	(111) p.57
1462-1466	83 s.	Lombardy	C	(111) p.57
1467-1471	82 s.	Lombardy	C	(111) p.57
1477.11.27	63 s.	Milan	C	(450) III p.23

The Venetian ducat in soldi and denari imperiali of Milan

Date	Rate	Place	Type	Reference
1311	19 s. 4 d.	Milan	B	(439) p.98
1375	84 s.	Piedmont	A	(110) p.500
1397	34 s.	Milan	A	(457) p238
1398	36 s.	Milan	A	(457) p238
1400-1406	32 s.	Lombardy	C	(111) p.58
1400	47 s.	Milan	C	(514) p.26
1404.07-08	37 s.	Milan	C	(458)
1404.07-08	43 s.	Milan	C	(458)
1405	41 s.	Milan	A	(457) p238
1405.06	40 s.	Milan	C	(458)
1405.06	40 s. 8 d.	Milan	C	(458)
1406	42 s.	Milan	A	(457) p238
1407	48 s. 6 d.	Milan	A	(457) p238
1407.09	49 s.	Milan	C	(458)
1407.09	49 s. 9 d.	Milan	C	(458)
1407	44 s. 6 d.	Lombardy	C	(111) p.59
1408-1411	48 s.	Lombardy	C	(111) p.59
1410.03-07	53 s. 6 d.	Milan	C	(458)
1410.03-07	54 s. 4 d.	Milan	C	(458)
1410.10-11	48 s.	Milan	C	(458)
1410.10-11	48 s. 5 d.	Milan	C	(458)
1412	49 s.	Lombardy	C	(111) p.59
1412	52 s.	Milan	A	(457) p238
1413-1421	50 s.	Lombardy	C	(111) p.59
1413	53 s.	Milan	C	(458)
1414	54 s.	Milan	A	(457) p238
1422	52 s.	Lombardy	C	(111) p.59
1423	53 s.	Lombardy	C	(111) p.59
1423	54 s.	Milan	C	(458)
1423	54 s. 6 d.	Milan	C	(458)
1424	54 s.	Lombardy	C	(111) p.59
1425	57 s.	Lombardy	C	(111) p.59
1426-1427	58 s.	Lombardy	C	(111) p.59
1426	57 s.	Milan	C	(458)
1426	59 s.	Milan	C	(458)
1427	55 s.	Milan	A	(457) p238
1428	56 s.	Milan	A	(457) p238
1428-1429	59 s.	Lombardy	C	(111) p.59
1430	59 s.	Milan	A	(457) p238
1431-1433	59 s.	Lombardy	C	(111) p.59
1434	61 s.	Lombardy	C	(111) p.59
1435	64 s.	Lombardy	C	(111) p.59
1436	60 s.	Milan	A	(457) p238
1436	64 s.	Lombardy	C	(111) p.60
1436	61 s. 6 d.	Milan	C	(458)
1436	62 s.	Milan	C	(458)
1437	61 s. 6 d.	Lombardy	C	(111) p.60
1437	63 s. 6 d.	Milan	A	(457) p238
1438	62 s.	Lombardy	C	(111) p.60
1439	62 s. 6 d.	Lombardy	C	(111) p.60
1440	63 s. 6 d.	Lombardy	C	(111) p.60
1441-1449	64 s.	Lombardy	C	(111) p.60
1442	64 s.	Milan	A	(457) p238
1450	65 s.	Lombardy	C	(111) p.60
1450.03.26	62 s. 6 d.	Milan	B	(81) p.73
1451-1452	66 s.	Lombardy	C	(111) p.60
1452	66 s.	Milan	O	(296) p.133
1452	66 s. 6 d.	Milan	M	(296) p.133
1452	67 s.	Milan	M	(296) p.133
1452	68 s.	Milan	M	(296) p.133
1452	68 s. 6 d.	Milan	M	(296) p.133
1453	67 s. 6 d.	Lombardy	C	(111) p.60

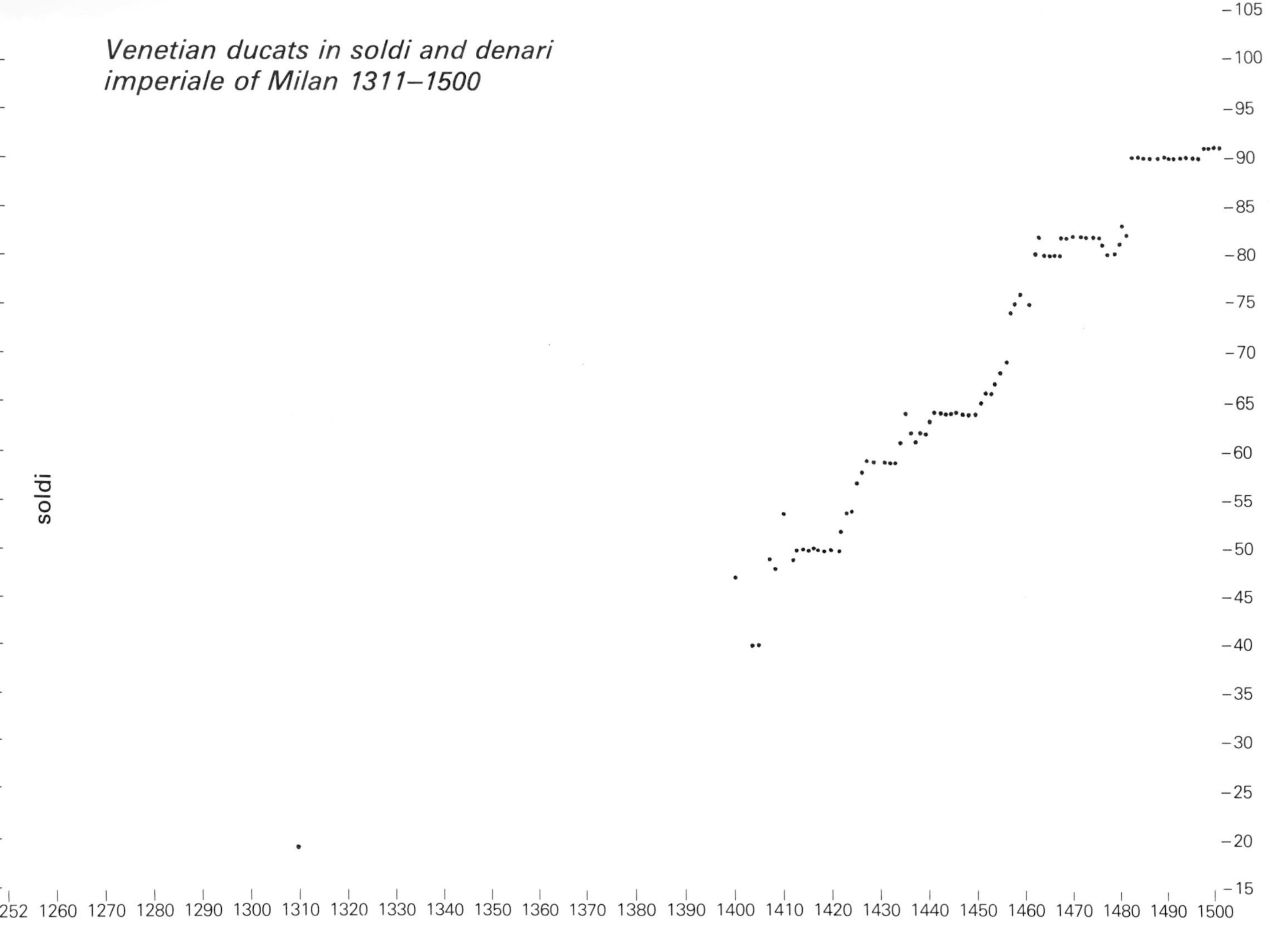
Venetian ducats in soldi and denari imperiale of Milan 1311–1500
soldi
100
95
90
85
80
75
70
65
60
55
50
45
40
35
30
25
20
15
105
1252
1260
1270
1280
1290
1300
1310
1320
1330
1340
1350
1360
1370
1380
1390
1400
1410
1420
1430
1440
1450
1460
1470
1480
1490
1500

THE VENETIAN DUCAT IN SOLDI AND DENARI IMPERIALI OF MILAN

Date	Rate	Place	Type	Reference
1454	70 s.	Milan	O	(296) p.133
1454	68 s.	Lombardy	C	(111) p.61
1454	64 s.	Milan	A	(296) p.133
1455	69 s.	Lombardy	C	(111) p.61
1455.01.02	70 s.	Rome	B	(81) p.77
1455	74 s.	Milan	C	(296) p.133
1456	74 s.	Lombardy	C	(111) p.61
1457	75 s.	Lombardy	C	(111) p.61
1458	76 s.	Lombardy	C	(111) p.61
1459	74 s.	Milan	C	(296) p.134
1459-1460	75 s.	Lombardy	C	(111) p.61
1461	80 s.	Lombardy	C	(111) p.61
1461.01.07	circa 74 s.	Milan	HC	(449) II p.87
1462	82 s.	Lombardy	C	(111) p.62
1463-1466	80 s.	Lombardy	C	(111) p.62
1467-1474	82 s.	Lombardy	C	(111) p.62
1468	64 s.	Milan	O	(296) p.132
1470.06.27	80 s.	Florence	B	(81) p.131
1475	81 s.	Lombardy	C	(111) p.62
1476-1477	80 s.	Lombardy	C	(111) p.62
1478	81 s.	Lombardy	C	(111) p.62
1479	83 s.	Lombardy	C	(111) p.62
1479.10	84 s.	Milan	C	(449) II p.248
1479.10	85 s.	Milan	C	(420) II p.248
1480	82 s.	Milan	C	(449) II p.248
1480	83 s. 3 d.	Milan	C	(449) II p.248
1480	84 s.	Lombardy	C	(111) p.63
1481-1495	90 s.	Lombardy	C	(111) p.63
1488	88 s.	Milan	C	(296) p.134
1496-1500	91 s.	Lombardy	C	(111) p.64
1500	90 s.	Milan	C	(296) p.134

The lira imperiale in other currencies

The following rates were mostly expressed in terms of imperial money, without any indication whether the imperial money was that of Milan or not. It may be assumed that it was probably of Milan.

The lira imperiale of Milan in soldi and denari of Lucca

Date	Rate	Place	Type	Reference
1184	34 s. 3 d.	Lucca	H	(241) p.605
1185	120 s. lucchese novi	Curia	B	(385) p.101

The lira imperiale in soldi and denari pisani (of Pisa)

Date	Rate	Place	Type	Reference
1185	30 s.	Curia	B	(385) p.101
1202	55 s. 8 d.	Curia	B	(385) p.100
1202	51 s. 8 d.	Milan?	H	(241) p.606

The lira imperiale in soldi bolognini (of Bologna)

Date	Rate	Place	Type	Reference
1191.02.11	60 s.	Bologna?	O	(241) p.586
1243.05.27	60 s.	Bologna	C	(118) III p.7

The lira imperiale in soldi ferrarini (of Ferrara)

Date	Rate	Place	Type	Reference
1191.02.11	60 s.	Ferrara	O	(241) p.586
1270	60 s.	Ferrara	C	(278) IA p.10

The lira imperiale of Milan in soldi and denari of Venice

Date	Rate	Place	Type	Reference
1172	40 s.	Frejus	C	(412) p.92
1190-1212	97 s. 7 d.	Venice	C	(412) p.93
1410.05.13	120 s.	Venice	C	(258) p.157

The lira imperiale in soldi and denari of Verona

Date	Rate	Place	Type	Reference
1165	100 s.	Verona?	H	(241) p.605
1165	100 s.	Italy	B	(385) p.102
1185	100 s.	Curia	B	(385) p.101
1228	102 s.	Padua	C	(412) p.93

The lira imperiale in soldi of mediatini (half-grossi) of Verona

Date	Rate	Place	Type	Reference
1228	40 s.	Verona	C	(412) p.68

The lira imperiale in soldi and denari of Mantua

Date	Rate	Place	Type	Reference
1160	40 s.	Mantua?	O	(241) p.606
1197.04.24	40 s.	Mantua?	O	(241) p.606

The lira imperiale in soldi cremonienses (of Cremona)

Date	Rate	Place	Type	Reference
1165	80 s.	Cremona?	O	(241) p.593
1185	80 s.	Curia	B	(385) p.101

The lira imperiale in soldi of Brescia

Date	Rate	Place	Type	Reference
1184	20 s.	Milan?	O	(241) p.856

The lira imperiale in soldi of papienses (of Pavia)

Date	Rate	Place	Type	Reference
circa 1155-1161	40 s.	Noceto	O	(112) p.34
1179	50 s.	Pavia	O	(241) p.604
1185	80 s.	Curia	B	(385) p.100

he lira imperiale in soldi and denari genovese (of Genoa)

ate	Rate	Place	Type	Reference
184	20 s. 6 d.	Genoa	B	(187A) f.1062
191.09.23	31 s. 7 1/2 d.	Genoa	C	(104) p.200
200	30 s. 7 d.	Genoa	B	(187A) f.1062
200.11.07	32 s. 7 1/2 d.	Milan	B	(234) p.8
201.06.20	32 s. 4 d.	Genoa	C	(104) p.200
216.07.09	30 s. 6 d.	Genoa	B	(274) II p.47
216	30 s. 6 d.	Genoa	B	(187A) f.1063
254	23 s. 10 d.	Genoa	B	(187A) f.1029
254.05.31	23 s. 9 d.	Genoa	M	(381) p.348
252	24 s. 10 d.	Genoa	B	(187A) f.1065
254	24 s.	Genoa	B	(187A) f.1066
287	21 s. 4 d.	Genoa	B	(187A) f.1068
269	20 s. 6 d.	Genoa	B	(187A) f.1069
291	21 s. 8 d.	Genoa	B	(187A) f.1068

The lira imperiale in sous provinois of Champagne

Date	Rate	Place	Type	Reference
1185	30 s.	Curia	B	(385) p.101

For the marc of écus in lire and soldi imperiali see under GENEVA p.135
For the livre tournois in soldi and denari imperiali see under FRANCE p.183

PAVIA

Pavia possessed one of the four old-established mints in Italy, and its denari papienses were for long the dominant currency, not only of Lombardy, but also as far south as Rome. However, from the mid-twelfth century its importance waned rapidly as many more mints were opened in all parts of Italy. Even in Lombardy the papienses were rapidly replaced as the dominant currency by the new imperiali.

The lira of Pavia in soldi and denari provisini of Rome

Date	Rate	Place	Type	Reference
1164	40 s.	Rome	O	(83) p.50
1299	90 s. 7 d.	Curia	HC	(179) p.98

The lira of Pavia in soldi and denari of Verona

Date	Rate	Place	Type	Reference
1165	40 s.	Curia	O	(385) p.102

The lira of Pavia in soldi and denari of Genoa

Date	Rate	Place	Type	Reference
1162.05.11	13 s.	Pavia	C	(381) p.332
1164	14 s.	Genoa	C	(93) p.46

See also the lira of Genoa in soldi and denari of Pavia under GENOA p.107

The lira of Pavia in sous and deniers provinois of Champagne

Date	Rate	Place	Type	Reference
1195	45 s.	Rome	O	(83) p.52

For the lira of Lucca in soldi and denari of Pavia see under LUCCA p.40.
For the lira imperiale in soldi of Pavia see under MILAN p.103
For the besant in soldi and denari of Pavia see under BESANT p.294

ASTI

Asti, in the hinterland of Genoa, was also important enough in the twelfth century to receive an imperial mint privilege from Conrad III, in 1140. It was the home town of many of the Lombard bankers, the most important of whom, the Malabayla, were considerable enough to provide banking services for the papacy in the fourteenth century after the collapse of the Bardi and the Peruzzi. The denaro astensis had therefore an unexpectedly wide circulation.

The Florentine florin in soldi and denari astenses (of Asti)

Date	Rate	Place	Type	Reference
1274-1280	20 s.	Rome	B	(439) p.72
1274-1280	21 s.	Rome	B	(439) p.72
1278-1282	20 s.	Curia	B	(439) p.897
1278-1282	21 s.	Curia	B	(439) p.897
1290	20 s.	Asti	C	(111) p.50
1295	24 s. 6 d.	Asti	C	(111) p.50
1309	35 s.	Piedmont	A	(110) p.491
1321	40 s.	Avignon	B	(439) p.72
1322-1323	41 s.	Asti	C	(111) p.50
1342	32 s.	Asti	C	(111) p.50
1356	45 s.	Asti	C	(111) p.50
1404	92 s.	Asti	C	(111) p.51

Asti began to strike a grosso astensis under the lordship of the marquises of Montferrat, in the second half of the fourteenth century. This replaced the, by then much enfeebled, denaro astensis as the base of the money of account of Asti in the fifteenth century.

The Florentine florin in grossi and quartari astenses (of Asti)

Date	Rate	Place	Type	Reference
1400	11 gr. 2 q.	Asti	C	(111) p.51
1401	12 gr.	Asti	C	(111) p.51
1402	12 gr. 2 q.	Asti	C	(111) p.51
1404	13 gr.	Asti	C	(111) p.51
1406	13 gr. 1 q.	Asti	C	(111) p.51
1408	13 gr. 2 q.	Asti	C	(111) p.51
1410	14 gr. 1 q.	Asti	C	(111) p.51
1412	14 gr. 2 q.	Asti	C	(111) p.51
1414	15 gr.	Asti	C	(111) p.51
1415	16 gr.	Asti	C	(111) p.51
1416	17 gr.	Asti	C	(111) p.51
1418	22 gr.	Asti	C	(111) p.51
1419	24 gr.	Asti	C	(111) p.51
1420	25 gr.	Asti	C	(111) p.51
1420	16 gr.	Asti	C	(111) p.51
1422	18 gr.	Asti	C	(111) p.51
1423	18 gr. 2 q.	Asti	C	(111) p.51
1424	18 gr.	Asti	C	(111) p.51
1425	19 gr.	Asti	C	(111) p.51
1426	19 gr. 3 q.	Asti	C	(111) p.51
1427	19 gr.	Asti	C	(111) p.51
1430	20 gr.	Asti	C	(111) p.51
1436	20 gr. 1 q.	Asti	C	(111) p.51
1437	21 gr. 2 q.	Asti	C	(111) p.51
1439	20 gr. 3 q.	Asti	C	(111) p.51
440	21 gr.	Asti	C	(111) p.51
447	21 gr. 2 q.	Asti	C	(111) p.51
448	22 gr.	Asti	C	(111) p.51
451	22 gr. 2 q.	Asti	C	(111) p.51
452	23 gr.	Asti	C	(111) p.51
455	24 gr.	Asti	C	(111) p.51
457	25 gr.	Asti	C	(111) p.51
458	26 gr.	Asti	C	(111) p.51
459	26 gr. 2 q.	Asti	C	(111) p.51
460	27 gr.	Asti	C	(111) p.51
463	27 gr. 2 q.	Asti	C	(111) p.51
466	28 gr.	Asti	C	(111) p.51
470	30 gr.	Asti	C	(111) p.51
474	32 gr.	Asti	C	(111) p.51
475	33 gr.	Asti	C	(111) p.51
476	30 gr.	Asti	C	(111) p.51
477	31 gr. 2 q.	Asti	C	(111) p.51
478	32 gr.	Asti	C	(111) p.51
483	33 gr. 2 q.	Asti	C	(111) p.51
484	34 gr.	Asti	C	(111) p.51
485	37 gr.	Asti	C	(111) p.51
487	39 gr.	Asti	C	(111) p.51
490	40 gr.	Asti	C	(111) p.51

THE FLORENTINE FLORIN IN GROSSI AND QUARTARI ASTENSES

Date	Rate	Place	Type	Reference
1491	41 gr.	Asti	C	(111) p.51
1492	38 gr.	Asti	C	(111) p.51
1493	39 gr.	Asti	C	(111) p.51
1494	41 gr.	Asti	C	(111) p.51
1495	42 gr.	Asti	C	(111) p.51
1500	43 gr.	Asti	C	(111) p.51

For the gros tournois in denari of Asti see under FRANCE p.188

GENOA

Until the twelfth century the Genoese, like most northern Italians, used the denari of Pavia. In 1139, by a privilege granted by the Emperor Conrad III, they began to strike their own denari genovesi. Because of the extent of Genoese trade, and the wealth of surviving notarial records, we have a relatively large number of rates for the Genoese lira in other currencies. The longish run of rates between Genoa and the Champagne Fairs from 1191 and 1286 appears below under CHAMPAGNE FAIRS, in terms of soldi and denari of Genoa against the livre of provinois. It appears there because it was normal to quote irregular amounts of Genoese money against round sums in the money of Provins. The rather shorter run of rates between Genoa and the kingdom of Sicily between 1158 and 1254 appear above, under SICILY for the same reason — it was normal to quote in terms of soldi and denari of Genoa against the (then gold) uncia of Sicily. For the same reason the single rate of exchange between the money of Genoa and that of Pavia appear under Pavia, and the handful of rates against imperiali appear under MILAN. Most of the rates derived from the notarial records follow here. These concern other currencies of northern Italy, Provence and southern France. It ought to be pointed out that although these rates seem few in relation to the extent of the surviving notarial records, it is because the majority of notarised documents which concerned exchange did not specify the rate at which the exchange was to be undertaken, but took it for granted.

The lira of Genoa in soldi and denari of Lucca

Date	Rate	Place	Type	Reference
1183	35 s. 10 d.	Genoa	B	(187A) f.1062
1201	35 s. 5 d.	Genoa	HC	(104)
1214	37 s. 10 d.	Genoa	B	(187A) f.1062
1216.07.30	35 s. 5 d.	Genoa	BH	(274) II p.61
1251.04.07	36 s. 5 1/2 d.	Lucca	A	(48)
1254	36 s. 8 d.	Genoa	B	(187A) f.1066
1254.02.14	36 s. 5 d.	Lucca	A	(48)
1268	38 s. 9 d.	Genoa	B	(187A) f.1067
1287	74 s.	Genoa	B	(187A) f.1067
1291	56 s.	Genoa	B	(187A) f.1068

The lira of Genoa in soldi and denari of Pisa

Date	Rate	Place	Type	Reference
1213	26 s. 8 d.	Genoa	B	(187A) f.1062
1214	40 s.	Genoa	B	(187A) f.1062
1216.07.09	37 s. 6 d.	Genoa	HB	(274) II p.47
1216.08.31	37 s. 6 d.	Genoa	HB	(445) II p.77
1216.11.25	35 s.	Genoa	HB	(274) II p.162
1216.12.06	35 s. 10 d.	Genoa	HB	(274) II p164
1225.08.01	35 s.	Genoa	HB	(274) II p.227
1234.08.22	38 s. 4 d.	Genoa	HC	(60) p.11
1227	37 s.	Genoa	B	(187A) f.1062
1268	39 s. 2 d.	Genoa	B	(187A) f.1067
1277	37 s.	Florence	B	(187A) f.1069
1299.01	55 s.	Sassari (Sardinia)	A	(70) p.280
1299.03	55 s.	Gallura (Sardinia)	A	(70) p.280
1300.04	55 s.	Sassari (Sardinia)	A	(70) p.280
1300.06	56 s. 2 d.	Gallura (Sardinia)	A	(70) p.280
1300.07	55 s.	Sassari (Sardinia)	A	(70) p.280

THE LIRA OF GENOA IN SOLDI AND DENARI OF PISA

Date	Rate	Place	Type	Reference
1301.09	55 s.	Sassari (Sardinia)	A	(70) p.280
1301.09	55 s. 5 d.	Sassari (Sardinia)	A	(70) p.280

The lira of Genoa in soldi and denari of Siena

Date	Rate	Place	Type	Reference
1226.12.04	35 s. 5 d. senesi boni	Bologna	L	(381) p.339

The lira of Genoa in soldi and denari of Bologna

Date	Rate	Place	Type	Reference
1225.10.02	45 s. 5 d.	Genoa	HB	(274) II p.282
1277	43 s.	Genoa	B	(187A) f.1069

The lira of Genoa in soldi and denari of Venice

Date	Rate	Place	Type	Reference
1200	54 s. 8 d.	Genoa	B	(187A) f.1063
1202	49 s. 1 d.	Genoa	B	(412) p.93

The lira of Genoa in soldi and denari of Verona

Date	Rate	Place	Type	Reference
1190	63 s. 2 d.	Genoa?	H	(241) p.605

The lira of Genoa in soldi and denari of Piacenza

Date	Rate	Place	Type	Reference
1200	39 s. 6 d.	Genoa	B	(187A) f.1063

The lira of Genoa in soldi and denari of Pavia

Date	Rate	Place	Type	Reference
1248	31 s. 8 d.	Genoa	B	(187A) f.1064

See also the lira of Pavia in soldi and denari of Genoa under PAVIA p.104

The lira of Genoa in sous and deniers raymondins of Provence

Date	Rate	Place	Type	Reference
1248	48 s.	Genoa	B	(187A) f.1064

The lira of Genoa in sous and deniers royaux coronats of Provence

Date	Rate	Place	Type	Reference
1200	21 s. 2 d.	Genoa	B	(187A) fo.1063
1216.03.24	21 s. 6 d.	Marseille	HB	(274) II p.10
1216.06.15	20 s. 6 d.	Marseille	HB	(274) II p.25
1282	17 s. 8 d.	Genoa	B	(187A) fo 1067
1292	17 s. 9 d.	Genoa	B	(187A) f.1069

The lira of Genoa in sous tournois of Provence

Date	Rate	Place	Type	Reference
1264	15 s.	Marseille	C	(43) p.190

The lira of Genoa in sous and deniers of the mixed money of Marseille

Date	Rate	Place	Type	Reference
1248	24 s. 8 d.	Genoa	B	(187A) f.1064
1248.03.23	21 s.	Genoa-Finali	B	(45) no.147
1248.03.27	23 s. 7 d.	Marseille-Genoa	B	(45) no.183
1248.03.27	20 s. 11 d.	Marseille-Genoa	B	(45) no.193
1248.03.28	22 s. 2 1/2 d.	Marseille-Sardinia	B	(45) no.214
1248.03.30	21 s. 5 d.	Marseille-Genoa	B	(45) no.249
1248.03.30	21 s.	Marseille-Genoa	B	(45) no.263
1248.03.30	23 s. 4 d.	Marseille-Sardinia	B	(45) no.280
1248.04.03	23 s. 6 d.	Marseille-Finali	B	(45) no.361
1248.04.07	23 s.	Marseille-Genoa	B	(45) no.416
1248.04.11	24 s.	Marseille	ML	(45) no.456
1248.04.14	25 s.	Marseille-Genoa	B	(45) no.497
1248.04.18	26 s.	Marseille-Genoa	B	(45) no.553
1248.05.08	25 s. 9 d.	Marseille	C	(45) no.700
1248.06.02	26 s.	Marseille-Genoa	B	(45) no.841
1248.06.20	23 s.	Marseille-Varaginem	B	(45) no.917

The lira of Genoa in sous and deniers melgorians

Date	Rate	Place	Type	Reference
1248.04.14	13 s. 4 d.	Genoa	L	(45) no.508
1248.04	13 s. 4 d.	Genoa	HB	(45) II p.71
1268	15 s. 3 d.	Genoa	B	(187A) f.1066

The lira of Genoa in sous and deniers provinois of Champagne

Date	Rate	Place	Type	Reference
1191	18 s. 8 d.	Genoa	B	(187A) f.1062
1191.05.14	15 s.	Troyes-Genoa	B	(381) p.337
1191.06.20	13 s. 4 d.	Troyes-Genoa	B	(381) p.337
1197.03.09	16 s.	Troyes	B	(381) p.338
1197.12.16	16 s.	Lagny-Genoa	B	(381) p.338
1227	15 s. 3 d.	Genoa	B	(187A) f.1062
1250	13 s. 4 d.	Genoa	B	(187A) f.1064
1252	14 s. 1 d.	Genoa	B	(187A) f.1065
1264	13 s. 4 d. fortium	Genoa	B	(187A) f.1066
1268	12 s.	Genoa	B	(187A) f.1066
1277	12 s.	Genoa	B	(187A) f.1066
1287	12 s.	Genoa	B	(187A) f.1068
1252	14 s. 9 d.	Genoa	B	(187A) f.1069
1268	12 s. 7 d.	Pisa	B	(187A) f.1070
1268	12 s.	Genoa	B	(187A) f.1069
1272	12 s.	Genoa	B	(187A) f.1069
1282	12 s.	Provins	B	(187A) f.1070
1292	12 s.	Provins	B	(187A) f.1070

See also the livre of Provins in soldi and denari of Genoa under CHAMPAGNE FAIRS p.164

The lira of Genoa in sous and deniers tournois of France

Date	Rate	Place	Type	Reference
1228.05.20	14 s. 1 1/2 d.	Paris	M?	(381) p.339
1248	19 s. 2 d.	Genoa	B	(187A) f. 1063
1248	17 s. 2 d.	Montpellier-Genoa	B	(187A) f.1064
1248	13 s. 4 d.	Aigues-Mortes-Genoa	B	(187A) f.1064
1248	17 s. 9 d.	Genoa	B	(187A) f.1064
1248	28 s. 4 d.	Genoa	B	(187A) f.1064
1250	17 s. 4 d.	Genoa	B	(187A) f.1064
1250	13 s. 4 d.	Genoa	B	(187A) f.1064
1253	13 s. 4 d.	Genoa	B	(187A) f.1065
1253	12 s. 7 1/2 d.	Genoa	B	(187A) f.1065
1253	13 s. 7 1/2 d.	Genoa	B	(187A) f.1065
1253	14 s. 7 d.	Genoa	B	(187A) f.1065
1253	14 s. 1 d.	Genoa	B	(187A) f.1066
1253.11.18	13 s. 4 d.	Genoa	M	(381) p.347

THE LIRA OF GENOA IN SOUS AND DENIERS TOURNOIS OF FRANCE

Date	Rate	Place	Type	Reference
1253.11.25	13 s. 4 d.	Genoa	M	(381) p.340
1253.12.06	14 s. 1 1/2 d.	Paris-Genoa	B	(381) p.341
1268	14 s. 1 d.	Genoa	B	(187A) f.1066
1286	13 s. 4 d.	Genoa	B	(187A) f.1067
1287	13 s. 8 1/2 d.	Genoa	B	(187A) f.1068
1291	26 s. 8 d.	Genoa	B	(187A) f.1068
1291	14 s. 6 d.	Genoa	B	(187A) f.1069
1270	13 s.	Genoa	B	(187A) f.1070

See also the livre tournois in soldi and denari of Genoa under FRANCE p.183

The lira of Genoa in aspers

Date	Rate	Place	Type	Reference
1286-1287	30 asperi baricati	Caffa?	C	(308) p.33
1289-1290	32-30 asperi baricati	Genoa	C	(308) p.33
1289-1290	36 asperi baricati	Caffa	C	(308) p.33
1299	30 7/10 asperi baricati	Genoa	C	(308) p.33
1348	15 1/5 aspers	Genoa	C	(187B) f.757
1409	8 aspers	Genoa	C	(187B) f.757
1416	circa 5 aspers	Genoa	C	(187B) f.757

The lira of Genoa in good zigliati of Chios

Date	Rate	Place	Type	Reference
1479.09.15	88 gr.	Chios	O	(5) p.245

The lira of Genoa in besants (unspecified)

Date	Rate	Place	Type	Reference
1192	4 1/2 besants	Genoa	A	(187A) f.1042
1264	5 besants	Genoa	A	(187A) f.1045
1267	5 besants	Genoa	A	(187A) f.1045

For the lira of Lucca in soldi and denari of Genoa see under LUCCA p.40
For the uncia of Sicily in soldi and denari of Genoa see under SICILY pp.59 and 66
For the uncia of Naples in soldi and denari of Genoa see under NAPLES p.64
For the lira imperiale in soldi and denari of Genoa see under MILAN p.103
For the gold morabetino and the dobla in soldi and denari of Genoa see under CASTILE pp.157 and 161
For the pound sterling in soldi and denari of Genoa see under ENGLAND p.208
For the hyperpyron in soldi and denari of Genoa see under BYZANTIUM p.288
For the sommo of Caffa in lire, soldi and denari of Genoa see under BLACK SEA p.290
For the florin and ducat of Chios in lire and soldi of Genoa see under CHIOS p.293
For the besant in soldi and denari of Genoa see under BESANT p.294
For the Syrian besant in soldi and denari of Genoa see under SYRIA p.295
For the besant of Acre in soldi and denari of Genoa see under ACRE p.297
For the white besant in soldi and denari of Genoa see under CYPRUS p.299
For the besant of Alexandria in soldi and denari of Genoa see under EGYPT p.306
For the besant of millarenses in soldi and denari of Genoa see under TUNIS p.309
For the dinar and dobla of Tunis in soldi and denari of Genoa see under TUNIS pp.311-12
For the uncia of Paiola gold in soldi and denari of Genoa see under PAIOLA GOLD p.312

The genovino d'oro or florin of Genoa

The Genoese began to strike genovini d'oro in 1252, the same year as the Florentines began to strike their florins, at the same fineness and at almost the same weight (Genoese 3.53 grams; Florentine 3.52 grams) The gold genovini were in consequence frequently known as fiorini. They had an initial value of 8 soldi of genovini piccoli. In the following listing genovini d'oro and fiorini d'oro have been mixed together, the rates for genovini being indicated by a G. From around 1415 onwards the genovino d'oro was more frequently known as a 'ducat', than as a 'florin'. Like that of the Florentine florin the weight of the gold genovino fluctuated in the fifteenth century between 3.45 grams and 3.57 grams. The upper figure is slightly above that of the dominant gold coin of the fifteenth century, the Venetian ducat (3.56 grams). For further details of Genoese coinage see Giovanni Pesce & Guiseppe Felloni, Le monete Genovese (381).

The Genoese and Florentine florins in soldi and genovini piccoli of Genoa

Nearly all of these rates probably refer to the Genoese rather than the Florentine florin, those marked G certainly do so.

Date	Rate	Place	Type	Reference
1252G	8 s.	Genoa	O	(381) p.58
1262G	11 s. 6 d.	Genoa	C	(111) p.41
1275.01.10G	13 s. 8 d.	Genoa	L	(381) p.348
1276G	14 s. 3 1/2 d.	Genoa	B	(187A) f.1051
1276G	14 s.	Genoa	C	(111) p.41
1276G	13 s. 10 d.	Genoa	C	(381) p.331
1276.03.03G	14 s. 1 d.	Genoa	L	(381) p.348
1277G	14 s. 1 d.	Genoa	C	(381) p.331
1277.05.27G	14 s. 1 d.	Genoa	L	(381) p.348
early 1281	14 s. 2 d.	Genoa	B	(187A) f.1051
1281	14 s. 4 d.	Genoa	B	(187A) f.1051
1281G	14 s. 6 d.	Genoa	C	(381) p.331
1281.02.03G	14 s. 8 d.	Genoa	M	(381) p.349
1281.10.10G	14 s. 4 d.	Genoa	M	(381) p.349
1282-1287G	14 s. 3 d.	Genoa	C	(111) p.41
1282G	14 s. 2 d.	Genoa	C	(381) p.331
1282.01.27	14 s. 2 d.	Genoa	M	(381) p.349
1284-1286G	20 s.	Curia	B	(439) p.897
1287	14 s. 4 d.	Genoa	C	(187A) f.1051
1291	14 s. 6 d.	Genoa	C	(111) p.41
1292	14 s. 5 d.	Genoa	C	(111) p.41
1302-1304	17 s. 2 d.	Curia	B	(439) p.899
1302	17 s. 2 d.	Genoa	C	(111) p.41
1306-1310	20 s.	Genoa	C	(111) p.65
1306	20 s.	Curia	B	(439) p.899
1309	20 s.	Genoa	B	(187A) f.1051
1309	20 s.	Genoa	L	(381) p.350
1310	20 s.	Curia	B	(439) p.899
1311G	21 s. 6 d.	Genoa	C	(111) p.42
1312	21 s. 6 d.	Rome	B	(439) p.95
1318-1320	22 s. 1 d.	Narbonne	C	(459) p.239
1318	23 s.	Curia	B	(439) p.900
1321G	24 s.	Genoa	C	(111) p.42
1321	24 s.	Avignon	B	(439) p.95
1326G	27 s.	Genoa	C	(111) p.42
1327G	21 s. 4 d.	Genoa	C	(111) p.42
1327	27 s.	Curia	B	(439) p.901
1328	25 s.	Avigliana	C	(119) p.143
1330	25 s.	Avignon	B	(439) p.95
1330G	24 s. 9 d.	Genoa	C	(111) p.42
1330	24 s. 9 d.	Avignon	B	(439) p.95
1331G	25 s. 5 d.	Genoa	C	(111) p.42
1335-1340	25 s.	Curia	B	(439) p.902
1335-1404G	25 s.	Genoa	C	(111) p.42
1336.03.02	25 s.	Genoa	B?	(334) p.169

In the 1320s and 1330s the commercial rate was frequently around 25 soldi di genovini piccoli. After 1340 the commercial rate occasionally varied, but it normally coincided with the official rate for the genovino which remained at 25 soldi, until 1405. Rates that diverge can generally be accounted for by particular circumstances. These are indicated by CM=Cambio Marittimo and R=Re-exchange, including an interest element (186).

Date	Rate	Place	Type	Reference
1340-1405	25 s.	Genoa	C	(186) ledgers
1341-1405	25 s.	Genoa	O	(381) p.328
1343.03.11	30 s.	Genoa	CM	(297) I p.140
1343.03.28	30 s.	Genoa	CM	(297) I p.148
1343.11.07	25 s.	Genoa	B	(297) I p.181
1344.12.29	28 s.	Genoa	R	(297) I p.202
1345.02.01	25 s.	Genoa	B	(297) I p.207
1345.02.09	30 s.	Genoa	CM	(297) I p.222
1345.02.10	28 s.	Genoa	CM	(297) I p.224
1345.11.17	25 s.	Genoa	B	(297) I p.234

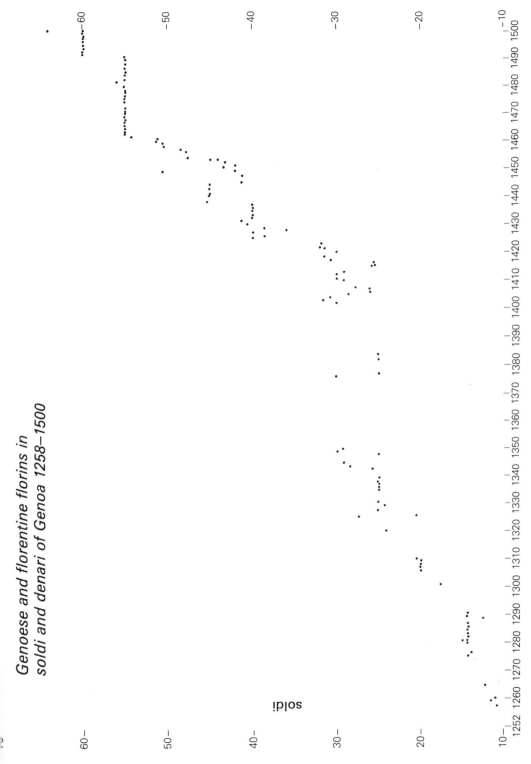

Genoese and florentine florins in
soldi and denari of Genoa 1258–1500
soldi
60
50
40
30
20
10
70
1252
1260
1270
1280
1290
1300
1310
1320
1330
1340
1350
1360
1370
1380
1390
1400
1410
1420
1430
1440
1450
1460
1470
1480
1490
1500

THE GENOESE AND FLORENTINE FLORINS IN SOLDI AND GENOVINI PICCOLI OF GENOA

Date	Rate	Place	Type	Reference
1347	25 s.	Genoa	C	(125) Notary
1348	25 s.	Curia	B	(270) p.902
1349	25 s.	Genoa	A	(338) I no.16
1349.03.30	30 s.	Genoa	CM	(297) I p.313
1349-1373	25 s.	Genoa	B	(338) p.48
1350-1399	25 s.	Genoa	C	(438) p.187
1350.02.08	29 s.	Genoa	R	(297) I p.326
1350.04.13	28 s.	Genoa	CM	(297) I p.345
1356	25 s.	Genoa	C	(125) Notary
1365	25 s.	Genoa	O	(125) Mint
1373	25 s.	Genoa	A	(338) I no.16
1376.01.26	30 s.	Genoa	CM	(297) II p.462
1376-1377	25 s.	Genoa	A	(122)
1380	25 s.	Genoa	A	(125) Magistri Rationali
1382.03.20	25 s.	Genoa	C	(121) p.654
1382.03.21	25 s.	Spezia	C	(121) p.654
1382.03.22	25 s.	Lerici	C	(121) p.654
1382.03.23	25 s.	Livorno	C	(121) p.654
1382.03.26	25 s.	Civitavecchia	C	(121) p.654
1382.11.21	25 s.	Genoa	C	(121) p.654
1384G	25 s.	Genoa	C	(23) p.110
1394.06.27	24 s.	Rome	C	(243) p.202
1399.02.10G	25 s.	Genoa	O	(213) p.95
1402	25 s. 3 1/4 d.	Malaga	HC	(332) p.32
1404G	28 s.	Genoa	C	(381) p.331
1404-1405	25 s.	Genoa	O	(381) p.328
1405.06.26G	26 s.	Genoa	A	(120) pp.57, 91
1406.07.21G	29 s. 6 d.	Genoa	A	(120) p.57
1407.08.17G	25 s. 9 d.	Genoa	A	(120) p.57
1407-1409G	27 s.	Genoa	C	(381) p.331
1408.01.08G	27 s. 6 d.	Genoa	C	(120) p.57
1408.04.01G	27 s.	Genoa	C	(120) p.57
1410G	29 s.	Genoa	C	(381) p.331
1411G	30 s.	Genoa	C	(381) p.331
1411.01-10G	30 s.	Genoa	O	(381) p.328
1412.01-05G	30 s.	Genoa	O	(381) p.328
1412 from 06G	29 s.	Genoa	O	(381) p.328
1412G	30 s.	Genoa	C	(111) p.42
1413G	29 s.	Genoa	C	(381) p.331
1413.04G	29 s.	Genoa	O	(381) p.328
1415G	26 s. 6 d.	Genoa	C	(381) p.331
1416-1417G	26 s.	Genoa	C	(381) p.331
1418G	31 s.	Genoa	C	(381) p.331
1419G	32 s.	Genoa	C	(381) p.331
1420G	30 s.	Genoa	C	(381) p.331
1420.01-02G	32 s.	Genoa	O	(381) p.328
1420.03G	31 s.	Genoa	O	(381) p.328
1420 from 04.01G	30 s.	Genoa	O	(381) p.328
1420.11G	32 s.	Genoa	O	(381) p.328
1421G	33 s.	Genoa	C	(381) p.331
1421.05G	32 s.	Genoa	O	(381) p.328
1421G	32 s.	Genoa	C	(111) p.42
1422-1423G	33 s. 6 d.	Genoa	C	(381) p.331
1423 from 02.01G	33 s.	Genoa	O	(381) p.329
1423.12G	34 s.	Genoa	O	(381) p.329
1425	40 s.	Genoa	C	(381) p.331
1425 until 11.10G	38 s.	Genoa	O	(381) p.329
1425 from 11.11G	37 s.	Genoa	O	(381) p.329
1425 from 12.11G	36 s.	Genoa	O	(381) p.329
1426G	38 s. 3 d.	Genoa	C	(381) p.331
1426 from 09G	37 s.	Genoa	O	(381) p.329
1427.07.25G	40 s.	Genoa	C	(247) p.615
1427.07-1428.11G	38 s.	Genoa	O	(381) p.329
1427.12.09G	32 s.	Genoa	C	(247) p.615
1427G	39 s.	Genoa	C	(381) p.331
1428G	38 s. 3 d.	Genoa	C	(381) p.331
1429.01.11	38 s.	Genoa	C	(144) p.160
1429G	39 s. 9 d.	Genoa	C	(381) p.331
1429G	36 s.	Genoa	C	(111) p.42
1429.01.11-05.31G	38 s.	Genoa	O	(381) p.329
1429.06.01G	37 s.	Genoa	O	(381) p.329

THE GENOESE AND FLORENTINE FLORINS IN SOLDI AND GENOVINI PICCOLI OF GENOA

Date	Rate	Place	Type	Reference
1429 from 08.15G	36 s.?	Genoa	O	(381) p.329
1429.09G	37 s.?	Genoa	O	(381) p.329
1430G	41 s. 3 d.	Genoa	C	(381) p.331
1430.02-05G	39 s.	Genoa	O	(381) p.329
1430.08-09G	40 s.	Genoa	O	(381) p.329
1430.10.11-1431.01.31G	38 s.	Genoa	O	(381) p.329
1430.10-12G	38 s.	Genoa	C	(381) p.330
1431.02.01-04.30G	37 s.	Genoa	O	(381) p.329
1431.05.01G	36 s.	Genoa	O	(381) p.329
1431	42 s. 9 d.	Genoa	C	(381) p.331
1431.01-03G	38 s.	Genoa	O	(381) p.329
1431.06-1432G	40 s.	Genoa	O?	(381) p.329
1432-1434G	40 s.	Genoa	C	(381) p.331
1433.07.05G	40 s.	Genoa	C	(247) p.615
1434-1437G	40 s.	Genoa	C	(111) p.42
1434G	40 s.	Genoa	C	(247) p.615
1436G	42 s.	Genoa	C	(381) p.331
1436.05.31G	40 s.	Genoa	O	(381) p.330
1437.10.06	40 s.	Bruges	O	(143) p.414
1437.12	40 s.	Genoa	O	(338) p.48
1437.12	40 s.	Genoa	A	(338) I no.16
1437G	40 s.	Genoa	C	(247) p.615
1438G	45 s. 9 d.	Genoa	C	(381) p.331
1440-1444G	45 s.	Genoa	C	(111) p.43
1440G	43 s.	Genoa	C	(381) p.331
1441G	43 s. 3 d.	Genoa	C	(381) p.331
1445.02.04G	42 s.	Genoa	O	(144) p.163
1445G	39 s.	Genoa	C	(247) p.615
1447G	42 s. 6 d.	Genoa	C	(111) p.43
1447.01.24	42 s. 6 d.	Genoa	O	(381) p.329
1449.11.19G	43 s.	Genoa	C	(247) p.615
1449G	43 s.	Genoa	C	(247) p.615
1450.09.28G	44 s.	Genoa	C	(247) p.615
1451.06.18G	43 s.	Genoa	C	(247) p.615
1451G	47 s.	Genoa	C	(111) p.43
1452.06.06G	44 s.	Genoa	C	(247) p.615
1453.02.06G	45 s.	Genoa	C	(247) p.616
1454.03.11G	47 s.	Genoa	C	(247) p.616
1454.05.18-12.01G	47 s.	Genoa	O	(381) p.329
1454.06.12G	47 s.	Genoa	C	(247) p.616
1454 from 12.01G	44 s.	Genoa	O	(381) p.329
1454-1455G	50 s.	Genoa	C	(111) p.43
1455.04.30G	47 s.	Genoa	C	(247) p.616
1455.06.14G	47 s.	Genoa	C	(247) p.616
1455.08.07G	47 s.	Genoa	C	(247) p.616
1455.09.17G	47 s.	Genoa	C	(247) p.616
1455	47 s.	Genoa	HC	(461) p.377
1456.02.10G	47 s.	Genoa	C	(247) p.616
1456.03.07G	47 s. 5 d.	Genoa	C	(247) p.616
1456.03.17G	47 s. 6 d.	Genoa	C	(247) p.616
1456.03.27G	47 s. 10 d.	Genoa	C	(247) p.616
1456.10.15G	51 s.	Genoa	C	(247) p.616
1456.11.27G	51 s.	Genoa	C	(247) p.616
1456-1460	50 s. 9 d.	Genoa	HC	(461) p.377
1457.03.28-10.23G	51 s.	Genoa	C	(247) p.616
1457.06.01G	51 s.	Genoa	C	(247) p.616
1457	51 s.	Genoa	C	(247) p.616
1458.01.07G	51 s.	Genoa	C	(247) p.616
1458.04.01G	51 s.	Genoa	C	(247) p.616
1458.09.23G	51 s.	Genoa	C	(247) p.616
1458.11.23G	51 s.	Genoa	C	(247) p.616
1459G	51 s.	Genoa	C	(111) p.43
1459.01-03G	51 s.	Genoa	C	(247) p.616
1459.02.06G	52 s.	Genoa	C	(247) p.616
1459.02.17G	52 s.	Genoa	C	(247) p.616
1459.03.29G	52 s.	Genoa	C	(247) p.616
1459.09.17G	52 s. 6 d.	Genoa	C	(247) p.616
1459.12.04G	52 s.	Genoa	C	(247) p.616
1460-1461	53 s.	Genoa	C	(111) p.43
1460	53 s.	Genoa	O	(338) III no.9
1460.01.16-03.10G	51 s.	Genoa	C	(247) p.616
1460.02.04G	52 s. 6 d.	Genoa	C	(247) p.616

THE GENOESE AND FLORENTINE FLORINS IN SOLDI AND GENOVINI PICCOLI OF GENOA

Date	Rate	Place	Type	Reference
1460.05.10G	52 s.	Genoa	C	(247) p.616
1460.09.02G	54 s.	Genoa	C	(247) p.616
1460.11	51 s.	Genoa	O	(338) p.49
1460.12.11G	54 s. 6 d.	Genoa	C	(247) p.616
1460G	53 s.	Genoa	O	(338) p.9
1461.04.07G	55 s.	Genoa	C	(247) p.616
1461.05.13G	54 s.	Genoa	C	(247) p.616
1461.05.15G	54 s.	Genoa	C	(247) p.617
1461.06.09G	54 s.	Genoa	C	(247) p.617
1461.07.14G	55 s.	Genoa	C	(247) p.617
1461.09.26G	54 s.	Genoa	C	(247) p.617
1461.10.12G	54 s.	Genoa	C	(247) p.617
1461.11.21G	54 s.	Genoa	C	(247) p.617
1461-1467	54 s. 10 d.	Genoa	C	(461) p.377
1462.04.30G	55 s.	Genoa	C	(247) p.617
1462.05.31G	55 s.	Genoa	C	(247) p.617
1462.08.09G	55 s.	Genoa	C	(247) p.617
1462.10.06G	55 s.	Genoa	C	(247) p.617
1463.01.14G	55 s.	Genoa	C	(247) p.617
1463.03.29G	55 s.	Genoa	C	(247) p.617
1463.05.10G	55 s.	Genoa	C	(247) p.617
1463.05.26G	55 s.	Genoa	C	(247) p.617
1463.08.02G	55 s.	Genoa	C	(247) p.617
1464.05.11G	55 s.	Genoa	C	(247) p.617
1464.06.20G	55 s.	Genoa	C	(247) p.617
1464.06.23G	55 s.	Genoa	C	(247) p.617
1464.10.09G	55 s.	Genoa	C	(247) p.617
1464.10.22G	55 s.	Genoa	C	(247) p.617
1464.11.05G	55 s.	Genoa	C	(247) p.617
1464.11.08G	55 s.	Genoa	C	(247) p.617
1464.12.12G	55 s.	Genoa	C	(247) p.617
1465.01.17G	55 s.	Genoa	C	(247) p.617
1465.01.21G	55 s.	Genoa	C	(247) p.617
1465.03.23-1471.07	55 s.	Genoa	C	(247) p.617
1473G	51 s.	Genoa	C	(111) p.43
1474-1481G	55 s.	Genoa	C	(381) p.331
1479.09G	55 s.	Genoa	C	(450) I p.248
1480G	56 s.	Genoa	C	(111) p.43
1481.09.18G	55 s.	Genoa	O	(381) p.329
1481.09	55 s.	Genoa	A	(338) I no.16
1481-1489	55 s.	Genoa	O	(338) p.49
1488.12.16-1489.01.15	55 s.	Genoa	O	(381) p.329
1489.06.16G	55 s.	Genoa	O	(381) pp.329-30
1490.02G	57 s.	Genoa	A	(338) I no.16
1490.02.26	60 s.	Genoa	O	(381) p.329
1490.02	60 s.	Genoa	A	(338) I no.16
1490.06.14G	60 s.	Genoa	O	(381) p.329
1490-1493	60 s.	Genoa	O	(338) p.49
1490-1500	60 s.	Genoa	C	(111) p.43
1491.03	56 s.	Genoa	A	(338) I no.16
1491.10.05G	60 s.	Genoa	O	(381) p.329
1492.02.08G	60 s.	Genoa	O	(381) p.329
1495.11	60 s.	Genoa	A	(338) I no.16
1495.11	56 s.	Genoa	A	(338) I no.16
1498.05.08	64 s.	Genoa	C	(247) p.617

The Venetian ducat in soldi and denari of Genoa

Date	Rate	Place	Type	Reference
1376.05.05	30 s.	Genoa	B	(297) II p.475
1400	25 s.	Genoa	C	(243) p.184
1407.10.06	27 s. 6 d.	Genoa	A	(120) p.57
1448	50 s.	Genoa	O	(338) III no.1
1460.11	51 s.	Genoa	A	(338) I no.16
1483	55 s.	Genoa	O	(338) III no.3
1490	60 s.	Genoa	O	(338) III no.5
1493	60 s.	Genoa	O	(338) III no.7
1497-8	60 s.	Genoa	O	(338) III no.8
1500	60 s.	Genoa	O	(338) p.96

The genovino of 25 soldi

For a long time in the fourteenth century, the gold genovino had a market value of 25 soldi in genovini piccoli. When the market value of the gold genovino in genovini piccoli had moved on, the official rate for the genovino remained at 25 soldi. An accounting genovino survived into the fifteenth century linked to the internal money of account at a perpetual rate of 25 soldi di genovini piccoli. Long-distance exchanges with Genoa were frequently quoted in terms of this accounting genovino of 25 soldi. Pegolotti already refers to the practice (177) pp. 222-4. Exchange from Genoa to England was quoted in terms of the number of sterlings or pence sterling to this genovino. Parts of a penny or sterling were either quoted as fractions, or as mites, at 24 mites to the penny. All rates are expressed here in pence and mites.

The genovino of 25 soldi in English sterlings (pence) and mites

Date	Rate	Place	Type	Reference
1436.03.01-10	23 d. 12 m.	Genoa	B	(38) p.380
1436.03.01-10	23 d. 6 m.	Genoa	B	(38) p.380
1436.03.01-10	23 d. 18 m.	Genoa	B	(38) p.380
1436.03.11-20	23 d. 6 m.	Genoa	B	(38) p.380
1436.03.11-20	25 d. 6 m.	London	B	(38) p.380
1436.08.11-20	26 d. 12 m.	London	B	(38) p.380
1436.08.21-09.20	26 d.	London	B	(38) p.380
1437.03.21-31	24 d.	Genoa	B	(38) p.380
1437.03.21-31	24 d. 6 m.	Genoa	B	(38) p.380
1437.12.21-31	22 d. 18 m.	Genoa	B	(38) p.380
1438.07.11-20	22 d. 12 m.	Genoa	B	(38) p.380
1438.09.11-20	22 d.	Genoa	B	(38) p.380
1438.10.11-20	22 d.	Genoa	B	(38) p.380
1439.02.01-10	24 d. 8 m.	London	B	(38) p.380
1439.02.01-10	24 d. 16 m.	London	B	(38) p.380
1439.04.01-10	23 d. 8 m.	London	B	(38) p.380
1439.04.11-20	22 d. 6 m.	Genoa	B	(38) p.380
1439.04.11-20	22 d. 12 m.	Genoa	B	(38) p.380
1439.05.01-10	22 d. 3 m.	Genoa	B	(38) p.380
1439.05.01-10	24 d. 2 m.	London	B	(38) p.380
1439.05.11-20	22 d. 3 m.	Genoa	B	(38) p.380
1439.05.11-20	22 d. 20 m.	Genoa	B	(38) p.380
1439.06.01-10	23 d. 8 m.	London	B	(38) p.380
1439.06.11-20	23 d. 8 m.	London	B	(38) p.380
1439.06.11-20	22 d. 12 m.	London	B	(38) p.380
1439.06.21-30	23 d. 10 m.	Genoa	B	(38) p.380
1439.06.21-30	23 d. 12 m.	Genoa	B	(38) p.380
1439.07.11-20	22 d. 12 m.	Genoa	B	(38) p.380
1439.09.11-20	22 d. 16 m.	Genoa	B	(38) p.380
1439.12.11-20	23 d. 18 m.	Genoa	B	(38) p.380
1439.12.11-20	23 d. 16 m.	Genoa	B	(38) p.380
1439.12.11-20	23 d. 20 m.	Genoa	B	(38) p.380
1439.12.11-20	24 d. 6 m.	London	B	(38) p.380
1439.12.21-31	23 d. 15 m.	Genoa	B	(38) p.380
1441.07.14	25 d. 8 m.	Genoa	B	(154) V p.642
1453.10.04	22 d. 18 m.	London	B	(137) p.122
1455.11.25	22 d. 6 m.	London	B	(246)p.51
1455.12.01	22 d. 14 m.	London	B	(246) p.51
1456.01.16-02.25	22 d. 19 m.	London	B	(246) p.51
1456.03.17-21	22 d. 18 m.	London	B	(246) p.51
1456.04.12-06.06	22 d. 17 m.	London	B	(246) p.51
1456.06.06	22 d. 12 m.	London	B	(246) p.51
1456.06.17	22 d.	London	B	(246) p.51
1456.09.11	22 d. 12 m.	London	B	(246) p.51
1456.09.15	22 d. 4 m.	London	B	(246) p.51
1456.12.14	22 d. 8 m.	London	B	(246) p.51
1457.01.06	22 d. 12 m.	London	B	(246) p.51
1457.04.26-29	23 d. 12 m.	London	B	(246) p.51
1457.05.02	23 d. 14 m.	London	B	(246) p.51
1457.05.14	23 d. 16 m.	London	B	(246) p.51
1457.06.10	23 d. 17 m.	London	B	(246) p.51
1457.06.26-08.14	23 d. 16 m.	London	B	(246) p.51
1457.10.12	23 d. 21 m.	London	B	(246) p.51
1457.11.23-12.03	24 d.	London	B	(246) p.51
1457	24 d.	London	C	(247) p.85

THE GENOVINO OF 25 SOLDI IN ENGLISH STERLINGS (PENCE) AND MITES

Date	Rate	Place	Type	Reference
1458.01.12-14	24 d. 3 m.	London	B	(246) p.51
1458.01.17	24 d. 5 m.	London	B	(246) p.51
1458.02.10	24 d.	London	B	(246) p.51
1458.02.07	24 d. 6 m.	London	B	(246) p.51
1458.02.15	24 d. 6 m.	London	B	(246) p.51
1458.02.18	24 d. 9 m.	London	B	(246) p.51
1458.03.20-30	24 d. 16 m.	London	B	(246) p.51
1458.04.20	24 d. 18 m.	London	B	(246) p.51
1458.06.13	25 d.	London	B	(246) p.51
1458.06.18	24 d. 19 m.	London	B	(246) p.51
1458.07.11	25 d. 2 m.	London	B	(246) p.51
1458.07.12	25 d.	London	B	(246) p.51
1458.07.14-17	25 d.	London	B	(246) p.52
1458.07.20	24 d. 12 m.	London	B	(246) p.52
1458.09.02	24 d. 22 m.	London	B	(246) p.52
1459.01.07	25 d. 6 m.	London	B	(246) p.52
1459.01.09	25 d. 3 m.	London	B	(246) p.52
1459.04.07	25 d. 12 m.	London	B	(246) p.52

SAVONA

From 1350 Savona issued florins intended to be identical in weight and fineness to those of Genoa and Florence.

For the florin of Savona in soldi and denari of Bologna see under BOLOGNA p.76

SECTION IV
ARELATE

From the tenth century the Rhône valley formed the core of the kingdom of Arles or Burgundy. In the later middle ages the German emperors were the nominal, but distant, rulers of this kingdom and it no longer had much political significance. I have nevertheless found it convenient to bring together the currencies of this area which was never Italy and not yet France. Under this heading will be found the moneys of Provence, both of the marquisate and the county, with that of Marseille; papal moneys, both for the Comtat Venaissin and for Avignon; the moneys of Vienne and Dauphiné; and the money of Savoy, with those of Geneva, Lausanne and Fribourg. The moneys of the Arelate are followed by the money of Melgueil which, in the twelfth century was in common use throughout Languedoc and Catalonia, from the Rhône to the Ebro.

MARQUISATE OF PROVENCE

The counts of Toulouse, as marquises of Provence, struck deniers raymondins, or raimondensium, at Pont-de-Sorgues between 1148 and 1249, which circulated widely in western Provence.

The livre raymondin in sous and deniers royaux coronats

Date	Rate	Place	Type	Reference
1252	10 s.	Puget nr. La Verdière	A	(18) p.320
1253	10 s.	Arles	A	(414) p.117

The livre raymondin in sous and deniers of the mixed money of Marseille

Date	Rate	Place	Type	Reference
1248.03	10 s.	Marseille	C	(45) no.307
1248.04.15	10 s. 8 d.	Marseille	C	(45) no.535
1248.05.13	10 s.	Marseille	L	(45) no.715
1248.06.05	10 s.	Marseille	M	(45) no.853

The livre raymondin in sous and deniers viennois

Date	Rate	Place	Type	Reference
1235-7	10 s.	Fréjus/Sisteron	A	(18) p.53

For the lira of Genoa in sous and deniers raymondins see under GENOA p.107

COUNTY OF PROVENCE

In 1186 the then count of Provence, Alfonso I, who was also king of Aragon, ordered the striking of a denier neuf, on the obverse of which he was to appear crowned in profile. These deniers of Provence were in consequence known as royaux coronats or in Latin, regalium coronatorum. After the death of the last Aragonese count in 1245 his successor, Charles of Anjou, struck deniers tournois provençaux until 1267, after he had himself became a king, of Sicily, when the mint of the counts of Provence again struck deniers royaux. This money of the Angevin counts of Provence, was also called, from the city where it was minted, royal money of Marseille, in Latin, regalium Massilie, but should not be confused with the independently minted mixed money of Marseille (see below p.120).

The Florentine florin in sous and deniers royaux coronats

Date	Rate	Place	Type	Reference
1263-1264	12 s. 6 d.	Marseille	C	(43) p.212
1263-1264	12 s.	Marseille	C	(43) p.212
1290	circa 10 s. 6 d.	Curia	B	(439) p.898
1301	20 s. 6 d.	Curia	B	(439) p.898

In 1302 the coronats were replaced by improved coronats reforciats, sometimes simply known as reforciats worth two of the previous coronats.

Date	Rate	Place	Type	Reference
1316.12.03	18 s.	Avignon	M	(439) p.49
1318.01.01	13 s.	Provence	A	(414) p.138
1318.01.15	14 s. 8 d.	Provence	A	(414) p.138
1318.01.25	14 s. 10 d.	Provence	A	(414) p.138
1318.01.31	14 s. 11 d.	Provence	A	(414) p.138
1318.02.16	15 s.	Provence	A	(414) p.138
1318.04.10	15 s. 3 d.	Provence	A	(414) p.138
1319	15 s. 7 d.	Curia	M	(439) p.86
1320	16 s. 1 d.	Curia	M	(439) p.86
1323	16 s. 10 d.	Curia	M	(439) p.900
1326-1327	17 s. 11 d.	Curia	M	(439) p.901
1326-1327	18 s.	Curia	M	(439) p.901
1330.11.11-12.22	13 s. 3 d.	Forcalquier	C	(341) p.142
1330	14 s.	Curia	M	(439) p.87
1332.04.02	13 s. 6 d.	Forcalquier	C	(341) p.161
1332.04.02-06.06	13 s.	Forcalquier	C	(341) p.162
1333-1334	13 s. 6 d.	Curia	M	(439) p.901
1333-1334	14 s. 6 d.	Curia	M	(439) p.901
1334.08.16	12 s. 8 d.	Avignon	M	(217) p.98
1335	13 s.	Curia	M	(440) p.35
1336	12 s. 8 d.	Curia	M	(440) p.32
1336	13 s.	Curia	M	(439) p.902
1337.04.07	12 s. 10 d.	Curia	M	(440) p.72
1337.06.12	13 s.	Curia	M	(440) p.71
1337.08.12	14 s. 6 d.	Curia	M	(440) p.70
1337	15 s. 6 d.	Curia	M	(440) p.55
1338.02.05	15 s.	Curia	M	(440) p.87
1339.01	16 s.	Curia	M	(440) p.96
1339.04.22	17 s. 4 d.	Curia	M	(440) p.107
1339	17 s.	Curia	M	(440) p.902
1339	20 s. 6 d.	Curia	M	(439) p.902
1340.01.19	15 s. 6 d.	Curia	M	(216) p.154
1340	17 s.	Curia	M	(439) p.902
1340	16 s.	Curia	M	(439) p.902
1341.06.25	17 s. 6 d.	Curia	M	(216) p.179
1341	15 s. 3 d.	Curia	M	(440) p.149
1342.11.03	18 s.	Curia	M	(440) p.220
1343	16 s.	Curia	C	(19) p.175
1343	16 s. 2 d.	Curia	M	(440) p.239
1345.05.18	16 s.	Curia	M	(440) p.264
1347.05.18	16 s.	Curia	M	(347) p.537
1348	16 s.	France	C	(431) p.15
1348	17 s. 6 d.	Curia	M	(439) p.902
1350.10.25	20 s.	Curia	M	(347) p.592
1350.11.08	16 s.	Curia	M	(347) p.592
1351.06.06	12 s. 6 d.	Curia	M	(347) p.616
1354.12.12	16 s.	Curia	M	(251) p.80
1355.10.24	16 s.	Curia	M	(251) p.107
1355.11.27	16 s.	Curia	M	(251) p.121
1356.02.10	16 s.	Curia	M	(251) p.156
1361.03.20	16 s.	Curia	M	(251) p.349
1369	16 s.	S. France	C	(501) p.7

The livre of royaux coronats in sous and deniers tournois of Provence

Date	Rate	Place	Type	Reference
1263.12.25-1264.12.25	24 s.	Provence	O	(414)
1264.12.25-1265.12.25	25 s.	Provence	O	(414)
1265.12.25-1267.08.26	26 s.	Provence	O	(414)

The livre of royaux coronats in soldi and denari of Pisa

Date	Rate	Place	Type	Reference
1248.03.30	28 s. 4 d.	Marseille-Pisa	B	(45) no.325
1248.05.01	28 s. 4 d.	Marseille-Pisa	B	(45) I p.397
1248.05.22	28 s. 9 d. old money	Marseille-Pisa or Volterra	B	(45) no.763
1248.05.22	30 s. old money	Marseille-San Gimignano	B	(45) no.764
1248.05.22	30 s.	Marseille-Pisa Gimignano	B	(45) no.765
1248.06	30 s. old money	Marseille-San Gimignano	B	(45) II p.184
1248.07.23	34 s. 2 d.	Marseille-Pisa	B	(45) no.1008

The livre of royaux coronats in sous and deniers tournois of France

Date	Rate	Place	Type	Reference
1268	16 s.	Provence	O	(414) p.85
1337	10 s.	Provence	O	(414) p.85
1400	8 s.	Provence	O	(414) p.85

For the uncia of Sicily in sous and deniers royaux coronats see under SICILY p.61
For the lira of Genoa in sous and deniers royaux coronats see under GENOA p.107
For the cameral florin in sous and deniers royaux coronats see under CAMERAL FLORIN p.124
For the florenus sentencie in moneys of Provence see under FLORENUS SENTENCIE p.125
For the livre of mixed money of Marseille in sous and deniers royaux coronats see under MARSEILLE p.120
For the livre raymondin in sous and deniers royaux coronats see under MARQUISATE OF PROVENCE p.117
For the livre viennois in sous and deniers royaux coronats see under VIENNOIS p.131
For the libra of Valencia in sous and deniers royaux coronats see under VALENCIA p.147
For the livre of Provins in sous and deniers royaux coronats see under CHAMPAGNE FAIRS p.166
For the besant of Acre in sous and deniers royaux coronats see under ACRE p.297
For the besant of Alexandria in sous and deniers royaux coronats see under EGYPT p.307
For the besant of millarenses in sous and deniers royaux coronats see under TUNIS p.311

Tournois of Provence

After the death of the last Aragonese count in 1245 his successor, Charles of Anjou, struck deniers tournois provençaux.

For the livre of royaux coronats in sous and deniers tournois of Provence see above p.118
For the lira of Genoa in sous and deniers tournois of Provence see under GENOA p.107
For the livre viennois in sous and deniers tournois of Provence see under VIENNOIS p.131

The florin of Provence

The florin of Provence in sous of Avignon

Date	Rate	Place	Type	Reference
1362-1382	24 s.	Avignon	A	(353) p.106

Gros of Provence

Robert of Anjou (1309-43) had gros struck for Provence, which like the deniers coronats had as their obverse type the crowned profile head of the king. These silver robertins or robertini were a very ephemeral money, since they were replaced in 1330 by heavier gros known as gillats or iulhats, which were identical, apart from the comital title, with the gigliati (or carlini) which Robert was already having struck in his kingdom of Naples. Some of the Curial entries under Neapolitan carlini (above pp.63) may well refer to Provençal iulhats.

The Florentine florin in gros of Robert, king of Naples

Date	Rate	Place	Type	Reference
1327	22 gros	Curia	M	(439) p.901
1328	24 gros	Curia	M	(439) p.901
1331-1334	24 gros	Curia	M	(439) p.901

MARSEILLE

Between 1221 and 1243 the Marseillais struggled for independence from their count, Raymond Berengar V of Provence. Towards the end of this period they struck their own coinage of gros and deniers (menuts), and continued to do so for some time after they had made peace with the count in 1243. This combined coinage of marseillais gros and marseillais menuts was known as moneta mescla or meslata, the mixed money of Marseille. In 1248 the royaux coronats were still not current in Marseille, but by 1251 the mixed money of Marseille had been demonetised, and was only worth a third of the royaux coronats (43)

The livre of mixed money of Marseille in soldi and denari of Pisa

Date	Rate	Place	Type	Reference
1248.04.07	circa 29 s. 3 d.	Marseille	A	(45) no.407
1248.05.23	28 s. 4 d.	Marseille-Pisa	B	(45) no.771

The livre of mixed money of Marseille in sous and deniers royaux coronats

Date	Rate	Place	Type	Reference
1248.04.15	11 s. 6 d.	Marseille	L	(45) no.516

The livre of mixed money of Marseille in besants and millarenses of Tunis

10 millarenses = 1 besant

Date	Rate	Place	Type	Reference
1248.04-07	3b.	Marseille	C	(43) p.491
1248.04-07	3b. 1m.	Marseille	C	(43) p.491
1248.04-07	3b. 2m.	Marseille	C	(43) p.491
1248.04-07	3b. 3m.	Marseille	C	(43) p.492
1248.04-07	3 1/3 b.	Marseille	C	(43) p.492
1248.04-08	3b. 6m.	Marseille	C	(43) p.492

See also the besant of millarenses in the mixed money of Marseille under TUNIS p.311

For the uncia of Sicily in the mixed money of Marseille see under SICILY p.62
For the lira of Genoa in the mixed money of Marseille see under GENOA p.108
For the livre raymondin in the mixed money of Marseille see MARQUISATE OF PROVENCE p.117
For the livre of Provins in the mixed money of Marseille see under CHAMPAGNE FAIRS p.166
For the livre tournois in the mixed money of Marseille see under FRANCE p.183
For the besant of Acre in the mixed money of Marseille see under ACRE p.298

NICE

The Florentine florin in soldi and denari niciensis of Nice

Date	Rate	Place	Type	Reference
1352	32 s.	Genoa	C	(187B) f.764

PAPAL MONEYS

Papal money presents a number of problems of identification, and it is not altogether certain that all the rates below have been listed under the correct headings.

COMTAT VENAISSIN

The Comtat Venaissin came under papal rule in 1274, but it was not until about 1300 that Boniface VIII began to have money minted there. References to sums in papal money, papales or paparini, can therefore, also mean money of the Comtat Venaissin. They have therefore, been listed here, but carefully distinguished. Clementini parvi, deniers issued for Clement V (pope 1305-14), have similarly been distinguished.

The Florentine florin in money of the Venaissin

Date	Rate	Place	Type	Reference
1301	23 s.	Curia	B	(439) p.898
1302	25 s.	Curia	B	(439) p.899
1316	17 s. 6 d.	Curia	M	(439) p.900
1316	18 s.	Curia	M	(439) p.900
1317	23 s. 10 d. papales	Curia	C	(111) p.92
1318	23 s.	Curia	M	(439) p.900
1318	23 s. 10 d.	Curia	M	(439) p.900
1318	24 s.	Curia	M	(439) p.900
1318	24 s. papales	Curia	C	(111) p.92
1319	24 s. 6 d.	Curia	M	(439) p.900
1319	23 s.	Curia	M	(439) p.900
1319	24 s.	Curia	M	(439) p.900
1324	26 s. clementini parvi	Curia	M	(439) p.901
1325	26 s. 2 clementini parvi	Carpentras	C	(425) p.71
1326-1327	circa 26 s. clementini parvi	Curia	M	(439) p.901
1332	35 s. clementini parvi	Curia	M	(439) p.901
1334	23 s. 8 d.	Curia	M	(439) p.901
1337-1338	23 s. 8 d.	Curia	M	(439) p.902

The sou of paparini of the Venaissin in deniers viennois

Date	Rate	Place	Type	Reference
1319.09.25	10 d.	Pont-de-Sorgues	A	(51) p.147

The sou of paparini of the Venaissin in deniers tournois

Date	Rate	Place	Type	Reference
1319.09.25	8 d.	Pont-de-Sorgues	A	(51) p.147

The Florentine florin in Iohanneti current in the Venaissin

Date	Rate	Place	Type	Reference
1334	35 s.	Curia	M	(439) p.901
1334	36 s.	Curia	M	(439) p.901
1337-1338	39 s.	Curia	M	(439) p.902

For the écu au soleil in gros de comte see under FRANCE p.194

AVIGNON

Both Clement V and John XXII regarded their stay at Avignon as temporary. It was not until 1336 that Pope Benedict XII acquired a permanent residence there, by buying the palace of the bishop and rebuilding it. Over the next few years, the whole papal administration was definitively moved into Avignon. The mint was transferred there from Pont-de-Sorgues in the Comtat Venaissin. Papal money begins to be referred to as money of Avignon at this period, although the sovereignity of the city of Avignon was not purchased until Pope Clement VI did so in 1348. Some of the following rates are derived from Curial accounts, which being compiled in Avignon, quite naturally simply referred to papal money as 'current money'.

The Florentine florin in sous and deniers of Avignon

Date	Rate	Place	Type	Reference
1340	27 s.	Curia	M	(439) p.902
1340.09.18	27 s.	Curia	M	(440) p.123
1340	26 s. 6 d.	Curia	M	(440) p.122
1341	25 s. 4 d.	Curia	M	(440) p.141
1341	26 s.	Curia	M	(439) p.902
1341	25 s. 6 d.	Curia	M	(439) p.902
1342.06.19	25 s.	Curia	M	(440) p.189
1342.06.19	25 s. 6 d.	Curia	M	(440) p.187
1342.11.27	24 s.	Curia	M	(440) p.215
1343.02.25	24 s. 6 d.	Curia	M	(440) p.224
1343.09.18	24 s. 6 d.	Curia	M	(440) p.237
1344.10	23 s. 10 d.	Curia	M	(440) p.272
1344	25 s.	Curia	M	(440) p.255
1346.06.08	23 s. 6 d.	Curia	M	(347) V p.374
1346.06.24	25 s.	Curia	M	(440) p.354
1347.12.12	24 s.	Curia	M	(347) V p.398
1348-1356	24 s.	Curia	M	(439) p.902
1349.02.06	24 s.	Curia	M	(347) p.418
1349.10.19	25 s.	Curia	M	(347) p.430
1350.11.08	24 s.	Curia	M	(347) p.596
1351.01.10	24 s.	Curia	M	(347) p.615
1352.03.07	24 s.	Curia	M	(440) p.477
1352.03.10	24 s.	Curia	M	(1540 p.602
1352	24 s.	Curia	M	(439) p.42
1358.10.31	24 s.	Curia	M	(251) p.245
1363.04.15	25 s.	Curia	M	(441) p.80
1363.06.19	24 s.	Curia	M	(441) p.77
1363.06.30	26 s.	Curia	M	(441) p.76
1364.02.12	24 s.	Curia	M	(441) p.95
1366.12.31	26 s. 2 d.	Curia	M	(441) p.191
1367.01.16	25 s.	Curia	M	(441) p.205
1367.04.06	26 s.	Curia	M	(441) p.187
1367.05.05	26 s. 6 d.	Curia	M	(441) p.203
1367.05.09	26 s.	Curia	M	(441) p.225
1368.03	24 s.	Curia	M	(441) p.262
1369.06.22	26 s.	Paris-Curia	B	(28) p.675
1372	27 s. 6 d.	Avignon	M	(439) p.57
1373	27 s. 6 d.	Curia	M	(441) p.377

THE FLORENTINE FLORIN IN SOUS AND DENIERS OF AVIGNON

Date	Rate	Place	Type	Reference
1376.09.10	27 s. 6 d.	Avignon	C	(343) p.152
1376.09.15	28 s.	Avignon	C	(343) p.154
1376.11.09	28 s.	Avignon	C	(268) p.202
1376	27 s. 10 d.	Avignon	C	(343) p.155
1376	28 s.	Livorno	B	(439) p.52
1378	30 s.	Avignon	C	(182) p.36
1393	30 s.	Avignon	C	(182) p.36

For the florin of Provence in sous of Avignon see under PROVENCE p.119
For the livre viennois in sous and deniers papales see under VIENNOIS p.131
For the florin of Aragon in sous and deniers of Avignon see under ARAGON p.152
For the rheingulden in sous and deniers of Avignon see under RHINELAND p.250

Papal gros

As well as deniers, successive popes, from Clement V (1305-14) onwards, also had gros struck for them in the Comtat Venaissin and later in Avignon, which went under various names.

The Florentine florin in silver paparini

Date	Rate	Place	Type	Reference
1320	circa 14 gr.	Curia	M	(439) p.900

The Florentine florin in silver clementini (Clement V 1305-14)

Date	Rate	Place	Type	Reference
1333-1334	19 1/2 gr.	Curia	M	(439) p.901

The Florentine florin in new silver clementini (Clement VI, 1342-52)

Date	Rate	Place	Type	Reference
1344	10 gr.	Curia	M	(439) p.902
1344	12 gr.	Curia	M	(439) p.902
1351.12.20	10 gr.	Curia	M	(347) p.450

In 1378 the Avignon gros was valued as 2 sous of Avignon money (182) p.36, and this value seems to have remained steady for some time, for in 1390 the cameral florin, then still reckoned as 28 sous of Avignon money, was valued at 14 Avignon gros in Piedmont (110) p.504.

The cameral florin

In 1322 John XXII began the minting of papal florins. These were initially almost deceptively similar to Florentine florins and were known as florins de la Chambre. They were modified under Urban V. (181) p.172. The cameral florin's value was expressed variously as in 'current money', 'papal money', and 'money of Avignon'.

The cameral florin in sous and deniers of Avignon

Date	Rate	Place	Type	Reference
1339	20 s. 6 d.	Avignon	C	(364) p.9
1340	19 s.	Avignon	C	(364) p.9
1342-1358	24 s.	Curia	C	(111) p.92
1343-1346	24 s.	Avignon	C	(364) p.9
1362.01	24 s.	Avignon	M	(251) p.385
1362.05	24 s.	Curia	M	(251) p.403
1364.09.30	25 s. 7 d.	Curia	M	(441) p.103
1364.11.27	20 s.	England	B	(311) p.225
1364-1367	26 s.	Curia	C	(111) p.92
1365.01.08	26 s.	Curia	M	(441) p.112
1365.04.30	26 s.	Curia	M	(441) p.108
1365.06.25	26 s.	Curia	M	(441) p.122
1365.12.23	26 s.	Curia	M	(441) p.154
1367.01.07	26 s. 3 d.	Curia	M	(441) p.204
1367.06.05	26 s.	Viterbo	C	(268) p.24

THE CAMERAL FLORIN IN SOUS AND DENIERS OF AVIGNON

Date	Rate	Place	Type	Reference
1367.06.15	26 s.	Viterbo	C	(268) p.26
1367.06.18	26 s.	Viterbo	C	(268) p.28
1367.06.30	26 s. 6 d.	Viterbo	C	(268) p.32
1367.06.30	24 s.	Viterbo	C	(268) p.33
1367.12.01	27 s.	Viterbo	C	(268) p.101
1368.09.30	27 s. 6 d.	Florence	B	(24) p.295
1368.09.22-1369.06.04	26 s.	Venaissin	O	(400) p.178
1368	28 s.	Curia	C	(111) p.92
1369.10.13	28 s.	Curia	M	(441) p.263
1369.11.03	28 s.	Curia	M	(441) p.267
1369	26 s.	Curia	C	(111) p.92
1369	28 s.	Curia	C	(111) p.92
1370.08.27	28 s.	Curia	M	(441) p.283
1370	27 s. 6 d.	Curia	C	(111) p.93

The cameral florin in sous and deniers royaux coronats

Date	Rate	Place	Type	Reference
1331	13 s. 4 d.	Pont-de-Sorgues	A	(51) p.173
1332	13 s. 4 d.	Pont-de-Sorgues	A	(51) p.174
1333	13 s. 4 d.	Pont-de-Sorgues	A	(51) p.174
1334	13 s. 4 d.	Pont-de-Sorgues	A	(51) p.174

The cameral florin in sous and deniers viennois

Date	Rate	Place	Type	Reference
1323.06.10	20 s. 8 d.	Pont-de-Sorgues	A	(51) p.171
1323.07.10	21 s. 5 d.	Pont-de-Sorgues	A	(51) p.171
1323.08.02	21 s. 8 d.	Pont-de-Sorgues	A	(51) p.171
1323.09.24	21 s. 11 d.	Pont-de-Sorgues	A	(51) p.171
1323.10.22	21 s. 9 d.	Pont-de-Sorgues	A	(51) p.171
1323.12.21	22 s. 1 d.	Pont-de-Sorgues	A	(51) p.171
1324.03.17	21 s. 8 d.	Pont-de-Sorgues	A	(51) p.171
1324.10.16	20 s. 10 d.	Pont-de-Sorgues	A	(51) p.171
1324.12.11	21 s. 8 d.	Pont-de-Sorgues	A	(51) p.171
1325.01.19	21 s. 9 d.	Pont-de-Sorgues	A	(51) p.171
1325.02.26	22 s. 1 d.	Pont-de-Sorgues	A	(51) p.171
1325.04.06	21 s. 10 d.	Pont-de-Sorgues	A	(51) p.172
1325.06.03	22 s. 2 d.	Pont-de-Sorgues	A	(51) p.172
1325.07.23	21 s. 8 d.	Pont-de-Sorgues	A	(51) p.172
1325.08.13	22 s. 3 d.	Pont-de-Sorgues	A	(51) p.172
1325.09.26	21 s. 10 d.	Pont-de-Sorgues	A	(51) p.172
1325.11.08	22 s. 3 d.	Pont-de-Sorgues	A	(51) p.172
1325.12.16	21 s. 6 d.	Pont-de-Sorgues	A	(51) p.172
1326.01.02	22 s.	Pont-de-Sorgues	A	(51) p.172
1326.02.24	20 s. 8 d.	Pont-de-Sorgues	A	(51) p.172
1326.05.07	21 s. 8 d.	Pont-de-Sorgues	A	(51) p.172
1326.06.07	22 s. 6 d.	Pont-de-Sorgues	A	(51) p.172
1326.12.09	22 s. 7 d.	Pont-de-Sorgues	A	(51) p.172
1327.02.10	24 s.	Pont-de-Sorgues	A	(51) p.172
1327.07.04	23 s. 8 d.	Pont-de-Sorgues	A	(51) p.172
1327.09.03	23 s. 2 d.	Pont-de-Sorgues	A	(51) p.172
1327.11.03	28 s.	Pont-de-Sorgues	A	(51) p.172
1328.01.31	31 s.	Pont-de-Sorgues	A	(51) p.172
1328.03.04	31 s. 3 d.	Pont-de-Sorgues	A	(51) p.172
1328.05.01	30 s. 10 d.	Pont-de-Sorgues	A	(51) p.172
1328.06.06	30 s. 9 d.	Pont-de-Sorgues	A	(51) p.172
1328.07.14	29 s. 10 d.	Pont-de-Sorgues	A	(51) p.172
1328.08.04	31 s. 7 d.	Pont-de-Sorgues	A	(51) p.172
1329.01.07	31 s. 9 d.	Pont-de-Sorgues	A	(51) p.173
1329.02.09	31 s. 9 d.	Pont-de-Sorgues	A	(51) p.173
1329.06.02	33 s. 4 d.	Pont-de-Sorgues	A	(51) p.173
1330.05.12	30 s. 11 d.	Pont-de-Sorgues	A	(51) p.173
1330.06.04	30 s. 8 d.	Pont-de-Sorgues	A	(51) p.173
1330.07.13	30 s. 5 d.	Pont-de-Sorgues	A	(51) p.173

The cameral florin in sous and deniers valosii
1 sous of valosii = 2 sous parisis

Date	Rate	Place	Type	Reference
1330.09.07	10 s. 3 d.	Pont-de-Sorgues	A	(51) p.173

In the 1360s the cameral florin became a unit of account, so that sums could be expressed in sous and deniers of the cameral florin.

The Florentine florin in sous and deniers of the Cameral florin

Date	Rate	Place	Type	Reference
1367.05.26	26 s. 10 1/2 d.	Rhodes	A	(312)
1367.11.26	27 s. 7 d.	Rhodes	A	(312)

The florenus sentencie

In 1352 Clement VI decided that the archbishop of Arles, the bishop of St Paul and the prince of Orange ought not to strike florins of worse gold than 23.7/8 carats fine, or lighter than 64 to the papal mark (i.e. 3.49 grams). The florins struck in accordance with this papal decision or sentence were known as 'florins de la sentence' or 'floreni sentencie' (414). The florenus sentencie also appears in papal accounts of the 1350s and early 1360s as an accounting unit of 24 sous of Avignon, then normally also the value of Florentine and cameral florins. See above pp.122 and 123.

The florenus sentencie in money of Provence

Date	Rate	Place	Type	Reference
1356.09.15	16 s.	Curia	A	(251) p.158

The florenus sentencie in parve monete Provincie

Date	Rate	Place	Type	Reference
1356.11.21	32 s.	Curia	A	(251) p.158

The florenus sentencie in monete Francie (? = sous and deniers tournois)

Date	Rate	Place	Type	Reference
1359.05.17	24 s.	Curia	A	(251) p.271

Current florins and gros, cameral florins and papal francs

From 1371 onwards Gregory XI began to issue a new, lighter, florin, known as commune or courant. In the following year similar florins began to be minted in Provence. The new current florin was valued at 24 sous of Avignon, or 12 gros of Provence. They came to be known as 'florins de 12 gros'. Reckoning in florins and gros was already common in southern France (see below p.131). The 'gros de florin' now became the twelfth part of the new papal florin, and reckoning in florin and gros became normal at Avignon, in the Comtat Venaissin and in Provence. In the Comtat Venaissin they were still using florins and gros at the end of the fifteenth century (277) pp.1130-1, and still keeping to the relationship of 12 gros to the florin. Light, current florins, 'fiorini correnti', continued to be struck at Avignon and in Provence from time to time. For example, when the great schism began, and Clement VII returned to Avignon in 1379, he had florins of St Clement florins clémentins struck, which were current florins of 12 gros, or 24 sous. In Provence florins of 12 gros continued to be struck until Louis III (count 1417-34).

Cameral florins, 'fiorini di camera', continued to be used as units of account, deriving their value from the current florin. In the 1370s and 1380s the cameral florin was a unit of 14 gros or 28 sous. By 1396 the cameral florin had come to mean 14 1/2 gros or 29 sous and remained a multiple of 29/24ths of the current florin into the fifteenth century.

Meanwhile, the use of the franc-gros accounting system in southern France (see below p.192) resulted in the adoption of a variant of it at Avignon. The 'franchi papali', referred to from 1385, were multiples of 15 grossi fiorinati, or 30 'soldi a monetta di grossi fiorinati', for the money of Avignon had become fossilized at 2 sous to the gros de florin (178). Papal francs therefore also took their value from the current florin, and were a multiple of 30/24ths of them.

Gros, current florins, cameral florins, and papal francs were used for different purposes. In his notebook, corrected in 1442, Uzzanno (373) noted that banks in Avignon kept their accounts in small, i.e. current, florins, 'pitteti' or 'correnti', of 12 gros; that cloth merchants sold cloth at so many gros per palme; that exchange dealings from Avignon to Florence, Pisa and Genoa were quoted in cameral florins, fiorini di camera, and that exchange dealings from Avignon to Montpellier, Bruges and Barcelona were quoted in papal francs. The accounts of Manelli bank at Avignon in 1427-31 partially illustrate Uzzanno's division of function. They used the cameral florin for exchange dealings with Florence and the papal franc for exchange dealings with Barcelona, Valencia, and Montpellier, but used the florin of 12 gros for exchange dealings with Bruges, see rates from (519) below.

The cameral florin in soldi and denari affiorini of Florence

In this table the two dates given are those of the drawing and the acceptance of the bills.

Date	Rate	Place	Type	Reference
1427.07.30-08.18	22 s. 1 1/2 d.	Avignon-Florence	B	(519) f.61
1427.10.30-11.19	23 s. 2 1/2 d.	Avignon-Florence	B	(519) f.61v
1427.11.13-12.18	23 s. 2 1/2 d.	Avignon-Florence	B	(519) f.61v
1427.12.07	23 s. 2 1/2 d.	Florence-Avignon	B	(519) f.42v
1427.12.22	23 s.	Florence-Avignon	B	(519) f.42v
1427.12.22	22 s. 10 1/2 d.	Florence-Avignon	B	(519) f.43
1428.01.28-02.05	22 s. 4 1/4 d.	Florence-Avignon	B	(519) f.43v
1428.02.23-03.22	22 s. 5 3/4 d.	Florence-Avignon	B	(519) f.44
1428.03.03-03.21	22 s. 5 3/4 d.	Avignon-Florence	B	(519) f.63
1428.04.06-05.02	21 s. 11 1/2 d.	Avignon-Florence	B	(519) f.63v
1428.05.12-05.25	22 s.	Florence-Avignon	B	(519) f.44v
1428.05.18	22 s. 1 1/2 d.	Avignon-Florence	B	(519) f.64
1428.08.27-09.09	22 s. 1 1/2 d.	Florence-Avignon	B	(519) f.45
1428.09.09-09.23	22 s. 1/2 d.	Florence-Avignon	B	(519) f.45
1428.10.12-11.30	22 s. 1/2 d.	Florence-Avignon	B	(519) f.45
1429.04.08-04.26	23 s. 1 3/4 d.	Florence-Avignon	B	(519) f.46v
1429.04.13-05.05	23 s. 1/2 d.	Florence-Avignon	B	(519) f.47
1429.06.27-07.17	23 s. 9 1/4 d.	Avignon-Florence	B	(519) f.66v
1429.07.15-08.07	23 s.	Florence-Avignon	B	(519) f.47v
1429.08.05-09.25	22 s. 11 1/2 d.	Florence-Avignon	B	(519) f.47v
1429.08.23-09.23	22 s. 9 d.	Florence-Avignon	B	(519) f.47v
1429.11.11-12.10	21 s. 11 1/2 d.	Florence-Avignon	B	(519) f.48
1429.12.08	22 s.	Florence-Avignon	B	(519) f.48
1430.01.28-02.29	21 s. 6 d.	Florence-Avignon	B	(519) f.48v
1430.03.16-03.31	22 s.	Florence-Avignon	B	(519) f.49v
1430.04.17-05.11	20 s. 10 1/4 d.	Florence-Avignon	B	(519) f.50
1430.06.15-07.20	20 s. 5 d.	Avignon-Florence	B	(519) f.69
1430.06.15-07.20	20 s. 6 3/4 d.	Avignon-Florence	B	(519) f.69
1430.05.23-06.26	20 s. 5 d.	Florence-Avignon	B	(519) f.50
1430.07.14	20 s. 3 1/2 d.	Avignon-Florence	B	(519) f.68v

The papal franc in sueldos and dineros of Barcelona

In this table the two dates given are those of the drawing and the acceptance of the bills. I have selected the first bills drawn each month in each direction from a much larger body of material.

Date	Rate	Place	Type	Reference
1427.08.15-08.28	12 s. 1 d.	Barcelona-Avignon	B	(519) f.41v
1427.09.02-09.17	12 s. 1 1/2 d.	Barcelona-Avignon	B	(519) f.41
1427.10.14-10.22	11 s. 11 d.	Barcelona-Avignon	B	(519) f.41v
1427.11.20-12.13	12 s. 3 d.	Barcelona-Avignon	B	(519) f.42v
1427.12.06-12.24	12 s. 1 1/2 d.	Barcelona-Avignon	B	(519) f.43
1428.01.21-02.01	12 s. 2 1/4 d.	Barcelona-Avignon	B	(519) f.43v
1428.02.01-02.10	12 s. 1 1/2 d.	Barcelona-Avignon	B	(519) f.43v
1428.04.19-05.02	11 s. 9 1/2 d.	Barcelona-Avignon	B	(519) f.44
1428.05.18-05.27	11 s. 7 d.	Avignon-Barcelona	B	(519) f.64
1428.05.30-06.22	11 s. 5 1/2 d.	Avignon-Barcelona	B	(519) f.64v

THE PAPAL FRANC IN SUELDOS AND DINEROS OF BARCELONA

Date	Rate	Place	Type	Reference
1428.06.10-06.17	11 s. 11 d.	Avignon-Barcelona	B	(519) f.64v
1428.06.17	11 s. 11 d.	Barcelona-Avignon	B	(519) f.44v
1428.09.19	11 s. 10 d.	Barcelona-Avignon	B	(519) f.45
1428.10.26-11.12	11 s. 9 d.	Barcelona-Avignon	B	(519) f.45
1428.12.17	11 s. 9 d.	Avignon-Barcelona	B	(519) f.65
1429.01.02-01.10	12 s.	Avignon-Barcelona	B	(519) f.65
1429.01.21	12 s. 1 d.	Barcelona-Avignon	B	(519) f.45v
1429.02.21-03.27	12 s. 10 d.	Barcelona-Avignon	B	(519) f.46v
1429.02.27-03.10	12 s. 5 1/2 d.	Avignon-Barcelona	B	(519) f.65v
1429.03.01-03.17	12 s. 5 1/2 d.	Avignon-Barcelona	B	(519) f.65v
1429.03.10-03.17	12 s. 5 d.	Barcelona-Avignon	B	(519) f.46
1429.04.05-04.13	12 s. 7 1/2 d.	Barcelona-Avignon	B	(519) f.46v
1429.05.10-05.22	11 s. 8 1/2 d.	Barcelona-Avignon	B	(519) f.47
1429.06.09-06.23	12 s. 8 d.	Avignon-Barcelona	B	(519) f.66v
1429.06.12-06.23	12 s. 8 d.	Barcelona-Avignon	B	(519) f.47v
1429.08.02-08.12	12 s.	Avignon-Barcelona	B	(519) f.66v
1429.08.08-08.17	12 s.	Barcelona-Avignon	B	(519) f.47
1429.09.22-10.02	11 s. 9 1/3 d.	Barcelona-Avignon	B	(519) f.48
1429.10.13-10.21	11 s. 10 d.	Avignon-Barcelona	B	(519) f.67
1429.11.03-11.17	11 s. 8 d.	Barcelona-Avignon	B	(519) f.48
1429.11.21	11 s. 8 1/2 d.	Avignon-Barcelona	B	(519) f.67
1429.12.01-12.17	11 s. 7 1/3 d.	Barcelona-Avignon	B	(519) f.48v
1430.01.02-01.09	11 s. 6 d.	Barcelona-Avignon	B	(519) f.48v
1430.02.06-02.27	11 s. 8 1/2 d.	Barcelona-Avignon	B	(519) f.49
1430.03.05-03.18	11 s. 9 1/2 d.	Barcelona-Avignon	B	(519) f.49
1430.03.12-03.27	11 s. 9 1/2 d.	Avignon-Barcelona	B	(519) f.67v
1430.04.28-05.10	11 s. 8 1/3 d.	Barcelona-Avignon	B	(519) f.49v
1430.05.11	11 s. 9 1/3 d.	Barcelona-Avignon	B	(519) f.49v
1430.05.16-05.30	11 s. 6 d.	Avignon-Barcelona	B	(519) f.68
1430.06.12	11 s. 8 d.	Avignon-Barcelona	B	(519) f.68
1430.06.24-07.28	12 s. 2 d.	Barcelona-Avignon	B	(519) f.50
1430.07.12-07.24	12 s. 3 d.	Avignon-Barcelona	B	(519) f.69

The papal franc in sous and deniers tournois

In this table the two dates given are those of the drawing and the acceptance of the bills. I have selected the first bills drawn each month in each direction from a much larger body of material

Date	Rate	Place	Type	Reference
1427.08.25-27	29 s. 3 1/4 d.	Avignon-Montpellier	B	(519) f.61
1427.08.31-09.03	29 s. 3 1/4 d.	Avignon-Montpellier	B	(519) f.61
1427.09.23	29 s. 1 3/4 d.	Montpellier-Avignon	B	(519) f.41
1427.10.05	28 s. 9 1/2 d.	Montpellier-Avignon	B	(519) f.41v
1427.10.16	28 s. 3 1/2 d.	Avignon-Montpellier	B	(519) f.61
1427.11.01	28 s. 3 1/2 d.	Montpellier-Avignon	B	(519) f.42
1427.11.02-06	28 s. 6 3/4 d.	Avignon-Montpellier	B	(519) f.61
1427.12.02	28 s. 8 1/2 d.	Avignon-Montpellier	B	(519) f.61v
1427.12.22-24	28 s. 6 3/4 d.	Montpellier-Avignon	B	(519) f.43
1428.01.03-07	28 s. 6 3/4 d.	Montpellier-Avignon	B	(519) f.43
1428.01.21-28	28 s. 6 3/4 d.	Avignon-Montpellier	B	(519) f.62
1428.02.01-04	28 s. 8 1/2 d.	Avignon-Montpellier	B	(519) f.62
1428.02.10	28 s. 3 d.	Montpellier-Avignon	B	(519) f.43v
1428.03.05-07	28 s. 5 1/4 d.	Avignon-Montpellier	B	(519) f.62v
1428.04.02-06	28 s. 1 d.	Avignon-Montpellier	B	(519) f.63
1428.04.22-23	75 s. 6 1/4 d.	Montpellier-Avignon	B	(519) f.44
1428.05.07	27 s. 6 1/4 d.	Avignon-Montpellier	B	(519) f.63v
1428.05.10-12	27 s. 6 1/4 d.	Montpellier-Avignon	B	(519) f.44v
1428.05.13-24	27 s. 9 1/3 d.	Avignon-Montpellier	B	(519) f.64
1428.06.06-09	28 s. 9 3/4 d.	Montpellier-Avignon	B	(519) f.44v
1428.06.22-25	28 s. 9 1/4 d.	Avignon-Montpellier	B	(519) f.64v
1428.07.08	28 s. 8 1/2 d.	Avignon-Montpellier	B	(519) f.64v
1428.10.08-10	29 s. 5 d.	Avignon-Montpellier	B	(519) f.65
1429.01.26-30	29 s. 2 1/2 d.	Montpellier-Avignon	B	(519) f.45v
1429.02.15-17	27 s. 6 1/4 d.	Montpellier-Avignon	B	(519) f.46
1429.03.29-04.01	27 s. 4 3/4 d.	Montpellier-Avignon	B	(519) f.46v
1429.05.10-12	26 s. 9 d.	Avignon-Montpellier	B	(519) f.66
1429.05.19-22	26 s. 6 1/2 d.	Montpellier-Avignon	B	(519) f.47
1429.06.12-15	32 s. 5 d.	Montpellier-Avignon	B	(519) f.47
1429.07.08-10	26 s. 9 3/4 d.	Montpellier-Avignon	B	(519) f.47v

THE PAPAL FRANC IN SOUS AND DENIERS TOURNOIS

Date	Rate	Place	Type	Reference
1429.08.26-28	29 s. 9 1/3 d.	Montpellier-Avignon	B	(519) f.47v
1429.10.05-09	28 s. 4 1/3 d.	Montpellier-Avignon	B	(519) f.48
1429.10.05-09	31 s. 2 1/2 d.	Montpellier-Avignon	B	(519) f.48
1429.10.19-21	30 s. 5 1/3 d.	Montpellier-Avignon	B	(519) f.48
1430.02.12-14	31 s. 7 d.	Montpellier-Avignon	B	(519) f.48v
1430.03.03-06	30 s. 9 d.	Montpellier-Avignon	B	(519) f.49
1430.04.09-13	31 s. 1/2 d.	Avignon-Montpellier	B	(519) f.68
1430.06.05-14	30 s. 7 d.	Montpellier-Avignon	B	(519) f.50

The florin of 12 gros (fiorino pitteto) in groten and miten of Flanders

(24 miten = 1 groot) In this table the two dates given are those of the drawing and the acceptance of the bills.

Date	Rate	Place	Type	Reference
1428.03.12-04.08	29 gr. 20 m.	Bruges-Avignon	B	(519) f.44
1429.11.13-27	31 gr. 20 m.	Avignon-Bruges	B	(519) f.67
1430.04.20-05.16	32 gr.	Bruges-Avignon	B	(519) f.50
1431.01.31	32 gr. 12 m.	Avignon-Bruges	B	(519) f.67v
1431.06.09	31 gr. 20 m.	Avignon-Bruges	B	(519) f.68
1431.05.07-07.11	31 gr. 21 m.	Avignon-Bruges	B	(519) f.68v

100 Curial florins in Hungarian ducats

Date	Rate	Place	Type	Reference
1376.08?	102 ducats	Eichstatt-Curia	B	(472) I p.195

100 Cameral florins in Venetian ducats

Date	Rate	Place	Type	Reference
1494	102 1/2 ducats	Rome?	H	(360) p.43

100 Cameral florins in rheingulden

Date	Rate	Place	Type	Reference
1494	128 1/4 rhg.	Rome	M	(360) p.43

VIENNOIS

Viennois was the principal money of account in the Rhône valley until the adoption of the florin-gros system of reckoning in the mid-fourteenth century (see below p.131). Reckoning in viennois was the normal means of accounting not only in the principalities in which it was issued, but also in the county of Forez until the 1320s, and in the Comtat Venaissin and at Avignon, despite the papal coinages issued there, and was one of the most used currencies in the county of Provence. The deniers viennois originated at Vienne where they were struck for the archbishops from the later Carolingian period. From the eleventh century deniers viennois were also struck for the counts of Savoy who became their principal issuers from a large number of mints in their growing territories. The counts of Savoy went on striking viennois until 1533. The Dauphins minted at Romans from 1342, and at Vienne itself from 1405. A number of other rulers in the region, such as the bishops of Gap, Geneva, Grenoble and St Jean de Maurienne also produced deniers inspired by the viennois.

The Florentine florin in sous and deniers viennois

Date	Rate	Place	Type	Reference
1275	12 s. 6 d.	Curia	B	(439) p.897
1276	12 s.	Curia	B	(439) p.897
1276	13 s.	Curia	B	(439) p.897

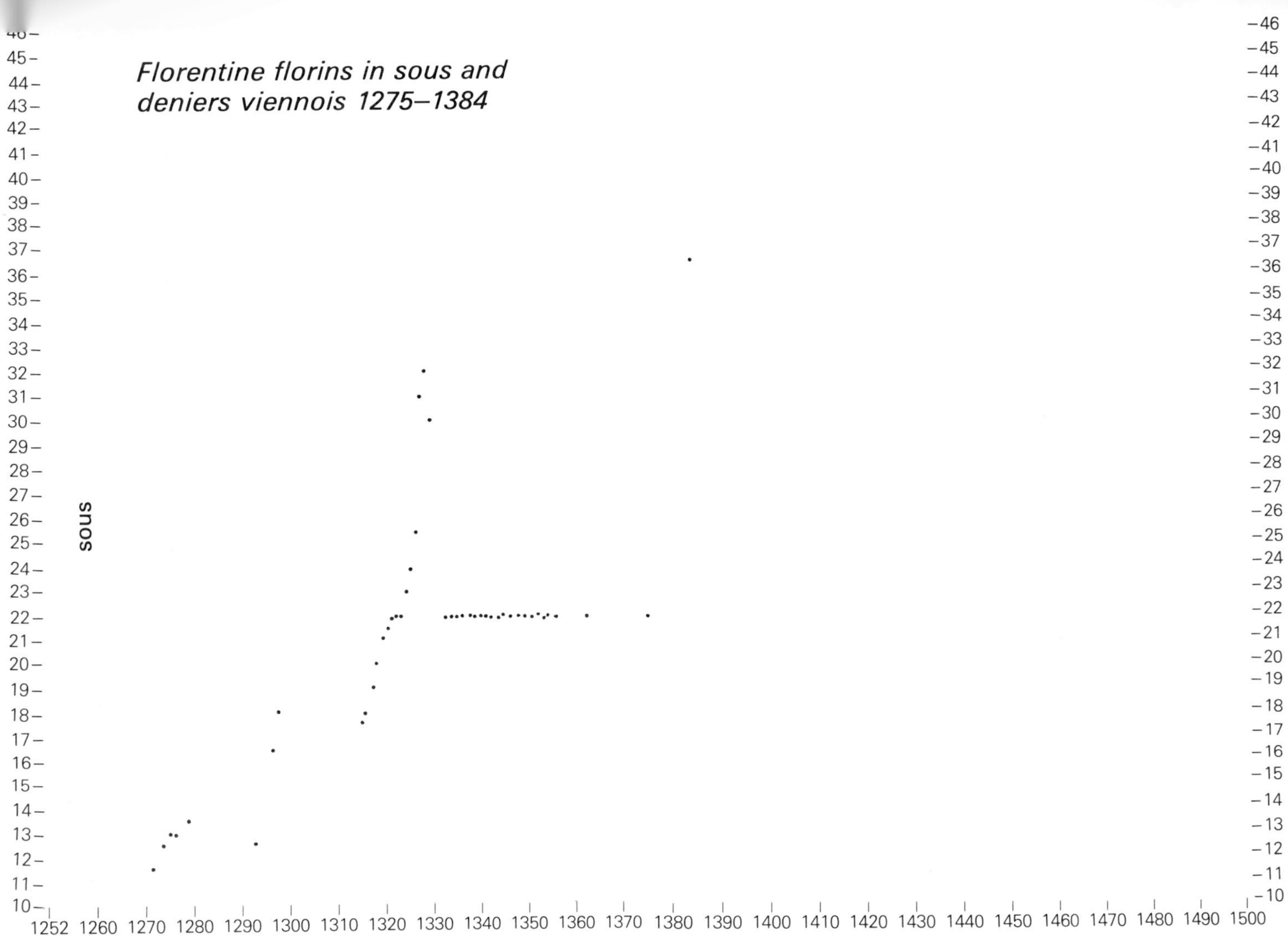

Florentine florins in sous and deniers viennois 1275–1384

sous

THE FLORENTINE FLORIN IN SOUS AND DENIERS VIENNOIS

Date	Rate	Place	Type	Reference
1277	12 s. 6 d.	Curia	B	(439) p.897
1277	13 s.	Curia	B	(439) p.897
1280	13 s. 6 d.	Curia	B	(439) p.897
1294	12 s. 8 d.	Piedmont	A	(110) p.488
1297	16 s. 6 d.	Piedmont	A	(110) p.488
1298	18 s.	Piedmont	A	(110) p.488
1316.12	17 s. 6 d.	Avignon	M	(439) p.128
1316	17 s. 11 d.	Curia	M	(439) p.900
1317.01	17 s. 8 d.	Avignon	M	(439) p.128
1317.03	17 s. 11 d.	Avignon	M	(439) p.128
1317.06	18 s.	Avignon	M	(439) p.128
1317.09	18 s. 6 d.	Avignon	M	(439) p.128
1318.02.03	18 s. 9 d.	Avignon	M	(439) p.50
1318.03.31	19 s.	Avignon	M	(439) p.50
1318.05.05	19 s. 6 d.	Avignon	M	(439) p.51
1318.09.08	19 s. 3 d.	Avignon	M	(439) p.54
1318.11.10	20 s.	Avignon	M	(439) p.52
1319.01	20 s.	Avignon	M	(439) p.128
1319.03.09	20 s. 6 d.	Avignon	M	(439) p.53
1319.06.22	21 s.	Avignon	M	(439) p.53
1319.08.24	21 s.	Avignon	M	(439) p.55
1319.09.07	21 s. 6 d.	Avignon	M	(439) p.55
1319.09	21 s. 6 d.	Avignon	M	(439) p.128
1320	19 s. 4 1/2 d.	Avignon	M	(439) p.128
1320	21 s. 3 d.	Avignon	M	(439) p.128
1321.08.16	21 s. 6 d.	Avignon	M	(439) p.70
1321.09.18	21 s. 8 d.	Avignon	M	(439) p.68
1322.01.22	21 s. 10 d.	Avignon	M	(439) p.68
1322.03.12	22 s.	Avignon	M	(439) p.69
1322.03-1323.04	22 s.	Avignon	M	(439) p.128
1322.10.13	22 s.	Avignon	M	(439) p.72
1323.05.14	21 s.	Avignon	M	(439) p.76
1323.07	21 s. 6 d.	Avignon	M	(439) p.128
1323.07	22 s.	Avignon	M	(439) p.128
1323.08.19	22 s.	Avignon	M	(439) p.79
1324.01.10	18 s.	Avignon	M	(439) p.84
1324.05.12	22 s. 6 d.	Avignon	M	(439) p.80
1324.05 & 06 & 09	22 s. 6 d.	Avignon	M	(439) p.128
1324	22 s. 3 d.	Avignon	M	(439) p.48
1325	22 s. 6 d.	Avignon	M	(439) p.128
1325	23 s.	Avignon	M	(439) p.128
1326.07 & 11	23 s.	Avignon	M	(439) p.128
1326.07 & 11	24 s.	Avignon	M	(439) p.128
1326.11	23 s. 6 d.	Avignon	M	(439) p.128
1326.12	24 s. 6 d.	Avignon	M	(439) p.129
1326	24 s.	Avignon	M	(439) p.128
1327.03	25 s.	Avignon	M	(439) p.129
1327.06	26 s.	Avignon	M	(439) p.129
1327.07	26 s. 6 d.	Avignon	M	(439) p.129
1327	25 s. 6 d.	Avignon	M	(439) p.129
1328?	28 s.	Lyons	C	(193) p.611
1328	31 s.	Curia	M	(439) p.901
1328	31 s. 6 d.	Curia	M	(439) p.901
1329	32 s.	Curia	M	(439) p.901
1329	33 s.	Curia	M	(439) p.901
1330.04	30 s. 7 d.	Avignon	M	(439) p.129
1330.07	31 s.	Avignon	M	(439) p.129

Some of the rates from the 1330s and 1340s may not be for Florentine florins, but for the florin of Dauphiné, see below p.132

Date	Rate	Place	Type	Reference
1333	22 s.	Curia	M	(439) p.49
1333	25 s. 2 d.	Curia	M	(439) p.49
1334	22 s.	Curia	M	(439) p.901
1335	22 s.	Curia	M	(440) p.24
1336-1356	22 s.	Curia	M	(439) p.902
1337	22 s.	Curia	M	(440) p.67
1340.06.03	22 s.	Curia	M	(440) p.112
1347.08	29 s.	Lyons	A	(192) p.585
1349.01	24 s.	Avignon	M	(439) p.129
1351.11	37 s. 1 d.	Montbrison	C	(193) p.613
1363.11.25	22 s.	Curia	M	(441) p.71

THE FLORENTINE FLORIN IN SOUS AND DENIERS VIENNOIS

Date	Rate	Place	Type	Reference
1375.04.21	22 s.	Curia	M	(441) p.599
1384	36 s. 6 3/4 d.	Piedmont	HC	(461) p.377

The livre viennois in sous royaux coronats of Provence

Date	Rate	Place	Type	Reference
1257.09.22	20 s.	Marseille	C	(43) p.209

The livre viennois in sous and deniers tournois of Provence

Date	Rate	Place	Type	Reference
1264	17 s. 2 d.	Marseille	C	(43) p.231

The livre viennois in sous and deniers papales

Date	Rate	Place	Type	Reference
1430.07.29	40 s.	Romans	O	(430) iii, 91-92

The livre viennois in sous and deniers delphinales of Dauphiné

Date	Rate	Place	Type	Reference
1430.07.29	40 s.	Romans	O	(430) iii, 91-92

The livre viennois in sous of Geneva

Date	Rate	Place	Type	Reference
1301	15 s.	Piedmont	A	(110) p.489

The livre viennois in sous and deniers tournois

Date	Rate	Place	Type	Reference
1422?	20 s. 10 d.	Dijon	A	(516) f.33r

See also the livre tournois in sous and deniers viennois under FRANCE p.183

For the livre raymondin in sous and deniers viennois see under MARQUISATE OF PROVENCE p.117
For the sou of paparini in deniers viennois see under COMTAT VENAISSIN p.121
For the cameral florin in sous and deniers viennois see under AVIGNON p.124
For the florin parvi ponderis in sous and deniers viennois see under DAUPHINÉ p.132
For the livre of Provins in sous and deniers viennois see under CHAMPAGNE FAIRS p.166
For the gros tournois in sous and deniers viennois see under FRANCE p.188
For the pound sterling in sous and deniers viennois see under ENGLAND p.208

DAUPHINÉ

Accounting in florins and gros

Throughout the Rhône valley, in Provence, and in much of southern France, accounting from the late 1330s was frequently carried out in florins and gros. The florin used as the basis for this system of accounting was not the florentine florin, but the imitative florin of Dauphiné first issued in 1327 which was sufficiently lighter than the florentine florin to be called the florin 'parvi ponderis'. Floreni parvi ponderis were also minted in Piedmont. The 'gros de florin' was reckoned as one twelfth part of these florins. The florin and gros system of accounting began to be used in Dauphiné itself around 1337, at the very

time that the florin of Dauphiné was about to cease and at Vienne itself to be worth twelve actual gros tournois, in other words, a sou of gros. This accounting system spread to the Lyonnais by 1342, Franche Comté by 1344, Forez by 1345, Bresse by 1348, Savoy by 1350, Toulouse and Burgundy by 1356, Lorraine by 1360, and Périgord by 1365. It stopped being used officially by the count's administration in Forez in 1360, but continued in use by private individuals in Toulouse to the 1390s, and in Forez, in the Lyonnais and in Savoy well into the fifteenth century and in Dauphiné itself until the sixteenth century (193) pp.571-614 and (509) pp.322-5. In France this system of accounting partially gave way to reckoning in francs and gros from the 1360s. See below under France, Francs, p.192.
See also above, p.125 for accounting in gros and florins at Avignon

The florin parvi ponderis in sous and deniers viennois

Date	Rate	Place	Type	Reference
1358-1369	24 s.	Lyons	A	(192) p.594

The florin parvi ponderis in sous and deniers tournois

Date	Rate	Place	Type	Reference
1346.01.31	16 s. 6 d.	Curia	C	(347) p.511
1356.08.22	17 s.	Auvergne	A	(53)

For the livre viennois in sous and deniers delphinales see under VIENNOIS p.131

SAVOY

Until the fourteenth century reckoning was normally carried out in livres, sous and deniers as elsewhere, but by 1350 this mean of accounting began to be supplemented by the florin-gros system of accounting imported from Dauphiné, see above pp.131-2. In the fifteenth century the Savoy lands continued to use this system in which the florin was worth 12 notional gros. In the Vaud the gros was reckoned as 16 deniers (322).

The gros of Savoy

In addition there was also an actual gros of Savoy also known as the plappart, or the ambrosaine (like the Milanese grosso), which was used in Geneva (see below pp.133 and 134) and Fribourg.

The gros of Savoy in deniers lausannois petits of Fribourg (See also below p.136)

Date	Rate	Place	Type	Reference
1426	13 d.	Fribourg	A	(354) p.227
1427	13 d.	Fribourg	A	(354) p.227
1429.07-12	12 d.	Fribourg	A	(354) p.227
1431.07-12	11 1/2 d.	Fribourg	A	(354) p.227
1433	11 1/2 d.	Fribourg	A	(354) p 227
1437	12 d.	Fribourg	A	(354) p.227
1440	12 1/2 d.	Fribourg	A	(354) p.227
1442.01-06	12 d.	Fribourg	A	(354) p.227
1442.07-12	13 d.	Fribourg	A	(354) p.227
1446	12 d.	Fribourg	A	(354) p.227
1250	13 d.	Fribourg	A	(354) p.227
1451	12 d.	Fribourg	A	(354) p.227
1452	12 1/2 d.	Fribourg	A	(354) p.227
1454	12 d.	Fribourg	A	(354) p.227
1455	12 d.	Fribourg	A	(354) p.227
1456	12 d.	Fribourg	A	(354) p.227
1459.07-12	14 d.	Fribourg	A	(354) p.227
1460	15 d.	Fribourg	A	(354) p.227
1461	15 d.	Fribourg	A	(354) p.227
1462	15 d.	Fribourg	A	(354) p.227
1465	15 d.	Fribourg	A	(354) p.227

THE GROS OF SAVOY IN DENIERS LAUSANNOIS PETITS OF FRIBOURG

Date	Rate	Place	Type	Reference
1466	15 d.	Fribourg	A	(354) p.227
1467	15 d.	Fribourg	A	(354) p.227
1469	15 d.	Fribourg	A	(354) p.227
1471	15 d.	Fribourg	A	(354) p.227
1472	15 d.	Fribourg	A	(354) p.227
1474	15 d.	Fribourg	A	(354) p.227
1475.01-06	15 d.	Fribourg	A	(354) p.227
1475.07-12	16 1/2 d.	Fribourg	A	(354) p.227
1476.01-06	15 d.	Fribourg	A	(354) p.227
1476.07-12	15 d.	Fribourg	A	(354) p.227
1477.01-06	15 d.	Fribourg	A	(354) p.227

For the rheingulden in gros of Savoy see under RHINELAND p.251
For the Florentine florin in Savoy gros in Geneva see under GENEVA p.134

The ducat of Savoy

The ducat of Savoy was not minted before 1430. It weighed 3.5 grams fine gold, which made it equivalent to the Venetian ducat.

The ducat of Savoy in Savoy gros of Geneva

Date	Rate	Place	Type	Reference
1449.01-06V	22 gr.	Geneva	A	(354) p.278
1450.07-12	22 gr.	Geneva	A	(354) p.278
1451.07-12	22 1/2 gr.	Geneva	A	(354) p.279
1451.07-12	23 gr.	Geneva	A	(354) p.279
1452.10.28-1453.01.06	23 gr.	Geneva	A	(354) p.238
1453.08.01-10.27	23 1/2 gr.	Geneva	A	(354) p.238
1453.10.28-1454.01.05	25 gr.	Geneva	A	(354) p.238
1454.01.06	25 1/2 gr.	Geneva	A	(354) p.238
1454.01-06	26 gr.	Geneva	A	(354) p.279
1455.07-12	25 gr.	Geneva	A	(354) p.279
1458.07-12	26 gr.	Geneva	A	(354) p.280
1473.07-12	27 gr.	Geneva	A	(354) p.281
1474.02	28 gr.	Geneva	A	(354) p.281
1475.01-06	30 gr.	Geneva	A	(354) p.282

The ducat of Savoy in sols and deniers lausannois petits of Fribourg

Date	Rate	Place	Type	Reference
1433.04.12	33 s.	Fribourg	A	(354) p.276
1433.07-12	34 s. 3 d.	Fribourg	A	(354) p.276
1434.03.28	35 s. 1/4 d.	Fribourg	A	(354) p.276
1437.07-12	36 s.	Fribourg	A	(354) p.277
1437.03.31	36 s.	Fribourg	A	(354) p.277
1438.03.06	35 s.	Fribourg	A	(354) p.277
1438.07-12	36 s.	Fribourg	A	(354) p.277
1440.01-06	36 s.	Fribourg	A	(354) p.277
1440.11.03	36 s.	Fribourg	A	(354) p.277
1441.04.16	36 s. 6 d.	Fribourg	A	(354) p.277
1441.07-12	36 s.	Fribourg	A	(354) p.277
1442.04.01	34 s. 9 d.	Fribourg	A	(354) p.278
1443.07-12	36 s.	Fribourg	A	(354) p.278
1444.04.12	36 s. 4 d.	Fribourg	A	(354) p.278
1445.03.28	36 s. 8 d.	Fribourg	A	(354) p.278
1446.04.17	37 s.	Fribourg	A	(354) p.278
1447.04.09	36 s.	Fribourg	A	(354) p.278
1450.07-12	37 s. 8 1/2 d.	Fribourg	A	(354) p.278
1451.07-12	38 s. 7 d.	Fribourg	A	(354) p.279
1452.10.28-1453.01.06	38 s. 4 d.	Fribourg	A	(352) p.238
1453.01-06	38 s. 4 d.	Fribourg	A	(354) p.279
1453.07-12	38 s. 4 d.	Fribourg	A	(354) p.279
1453.08.01-10.27	39 s. 2 d.	Fribourg	A	(352) p.238
453.10.28-1454.01.05	41 s. 8 d.	Fribourg	A	(210) p.238
454.01.06	42 s. 6 d.	Fribourg	A	(210) p.238
454.01-06	43 s. 4 d.	Fribourg	A	(354) p.279
454.07-12	40 s.	Fribourg	A	(354) p.279
455.07-12	41 s. 8 d.	Fribourg	A	(354) p.279

THE DUCAT OF SAVOY IN SOLS AND DENIERS LAUSANNOIS PETITS OF FRIBOURG

Date	Rate	Place	Type	Reference
1456.01-06	42 s. 4 d.	Fribourg	A	(354) p.279
1458.05	43 s. 4 d.	Fribourg	A	(354) p.280
1458.07.12	43 s. 4 d.	Fribourg	A	(354) p.280
1464.07-12	45 s.	Fribourg	A	(354) p.280
1466.01-06	45 s.	Fribourg	A	(354) p.280
1466.07-12	45 s.	Fribourg	A	(354) p.281
1467.01-06	45 s.	Fribourg	A	(354) p.281
1467.07-12	45 s.	Fribourg	A	(354) p.281
1468.01-06	45 s.	Fribourg	A	(354) p.281
1468.10-11	45 s.	Fribourg	A	(210) p.281
1469.07-12	45 s.	Fribourg	A	(354) p.281
1470.01-06	45 s.	Fribourg	A	(354) p.281
1471.07-12	45 s.	Fribourg	A	(354) p.281
1472.04	45 s.	Fribourg	A	(354) p.281
1472.07-12	45 s.	Fribourg	A	(354) p.281
1473.01-06	45 s.	Fribourg	A	(354) p.281
1473.07-12	45 s.	Fribourg	A	(354) p.281
1474.02	46 s. 8 d.	Fribourg	A	(354) p.281
1474.07-12	50 s.	Fribourg	A	(354) p.281
1475.01-06	50 s.	Fribourg	A	(354) p.282
1475.07-12	50 s.	Fribourg	A	(354) p.282
1476.01-06	50 s.	Fribourg	A	(354) p.282
1477.07-12	53 s. 4 d.	Fribourg	A	(354) p.282
1478.08	53 s. 4 d.	Fribourg	A	(354) p.282
1479.07-12	53 s. 4 d.	Fribourg	A	(354) p.282
1481.02	53 s. 4 d.	Fribourg	A	(354) p.282

GENEVA

From the eleventh century, the bishops of Geneva struck deniers of the same general type as the deniers of the archbishops of Vienne, although from the twelfth century they substituted the head of St Peter for that of St Maurice. They continued to strike deniers and oboles in prolific quantities for much of the later middle ages when the bishopric fell under the influence of the counts of Savoy. Geneva also became the venue for some of the most important fairs of the later middle ages.

The Florentine florin in sous and deniers of Geneva

Date	Rate	Place	Type	Reference
1318	12 s.	Curia	B	(439) p.900
1318	13 s.	Curia	B	(439) p.900
1371	12 s.	Geneva	B	(270) p.192
1379.10.22-1390.05.12	12 s.	Fribourg	B	(4) I p.40

For the livre viennois in sous of Geneva see under VIENNOIS p.131

The Florentine florin in Savoy gros of Geneva

Date	Rate	Place	Type	Reference
1464.01.06	27	Geneva	A	(354) p.281
1466.01.06	27	Geneva	A	(354) p.281

Écus and marcs of écus

In the early fifteenth century, Libro di Mercatantie et Usanze de Paesi (57), Geneva was noted as exchanging with Venice, Genoa, Milan, Avignon, Barcelona, London and Bruges, but not with Florence. This perhaps reflects the scope of the fairs. However, this does not produce a vast number of rates into and out of the money of Geneva, for quotations against Geneva were made in terms of the écu described as the 'schude de 66 per marcho' for example, sterling was quoted in this notebook from Geneva to London at 44 to 48 pence sterling to the écu, and from London to Geneva at 42 to 46 pence sterling to the écu. By the 1440s and 1450s quotation was in terms of marcs of gold écus 'ad rationem 64 per marcha'.

The marc of écus at 64 to the marc, in lire and soldi imperiali

Date	Rate	Place	Type	Reference
1444.05.21	224 li.	Milan-Geneva	B	(81) p.60
1453.08.25	206 li.	Milan-Geneva	B	(81) p.76
1453.11.26	224 li. 10 s.	Milan-Geneva	B	(81) p.76
1454.05.21	224 li.	Milan-Geneva	B	(81) p.76
1455.11.28	246 li.	Milan-Geneva	B	(81) p.79
1456.11.19	240 li.	Milan-Geneva	B	(81) p.81
1457.08.23	244 li.	Milan-Geneva	B	(81) p.83
1458.02.01	240 li.	Milan-Geneva	B	(81) p.84
1458.04.29	241 li.	Milan-Geneva	B	(81) p.87
1458.08.22	243 li.	Milan-Geneva	B	(81) p.88
1458.11.27	240 li.	Milan-Geneva	B	(81) p.89
1459.02.01	240 li.	Milan-Geneva	B	(81) p.90
1459.04.25	243 li.	Milan-Geneva	B	(81) p.90
1459.08.24	247 li.	Milan-Geneva	B	(81) p.91

The écu in sous and deniers of Geneva

A few rates do survive linking the écu, used for international exchange, with the local currency of Geneva

Date	Rate	Place	Type	Reference
1463-1467	25 s.	Geneva	M	(54) II p.573
1468	26 s.	Geneva	M	(54) II p.573
1469-1477	28 s.	Geneva	M	(54) II p.573
1478-1483	30 s.	Geneva	M	(54) II p.573
1484	31 s.	Geneva	M	(54) II p.573
1485	32 s.	Geneva	M	(54) II p.573
1486-1488	36 s.	Geneva	M	(54) II p.573
1489-1497	38 s.	Geneva	M	(54) II p.573

LAUSANNE

The bishops of Lausanne struck their own deniers from at least the beginning of the eleventh century, and the livre of Lausanne was being used for accounting by 1100. It became the principal currency of the Pays de Vaud and of Fribourg, until the latter minted its own derivative coinage in 1420.

The Florentine florin in sous and deniers of Lausanne

Date	Rate	Place	Type	Reference
1316	12 s.	Lausanne	C	(355) p.393
1318.09.01	12 s. 8 d.	Yverdon	B	(309) II p.337
1344	15 s. 2 d.	Chillon	H	(461) p.375
1356.02.05-20	13 s. 6 d.	Fribourg	B	(4) I p.3
1356.03.10-11	13 s. 6 d.	Fribourg	B	(4) I p.3
1368	14 s.	Lausanne	B	(270) p.193
1372.09.23	13 s. 6 d.	Fribourg	B	(4) I p.19
1373.05.09	12 s. 3 d.	Fribourg	B	(4) I p.20
1384.01.28	14 s.	Fribourg	B	(4) I p.29
1384.05.12	14 s.	Fribourg	B	(4) I p.30
1385.04.30	14 s.	Fribourg	B	(4) I p.33
1386.03.12	14 s.	Fribourg	B	(4) I p.34
1390.02.02	15 s.	Fribourg	B	(4) I p.39
1390.08.09	16 s.	Fribourg	B	(4) I p.41
1390.10.05	15 s.	Fribourg	B	(4) I p.41
1391.05.06	15 s.	Fribourg	B	(4) I p.43
1391.09.14-1392.05.20	15 s.	Fribourg	B	(4) I p.43
1392.07.26	16 s.	Fribourg	B	(4) I p.46
1392.11.09	15 s.	Fribourg	B	(4) I p.46
1393.09.03	16 s.	Fribourg	B	(4) I p.48

THE FLORENTINE FLORIN IN SOUS AND DENIERS OF LAUSANNE

Date	Rate	Place	Type	Reference
1394.06.28	14 s.	Fribourg	B	(4) I p.51
1394.06.30	15 s.	Fribourg	B	(4) I p.51
1394.09.05	14 s.	Fribourg	B	(4) I p.52
1394.10.07	16 s.	Fribourg	B	(4) I p.52
1394.10.08	15 s.	Fribourg	B	(4) I p.53
1395.05.05	16 s.	Fribourg	B	(4) I p.54
1395.09.20	15 s.	Fribourg	B	(4) I p.56
1395.11.12	16 s.	Fribourg	B	(4) I p.56
1396.09.02	14 s.	Fribourg	B	(4) I p.69
1397.08.05	15 s.	Fribourg	B	(4) I p.62
1397.09.15	16 s.	Fribourg	B	(4) I p.64
1397.10.13	15 s.	Fribourg	B	(4) I p.65
1397	15 s.	Fribourg	H	(461) p.378
1398.01.18	16 s.	Fribourg	B	(4) I p.42
1398.03.15	15 s.	Fribourg	B	(4) I p.67
1398.08.28	15 s.	Fribourg	B	(4) I p.68
1399.07.08	16 s.	Fribourg	B	(4) I p.71
1400.05.05	17 s.	Fribourg	B	(4) I p.74
1400.05.22	18 s. 6 d.	Fribourg	B	(4) I p.74
1400.08.13	17 s.	Fribourg	B	(4) I p.75
1400.10.12	17 s.	Fribourg	B	(4) I p.75
1402.03.02	18 s.	Fribourg	B	(4) I p.78
1402.04.10	16 s.	Fribourg	B	(4) I p.79
1404-1405	18 s.	Fribourg	A	(352) p.27
1405.12.15	18 s.	Fribourg	B	(4) I p.95
1406	15 s.	Fribourg	A	(352) p.27
1406.08.19	18 s.	Fribourg	B	(4) I p.96
1407	15 s.	Fribourg	A	(352) p.27
1407-1410	18 s.	Fribourg	A	(352) p.27
1411	17 s. 6 d.	Fribourg	A	(352) p.27
1412	14 s.	Fribourg	A	(352) p.27
1415	14 s.	Fribourg	A	(352) p.27
1415	18 s.	Fribourg	A	(352) p.27
1416	17 s. 3 d.	Fribourg	A	(352) p.27
1417	17 s. 6 d.	Fribourg	A	(352) p.27

For the livre tournois and the gros tournois in sols and deniers lausannois see under FRANCE pp.184 and 188
For the rheingulden in sols and deniers lausannois see under RHINELAND p.251

FRIBOURG

In 1420 the authorities of Fribourg (Freiburg im Üchtland) instituted their own money of account ostensibly to protect their good money from the weaker Savoyard or Lausanne currencies circulating freely in Fribourg. However the new money of Fribourg was actually weaker rather than stronger than that of Lausanne. From 1452, the convenient exchange ratio of 3 to 5, i.e. 12 deniers 'forts' of Lausanne and Savoy for 20 deniers 'faibles' of Fribourg, put the florin of account of Savoy (= 12 gros) on a level with the livre of lausannois petits of Fribourg.

The Florentine florin in sols and deniers lausannois petits of Fribourg

Date	Rate	Place	Type	Reference
1422.07-12	29 s. 8 d.	Fribourg	A	(354) p.275
1428.01-06	36 s.	Fribourg	A	(354) p.276
1429.01-06	33 s.	Fribourg	A	(354) p.276
1432.01-06	32 s.	Fribourg	A	(354) p.276
1433.01-06	32 s.	Fribourg	A	(354) p.276
1433.07-12	34 s.	Fribourg	A	(354) p.276
1434.01-06	32 s.	Fribourg	A	(354) p.276
1435.01-06	32 s.	Fribourg	A	(354) p.277
1435.01-06	34 s.	Fribourg	A	(354) p.277
1436.01-06	32 s.	Fribourg	A	(354) p.277
1436.01-06	34 s.	Fribourg	A	(354) p.277
1438.01-06	32 s.	Fribourg	A	(354) p.277
1438.01-06	34 s.	Fribourg	A	(354) p.277

THE FLORENTINE FLORIN IN SOLS AND DENIERS LAUSANNOIS PETITS OF FRIBOURG

Date	Rate	Place	Type	Reference
1439.01-06	32 s.	Fribourg	A	(354) p.277
1439.01-06	34 s.	Fribourg	A	(354) p.277
1439.01-06	34 s.	Fribourg	A	(354) p.277
1440.01-06	34 s.	Fribourg	A	(354) p.277
1440.07-12	33 s. 6 d.	Fribourg	A	(354) p.277
1442.01-06	34 s.	Fribourg	A	(354) p.278
1443.01-06	34 s.	Fribourg	A	(354) p.278
1444.01-06	34 s.	Fribourg	A	(354) p.278
1445	34 s.	Fribourg	A	(354) p.278
1446	34 s.	Fribourg	A	(354) p.278
1464.01-06	35 s.	Fribourg	A	(354) p.281
1465.01-06	35 s.	Fribourg	A	(354) p.281
1466.01-06	35 s.	Fribourg	A	(354) p.281
1467.01-06	35 s.	Fribourg	A	(354) p.281

The Venetian ducat in sols and deniers lausannois petits of Fribourg

Date	Rate	Place	Type	Reference
1423.01-06	35 s. 6 d.	Fribourg	A	(354) p.275
1428.05	37 s. 2 1/2 d.	Fribourg	A	(354) p.276
1430.07-12	33 s.	Fribourg	A	(354) p.276
1439.08.25	36 s.	Fribourg	A	(354) p.277
1449.01-06	37 s. 8 1/2 d.	Fribourg	A	(354) p.278

The Hungarian ducat in sols and deniers lausannois petits of Fribourg

Date	Rate	Place	Type	Reference
1447.07-12	36 s.	Fribourg	A	(354) p.278

For the ducat of Savoy in sols and deniers of Fribourg see under SAVOY p.133
For the rheingulden in sols and deniers of Fribourg see under RHINELAND p.251

MELGORIAN

In the south of France the Melgorian deniers issued by the counts of Melgueil or Mauguio, came to dominate the trade of the whole coastal plain of Languedoc in the twelfth century. They became not only the official coinage of the fast growing nearby city of Montpellier, but were so successful that independent coinages ceased to be issued to the west at Béziers, Narbonne and Carcassonne, and to the east at Uzés, Nîmes, and St Gilles in the Rhône delta. All these had stopped by the early thirteenth century, when the Melgorian deniers were the common currency from Provence to Toulouse. They even circulated to a considerable extent beyond the Pyrennées in Catalonia. They also circulated widely in Majorca after its conquest in 1229. They were also the standard by which other currencies were valued. The money of Béziers, before it ceased, was reckoned as equal to the Melgorian in 1179 (165) p.24 and perhaps as early as 1097 (39) p.67. The tolzas of Toulouse, were reckoned as double the melgorians in 1180 and 1197 (165) p.26, and in 1202 and 1208 (39) p.106.

In the mid-thirteenth century a French royal mint was opened at Sommières, a few miles from Montpellier, to strike deniers tournois in deliberate competition with Melgorian deniers, which gradually lost their dominance in Languedoc. In 1282 a French royal ordinance effectively destroyed the Melgorian denier as a trading currency by specifically limiting the circulation of Melgorian deniers to the diocese of Maguelonne, whose bishops had acquired the county of Melgueil. The circulation of other 'feudal' coin had already been theoretically limited for a generation to the fief of the issuer, whilst royal coin was free to circulate throughout the kingdom. After the royal acquisition of Montpellier itself in 1293 the mint at Sommières was moved there. Later in the middle ages the Montpellier mint was one of the two most prolific mints in France outside Paris. As well as this, Montpellier was the only banking place in France, apart from Paris, much used by the Tuscan bankers. The bishop of Maguelonne retained his theoretical right of coinage, but money tournois was the common coinage of Languedoc in the fourteenth century. By the middle of that century Melgorian money even ceased to be used for accounts in Montpellier itself. Reckoning was carried out in tournois instead. I have found no quotations for the Florentine florin in Melgorian money and all the quotations between Melgorian money and other currencies have been included under other headings e.g. the money of Genoa, Barcelona, Provins and Tournois.

For the lira of Genoa in sous and deniers melgorians see under GENOA p.108
For the libra of Barcelona in sous and deniers melgorians see under BARCELONA p.146
For the libra of Valencia in sous and deniers melgorians see under VALENCIA p.147
For the livre of Provins in sous and deniers melgorians see under CHAMPAGNE FAIRS p.166
For the livre tournois in sous and deniers melgorians see under FRANCE p.181
For the pound sterling in sous and deniers melgorians see under ENGLAND p.208
For the besant of Acre in sous and deniers melgorians see under ACRE p.298

SECTION V
IBERIAN PENINSULA

THE KINGDOMS OF THE CROWN OF ARAGON

THE COUNTY OF BARCELONA (CATALONIA)

Dineros were issued by the counts of Barcelona from the eleventh century onwards and were continued by them as a separate coinage even after they acquired the kingdom of Aragon by marriage. Despite attempts at reform they were gradually debased until in 1256, when their alloy was stabilised at one quarter silver. This fineness of a quarter or 3/12 was expressed at the time as 3 dineros (in the sueldo being understood) and they were hence sometimes called ternals or dineros de tern.

The Florentine florin in sueldos and dineros of Barcelona

Date	Rate	Place	Type	Reference
1276-1285	11 s.	Catalonia	O	(211) p.237
1280-1282	13 s. 9 d.	Curia	B	(439) p.897
1310-1311	11 s.	Curia	B	(439) p.899
1311.10.21	16 s.	Barcelona	A	(298) I p.113
1318-1320	17 s. 7 d.	Narbonne	C	(459) p.103
1319-1321	15 s.	Curia	B	(439) p.900
1319-1321	16 s.	Curia	B	(439) p.900
1319-1321	17 s.	Curia	B	(439) p.900
1319-1321	18 s.	Curia	B	(439) p.900
1320	17 s.	Curia	B	(439) p.900
1320	18 s.	Curia	B	(439) p.900
1321.12.24	16 s. 10 d.	Spain	B	(217) p.75
1322-1323	15 s.	Curia	B	(439) p.900
1322-1323	18 s.	Curia	B	(439) p.900
1324	18 s.	Barcelona	B	(163) p.530
1328	17 s. 6 d.	Avignon	B	(439) p.74
1328	18 s.	Avignon	B	(439) p.74
1328	15 s. 2 d.	Avignon	B	(439) p.75
1328	18 s.	Curia	B	(439) p.53
1329.01.07	17 s. 6 d.	Toledo	B	(217) p.86
1329	15 s.	Avignon	B	(439) p.74
1329	15 s. 8 d.	Avignon	B	(439) p.74
1332	15 s. 4 d.	Cagliari	O	(36) p.75
1332.11.14	15 s.	Barcelona	O	(82) II p.198
1334	18 s.	Barcelona	A	(163) p.530
1334	15 s. 6 d.	Cagliari	O	(36) p.75
1334-1342	14 s. 7 d.	Barcelona	B	(321) p.442
1334-1342	14 s.	Barcelona	B	(321) p.467
1335	14 s. 10 d.	Curia	B	(439) p.902
1336	14 s. 9 d.	Castile	B	(439) p.52
1338.12.23	15 s. 2 d.	Curia	B	(216) p.136
1341.08.14	15 s. 6 d.	Curia	B	(216) p.182
1345.10.28	15 s.	Curia	B	(347) p.362
1348.04.03	11 s. 6 d.	Curia	B	(440) p.404
1348	14 s.	Curia	B	(439) p.902
1348	15 s.	Curia	B	(439) p.902
1350.11.13	12 s.	Curia	B	(347) p.441
1354.06.20	12 s.	Curia	B	(251) p.56
1365	14 s.	Avignon	B	(439) p.75
1370	12 s.	Barcelona	C	(434) p.233
1370	16 s. 6 d.	Navarre	B	(439) p.83
1376	12 s. 8 d.	Barcelona	B	(433) P.29
1378	16 s. 8 d.	Cagliari	B	(319) p.8
1384.09.07	14 s.	Genoa	C	(23) p.102
386	15 s.	Barcelona	O	(82) p.339
388.06.21	12 s. 8 d.	Barcelona	B	(434) p.234
388.07.21	12 s. 8 d.	Barcelona	B	(434) p.234
389.06.19	13 s. 6 d.	Barcelona	B	(138) p.137
389.11.29	12 s. 10 d.	Barcelona	B	(138) p.138
390.01.03	13 s. 2 d.	Barcelona	B	(138) p.138
392.02.29	15 s. 1 1/2 d.	Barcelona	B	(138) p.139

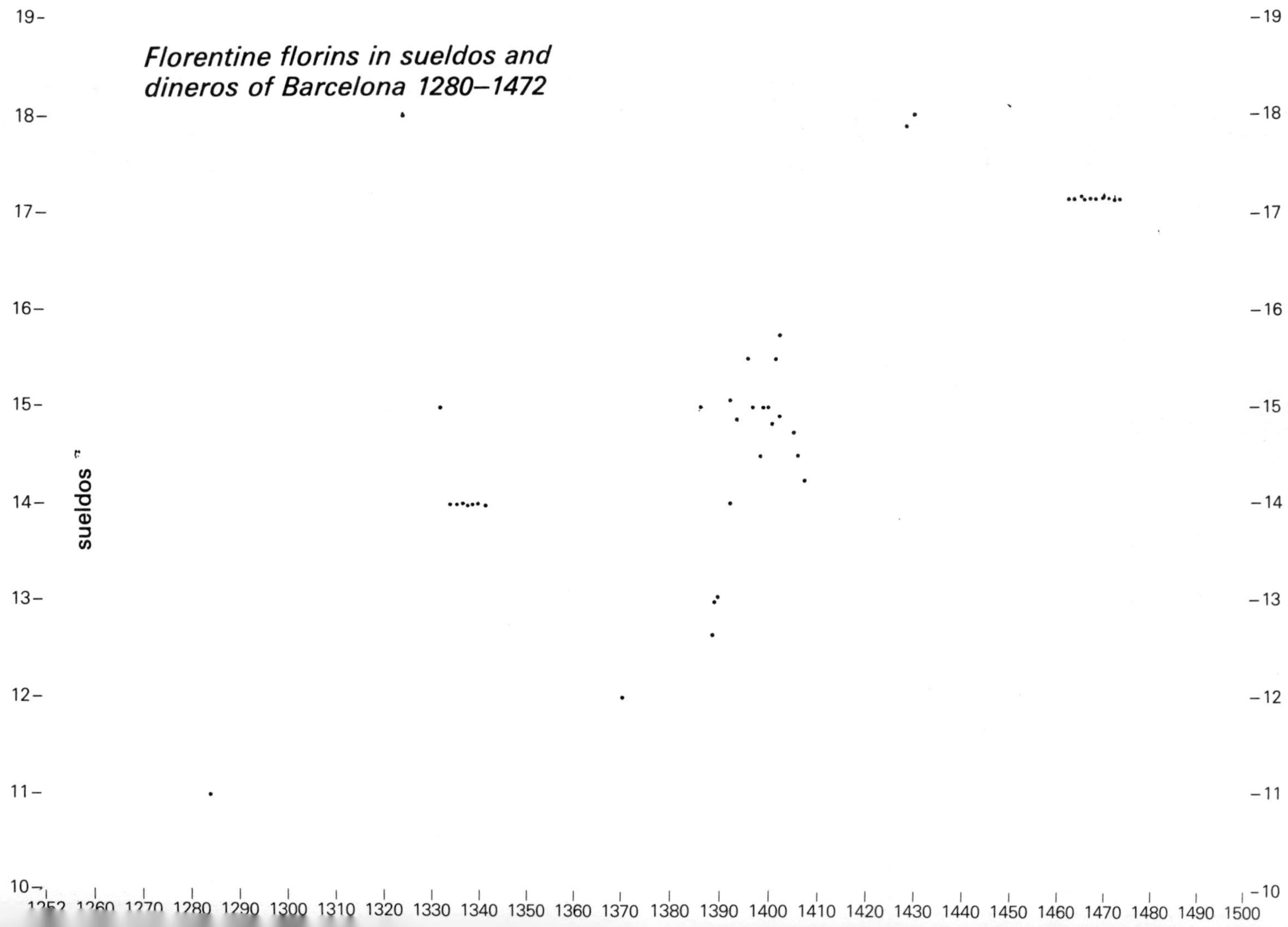

Florentine florins in sueldos and dineros of Barcelona 1280–1472

THE FLORENTINE FLORIN IN SUELDOS AND DINEROS OF BARCELONA

Date	Rate	Place	Type	Reference
1393.02.27	14 s. 2 d.	Barcelona	B	(138) p.140
1393.06.06-13	14 s.	Barcelona	B	(138) p.140
1394.01.24-09.22	14 s. 10 d.	Barcelona	B	(138) p.141
1394.10.13	14 s. 11 d.	Barcelona	B	(138) p.141
1396.03.09	15 s. 3 d.	Barcelona	B	(24) p.333
1396.03.29	15 s. 6 d.	Barcelona	B	(24) p.334
1396.04.22	15 s. 5 d.	Barcelona	B	(24) p.335
1397.03.12	14 s. 7 d.	Barcelona	B	(138) p.143
1397.03.15	14 s. 6 d.	Genoa	B	(24) p.338
1397.03.27	14 s. 8 d.	Barcelona	B	(138) p.143
1397.06.28	15 s. 2 d.	Barcelona	B	(138) p.144
1397.07.27	15 s. 4 d.	Barcelona	B	(138) p.144
1397.08.10	15 s. 3 d.	Barcelona	B	(138) p.144
1397.08.16	15 s. 2 d.	Barcelona	B	(138) p.144
1397.08.27	15 s. 3 d.	Barcelona	B	(138) p.144
1397.09.07-09	15 s.	Barcelona	B	(138) p.144
1397.12.30	15 s. 2 d.	Barcelona	B	(138) p.144
1398.02.04	15 s. 4 d.	Barcelona	B	(138) p.144
1398.02.21	15 s. 3 d.	Barcelona	B	(138) p.144
1397.03.14-17	14 s. 9 d.	Barcelona	B	(138) p.144
1398.04.26	14 s. 10 d.	Barcelona	B	(138) p.145
1398.05.08	14 s. 8 d.	Barcelona	B	(138) p.145
1398.05.31	14 s. 9 d.	Barcelona	B	(138) p.145
1398.06.14	14 s. 5 d.	Barcelona	B	(138) p.145
1398.07.08	14 s. 4 d.	Barcelona	B	(138) p.145
1398.07.25	14 s. 8 d.	Barcelona	B	(138) p.145
1398.08.03-06	14 s. 9 d.	Barcelona	B	(138) p.145
1398.08.27	14 s. 6 d.	Barcelona	B	(138) p.145
1398.09.11-14	14 s. 5 d.	Barcelona	B	(138) p.145
1398.10.02-10	14 s.	Barcelona	B	(138) p.145
1398.10.28	13 s. 8 d.	Barcelona	B	(138) p.145
1399.01.02	14 s. 9 d.	Barcelona	B	(138) p.145
1399.01.23	14 s. 11 d.	Barcelona	B	(138) p.145
1399.02.11	14 s. 10 d.	Barcelona	B	(138) p.145
1399.02.13	14 s. 8 d.	Barcelona	B	(138) p.145
1399.02.27-03.05	14 s. 6 1/2 d.	Barcelona	B	(138) p.145
1399.03.26-04.07	14 s. 9 d.	Barcelona	B	(138) p.145
1399.04.16-04.24	15 s. 1 d.	Barcelona	B	(138) p.145
1399.04.16-24	14 s. 11 d.	Barcelona	B	(138) p.145
1399.05.15	15 s. 1 d.	Barcelona	B	(138) p.145
1399.05.21	15 s.	Barcelona	B	(138) p.146
1399.06.06-18	15 s. 1 d.	Barcelona	B	(138) p.146
1399.06.06-18	15 s. 1 1/2 d.	Barcelona	B	(138) p.146
1399.06.19	14 s. 11 d.	Barcelona	B	(138) p.146
1399.06.28-07.08	14 s. 10 d.	Barcelona	B	(138) p.146
1399.07.14	14 s. 10 1/2 d.	Barcelona	B	(138) p.146
1399.07.19	14 s. 11 d.	Barcelona	B	(138) p.146
1399.07.24	15 s.	Barcelona	B	(138) p.146
1399.08.08	14 s. 11 d.	Barcelona	B	(138) p.146
1399.08.20-27	14 s. 11 1/2 d.	Barcelona	B	(138) p.146
1399.09.06	14 s. 11 d.	Barcelona	B	(138) p.146
1399.09.15-27	14 s. 7 d.	Barcelona	B	(138) p.146
1399.10.15	14 s. 8 1/2 d.	Barcelona	B	(138) p.146
1399.10.29	14 s. 9 d.	Barcelona	B	(138) p.146
1399.11.19	15 s. 1 d.	Barcelona	B	(138) p.146
1399.11.24-12.04	15 s. 2 d.	Barcelona	B	(138) p.146
1399.12.10-11	15 s. 1 d.	Barcelona	B	(138) p.146
1399.12.16-20	15 s. 1 1/2 d.	Barcelona	B	(138) p.146
1399.12.24	15 s. 2 d.	Barcelona	B	(138) p.146
1400.01.01-21	15 s. 3 d.	Barcelona	B	(138) p.147
1400.01.29	15 s. 3 1/2 d.	Barcelona	B	(138) p.147
1400.02.03	15 s. 4 d.	Barcelona	B	(138) p.147
1400.02.04-05	15 s. 4 1/2 d.	Barcelona	B	(138) p.147
1400.02.06	15 s. 4 d.	Barcelona	B	(138) p.147
1400.02.19	15 s. 4 1/2 d.	Barcelona	B	(138) p.147
1400.02.20	15 s. 5 d.	Barcelona	B	(138) p.147
1400.02.26	15 s. 4 d.	Barcelona	B	(138) p.147
1400.02	15 s. 4 d.	Barcelona	B	(138) p.57
1400.03.04-15	15 s. 4 1/2 d.	Barcelona	B	(138) p.147
1400.03.22	15 s. 5 1/2 d.	Barcelona	B	(138) p.147
1400.04.05-14	15 s. 6 d.	Barcelona	B	(138) p.147
1400.04.15	15 s. 6 1/2 d.	Barcelona	B	(138) p.147

THE FLORENTINE FLORIN IN SUELDOS AND DINEROS OF BARCELONA

Date	Rate	Place	Type	Reference
1400.04.24-05.05	15 s. 6 d.	Barcelona	B	(138) p.147
1400.05.11-20	15 s. 5 1/2 d.	Barcelona	B	(138) p.147
1400.05.27-29	15 s.	Barcelona	B	(138) p.147
1400.06.01	15 s. 1 d.	Barcelona	B	(138) p.147
1400.06.05-19	15 s. 1 1/2 d.	Barcelona	B	(138) p 147
1400.06.26-28	15 s.	Barcelona	B	(138) p.147
1400.07.05	14 s. 11 d.	Barcelona	B	(138) p.147
1400.07.14	14 s. 10 d.	Barcelona	B	(138) p.147
1400.07.23	14 s. 9 d.	Barcelona	B	(138) p.148
1400.07.31	14 s. 6 d.	Barcelona	B	(138) p.148
1400.08.04	14 s. 5 d.	Barcelona	B	(138) p.148
1400.08.20-30	14 s. 4 d.	Barcelona	B	(138) p.148
1400.09.18	13 s. 9 d.	Barcelona	B	(138) p.148
1400.09.28	13 s. 10 d.	Barcelona	B	(138) p.148
1400.10.06	14 s.	Barcelona	B	(138) p.148
1400.10.15	14 s. 5 d.	Barcelona	B	(138) p.148
1400.10.22	14 s. 6 d.	Barcelona	B	(138) p.148
1400.11.02	14 s. 4 d.	Barcelona	B	(138) p.148
1400.12.31	14 s. 3 d.	Barcelona	B	(138) p.148
1401.01.10	14 s. 5 d.	Barcelona	B	(138) p.148
1401.01.28	14 s. 4 1/2 d.	Barcelona	B	(138) p.148
1401.02.02	14 s. 5 1/2 d.	Barcelona	B	(138) p.148
1401.02.06	14 s. 5 d.	Barcelona	B	(138) p.148
1401.02.19-27	14 s. 4 1/2 d.	Barcelona	B	(138) p.148
1401.04.07	14 s. 8 d.	Barcelona	B	(138) p.148
1401.04.15	14 s. 10 d.	Barcelona	B	(138) p.148
1401.04.28	15 s.	Barcelona	B	(138) p.148
1401.05.05-20	14 s. 11 1/2 d.	Barcelona	B	(138) p.148
1401.05.31	14 s. 11 d.	Barcelona	B	(138) p.148
1401.06.10	14 s. 11 1/2 d.	Barcelona	B	(138) p.149
1401.06.14-16	15 s.	Barcelona	B	(138) p.149
1401.07.01-06	15 s. 1 d.	Barcelona	B	(138) p.149
1401.07.15-25	14 s. 11 d.	Barcelona	B	(138) p.149
1401.07.28	15 s.	Barcelona	B	(138) p.149
1401.08.11	14 s. 11 d.	Barcelona	B	(138) p.149
1401.08.16	14 s. 10 d.	Barcelona	B	(138) p.149
1401.08.26	14 s. 6 d.	Barcelona	B	(138) p.149
1401.09.01-06	14 s. 8 d.	Barcelona	B	(138) p.149
1401.09.13	14 s. 10 d.	Barcelona	B	(138) p.149
1401.09.28	14 s. 9 d.	Barcelona	B	(138) p.149
1401.10.04-19	14 s. 8 d.	Barcelona	B	(138) p.149
1401.10.28	14 s. 9 d.	Barcelona	B	(138) p.149
1401.10.30	14 s. 9 1/2 d.	Barcelona	B	(138) p.149
1401.11.02	14 s. 9 d.	Barcelona	B	(138) p.149
1401.12.05	15 s. 1 d.	Barcelona	B	(138) p.149
1401.12.12	15 s. 5 d.	Barcelona	B	(138) p.149
1401.12.30	15 s. 6 d.	Barcelona	B	(138) p.149
1402.01.02-11	15 s. 6 1/2 d.	Barcelona	B	(138) p.149
1402.01.27	15 s. 7 d.	Barcelona	B	(138) p.149
1402.02.04-12	15 s. 6 d.	Barcelona	B	(138) p.149
1402.02.28	15 s. 7 d.	Barcelona	B	(138) p.149
1402.03.09	15 s. 8 d.	Barcelona	B	(138) p.149
1402.03.18	15 s. 8 d.	Barcelona	B	(138) p.150
1402.03.28	15 s. 9 d.	Barcelona	B	(138) p.150
1402.04.06-10	15 s. 8 d.	Barcelona	B	(138) p.150
1402.04.15	15 s. 8 1/2 d.	Barcelona	B	(138) p.150
1402.04.23	15 s. 8 d.	Barcelona	B	(138) p.150
1402.05.13-16	15 s. 5 1/2 d.	Barcelona	B	(138) p.150
1402.05.31	15 s. 6 d.	Barcelona	B	(138) p.150
1402.06.13-19	15 s. 7 d.	Barcelona	B	(138) p.150
1402.07.01	15 s. 9 d.	Barcelona	B	(138) p.150
1402.07.12	15 s. 9 1/2 d.	Barcelona	B	(138) p.150
1402.07.20-08.05	15 s. 10 1/2 d.	Barcelona	B	(138) p.150
1402.08.12	15 s. 11 d.	Barcelona	B	(138) p.150
1402.08.21	15 s. 9 1/2 d.	Barcelona	B	(138) p.150
1402.08.30-09.07	15 s. 9 d.	Barcelona	B	(138) p.150
1402.09.13-28	15 s. 10 d.	Barcelona	B	(138) p.150
1402.04.28-10.10	15 s. 11 d.	Barcelona	B	(138) p.150
1402.10.24	15 s. 6 d.	Barcelona	B	(138) p.150
1402.11.01	15 s. 6 1/2 d.	Barcelona	B	(138) p.150
1402.11.16	15 s. 8 d.	Barcelona	B	(138) p.150
1402.12.16	15 s. 9 d.	Barcelona	B	(138) p.151

THE FLORENTINE FLORIN IN SUELDOS AND DINEROS OF BARCELONA

Date	Rate	Place	Type	Reference
1402.12.20	15 s. 8 1/2 d.	Barcelona	B	(138) p.151
1402	18 s. 2 d.	Malaga	C	(332) p.32
1403.01.16	15 s. 11 d.	Barcelona	B	(138) p.151
1403.01.23	16 s.	Barcelona	B	(138) p.151
1403.02.11	15 s. 6 d.	Barcelona	B	(24) p.347
1403.02.14	16 s. 3 d.	Barcelona	B	(138) p.151
1403.02.21-26	16 s. 2 d.	Barcelona	B	(138) p.151
1403.03.01	16 s. 2 1/2 d.	Barcelona	B	(138) p.151
1403.03.20	16 s. 4 d.	Barcelona	B	(138) p.151
1403.03.30	16 s. 4 1/2 d.	Barcelona	B	(138) p.151
1403.04.07-24	16 s. 3 d.	Barcelona	B	(138) p.151
1403.05.03	16 s. 2 d.	Barcelona	B	(138) p.151
1403.05.08	16 s. 1 d.	Barcelona	B	(138) p.151
1403.05	16 s. 1/2 d.	Barcelona	B	(138) p.151
1403.05.30	15 s. 10 d.	Barcelona	B	(138) p.151
1403.06.13	15 s. 10 1/2 d.	Barcelona	B	(138) p.151
1403.06.15	15 s. 10 d.	Barcelona	B	(138) p.151
1403.06.24	15 s. 9 d.	Barcelona	B	(138) p.151
1403.06.30	15 s. 8 d.	Barcelona	B	(138) p.151
1403.07.04-08	15 s. 7 d.	Barcelona	B	(138) p.151
1403.07.25	15 s. 6 d.	Barcelona	B	(138) p.151
1403.08.03-08	15 s. 6 1/2 d.	Barcelona	B	(138) p.151
1403.08.19-23	15 s. 6 d.	Barcelona	B	(138) p.151
1403.08.30	15 s. 5 d.	Barcelona	B	(138) p.151
1403.09.04	15 s. 3 d.	Barcelona	B	(138) p.151
1403.09.15-16	15 s. 1 d.	Barcelona	B	(138) p.151
1403.10.02	15 s.	Barcelona	B	(138) p.151
1403.10.18	15 s. 2 1/2 d.	Barcelona	B	(138) p.151
1403.10.22	15 s. 3 1/2 d.	Barcelona	B	(138) p.152
1403.10.27	15 s.	Barcelona	B	(138) p.152
1403.11.15	14 s. 10 d.	Barcelona	B	(138) p.152
1403.11.26	14 s. 9 1/2 d.	Barcelona	B	(138) p.152
1403.12.04	14 s. 8 d.	Barcelona	B	(138) p.152
1403.12.20	15 s. 1 d.	Barcelona	B	(138) p.152
1404.01.03	15 s.	Barcelona	B	(138) p.152
1404.01.09	14 s. 10 d.	Barcelona	B	(138) p.152
1404.01.10	14 s. 11 1/2 d.	Barcelona	B	(138) p.152
1404.01.29	15 s. 3 1/2 d.	Barcelona	B	(138) p.152
1404.02.07-19	15 s. 4 d.	Barcelona	B	(138) p.152
1404.02.29	15 s. 4 1/2 d.	Barcelona	B	(138) p.152
1404.03.07	15 s. 4 d.	Barcelona	B	(138) p.152
1404.04.06	15 s. 5 1/2 d.	Barcelona	B	(138) p.152
1404.04.22	15 s.	Barcelona	B	(138) p.152
1404.04.29	14 s. 11 d.	Barcelona	B	(138) p.152
1404.05.12	14 s. 6 1/2 d.	Barcelona	B	(138) p.152
1404.05.23	14 s. 9 d.	Barcelona	B	(138) p.152
1404.05.31	14 s. 10 d.	Barcelona	B	(138) p.152
1404.06.12	14 s. 7 d.	Barcelona	B	(138) p.152
1404.06.18	14 s. 7 1/2 d.	Barcelona	B	(138) p.152
1404.06.27	14 s. 7 d.	Barcelona	B	(138) p.152
1404.07.07	14 s. 6 1/2 d.	Barcelona	B	(138) p.152
1404.07.14	14 s. 7 d.	Barcelona	B	(138) p.152
1404.07.22	14 s. 9 d.	Barcelona	B	(138) p.152
1404.08.02	14 s. 6 d.	Barcelona	B	(138) p.153
1404.08.19	14 s. 4 d.	Barcelona	B	(138) p.153
1404.08.20	14 s. 3 d.	Barcelona	B	(138) p.153
1404.08.24	14 s. 4 d.	Barcelona	B	(138) p.153
1404.09.04	14 s. 7 d.	Barcelona	B	(138) p.153
1404.09.13	14 s. 9 1/2 d.	Barcelona	B	(138) p.153
1404.09.20	14 s. 7 1/2 d.	Barcelona	B	(138) p.153
1404.09.30	14 s. 6 d.	Barcelona	B	(138) p.153
1404.10.03	14 s. 8 d.	Barcelona	B	(138) p.153
1404.10.16	14 s. 6 d.	Barcelona	B	(138) p.153
1404.10.24-27	14 s. 8 1/2 d.	Barcelona	B	(138) p.153
1404.11.06	14 s. 5 d.	Barcelona	B	(138) p.153
1404.11.20	14 s. 6 d.	Barcelona	B	(138) p.153
1404.11.27	14 s. 10 1/2 d.	Barcelona	B	(138) p.153
1404.12.12-1405.01.05	14 s. 8 d.	Barcelona	B	(138) p.153
1405.01.08	14 s. 8 1/2 d.	Barcelona	B	(138) p.153
1405.01.24	14 s. 9 1/2 d.	Barcelona	B	(138) p.153
1405.01.26	14 s. 9 d.	Barcelona	B	(138) p.153
1405.02.18	15 s. 1 d.	Barcelona	B	(138) p.153

THE FLORENTINE FLORIN IN SUELDOS AND DINEROS OF BARCELONA

Date	Rate	Place	Type	Reference
1405.03.19	14 s. 10 d.	Barcelona	B	(138) p.153
1405.03.24	14 s. 11 d.	Barcelona	B	(138) p.153
1405.04.01-14	15 s.	Barcelona	B	(138) p.153
1405.04.28	14 s. 10 d.	Barcelona	B	(138) p.153
1405.05.12-13	14 s. 7 d.	Barcelona	B	(138) p.153
1405.05.25	14 s. 3 d.	Barcelona	B	(138) p.153
1405.06.01	14 s. 5 d.	Barcelona	B	(138) p.154
1405.06.10-15	14 s. 7 d.	Barcelona	B	(138) p.154
1405.06.21-07.29	14 s. 6 d.	Barcelona	B	(138) p.154
1405.08.05	14 s. 8 1/2 d.	Barcelona	B	(138) p.154
1405.09.10	14 s. 6 d.	Barcelona	B	(138) p.154
1405.10.12	14 s. 9 d.	Barcelona	B	(138) p.154
1405.11.10	14 s. 11 d.	Barcelona	B	(138) p.154
1405.11.16	14 s. 9 d.	Barcelona	B	(138) p.154
1405.11.18	14 s. 10 d.	Barcelona	B	(138) p.154
1406.02.13	14 s. 6 d.	Barcelona	B	(138) p.154
1406.05.10	14 s. 5 d.	Barcelona	B	(138) p.154
1408.09.20	14 s. 2 1/2 d.	Barcelona	B	(138) p.154
1408.10.06	13 s.	Cagliari	O	(36) p.92
1408.12.01	15 s.	Cagliari	O	(36) p.92
1423.05.01	16 s.	Alghero	M	(117) p.41
1423.06.08	15 s. 8 d.	Barcelona	M	(117) p.41
1428.10.19	17 s. 11 d.	Valencia	B	(81) p.41
1430.06.17	18 s.	Rome	C	(285) p.264
1462-1472	17 s. 3 d.	Barcelona	C	(456) p.238

The florin of Genoa (Genovino d'oro) in sueldos and dineros of Barcelona

Date	Rate	Place	Type	Reference
1423.05.01	16 s.	Alghero	M	(117) IV p.41
1423.06.08	15 s. 8 d.	Barcelona	M	(117) IV p.41

The Venetian ducat in sueldos and dineros of Barcelona

Date	Rate	Place	Type	Reference
1385-1405	15 s.	Barcelona	B	(243) p.206
1394.02.28	15 s.	Avignon	B	(243) p.206

Between 1398 and 1405 I have selected the first bill drawn each month from a much larger body of material drawn from Datini archive. Lane and Mueller will publish bill rates from Venice to Barcelona between February 1399 and February 1411 from the Datini archive (284) II.

Date	Rate	Place	Type	Reference
1398.03.17	15 s. 4 d.	Barcelona-Venice	B	(138) p.144
1399.06.28	15 s. 10 1/2 d.	Barcelona-Venice	B	(138) p.146
1399.07.03-14	15 s. 10 d.	Barcelona-Venice	B	(138) p.146
1399.10.21-29	15 s. 6 d.	Barcelona-Venice	B	(138) p.146
1399.11.19-24	16 s.	Barcelona-Venice	B	(138) p.146
1399.12.04	15 s. 11 d.	Barcelona-Venice	B	(138) p.146
1400.01.01-29	16 s.	Barcelona-Venice	B	(138) p.147
1400.02.03	16 s. 1 1/2 d.	Barcelona-Venice	B	(138) p.147
1400.03.04-15	16 s. 2 1/2 d.	Barcelona-Venice	B	(138) p.147
1400.04.05	16 s. 4 d.	Barcelona-Venice	B	(138) p.147
1400.05.05	16 s. 6 d.	Barcelona-Venice	B	(138) p.147
1400.06.01	16 s. 1 d.	Barcelona-Venice	B	(138) p.147
1400.07.05	16 s.	Barcelona-Venice	B	(138) p.147
1400.08.04	15 s. 4 d.	Barcelona-Venice	B	(138) p.148
1400.09.07	15 s. 1 d.	Barcelona-Venice	B	(138) p.148
1400.10.06	15 s.	Barcelona-Venice	B	(138) p.148
1400.12.31-1401.01.10	14 s. 11 d.	Barcelona-Venice	B	(138) p.148
1401.01.28-02.06	15 s.	Barcelona-Venice	B	(138) p.148
1401.02.19	14 s. 11 d.	Barcelona-Venice	B	(138) p.148
1401.04.07	15 s. 5 d.	Barcelona-Venice	B	(138) p.148
1401.05.20-31	15 s. 8 d.	Barcelona-Venice	B	(138) p.148
1401.06.15	15 s. 9 d.	Barcelona-Venice	B	(138) p.148
1401.07.01-06	16 s.	Barcelona-Venice	B	(138) p.149
1401.08.11	15 s. 8 d.	Barcelona-Venice	B	(138) p.149
1401.09.01-06	15 s. 8 d.	Barcelona-Venice	B	(138) p.149
1401.10.04	15 s. 8 d.	Barcelona-Venice	B	(138) p.149

THE VENETIAN DUCAT IN SUELDOS AND DINEROS OF BARCELONA

Date	Rate	Place	Type	Reference
1401.11.02	15 s. 9 d.	Barcelona-Venice	B	(138) p.149
1401.12.05-12	16 s.	Barcelona-Venice	B	(138) p.149
1402.01-02-11	16 s. 2 d.	Barcelona-Venice	B	(138) p.149
1402.02.04	16 s. 3 1/2 d.	Barcelona-Venice	B	(138) p.149
1402.03.09	16 s. 7 d.	Barcelona-Venice	B	(138) p.149
1402.04.06-23	16 s. 8 d.	Barcelona-Venice	B	(138) p.150
1402.05.13	16 s. 5 1/2 d.	Barcelona-Venice	B	(138) p.150
1402.06.13	16 s. 6 1/2 d.	Barcelona-Venice	B	(138) p.150
1402.07.01-12	16 s. 7 1/2 d.	Barcelona-Venice	B	(138) p.150
1402.08.12	16 s. 8 d.	Barcelona-Venice	B	(138) p.150
1402.09.07-10.03	16 s. 7 d.	Barcelona-Venice	B	(138) p.150
1402.10.10	16 s. 6 1/2 d.	Barcelona-Venice	B	(138) p.150
1402.12.16	16 s. 8 d.	Barcelona-Venice	B	(138) p.151
1403.01.16-23	17 s.	Barcelona-Venice	B	(138) p.151
1403.02.14	17 s. 4 d.	Barcelona-Venice	B	(138) p.151
1403.03.01	17 s. 4 d.	Barcelona-Venice	B	(138) p.151
1403.04.07	17 s. 2 d.	Barcelona-Venice	B	(138) p.151
1403.05.03	17 s. 2 d.	Barcelona-Venice	B	(138) p.151
1403.06.13	16 s. 10 d.	Barcelona-Venice	B	(138) p.151
1403.07.04	16 s. 7 1/2 d.	Barcelona-Venice	B	(138) p.151
1403.08.03-08	16 s. 7 d.	Barcelona-Venice	B	(138) p.151
1403.09.04	16 s. 1 d.	Barcelona-Venice	B	(138) p.151
1403.09.15-16	15 s. 10 d.	Barcelona-Venice	B	(138) p.151
1403.10.02	15 s. 8 d.	Barcelona-Venice	B	(138) p.151
1403.11.15	15 s. 9 d.	Barcelona-Venice	B	(138) p.152
1403.12.04	15 s. 8 d.	Barcelona-Venice	B	(138) p.152
1404.01.03-09	15 s. 10 d.	Barcelona-Venice	B	(138) p.152
1404.02.29-03.07	16 s. 4 1/2 d.	Barcelona-Venice	B	(138) p.152
1404.04.06	16 s. 6 d.	Barcelona-Venice	B	(138) p.152
1404.05.12	15 s. 9 1/2 d.	Barcelona-Venice	B	(138) p.152
1404.06.12-18	15 s. 10 d.	Barcelona-Venice	B	(138) p.152
1404.07.07-14	15 s. 6 d.	Barcelona-Venice	B	(138) p.152
1404.08.02	15 s. 6 d.	Barcelona-Venice	B	(138) p.153
1404.09.04	15 s. 6 d.	Barcelona-Venice	B	(138) p.153
1404.10.03-16	15 s. 5 d.	Barcelona-Venice	B	(138) p.153
1404.11.06	15 s. 2 1/2 d.	Barcelona-Venice	B	(138) p.153
1404.12.12	15 s. 4 d.	Barcelona-Venice	B	(138) p.153
1405.01.08	15 s. 7 d.	Barcelona-Venice	B	(138) p.153
1405.02.18-24	15 s. 8 d.	Barcelona-Venice	B	(138) p.153
1405.03.19	15 s. 4 d.	Barcelona-Venice	B	(138) p.153
1405.04.01-14	15 s. 6 d.	Barcelona-Venice	B	(138) p.153
1405.05.12-13	15 s. 2 d.	Barcelona-Venice	B	(138) p.153
1405.06.01	14 s. 10 d.	Barcelona-Venice	B	(138) p.154
1405.07.06	15 s. 1 d.	Barcelona-Venice	B	(138) p.154
1405.08.05-15	15 s. 4 d.	Barcelona-Venice	B	(138) p.154
1405.10.12	15 s. 2 d.	Barcelona-Venice	B	(138) p.154
1405.11.10	15 s. 6 d.	Barcelona-Venice	B	(138) p.154
1406.02.13	15 s. 6 d.	Barcelona-Venice	B	(138) p.154
1406.05.10	15 s. 4 1/2 d.	Barcelona-Venice	B	(138) p.154
1408.09.20	15 s. 1 d.	Barcelona-Venice	B	(138) p.154
1423.05.01	16 s.	Alghero	M	(117) p.4
1423.06.08	15 s.	Barcelona	M	(117) p.41
1434	14 s.	Barcelona	C	(91) II p.590
1445	14 s. 8 d.	Barcelona	C	(91) II p.623
1447.07.18	16 s. 1/2 d.	Barcelona	B	(81) p.64
1447.07.21	16 s.	Barcelona	B	(81) p.65
1447.07.27	15 s. 10 d.	Barcelona	B	(81) p.65
1447.07.27	17 s. 1 d.	Barcelona	B	(81) p.42
1452	15 s.	Barcelona	C	(91) II p.623
1458-1459	16 s. 3 d.	Barcelona	B	(488) p.257
1458-1459	16 s. 2 4/5 d.	Barcelona	B	(488) p.257
1458-1459	16 s. 2 d.	Barcelona	B	(488) p.257
1459-1460	17 s. 5 1/4 d.	Barcelona	B	(488) p.257
1459-1460	15 s. 6 d.	Barcelona	B	(488) p.257
1460-1461	14 s. 8 d.	Barcelona	B	(488) p.257
1460-1461	14 s. 6 d.	Barcelona	B	(488) p.257
1460-1461	14 s. 2 d.	Barcelona	B	(488) p.257
1460-1461	14 s.	Barcelona	B	(488) p.257
1460-1461	13 s. 3 d.	Barcelona	B	(488) p.257
1462.02.18	22 s.	Barcelona	B	(81) p.103
1462.02.18	19 s. 4 d.	Barcelona	B	(81) p.104
1462.02.19	19 s. 3 d.	Barcelona	B	(81) p.104

THE VENETIAN DUCAT IN SUELDOS AND DINEROS OF BARCELONA

Date	Rate	Place	Type	Reference
1462.02.26	19 s. 4 d.	Barcelona	B	(81) p.105
1462.03.11	19 s.	Barcelona	B	(81) p.105
1462.04.09	19 s.	Barcelona	B	(81) p.107
1462.04.17	18 s. 10 d.	Barcelona	B	(81) p.108
1462.04.21	18 s. 11 d.	Barcelona	B	(81) p.108
1462.04.21	18 s. 9 d.	Barcelona	B	(81) p.108
1462.04.22	18 s. 10 d.	Barcelona	B	(81) p.108
1462.05.07	19 s.	Barcelona	B	(81) p.109
1462.05.28	18 s. 2 d.	Valencia	B	(81) p.110
1462.06.01	18 s. 2 d.	Valencia	B	(81) p.110
1462.06.19	18 s. 11 d.	Barcelona	B	(81) p.110
1463.10.13	18 s.	Valencia	B	(81) p.118
1464.07.24	17 s. 8 d.	Valencia	B	(81) p.122
1475.10	20 s.	Valencia	C	(450) II p.248
1479.06	21 s.	Valencia	C	(450) II p.248
1479.07	21 s. 10 d.	Saragossa	C	(450) II p.248
1480.08	20 s.	Valencia	C	(450) II p.248
1489.06.28	23 s.	Cagliari	C	(36) p.128

The libra of Barcelona in sueldos and dineros of Majorca

Date	Rate	Place	Type	Reference
1334-1342	30 s.	Barcelona	C	(321) p.479

The libra of Barcelona in sueldos and dineros alfonsinos of Sardinia

Date	Rate	Place	Type	Reference
1334-1342	31 s. 10 d.	Barcelona	C	(321) p.488
1334-1342	32 s.	Barcelona	C	(321) p.481
1463.08.31	65 s.	Cagliari	C	(300) p.175

See also the libra alfonsina in sueldos and dineros of Barcelona under SARDINIA p.155

The libra of Barcelona in sous and deniers melgorians of Melgueil

Date	Rate	Place	Type	Reference
1213	15 s.	Barcelona	H	(165) p.26
1260.12.28	16 s. 8 d.	Barcelona	M	(315) no.14

For the ducat of 10 carlini in sueldos and dineros of Barcelona see under NAPLES p.64
For the uncia of Sicily in sueldos and dineros of Barcelona see under SICILY p.66
For the florin of Sicily in sueldos and dineros of Barcelona see under SICILY p.66
For the papal franc in sueldos and dineros of Barcelona see under AVIGNON p.126
For the libra of Valencia in sueldos and dineros of Barcelona see under VALENCIA p.147
For the libra of iaccenses in sueldos and dineros of Barcelona see under ARAGON p.148
For the florin of Aragon in sueldos and dineros of Barcelona see under ARAGON p.148
For the gold morabetino and the dobla in sueldos and dineros of Barcelona see under CASTILE pp.156 and 160
For the dobla morisca in sueldos and dineros of Barcelona see under GRANADA p.162
For the rheingulden in sueldos and dineros of Barcelona see under RHINELAND p.254
For the ducat of Rhodes in sueldos and dineros of Barcelona see under RHODES p.293
For the besant (unspecified) in sueldos and dineros of Barcelona see under BESANT p.294
For the dinar in sueldos and dineros of Barcelona see under EGYPT p.307
For the besant of Alexandria in sueldos and dineros of Barcelona see under EGYPT p.307
For the dobla massamutino in sueldos and dineros of Barcelona see under TUNIS p.312

VALENCIA

In 1238 James I of Aragon conquered the Muslim kingdom of Valencia and from 1247 began to have dineros struck for it known as reales de Valencia. Although no further dineros were struck after the death of James I in 1276 until 1421, the money of Valencia remarkably survived for accounting purposes. This survival is partially accounted for by the market equivalence in James II's reign (1291-1327) of 18 of the surviving reales of Valencia with the sueldo jaquesa of Aragon. When John I in 1393 created a gros for Valencia, a real de plata, equivalent to a sueldo jaquesa. It was popularly known in Valencia as a dihuité, being 18 diners de moneda menuda de reals de Valencia.

The Venetian ducat in sueldos and dineros reales of Valencia

Date	Rate	Place	Type	Reference
1447.07.29	15 s. 8 d.	Barcelona	B	(81) p.42
1447.07.31	15 s. 9 d.	Barcelona	B	(81) p.42
1447.08.03	15 s. 8 d.	Barcelona	B	(81) p.67
1447	16 s. 10 d.	Barcelona	B	(81) p.67
1447.08.17	15 s. 7 d.	Barcelona	B	(81) p.68
1447.08.22	15 s. 8 d.	Barcelona	B	(81) p.68
1447.08.22	15 s. 7 d.	Barcelona	B	(81) p.69
1447.09.06	15 s. 6 d.	Barcelona	B	(81) p.69
1447.09.09	15 s. 4 d.	Barcelona	B	(81) p.70
1447.09.15	15 s. 3 d.	Barcelona	B	(81) p.70
1459.07.21	16 s. 6 d.	Valencia	B	(81) p.90

The libra of dineros reales of Valencia in sueldos ternales of Barcelona

Date	Rate	Place	Type	Reference
1247	30 s.	Valencia	O	(163) p.170

The libra of Valencia in sueldos and dineros alfonsinos of Sardinia

Date	Rate	Place	Type	Reference
1463.08.31	48 s.	Valencia	C	(300) p.175
1463.09.28	75 s.	Cagliari	C	(300) p.175

The libra of Valencia in sous royaux coronats of Provence

Date	Rate	Place	Type	Reference
1247	40 s.	Valencia	O	(163) p.170

The libra of Valencia in sous and deniers melgorians of Melgueil

Date	Rate	Place	Type	Reference
1247	26 s. 8 d.	Valencia	O	(163) p.170

For the florin of Sicily in sueldos and dineros of Valencia see under SICILY p.66
For the libra of iaccenses and the florin of Aragon in sueldos and dineros of Valencia see under ARAGON pp.148 and 149
For the dobla in sueldos and dineros of Valencia see under CASTILE p.161
For the livre tournois in sueldos and dineros of Valencia see under FRANCE p.184
For the dinar in sueldos and dineros of Valencia see under EGYPT p.307

ARAGON

The dinero iaccensis or jaquesa was issued by the kings of Aragon from Sancho Ramirez (1063-94) onwards. It took its name from the town of Jaca where it was first minted, although other mints were also used later.

The Florentine florin in sueldos and dineros iaccenses of Aragon

Date	Rate	Place	Type	Reference
1280-1282	9 s.	Curia	B	(439) p.897
1280-1282	10 s.	Curia	B	(439) p.897
1320	11 s. 6 d.	Curia	B	(439) p.900
1321	11 s. 6 d.	Curia	B	(439) p.900
1323-1334	11 s. 6 d.	Curia	B	(439) p.900
1335	10 s.	Curia	B	(439) p.902
1336	10 s. 6 d.	Curia	B	(439) p.902
1338	11 s. 6 d.	Curia	B	(439) p.902
1348-1351	11 s.	Curia	B	(439) p.902
1479.8.21	22 s.	Saragossa	B	(483) I p.39

The libra of iaccenses in sueldos and dineros of Barcelona

The money of Aragon remained separate from that of Barcelona after the union of the kingdom of Aragon and the county of Barcelona. Despite an attempt to make them equivalent in 1256, they continued to evolve differently and there was no permanently fixed relationship between them.

Date	Rate	Place	Type	Reference
1247	24 s.	Barcelona	C	(163) p.525
1308	30 s.	Aragon	O	(326) p.339
1310.04.03	30 s.	Aragon	O	(326) p.339
1310	35 s.	Barcelona	C	(163) p.525
1323	28 s.	Barcelona	C	(163) p.525

The libra of iaçcenses in sueldos and dineros reales of Valencia

Date	Rate	Place	Type	Reference
1247	16 s.	Valencia	O	(211) p.285
1310.04.03	30 s.	Valencia/Almeria	O	(326) VII p.339

For the florin of Sicily in sueldos and dineros iaccenses see under SICILY p.67
For the gold morabetino and the dobla in sueldos and dineros iaccenses see under CASTILE pp.156 and 161

FLORINS OF ARAGON

In 1346 Pedro IV of Aragon began to mint florins at Perpignan, in imitation of those of Florence. In 1369 he converted the 'florin de Perpignan' into the 'florì d'or d'Aragò'. He intended it to circulate throughout all his territories in common, although the silver coinages of the various Aragonese principalities were not unified. The florin of Aragon was minted at Barcelona and Tortosa in Catalonia, at Saragossa in Aragon, and at Valencia, as well as at Perpignan. At 3.48 grams the florin of Aragon was slightly lighter in weight than the prototype, the florin of Florence. It was however, only 18 carats fine, whereas the Florentine florin was as near to 24 carats fine as was technically practicable. It was therefore a piece of approximately 3/4 value of the Florentine florin. The florin of Aragon remained the standard gold coin of all the Aragonese dominions until 1475-6, when it was replaced by a 'ducado d'oro'.

The florin of Aragon in other Spanish currencies

The florin of Perpignan and the florin of Aragon in sueldos and dineros of Barcelona

Date	Rate	Place	Type	Reference
Mid-14th century	14 s.	Valencia	C	(163) p.528
1356.01	12 s.	Perpignan	C	(304) V p.696
1362	12 s.	Avignon	B	(439) p.75
1366	11 s.	Sardinia	C	(36) p.88
1368	11 s.	Curia	B	(439) p.75
1390.03.14	11 s.	Barcelona	C	(82) II p.350
1408.10.16	9 s.	Cagliari	O	(36) p.92

THE FLORIN OF ARAGON IN SUELDOS AND DINEROS OF BARCELONA

Date	Rate	Place	Type	Reference
1408.12.01	11 s.	Cagliari	O	(36) p.95
1462-1472	13 s.	Barcelona	C	(456) p.269
1462-1472	11 s.	Barcelona	C	(456) p.253
1484	13 s.	Rome	B	(439) p.75

The florin of Aragon in sueldos and dineros iaccenses

Date	Rate	Place	Type	Reference
1379-1384	9 s.	Aragon	C	(235) p.93
1385	9 s. 1 d.	Aragon	C	(235) p.93
1386	9 s. 2 d.	Aragon	C	(235) p.93
1387-1390	9 s. 4 d.	Aragon	C	(235) p.93
1391	9 s. 9 d.	Aragon	C	(235) p.93
1392-1399	10 s.	Aragon	C	(235) p.93
1396.12.08	10 s. 1 d.	Navarre	C	(421) p.495
1400-1401	10 s. 4 d.	Aragon	C	(235) p.93
1402-1406	10 s. 1 d.	Aragon	C	(235) p.93
1407-1415	9 s. 7 d.	Aragon	C	(235) p.93
1415.01.10	11 s.	Valencia	C	(351) p.71
1416-1417	10 s.	Aragon	C	(235) p.93
1418-1425	10 s. 2 d.	Aragon	C	(235) p.93
1426-1433	10 s. 4 d.	Aragon	C	(235) p.93
1434-1436	10 s. 6 d.	Aragon	C	(235) p.93
1437-1438	10 s. 9 d.	Aragon	C	(235) p.93
1439	10 s. 10 d.	Aragon	C	(235) p.93
1440	10 s. 11 d.	Aragon	C	(235) p.93
1441-1442	11 s.	Aragon	C	(235) p.93
1443-1446	10 s.	Aragon	C	(235) p.93
1447-1448	10 s. 6 d.	Aragon	C	(235) p.93
1449-1450	10 s. 9 d.	Aragon	C	(235) p.93
1451-1454	11 s.	Aragon	C	(235) p.93
1455-1457	11 s. 8 d.	Aragon	C	(235) p.93
1459-1461	12 s. 4 d.	Aragon	C	(235) p.93
1458	13 s.	Barcelona	C	(91) I p.479
1462	12 s. 6 d.	Aragon	C	(235) p.93
1463	12 s. 8 d.	Aragon	C	(235) p.93
1464-1465	13 s. 4 d.	Aragon	C	(235) p.93
1466-1476	14 s.	Aragon	C	(235) p.93
1477-1480	15 s.	Aragon	C	(235) p.93
1479.02.02	15 s.	Trujillo	B	(483) I p.1
1481-1500	16 s.	Aragon	C	(235) p.93

The florin of Aragon in sueldos reales of Valencia

Date	Rate	Place	Type	Reference
1433.03.17	22 s.	Rome	C	(287) p.123

The florin of Perpignan and the florin of Aragon in sueldos and dineros alfonsinos menuts of Sardinia

Date	Rate	Place	Type	Reference
1346	16 s. 6 d.	Sardinia	C	(318) p.340
1347	16 s. 6 d.	Sardinia	C	(318) p.340
1349	21 s. 1 d.	Sardinia	C	(318) p.340
1350	20 s. 1 d.	Sardinia	C	(318) p.340
1351	19 s.	Sassari	M	(319) p.16
1351	18 s.	Sardinia	M	(319) p.16
1354	18 s.	Sardinia	M	(319) p.16
1355	18 s.	Sardinia	M	(319) p.16
1356	18 s.	Sardinia	M	(319) p.16
1357	18 s.	Sardinia	O	(123) pp.164-168
1362	18 s.	Sardinia	M	(319) p.16
1362	20 s.	Cagliari	M	(319) p.16
1363	17 s. 3 d.	Sardinia	M	(319) p.16
1364	17 s. 6 d.	Sardinia	M	(319) p.16
1366	16 s. 6 d.	Sardinia	M	(319) p.16

THE FLORIN OF ARAGON IN SUELDOS AND DINEROS OF SARDINIA

Date	Rate	Place	Type	Reference
1367	16 s. 6 d.	Sardinia	M	(319) p.16
1367	14 s. 6 d.	Sardinia	A	(319) p.16
1369-1380	16 s. 6 d.	Sardinia	M	(319) p.16
1381-1399	18 s.	Sardinia	M	(319) p.16
1399	16 s. 6 d.	Cagliari	A	(319) p.16
1400	18 s.	Sardinia	M	(319) p.19
1401-5	18 s.	Sardinia	C	(318) p.340
1408.10.06	18 s.	Sardinia	O	(123) pp.164-168
1408.12.01	22 s.	Cagliari	O	(36) p.95
1414	22 s.	Sardinia	C	(318) p.340
1418	20 s.	Sardinia?	H	(318) p.340
1419.01.31	22 s.	Cagliari	O	(36) p.101
1428.10.01	24 s.	Cagliari	O	(36) p.106
1428	32 s.	Sardinia	O	(123) pp.164-168
1433	36 s.	Sardinia	O	(123) pp.164-168
1436	27 s.	Sardinia	O	(123) pp.164-168
1458	30 s. money of Cagliari	Sardinia	C	(123) pp.164-168
1480	33 s.	Cagliari	O	(36) pp.128

The florin of Aragon in maravedis

Date	Rate	Place	Type	Reference
1369	23 old m.	Castile	O	(492) II p.838
1390	23 old m.	Burgos	A	(314) p.144
1391	22 1/2 old m.	Burgos	A	(314) p.144
1392	45 m.	Burgos	A	(314) p.144
1393	45 m.	Burgos	A	(314) p.144
1394	45 m.	Burgos	A	(314) p.144
1395	45 m.	Burgos	A	(314) p.144
1396	45 m.	Burgos	A	(314) p.144
1397	22 1/4 old m.	Burgos	A	(314) p.144
1398	46-45 m.	Burgos	A	(314) p.144
1399	47-45 m.	Burgos	A	(314) p.144
1400	44 m.	Madrid	C	(280) p.95
1400	48 m.	Burgos	A	(314) p.144
1401	46 m.	Toledo	M	(256) p.35
1401	49 m.	Burgos	A	(314) p.144
1402	50 1/2 m.	Burgos	A	(314) p.144
1403	50 1/2 m.	Burgos	A	(314) p.144
1404	50 m.	Burgos	A	(314) p.144
1405.12.08	46 m.	Spain	C	(421) p.506
1405	50 1/2 m.	Burgos	A	(314) p.144
1406.03.13	50 m.	Spain	C	(421) p.508
1406	50 1/2 m.	Burgos	A	(314) p.144
1407	51 m.	Burgos	A	(314) p.144
1408	50 1/2 m.	Burgos	A	(314) p.144
1409	50 1/2 m.	Burgos	A	(314) p.144
1410	50 1/2 m.	Burgos	A	(314) p.144
1410.01.22	35 m.	Murcia	O	(337)
1411	50 1/2 m.	Burgos	A	(314) p.144
1412	52 m.	Burgos	A	(314) p.144
1413	50 1/2 m.	Burgos	A	(314) p.144
1414	50 1/2 m.	Burgos	A	(314) p.145
1415	50 1/2 m.	Burgos	A	(314) p.145
1416	50 m.	Burgos	A	(314) p.145
1417	50 1/2 m.	Burgos	A	(314) p.145
1418	51 m.	Burgos	A	(314) p.145
1418	50-50 1/2 m.	Toledo	A	(256) p.35
1419	51 m.	Burgos	A	(314) p.145
1420	51 1/2 m.	Burgos	A	(314) p.145
1421	52 m.	Burgos	A	(314) p.145
1422	52 m.	Burgos	A	(314) p.145
1423	52 m.	Burgos	A	(314) p.145
1424	51 1/2-52 m.	Toledo	A	(256) p.35
1424	52 1/4 m.	Burgos	A	(314) p.145
1425	52 m.	Burgos	A	(314) p.145
1426	52 1/4 m.	Burgos	A	(314) p.145
1426	53 m.	Toledo	A	(256) p.35
1427	52 1/4 m.	Burgos	A	(314) p.145

THE FLORIN OF ARAGON IN MARAVEDIS

Date	Rate	Place	Type	Reference
1428	52 1/2 m.	Toledo	A	(256) p.35
1428	53 m.	Burgos	A	(314) p.145
1429	53 m.	Toledo	A	(256) p.35
1429	53 1/2 m.	Burgos	A	(314) p.145
1430	53 m.	Burgos	A	(314) p.145
1430	52 m.	Madrid	C	(280) p.95
1431	54 1/2 m.	Burgos	A	(314) p.145
1431	52-56 m.	Toledo	A	(256) p.35
1432	55 1/2 m.	Burgos	A	(314) p.145
1432	56 m.	Toledo	A	(256) p.35
1433	59 1/2 m.	Burgos	A	(314) p.145
1434	62 2/3 m.	Burgos	A	(314) pp.144-146
1435	67 m.	Burgos	A	(314) pp.144-146
1436	67 1/2 m.	Burgos	A	(314) p.145
1437	69 2/3 m.	Burgos	A	(314) pp.144-146
1438	70 2/3 m.	Burgos	A	(314) p.145
1438	70 m.	Madrid	C	(280) p.95
1439	75 m.	Burgos	A	(314) p.145
1440	88 1/3 m.	Burgos	A	(314) p.145
1441	77 1/2 m.	Burgos	A	(314) p.145
1442	68 2/3 m.	Burgos	A	(314) p.145
1442.04.06	65 m.	Aragon	O	(484) p.713
1442.04.06	65 m.	Valladolid	O	(484) p.712
1443	68 1/5 m.	Burgos	A	(314) p.145
1443.11.09	51 m.	Aragon	O	(484) p.713
1444	80 m.	Burgos	A	(314) p.145
1444	77 1/2 m.	Burgos	A	(314) p.145
1444.12.05	50 m.	Aragon	O	(484) p.713
1445	80 m.	Burgos	A	(314) p.145
1446	84 1/3 m.	Burgos	A	(314) p.145
1447	87 1/5 m.	Burgos	A	(314) p.145
1448	95 3/5 m.	Burgos	A	(314) p.145
1449	101 2/5 m.	Burgos	A	(314) p.145
1449	100 m.	Toledo	A	(256) p.35
1449	110 m.	Toledo	A	(256) p.35
1450	100 m.	Madrid	C	(280) p.95
1451	106-110 m.	Toledo	A	(256) p.35
1451	106 2/3 m.	Burgos	A	(314) p.145
1452	106 2/3 m.	Burgos	A	(314) p.145
1453	106 2/3 m.	Burgos	A	(314) p.145
1454	106 2/3 m.	Burgos	A	(314) p.145
1454	110-111 m.	Toledo	A	(256) p.35
1455	106 2/3 m.	Burgos	A	(314) p.145
1455	110 m.	Madrid	C	(280) p.95
1456	110 m.	Madrid	C	(280) p.95
1456	116 m.	Madrid	C	(280) p.95
1456	113 3/5 m.	Burgos	A	(314) p.146
1457	118 2/3 m.	Burgos	A	(314) p.146
1457	117 m.	Madrid	C	(280) p.95
1457	125 m.	Madrid	C	(280) p.95
1458	110-132 m.	Toledo	A	(256) p.35
1458	120 m.	Madrid	C	(280) p.95
1458	125 m.	Burgos	A	(314) p.146
1458-1460	130 m.	Madrid	C	(280) p.95
1459	128 m.	Burgos	A	(314) p.146
1460	125 m.	Burgos	A	(314) p.146
1461	140 m.	Burgos	A	(314) p.146
1460-1461	140 m.	Madrid	C	(280) p.95
1461	150 m.	Madrid	C	(280) p.95
1462-1464	103 m.	Madrid	C	(280) p.95
1462	103 m.	Burgos	A	(314) p.146
1462	100 m.	Toledo	A	(256) p.35
1463	103 m.	Toledo	A	(256) p.35
1463	130 m.	Burgos	A	(314) p.146
1464	147 1/2 m.	Burgos	A	(314) p.146
1464-1465	150 m.	Madrid	C	(280) p.95
1465	155 m.	Burgos	A	(314) p.146
1465	160 m.	Toledo	A	(256) p.35
1466	170 m.	Burgos	A	(314) p.146
1466	180 m.	Toledo	A	(256) p.35
1467	173 1/3 m.	Burgos	A	(314) p.146
1468	180 m.	Burgos	A	(314) p.146

THE FLORIN OF ARAGON IN MARAVEDIS

Date	Rate	Place	Type	Reference
1469	190 m.	Burgos	A	(314) p.146
1470	200 m.	Burgos	A	(314) p.146
1470	225 m.	Toledo	A	(256) p.35
1471	210 m.	Madrid	C	(280) p.95
1471	225-230 m.	Toledo	A	(256) p.35
1472	210 m.	Burgos	A	(314) p.146
1473	230 m.	Toledo	A	(256) p.35
1473	210 m.	Burgos	A	(314) p.146
1474	216 2/3 m.	Burgos	A	(314) p.146
1475	200 m.	Madrid	C	(280) p.95
1475	235 m.	Burgos	A	(314) p.146
1476	245 m.	Burgos	A	(314) p.146
1477	245 m.	Burgos	A	(314) p.146
1478	260 m.	Burgos	A	(314) p.146
1480-1486	265 m.	Madrid	C	(280) p.95
1493	267 m.	Spain	C	(98) p.99

The florin of Aragon in sueldos and dineros of Navarre

Date	Rate	Place	Type	Reference
1386.02	37 s. 6 d.	Navarre	O	(490) p.61
1386.02	37 s.	Navarre	O	(490) p.61
1393.07.21	26 s.	Spain	C	(421) p.486
1398.01.14	26 s. 8 d.	Spain	C	(421) p.497
1400.05.20	26 s. 8 d.	Navarre	C	(421) p.499
1405.09.03	28 s.	Spain	C	(421) p.505

The florin of Aragon in non-Spanish currencies

The florin of Perpignan and the florin of Aragon in sous and deniers of Avignon

Date	Rate	Place	Type	Reference
1362.01	22 s.	Curia	B	(251) p.385
1372.03.06	19 s. 10 d.	Curia	B	(441) p.355
1372	20 s. 1 d.	Avignon	B	(439) p.57
1373	20 s. 4 d.	Curia	B	(441) p.377
1376.01.27	20 s.	Avignon	B	(268) p.221
1376.10.02	20 s.	Avignon	C	(343) p.136
1376	20 s.	Avignon	C	(343) p.154
1378	21 s. 6 d.	Avignon	C	(182) p.36

The florin of Aragon in sous and deniers of Narbonne

Date	Rate	Place	Type	Reference
1381	16 s. 11 1/4 d.	Narbonne	B	(42) p.3
1386.01.23	13 s. 9 d.	Narbonne	B	(42) p.95
1390	13 s. 9 d.	Narbonne	B	(42) p.221

DUCATS OF ARAGON

The ducado d'oro was introduced by John II in 1477 as the new standard gold coin for all the Aragonese dominions. It was officially worth two of the florins of Aragon. By 1483 it had become the pound unit of a money of account and was called by Italians the 'lira spagnuola' (489) p.28.

For the uncia of Sicily in ducats of Aragon see under SICILY p.66

MAJORCA

In 1229 James I of Aragon conquered the Balearic Islands from the Muslims and erected them into the kingdom of Majorca. Throughout the thirteenth century a wide variety of outside coinages, such as the southern French deniers melgorians, were used in the islands as well as dirhams (millarenses) surviving from before the conquest. In the thirteenth century accounting continued in besants of 10 millarenses, as in north Africa. For this accounting system see BARBARY p.309. On the death of James I in 1276, the kingdom of Majorca was separated from the kingdom of Aragon and passed to his younger son James II of Majorca. It was only in 1300 that he began to mint his own money, This consisted of a base silver dinero known as a 'real senar' or 'menut', its half, a 'doblenc' or double dinero, and a fine silver 'royal d'argent' worth 16 dineros menudos. Although the kingdom of Majorca was reunited with the kingdom of Aragon in 1343, it retained a separate coinage until the eighteenth century.

The Florentine florin in sueldos and dineros reales of Majorca

Date	Rate	Place	Type	Reference
1320-1328	21 s.	Avignon	B	(439) p.98
1323	21 s. 8 d.	Barcelona	C	(163) p.529
1340.09.06	24 s. 9 d.	Majorca	C	(315) no.93
1358	20 s.	Avignon	B	(439) p.99

The besant of silver (10 millarenses) in soldi of Genoa

Date	Rate	Place	Type	Reference
1243.08	6 s.	Majorca-Genoa	B	(524)

For the uncia of Sicily in sueldos and dineros of Majorca see under SICILY p.66
For the libra of Barcelona in sueldos and dineros of Majorca see under BARCELONA p.146
For the gold morabetino in sueldos and dineros of Majorca see under CASTILE p.156
For the dinar in sueldos and dineros of Majorca see under EGYPT p.307

SARDINIA

In 1297 Pope Boniface granted the kingdom of Sardinia to James II of Aragon. However the effective conquest of Sardinia by the Aragonese did not begin until 1324 and it took a generation of continuous warfare to achieve it.

When the Aragonese landed the currency consisted of Genoese and Pisan silver and billon coins and gold coins of Florence and Genoa. They introduced two new coins, billon dineros and silver grossos or reyal majors. The grossos were initially identical in value with the croats of Barcelona, which also circulated in Sardinia. In the reign of the next ruler Alfonso IV of Aragon (1327-36) the new coins were called alfonsinos menuts and alfonsinos de plata, and kept these names after his death. The dineros alfonsinos (menuts) were the basis of the money of account, although the commonest coins were the silver alfonsinos or groats which were initially worth 18 dineros. These were minted from local ore in vast quantities for export, in particular to Naples where they were transformed into carlini.

Until the rich silver mines of Iglesias were exhausted later in the fourteenth century, a very considerable amount of coin was minted in Sardinia, which passed in large quantities through trade to Italy, north Africa and Cyprus. Silver alfonsinos were known to the Spaniards as 'tarines de plata', but to Italians as grossi 'anfrusini'. Monetary values were usually expressed in pounds of 240 menuts (moneta alfonsina minuta), occasionally in gold florins of Florence and Genoa and towards the end of the fourteenth century increasingly in gold florins of Aragon.

The silver alfonsino or reyal major in dineros alfonsinos (menuts) of Sardinia

Date	Rate	Place	Type	Reference
1326	16 d.	Sardinia	O	(123) p.162
1330.04.03	18 d.	Sardinia	O	(326) p.345
circa 1338	18 d.	Sardinia	O	(123) p.162
1339-1341	18 d.	Sardinia	O	(123) p.162
until 1358	18 d.	Sardinia	O	(123) p.162
1408	24 d.	Sardinia	O	(123) p.162
1419	36 d.	Sardinia	O	(123) p.162
1442	36 d.	Sardinia	O	(123) p.162
1492	48 d.	Sardinia	O	(123) p.162

The Florentine florin and the Venetian ducat in sueldos and dineros alfonsinos (menuts) of Sardinia

Where unit is Ducat D

Date	Rate	Place	Type	Reference
1324-1326	26 s. 2 d.	Sardinia	C	(318) p.341
1326	26 s. 2 d.	Sardinia	O	(123) pp.164-168
1331	26 s. 6 d.	Sardinia	O	(123) pp.164-168
1331-1333	24 s. 6 d.	Sardinia	C	(318) p.341
1332	23 s. 3 d.	Cagliari	O	(36) p.75
1334	24 s. 3 d.	Sardinia	O	(123) pp.164-168
1334	24 s. 3 d.	Sardinia	C	(318) p.341
1334	23 s. 3 d.	Cagliari	O	(36) p.75
1334-1342	22 s. 1 3/4 d.	Sardinia	C	(387) p.476
1346	25 s. 6 d.	Sassari	C	(123) pp.164-168
1346	19 s.	Sassari	C	(123) pp.164-168
1346	19 s. 6 d.	Sassari	C	(123) pp.164-168
1347	20 s.	Sardinia	O	(123) pp.164-168
1347	21 s. 1 d.	Sardinia	C	(123) pp.164-168
1349	20 s.	Sardinia	O	(123) pp.164-168
1351	19 s. 6 d.	Sardinia	O	(123) pp.164-168
1351	19 s. 6 d.	Sardinia	A	(319) p.17
1355	19 s. 6 d.	Sardinia	O	(123) pp.164-168
1357	18 s.	Sardinia	O	(123) pp.164-168
1361	19 s.	Sassari	C	(123) pp.164-168
1361	19 s. 6 d.	Sardinia	A	(319) p.17
1362	20 s.	Sardinia	O	(123) pp.164-168
1363	20 s.	Sardinia	O	(123) pp.164-168
1363	19 s. 4 d.	Sassari	C	(123) pp.164-168
1364	20 s.	Sardinia	A	(319) p.17
1365	20 s.	Sardinia	O	(123) pp.164-168
1365	21 s.	Sardinia	O	(123) pp.164-168
1367	22 s.	Sardinia	O	(123) pp.164-168
1369	25 s.	Sardinia	O	(123) pp.164-168
1371	25 s.	Sardinia	A	(319) p.17
1378	24 s. 9 d.	Alghero	C	(123) pp.164-168
1378	25 s.	Sardinia	A	(319) p.17
1381	25 s.	Sardinia	O	(123) pp.164-168
1382	15 s.	Sardinia	A	(319) p.17
1389	25 s.	Sardinia	O	(123) pp.164-168
1390	25 s.	Sardinia	O	(123) pp.164-168
1391	25 s.	Sardinia	A	(319) p.17
1392	23 s. 5 d.	Cagliari	O	(36) p.75
1405	26 s.	Sardinia	O	(123) pp.164-168
1408.10.16	26 s.	Cagliari	O	(36) p.75
1408.12.01	30 s.	Cagliari	O	(36) p.75
1414.02.08D	25 s.	Cagliari	O	(36) p.75
1414	30 s.	Sardinia	O	(123) pp.164-168
1414	32 s.	Sardinia	O	(123) pp.164-168
1428.10.01	24 s.	Cagliari	H	(36) p.106

In the 1430s the coinage was increasingly debased, and to make matter worse, the different mints in the island issued coins on different standards. By 1451 the pounds of Sassari and Bosa were worth 20% less than the pound of Cagliari, and the pound of Alghero was worth 26% less (123) p.171. The following entries all refer to the money of Cagliari.

THE FLORIN AND THE DUCAT IN SUELDOS AND DINEROS OF SARDINIA

Date	Rate	Place	Type	Reference
1434	50 s.	Sardinia	O	(123) pp.164-168
1434-1435	55 s.	Sardinia	O	(123) pp.164-168
1435D	48 s.	Cagliari	O	(36) p.114
1438	48 s.	Sardinia	O	(123) pp.164-168
1441	50 s.	Cagliari	O	(36) p.114
1446	46 s. 2 d.	Cagliari	O	(36) p.114
1456-1408	46 s.	Sardinia	O	(123) pp.164-168
1472D	60 s.	Cagliari	O	(36) p.126
1480D	56 s.	Sardinia	O	(123) pp.164-168
1489.06.28D	56 s.	Cagliari	C	(36) p.128
1492.02D	48 s.	Cagliari	O	(36) p.130
1492.04	56 s.	Cagliari	C	(36) p.130
1500-1503	56 s.	Sassari	C	(36) p.141

The libra alfonsina in sueldos and dineros of Barcelona

Date	Rate	Place	Type	Reference
1334-1342	11 s. 1 d.	Barcelona	C	(321) p.482
1334-1342	11 s. 8 d.	Barcelona	C	(321) p.484

These rates are inconsistant with those given by the same source for the libra of Barcelona in sueldos and dineros alfonsinos, see under BARCELONA p.146

For the libra of Valencia in sueldos and dineros alfonsinos see under VALENCIA p.147
For the florin of Aragon in sueldos and dineros alfonsinos see under ARAGON p.149

CASTILE

The gold morabetino or maravedi

The gold dinars of the Al-Moravid rulers of north Africa and Muslim Spain were also much used in Christian Spain, where they were known as morabetinos or maravedis (i.e. of the Moravids). When the striking of gold maravedis ceased in Muslim Spain around 1170, the kings of Castile, Leon and Portugal very soon began to strike Christian maravedis, sometimes called morabetinos anfusinos. The issue of these Christian gold maravedis came to an end about 1221, but occasional reckoning in them continued for much of the thirteenth century.

The gold dinar of the Al-Moravids and their successors, both Muslim and Christian, circulated widely, not only in north Africa and the kingdoms of Spain, but also in other parts of the western Mediterranean. A number of sporadic references therefore survive to their value in widely scattered places. These are not always to the same pieces, since the various issues of morabetinos did not always keep precisely to the same standard. The original almoravid gold dinar was valued at ten silver dirhams in Andalusia.

The last Muslim morabetinos were struck in Murcia in 1170, and the last Christian ones in Castile around 1221. From the 1240s it is not always clear whether the morabetino in Castile and Leon was any longer an actual gold coin, or merely an accounting multiple. By 1252, there is some evidence to suggest that a distinction was being made between the short maravedi (curtis) meaning 90 dineros in Castile and the long maravedi (longis) meaning 96 dineros in Leon.

The gold morabetino in other Spanish currencies

The gold morabetino in sueldos and dineros of Castile

Date	Rate	Place	Type	Reference
1134	5 s.	Castile	A	(211) p.317
1172	6 s.	Castile	A	(211) p.317
circa 1222 (Ferdinand III)	7 s. 6 d.	Castile	O	(201) p.150
1228	15 s. pepiones	Castile	A	(211) p.328
1228	7 s. 6 d. moneda nueva	Castile	A	(211) p.328

This moneda nueva was later known as burgales, (from the Burgos mint) and was worth double the previous money (pepiones). It continued to be struck until 1258.

1241	15 s. pepiones	Castile	A	(211) p.329
1244	7 s. 6 d. burgaleses	Castile	A	(211) p.334
1252	15 s. pepiones	Castile	A	(211) p.334
1252	7 s. 6 d. burgaleses	Castile	A	(211) p.334
1258	7 s. 6 d. prietos negros	Castile	A	(211) p.336
1271	5 s. segundos prietos blancoś	Castile	A	(211) p.336
1276	7 s. 6 d. moneda nueva blanca alfonsa	Castile	A	(211) p.336
1277	7 s. 6 d. blancos	Castile	A	(211) p.338
1279	7 s. 6 d. blancos	Castile	A	(211) p.338
1282	5 s. novenes alfons-ines or cornados novénes	Castile	A	(211) p.338

The gold morabetino in sueldos and dineros legionenses or leoneses (of Leon)

Date	Rate	Place	Type	Reference
1184	8 s.	Leon	A	(211) p.326
1252	8 s.	Leon	A	(211) p.328
1280	8 s. alfonsinos blancos	Leon	A	(211) p.329

The gold morabetino in sueldos and dineros of Barcelona

Date	Rate	Place	Type	Reference
1202	7 s.	Catalonia	A	(211) p.226
(1276-1285) Pedro III	10 s. 6 d.	Catalonia	O	(211) p.237

The gold morabetino in sueldos and dineros iaccenses of Aragon

Date	Rate	Place	Type	Reference
1152	5 s.	Aragon	?	(211) p.270
1171	7 s.	Aragon	O	(211) p.270
1197.04.18	9 s.	Aragon	A	(39) p.86 n.1
1222.12.10	7 s. 8 d.	Aragon	C	(253) p.91

The gold morabetino in sueldos reales of Majorca

Date	Rate	Place	Type	Reference
1300	8 s.	Majorca	?	(211) p.285

The gold morabetino in non-Spanish currencies

The gold morabetino in soldi and denari of Lucca

Date	Rate	Place	Type	Reference
1180-1200	5 s.	Curia	C	(385) p.110
1187	5 s.	Curia	C	(385) p.100
1291.01.16	37 s.	Pistoia	C	(179) p.60

The gold morabetino in soldi of Pisa

Date	Rate	Place	Type	Reference
1291.02.10	32 s.	Lucca	C	(179) p.68

The gold morabetino in soldi of Verona

Date	Rate	Place	Type	Reference
1180-1200	12 s.	Curia	C	(385) p.110
1180-1200	20 s.	Curia	C	(385) p.110

The Almoravid gold morabetino in soldi and denari of Genoa

Date	Rate	Place	Type	Reference
1147	more than 5 s. 8 d.	Genoa	A	(381) p.342

The gold morabetino in sous provinois of Champagne

Date	Rate	Place	Type	Reference
1180-1200	5 s.	Curia	C	(385) p.110

The gold morabetino in sous tournois of France

Date	Rate	Place	Type	Reference
1180-1200	5 s.	Curia	C	(385) p.110
1309-1310	11 s. 6 d.	Curia	C	(439) p.64
1338.05.04	15 s.	Curia	C	(215) p.27

The gold morabetino in sous of Anjou

Date	Rate	Place	Type	Reference
1180-1200	7 s.	Curia	C	(385) p.110

The gold morabetino in shillings sterling of England

Date	Rate	Place	Type	Reference
1180-1200	3 s.	Curia	C	(385) p.110

The maravedi

Until the thirteenth century sums of money were reckoned in Castile, as elsewhere, in libras, sueldos and dineros, based on actual dineros, issued by the kings of Castile from Ferdinand I (1035-65) onwards. From the thirteenth century onwards sums of money were reckoned rather differently in Castile from elsewhere, in maravedis of 10 dineros instead. The way that this transformation took place is rather curious.

Nearly forty years after the last gold morabetinos or maravedis had been minted, Alfonso X of Castile and Leon had an issue of large silver coins struck in 1258 which came to be called maravedis de plata. The old gold maravedi was valued at six of these new maravedis de plata, each of which, in its turn, was valued at 15 of the current Castilian dineros prietos. Castilian society was not yet ready to use such large silver coins and their issue seems to have been very limited. A certain number of them remained in circulation. The value of the silver maravedi in dineros at first varied as the dineros changed. When the dinero was improved in 1271 the silver coin was worth only ten of them. When the dinero was debased in 1276, the maravedi's value changed back to fifteen dineros. When the dineros nuevos were issued in 1282, the maravedi was valued at ten dineros again. After this so few actual silver maravedis survived, that, however much the dinero changed, the maravedi always meant a unit of ten dineros.

When Pegolotti compiled his notebook in the early fourteenth century, he explained in his entry for Seville 'i quali marobottini non è moneta che si veggia' (177) p.271. Very occasionally reckoning in sueldos and dineros continued alongside that in maravedis and dineros until the end of the fourteenth century at least. For further details of the complexity of Castilian money, and indeed all Spanish moneys, see O. Gil Farres, Historia de la Moneda Espanola (211).

The Florentine florin in maravedis and dineros
10 dineros = 1 maravedi

Date	Rate	Place	Type	Reference
1291.02.22	5 m. 8 d.	Florence	A	(179) p.65
1311-1335	20 m.	Curia	B	(439) pp.99, 899-902
1358	25 m.	Avignon	B	(439) p.100
1369	25 m.	Castile	O	(492) II p.838
1369	45 m.	Castile	H	(461) p.376
1438	103 m.	Castile	O	(211) p.361
1445	130 m.	Toledo	A	(256) p.35
1459	166 m.	Toledo	A	(256) p.35

The Venetian ducat in maravedis and dineros
10 dineros = 1 maravedi

Date	Rate	Place	Type	Reference
1400	66 m.	Madrid	C	(280) p.95
1424	79 m. 5 d.	Toledo	A	(256) p.35
1425	77 m.	Toledo	A	(256) p.35
1430	73 m.	Madrid	C	(280) p.95
1431	81 m.	Toledo	A	(256) p.35
1438	105 m.	Madrid	O	(280) p.95
1443	110 m.	Burgos	A	(314) p.144
1444	110 m.	Burgos	A	(2909 p.144
1450	150 m.	Madrid	C	(280) p.95
1451	160 m.	Burgos	A	(314) p.144
1452	165 m.	Burgos	A	(314) p.144
1455	165 m.	Madrid	C	(280) p.95
1455	175 m.	Spain	C	(421) p.242
1455	176 m.	Spain	C	(421) p.242
1458	210-250 m.	Toledo	A	(256) p.35
1464-1465	230 m.	Madrid	C	(280) p.95
1464-1465	260 m.	Madrid	C	(280) p.95
1471	315 m.	Madrid	C	(280) p.95
1471	350 m.	Toledo	A	(256) p.35
1475	380 m.	Toledo	A	(256) p.35
1480	375 m.	Castile	O	(211) p.36
1480-1486	375 m.	Madrid	C	(280) p.95
1497	375 m.	Spain	C	(303) p.576

For the florin of Aragon in maravedis see under ARAGON p.150
For the dobla morisca in maravedis and dineros see under GRANADA p.162
For the livre tournois in sueldos and dineros burgaleses see under FRANCE p.184
For the dinar in maravedis see under EGYPT p.307

The real de plata

After the failure as a coin of the silver maravedi in the mid-thirteenth century, there was no attempt to create a coinage of silver groats in Castile for another hundred years. It was Peter I (1350-69) who introduced a successful coinage of groats into Castile. They were known initially as 'coronas' or 'reales'. It was the latter name which stuck to these pieces, which went on being struck of good silver and at the same weight for the remainder of the middle ages. Over the next century and a half the dinero was frequently debased and particularly in times of civil war. As a consequence the maravedi, as a unit of ten dineros, came to be not only a smaller and smaller unit, but a particularly unstable one. It was therefore only natural that Castilians should turn to the real as a stable unit for accounting alongside the maravedi. The relationship between the two is itself illuminating.

The real de plata in maravedis
10 dineros = 1 maravedi

Initial value 3m.

Date	Rate	Place	Type	Reference
1373	3 m.	Castile	0	(492) II p.843
1386	4 m. de novenes	Castile	0	(211) p.355
1390	7 m. 8 d.	Castile	0	(37) p.356
1390	7 m.	Castile	0	(211) p.356
1391	3 m. de moneda vieja	Castile	0	(211) p.357
1400	6-8 m.	Castile	?	(280) p.95
1406	8 m. moneda nueva	Castile	?	(211) p.365
1418	6 m.	Toledo	A	(256) p.35
1426	6 m.	Toledo	A	(256) p.35
1430	8-10 m.	Castile	?	(280) p.95
1438	8 m. 5d.	Castile	0	(211) p.361
1442	8 m.	Castile	0	(211) p.369
1442.07.07	9 m. 5d.	Aragon	0	(484) p.713
1449.02.22	12 m.	Aragon	0	(484) p.713
1450-1455	15 m.	Castile	?	(280) p.95
1454	15 m.	Castile	0	(211) p.365
1457	17 m. 5d.	Toledo	A	(256) p.35
1458	20 m.	Toledo	A	(256) p.35
1460	21 m.	Toledo	A	(256) p.35
1461	21 m.	Castile	?	(280) p.95
1462	16 m.	Castile	0	(211) p.369
1462	16 m.	Toledo	A	(256) p.35
1463	16 m.	Toledo	A	(256) p.35
1463-1464	16-20 m.	Castile	?	(280) p.95
1465	20 m.	Castile	0	(211) p.370
1471	31 m.	Castile	0	(211) p.370
1471	31 m.	Toledo	A	(256) p.35
1472	31 m.	Toledo	A	(256) p.35
1473	30-32 m.	Toledo	A	(256) p.35
1475	30 m.	Castile	0	(211) p.375
1480	31 m.	Castile	0	(211) p.376
1480-1486	31 m.	Castile	?	(280) p.95
1490s	34 m.	Castile	?	(379) p.284
1497	34 m.	Castile	0	(211) pp.377, 387

The dobla

The Mazmuda or Almohads who succeeded the Almoravids in Spain and north Africa issued the Mazmudina which was a lighter dinar than that of their predecessors. Their standard coin was, however the double dinar, known to Christian Spaniards as the dobla. It was struck in Spain from Abdelmumin (1129-62) to the fall of Granada (1492), initially at a weight of 4.6 grams. It was copied by the kings of Castile from Ferdinand III (1217-52) onwards. Castilian doblas were obviously not common until the reign of Alfonso XI (1312-50), since only four survive from earlier reigns. However, plentiful quantities of doblas were minted from the reign of Alfonso XI and it rapidly became the standard gold coin of Castile. In Alfonso XI's reign Pegolotti noted 'Fannosi i pagamenti in Sobilia e per Ispagna in più di double d'oro' (177) p.271. Just over a century later Uzzanno noted down 'Da Genova a Sibilia si cambia soldi di genovini contra dobbre d'oro.' Giovanni da Uzzanno, La Pratica della mercatura (373). With variants such as the dobla de la banda and the castellano de oro, the dobla lasted until 1497 when it was replaced by a ducado.

The dobla in other Spanish currencies

The dobla in maravedis and dineros
10 dineros = 1 maravedi

Date	Rate	Place	Type	Reference
1292-1293	20 m. 5 d.	Spain	C	(163) p.528
1309	24 m.	Barcelona	C	(163) p.529
1318-1319	23 m.	Castile	B	(439) p.52
1334	25 m.	Castile	B	(439) p.52
1355	36 m.	Castile	0	(211)

THE DOBLA IN MARAVEDIS AND DINEROS

Date	Rate	Place	Type	Reference
1369	38 m.	Castile	O	(492) II p.838
1373	35 m.	Castile	O	(492) II p.838
1384dobla castellana	37 m.	Castile	?O	(211) p.355
1386	36 m.	Castile	?O	(211) p.355
1390	95 m.	Castile	O	(211) p.356
(1390-1406) Henry III	35 m. (*)	Castile	?O	(211) p.357
(*) maravedis de moneda vieja, i.e. pre-inflation of later 1380s				
1400	74 m.	Castile	C	(279) p.785
1410.01.22	58 m.	Murcia	O	(337)
1430	94 m.	Castile	C	(279) p.785
1450	100 m.	Castile	C	(279) p.785

The dobla de la banda in maravedis

The dobla de la banda was modelled on the dobla of Granada, see below p.162, and was introduced between 1406 and 1415.

Date	Rate	Place	Type	Reference
When introduced	90 m.	Castile	O	(211) p.360
1418	80 m.	Toledo	A	(256) p.35
1424	100 m.	Toledo	A	(256) p.35
1425	97 m.	Toledo	A	(256) p.35
1426	100 m.	Toledo	A	(256) p.35
1427	100-103 m.	Toledo	A	(256) p.35
1428	100 m.	Toledo	A	(256) p.35
1429	102-105 m.	Toledo	A	(256) p.35
1430	104 m.	Castile	C	(279) p.785
1431	110 m.	Toledo	A	(256) p.35
1434	103 m.	Castile	O	(211) p.360
1438	111 m.	Castile	O	(211) p.361
1441	100 m.	Aragon	O	(484) p.712
1442.04.06	100 m.	Valladolid	O	(484) p.712
1445	120 m.	Toledo	A	(256) p.35
1445.10.02dobla cruzada	115 m.	Aragon	O	(484) p.713
1448.12.24	140 m.	Aragon	O	(484) p.713
1449	143-150 m.	Toledo	A	(256) p.35
1450	150 m.	Castile	C	(279) p.785
1451	148-150 m.	Toledo	A	(256) p.35
1454	150 m.	Toledo	A	(256) p.35
1454	152 m.	Toledo	A	(256) p.35
1454.01.08	152 m.	Aragon	O	(484) p.713
1455	155 m.	Toledo	A	(256) p.35
1456	160 m.	Toledo	A	(256) p.35
1457	160 m.	Toledo	A	(256) p.35
1458	170-176 m.	Toledo	A	(256) p.35
1460	188 m.	Toledo	A	(256) p.35
1461	190 m.	Toledo	A	(256) p.35
1462	150 m.	Castile	O	(211) p.370
1462	150 m.	Toledo	A	(256) p.35
1464	180-206 m.	Toledo	A	(256) p.35
1465	200 m.	Castile	O	(211) p.370
1466	230 m.	Toledo	A	(256) p.35
1467	242 m.	Toledo	A	(256) p.35
1469	260 m.	Toledo	A	(256) p.35
1473	300 m.	Toledo	A	(256) p.35
1475.02.20	335 m.	Castile	O	(211) p.375
1480	365 m.	Castile	O	(211) p.376
1490	365 m.	Seville	O	(379) p.284

The dobla in sueldos and dineros of Barcelona

Date	Rate	Place	Type	Reference
(1276-1285) Peter III	14 s. 6 d.	Barcelona	O	(211) p.237
1285	15 s.	Barcelona	C	(163) p.528
1292-1293	17 s. 1 d.	Spain	C	(163) p.528
1294	15 s.	Barcelona	C	(163) p.528
1304	20 s.	Barcelona	C	(163) p.529
1307	21 s. 6 d.	Barcelona	C	(163) p.529

THE DOBLA IN SUELDOS AND DINEROS OF BARCELONA

Date	Rate	Place	Type	Reference
1308	20 s.	Barcelona	C	(163) p.529
1308	21 s.	Barcelona	C	(163) p.529
1309.06.10	20 s.	Barcelona	C	(82) II p.122
1309	20 s.	Barcelona	C	(163) p.529
1328	22 s.	Curia	B	(439) p.53
1336	18 s. 3 d.	Castile	B	(439) p.52
1341.08.14	19 s. 6 d.	Curia	B	(216) p.182

The dobla in sueldos and dineros reales of Valencia

Date	Rate	Place	Type	Reference
1288	14 s.	Valencia	C	(163) p.528
1288	15 s.	Valencia	C	(163) p.528
1302	16 s.	Barcelona	C	(163) p.528
1420.04.19	17 s.	Valencia	B	(81) p.34
1421.01.30	16 s. 6 d.	Valencia	B	(81) p.35
1422.05.20	16 s. 6 d.	Barcelona	B	(81) p.37
1423.08.03	16 s. 8 d.	Valencia	B	(81) p.39
1424.09.18	16 s. 8 d.	Barcelona	B	(81) p.40

The dobla in sueldos and dineros iaccenses

Date	Rate	Place	Type	Reference
1336	13 s. 2 d.	Castile	B	(439) p.52

The dobla in sueldos and dineros of Navarre

Date	Rate	Place	Type	Reference
1386.02	64 s. 9 d.	Navarre	C	(490) p.62
1395.06.24	46 s. 4 d.	Navarre	C	(421) p.490

The dobla in non-Spanish currencies

The dobla in soldi and denari of Genoa

Date	Rate	Place	Type	Reference
1248	12 s.	Genoa	A	(187A) f.1047
1253	15 s. 9 d.	Genoa	A	(187A) f.1048
1261	15 s. 4 d.	Genoa	A	(187A) f.1048
1268	14 s. 8 1/2 d.	Genoa	A	(187A) f.1048
1273	20 s.	Genoa	A	(187A) f.1048
1285	21 s.	Genoa	A	(187A) f.1048
1287	21 s. 11 d.	Genoa	A	(187A) f.1048
1287	19 s. 5 d.	Genoa	A	(187A) f.1048
1288	20 s.	Genoa	A	(187A) f.1048
1291	22 s.	Genoa	A	(187A) f.1048
1291	25 s.	Tunis	A	(187A) f.1048
1291	24 s.	Bougie	A	(187A) f.1048
1291	20 s.	Genoa	A	(187A) f.1048
1291	16 s. 11 d.	Genoa	A	(187A) f.1047
1291	18 s. 11 d.	Majorca	A	(187A) f.1048
1292	15 s. 6 d.	Genoa	A	(187A) f.1048
1293	20 s. 6 d.	Genoa	A	(187A) f.1048

The dobla in carats of Alexandria

Date	Rate	Place	Type	Reference
1400.08.02	25 1/2 carats	Seville-Alexandria	B	(523) no.1003

GRANADA

For the accounting system in the Muslim kingdom of Granada see under BARBARY p.309. The double dinars of the Nasrid kings of Granada circulated widely in Christian Spain where they were known as doblas moriscas

The dobla morisca in sueldos and dineros of Barcelona

Date	Rate	Place	Type	Reference
1308	20 s.	Aragon	O	(326) p.339
1423.05.01	18 s.	Alghero	M	(117) II p.41
1423.06.08	16 s. 6 d.	Barcelona	M	(117) II p.41

The dobla morisca in maravedis and dineros of Castile
1 maravedi = 10 dineros

Date	Rate	Place	Type	Reference
1330-1334	36 m.	Murcia	C	(211) p.347
1369	36 m.	Castile	O	(492) II p.838
1373	32 m.	Castile	O	(492) II p.843
1384	35 m.	Castile	?O	(211) p.355
1398.09.03	57 m. 6 d.	Seville	M	(523) no.794
1400	70 m.	Castile	H	(279) p.785
1430	104 m.	Castile	H	(279) p.785
1447.03.09dobla vieja	130 m.	Aragon	O	(484) p.713
1450	150 m.	Castile	H	(279) p.785
1465	200 m.	Castile	H	(279) p.785
1480	445 m.	Castile	H	(279) p.785
1486	445 m.	Castile	H	(279) p.785

PORTUGAL

The kings of Portugal, from the very first (Alfonso I crowned 1139), struck dinheiros which provided the basis for the money of account until the fourteenth century. Under Ferdinand I (1367-83), larger reis began to be struck, as they were in Castile at the same time. These reis eventually provided an alternative method of accounting. Sometime in the first half of the fifteenth century the anonymous Italian compiler of a Libro de Mercatantie noted under Lisbon 'Vendevixi, merchantie e cambiarixi a reali' without any reference to dinheiros. At that time a ducat was worth 130 reis. In the same period Antonio Marabotti wrote from Lisbon in November 1424 that exchange was undertaken in 'corone correnti', which were 16% less than the actual 'corona d'oro' (an escudo of the écu à la couronne type). Giovanni Uzzanno, when incorporating this information in his notebook explained that 70 reis were worth one corona. When Marabotti wrote the exchanges were such that for each corona given in Lisbon, 42 to 46 groten would be paid in Bruges, and that in order that a hundred cameral florins be paid at the Curia, it was necessary to pay 105 to 108 corone in Lisbon.

The Florentine florin in soldos and dinheiros of Portugal

Date	Rate	Place	Type	Reference
1336.09.11	60 s.	Curia	B	(216) p.111
1359.12.14	70 s.	Curia	B	(251) p.275
1361.09.30	60 s.	Barcelona-Curia	B	(251) p.359
1466	55 s. 3 d.	Portugal	C	(245) XXII p.95

The Venetian ducat in reis of Portugal

Date	Rate	Place	Type	Reference
1465	300 reis	Porto	C	(245) XXII p.91
1466	350 reis	Portugal	C	(245) XXII p.94

NAVARRE

Dineros were minted in Navarre from around 1086 during the period when Navarre and Aragon were united under a single ruler. After the division of the two kingdoms in 1134 the money of Navarre and that of Aragon evolved separately. The dineros of Navarre had come to be known as sanchetes by the early thirteenth century. The seventh and last Sancho of Navarre died in 1234. Under Charles II the Bad (1347-87), the old sanchetes were replaced, first by tornés in imitation of the French tournois, and then after 1355 by a dinero carlin. These carlines formed the basis of the money of account for the remainder of the middle ages.

The Florentine florin and the ducat in sueldos and dineros carlines of Navarre

H = Hungarian ducat; D = Unspecified ducat

Date	Rate	Place	Type	Reference
1361	12 s.	Navarre	A	(73) p.76
1386.02H	42 s.	Navarre	O	(490) p.64
1386.02	44 s. 4 d.	Navarre	O	(490) p.63
1386.02D	46 s. 6 d.	Navarre	O	(490) p.63
1390-1406H	26 s.	Spain	C	(421) p.153
1390-1406	36 s.	Spain	C	(421) p.153
1390-1406	40 s.	Spain	C	(421) p.153
1392.06.17D	36 s.	Spain	C	(421) p.482
1392.07.04	30 s.	Spain	C	(421) p.483
1392	29 s.	Spain	C	(421) p.480
1393.07.05	36 s.	Navarre	C	(421) p.487
1396.06.17D	38 s.	Navarre	C	(421) p.495

The libra of sanchetes of Navarre in sous and deniers tournois

Date	Rate	Place	Type	Reference
1275-1280	20 s. 8 d.	Aragon	A	(419) II p.283

For the florin of Aragon in sueldos and dineros of Navarre see under ARAGON p.152
For the dobla of Castile in sueldos and dineros of Navarre see under CASTILE p.161

SECTION VI
FRANCE

By the end of the twelfth century a handful of the more successful of the multitude of local feudal coinages came to dominate the currency of wide areas of France. The deniers of Provins did so in eastern France, the deniers of Tours in western France, those of Paris in northern France, and of Melgueil in southern France.

CHAMPAGNE FAIRS

MONEY OF PROVINS

In eastern France the deniers of Provins, one of the four great fair towns of Champagne, circulated not merely in the vicinity of Provins, but much further afield, first overwhelming the money of Troyes and Meaux, and then gradually becoming the basis of money of account which became standard not only for the whole of Champagne and all its fairs, but also for the Chalonnais, the Barrois and Lorraine. The deniers provinois increased from regional to international importance, in parallel with the fairs, from the reign of Henry I, count of Champagne 1152-80. Through the fairs the mint at Provins was abundantly supplied with silver, some of which was brought by merchants in ingots from Germany. From the fairs the deniers provinois travelled outwards along the trade routes, particularly to Italy. By the 1170s these deniers, known in central Italy as denari provisini, had become the dominant currency of that area. When the senate of Rome, by arrangement with the pope, began to mint denari, it was in imitation of these deniers of Champagne. (See above, p.67)

When the money of Tours became the national coinage of France, in the thirteenth century, the denier provinois was reduced in silver content to bring it into conformity with the denier tournois. This probably took place in 1224 (373) pp.13 and 58. Later in the century when Philip IV of France married the heiress of Champagne, tournois money was minted in Champagne itself, in place of provinois. Because of the importance of the fairs, a very large number of early exchange quotations survive particularly among the notarial records of Genoa.

The Florentine florin in sous and deniers of Provins

Date	Rate	Place	Type	Reference
1265.09-10	8 s. 1 d.	Provins	B	(374) p.57
Contemporary comment that the rate at St Ayoul fair, 6 weeks from 14 September, higher than normal, because of the Crusade of Charles of Anjou against Manfred				
1265.11.29	7 s. 9 d.	Troyes	B	(374) p.57

The livre of Provins in soldi and denari of Genoa

Date	Rate	Place	Type	Reference
1191.03.11	28 s. 4 d.	Genoa	C	(104) p.210
1191.03.14	26 s. 8 d.	Genoa	C	(104) p.210
1191.06.20	30 s.	Genoa	C	(104) p.210
1191.06.24	28 s. 4 d.	Genoa	C	(104) p.210
1191.09.12	25 s.	Genoa	C	(104) p.210
1191.12.10-13	25 s.	Genoa	C	(104) p.210
1191.12.19	28 s. 4 d.	Genoa	C	(104) p.210
1192.03.06-1193.07.16	28 s. 4 d.	Genoa	C	(104) p.210
1244.02.27	26 s. 11 d.	Genoa	B	(154) III p.273
1244.03.05	27 s. 1 d.	Genoa	B	(154) III p.276
1245.12.11	26 s. 7 d.	Genoa	B	(154) III p.293
1248.01.03	26 s. 8 d.	Genoa	B	(154) III p.300
1250.02.14	27 s. 2 d.	Genoa	B	(154) III p.311
1251.06.10	33 s. 4 d.	Genoa	B	(154) III p.357
1251.11.08	25 s. 4 d.	Genoa-Bar	B	(103) p.139
1251.11.13	27 s. 4 d.	Genoa-Bar	B	(103) p.140
1252.06.10	27 s. 7 d.	Genoa	B	(154) III p.398

THE LIVRE OF PROVINS IN SOLDI AND DENARI OF GENOA

Date	Rate	Place	Type	Reference
1252.06.18	27 s. 8 d.	Genoa	B	(154) III p.402
1252.10.31	28 s. 4 d.	Genoa	B	(154) II p.418
1252.11.01	28 s. 4 d.	Genoa	B	(154) III p.419
1252.12.12	27 s. 4 d.	Genoa	B	(154) III p.421
1253.12.09	31 s. 8 d.	Genoa	B	(154) III p.498
1254.04.21	29 s. 2 d.	Genoa	B	(154) III p.511
1257.01.12	33 s. 4 d.	Genoa	B	(154) III p.536
1259.05.12	31 s. 8 d.	Genoa	B	(154) III p.562
1259.05.21	33 s. 4 d.	Genoa	B	(154) III p.568
1259.05	30 s. 5 d.	Genoa	B	(154) III p.569
1259.10.30	33 s. 7 1/2 d.	Genoa	B	(154) III p.596
1259.11.15	31 s. 8 d.	Genoa	B	(154) III p.605
1262.09.04	28 s.	Troyes	B	(374) p.30
1264.02.28	30 s.	Genoa	B	(154) IV p.677
1267.06.23	31 s. 11 d.	Genoa	B	(154) IV p.693
1274.03.02	33 s. 4 d.	Genoa	B	(154) IV p.716
1274.03.23	31 s. 1 d.	Genoa	B	(154) IV p.723
1277.05	30 s.	Genoa	B	(154) IV p.753
1286.09.06	33 s. 4 d.	Genoa	B	(153) p.29

See also the lira of Genoa in sous and deniers of Provins under GENOA p.108

The livre of Provins in soldi and denari of Lucca

Date	Rate	Place	Type	Reference
1242	46 s. 3 d.	Lucca	H	(47)
1247-8	47 s. 11 d.	Lucca	H	(47)
1253	55 s.	Lucca	H	(47)
1268.06.16	55 s.	Lucca	C	(118) III p.23
1273	55 s. 9 1/2 d.	Lucca	H	(47)
1279	69 s. 9 1/2 d.	Lucca	H	(47)
1284	74 s. 9 1/2 d.	Lucca	H	(47)
1290	76 s. 8 d.	Lucca	H	(47)
1298	57 s. 6 d.	Lucca	H	(47)

The livre of Provins in soldi and denari of Pisa

Date	Rate	Place	Type	Reference
1248.03.18	43 s. 4 d.	Bar	B	(45) no.92
1248.04	43 s. 4 1/4 d.	Bar-Marseille	B	(45) I p.299
1248.05.29	46 s. 8 d.	Pisa	B	(45) no.815
1248.05.29	46 s. 8 d.	Provins-Marseille	B	(45) II pp.207-210
1282.03.16	40 s.	Tuscany	C	(226) p.236

The livre of Provins in soldi and denari of Siena

Date	Rate	Place	Type	Reference
1248.05.29	47 s. 6 d.	Siena-Marseille	B	(45) II p.208
1262.09.04	52 s. 6 1/2 d.	Troyes-Siena	B	(374) pp.32-33
1265.11.29	66 s. 8 d.	Troyes-Siena	B	(374) p.57

The livre of Provins in soldi and denari provisini of Rome

Date	Rate	Place	Type	Reference
1191.05.12	30 s.	Rome	A	(203) III pp.47 and 98
1195	27 s. 6 d.	Curia	A	(179) p.98 and (83) p.55
1208.08.05	26 s. 8 d.	Campania	O	(479) I p.42

THE LIVRE OF PROVINS IN SOUS AND DENIERS OF PROVENCE

The livre of Provins in sous and deniers royaux coronats of Provence

Date	Rate	Place	Type	Reference
1248.04	34 s.	Bar	B	(44) p.126
1248.04	33 s. 6 d.	Bar	B	(44) p.124
1253	23 s. 6 d.	Marseille	C	(43) p.209

The livre of Provins in mixed money of Marseille

Date	Rate	Place	Type	Reference
1248.03.18	34 s.	Marseille	B	(45) no.79
1248.03.18	33 s. 6 d.	Marseille-Bar	B	(45) no.81
1248.03.23	33 s. 5 d.	Marseille-Bar	B	(45) no.100
1248.03.23	34 s.	Marseille-Bar	B	(45) no.150
1248.04.01	31 s.	Marseille-Bar	B	(45) no.340
1248.04.01	31 s.	Marseille-Bar	B	(45) no.351
1248.04.04	31 s.	Marseille-Bar	B	(45) no.375
1248.04.04	32 s.	Marseille-Provins	B	(45) no.377
1248.04.09	34 s.	Marseille-Provins	B	(45) no.424
1248.04.14	31 s. 5 d.	Marseille-Provins	B	(45) no.498
1248.04.18	30 s. 9 d.	Marseille-Provins	B	(45) no.557
1248.04.27	30 s.	Marseille-Provins	B	(45) no.615
1248.04.29	30 s.	Marseille-Provins	B	(45) no.625
1248.05.08	29 s.	Marseille-Provins	B	(45) no.667
1248.05.13	31 s. 7 d.	Marseille-Provins	B	(45) no.717
1248.05.23	29 s. 2 d.	Marseille-Provins	B	(45) no.770
1248.05.23	30 s.	Marseille-Provins	B	(45) no.772
1248.05.26	31 s. 7 d.	Marseille-Provins	B	(45) no.793
1248.05.27	31 s. 2 d.	Marseille-Provins	B	(45) no.800
1248.06.27	29 s.	Marseille-Troyes	B	(45) no.929
1248.07.18	28 s.	Marseille-Troyes	B	(45) no.995

The livre of Provins in sous and deniers viennois

Date	Rate	Place	Type	Reference
1248.04.18	21 s. 1 d.	Provins	B	(45) no.550
1248.04.18	21 s. 6 d.	Provins	B	(45) II p.93

The livre of Provins in sous and deniers melgorians

Date	Rate	Place	Type	Reference
1248.04	20 s. 2 3/4 d.	Provins	B	(45) II p.151
1248.05.08	20 s. 2 d.	Montpellier-Provins	B	(45) no.691

The livre of Provins in sous and deniers parisis

Date	Rate	Place	Type	Reference
1202-1203	14 s. 11 d.	Lagny	A	(307) p.CLII
1202-1203	14 s. 8 1/2 d.	Moret et Samois	A	(307) p.164
1262.09.04	15 s. 10 d.	Troyes-Arras	B	(374) p.33
1262.09.04	15 s. 1 d.	Troyes-Arras	B	(374) p.33
1262.09.04	16 s.	Troyes	B	(374) p.30

The livre of Provins in sous and deniers Châlonnais (of Châlons-sur-Marne)

Date	Rate	Place	Type	Reference
Time Henry I (1152-80)	16 s.	Champagne	A	(39) p.130

The livre of Provins in sous and deniers of Auxerre

Date	Rate	Place	Type	Reference
1219	circa 20 s. 7 3/4 d.	Auxerre	A	(39) p.143

310 livres of Provins reckoned as equal to 320 livres of Auxerre

The livre of Meaux in sous and deniers of Vermandois

The money of Provins was reckoned as equal to those of Troyes and Meaux.

Date	Rate	Place	Type	Reference
1141	13 s. 4 d.	Vermandois	A	(39) p.148

For the lira imperiale in sous and deniers of Provins see under MILAN p.104
For the lira of Pavia in sous and deniers of Provins see under PAVIA p.104
For the gold morabetino in sous and deniers of Provins see under CASTILE p.157
For the livre tournois in sous and deniers of Provins see under FRANCE p.182
For the pound sterling in sous and deniers of Provins see under ENGLAND p.208

ROYAL CURRENCIES OF FRANCE

PARISIS

At the beginning of the twelfth century the deniers parisis of the Capetians were still only the money of Paris, but Louis VII (1137-80), by closing most of the other mints in the royal domain, ensured that it became the money of the whole Île-de-France. It was under Philip II Augustus (1180-1223) that it began to be minted on a considerable scale and became the common coin of much of northern France. He had deniers parisis struck not only in Paris itself, but also at the then important channel port of Montreuil-sur-Mer, and when he inherited Artois and Peronne in 1191, also at Arras, St Omer and Peronne. Imitative deniers parisis were soon struck by the counts of St Pol, of Ponthieu, of Boulogne, of Dreux and of Bar, by the countess of Vermandois and by the archbishop of Rheims. The independent coinages of the bishops of Beauvais, of Laon, and of Noyon all came to an end by 1220, so that the deniers parisis were used commonly for both payment and accounting from Orleans to Flanders in the first quarter of the thirteenth century.

This was the high water mark of money parisis, for successive kings of France preferred the money tournois of western France more and more and even began to mint it in some northern French mints in place of money parisis. Money parisis came to assume a subordinate role to money tournois, to which it came to be linked at a fixed rate of 16 sous parisis to the livre tournois. See below p.172.

Deniers parisis continued to be struck alongside deniers tournois until the end of the middle ages, but their importance diminished to such an extent that no quotations of the florin in money parisis have been found later than the end of the fourteenth century. However, some reckoning continued to be carried out in parisis, for example in the 1420s by the anonymous citizen of Paris in his Journal (63). In the second half of the fifteenth century the use of money parisis was largely confined to royal alms giving. The quotations below often appear very erratic. This is partially because of the violence of the changes in royal French money from Philip IV onwards, but it is also partially because some the the quotations may well refer to non-royal money parisis — for example, that struck by the counts of Flanders, see below p.214.

Paris as an exchange place

In an arithmetic book of 1328 accounting at Paris was assumed to be in parisis, as opposed to tournois in Montpellier. I owe this reference to Prof. Warren van Egmond. The same distinction, possibly by then outdated, was made a hundred years later by Uzzanno (373) p.162. Uzzanno also tells us (p.100) that the couriers from Florence took 20 to 22 days, and that bills drawn on Florence, Venice, Milan, Genoa and Pisa were due for payment in Paris 2 months after drawing, and the same in the opposite directions. Bills from London were due a month after drawing, from Montpellier 30 days after drawing, from Barcelona 30 days from sight, from Bruges, 10 days from sight (373) pp.101-2.

In 1396 Ricci anticipated that money would normally be scarce in Paris in and around fair times: Lendit, 15-24 June, and St Andrew, starting 1 December (55) p.116, and Uzzanno follows him.

The Florentine florin in sous and deniers parisis

Date	Rate	Place	Type	Reference
1280-1286	8 s. 4 d.	Curia	B	(439) p.898
circa 1287-1289	8 s.	Curia	B	(439) p.898
1290-1292	8 s.	Curia	B	(439) p.898
1295 until 07.01	8 s.	France	O	(148) p.435
1295 from 07.01	8 s. 2 1/2 d.	France	O	(148) p.435
1296	8 s. 6 d.	Curia	B	(439) p.898
1296	8 s. 9 1/2 d.	Curia	B	(439) p.898
1296	12 s.	France	C	(184) p.37
1296.02.10	11 s.	France	C	(184) p.77
1296.02.11	12 s.	France	C	(184) p.52
1296.02.16	8 s. 6 d.	France	O	(148) P.435
1296.07.04	8 s. 9 d.	France	O	(148) p.435
1305.05.27	26 s. 6 d.	France	C	(185) p.328
1306	34 s.	France	C	(152) p.71
1306	10 s. 6 d.	Piedmont	A	(110) p.490
1307	11 s.	Piedmont	A	(110) p.490
1309	32 s.	Mons	A	(389) II p.145
1312.10.04	15 s. 4 d.	Tournai	C	(231) p.334
1312.10.26	16 s.	Tournai	C	(231) p.335
1313	14 s.	Mons	A	(389) II p.144
1313	16 s.	Mons	A	(389) II p.144
1313.02.02	16 s. 3 d.	Tournai	C	(231) p.335
1313.05.03	18 s.	Tournai	C	(231) p.335
1315	11 s.	France	A	(316) II p.133
1315	8 s. 3 d.	France	O	(430) I p.195
1315.12.08	11 s.	Aire	A	(69)
1316	12 s.	France	O	(162) p.325
1316.04.11	14 s. 3 d.	Tournai	C	(231) p.335
1316.12.25	11 s. 6 d.	Tournai	C	(231) p.336
1319-1323	13 s.	Avignon	M	(439) p.106
1320	13 s. 4 d.	France	C	(316) II p.151
1320.05.28	13 s.	Forez	A	(69)
1321	13 s.	Curia	M	(439) p.900
1322.01.18	13 s. 4 d.	Paris	C	(118) III p.194
1322.05.01	14 s. 4 d.	Paris	C	(118) III p.195
1322.10.30	13 s. 4 d.	France	O	(228) p.243
1323	13 s.	Curia	M	(439) p.900
1323	12 s. 4 d.	Tournai	C	(231) p.337
1324	13 s. 8 d.	Tournai	C	(231) p.337
1325	14 s.	France	C	(324) p.130
1325	14 s. 6 d.	Holland	A	(455) I p.134
1325.07	14 s.	France	O	(228) p.248
1325.12-1326.01	14 s. 6 d.	France	O	(228) p.248
1326	14 s. 4 d.	Paris	A	(455) I p.178
1327	17 s. 4 d.	Piedmont	A	(110) p.494
1328.01.02	13 s. 4 d.	Cambrai	B	(28) p.21
1328.01.23	20 s.	Cambrai	B	(28) p.29
1328	20 s. 6 d.	Avignon	M	(439) p.106
1328	21 s. 6 d.	France	A	(455) I p.407
1328.07.06	22 s.	Cambrai	B	(28) p.30
1328	22 s. 6 d.	Cambrai	B	(28) p.34
1329.10.05	22 s.	Cambrai	B	(28) p.36
1329.12.07	10 s.	Cambrai	B	(28) p.32
1329.12.18	12 s.	Cambrai	B	(28) p.23
1329-1330	10 s.	France	C	(327) p.110
1330-1331	10 s.	Cambrai	B	(28) p.24
1330	16 s.	Curia	M	(439) p.901
1330	21 s.	Curia	M	(439) p.67
1331-1334	10 s.	Curia	M	(439) p.901
1331	10 s.	France	O	(430) I p.217
1331.07.28	12 s.	Bruges	A	(212) I p.437
1331.09.21	12 s.	Bruges	A	(212) I p.437
1332.03.21	12 s.	Bruges	A	(212) I p.445
1332.11.10	10 s.	Cambrai	B	(28) p.41
1333	20 s. 8 d.	Cambrai	B	(28) p.42
1333.10.01	12 s.	Cambrai	B	(28) p.40

Florentine florins in sous and deniers parisis of France 1280–1400

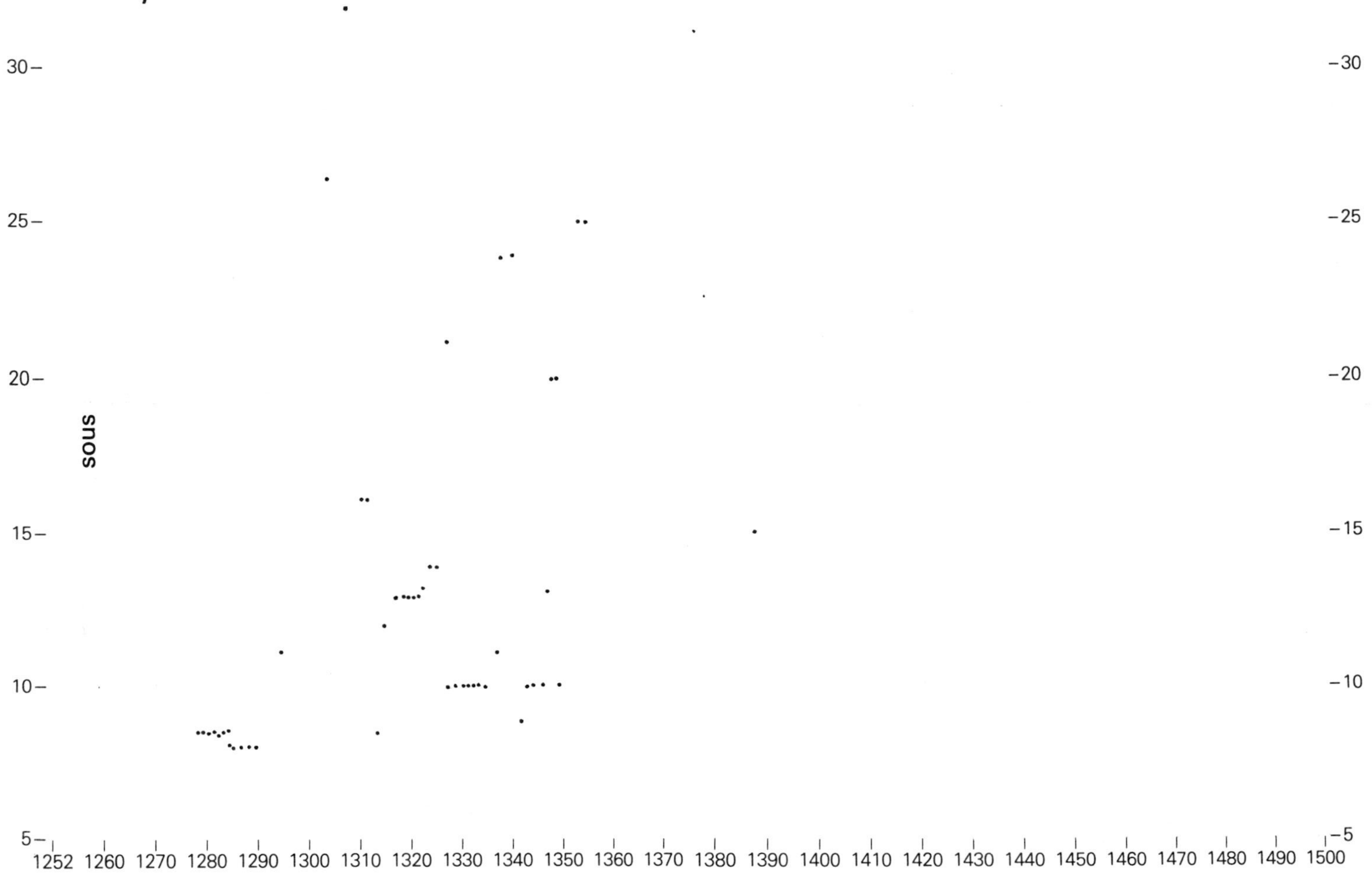

THE FLORENTINE FLORIN IN SOUS AND DENIERS PARISIS

Date	Rate	Place	Type	Reference
1334-1336	10 s. 5 d.	Curia	M	(439) p.45
1334	12 s.	Flanders	C	(327) p.111
1336.05.14	10 s.	Curia	M	(440) p.49
1337.12	11 s. 2 d.	Avignon	M	(439) p.106
1338	25 s. 4 d.	Mons	A	(389) II p.144
1339	24 s.	Avignon	M	(439) p.106
1339-1340	32 s. 6 d.	Mons	A	(389) II p.144
1339-1340	36 s.	Mons	A	(389) II p.144
1340	30 s.	Avignon	M	(439) p.106
1340.01	20 s.	Curia	M	(216) p.154
1341.02.08	24 s.	Avignon	M	(439) p.106
1342	44 s. in minuta moneta debili	Thérouanne	B	(28) p.90
1342	50 s.	Mons	A	(389) II p.144
1343	68 s.	Mons	A	(389) II p.144
1343	9 s. 6 d.	France	O	(430) I p.243
1343.01.30	10 s.	Curia	C	(347) p.4
1343.12.26	16 s. 6 d.	Thérouanne	B	(28) p.110
1344	44 s.	Mons	A	(389) II p.144
1344	16 s. 8 d.	Mons	A	(389) II p.144
1344.01.04	10 s. 5 d.	Thérouanne	B	(28) p.110
1344.04.09	16 s. 6 d.	Thérouanne	B	(28) p.87
1344.07.22	10 s. 5 1/2 d.	Thérouanne	B	(28) p.137
1344.09.30	13 s. 2 d.	Thérouanne	B	(28) p.113
1344.10.26	10 s. 7 d.	Thérouanne	B	(28) p.117
1344.11.04-12	16 s. 6 d.	Thérouanne	B	(28) p.89
1344.11.29	19 s.	Thérouanne	B	(28) p.124
1344.12.10	10 s.	Thérouanne	B	(28) p.124
1345.01.28	10 s. 12(sic) d.	Thérouanne	B	(28) p.104
1345.06.07	10 s.	Thérouanne	B	(28) p.124
1345-1346	16 s. 8 d.	Mons	A	(389) II p.144
1345-1346.01.09	16 s.	Thérouanne	B	(28) p.137
1346	13 s. 6 d.	Thérouanne	B	(28) p.147
1346	13 s. 4 d.	Thérouanne	B	(28) p.148
1346.06.13	10 s.	France	O	(430) p.248
1346.07	10 s. 6 d.	France	O	(50) Annexe 8
1346.07	13 s.	Thérouanne	B	(28) p.142
1346.10.14	22 s.	Thérouanne	B	(28) p.140
1346.10.19	15 s.	Thérouanne	B	(28) p.126
1346.11.20	22 s. 6 d.	Thérouanne	B	(28) p.149
1347-1348	17 s.	Mons	A	(389) II p.144
1347.05	13 s. 6 d.	Thérouanne	B	(28) p.126
1347.05.19	17 s.	Thérouanne	B	(28) p.130
1347.08.30	22 s. 6 d.	Thérouanne	B	(28) p.125
1347.10.08	10 s. 6 d.	Thérouanne	B	(28) p.141
1348.09.22	20 s.	Curia	C	(347) p.411
1349.04.21	22 s. 6 d.	Thérouanne	B	(28) p.129
1349.06	20 s.	Avignon	M	(439) p.106
1349.10.16	20 s.	Thérouanne	B	(28) p.128
1350	10 s.	France	C	(162) p.324
1351-1352	32 s.	Thérouanne	B	(28) p.257
1354	25 s.	Avignon	M	(439) p.107
1355-1356	19 s.	Mons	A	(389) II p.144
1355-1356	18 s.	Mons	A	(389) II p.144
1355.02.28	25 s.	Curia	M	(440) p.587
1355.03	13 s. 6 d.	France	O	(50) Annexe 8
1356-1357	17 s.	Languedoc	C	(50) Annexe 8
1379.02.02	10 s.	Dijon	A	(29)
1388	15 s.	Thérouanne	B	(28) p.442

The livre parisis in other French currencies

The livre parisis in sous and deniers of Artois

Date	Rate	Place	Type	Reference
1180	20 s.	France	A	(39) p.149

The livre parisis in sous and deniers of Beauvais

Date	Rate	Place	Type	Reference
1179	16 s.	Beauvais	A	(39) p.152
1190s	18 s.	Beauvais	A	(39) p.152
1212-1214	20 s.	Beauvais	A	(39) p.152
1214 or 1215	circa 17 s. 10 d.	France	H	(165) p.24
1215	circa 18 s. 6 d.	Senlis	H	(165) p.24
1222	16 s.	Senlis	H	(165) p.24

See also the livre of Beauvais in sous and deniers parisis, below p.195

The livre parisis in sous and deniers of Chartres

Date	Rate	Place	Type	Reference
1198	21 s.	Chartres	H	(165) p.24
1201	21 s.	Chartres	H	(165) p.24

The livre parisis in sous and deniers of Dreux

Date	Rate	Place	Type	Reference
1208	circa 22 s. 3 d.	Chartres	H	(165) p.25

(the livre of Dreux was reckoned at 18 sous parisis)

The livre parisis in sous and deniers of Noyon

Date	Rate	Place	Type	Reference
1198	30 s.	Noyon	O	(39) pp.202-203

The livre parisis in sous and deniers of Tournai

Date	Rate	Place	Type	Reference
1202	40 s.	France	H	(165) p.27

For the uncia of Sicily in sous and deniers parisis see under SICILY p.62
For the uncia of Naples in sous and deniers parisis see under NAPLES p.65
For the livre of Provins in sous and deniers parisis see under CHAMPAGNE FAIRS p.166
For the livre tournois in sous and deniers parisis see below p.173
For the gros tournois in deniers parisis see below p.185
For the écu and the franc in sous and deniers parisis see below pp.190 and 192
For the livre of Gien in sous and deniers parisis see below p.196
For the livre angevin in sous and deniers parisis see below p.194
For the pound sterling in sous and deniers parisis see under ENGLAND p.209

Valosii

By the 1320s the denier parisis had become so insignificant a piece that the double parisis (2d.) became the standard small coin for money parisis. The doubles parisis were also known as valosii. Sometimes they were themselves used as deniers rather than doubles. This meant that a florin could equally be reckoned in 1328 at ten sous of valosii or at twenty sous of parisis.

The Florentine florin in sous and deniers valosii

Date	Rate	Place	Type	Reference
1326	7 s. 6 d.	Curia	M	(439) p.901
326	8 s.	Curia	M	(439) p.901
327	9 s.	Curia	M	(439) p.901
328	10 s.	Curia	M	(439) p.901
329	10 s.	Curia	M	(439) p.901
329	11 s.	Curia	M	(439) p.901
335-1337	10 s.	Curia	M	(439) p.902

The livre of valosii in sous of Bordeaux

Date	Rate	Place	Type	Reference
1329	70 s.	France	O	(162) p.240

For the cameral florin in sous and deniers valosii see under AVIGNON p.125

TOURNOIS

In 1204 Philip Augustus enormously increased the scope of his kingship by confiscating Normandy and many of the extensive Plantagenet lands in western France from John of Anjou, who was also king of England. Philip put his authority behind the most successful of the coinages already circulating in the newly conquered lands in western France. These were the deniers minted at Tours by the abbey of St Martin which had already been struck in very considerable quantities in the previous half century. Philip brought the independent coinages of Maine and Anjou to an end, and the mint at Tours was brought directly under his own administration. In the years that followed the lighter money tournois was preferred to the heavier money parisis, which was also under royal control, so that tournois became the national coinage of France, struck not merely at Tours, but at the increasing number of mints under royal control throughout France. In northern France tournois replaced parisis, in eastern France it replaced provinois, and in southern France it replaced melgorian. In the third decade of the fourteenth century the kings of France bought back the right of minting from a number of their feudatories, so that in the later middle ages the only effective non-royal coinages in France were those issued by a handful of the greatest near autonomous princes, whose actions were not amenable to royal control, such as the duke of Brittany, or the duke of Guyenne, who was also king of England. Money tournois was also used in Hainault (see below pp.230-2) and diverged gradually from French royal money tournois. We hope no Hainault rates are in the following tables.

The livre tournois in sous and deniers parisis

Date	Rate	Place	Type	Reference
1120	13 s. 4 d.	France	H	(148) p.435
1221	16 s. 8 d.	France	A	(165) p.27
1221	16 s.	France	A	(165) p.27
1222	16 s.	Châteauroux	A	(165) p.27

Since both the denier tournois and the denier parisis were royal coinages by the 1220s, the kings of France were able to keep them in a fixed relationship for the rest of the middle ages. From the 1220s onwards the livre tournois was always worth 16 sous parisis, or, put the other way round, the livre parisis was always worth 25 sous tournois. See above p.167.

The Florentine florin in sous and deniers tournois of France

In fourteenth century France 'florin' for a time meant any gold coin, so that the coin that we know as the masse d'or was sometimes described as the 'fleurin de 35 au marc', our chaise d'or as the 'florin à la chaire', our mantelet as the 'fleurin au mantelet', our denier d'or à la Reine as the 'fleurin à la Reyne' and so forth. In addition the light weight florins of Piedmont and Dauphiné, florins parvi ponderis, circulated widely in southern France (see above pp.131-2), as did the various florins issued by the popes at Avignon (see above pp.123-6). Usually some additional description makes it clear which florin is meant, but this is not always the case, and some of the florins in the following table are almost certainly not Florentine.

Date	Rate	Place	Type	Reference
1265	8 s.	Curia	B	(439) p.896
1265.09-11	8 s. 2 d.	Provins (fair)	C	(227) 1922 p.185
This rate was considered high because of Charles of Anjou's crusade. The rate was expected to fall to 7s. 9d. at the fair of St Remy at Troyes.				
1267-1268	8 s. 6 d.	Paris	O	(193) p.277
Fixed by Alphonse de Poitiers to aid seneschals with accounts.				
1268	8 s. 6 d.	Curia	B	(439) p.896
1274-1278	10 s. 3 d.	Curia	B	(439) p.897
1283	10 s. 3 d.	Provence	B	(309) II p.143

Florentine florins in sous and deniers tournois of France 1265–1500

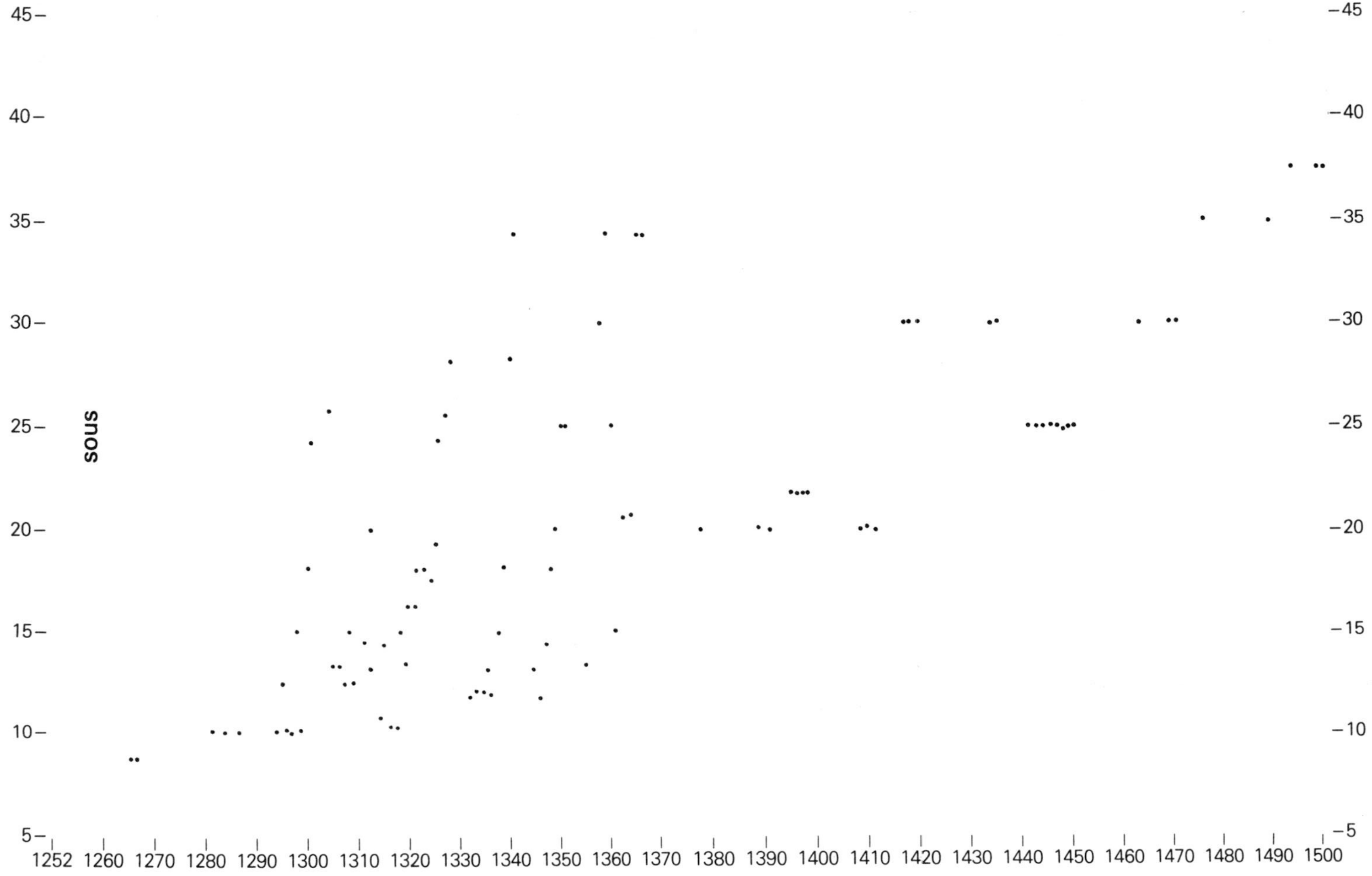

sous

45 40 35 30 25 20 15 10 5

1252 1260 1270 1280 1290 1300 1310 1320 1330 1340 1350 1360 1370 1380 1390 1400 1410 1420 1430 1440 1450 1460 1470 1480 1490 1500

THE FLORENTINE FLORIN IN SOUS AND DENIERS TOURNOIS OF FRANCE

Date	Rate	Place	Type	Reference
1285	10 s.	France	C	(151) p.244
1287	10 s.	Burgundy	?	(382) 4836
1288	10 s.	Curia	B	(270) p.898
1288	10 s.	Champagne	B	(443) p.304
1292	10 s.	Curia	B	(270) p.898
1292	10 s. 6 d.	Curia	B	(439) p.898
1293.06.13	10 s.	Tarascon	B	(118) II no.182
1294	10 s.	Curia	B	(439) p.898
1295.05.15	10 s.	Bourges	B	(226) CXLIV p.21
1296	10 s.	Curia	B	(439) p.898
1296	12 s. 6 d.	France	C	(151) p.244
1296.03.31?	15 s.	France	O?	(184) p.77
1296.05.08	13 s. 6 d.	France	O?	(184) p.38
1296.12.08	10 s. 6 d.	Rheims	B	(309) II p.305
1297	10 s.	Sens	B	(309) II p.305
1297.10.07	10 s. 4 d.	Bourgdieu	B	(309) II p.305
1297.12	10 s. 6 d.	Arras	B	(309) II p.305
1298.05	10 s. 6 d.	France	O?	(185) p.26
1298.09.05	10 s. 6 d.	Tours	B	(309) II p.306
1298-1299	15 s.	France	C	(151) p.244
1299	19 s. 5 d.	Provence	C	(96) II p.716
1299	19 s.	Provence	C	(96) II p.710
1299.09.25	10 s. 6 d.	Venaissin	A	(118) II no.693
1300	19 s.	Provence	C	(96) II p.738
1300	18 s.	Provence	C	(96) II p.746
1300.01.01	10 s. 6 d.	Venaissin	B	(309) I p.305
1300.07.12	10 s.	Bourges	B	(226) CXLIV p.25
1301	18 s. 9 d.	France	C	(151) p.244
1301.07.05	18 s. 10 d.	France	O	(228) p.95
1302 (St Rémi)	23 s. 6 d.	Troyes	C	(89) pp.359-360
1302	25 s. 6 d.	Troyes (fair)	C	(89) pp.359-360
1302	circa 19 s.	Curia	B	(439) p.899
1304-1305?	42 s. 6 d.	France	C	(151) p.244
1304	25 s.	Curia	B	(439) p.899
1305	26 s. 6 d.	Curia	B	(439) p.899
1305.07.30	26 s. 6 d.	France	HA	(128) p.225
1306-1307	13 s. 9 d.	France	C	(151) p.244
1306	13 s.	Piedmont	A	(110) p.490
1307	13 s.	Curia	B	(439) p.899
1307	14 s.	Curia	B	(439) p.899
1307	13 s. 6 d.	Poitiers	H	(461) p.374
1308-1309	10 s.	Curia	A	(229) p.XVIII
1308	10 s.	Curia	B	(439) p.899
1308	10 s. 6 d.	Curia	B	(439) p.899
1308	13 s. 10 d.	Curia	B	(439) p.899
1308	12 s. 6 d.	France	C	(151) p.244
1309-1310	10 s. 6 d.	Curia	A	(439) p.64
1309	14 s. 6 d.	Curia	A	(439) p.64
1309	14 s.	Piedmont	A	(110) p.491
1309	15 s.	France	C	(151) p.244
1309	15 s.	Hainault	A	(208) p.40
1310.01.26	12 s.	France	O?	(208) p.65
1310.04.16	12 s.	France	O?	(152) p.67
1310.10.17	10 s. 6 d.	Avignon	B	(179) p.18
1310.11.10	12 s. 6 d.	France	O?	(152) p.42
1310.12.17	12 s. 6 d.	France	C	(152) p.68
1311.01	17 s.	England	B	(426) p.85
1311.02	17 s. 4 d.	England	B	(426) p.87
1311.02	17 s. 2 d.	England	B	(426) p.92
1311.03	17 s.	England	B	(426) p.93
1311.07.19	10 s.	Aix-en-Provence	B	(226) CXLIV p.10
1312	13 s. 4 d.	Curia	B	(269) p.135
1312	13 s. 6 d.	Curia	M	(439) p.899
1312.02-03	17 s. 5 d.	England	B	(426) p.109
1312.03	17 s. 4 d.	England	B	(426) p.94
1312.06.24	14 s. 6 d.	Tournai	C	(231) p.334
1312.06	17 s. 2 1/2 d.	England	B	(426) p.100
1312.07.22	15 s.	Tournai	C	(231) p.334
1313	22 s.	Tournai	C	(231) p.335
1313.04.22	17 s.	Tournai	C	(231) p.335
1313.08.18	20 s.	Montbrison	B	(193) p.611
1313.09.15	13 s.	Tournai	C	(231) p.335

THE FLORENTINE FLORIN IN SOUS AND DENIERS TOURNOIS OF FRANCE

Date	Rate	Place	Type	Reference
1314.10	12 s. 2 1/2 d.	France	O?	(131) p.570
1314.10(72 to mark)	11 s. 6 d.	France	O?	(131) p.570
1316	14 s.	Tournai	C	(231) p.335
1316	14 s.	Curia	M	(439) p.900
1316.11.01	14 s. 2 d.	Tournai	C	(231) p.336
1317-1320	15 s.	Trier	B	(267) p.38
1317	14 s. 5 d.	Curia	A	(439) p.48
1317	16 s.	Arles	O?	(400) p.176
1317	15 s.	Metz	B	(309) I p.240
1317.02.16	10 s. 6 d.	Tours	B	(309) II p.307
1317.04.02	14 s. 2 d.	Carcassonne	A	(69)
1317.04.18	10 s. 6 d.	Bourges	B	(309) II p.307
1317.06.01	10 s. 6 d.	Arras	B	(309) II p.307
1317.06.25	14 s. 6 d.	Carcassonne	A	(69)
1317.11.19	10 s. 6 d.	Venaissin	C	(118) III p.137
1317.11.30	10 s. 7 d.	Sens	BH	(309) II p.307
1318.02.10	15 s. 2 d.	Avignon	A	(439) p.50
1318.03.21	16 s. 3 d.	France	A	(69)
1318.05.04	10 s. 6 d.	Rouen	B	(309) II p.507
1318.05.23	10 s. 6 d.	Rheims	B	(309) II p.307
1319	16 s. 4 d.	Curia	A	(439) p.48
1319	14 s. 2 d.	Avignon	A	(439) p.82
1319.01.07-1320	14 s. 4 3/4 d.	Florence	C	(224) p.45
1319.04.03	15 s.	France	A	(228) p.241
1319.04.05	15 s.	France	A	(69)
1320	16 s.	Narbonne	A	(459) p.93
1320	16 s. 1 d.	Narbonne	A	(459) p.95
1320	16 s. 4 d.	Narbonne	A	(459) p.96
1320	16 s. 6 d.	Narbonne	A	(459) p.104
1320	16 s. 8 d.	Narbonne	A	(459) p.106
1320	16 s. 3 d.	Narbonne	A	(459) p.238
1320	16 s. 6 d.	Curia	M	(439) p.900
1320	19 s. 2 d.	Curia	M	(439) p.900
1320.07.01-1321.01.01	13 s. 8 d.	Champagne	M	(316) II p.151
1320.07.01-1321.01.01	13 s. 6 d.	Normandy	M	(316) II p.151
1320.07.01-1321.01.01	13 s. 4 d.	Paris(Trésor)	M	(316) II p.151
1321.03.10	17 s.	Avignon	A	(439) p.42
1321.08.16	16 s. 8 d.	Avignon	A	(439) p.70
1321.11.27	17 s. 6 d.	Avignon	A	(439) p.70
1321.11.27	16 s. 9 d.	Avignon	A	(439) p.70
1321-1322	16 s. 8 d.	France	C	(327) p.337
1322.01.26	16 s. 8 d.	Avignon	A	(439) p.71
1322.01.11	17 s. 4 d.	Burgundy	C	(200) p.171
1322.04.30	13 s. 4 d.	Florence	L	(118) II no.977
1322.10.30	16 s. 8 d.	France	O	(228) p.243
1322.12.03	15 s. 3 1/8 d.	France	O	(504) p.236
1322.12.03	14 s. 9 1/2 d.	France	O	(504) p.236
1323.01.06	17 s.	Avignon	A	(439) p.75
1324	17 s. 6 d.	Curia	M	(439) p.901
1324.01-06	17 s. 6 d.	Hainault	A	(208) p.41
1324.01.10	22 s.	Avignon	A	(439) p.191
1324.05.21	17 s.	Cadajoue	A	(69)
1324.05.25	17 s. 6 d.	Metz	B	(309) II p.383
1325	18 s.	Curia	M	(439) p.901
1325	21 s.	Carpentras	B	(426) p.80
1325.02.06	21 s. 9 d.	Carpentras	B	(426) p.91
1325.12-1326.01	18 s.	France	O	(228) p.248
1326	17 s. 11 d.	Arles	C	(400) p.175
1326	19 s. 6 d.	Curia	M	(439) p.901
1326	20 s.	Curia	M	(439) p.901
1327.12.21	24 s.	Dombes	B	(193) p.611
1327	19 s.	Curia	M	(439) p.901
1327	27 s. 4 d.	Cambrai	B	(28) p.10
1328	26 s.	Curia	M	(439) p.901
1328	25 s.	Curia	M	(439) p.901
1328	25 s. 7 d.	Cambrai	B	(28) p.3
1329	27 s. 6 d.	Cambrai	B	(28) p.64
1329	28 s. 6 d.	Hainault	A	(208) p.41
1329.12.04	28 s.	France	O	(430) I p.214
1330	25 s.	Beaune	O	(384) p.19 no.66
1330.01	21 s.	Hainault	A	(208) p.42
1330.05	13 s. 4 d.	Hainault	A	(208) p.42

THE FLORENTINE FLORIN IN SOUS AND DENIERS TOURNOIS OF FRANCE

Date	Rate	Place	Type	Reference
1330.07-12	13 s.	Hainault	A	(208) p.42
1331	27 s.	Curia	M	(439) p.901
1331	12 s.	Curia	M	(439) p.901
1332	12 s. 6 d.	Languedoc	C	(50) Annexe 8
1332.11.10	13 s.	Cambrai	B	(28) p.41
1332-1333	12 s. 7 d.	Tournai	A	(232) p.481
1333	12 s. 6 d.	Cambrai	B	(28) p.64
1333	13 s.	Cambrai	B	(28) p.64
1333	12 s. 2 d.	France	C	(231) p.321
1334	12 s. 6 d.	Curia	M	(439) p.901
1334	13 s.	Curia	M	(439) p.901
1334.02.09-1335	25 s. 6 d.	Hainault	O?	(327) p.114
1335	12 s.	Curia	M	(440) p.34
circa 1335	12 s.	Burgundy	A	(382) 7640
1335	12 s. 8 d.	Languedoc	C	(50) Annexe 8
1335	13 s.	France	C	(231) p.321
1335.02.14	10 s. 6 d.	Curia	B	(216) p.12
1335.05.16	12 s. 8 d.	Curia	B	(216) p.99
1335.05.17	12 s. 8 1/2 d.	Curia	B	(216) p.99
1335.08.14	12 s. 6 d.	Curia	B	(216) p.101
1335.10.05	12 s. 9 d.	Curia	B	(216) p.107
1335.12.26	12 s. 6 d.	Moulins	B	(193) p.611
1336	14 s.	France	C?	(231) p.321
1336	13 s.	France	O	(162) p.325
1336.03	12 s. 10 d.	Curia	B	(216) p.106
1336.08.31	13 s.	Curia	M	(440) p.50
1336.11.07	12 s. 8 d.	Curia	B	(216) p.113

With the opening of the Hundred Years War France entered a period of extreme monetary instability. Between 1 February 1337 and 5 December 1360 there were no less than 85 changes in the coinage. These were mostly debasements, but were punctuated by 16 attempts to return to stronger money. As a consequence accounting became chaotic. Frenchmen sometimes tried to continue to reckon in good, pre-war, tournois, 'bone mon. Francie'. At other times they allowed themselves to reckon in the debased tournois of the moment, 'minuta moneta debili currenti'. The wide variety of exchange rates recorded here from the 1330s to the 1360s reflects not only the 85 changes in the coinage itself, but also the attempts to preserve some continuing standard for accounting, despite these wild oscillations in the silver content of the tournois.

Date	Rate	Place	Type	Reference
1337-1338	15 s.	France	C?	(231) p.321
1337-1339	15 s.	France	C?	(127) p.212
1337-1339	16 s. 8 d.	France	C?	(127) p.213
1337-1339	15 s. 9 d.	Avignon	C?	(127) p.231
1337	14 s. 6 d.	Languedoc	C	(50) Annexe 8
1337	15 s.	Curia	M	(439) p.902
1337	15 s.	Cîteaux	A	(264) p.138
1337.02.13	13 s.	Curia	B	(216) p.116
1337.02.24	12 s.	Curia	B	(216) p.117
1337.04	14 s.	Hainault	A	(208) p.42
1337.06.21	13 s.	Curia	B	(216) p.120
1337.07.03	14 s.	Curia	B	(216) p.120
1337.09.29	12 s. 6 d.	Montbrison	B	(193) p.611
1337.10.14	13 s.	Aix-en-Provence-Curia	B	(216) p.214
1338	15 s.	Cîteaux	A	(264) p.138
1338.01.13	13 s.	Curia	B	(216) p.125
1338.02.09	15 s.	Curia	B	(216) p.126
1338.02.23	14 s. 4 d.	Curia	B	(216) p.126
1338.06.25	16 s.	Curia	B	(216) p.131
1338.08.14	13 s.	Curia	B	(216) p.132
1338.12.25	15 s. 6 d.	Curia	B	(216) p.136
1339	15 s.	Cîteaux	A	(264) p.138
1339	17 s.	Curia	M	(439) p.902
1339	13 s.	Curia	M	(439) p.902
1339	18 s.	France	C?	(231) p.321
1339	31 s.	Languedoc	C	(50) Annexe 8
1339.03.05	13 s. 6 d.	Curia	B	(216) p.141
1339.03.05	12 s. 6 d.	Curia	B	(216) p.141
1339.08.21	19 s. 6 d.	Curia	M	(440) p.104
1339.08.22	19 s. 9 d.	Curia	M	(440) p.104
1340	30 s.	Cîteaux	A	(264) p.138
1340	28 s.	France	C?	(231) p.321

THE FLORENTINE FLORIN IN SOUS AND DENIERS TOURNOIS OF FRANCE

Date	Rate	Place	Type	Reference
1340(70 to mark)	30 s.	France	O	(50) Annexe 8
1340(72 to mark)	28 s. 6 d.	France	A	(50) Annexe 8
1341	30 s.	Cîteaux	A	(264) p.138
1341	34 s.	France	C?	(231) p.321
1341	50 s.	Cîteaux	A	(264) p.138
1341.02.14	16 s. 6 d.	Curia	B	(216) p.46
1342	46 s.	France	C?	(231) p.321
1342	50 s.	Cîteaux	A	(264) p.138
1342.01.03	10 s. 6 d.	Curia	B	(216) p.49
1342.01.24	38 s.	Curia	M	(440) p.142
1342.02.09	28 s. 4 d.	Curia	B	(216) p.190
1342.03	43 s. 3 d.	Languedoc	C	(50) Annexe 8
1342.03.05	12 s. 6 d.	Curia	B	(216) p.50
1342.07.05(70 to mark)	48 s.	France	O	(50) Annexe 8
1342.07.05(72 to mark)	46 s. 8 d.	France	O	(50) Annexe 8
1342.07.11	42 s. 6 d.	Thérouanne	B	(28) p.77
1342.06.24-1343.06.23	53 s. 6 d.	Tournai	A	(232) p.527
1343	16 s.	Arles	C?	(400) p.175
1343	53 s.	France	C?	(231) p.321
1343	48 s.	Cîteaux	A	(264) p.138
1343	57 s. 6 d.	Cîteaux	A	(264) p.138
1343.02.08	12 s.	Curia	C	(347) p.4
1343.03.24	50 s.	Curia	M	(440) p.207
1343.06.15	17 s.	Thérouanne	B	(28) p.105
1343.06.24	55 s.	Tournai	A	(232) p.537
1343.07.15	40 s. minuta moneta debili currenti	Thérouanne	B	(28) p.90
1343.08.20	56 s.	Curia	M	(440) p.235
1343.10.26 First return to stronger money				
1344	12 s. 6 d.	Cîteaux	A	(264) p.138
1344	12 s. 6 d.	Curia	M	(440) p.269
1344.01.02	55 s.	Curia	C	(347) p.477
1344.01.05	35 s. monete Francie debilis	Curia	M	(440) p.239
1344.01.05	11 s. 4 d. bone monete Francie	Curia	M	(440) p.239
1344.03.03	10 s. 6 d.	Curia	C?	(347) p.8
1344.06.06	55 s.	Curia	C	(347) p.489
1344.11	12 s. 8 d.	Curia	M	(440) p.270
1345-1346	12 s. 6 d.	Cîteaux	A	(264) p.138
1345-1346	13 s.	France	C	(231) p.321
1345.05.03	12 s. 6 d.	Forez	C	(193) p.612
1346.05.10	12 s. 10 d.	Curia	C	(347) p.368
1346.06.13	12 s. 6 d.	France	C	(504) p.238
1346.11.18	12 s. 10 d.	Curia	M	(440) p.316
1346-1347	25 s.	Cîteaux	A	(264) p.138
1347	14 s.	France	C	(231) p.321
1347	25 s.	Cîteaux	A	(264) p.138
1347.12.04	26 s.	Curia	M	(440) p.358
1347-1348	25 s.	Cîteaux	A	(264) p.138
1347.11.11-1348.11.11	22 s.	Dijon	A	(29)
1347.11.11-1348.11.11	24 s.	Dijon	A	(29)
1348	17 s.	Curia	M	(439) p.903
1348	18 s. 6 d.	France	C	(231) p.321
1348.10.29	16 s.	Violay	M?	(192) 1963 p.585
348.11.11-1349.07.25	28 s.	Dijon	C	(29)
349	20 s.	France	C	(231) p.321
349	22 s. 8 d.	Forez	A	(193) p.585
349.02.21	10 s. 6 d.	Curia	C	(347) p.32
349.09	24 s.	Languedoc	C	(50) Annexe 8
350	15 s.	Burgundy	A	(100)
350.05.04	25 s.	Curia	C	(347) p.585
351.06.01	24 s.	Curia	C	(347) p.447
351.06.18	21 s.	Curia	C	(347) p.609
351.09.07	12 s. 7 d.	Curia	C	(347) p.448
351.10.31	25 s.	Curia	C	(347) p.606
352	21 s.	Curia	M	(440) p.494
352.04.02	12 s. 6 d.	Curia	C	(347) p.618
352.07	25 s.	Curia	A	(251) p.31
352.12.17	19 s.	Curia	M	(440) p.497

Date	Rate	Place	Type	Reference
1353.02.21	10 s. 6 d. turonensis parvorum	Curia	A	(251) p.4
1353.06	40 s.	Curia	A	(251) p.31
1353.09.12	40 s. monete Francie	Curia	C	(251) p.24
1353.09.24	48 s. monete Francie	Curia	C	(251) p.21
1353.10.03	40 s.	Curia	A	(251) p.31

1353.10.05 Major return to stronger money.

Date	Rate	Place	Type	Reference
1353.02.16-1354.02.15	10 s. 6 d. turonensis parvorum	Curia	A	(251) p.41
1355	10 s. 6 d.	Curia	C	(252) p.83
1355.03.22	13 s. 10 d.	France	O	(430) p.357
1356-7(72 to mark)	17 s.	Languedoc	C	(50) Annexe 8
1356-7	18 s.	Languedoc	C	(50) Annexe 8
1356-7	23 s.	Languedoc	C	(50) Annexe 8
1356-7	24 s.	Languedoc	C	(50) Annexe 8
1356-7	13 s. 9 d.	Languedoc	C	(50) Annexe 8
1356-7	13 s.	Languedoc	C	(50) Annexe 8
1356-7	20 s.	Languedoc	C	(50) Annexe 8
1356.09.09	20 s.	Toulouse	A	(509) p.317
1356.11.11-1357.11.11	15 s.	Dijon	C	(394) II 220
1356.12.29	20 s.	Toulouse	A	(509) p.317
1357	25 s.	Beaune	A	(384) p.19 no.66
1357.01.03	22 s.	Toulouse	A	(509) p.317
1357.02.23	20 s.	Toulouse	A	(509) p.317
1357 Lent	22 s.	Montauban	A	(509) p.317
1357.03.23-27	22 s.	Toulouse	A	(509) p.317
1357.05	20 s.	Languedoc	C	(50) Annexe 8
1357.06.02	33 s.	Montauban	C	(191) XX p.49
1357.08.02	43 s.	Montauban	C	(191) XX p.49
1357.08.24	24 s.	Toulouse	A	(509) p.317
1357.10	24 s.	Languedoc	C	(50) Annexe 8
1358	22 s. 6 d.	Forez	A	(192) p.59
1358.02	24 s.	Languedoc	C	(50) Annexe 8
1358.02.01	24 s.	Toulouse	A	(509) p.317
1358.02.21	24 s.	Toulouse	A	(509) p.317
1358.04.02	25 s.	Toulouse	A	(509) p.317
1358.04.03-15	25 s.	Montauban	C	(191) XX p.49
1358.05.05	27 s.	Montauban	C	(191) XX p.49
1358.05.17	32 s.	Toulouse	A	(509) p.317
1358.05.18	28 s.	Montauban	C	(191) XX p.49
1358.05.20	30 s.	Montauban	A	(509) p.317
1358.05.24-26	20 s.	Toulouse	A	(509) p.317
1358.05.31	32 s.	Montauban	A	(509) p.317
1358.06	30 s.	Montauban	C	(191) XX p.49
1358.06.26	43 s.	Toulouse	A	(509) p.317
1358.08.09	40 s.	Curia	B	(252) p.239
1358.08.11	20 s.	Toulouse	A	(509) p.317
1358.08.15	42 s.	Montauban	C	(191) XX p.49
1358.09.11	20 s.	Toulouse	A	(509) p.317
1358.11.02	25 s.	Toulouse	A	(509) p.317
1358.11.05	41 s.	Toulouse	A	(509) p.317
1358.11.24	24 s.	Toulouse	A	(509) p.317
1358.12.01-11	25 s.	Montauban	C	(191) XX p.49
1358.12.16	25 s.	Toulouse	A	(509) p.317
1358.12.19	30 s.	Montauban	C	(191) XX p.49
1359.01.26	48 s.	Montauban	C	(191) XX p.49
1359.01.27	20 s.	Toulouse	A	(509) p.317
1359.02.03	48 s.	Toulouse	A	(509) p.317
1359.03.30	48 s.	Montauban	C	(191) XX p.49
1359.08.06	48 s.	Montauban	C	(191) XX p.49
1359.12.08	34 s.	Montauban	C	(191) XX p.49
1360.02.18-05.31	25 s.	Montauban	C	(191) XX p.49
1360.06.24	15 s.	Dijon	C	(394) II p.235
1360.10.08-12	26 s.	Montauban	C	(191) XX p.49

1360.12.05 End of period of frequent changes in the coinage

Date	Rate	Place	Type	Reference
1361.01.12-05.02	15 s.	Montauban	C	(191) XX p.49
1361.02.16	20 s.	Toulouse	A	(509) p.317
1361.03	16 s.	Languedoc	C	(50) Annexe 8

THE FLORENTINE FLORIN IN SOUS AND DENIERS TOURNOIS OF FRANCE

Date	Rate	Place	Type	Reference
1361.03	16 s. 3 d.	Languedoc	C	(50) Annexe 8
1361.03	16 s. 6 d.	Languedoc	C	(50) Annexe 8
1361.03.13	20 s.	Toulouse	A	(509) p.317
1361.05.29	20 s.	Toulouse	A	(509) p.317
1361.06.07	30 s.	Toulouse	A	(509) p.317
1361.07.13	20 s.	Toulouse	A	(509) p.317
1361.11	22 s. 9 d.	Curia	C	(252) p.374
1362	16 s.	Languedoc	C	(50) Annexe 8
1362.01	12 s. 8 d.	Beaune	O	(384) no.82
1362.03	30 s.	Curia	C	(252) p.392
1362.03.15-04.25	22 s.	Montauban	C	(191) XX p.49
1363-1364	21 s. 8 d.	Nevers	A	(193) p.546
1365.06.23	34 s.	Marseille	O	(414) p.155
1371.01.01	16 s. 8 d.	Burgundy	C	(200) p.250
1371.07	16 s.	Toulouse	A	(509) p.322
1375	14 s. 11 3/4 d.	Perpignan	H	(461) p.376
1375.11.11-1376.11.11	16 s. 8 d.	Dijon	A	(29)
1377.08	16 s. 8 d.	Toulouse	A	(509) p.322
1378	20 s.	Avignon	M	(182) p.36
1378.05.13	16 s. 8 d.	Dijon	C	(29)
1381	12 s. 6 d.	Dijon	A	(29)
1381.10-1382.10	16 s. 6 d.	Toulouse	A	(509) p.322
1382	12 s. 8 d.	Dijon	A	(29)
1382-1383	16 s. 8 d.	Dijon	R	(29)
1389	19 s. 8 3/4 d.	Paris	H	(461) p.386
1391	19 s. 8 3/4 d.	Orleans	H	(461) p.386
1392.02.22	16 s. 8 d.	Dijon	A	(29)
1393.11.04	20 s. 5 1/2 d.	Paris-Genoa	B	(140) p.9
1395-1398	22 s.	France	C	(113) p.393
1397?	16 s. 8 d.	Dijon	A	(29)
1400.08.31-11.11	16 s. 8 d.	Dijon	A	(29)
1400	16 s. 7 1/2 d.	Dijon	A	(29)
1409-1410	20 s. 7 d.	Orleans	H	(461) p.386
1412	20 s. 6 3/4 d.	Orleans	H	(461) p.386
1417-1420	30 s.	Orleans	H	(461) p.386
1434-1435	30 s. 1/2 d.	Orleans	H	(461) p.387
1441-1442	25 s.	Orleans	H	(461) p.387
1448	25 s.	Orleans	H	(461) p.387
1449-1450	25 s.	Orleans	H	(461) p.387
1450	25 s.	Moissac	C	(281) XXXI p.142
1463	29 s. 9 1/2 d.	Orleans	H	(461) p.388
1469-1470	29 s. 9 1/2 d.	Orleans	H	(461) p.388
1475	34 s. 2 3/4 d.	Orleans	H	(461) p.388
1485.05.19	41 s. 8 d.	Cambrai	B	(68) p.19
1488	34 s. 2 3/4 d.	Lyons	H	(461) p.388
1493.08.31	37 s. 6 d.	France	C	(411) p.378
1493.11.13	33 s. 4 d.	Thérouanne	B	(68) p.116
1497	37 s. 6 d.	Orleans	H	(461) p.388
1498.03.11	37 s. 6 d.	France	C	(411) p.378
1498	37 s.	Curia	B	(439) p.42
1498	37 s. 6 d.	Troyes	H	(461) p.388
1500	38 s. 9 d.	England	O	(362) p.339

The livre tournois in soldi and denari affiorino of Florence

Very occasionally the rate between florins and tournois was expressed the other way round. This can be simply translated back into the familiar form of sous and deniers tournois to the florin on the basis of 29 soldi affiorino to each florin. The first rate below, for example, is equivalent to saying that the florin equalled 15 s. 15 1/2 d. tournois.

Date	Rate	Place	Type	Reference
318.09.17	37 s. 6 d.	Provins	A	(424) p.80
318	37 s. 10 d.	Provins	A	(424) p.94
319.02.01	36 s. 8 d.	Provins	A	(424) p.80
319	37 s. 6 d.	Troyes	A	(424) p.86
319	37 s.	Troyes	A	(424) p.88
319	38 s. 4 d.	Troyes	A	(424) p.97
319	36 s. 8 d.	Champagne	A	(424) p.90

The Venetian ducat in sous and deniers tournois

Date	Rate	Place	Type	Reference
1310.04.28	12 s.	France	C	(152) p.68
1310.11.10	12 s.	France	C	(152) p.42
1470.01.04	28 s. 9 d.	France	O	(258) p.138
1472.11.18	30 s. 3 d.	Rouen	M	(348) p.381

The livre tournois in other French currencies

Other French currencies are arranged alphabetically

The livre tournois in sous and deniers angevin (of Anjou)

Date	Rate	Place	Type	Reference
1200	20 s.	Normandy	A	(165) p.23
1265	25 s.	England	O	(399) p.41

The livre tournois in sous and deniers arnaldenses (of Agen)

Date	Rate	Place	Type	Reference
1252	24 s.	Agen	A	(447) p.37
1301	25 s.	England	O	(399) p.42

The livre tournois in sous and deniers blésois (of Blois)

Date	Rate	Place	Type	Reference
1315	23 s. 4 d.	France	O	(52) p.464
1318.06.24	32 s. 3 d.	Blois	A	(52) p.464
1319	32 s.	Blois	A	(52) p.464
1319	30 s.	Blois	A	(52) p.464

The livre tournois in sous bordelais or burdegals (of Bordeaux)

Date	Rate	Place	Type	Reference
1252.03	26 s. 1 d.	Toulouse	A	(195) p.473
1310-1317	25 s.	England	O	(399) p.42
1329	28 s. debilium	Paris	O	(162) Valozius
1330s	25 s. nouveau	Midi	?	(87) p.415

The livre tournois in sous and deniers bretons

Date	Rate	Place	Type	Reference
1265	25 s.	Brittany	O	(227) p.179
1373-1386	20 s.	Brittany	A	(260) p.56
early 15th century	20 s.	Brittany	A	(260) p.56
1420	30 s.	Brittany	A	(260) p.56
1433	24 s.	Brittany	A	(260) p.57
1433	22 s. 7 d.	St Brice en Coglès (Ille-et-Vilaine)	A	(262) p.160
1457	23 s. 4 d.	Brittany	A	(260) p.57
1467	16 s. 8 d.	Brittany	A	(260) p.57
1468-1470	16 s. 8 d.	Brittany	A	(260) p.57
1479.02.24	16 s. 6 d.	St Brice en Coglès	A	(262) p.160
1480.01.21	16 s. 8 d.	St Brice en Coglès	A	(262) p.160
1491	16 s. 8 d.	Brittany	O	(260) p.57
1494.01.15	16 s. 8 d.	St Brice en Coglès	A	(262) p.160
1494.02.08	16 s. 8 d.	St Brice en Coglès	A	(262) p.160
1494.07.22	16 s. 8 d.	St Brice en Coglès	A	(262) p.160
1494.09.24	16 s. 8 d.	St Brice en Coglès	A	(262) p.160

THE LIVRE TOURNOIS IN SOUS AND DENIERS OF CAHORS

The livre tournois in sous and deniers caorcin or caturcensis (of Cahors)

Date	Rate	Place	Type	Reference
1251	40 s.	Toulouse	A	(195) p.473
1253	40 s.	Toulouse	A	(195) p.473
1253	35 s. 8 1/2 d.	Toulouse	A	(195) p.473
1255	35 s. 1 d.	Toulouse	A	(195) p.473
1256	36 s. 8 d.	Toulouse	A	(195) p.473
1265	41 s. 8 d.	Carcassonne	O	(227) p.178
1269	40 s.	Toulouse	A	(195) p.473
1269.11.02	35 s. 8 1/2 d.	Toulouse	A	(195) p.473
1295	30 s.	Carcassonne	O	(227) p.178

The livre tournois in sous and deniers chapotensis (of Bigorre)

Date	Rate	Place	Type	Reference
1301	25 s.	France	A	(162) II p.287
1307	25 s.	France	A	(162) II p.287
1307.05	25 s.	France	A	(69)
1313	25 s.	Gascony	A	(290) IIC p.328
1313.10.28	25 s.	Gascony	A	(486) p.218
1317	25 s.	Gascony	A	(290) IIC p.328

The livre tournois in sous and deniers of Clermont

Date	Rate	Place	Type	Reference
1315	21 s. 8 d.	France	C?	(61) p.20

The livre tournois in sous estevenantes of Besançon

Date	Rate	Place	Type	Reference
1422?	18 s.	Dijon	A	(516) f.33r

The livre tournois in sous of Lyons

Date	Rate	Place	Type	Reference
1315	20 s.	Lyons	C?	(380) p.534
1343	10 s. new deniers	Chamazel (Forez)	R	(192) p.591

The livre tournois in sous and deniers mansois (of Maine)

Date	Rate	Place	Type	Reference
1265	12 s. 6 d.	France	O	(227) p.179
1265.11.29	12 s. 6 d.	Troyes	M	(374) p.57

The livre tournois in sous and deniers of Meaux

Date	Rate	Place	Type	Reference
1224?	22 s. 6 d.	Meaux	H	(165) p.26

The livre tournois in sous and deniers melgorians (of Melgueil)

Date	Rate	Place	Type	Reference
1251	21 s. 9 d.	Toulouse	A	(195) p.473
1252	23 s.	Toulouse	A	(195) p.473
1265	23 s. 4 d.	Montpellier	O	(227) 1924 p.177
1265	23 s.	Montpellier	O	(227) 1924 p.177
1269	20 s. 10 d.	Toulouse	A	(195) p.473
1283.07	22 s.	Aragon	B	(419) II p.302
1315	21 s. 8 d.	France	O	(171) II 456-457

The livre tournois in sous of Metz

Date	Rate	Place	Type	Reference
1298-1300	10 s.	Metz?	H	(445) p.259
1345	20 s.	Metz?	H	(445) p.259
1381-1384	20 s.	Metz?	H	(445) p.259
1388-1389	20 s.	Metz?	H	(445) p.259
1395-1398	10 s.	Pont-a-Mousson	A	(113) p.381

The livre tournois in sous Nantais (of Nantes)

Date	Rate	Place	Type	Reference
1265	25 s.	France	O	(258) p.58

The livre tournois in sous of Narbonne

Date	Rate	Place	Type	Reference
1387	20 s.	Narbonne	B	(42) p.131

The livre tournois in sous and deniers of Périgord

Date	Rate	Place	Type	Reference
1315	26 s. 8 d.	Périgueux	M	(69)
1346	38 s. 3 3/4 d.	Périgueux	C	(114) p.162

The livre tournois in sous and deniers poitevins or pictavensis (of Poitou)

Date	Rate	Place	Type	Reference
1249.06	20 s. 5 d.	Toulouse	A	(195) p.474
1268.09	20 s. 7 d.	Toulouse	A	(195) p.474
1268.11	20 s.	Toulouse	A	(195) p.474
1291	23 s. 5 1/4 d.	Anjou	B	(179) II p.198

The livre tournois in sous and deniers provinois (of Champagne)

See above p.164

The livre tournois in sous and deniers rodan (of Rodez)

Date	Rate	Place	Type	Reference
1297	30 s.	Najac (Aveyron)	A	(69)
1307-1308	30 s.	Najac (Aveyron)	A	(69)
1316	30 s.	Najac (Aveyron)	A	(69)
1324	30 s.	Najac (Aveyron)	A	(69)

The livre tournois in sous and deniers of Toulouse

Date	Rate	Place	Type	Reference
13th century generally	10 s.	Toulouse	A	(195) p.474
1304.04.16	10 s.	Nimes	A	(69)
1380.10	10 s.	Toulouse	A	(509) p.322

The livre tournois in non-French currencies before 1300

The livre tournois in soldi and denari of Pisa

Date	Rate	Place	Type	Reference
1248.04.15	43 s. 4 1/4 d.	Paris	B	(44) p.114
1248.03.23	44 s. 10 d.	Pisa-Paris	B	(45) no.159
1248.07.01	40 s.	Marseille	C	(45) no.939

The livre tournois in soldi and denari imperiali of Milan

Date	Rate	Place	Type	Reference
1298	29 s. 6 d.	Champagne-Venice	B	(393) I p.227

The livre tournois in soldi and denari of Genoa

Date	Rate	Place	Type	Reference
1250.11.14	37 s. 8 d.	France	O	(432) p.295
1253.07.15	29 s. 2 d.	France	O	(432) p.298
1262.01.30	27 s. 9 1/3 d.	Genoa	B	(154) IV p.627
1298.10.29	22 s. 6 d.	Genoa	B	(154) II p.140

See also the lira of Genoa in sous and deniers tournois under GENOA p.108

The livre tournois in sous and deniers of the mixed money of Marseille

Date	Rate	Place	Type	Reference
1246	35 s.	Provence	O?	(414) p.109
1248.03.21	36 s. 1 d.	Marseille	C	(45)
1248.03.23	35 s.	Marseille	C	(45) no.136
1248.04.01	25 s.	Marseille	L	(45) no.344
1248.04.07	25 s.	Marseille	B	(45) no.396
1248.04.18	30 s.	Marseille-Provins	B	(45) no.564
1248.05.26	32 s.	Marseille	C	(45) no.789
1248.05.27	32 s.	Marseille-Provins	B	(45) no.806
1248.06.03	25 s.	Marseille	B	(45) no.852
1248.07.01	40 s.	Marseille	C	(45) no.939
1248.07.08	25 s. 6 d.	Marseille	B	(45) no.959
1248.07.15	23 s.	Marseille	B	(45) no.975
1248.07.15	27 s.	Marseille	B	(45) no.976
1248.07.23	25 s.	Marseille	L	(45) no.1003
1248.07.23	20 s.	Marseille-Aigues-Mortes	B	(45) no.1013
1248.07.27	20 s.	Marseille-Aigues-Mortes	B	(45) no.1019
1248.07.28	28 s.	Marseille-Provins	B	(45) no.1028
1248.07.29	27 s. 5 d.	Marseille	L	(45) no.1031
1268	23 s. 4 d.	Marseille	C	(17) I p.324
1301	25 s.	Provence	O?	(414) p.109

It is not clear if these last two references are to the mixed money of Marseille or the royal money of Marseille — see above pp.117 and 120

The livre tournois in sous and deniers viennois

Date	Rate	Place	Type	Reference
1249.02	23 s. 1 d.	Toulouse	A	(195) p.474
1249.08	24 s. 1 d.	Toulouse	A	(195) p.474
1251	22 s. 7 d.	Toulouse	A	(195) p.474
1252.02	23 s. 1 d.	Toulouse	A	(195) p.474
1253.05	24 s. 1 d.	Toulouse	A	(195) p.474
1254.02	24 s. 1 d.	Toulouse	A	(195) p.474
1254.02	23 s. 1 d.	Toulouse	A	(195) p.474
1255.05	24 s. 1 d.	Toulouse	A	(195) p.474
1255.05	23 s. 1 d.	Toulouse	A	(195) p.474
1255.05-1256.02	23 s. 4 d.	Toulouse	A	(195) p.474
1256.02	26 s. 8 d.	Toulouse	A	(195) p.474
1256.05	24 s. 1 d.	Toulouse	A	(195) p.474
1256.02	25 s.	Toulouse	A	(195) p.474
1257.05	24 s. 1 d.	Toulouse	A	(195) p.474
1284	25 s.	Piedmont	A	(110) p.487
1310-1313	25 s.	Paris	O	(171) III p.103
1319.09.25	25 s.	Pont-de-Sorgues	A	(51) p.147
1343	20 s.	Chalmazel (Forez)	A	(192) p.591
1430.07.29	16 s.	Romans	O	(430) III 91-92

See also the livre viennois in sous and deniers tournois under VIENNOIS p.131

The livre tournois in sous and deniers of Lausanne

Date	Rate	Place	Type	Reference
1275	18 s. 5 3/4 d.	Lausanne	HO	(355) p.385

The livre tournois in sueldos and dineros reales of Valencia

Date	Rate	Place	Type	Reference
1317.08.11	21 s. 8 d.	Montpellier	C	(415) p.190

The livre tournois in sueldos and dineros burgaleses of Castile

Date	Rate	Place	Type	Reference
1280	60 s. 7 d.	Aragon	C	(419) II p.291

The livre tournois in sous and deniers artésians (of Artois)

Date	Rate	Place	Type	Reference
1253	24 s.	Toulouse	A	(195) p.473
1256	24 s.	Toulouse	A	(195) p.473
1257	25 s. 3 1/2 d.	Toulouse	A	(195) p.473
1258	25 s.	Toulouse	A	(195) p.473
1259	25 s. 11 d.	Toulouse	A	(195) p.473
1260	25 s.	Toulouse	A	(195) p.473
1260	25 s. 3 1/2 d.	Toulouse	A	(195) p.473
1269	23 s. 4 d.	Toulouse	A	(195) p.473
1269	23 s. 3 d.	Toulouse	A	(195) p.473
1310	16 s.	France	C	(152) p.75

For the uncia of Sicily in sous and deniers tournois see under SICILY p.62
For the livre of royaux coronats in sous and deniers tournois see under PROVENCE p.119
For the sou of paparini in deniers tournois see under COMTAT VENAISSIN p.121
For the papal franc in sous and deniers tournois see under AVIGNON p.127
For the florin parvi ponderis in sous and deniers tournois see under DAUPHINÉ p.132
For the gold morabetino in sous and deniers tournois see under CASTILE p.157
For the libra of Navarre in sous and deniers tournois see under NAVARRE p.163
For the pound sterling in sous and deniers tournois see under ENGLAND p.209
For the livre of Liège in sous tournois see under LIÈGE p.232
For the mark of Danish pfennige in sous and deniers tournois see under DENMARK p.282
For the besant (unspecified) in sous and deniers tournois see under BESANT p.295
For the saracen besant in sous and deniers tournois see under ACRE p.298
For the besant of millarenses in sous and deniers tournois see under TUNIS p.311

THE GROS TOURNOIS

The gros tournois was the first successful large silver coin to be issued outside Italy. It was first struck by St Louis in 1266 and was initally valued at 12d. (one sou) tournois. It weighed 4.22 grams of nearly pure silver. Its weight and fineness remained unchanged until 1322, although its value in money tournois had risen and fallen erratically from 1290 onwards as Philip IV altered the silver content of the denier tournois (see below). Gros tournois were widely used for payments not only in France, but very soon in Italy also. In 1296 over 30%, by value, of papal taxation in the diocese of Pisa was paid to the papal collectors in gros tournois. By the end of the thirteenth century they were also widely used in the Low Countries, and from the 1290s onwards were being imitated by such princes as the duke of Brabant and the count of Holland. After 1329 the weight of the French gros tournois frequently changed, and its issue ceased in 1364. Exchange quotations after this date are rare, and ceased altogether before the end of the fourteenth century. Some of these rates may apply to the imitative florins struck in Dauphiné and elsewhere in the Rhône valley from the first half of the fourteenth century, which had a wide circulation in the southern France. They were initially struck at the same weight and fineness as their Florentine prototypes, but were very soon reduced in weight. These lighter Delphinal florins were not always distinguished in documents.

Various accounting systems were based on the gros. A 'livre de gros' was in use in Forez in the 1330s and 1340s (193). The light florin of Dauphiné equalled the sou in this system. An accounting system of 12 notional gros to the Delphinal florin was in use in Dauphiné itself by 1337, and was adopted in much of southern France in the fourteenth and fifteenth century, so that some of the 12 gros entries may relate to this accounting system. See above, under DAUPHINÉ pp.131-2. Confusingly, a different florin-gros system was used in Burgundy, in which 10 notional gros were reckoned to the florin. It is described in a ready reference book compiled for the ducal chambre des comptes at Dijon around 1422 (516) f.33r, although it is notorious that such books frequently incorporated outdated information in case it might possibly be needed again. In 1378 it was actually in use in Dijon (29) and in the accounts of the bursar of Cîteaux (265). The florin-gros system of accounting was succeeded in some places from the late 1360s by a franc-gros system of accounting, see below p.192. There are hints that, in Toulouse at least, this was in turn temporarily succeeded, in the crisis years of 1417-22, by an écu-gros system, in which 18 notional 'gros d'écu' made up the écu (193) p.599.

The gros tournois in deniers tournois

Date	Rate	Place	Type	Reference
1266.08	12 d.	France	O	Initial Value
1290	12 d.	France	O	(228) p.87
1290.02	12 d.	Paris	A	(265)
1290.04.05	13 d.	Ypres	M	(145) p.71
1290.04.09	13 d.	Paris	A	(149) pp.233-234
1296.06.23	15 d.	France	C	(184) p.38
1299.04.10	16 1/2 d.	France	O	(228) p.94
1299.09.09	14 d.	Liège	O	(228) p.94
1301.07.05	20 d.	France	O	(228) p.95
1302	25 7/8 d.	Lagny (fair)	C	(89) pp.359-360
1310 gros of St Louis	15 d.	Burgundy	A	(227) 1925 p.220
1315 gros of St Louis	14 d.	Millau	A	(69)
1316.01.15	12 d.	France	O	(228) p.237
1320.05.28	15 d.	Forez	A	(69)
1323.02.18	15 d.	Avignon	M	(439) p.911
1326.02.02	16 1/4 d.	France	O	(228) p.248
1327.03.16	16 1/2 d.	Curia	O	(228) p.250
1329.12.26	18 d.	France	O	(430) I p.215
1330.04.08	12 d.	France	O	(430) I p.216
1332.03.16	12 d.	Montbrison	L	(192) p.583
1337.06.21	13 d.	Curia	M	(216) p.120
1338.02.09	15 d.	Curia	M	(216) p.126
1362.01	16 d.	Beaune	A	(384) no.82
1364	15 d.	Saint-Jacques d'Arnay	A	(199) p.330
1365-1383	15 d.	Toulouse	A	(509) p.322
1370.12 old gros	20 d.	Beaune	A	(384) no.123
1443.10.26	15 d.	France	O	(327) p.116

The gros tournois in deniers parisis
4d. parisis = 5d. tournois

Date	Rate	Place	Type	Reference
1278.11.25	10 d.	Ypres	M	(145) p.71
1288.02	10 d.	France	O	(228) p.86
1289	10 d.	Artois?	H	(410) p.145
1290.01.31	10 d.	Ypres	M	(145) p.71
1290.03.01	10 d.	Ypres	M	(145) p.71
1295	10 1/2 d.	Artois?	H	(410) p.145
1290	10 1/2	France	H	(148) p.435
1296.06.12	12 d.	France	C	(184) p.38
1307.02.14	31 1/2 d. weak money	London	A	(35) I p.268
1312	12 d.	Artois?	H	(410) p.145
1315.12.08	10 1/2 d.	Aire	A	(69)
1318	12 d.	Provins	B	(424) p.79
1322.10.15	12 d.	France	O	(228) p.243
1322-1325	12 d.	France	C	(324) p.136
1326.02.02	13 d.	France	O	(228) p.248
1326-1329	12 d.	France	C	(327) p.112

Date	Rate	Place	Type	Reference
1335.05.16-10.05	13 d.	Curia	M	(216) pp.99, 102
1339	10 d.	England	C	(80) 1338-1340, p.370
1346.06.13	12 d.	France	O	(430) I p.248
1381	16 d.	France	C	(160) p.6
1443.10.26	12 d.	France	O	(327) p.116

The Florentine florin in gros tournois of France

In the following rates between the Florentine florin and the gros tournois parts of a gros are expressed in various ways. They were most simply expressed in sterlings (reckoned in northern France and the Low Countries as one third of a gros tournois), in mites (one twenty-fourth) or deniers tournois (variable, see the above list). Apart from the last group, these rates have been reduced to fractions, but the original form of the rate can be easily recognized.

Date	Rate	Place	Type	Reference
1274-1278	9 gr.	Rome	B	(439) pp.122-5
1274-1278	10 gr.	Rome	B	(439) pp.122-5
1280-1290	10 gr.	Rome	B	(193) p.277
1282	9 2/3 gr.	Curia	B	(270) p.897
1282	10 gr.	Curia	B	(439) p.897
1288-1301	10 gr.	Curia	B	(439) p.898
1293	8 3/4 gr.	Piedmont	A	(110) p.488
1300	11.1/2 gr.	Piedmont	A	(110) p.488
1302-1307	12 gr.	Curia	B	(439) p.899
1302	10 gr.	Rome	B	(439) p.122
1312.07.07	13 1/2 gr.	Bruges	B	(426) p.122
1312.07.08	14 gr.	Bruges	B	(426) p.122
1312.11	13 1/2 gr.	Flanders	B	(426) p.123
1314.01.25	13 gr.	Tournai	C	(231) p.335
1314.04.07	12 1/2 gr.	Tournai	C	(231) p.335
1314.06.09	12 gr.	Tournai	C	(231) p.335
1314.07.22	11 gr.	Tournai	C	(231) p.335
1314.12.19	12 gr.	Tournai	C	(231) p.335
1315	12 1/3 gr.	Tournai	C	(231) p.335
1316	13 gr.	Curia	M	(439) p.900
1316.02.02	12 1/2	Tournai	C	(231) p.335
1316.05.15	12 1/2 gr.	Tournai	C	(231) p.335
1317	12 1/2 gr.	Champagne	B	(439) pp.122-5
1317.02.02	12 gr.	Tournai	C	(231) p.336
1317.04.03	12 1/3 gr.	Tournai	C	(231) p.336
1317.05.03	12 1/2 gr.	Tournai	C	(231) p.336
1317-1320	13 gr.	France	O	(228) p.239
1317-1320	13 gr.	Cologne	C	(267) p.38
1318	13 gr.	Avignon	M	(439) pp.122-5
1318.02.02	13 gr.	Tournai	C	(231) p.336
1318.09.01	13 gr. 18 d.tournois	Bern	B	(309) II p.337
1320 until 05	10 1/8 gr.	Tournai	C	(231) p.336
1320.05-12	13 gr.	Tournai	C	(231) p.336
1320.12.29	13 gr.	Venaissin	M	(309) II p.17
1321-1325	13 gr.	Curia	M	(439) p.900
1321-1325	13 1/2 gr.	Curia	M	(439) p.900
1323-1324	13 gr.	Forez	B	(193) p.578
1323	13 1/3 gr.	Flanders	C	(231) p.337
1324	13 1/2 gr.	Tournai	C	(231) p.337
1325	13 gr.	Carpentras	B	(425) p.63
1325	13 gr. 6 d. tournois	Carpentras	B	(425) p.67
1325	13 gr.	Curia	M	(439) p.901
1325.10.18	11 2/5 gr.?	Venice	C	(298) I p.268
1326-1329	13 1/3 gr.	Curia	M	(439) p.901
1327	12 1/3 gr.	Flanders	A	(455) I p.310
1328	13 2/3 gr.	Cambrai	B	(28) p.14
1330	13 1/3 gr.	Cambrai	B	(28) p.67
1331-1334	12 gr.	Curia	M	(439) p.901
1331-1334	12 1/2 gr.	Curia	M	(439) p.901
1335.05.20	12 gr.	Brussels	O	(497) p.34
1335.09.04	12 gr.	Curia	B	(216) p.102
1336-1353	12 gr.	Curia	M	(439) p.902
1342	12 1/2 gr.	Curia	M	(439) p.49

THE FLORENTINE FLORIN IN GROS TOURNOIS OF FRANCE

Date	Rate	Place	Type	Reference
1346	12 1/2 gr.	Piedmont	A	(110) p.497
1347.05.07	10 gr. 5 d. tournois	Curia	B	(347) p.535
1350-1352.11.29	10 gr.	Curia	B	(347) p.454
1353 07.05	10 gr.	Curia	M	(251) p.6
1353	12.1/2 gr.	Piedmont	A	(110) p.498
1358.03.20	12 gr.	Brabant	O	(115) p.21
1359.12.06	9 gr.	Curia	C	(251) p.258
1363.02.10	9 1/3 gr.	Curia	C	(441) p.319
1363.12.23	9 gr.	Curia	C	(441) p.57
1365.02.21	10 1/3 gr.	Curia	C	(441) p.328
1365-1368.10	12 gr.	Toulouse	A	(509) p.322
1366	13 gr.	Piedmont	A	(110) p.499
1366.06.12-1368.01.22	12 1/2 gr.	Orient	A	(49) p.278
1368.10-1371.07	13 gr.	Toulouse	A	(509) p.322
1370.09.06	12 gr.	Curia	C	(441) p.283
1372.07	11 gr.	Toulouse	A	(509) p.322
1375.11	14 gr.	Toulouse	A	(509) p.322
1378	10 gr.	Dijon	A	(29)
1380	13 3/4 gr.	Piedmont	A	(110) p.502
1383.08	13 gr.	Toulouse	A	(509) p.322
1390	14 gr.	Piedmont	A	(110) p.503

The gros tournois in other French currencies

Other French currencies are arranged alphabetically.

The gros tournois in deniers digenois (of Dijon)

Date	Rate	Place	Type	Reference
1380	16 d.	Burgundy	A	(423) p.224

The gros tournois in deniers estevenantes of Besançon

Date	Rate	Place	Type	Reference
1331	15 d.	Besançon	O	(408) p.58
1342	20 d.	Besançon	O	(408) p.58

The gros tournois in non-French currencies

The gros tournois in denari of Florence

Date	Rate	Place	Type	Reference
1297	50 d.	Piedmont	A	(110) p.488

The gros tournois in denari of Lucca

Date	Rate	Place	Type	Reference
1297	49 d.	Piedmont	A	(110) p.488

The gros tournois in denari of Pisa

Date	Rate	Place	Type	Reference
1297	50 d.	Rome	B	(439) p.109

The gros tournois in denari of Siena

Date	Rate	Place	Type	Reference
1279.08	43 d.	Siena	B	(10) p.123

The gros tournois in denari of Cortona

Date	Rate	Place	Type	Reference
1278.03.01	57 d.	Viterbo	C	(108) V p.339

The gros tournois in soldi and denari provisini of Rome

Date	Rate	Place	Type	Reference
1274-1280	2 s.	Rome	B	(226) CXXVIII, 28
1285	2 s. 7 d.	Rome	B	(439) pp.122-125
1286	2 s. 6 d.	Rome	C	(401) p.306

The gros tournois in soldi and denari of Venice

Date	Rate	Place	Type	Reference
1274-1280	2 s.	Rome	B	(226) CXXVIII, 28

The gros tournois in denari of Asti

Date	Rate	Place	Type	Reference
1274-1280	25 d.	Rome	B	(439) p.72

The gros tournois in deniers viennois

Date	Rate	Place	Type	Reference
1274-1280	16 d.	Rome	A	(439) p.128
1336	17 d.	Grenoble	A	(192) p.595
1348	25 d.	Dauphiné	A	(192) p.595
1348	17-20 d.	Dauphiné	A	(192) p.595

The gros tournois in deniers of Lausanne

Date	Rate	Place	Type	Reference
1289	12 d.	Piedmont	A	(110) p.487

The gros tournois in sterlings

Date	Rate	Place	Type	Reference
1291	3 d.	Ypres	M	(145) p.71

The gros tournois in deniers of Artois

Date	Rate	Place	Type	Reference
1286.03.12	10 d.	Ypres	M	(145) p.71

The gros tournois in deniers tournois of Hainault

Date	Rate	Place	Type	Reference
1323.12.22	16 d.	Brabant-Hainault	O	(204) p.74
1326	more than 16 d.	Brabant-Hainault	A	(204) p.74
1326	17 d.	Brabant-Hainault	A	(204) p.78
1326	18 d.	Brabant-Hainault	A	(204) p.78
1329	26 d.	Brabant-Hainault	A	(204) p.78
1329-1330	13 d.	Brabant-Hainault	O	(204) p.78
1335	13 d.	Brabant-Hainault	A	(204) p.80
1335	14 d.	Brabant-Hainault	A	(204) p.80

The gros tournois in schillinge and pfennige of Lübeck

Date	Rate	Place	Type	Reference
1305	9 pf.	Lübeck	H	(462) p.197
1353.09.18 old gros	9 s.	Denmark	L	(346) II no.421

For the mark of Danish pfennige in gros tournois see under DENMARK p.282
For the besant (unspecified) in gros tournois see under BESANT p.295

ÉCUS AND FRANCS

In France, exchange rates were also quoted in terms of gold as well as in moneys of account based on deniers.

The écu

The first French gold coin to be struck in really large quantities was the 'chaise à l'écu', sometimes simply called the 'écu'. This weighted over four and a half grams, and was first issued in 1337 by Philip VI on the eve of war with Edward III.

The gold écu or chaise à l'écu in sous and deniers tournois

Date	Rate	Place	Type	Reference
1337.01.01	20 s.	France	O	(327) p.116
1337.06.21	21 s.	Curia	B	(216) p.120
1337-1339	20 s.	France	C	(127) p.212
1338	20 s.	Cîteaux	A	(264) p.138
1339.05.24	22 s.	Curia	M	(440) p.108
1339-1340	36 s.	Mons	A	(389) II p.144
1340.01.29	40 s.	France	O	(327) p.116
1340.02.02	27 s. 6 d.	Tournai	A	(207) p.117
1340.08	40 s.	Tournai	A	(207) p.117
1340.12.25	41 s.	Tournai	A	(207) p.117
1341	40 s.	Cîteaux	A	(264) p.138
1341.03.18	44 s.	Tournai	A	(207) p.117
1341.04.15	45 s.	Tournai	A	(207) p.117
1341.06.24	47 s. 6 d.	Tournai	A	(207) p.117
1341.09.14	49 s. 6 d.	Tournai	A	(207) p.117
1341.11.11	50 s. 6 d.	Tournai	A	(207) p.117
1342.01.16	52 s.	Tournai	A	(207) p.117
1342.02.13	54 s. 6 d.	Tournai	A	(207) p.117
1342.04.25	56 s. 6 d.	Tournai	A	(207) p.117
1342.07.01	62 s. 6 d.	Tournai	A	(207) p.117
1342	62 s. 6 d.	Cîteaux	A	(264) p.138
1342.10.01	64 s.	Tournai	A	(207) p.117
1342.11.01	64 s. 6 d.	Tournai	A	(207) p.117
1342.12.14	66 s.	Tournai	A	(207) p.117
1343	60 s.	Cîteaux	A	(264) p.138
1343.01.15	68 s.	Tournai	A	(207) p.117
1343.04.10	56 s.	France	O	(183) p.56
1343.04.13	70 s.	Tournai	A	(207) p.117
1343.07.22	72 s.	Tournai	A	(207) p.117
1343.09.14	72 s. 6 d.	Tournai	A	(207) p.117
1343.10.26	16 s. 8 d.	France	O	(327) p.116
1343.12.25	16 s. 8 d.	Tournai	A	(207) p.117
1344.02.02	16 s. 8 d.	Tournai	A	(207) p.117
1344.02.24	16 s. 4 d.	Curia	M	(440) p.240
1344.04.11	16 s. 9 d.	Tournai	A	(207) p.117
1344.06.24	16 s. 10 d.	Tournai	A	(207) p.117
1344.10.29	16 s. 8 d.	Curia	C	(347) p.490
1344.12.25	17 s.	Tournai	A	(207) p.117
1345.06.24	17 s. 6 d.	Tournai	A	(207) p.117
1346.01.30	20 s.	Curia	C	(347) p.528
1346.05.10	16 s.	Curia	C	(347) p.368
1346.06.27	17 s. 6 d.	Curia	C	(347) p.521
1346.07.17	20 s.	France	O	(183) p.56
1346.07.22	17 s. 8 d.	Tournai	A	(207) p.117
1347.02.10	17 s. 10 d.	Curia	C	(347) p.522
1347.05.07	16 s. 8 d.	Curia	C	(347) p.535

THE GOLD ÉCU IN SOUS AND DENIERS TOURNOIS

Date	Rate	Place	Type	Reference
1347.12.04	33 s. 6 d.	Curia	M	(440) p.358
1348.02.28	31 s.	Curia	C	(347) p.403
1348.06.25-1348.06.24	25 s.	Tournai	A	(232) p.190
1349.05.06	25 s.	France	O	(183) p.56
1349.10.19	23 s.	Curia	C	(347) p.430
1350.02.11	32 s.	Curia	C	(347) p.433
1350-1351	19 s. 6 d.	France	C	(452) p.180
1352.09.22	25 s.	France	O	(183) p.56
1352.04.10	23 s.	Montauban	C	(509) p.316
1352.04.15	12 s.	Montauban	C	(509) p.316
1352.05.15	20 s.	Toulouse	C	(509) p.316
1352.06	20 s.	Toulouse	C	(509) p.316
1352.06	34 s.	Toulouse	C	(509) p.316
1352.07.20	20 s.	Montauban	C	(509) p.316
1352.07.25	22 s.	Montauban	C	(509) p.316
1353-1357	27 s.	France	C	(452) p.180
1353.06	40 s.	Toulouse	C	(509) p.316
1353.06.19	40 s.	Montauban	C	(509) p.316
1353.06.24	42 s.	Montauban	C	(509) p.316
1353.08	50 s.	Toulouse	C	(509) p.316
1353.08.24	50 s.	Montauban	C	(509) p.316
1353.09	50 s.	Toulouse	C	(509) p.316
1353.09.14	50 s.	Montauban	C	(509) p.316
1353.12	15 s.	Toulouse	C	(509) p.316
1353.12.20-25	15 s.	Montauban	C	(509) p.316
1354.01	15 s.	Toulouse	C	(509) p.316
1354.02	15 s.	Toulouse	C	(509) p.316
1354.02.04	18 s.	Montauban	C	(509) p.316
1354.03.09	22 s.	Toulouse	C	(509) p.316
1354.04.01-05.30	23 s.	Montauban	C	(509) p.316
1354.06.13	30 s.	Montauban	C	(509) p.316
1354.06.22	32 s.	Toulouse	C	(509) p.316
1354.10.05	44 s.	Toulouse	C	(509) p.316
1354.10.15	42 s.	Montauban	C	(509) p.316
1354.10.21	44 s.	Montauban	C	(509) p.316
1354.12.1 & 4	50 s.	Toulouse	C	(509) p.316
1354.12.07	52 s.	Montauban	C	(509) p.316
1355.01.04	17 s.	Montauban	C	(509) p.316
1355.01.08	12 s. 6 d.	Toulouse	C	(509) p.316
1355.02.15	17 s.	Toulouse	C	(509) p.316
1355.02-03	16 s.	Montauban	C	(509) p.316
1355.05.04	20 s.	Montauban	C	(509) p.316
1355.05.10	20 s.	Toulouse	C	(509) p.316
1355.06.01	21 s.	Montauban	C	(509) p.316
1355.06.05	21 s.	Toulouse	C	(509) p.316
1356.01.10	22 s.	Montauban	C	(509) p.316
1356.01.20	20 s.	Toulouse	C	(509) p.316
1356.02.14	16 s.	Toulouse	C	(509) p.316
1356.07.02	18 s.	Montauban	C	(509) p.316
1356.08.05	18 s.	Montauban	C	(509) p.316
1356.12.12	18 s.	Toulouse	C	(509) p.316
1356.12 écu of Philip VI	37 s. 6 d.	Auxerre	A	(383) p.4
1358	23 s.	France	C	(452) p.180
1359	25 s. 4 d.	S. France	C	(501) p.134
1360	32 s.	S. France	C	(501) p.79
1361.11	30 s.	Curia	C	(251) p.374
1362.08 old écu	29 s.	Curia	C	(251) p.419
1362.08 écu of Philip VI	25 s.	Curia	C	(251) p.419
1368.09.22-1369.06.04	20 s. 6 d.	Venaissin	O	(400) p.179

The écu or chaise à l'écu in sous and deniers parisis

Date	Rate	Place	Type	Reference
1337.01.01	16 s.	France	O	(327) p.116
1340.01.29	32 s.	France	O	(327) p.116
1343	13 s. 4 d.	France	O	(430) p.243
1343.10.26	13 s. 4 d.	France	O	(327) p.116
1346.07.17	16 s.	France	O	(327) p.116

Date	Rate	Place	Type	Reference
1348	16 s.	France	C	(127) p.373
1350.11.11	23 s.	Bruges	C	(212) II p.7

The écu in sous and deniers bretons

Date	Rate	Place	Type	Reference
1369-72	16s.	Brittany	A	(260) ducal household

The franc

The franc was the principal gold coin of France from the 1360s to the 1380s. There were two types of franc. The franc à cheval began to be issued in 1360, when it was a piece of 20 sous tournois or 16 sous parisis. It was a little heavier than the florin at 3.89 grams. It was replaced in 1365 by the slightly lighter franc à pied of 3.82 grams, which went on being issued for 20 years. During this period the silver and billon coinages of France also remained unchanged and the franc therefore retained the official value of a livre tournois. Nevertheless the actual gold franc did vary in value in sous and deniers tournois (see table below). The word franc, however, became an alternative term for the livre tournois, not only when gold francs of a different, higher, value were actually in circulation, but for long after 1385 when gold francs ceased to be struck, and gradually ceased to circulate. In 1419 and 1420, for example, the value of écus was expressed at Troyes in francs and sous (see below p.192) and in the immediately following years an anonymous citizen of Paris was recording prices in his journal in francs (63).

Lane and Mueller will publish bill rates from Venice to Paris from the Datini archive between July 1388 and February 1411 expressed in Venetian grossi per franc (284) II. In the notebook completed by Giovanni da Uzzanno in 1442 information is given for Paris and for Montpellier, the two Italian banking places in France. Uzzanno noted that payments from all places were paid in France in francs at the rate of twenty sous tournois, or sixteen sous parisis to the franc. He noted that exchange between Paris and Montpellier was quoted in terms of francs against francs, normally, naturally, at par, although sometimes slightly different. From either Paris or Montpellier to Avignon exchange was quoted in francs against francs, to Genoa and Florence in francs against florins, to Venice in francs against ducats and to Barcelona in francs against sueldos of Barcelona. From Paris to Bruges it was quoted in terms of francs against Flemish groten at around 38 to 40 groten to the franc, to London in sterlings, at around 37 to 39 to the franc. From Montpellier to Pisa, or from Paris to Lucca exchange was quoted in francs against florins, 'a fiorini'. In addition exchanges from Avignon to Bruges and Barcelona were also quoted in francs. By the time that da Uzzanno completed his notebook some of this information was undoubtedly out of date. A little of it was already incorporated in the notebook compiled at Genoa in 1396 by Saminiato de Ricci (55) who noted, p.101, that exchange from Montpellier and Paris and Bruges was quoted in francs, and from Avignon to Barcelona as well.

The franc in sous and deniers tournois

Date	Rate	Place	Type	Reference
1360 à cheval	20 s.	France	O	(183) p.56
1361.11	22 s. 2 d.	Curia	B	(251) p.374
1364-1365 Charles V franc	20 s.	Besançon	O	(408) p.59
1365.04.22 à pied	20 s.	France	O	(183) p.57
1367-1368	28 s.	France	C	(452) p.181
1370	20 s.	France	C	(302) p.179
1370.12	20 s.	Beaune	A	(384) no.123
1372-1373	34 s.	Florence	C	(452) p.181
1373-1374	36 s.	France	C	(452) p.181
1378.12.28	20 s.	St Chamond	C	(192) p.585
1384	20 s.	Burgundy	A	(199) p.429
1385	20 s.	Lyons	A	(192) p.585
1419.03	22 s. 6 d.	Burgundy	A	(349) p.52
1419.04	23 s. 4 d.	Burgundy	A	(349) p.52
1423.11	20 s.	France	O	(183) p.57

The franc in sous and deniers parisis

Date	Rate	Place	Type	Reference
1360.12.05	16 s.	France	O	Initial Value
1384.07.26	16 s.	France	C	(184) p.137
1387	16 s.	France	C	(161) p.113

These three quotations are all the equivalent of valuing the franc as the livre tournois.

The franc in other French currencies

The franc in sous and deniers estevenantes of Besançon

Date	Rate	Place	Type	Reference
1367	17 s. 6 d.	Besançon	O	(408) p.59

The franc in sous of Metz

Date	Rate	Place	Type	Reference
1364	12 s.	Metz	H	(445) p.259
1384	12 s.	Metz	H	(445) p.259
1394	12 s.	Metz	H	(445) p.259

The franc in sous and deniers narbonnais

Date	Rate	Place	Type	Reference
1382	16 s.	Narbonne	B	(42) p.22
1384	25 s.	Narbonne	B	(42) p.53

Francs and gros

Francs were used as units of account in two different ways. When used with sous and deniers tournois they were synonymous with livres tournois, see above p.191. They were also used with gros. Reckoning in francs and gros was particularly prevalent in those parts of southern France which had earlier been reckoning in florins and gros. Twelve gros had there generally equalled one florin. See above, under Dauphiné, pp.131-2. In the franc — gros accounting system sixteen gros generally equalled the franc, for example at Lyons in 1372 (192) p.594. The last gros tournois were minted in France between 1361 and 1365 and were officially valued at 15 d. tournois, or a sous parisis, which gave the 16:1 relationship. No gros tournois were struck after 1365, but it was only in the late 1360s that the franc — gros accounting system began to supercede the florin — gros system in south-western France. Wolff observed that francs and gros were the predominant means of reckoning in Toulouse from around 1370 to around 1404, although reckoning in florins and gros continued until around 1390 (509) p.324.

In Burgundy, however, where 10 gros were reckoned to the florin (see above p.185), 12 gros were reckoned to the franc, for example in the accounts of the bursar of Citeaux for 1378 (265) and were still so recorded in the quick reference book compiled for the ducal chambre des comptes at Dijon around 1422 (516) f.33r.

See above pp.125-6 for accounting in papal francs and gros at Avignon.

Écus à la couronne and au soleil

After the franc à pied, the principal gold coin in France was another quite different écu, the écu à la couronne, first struck for Charles VI in 1385. It remained the standard gold coin of France until 1475 when Louis XI had it slightly modified to become the écu au soleil which was to last well beyond the end of the middle ages.

The écu à la couronne in sous and deniers tournois

Date	Rate	Place	Type	Reference
1385.03.11	22 s. 6 d.	France	O	(183) p.57
1385.03.11	22 s. 6 d.	Toulouse	O	(509) p.329
1388.02.28	22 s. 6 d.	Toulouse	O	(509) p.329

THE ÉCU À LA COURONNE IN SOUS AND DENIERS TOURNOIS

Date	Rate	Place	Type	Reference
1394	22 s. 6 d.	Forez	A	(192) p.585
1394.07.29	22 s. 6 d.	Toulouse	C	(509) p.329
1399	34 s.	Hainault	A	(453) pp.331-332
1400	28 s.	Hainault	A	(453) pp.331-332
1401	30 s.	Hainault	A	(453) pp.331-332
1401	22 s. 6 d.	Forez	A	(192) p.587
1401	32 s.	Hainault	A	(453) pp.331-332
1402-1412	28 s.	Hainault	A	(453) pp.331-332
1411.11.02	22 s. 6 d.	Toulouse	C	(509) p.330
1413	30 s.	Hainault	A	(453) pp.331-332
1414	26 s.	Hainault	A	(453) pp.331-332
1416.10?	26 s. 8 d.	Toulouse	C	(509) p.330
1418	26 s.	Hainault	A	(453) pp.331-332
1419.03.07	30 s.	France	O	(183) p.57
1419.03.07	50 s.	Toulouse	O	(509) p.329
1419.05	2 francs 5 s.=45 s.	Troyes	C	(395) 1106
1419.08	2 francs 10 s.=50 s.	Troyes	C	(395) 989
1419.10	50 s.	Burgundy	A	(349) 524
1419	60 s.	Troyes	C	(395) 1000
1420.01-03	3 francs 10 s.	Troyes?	C	(395) 1106
1420.07.03	22 s. 6 d.	Dijon	O	(299) p.51
1420.12.19	22 s. 6 d.	France	O	(183) p.57
1422.02.27	23 s. 4 d.	Burgundy	O	(299) p.86
1422.05.21	20 s.	S. France	C	(481) p.444
1423.01 vieux	25 s.	France	O	(183) p.57
1424.08 vieux	25 s.	France	O	(183) p.57
1424.08.23	22 s. 6 d.	Toulouse	O	(509) p.336
1424.09.02	25 s.	Toulouse	O	(509) p.336
1435.09.15 vieux	30 s.	France	O	(183) p.57

Charles VII reformed the coinage on 28 January 1436

Date	Rate	Place	Type	Reference
1436.01.28 neuf	25 s.	France	O	(183) p.57
1448.01	27 s. 6 d.	France	O	(348) p.380
1448.01	29 s. 3 d.	Dieppe	M	(348) p.380
1448.01	30 s.	Rouen	M	(348) p.380
1448.01	30 s. 9 d.	Rouen	M	(348) p.380
1450s	30 s.	Normandy	M	(348) p.380
1462-1463	30 s. 7 1/2 d.	Normandy	M	(348) p.380
1472.11.18	28 s. 1 1/2 d.	Rouen	M	(348) p.381
1473.09.13	28 s. 6 d.	Harfleur	M	(348) p.382
1474.01.04	30 s. 3 d.	France	O	(183) p.57
1477	32 s. 1 d.	France	C	(184) p.183
1488.02	35 s.	France	H	(66) p.254

The écu au soleil in sous and deniers tournois

Date	Rate	Place	Type	Reference
1475.11.02	33 s.	France	O	(183) p.57
1475	33 s.	Pays de Vaud	A	(323) p.241
1487.07	36 s. 3 d.	France	O	(405) p.183
1488.04	36 s. 3 d.	France	O	(405) p.183
1493.08	36 s. 3 d.	France	O	(405) p.183
1494	36 s. 3 d.	Pays de Vaud	A	(323) p.241

The écus à la couronne and au soleil in other French currencies

The écu à la couronne in sous and deniers bretons

Some of these may be Breton écus rather than French

Date	Rate	Place	Type	Reference
1394.08	22 s. 6 d.	Brittany	O	(102) p.45
1405.01	22 s. 6 d.	Brittany	O	(102) p.45
1411-12	22 s. 6 d.	Brittany	O	(102) p.45
1422.07	22 s. 6 d.	Brittany	O	(102) p.45
1423.12	22 s. 6 d.	Brittany	O	(102) p.45

THE ÉCU À LA COURONNE IN SOUS AND DENIERS BRETONS

Date	Rate	Place	Type	Reference
1431-1433 escu de pays de franc	25 s.	Brittany	O	(102) p.45
1434-1436 escu de pays de franc	25 s.	Brittany	O	(102) p.45
1436-1437	25 s.	Brittany	O	(102) p.45
1441	25 s.	Brittany	A	(260)
1444-1445	25 s.	Brittany	O	(102) p.45
1446-1448	25 s.	Brittany	O	(102) p.45
1455-1458	25 s.	Brittany	O	(102) P.45
1456.06.02 neuf	22 s. 11 d.	Brittany	O	(102) p.45
1456.08.29 neuf	23 s. 4 d.	Brittany	O	(102) p.45
1457.03.19-07.12 neuf	23 s. 4 d.	Brittany	O	(102) p.45
1458	23 s. 4 d.	Brittany	O	(102) p.45
1458.06.12 vieux	25 s.	Brittany	O	(102) p.45
1460	23 s. 4 d.	Brittany	O	(102) p.45
1461.05.22 neuf	23 s. 4 d.	Brittany	O	(102) p.45
1463 neuf	22 s. 11 d.	Brittany	O	(102) p.45
1466-1467 neuf	22 s. 11 d.	Brittany	O	(102) p.45
1467.06.21 escu de pays	25 s.	Brittany	O	(102) p.45
1468 neuf	22 s. 11 d.	Brittany	O	(102) p.45
1472	22 s. 11 d.	Brittany	O	(102) p.45
1473 neuf	22 s. 11 d.	Brittany	O	(102) p.45
1476 neuf	22 s. 11 d.	Brittany	O	(102) p.45
1477	22 s. 11 d.	Brittany	O	(102) p.45

The écu au soleil in sous and deniers bretons

Date	Rate	Place	Type	Reference
1488	41s. 8d.	Brittany	O	(260)

The écu au soleil in gros de comte (of the Comtat Venaissin?)

Date	Rate	Place	Type	Reference
1486.07.24	36gr.	Isle-en-Venaissin	A	(277) pp.1130-1
1496.05.18	38gr.	Isle-en-Venaissin	A	(277) pp.1130-1

See also Geneva, pp.134-5 above, for the use of écus at the fairs.

NON-ROYAL CURRENCIES OF FRANCE

Arranged alphabetically

Agen, see Arnaldenses

Angevin (of Anjou), see under TOURNOIS p.180 and ENGLAND p.206

The livre angevin in sous and deniers parisis

Date	Rate	Place	Type	Reference
1202-1203	13 s. 11 d.	Pacy-sur-Eure	A	(307) p.CLXXII

For the gold morabetino in sous of Anjou see under CASTILE p.157

Angoulême, see Poitevin

Aquitaine, see under ENGLAND p.207

Arnaldenses (of Agen) see under TOURNOIS p.180

Artesian (of Artois), separate entry, in LOW COUNTRIES p.213

See also under TOURNOIS p.184, GROS TOURNOIS p.188, and PARISIS p.170

NON-ROYAL CURRENCIES OF FRANCE

Auxerre, see Gien
Around 1188 the livre of Auxerre was reckoned as equal to those of Nevers and Tonerre (39) p.138.

Avignon (papal money), separate entry in ARELATE p.122

Beauvais, see under PARISIS p.171

The livre of Beauvais in sous and deniers parisis

Date	Rate	Place	Type	Reference
1215	22 s. 6 d.	Beauvais	O	(39) p.151

Besançon, see Estevenante

Bigorre, see Chapotensis

Blésois (of Blois), see under TOURNOIS p.180

Bordelais or Burdegals (of Bordeaux), see under TOURNOIS p.180, valosii p.173, and ENGLAND pp.207-8

The Florentine florin in sous and deniers of Bordeaux

Date	Rate	Place	Type	Reference
1306	16 s.	Piedmont	A	(110) p.490
1307	16 s.	Curia	B	(439) p.899
1320	16 s.	Avignon	M	(439) p.82
1332-1333	16 s.	Curia	M	(439) p.901
1334	15 s.	Curia	M	(439) p.901

Bretons (of Brittany), see under TOURNOIS p.180 and under ÉCUS AND FRANCS p.191 and pp.193-4

Caorcin or Caturcensis (of Cahors), see under TOURNOIS p.181

Châlonnais (of Châlons-sur-Marne), see under PROVINOIS p.166

Chapotensis (of Bigorre), see under TOURNOIS p.181 and ENGLAND p.208

Chartres, see under PARISIS p.171

Clermont, see under TOURNOIS p.181
In 1239 the money of Clermont was worth double that of Le Puy (165) p.24.

Comtat Venaissin (papal money), separate entry in ARELATE p.121

Déols, see Gien

Digenois (of Dijon), see under GROS TOURNOIS p.187

The Florentine florin in sous and deniers of Dijon

Date	Rate	Place	Type	Reference
1375.11.11-1376.11.11	15 s.	Dijon	C	(29)
1382.11.01	15 s.	Dijon	A	(29)
1382-1383	15 s.	Dijon	A	(29)

The livre of Dijon in sous and deniers estevenantes of Besançon

Date	Rate	Place	Type	Reference
Louis VIII	circa 31 s. 6 d.	Burgundy	H	(165) p.25

Dreux, see under PARISIS p.171

Estevenante (of Besançon for Franche Comté), see under TOURNOIS p.187, GROS TOURNOIS p.187, and the franc p.192

The Florentine florin in sous and deniers estevenantes of Besançon

Date	Rate	Place	Type	Reference
1345	15 s. 3 d.	Besançon	O	(408) p.57
1345	15 s.	Besançon	O	(408) p.57
1347	16 s.	Besançon	O	(408) p.57

Franche Comté, see Estevenante

Gien

The livre of Gien in sous and deniers parisis

Date	Rate	Place	Type	Reference
1202	13 s. 4 d.	France	H	(165) p.25
1202	circa 12 s. 4 1/2 d.	Bourges	H	(147) pp.575-576
21 sous of Gien were accounted the same as 13 sous parisis				
1220	circa 18 s. 8 d.	Bourges	H	(147) pp.575-576

In 1210 the money of Déols and, in 1215, that of Nevers were reckoned as equal to the money of Gien (165) p.25. Around 1188 the money of Nevers was accounted as equal to the money of Auxerre and of Tonerre (39) p.138

Guingampois, see under ENGLAND p.207

Le Mans, see Mansois

Le Puy, see Clermont

Limoges, see Poitevin

Lyons, see under TOURNOIS p.181

Mansois (of Le Mans, for Maine), see under TOURNOIS p.181 and ENGLAND p.206

Marseille, separate entry in ARELATE p.120

Meaux, see under PROVINOIS p.167 and TOURNOIS p.181

Melgorian (of Melgueil), separate entry in ARELATE p.137

Metz, see under TOURNOIS p.182 and the franc p.192

Nantes, see under TOURNOIS p.182

Narbonne, see under TOURNOIS p.182 and the franc p.192
For the florin of Aragon in sous and deniers of Narbonne see under ARAGON p.152

Nevers, see under Auxerre and Gien

Normandy, see under Roumois p.206

Noyon, see under PARISIS p.171

Perigord, see under TOURNOIS p.182

Poitevin or pictavensis (of Poitou), see under TOURNOIS p.182
The coinages of Poitou, Angoulême and Limoges were all equivalent to each other (165) p.23.

Provence county, see Royaux coronats p.117

Provence marquisate, see Raymondins p.117

Provinois (of Provins), separate entry under CHAMPAGNE FAIRS p.164

Raymondins (of marquisate of Provence), separate entry in ARELATE p.117

Rodan (of Rodez), see under TOURNOIS p.182

Roumois (of Rouen, for Normandy), see under ENGLAND p.206

Royaux coronats (of county of Provence), separate entry in ARELATE p.117

Tonerre, see Auxerre and Gien

Tolza or toulousain (of Toulouse), see under TOURNOIS p.182

The Florentine florin in sous and deniers toulousain

Date	Rate	Place	Type	Reference
1380.10	8 s.	Toulouse	A	(509) p.322

Tournai, see under PARISIS p.171

Troyes, see under PROVINOIS p.167

Vermandois, see under PROVINOIS p.167

Viennois, separate entry in ARELATE p.128

SECTION VII
BRITISH ISLES

ENGLAND

The sterling money of England was one of the most stable in Europe and changed relatively little. In the early thirteenth century the penny sterling was nearly as large a coin as some of the new grossi then being introduced in Italy. As a consequence of the high value of the penny sterling, groats were not permanently introduced in England until the 1340s when they were valued at 4d. They never came to form the basis of a separate money of account. English money is therefore relatively simple to understand. Apart from the pound sterling (240 pence) and the shilling (12 pence), accounts also frequently used the mark sterling (160 pence or 13s. 4d.). As well as exchange rates which were quoted as 'so many sterlings to the florin', other rates were quoted as 'so many florins to the mark'. For the purposes of this listing these have all been converted into the form of sterlings to the florin. The principal English gold coin, a double florin called the noble, was not introduced until 1344, and retained until 1464 the value of 6s. 8d. (one third of a pound, or half a mark).

Since the noble remained stable at the same value for so long a time, sums were sometimes expressed in nobles. These can however easily be turned into pounds, shillings and pence sterling. Although the penny sterling was so heavy a coin, the only submultiples to be minted were half pennies and quarter pennies (farthings). However for accounting purposes mites were also used, reckoned at 24 to the penny, although no such coins were ever minted in England. The term 'mijt' was used in the Low Countries for the smallest coin issued there. The term was presumably borrowed by the English from the Low Countries.

The Florentine florin in shillings, pence and mites sterling
24 mites = 1 penny

Date	Rate	Place	Type	Reference
1277	2 s. 6 d.	Curia	B	(439) p.897
1278	2 s. 6 d.	Rome	B	(439) p.117
1280-1286	2 s. 6 d.	Curia	B	(439) p.897
1280-1286	2 s. 9 d.	Curia	B	(439) p.897
1294-1298	2 s. 10 d.	Curia	B	(439) p.898
1294-1298	2 s. 11 d.	Curia	B	(439) p.898
1301-1302	2 s. 8 d.	England	B	(439) p.117
1301	3 s. 1 d. 12 m.	England	B	(397) p.472
1301	3 s. 4 d.	England	B	(397) p.472
1302	3 s. 4 d.	England	A	(399) 1924 p.163
1302.01.02	3 s. 1 d.	London-Florence	B	(118) no.384
1302.01.05	3 s. 1 d. 22 m.	Florence	C	(118) III p.80
1302	3 s. 4 d.	England	O	(399) p.43
1305.05.08	2 s. 6 d. 11 m.	London	B	(35) I p.6
1305.06.07	2 s. 11 d. 12 m.	London	B	(35) I p.10
1305.06.18	2 s. 7 d. 5 m.	Genoa	B	(154) IV p.931
1305.07.02	2 s. 8 d.	London	B	(35) I p.12
1305.10.19	3 s. 4 d.	London	B	(35) I p.266
1306,1308	2 s. 8 d.	England	O	(399) p.43
1307	2 s. 10 d.	England	C	(413) I p.177
1307	2 s. 11 d. 12 m.	Paris	B	(309) I p.251
1308-1312	3 s. 3 d.	Curia	B	(439) p.899
1309	3 s. 4 d.	Rome	B	(309) II p.306
1310	3 s. 3 d.	Curia	B	(439) p.899
1310-1311	3 s. 3 d.	London-Curia	B	(397) p.476
1311.02.27	2 s. 8 d.	Dublin	B	(226) CXLIV p.47
1311.11.23	2 s. 8 d.	Armagh	B	(226) CXLIV p.14
1312.02.22	3 s. 5 d.	London-Florence	B	(118) no.622
1313.10.28-1317	3 s. 1 d. 12 m.	Curia	A	(486) p.218
1313	4 s.	London	L	(397) p.476
1314	3 s. 1 d.	London and Paris	C	(397) p.476
1316.07.15	3 s. 4 d.	England	B	(309) II p.70
1317	2 s. 8 d.	England	B	(439) p.117
1317	3 s. 5 d.	England	A	(397) p.476
1318.01.12	3 s. 3 d. 10 m.	York	B	(311) p.28
1318	3 s. 3 d.	Curia	B	(439) p.900
1318	3 s. 4 d.	Curia	B	(439) p.900
1319	3 s. 3 d.	Curia	B	(439) p.900

Florentine florins in english shillings and pence sterling 1277–1500

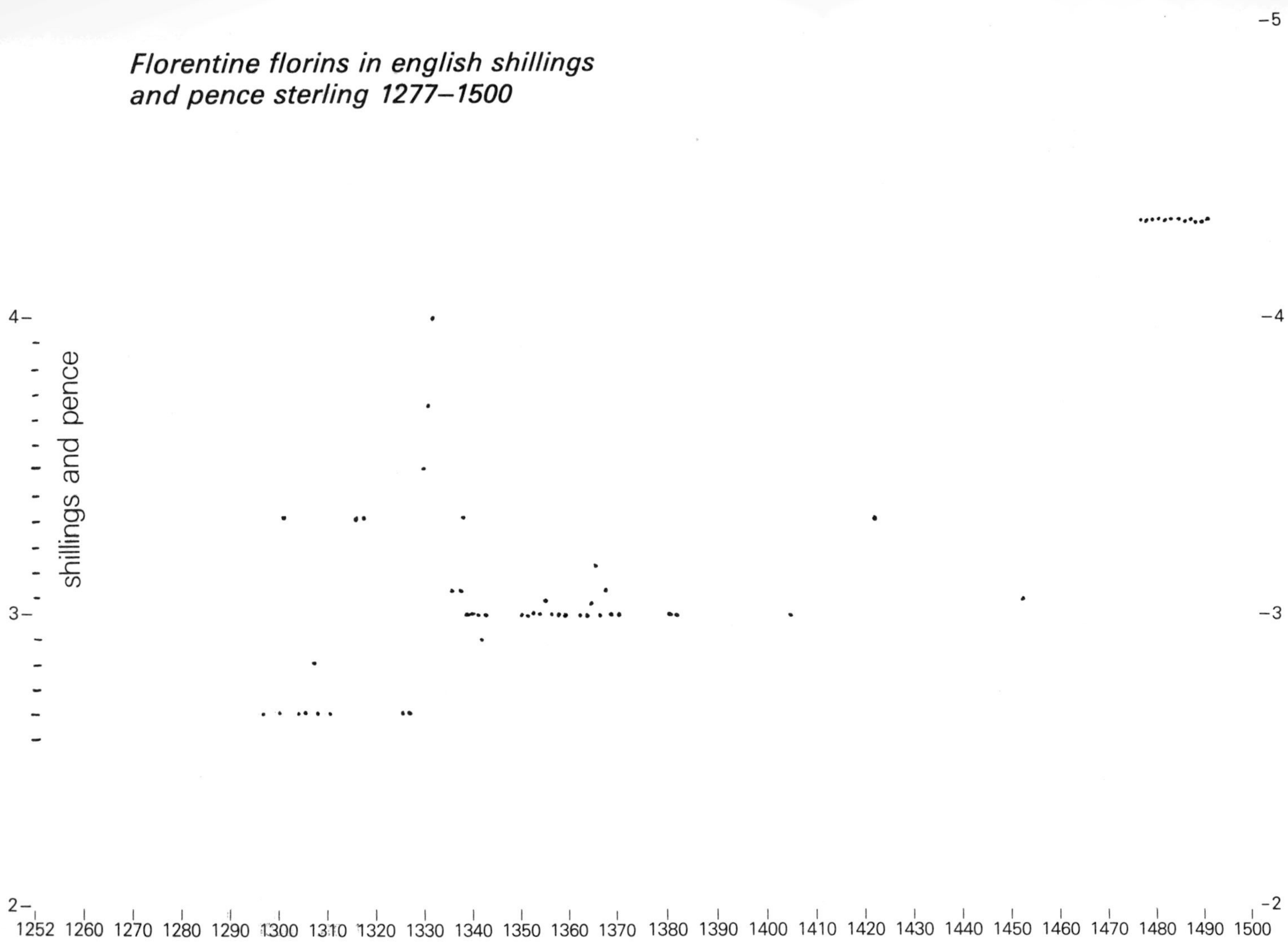

shillings and pence

2 3 4 5

1252 1260 1270 1280 1290 1300 1310 1320 1330 1340 1350 1360 1370 1380 1390 1400 1410 1420 1430 1440 1450 1460 1470 1480 1490 1500

Date	Rate	Place	Type	Reference
1319	3 s. 4 d. 12 m.	Curia	B	(439) p.900
1319.04.08	3 s. 5 d.	Curia	B	(397) p.476
1320	3 s. 3 d.	Curia	B	(439) p.900
1321-1333	3 s. 4 d.	Avignon	B	(439) p.117
1323	3 s. 5 d.	Avignon	B	(439) p.117
1324	3 s. 4 d.	Bordeaux	C	(397) p.476
1324.06	3 s. 2 d.	London	L	(397) p.476
1324.10	3 s. 3 d. 12 m.	London	L	(397) p.476
1324.10	3 s. 4 d.	London	L	(397) p.476
1325	3 s. 5 d. 12 m.	Curia	B	(397) p.476
1326	2 s. 8 d.	St Albans	B	(309) II p.258
1327	2 s. 8 d.	England	A	(399) p.163
1327.12.09	2 s. 8 d.	Exeter	B	(309) II p.262
1329	3 s. 5 d. 12 m.	Avignon	B	(439) p.117
1330	3 s. 6 d.	England	O	(399) p.42
1331	3 s. 8 d. 12 m.	London	C	(413) I p.177
1331	3 s. 4 d.	London-Curia	B	(397) p.477
1332	4 s.	England	C	(399) p.42
1332	3 s. 2 d.	London-Curia	B	(397) p.477
1333	3 s. 2 d.	Avignon	B	(439) p.117
1333	3 s. 2 d.	London-Curia	B	(397) p.477
1334	3 s. 2 d.	London-Curia	B	(397) p.477
1335.09.15	3 s. 4 d.	Curia	B	(216) p.15
1336	2 s. 11 d. 12 m.	London-Curia	B	(397) p.477
1336.04.04	3 s. 1 d.	England	B	(311) p.65
1336.04.15-1336.05.15	3 s. 1 d.	England	B	(311) p.65
1336.12.08-1337.03.19	2 s. 11 d. 12 m.	England	B	(311) p.65
1337	3 s.	England	C	(399) p.43
1337	3 s. 3 d.	London-Curia	B	(397) p.477
1337	3 s. 4 d.	London-Curia	B	(397) p.477
1337	3 s. 7 d.	Curia	A	(397) p.477
1338	3 s. 7 d.	Curia	A	(397) p.477
1338	3 s. 4 d.	London-Curia	B	(397) p.477
1338.04.00	3 s. 3 d.	England	B	(311) p.65
1338.08.09	3 s. 4 d.	England	B	(311) p.65
1338.11.22	4 s.	England	C	(79) 1337-1339 p.571
1339	3 s.	London-Curia	B	(397) p.477
1339.07.12	3 s.	England	C	(79) 1339-1341 p.198
1340	3 s. 2 d.	London-Curia	B	(397) p.477
1340.03.08	3 s. 2 d.	England	B	(311) p.66
1340.08.25	3 s.	England	C	(79) 1339-1341 p.622
1340.10.06-1341.10.06	3 s.	England	C	(79) 1339-1341 p.540
1341	3 s. 2 d.	London-Curia	B	(397) p.477
1342	3 s. 2 d.	Curia	B	(397) p.477
1342.03.01	2 s. 11 d.	England-Curia	B	(311) p.67
1342.04.18	2 s. 9 d.	England-Curia	B	(311) p.66
1343.07.02	3 s.	England	C	(79) 1343-1346 p.158
1344	2 s. 9 d.	London-Curia	B	(397) p.477
1344.06.20	2 s. 9 d.	Curia	B	(347) p.488
1345.04.03	2 s. 8 d. 12 m.	Curia	B	(347) p.504
1346.06.02-1348.12.11	2 s. 8 d.	Curia	B	(347) p.519
1350.06.12-1354.09.27	3 s. 12 m.	England	B	(311) p.91
1355.02.14	3 s.	Curia	B	(252) p.102
1355.06.05	3 s. 12 m.	England	B	(311) p.91
1355.09.25	3 s. 5 d.	Curia	B	(252) p.126
1356.01.02	3 s. 1 d.	England	B	(311) p.92
1356.01.10-1357.05.11	3 s.	England	B	(311) p.91
1357.07.03	2 s. 11 d.	England	B	(311) p.92
1358.02.12	3 s. 2 d.	England	B	(311) p.220
1358.11.15-1359.10.25	3 s.	England	B	(311) p.92
1359	2 s. 10 d.	England	C	(159) p.195
1360	3 s. 1 d.	Avignon	B	(439) p.117
1360	3 s.	Curia	B	(440) p.769
1362.03.00	3 s.	England	B	(311) p.141
1362.03.00	2 s. 11 d.	Curia	B	(252) p.395
1362	3 s.	England	C	(399) p.43
1363.04.18-1363.12.09	3 s.	England	B	(311) p.141

THE FLORENTINE FLORIN IN STERLING

Date	Rate	Place	Type	Reference
1363	3 s. 1 d. 6 m.	London	C	(413) I p.136
1364.04.22	3 s. 12 m.	England	B	(311) p.184
1364	3 s. 1 d.	Dublin	B	(311) p.214
1365.02.03	3 s. 2 d.	England	B	(311) p.225
1366.07.09	3 s.	England	B	(311) p.226
1367.07.03	3 s. 1 d.	England	B	(311) p.265
1368.02.18	3 s.	England	B	(311) p.266
1370.01.24	3 s. 18 m.	England	B	(311) p.322
1370	3 s.	England	C	(399) p.43
1376	3 s.	Avignon	B	(343) p.155
1380.10.13-1382.02.21	3 s.	London	C	(79) 1377-1381 p.476
1394.11.12	2 s. 10 d. 18 m.	Genoa	B	(297) II p.771
1405.03.19	3 s.	London	B	(77) I p.272

Easter 1412 English silver coinage reduced in weight by one-sixth.

Date	Rate	Place	Type	Reference
1422	3 s. 4 d.	England	B	(350) p.167
1453.10.04	3 s. 16 m.	London	B	(137) p.122
1476-1489	4 s. 4 d.	England	B	(350) p.167
1494	4 s. 5 d.	England	B	(350) p.167
1500	4 s. 7 d.	England	O	(361) p.339

For the genovino of 25 soldi in pence and mites sterling see under GENOA p.115

<u>he Venetian ducat in shillings, pence and mites sterling of England</u>
24 mites = 1 penny

Lane and Mueller will publish bill rates from Venice to London from April 1399 to January 1411 from the Datini archive (284) II.

ate	Rate	Place	Type	Reference
409.10.23	2 s. 6 d. 12 m.	London-Venice	B	(78) IV no.986
410.06.04	2 s. 6 d.	London-Sicily	B	(78) IV no.985
410.06.04	2 s. 5 d.	London-Sicily	B	(78) IV no.985
410.06.07	2 s. 5 d.	Venice	M	(78) IV no.988
410.06.07	2 s. 6 d. 12 m.	Venice	M	(78) IV no.988

Easter 1412 English silver coinage reduced in weight by one-sixth.

Date	Rate	Place	Type	Reference
436.03.11-20	3 s. 5 d. 8 m.	Venice	B	(38) p.378
436.03.11-20	3 s. 5 d. 12 m.	Venice	B	(38) p.378
436.04.01-10	3 s. 4 d.	Venice	B	(38) p.378
436.04.10-20	3 s. 8 d. 12 m.	London	B	(38) p.377
436.04.11-20	3 s. 4 d. 10 m.	Venice	B	(38) p.378
436.04.11-20	3 s. 5 d. 12 m.	Venice	B	(38) p.378
436.04.11-20	3 s. 3 d.	Venice	B	(38) p.378
36.05.11-1436.06.10	3 s. 3 d.	Venice	B	(38) p.378
36.08.01-10	3 s. 2 d. 16 m.	Venice	B	(38) p.379
36.08.11-1436.09.10	3 s. 3 d.	Venice	B	(38) p.379
36.09.01-10	3 s. 7 d.	London	B	(38) p.377
36.09.21-30	3 s. 8 d.	London	B	(38) p.377
36.09.21-30	3 s. 3 d.	Venice	B	(38) p.379
36.09.21-30	3 s. 3 d. 8 m.	Venice	B	(38) p.379
36.10.21-31	3 s. 4 d. 6 m.	Venice	B	(38) p.379
36.11.21-30	3 s. 4 d.	Venice	B	(38) p.379
36.12.11-20	3 s. 3 d. 12 m.	Venice	B	(38) p.379
36.12.21-31	3 s. 3 d.	Venice	B	(38) p.379
37.01.21-1437.03.31	3 s. 4 d.	Venice	B	(38) p.379
37.03.21-31	3 s. 6 d. 12 m.	London	B	(38) p.377
37.06.01-10	3 s. 6 d. 12 m.	London	B	(38) p.377
37.06.01-10	3 s. 6 d. 6 m.	London	B	(38) p.377
37.07.21-31	3 s. 7 d. 12 m.	London	B	(38) p.377
37.08.11-21	3 s. 7 d. 12 m.	London	B	(38) p.378
37.08.21-31	3 s. 6 d. 8 m.	Venice	B	(38) p.379
37.08.21-31	3 s. 6 d. 12 m.	Venice	B	(38) p.379
37.09.21-30	3 s. 6 d.	Venice	B	(38) p.379
37.10.11-20	3 s. 6 d. 14 m.	Venice	B	(38) p.379
37.11.11-20	3 s. 8 d. 6 m.	London	B	(38) p.378
37.11.11-20	3 s. 6 d.	Venice	B	(38) p.379
7.11.21-30?	3 s. 8 d. 16 m.	London	B	(38) p.378

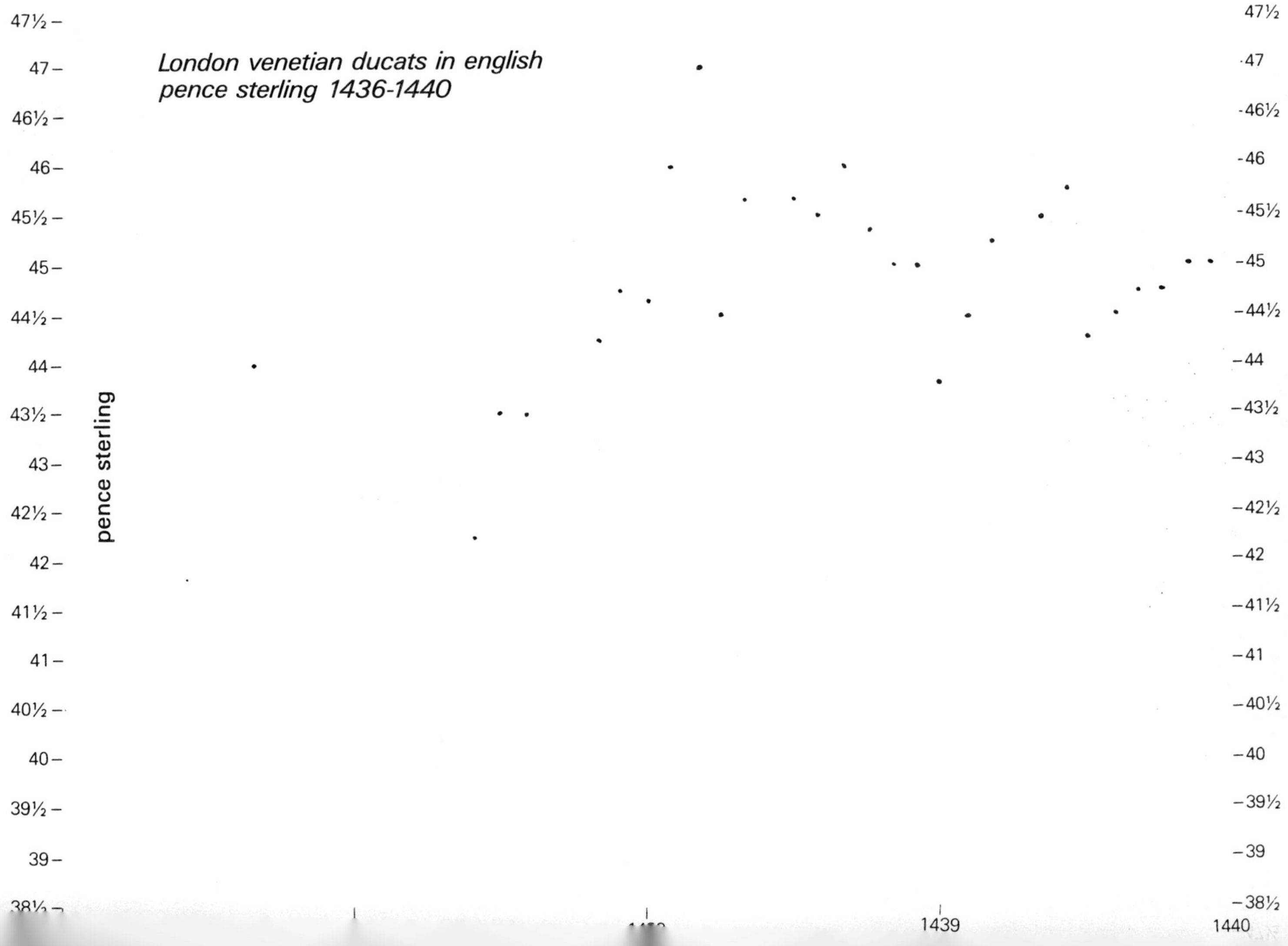

London venetian ducats in english pence sterling 1436-1440

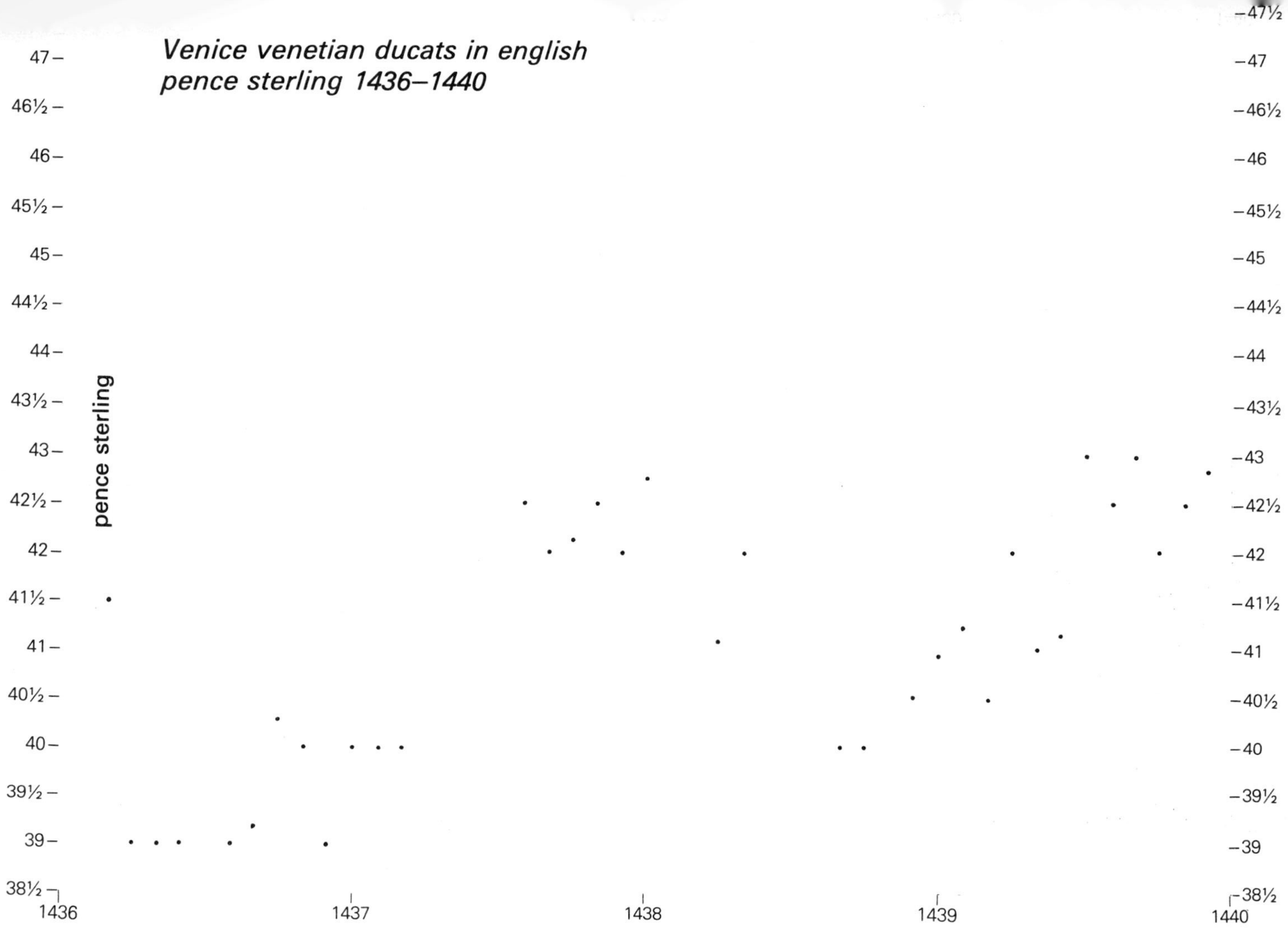

Venice venetian ducats in english pence sterling 1436–1440

Date	Rate	Place	Type	Reference
1437.11.21-30	3 s. 6 d.	Venice	B	(38) p.379
1437.11.21-30	3 s. 6 d. 12 m.	Venice	B	(38) p.379
1437.12.01-10	3 s. 8 d. 16 m.	London	B	(38) p.378
1437.12.11-20	3 s. 8 d. 18 m.	London	B	(38) p.378
1437.12.11-20	3 s. 6 d. 6 m.	Venice	B	(38) p.379
1437.12.11-20	3 s. 6 d. 18 m.	Venice	B	(38) p.379
1437.12.21-31	3 s. 6 d.	Venice	B	(38) p.379
1438.01.01-20	3 s. 8 d. 16 m.	London	B	(38) p.378
1438.01.01-10	3 s. 6 d. 16 m.	Venice	B	(38) p.379
1438.01.01-10	3 s. 7 d.	Venice	B	(38) p.379
1438.01.11-20	3 s. 6 d. 8 m.	Venice	B	(38) p.379
1438.01.21-31	3 s. 8 d. 18 m.	London	B	(38) p.378
1438.01.21-31	3 s. 6 d. 18 m.	Venice	B	(38) p.379
1438.02.11-20	3 s. 9 d.	London	B	(38) p.378
1438.02.21-28	3 s. 10 d.	London	B	(38) p.378
1438.03.01-10	3 s. 9 d. 8 m.	London	B	(38) p.378
1438.03.11-20	3 s. 11 d.	London	B	(38) p.378
1438.04.01-10	3 s. 10 d.	London	B	(38) p.378
1438.04.01-10	3 s. 10 d. 8 m.	London	B	(38) p.378
1438.04.01-10	3 s. 11 d.	London	B	(38) p.378
1438.04.01-10	3 s. 6 d. 12 m.	Venice	B	(38) p.379
1438.04.11-20	3 s. 8 d. 12 m.	London	B	(38) p.378
1438.04.11-20	3 s. 6 d. 12 m.	Venice	B	(38) p.379
1438.04.21-30	3 s. 5 d. 2 m.	Venice	B	(38) p.379
1438.05.01-10	3 s. 9 d. 21 m.	London	B	(38) p.378
1438.05.11-20	3 s. 9 d.	London	B	(38) p.378
1438.05.11-20	3 s. 10 d.	London	B	(38) p.378
1438.05.21-31	3 s. 8 d. 18 m.	London	B	(38) p.378
1438.05.21-31	3 s. 9 d.	London	B	(38) p.378
1438.05.21-31	3 s. 9 d. 16 m.	London	B	(38) p.378
1438.05.21-31	3 s. 6 d.	Venice	B	(38) p.379
1438.07.01-10	3 s. 9 d. 12 m.	London	B	(38) p.378
1438.07.01-10	3 s. 9 d. 16 m.	London	B	(38) p.378
1438.08.01-10	3 s. 9 d. 12 m.	London	B	(38) p.378
1438.09.01-10	3 s. 10 d.	London	B	(38) p.378
1438.09.01-1438.10.20	3 s. 4 d.	Venice	B	(38) p.379
1438.09.01-1438.10.20	3 s. 4 d. 18 m.	Venice	B	(38) p.379
1438.10.11-20	3 s. 9 d. 8 m.	London	B	(38) p.378
1438.11.01-20	3 s. 9 d.	London	B	(38) p.378
1438.11.11-20	3 s. 8 d. 6 m.	London	B	(38) p.378
1438.11.21-30	3 s. 9 d.	London	B	(38) p.378
1438.12.01-10	3 s. 8 d. 21 m.	London	B	(38) p.378
1438.12.01-10	3 s. 5 d. 8 m.	Venice	B	(38) p.379
1438.12.11-20	3 s. 4 d. 6 m.	Venice	B	(38) p.379
1438.12.21-31	3 s. 4 d. 12 m.	Venice	B	(38) p.379
1439.01.01-10	3 s. 8 d. 3 m.	London	B	(38) p.378
1439.01.11-20	3 s. 7 d. 20 m.	London	B	(38) p.378
1439.01.11-20	3 s. 7 d. 14 m.	London	B	(38) p.378
1439.01.11-20	3 s. 4 d. 21 m.	Venice	B	(38) p.379
1439.01.21-31	3 s. 7 d. 16 m.	London	B	(38) p.378
1439.02.01-10	3 s. 7 d. 16 m.	London	B	(38) p.378
1439.02.01-10	3 s. 5 d. 8 m.	Venice	B	(38) p.379
1439.02.01-10	3 s. 5 d. 6 m.	Venice	B	(38) p.379
1439.02.21-28	3 s. 8 d. 4 m.	London	B	(38) p.378
1439.02.21-28	3 s. 8 d. 12 m.	London	B	(38) p.378
1439.03.01-10	3 s. 8 d. 12 m.	London	B	(38) p.378
1439.03.01-10	3 s. 9 d.	London	B	(38) p.378
1439.03.01-10	3 s. 4 d. 8 m.	Venice	B	(38) p.379
1439.03.01-10	3 s. 4 d. 6 m.	Venice	B	(38) p.379
1439.03.11-20	3 s. 9 d. 6 m.	London	B	(38) p.378
1439.03.11-20	3 s. 4 d.	Venice	B	(38) p.379
1439.03.21-31	3 s. 4 d. 12 m.	Venice	B	(38) p.379
1439.04.01-10	3 s. 10 d. 12 m.	London	B	(38) p.378
1439.04.01-10	3 s. 10 d. 16 m.	London	B	(38) p.378
1439.04.21-31	3 s. 6 d.	Venice	B	(38) p.379
1439.05.01-10	3 s. 9 d. 16 m.	London	B	(38) p.378
1439.05.01-10	3 s. 5 d. 18 m.	Venice	B	(38) p.379
1439.05.11-20	3 s. 9 d. 18 m.	London	B	(38) p.378
1439.05.11-20	3 s. 9 d. 12 m.	London	B	(38) p.378
1439.05.11-20	3 s. 5 d.	Venice	B	(38) p.379
1439.06.01-10	3 s. 8 d. 12 m.	London	B	(38) p.378
1439.06.01-10	3 s. 8 d.	London	B	(38) p.378

THE VENETIAN DUCAT IN STERLING

Date	Rate	Place	Type	Reference
1439.06.11-20	3 s. 8 d. 6 m.	London	B	(38) p.378
1439.06.11-20	3 s. 9 d. 18 m.	London	B	(38) p.378
1439.06.11-20	3 s. 5 d. 8 m.	Venice	B	(38) p.379
1439.06.11-20	3 s. 6 d. 3 m.	Venice	B	(38) p.379
1439.06.21-30	3 s. 5 d. ?? m.	Venice	B	(38) p.379
1439.07.01-10	3 s. 6 d.	Venice	B	(38) p.379
1439.07.01-10	3 s. 7 d.	Venice	B	(38) p.379
1439.07.11-20	3 s. 8 d. 6 m.	London	B	(38) p.378
1439.07.11-20	3 s. 7 d.	Venice	B	(38) p.379
1439.07.21-1439.09.20	3 s. 8 d. 12 m.	London	B	(38) p.378
1439.08.01-10	3 s. 7 d.	Venice	B	(38) p.379
1439.08.01-10	3 s. 6 d.	Venice	B	(38) p.379
1439.08.21-1439.09.10	3 s. 6 d. 12 m.	Venice	B	(38) p.379
1439.09.11-20	3 s. 7 d.	Venice	B	(38) p.379
1439.09.21-30	3 s. 8 d. 12 m.	London	B	(38) p.378
1439.09.21-30	3 s. 8 d. 18 m.	London	B	(38) p.378
1439.09.21-1439.10.10	3 s. 7 d.	Venice	B	(38) p.379
1439.09.21-1439.10.10	3 s. 6 d.	Venice	B	(38) p.379
1439.10.01-10	3 s. 9 d. 6 m.	London	B	(38) p.378
1439.10.11-20	3 s. 8 d. 18 m.	London	B	(38) p.378
1439.10.11-20	3 s. 6 d. 18 m.	Venice	B	(38) p.379
1439.10.11-20	3 s. 6 d. 21 m.	Venice	B	(38) p.379
1439.10.21-31	3 s. 6 d. 16 m.	Venice	B	(38) p.379
1439.10.21-31	3 s. 6 d.	Venice	B	(38) p.379
1439.11.11-20	3 s. 9 d.	London	B	(38) p.378
1439.11.11-1439.12.20	3 s. 6 d. 12 m.	Venice	B	(38) p.379
1439.12.01-10	3 s. 9 d.	London	B	(38) p.378
1439.12.01-10	3 s. 9 d. 6 m.	London	B	(38) p.378
1439.12.11-20	3 s. 9 d.	London	B	(38) p.378
1439.12.21-31	3 s. 6 d. 12 m.	Venice	B	(38) p.379
1439.12.21-31	3 s. 6 d. 16 m.	Venice	B	(38) p.379
1444.08.11	3 s. 9 d.	Venice	B	(137) p.117
1444.11.24	3 s. 8 d.	London	B	(81) p.62
1444	3 s. 10 d.	London	C	(190) p.130
1444	3 s. 9 d.	London	B	(81) p.73
450.02.01	3 s. 9 d. 12 m.	Venice	B	(137) p.117
450.05.04	3 s. 7 d.	London	B	(81) p.73
453.09.04	3 s. 8 d. 6 m.	London	C	(78) I p.78
453.10.04	3 s. 4 d. 16 m.	London	B	(137) p.122
454.10.02	3 s. 9 d.	London	C	(78) I p.79
458.02.14	3 s. 8 d.	London	B	(81) p.85
458.11.06	3 s. 11 d. 6 m.	Venice	B	(137) p.117
459.02.07	3 s. 8 d.	London	B	(137) p.117
460.01.11	3 s. 11 d.	London	C	(78) I p.88
460.05.19	3 s. 11 d.	Venice	B	(137) p.117
460.09.30	3 s. 7 d.	London	B	(81) p.94
460.11.08	3 s. 11 d.	Venice	B	(137) p.117
461.02.09	3 s. 7 d. 18 m.	London	B	(137) p.117
461.03.20	3 s. 11 d.	London	B	(81) p.98
461.04.13	3 s. 6 d. 8 m.	London	B	(81) p.99
461.05.15	3 s. 10 d. 2 m.	Venice	B	(137) p.117
461.06.08	3 s. 10 d. 18 m.	Venice	B	(137) p.117
461.08.19	3 s. 7 d. 12 m.	London	B	(81) p.101
462.09.09	3 s. 7 d. 18 m.	London	B	(137) p.117
462.02.04	3 s. 8 d. 6 m.	London	B	(81) p.103
462.12.03	3 s. 10 d. 8 m.	Venice	B	(137) p.117
463.01.11	3 s. 5 d. 8 m.	London	C	(78) I p.113
463.01.11	3 s. 11 d.	Venice	C	(78) I p.113
463.03.04	3 s. 7 d.	London	B	(137) p.117
463.04.04	3 s. 11 d.	London	B	(81) p.114
463.04.04	3 s. 7 d.	London	B	(81) p.114
463.07.20	3 s. 11 d.	Venice	B	(137) p.117
463.10.22	3 s. 8 d.	London	B	(81) p.119
465.03.16	3 s. 9 d. 12 m.	Venice	M	(78) IV no.990
466.04.29	4 s. 2 d.	London	C	(78) I p.116
466.07.29	3 s. 10 d. 12 m.	London	C	(78) I p.116
468.09.05	4 s. 1 d.	London	C	(78) I p.122
469.06.27	4 s. 1 d. 18 m.	London	C	(78) I p.123
471.04.09	4 s. 2 d.	London	C	(78) I p.126
471.10.21	4 s. 2 d. 18 m.	London	C	(78) I p.130
473.08.11	4 s. 2 d.	London	C	(78) I p.131
473.12.11	4 s. 7 d.	Venice	B	(78) IV no.991

Date	Rate	Place	Type	Reference
1474.03.12	4 s. 2 d.	Venice	M	(78) IV no.991
1475.10.23	4 s. 3 d. 12 m.	London	C	(78) I p.134
1476.05.29	4 s. 3 d. 12 m.	London	C	(78) I p.137
1476.05.31	4 s. 8 d.	London	C	(78) I p.137
1477.04.02	4 s. 4 d. 12 m.	London	C	(78) I p.137
1477.10.22	4 s. 9 d.	Venice	B	(160) IV no.992
1478.01.23	4 s. 12 m.	London	M	(78) IV no.992
1481.07.31	4 s. 3 d. 18 m.	London	C	(78) I p.143
1497.12.18	4 s. 4 d.	London	C	(78) I p.340

English sterling money in related currencies

For Scottish currency, see below pp.211-2

Ireland

The pound sterling in shillings and pence of Ireland

Until 1460 Irish money was equivalent to English. After that date they diverged quite considerably.

Date	Rate	Place	Type	Reference
1467	40 s.	Dublin	O	(156) p.53
early 16th century	30 s.	Ireland	C	(156) p.56

Principalities in France whose rulers were also kings of England

Normandy

Since the kings of England were dukes of Normandy from 1066 to 1204 there was a need to evaluate sterling in Norman money. The money of Rouen was the key money of Normandy.

The pound sterling in sous and deniers roumois (of Rouen)

Date	Rate	Place	Type	Reference
1144-1151	40 s.	England?	?	(164) p.99
circa 1151	40 s.	Dieppe	?	(164) p.97

Early in the twelfth century the money of Rouen was interchangeable with that of Anjou (39) p.24. It was still so between 1159 and 1201 (164) p.98.

The livre of Rouen in sous mansois (of Maine)

Date	Rate	Place	Type	Reference
1106	10 s.	Préaux	?	(164) p.99

Angevin lands

Since the kings of England from Henry II to John were also counts of Anjou, Maine, and Touraine and overlords of Brittany as well as dukes of Normandy there was also a need to value sterling in the currencies used there.

The pound sterling in sous and deniers angevins (of Anjou)

Date	Rate	Place	Type	Reference
1186	81 s.	England	A	(164) p.99
1202.09.29-1203.09.29	80 s.	England	A	(391) p.21

See above, under Normandy and see also under TOURNOIS p.180 and PARISIS p.194
For the gold morabetino in sous of Anjou see under CASTILE p.157

The pound sterling in sous and deniers guingampois (of Guingamp in the county of Penthièvre in Brittany)

Date	Rate	Place	Type	Reference
1204	80 s.	France	H	(165) p.23

The pound sterling in sous and deniers mansois (of Maine)

Date	Rate	Place	Type	Reference
1204	40 s.	France	H	(165) p.23

See also above, under Normandy, p.206 and under TOURNOIS p.181

The pound sterling in sous and deniers of Tours

Date	Rate	Place	Type	Reference
1200	80 s.	Normandy	H	(165) p.23

(See below p.209 for Tournois after 1204)

Aquitaine

Since the kings of England were also dukes of Aquitaine (Guyenne and Gascony) from the twelfth century to the fifteenth, there was frequently a need to value sterling in the currencies used there.

The pound sterling in sous and deniers bordelais or burdegalensis (of Bordeaux)

Date	Rate	Place	Type	Reference
1236	80 s.	England	C	(399) p.41
1243	90 s.	England	C	(399) p.41
1318	120 s.	England	C	(399) p.42
1327.03.27-1331.07.22	160 s.	Bordeaux	A	(88) p.140

On 22 July 1330 a bordelais nouveau replaced the existing denier bordelais, but the new denier itself declined over the following years.

Date	Rate	Place	Type	Reference
1336-1337	120 s.	St Macaire	A	(406) p.81
1338-1338	160 s.	St Macaire	A	(406) p.81
1338-1339	240 s.	St Macaire	A	(406) p.81
1339-1340	240 s.	St Macaire	A	(406) p.81
1340-1341	300 s.	St Macaire	A	(406) p.81
1341-1342	400 s.	St Macaire	A	(406) p.81
1342-1343	400 s.	St Macaire	A	(406) p.81

In 1348 another new bordelais replaced the existing denier and accounts distinguish between monnaie petite or parvus, and bonne monnaie.

Date	Rate	Place	Type	Reference
1348	480 s. petite	Bordeaux	A	(88) p.143
1348	560 s. petite	Bordeaux	A	(88) p.143
1348.08	100 s.	Gascony	O	(406) p.102
1355.09	100 s.	Gascony	O	(406) p.102
1353	100 s.	Bordeaux	O	(85) p.398
1354-1355	100 s.	Aquitaine	A	(86) p.118
1355-1361	100 s. bonne	Bordeaux	A	(88) P.144
1356.07	67 s. 8 d.	Gascony	O	(406) p.102
1357	100 s.	Gascony	O	(406) p.102
1361.10	100 s.	Gascony	O	(406) p.102

A sterling guyennois was issued from November 1361 to at least 1390, at a value of 5d. bordelais. When first issued it was officially worth as much as the English sterling (88) pp.146-52.

Date	Rate	Place	Type	Reference
1361-1378	100 s.	Bordeaux (archbishop)	A	(88) p.144
1368.05.01	100 s.	Bordeaux	O	(84) p.472
1401-1413	150 s.	London	A	(493)
1413-1418	200 s.	London	A	(493)
1417	100 s.	England	C	(399) p.42
1418-1419	200 s.	London	A	(493)
1419-1423	200 s.	London	A	(493)

THE POUND STERLING IN SOUS AND DENIERS OF BORDEAUX

Date	Rate	Place	Type	Reference
1423-1427	200 s.	London	A	(493)
1427-1431	200 s.	London	A	(493)
1431-1435	200 s.	London	A	(493)
1435-1439	200 s.	London	A	(493)
1442-1446	255 s.	London	A	(493)
1446-1451	255 s.	London	A	(493)
1452-1453	255 s.	London	A	(493)

For the Florentine florin in sous and deniers of Bordeaux see under NON-ROYAL FRENCH CURRENCIES p.195
See also under TOURNOIS p.180 and valosii p.173

The pound sterling in livres and sous chapotensis (of Bigorre)

Date	Rate	Place	Type	Reference
1290	5 li. 10 s.	Bordeaux	A	(485) II p.7
1310	8 li.	Bordeaux	A	(162)
1312	8 li.	Bordeaux	A	(485) II p.7
1313.10.28-1317	5 li.	Curia?	A	(69)

English sterling money in other currencies before 1300

The pound sterling in soldi and denari of Lucca

Date	Rate	Place	Type	Reference
1230.1.26	180 s. 5 d.	Lucca	A	(48)

The pound sterling in soldi and denari provisini of Rome

Date	Rate	Place	Type	Reference
1285 old sterlings	160 s.	Rome	C	(401) p.338
1285 new sterlings	200 s.	Rome	C	(401) p.306

The pound sterling in soldi and denari of Genoa

Date	Rate	Place	Type	Reference
1252.03.06	98 s. 8 1/4 d.	Genoa	B	(154) V p.372
1253.03.26	117 s.	Genoa	B	(154) V p.436

The pound sterling in sous viennois

Date	Rate	Place	Type	Reference
1284	100 s.	Piedmont	A	(110) p.487
1301	105 s.	Piedmont	A	(110) p.489

The pound sterling in sous and deniers melgorians

Date	Rate	Place	Type	Reference
1244	49 s. 2 1/4 d.	Marseille	C	(43) p.266

The pound sterling in sous and deniers provinois of Champagne

Date	Rate	Place	Type	Reference
1262.09.04	90 s.	Troyes	B	(374) p.32
1262.09.04	88 s. 5 d.	Troyes	B	(374) p.36
13th.c	88 s. 6 d.	England	C	(443) p.287
1285	180 s.	Curia	B	(439) p.111

The pound sterling in sous and deniers parisis of France

Date	Rate	Place	Type	Reference
1265	90 s.	France	O	(430) I p.131
1268-1279	65 s.	Calais	C	(62) p.22
1269-1271	64 s.	Calais	C	(62) p.22
1285	66 s. 9 1/2 d.	France	C	(22) p.234
1286-1290	70 s.	Calais	C	(62) p.22
1295-1296	65 s.	Calais	C	(62) p.22
1297	65 s.	Calais	C	(62) p.22
1299	66 s. 8 d.	France	C	(185) p.149
1299	64 s.	France	C	(185) p.149

The pound sterling in sous and deniers tournois of France

Date	Rate	Place	Type	Reference
1204	80 s.	Italy	B	(385) p.105
1228	80 s.	England	C	(79) 1227-1231 p.116
1233	75 s.	England	C	(79) 1231-1234 p.305
1250	79 s. 6 d.	Rome	B	(439) p.116
1255	80 s.	England	B	(310) I p.295
1265	90 s.	France	C	(258) p.131
1265	80 s.	France	C	(258) p.58
1290.04.09	80 s.	Paris	A	(149) pp.233-4
1292	82 s. 6 d.	England	C?	(399) p.160
1297	83 s. 4 d.	England	C?	(399) p.160
1299	120 s.	England	C?	(399) p.160
1299	150 s.	England	C?	(399) p.160
1299	220 s.	England	C?	(399) p.160

The pound sterling in sous and deniers of Artois

Date	Rate	Place	Type	Reference
1265.06	70 s.	Flanders	C	(205) p.21
1275.06.27	48 s. 9 d.	Ypres	C	(145) p.71
1280.10.12	48 s. 9 d.	Ypres	C	(145) p.71
1281.01.25	48 s. 9 d.	Ypres	C	(145) p.71
1281.09.12	48 s. 9 d.	Ypres	C	(145) p.72
1281.09.25	48 s. 9 d.	Ypres	C	(145) p.72
1282.09.16	48 s. 9 d.	Ypres	C	(145) p.72
1282.10.25	48 s. 9 d.	Ypres	C	(145) p.72
1283.11.20	49 s. 7 1/2 d.	Ypres	C	(145) p.71
1284.04	49 s. 7 1/2 d.	Ypres	C	(145) p.71
1286.05.18	49 s. 7 1/2 d.	Ypres	C	(145) p.71
1288.05.26	49 s. 7 1/2 d.	Ypres	C	(145) p.71
1290.03.16	49 s. 7 1/2 d.	Ypres	C	(145) p.71

The pound sterling in sous and deniers of Flanders

Date	Rate	Place	Type	Reference
1270-1275	65 s.	Flanders	A	(74)
1281.01.26	66 s. 8 d.	Ypres	C	(145) p.72
1284.09.20	66 s. 8 d.	Ypres	C	(145) p.71
1285	65 s.	Ypres	A	(146)
1286.09.24	66 s. 8 d.	Ypres	C	(145) p.71

The pound sterling in schellingen and groten of Flanders

A large number of rates between English sterling and Flemish money groot survive from the fourteenth and fifteenth centuries, since Flanders was England's principal trading partner. However, these have not been included in this Handbook as adequate series exist between the florin and both English and Flemish money.

The pound sterling in sous and deniers of Brabant

Date	Rate	Place	Type	Reference
1270-5	60 s.	Brabant	A	(74)

The pound sterling in schellingen and penningen of Groningen

Date	Rate	Place	Type	Reference
1250	480 s.	Groningen	C	(462) p.196
1288	600 s.	Groningen	C	(462) p.196

The pound sterling in schillinge and pfennige of Cologne

Date	Rate	Place	Type	Reference
1208	20 s.	Utrecht	A	(242) p.108

English sterling money in currencies outside the general area of Tuscan exchanges after 1300

The pound sterling in weisspfennige of the Rhineland Monetary Union

Date	Rate	Place	Type	Reference
1372	120 wpf.	Rhineland	O	(416) p.305
1374	120 wpf.	Rhineland	O	(416) p.305
1374	135 wpf.	Rhineland	O	(416) p.305
1386	136 1/2 wpf.	Rhineland	O	(416) p.305

The pound sterling in schillinge and pfennige of Lübeck

Date	Rate	Place	Type	Reference
1260	54 s.	Lübeck	C	(462) V p.197
1368	60 s.	Lübeck	C	(291) p.64
1423	60 s.	Lübeck	C	(258) p.161

The pound sterling in mark, öre and pfennige of Denmark
1 mark = 8öre; 1 öre = 30 pfennige

Date	Rate	Place	Type	Reference
1296	10 mk.	Denmark	?	(462) p.195
1298	8 mk.	Denmark	?	(462) p.195
1313	16 mk.	Jütland	?	(462) p.195
1330	10 mk.	Schleswig	?	(462) p.195
1332	6 mk. 5 ö. 18 pf.	Schonen	?	(462) p.195
1357	6 mk.	Schonen	?	(462) p.195

See also the mark of Danish pfennige in shillings and pence sterling under DENMARK p.282

For the lira di grossi of Venice in shillings and pence sterling see under VENICE p.87
For the gold morabetino in shillings and pence sterling see under CASTILE p.157
For the gros tournois in sterlings see under FRANCE p.188
For the rheingulden in shillings and pence sterling see under RHINELAND p.255
For the besant in shillings and pence sterling see under BESANT p.295

SCOTLAND

As in England, accounting in Scotland was carried out not only in pounds, shillings and pence, but also in mark, here known as merks, of 13s. 4d. When they were first struck in the twelfth century Scottish pennies were identical in weight and fineness to English pennies. Like them they were known as sterlings and were interchangeable with them. It was not until 1367 that the silver content of the Scottish sterling was reduced below its English counterpart. Thereafter the money of Scotland increasingly diverged from that of England. Even in 1393 the Scottish government pretended that no divergence had taken place and in Scotland the official value of English and Scottish money remained the same. The English government, on the other hand, exaggerated the extent of the debasement and pretended that Scottish money had become worth very much less in term of English than a straightforward comparison of the silver content of the two coinages warranted. In 1374 and again in 1387 the English government ordered that 26s. 8d. of Scottish money be taken in England as equivalent to 20s. of English money, and in 1390 that 40s. of Scottish money be taken in England as equivalent to 20s. of English money.

As the two coinages diverged, the terminology used for the Scottish coinage also changed. It was no longer sufficient to specify 'sterling', and in the 1370s, 1380s and 1390s various attempts were made to distinguish Scottish currency from English sterling — 'sterlingys of the payement of Scotland', 'sterlings of usual money', 'sterlings of current money' and occasionally just 'monete currentis' or 'usual mone of the Kinrike of Scotland'. After the further debasement of 1393, terms which included 'sterling' gradually disappeared out of use for Scottish money, and by the end of the century it had become generally known as the 'usual (i.e. current) money of Scotland'. Only in correspondence with the papal curia did the term 'sterling' continue to be used. Papal clerks continued to use 'sterling' for Scottish money until well into the fifteenth century, although distinguishing the pre-1393 currency as 'old sterling'. For a full discussion of the terminology used to describe the Scottish currency see William W. Scott, 'Sterling and Usual Money of Scotland 1370-1415', Scottish Economic and Social History (1985). I am much indebted to W. Scott for the opportunity to read his article in advance of publication.

The Florentine florin in shillings and pence sterling of Scotland

Equivalents used by the papal camera in calculating payments due from Scottish bishoprics.

Date	Rate	Place	Type	Reference
1296	2 s. 8 d.	Curia	A	(340) p.147
1297	2 s. 8 d.	Curia	A	(340) p.147
1297.02.10	2 s. 8 d.	Brechin	B	(226) CXLIV p.23
1299	2 s. 8 d.	Curia	A	(340) p.147
1301	2 s. 8 d.	Curia	A	(340) p.147

The ducat (unspecified) in Scottish shillings and pence

Date	Rate	Place	Type	Reference
.488	16 s.	Scotland	A	(340) p.148
.497	15 s. 6 d.	Scotland	A	(340) p.148
.503	15 s. 6 d.	Scotland	A	(340) p.148

The pound sterling of England in shillings and pence sterling of Scotland

Date	Rate	Place	Type	Reference
irca 1150-circa 1350	20 s.	Scotland	H	(340) p.140
355	20 s.	Scotland	O	(340) p.140
357	20 s.	Scotland	O	(340) p.140
358	20 s.	Scotland	H	(340) p.140
365	more than 20 s.	Scotland	O	(340) p.140
366	20 s.	Scotland	O	(340) p.140
367	more than 20 s.	Scotland	O	(340) p.140
373	26 s. 8 d.	Scotland	H	(340) p.140
374	26 s. 8 d.	England	O	(399) p.162
385	23 s.	Scotland	O	(340) p.140
387	26 s. 8 d.	England	O	(340) p.140

THE POUND STERLING OF ENGLAND IN SHILLINGS AND PENCE STERLING OF SCOTLAND

Date	Rate	Place	Type	Reference
1387.07.30	26 s. 8 d.	London	C	(79) 1385-1389 p.441
1390	40 s.	England	O	(340) p.140
1393	more than 20 s.	Scotland	O	(340) p.140
1393	28 s. 6 d.	Scotland	O	(340) p.140
1397.11.19	40 s.	England	O	(79) 1396-1399 p.230
1398	40 s.	Scotland	O	(340) p.140
1422	30 s.	Scotland	A	(340) p.140
1424	20 s.	Scotland	O	(340) p.140
1430b.	40 s.	Scotland	A	(340) p.140
1430	48 s.	Scotland	A	(340) p.140
1434	45 s.	Scotland	A	(340) p.140
1434	54 s.	Scotland	A	(340) p.141
1451	40 s.	Scotland	O	(340) p.141
1452	66 s.	Scotland	O	(340) p.141
1452	60 s.	Scotland	O	(340) p.141
1466	50 s.	Scotland	O	(340) p.141
1467	64 s.	Scotland	O	(340) p.141
1467	60 s.	Scotland	O	(340) p.141
1467 in nobles	82 s. 6 d.	Scotland	O	(340) p.138
1468	70 s.	Scotland	O	(340) p.141
1468 in nobles	72 s.	Scotland	O	(340) p.138
1474 in nobles	80 s.	Scotland	A	(340) p.138
1474 in nobles	90 s.	Scotland	A	(340) p.138
1475	70 s.	Scotland	O	(340) p.141
1475 in nobles	93 s.	Scotland	O	(340) p.138
1483	100 s.	Scotland	A	(340) p.141
1483	100 s.	Curia	A	(340) p.139
1483	120 s.	Scotland	A	(340) p.141
1483 in nobles	180 s.	Scotland	A	(340) p.138
1485	100 s.	Scotland	A	(340) p.141
1485	120 s.	Scotland	A	(340) p.141
1485-1487	66 s. 8 d.	Scotland	A	(340) p.141
1485	60 s.	Scotland	A	(340) p.141
1486	60 s.	Scotland	A	(340) pp.139 and 141
1487	88 s.	Scotland	A	(340) p.141
1487	58 s. 9 d.	Scotland	A	(340) p.141
1487	86 s. 8 d.	Scotland	A	(340) p.141
1488	72 s.	Scotland	A	(340) p.141
1488-1489 in nobles	96 s.	Scotland	A	(340) p.138
1492	90 s.	Scotland	A	(340) p.141
1501	70 s.	Scotland	A	(340) p.139

<u>The pound sterling of England in Scottish merks and shillings
1 merk = 13s. 4d.</u>

Date	Rate	Place	Type	Reference
1483	5 mk.	Curia	A	(340) p.139
1485	5 mk.	Curia	A	(340) p.139
1487	6 2/3 mk.	Curia	A	(340) p.139
1487	4 2/7 mk.	Curia	A	(340) p.139
1487	6 1/3 mk.	Curia	A	(340) p.139
1488	4 mk.	Curia	A	(340) p.139
1501	3 mk.10 s.	Scotland	A	(340) p.139

SECTION VIII
LOW COUNTRIES

The moneys of account in the principalities of the Low Countries were particularly complex. This was partially because the region, although the second most commerically advanced area of Europe after Italy, took a long time to evolve a distinctive coinage of its own.′ Instead it borrowed the coinages of its neighbours, and of those who came to trade there. Fifteenth-century travellers contrasted Bruges, then the principal trading city of the Low Countries, with Venice. They pointed out that men of all nations came to Bruges and the men of Bruges stayed at home, whilst the Venetians travelled to all countries and foreigners relatively rarely came to Venice.

The currency in circulation in Bruges reflected this, for it was made up of the coinages of many countries. Furthermore, the rulers of the principalities of the Low Countries struck coins after the pattern of many 'foreign' coinages, imitating the sterlings and nobles of England; the deniers parisis, the gros tournois, the chaise à l'écu and the franc à cheval of France; the florin of Florence; and the gulden of the Rhineland electors. Moneys of account were developed on the basis of many of these adopted coinages.

ARTOIS

In the twelfth century Arras was the leading financial centre of the Low Countries and one of its leading textile towns. Small deniers were minted in Artois of the same sort as elsewhere in Flanders, with which Artois was then united. At the end of the twelfth century Philip Augustus of France acquired Artois and the Arras mint became the most prolific issuer of deniers parisis. In this way the use of money parisis was introduced into the Low Countries (see below p.214). In the thirteenth century the money of Flanders was still sometimes called artésian.

For the livre tournois, the gros tournois and the livre parisis in sous and deniers of Artois see under FRANCE pp.184, 188 and 170
For the pound sterling in sous and deniers of Artois see under ENGLAND p.209
For the sou of Brabant in deniers of Artois see under BRABANT p.229
For the sou of Holland in deniers of Artois see under HOLLAND p.233

FLANDERS

In Flanders there was a money of account based on the native deniers of Flanders; a money parisis based on Flemish deniers parisis; esterlins used for accounting based initially on Flemish sterlings; money groot based initially on Flemish versions of the gros tournois and later on Flemish groten; royales used for accounting based on the French gold royale or masse d'or (regalis ad massam); gulden used for accounting based initially on the rheingulden. Many of these came over time to be tied not to the coins after which many were named, but to the Flemish groot.

The small monnaies noires descended from the ancient deniers ended up being called 'miten', from the Latin 'minutus'. Twenty-four miten made one groot.

The Flemish sous parisis ended up fossilized as equivalent to one groot.

Derivative sterlings were minted in Flanders from the 1290s. The Flemish esterlin or sterling ended up as equivalent to one third of a groot. The Flemish mark sterling was worth 1/2 of the Flemish pond sterling; it was employed in Flanders and Artois from the 1150s and elsewhere as a money of account. The relationship 10 shillings to 1 mark appears to have distinguished the money mark from the mark weight (62) VIII p.24.

The royale or real ended up as a unit of 24 groten, and the electoral rheingulden as equal to 40 groten, and was used at that value as the pound of a system of accounting.

In addition there was a certain amount of reckoning in stuivers or patards in the fifteenth century. As a coin the stuiver began as a double groot, and remained so for accounting purposes.

The livre of Flanders in sous of Antwerp

Date	Rate	Place	Type	Reference
1187	10 s.	Flanders	A	(498) p.145

The livre of Flanders in sous of Brabant

Date	Rate	Place	Type	Reference
1187	10 s.	Flanders	A	(205) p.20

The livre of Flanders in sous of Liège

Date	Rate	Place	Type	Reference
1187	10 s.	Flanders	A	(205) p.20

The livre of Flanders in schillinge of Cologne

Date	Rate	Place	Type	Reference
1187	6 s.	Flanders	A	(205) p.20

For the pound sterling in sous and deniers of Flanders see under ENGLAND p.209

Flemish money parisis

In the thirteenth century the money of Flanders was still frequently called artésian, since the Arras mint had provided the standard for the various deniers of Flanders until Philip II of France took it over as the principal mint for striking deniers parisis. In 1180 before Philip II, the denier artésian of Flanders was already identical in value with the denier parisis. In 1259 it was still identical in value. It is not surprising that the deniers of Flanders came also to be called parisis. Pegolotii noted, (177) p.239, that 3 soldi of the 'moneta di pagamento' in Bruges were worth a silver 'grosso tornese'; and that sterlings also circulated which were worth a soldo of poor parisis, and that three sterlings were worth a gros tournois. From this it appears that the current money of Bruges was the same as his 'parigini fieboli'. These poor parisis were not French royal parisis, but the parisis which had been issued by the counts of Flanders themselves. Similarly the gros tournois involved were also those of the counts of Flanders. Pegolotti was working for the Bardi in the Low Countries for at least two years before his departure for their London branch in 1317. Presumably the information in the Bruges section of his notebook is most likely to refer to that period. The Flemish groot was frequently debased in the fourteenth century particularly under Louis de Male. It became worth only a sou of the old Flemish parisis before the latter passed out of existence as actual coins. In accounts at Bruges in 1386-7 and 1390-1, the groot was treated as equivalent to the sou parisis (212) III pp.143 and 153.

Florentine florin in current money (parisis) of Flanders

Date	Rate	Place	Type	Reference
1339.12.03	16 s. 6 d.	Thérouanne	B	(28) p.84
1340.06.28	16 s. 6 d.	Thérouanne	B	(28) p.84
1342.05.22	17 s.	Thérouanne	B	(28) p.101
1343.02.28	16 s. 8 d.	Thérouanne	B	(28) p.105
1345.12.17-1346.01.05	16 s. 6 d.	Thérouanne	B	(28) p.107
1346.06.29	22 s. 6 d.	Thérouanne	B	(28) p.148
1348.04	17 s. 6 d.	Thérouanne	B	(28) p.133

Flemish money groot

Derivative gros tournois were struck by the counts of Flanders, from Jean de Namur (count 1302-3), for twenty years. This was succeeded by a distinctive indigenous groot under Louis de Nevers (1322-46). Whether the original exchange rates were expressed in s. & d. groot (12 groten = 1 s. groot) in groten and sterlings (3 sterlings = 1 groot); in gulden and stuivers (2 groten = 1 stuiver; 20 stuivers = 1 gulden); or in groten and miten, they have all been reduced to groten and miten.

The Florentine florin in groten and miten of Flanders
24 miten = 1 groot

Date	Rate	Place	Type	Reference
1317	13 gr. 3 m.	Bruges	C	(258) p.260
1343.03.28	15 gr.	Genoa	B	(297) I p.148
1348.02.06	16 gr. 20 m.?	Genoa	B	(297) I p.281
1348.02.28	16 gr. 20 m.?	Curia	B	(347) p.551
1353-1354	19 gr. 2 m.	Bruges	B	(446) p.127
1354	20 gr.	Avignon	B	(446) p.130
1361	22 gr.	Navarre	C	(73) p.XXIII
1365	27 gr.	Avignon	B	(439) p.62
1367	24 gr. 14 m.	Antwerp	H	(461) p.385
1368	27 gr. 2 m.	Antwerp	H	(461) p.385
1368	27 gr.	Rome	B	(439) p.62
1369	27 gr. 13 m.	Antwerp	H	(461) p.385
1369	27 gr. 10 m.	Antwerp	H	(461) p385
1370.08.28	32 gr.	Bruges	B	(297) I p.LXXVIII
1370.08.28	31 gr. 4 m.	Bruges	B	(297) I p.78
1370.10.14	32 gr.	Genoa	B	(297) I p.437
1372.08.31	24 gr.	Genoa	B	(297) II p.448
1380	28 gr. 9 m.	Antwerp	H	(461) p.385
1382.04.10	31 gr. 9 m.	Genoa	B	(297) II p.529
1384.08.29	35 gr. 12 m.	Bruges	B	(138) p.106
1386-1387	34 gr.	Bruges	C	(212) III p.143
1389.11.03	42 gr. 7 m.	Bruges	B	(297) I p.78
1399.01.14-1400	33 gr. 12 m.	Bruges	B	(138) p.116
1399.02.19-1400	33 gr.	Bruges	B	(138) p.117
1399.03.13	33 gr.	Bruges	B	(138) p.117
1399.03.17-20	33 gr. 3 m.	Bruges	B	(138) p.117
1399.04.26	33 gr. 12 m.	Bruges	B	(138) p.114
1399.07.25	33 gr. 16 m.	Bruges	B	(138) p.115
1399.08.06	33 gr. 12 m.	Bruges	B	(138) p.115
1399.08.13	33 gr. 8 m.	Bruges	B	(138) p.115
1399.08.26	33 gr.	Bruges	B	(138) p.115
1399.10.21	32 gr. 12 m.	Bruges	B	(138) p.116
1400.03.26	33 gr. 12 m.	Bruges	B	(138) p.117
1400.05.19	31 gr. 12 m.	Bruges	B	(138) p.118
1400.08.08	31 gr.	Bruges	B	(138) p.118
1401.05.13	33 gr.	Bruges	B	(138) p.120
1407	32 gr.	Bruges	B	(138) p.69
1408.05.10	33 gr.	Genoa	B	(154) V no.24
1409.12.02	40 gr. 12 m.	Genoa-Bruges	B	(154) V p.36
1409	40 gr.	Genoa	C	(155) p.749
1412.03.15	33 gr.	London-Genoa	B	(154) V no.134
1412.07.07	33 gr.	Genoa-Bruges	B	(154) V no.145
1412.07.27	40 gr.	Bruges-Genoa	B	(154) V no.150
1412	40 gr.	Genoa	C	(155) p.749
1413.11.04-1413.11.08	39 gr. 12 m.	Genoa-Bruges	B	(154) V no.212
1414	39 gr.	Genoa	C	(155) p.749
1418.10.13	46 gr.	Bruges	B	(81) p.31
1420	33 gr.	Genoa	C	(155) p.749
1424.10.13	33 gr.	Bruges	C	(154) V no.296
1424.11.22	33 gr.	Bruges	C	(154) V no.296
1433 Reformed Flemish coinage became common coinage of Burgundian Netherlands				
1433.02.05	38 gr.	Genoa-Bruges	B	(154) V no.752
1440-1442	39 gr.	Genoa	C	(155) p.749
1440	53 gr. 18 m.	Holland	H	(461) p.386
1441.07.14	29 gr. 7 m.	Bruges-Genoa	B	(154) V no.815
1441	53 gr. 22 m.	Low Countries	H	(461) p.386
1453-1454	49 gr.	Holland	M	(522)
1455	52 gr. 12 m.	Zeeland	H	(461) p.386

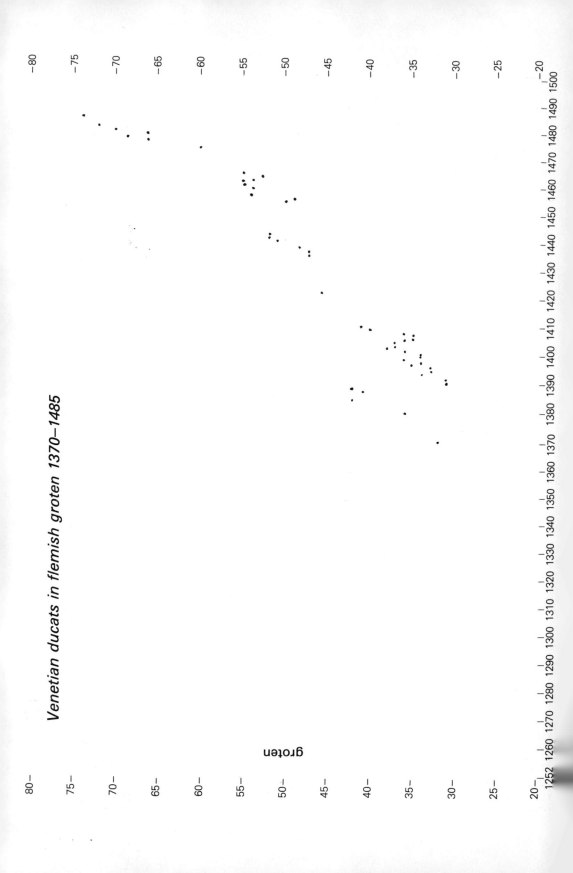

Venetian ducats in flemish groten 1370–1485

groten

80 75 70 65 60 55 50 45 40 35 30 25 20

1252 1260 1270 1280 1290 1300 1310 1320 1330 1340 1350 1360 1370 1380 1390 1400 1410 1420 1430 1440 1450 1460 1470 1480 1490 1500

THE FLORENTINE FLORIN IN GROTEN AND MITEN OF FLANDERS

Date	Rate	Place	Type	Reference
1466.05	41 gr.	Low Countries	C	(362) p.210
1467.07.31	34 gr. 8 m.	Bruges	C	(143) p.439
1467.10	42 gr.	Low Countries	C	(362) p.210
1474.10	48 gr.	Low Countries	C	(362) p.210
1474.10.27	60 gr.	Low Countries	C	(495) p.395
1485	74 gr.	Low Countries	C	(495) p.402
1493.01.07	60 gr.	Tournai	B	(68) p.108
1493.04	62 gr.	Low Countries	O	(362) p.339
1496-1499	76 gr.	Low Countries	O	(362) p.339

The florin of Genoa in groten and miten of Flanders

24 miten = 1 groot

Date	Rate	Place	Type	Reference
1345	30 gr.	Low Countries	M	(6) p.161
1370	32 gr.	Low Countries	M	(6) p.161
1389	42 gr. 7 m.	Low Countries	M	(6) p.161
1396.07	31 gr. 16 m.	Bruges	B	(138) p.53
1397.03	34 gr. 16 m.	Bruges	B	(138) p.53
1408	33 gr.	Low Countries	M	(6) p.161
1409	40 gr. 12 m.	Low Countries	M	(6) p.161
1412	33 gr.	Low Countries	M	(6) p.161
1412	40 gr.	Low Countries	M	(6) p.161
1414	39 gr. 12 m.	Low Countries	M	(6) p.161
1421	34 gr. 6 m.	Low Countries	M	(6) p.161
1424	33 gr.	Low Countries	M	(6) p.161
1433	38 gr.	Low Countries	M	(6) p.161
1441	29 gr. 7 m.	Low Countries	M	(6) p.161
1441.11.30	46 gr.	Low Countries	O	(6) p.161
1443.10.12	46 gr.	Low Countries	O	(6) p.161
1454.01.19	49 gr.	Low Countries	O	(6) p.162

The Venetian ducat in groten and miten of Flanders

24 miten = 1 groot

A certain number of these quotations were expressed in stuivers. These have been reduced to groten at the rate of 2 groten to every stuiver. Between 1388 and 1410 I have generally selected only the first bill drawn each month from a much larger body of material printed by De Roover from the Datini archive (138).

Date	Rate	Place	Type	Reference
1370.08.28	32 gr. 4 m.	Bruges	B	(297) I p.78
1384.09.29	36 gr.	Bruges-Venice	B	(138) p.106
1385-1405	42 gr.	Bruges	B	(243) p.206
1388.06.15	41 gr. 8 m.	Bruges-Venice	B	(138) p.106
1388.10.04	41 gr. 16 m.	Bruges-Venice	B	(138) p.106
1388.12.02	41 gr.	Bruges-Venice	B	(138) p.106
1389.02.22	42 gr. 10 m.	Bruges-Venice	B	(138) p.106
1389.03.19	42 gr. 16 m.	Bruges-Venice	B	(138) p.106
1389.04.26	42 gr. 18 m.	Bruges-Venice	B	(138) p.106
1390	31 gr. 12 m.	Flanders	O	(6) p.161
1391.03.27	52 gr.	Venice	B	(243) p.184
1391.12.01	33 gr. 14 m.	Bruges-Venice	B	(138) p.106
1392	32 gr. 12 m.	Flanders	O	(6) p.161
1392.01.08	31 gr. 18 m.	Bruges-Venice	B	(138) p.106
1392.01.10-02.01	32 gr.	Bruges-Venice	B	(138) p.106
1392.02.25-03.09	31 gr. 21 m.	Bruges-Venice	B	(138) p.106
1392.03.28	31 gr. 18 m.	Bruges-Venice	B	(138) p.106
1392.04.06	31 gr. 16 m.	Bruges-Venice	B	(138) p.106
1392.04.18-05.10	31 gr. 14 m.	Bruges-Venice	B	(138) p.107
1392.06.01	31 gr. 12 m.	Bruges-Venice	B	(138) p.107
1394.01.04	34 gr. 12 m.	Bruges-Venice	B	(138) p.107
1394.02.28	42 gr.	Avignon	C	(243) p.206
1395.01.05	34 gr. 20 m.	Bruges-Venice	B	(138) p.107
1395.03.05	34 gr. 12 m.	Bruges-Venice	B	(138) p.107
1395.04.01	34 gr. 12 m.	Bruges-Venice	B	(138) p.107
1395.05.04	34 gr. 12 m.	Bruges-Venice	B	(138) p.107
1395.07.05	33 gr. 16 m.	Bruges-Venice	B	(138) p.107
1395.07.12-29	33 gr. 6 m.	Bruges-Venice	B	(138) p.107

Date	Rate	Place	Type	Reference
1395.08.10	33 gr. 10 m.	Bruges-Venice	B	(138) p.107
1395.08.13-25	33 gr. 8m.	Bruges-Venice	B	(138) p.107
1395.09.27-28	33 gr. 16 m.	Bruges-Venice	B	(138) p.107
1395.10.11-27	34 gr.	Bruges-Venice	B	(138) p.107
1395.11.05	33 gr. 20 m.	Bruges-Venice	B	(138) p.108
1395.12.22-23	33 gr. 6 m.	Bruges-Venice	B	(138) p.108
1396.01.21	33 gr.	Bruges-Venice	B	(138) p.108
1396.02.27	33 gr. 12 m.	Bruges-Venice	B	(138) p.108
1396.02.28-03.29	33 gr. 12 m.	Bruges-Venice	B	(138) p.108
1396.04.08	33 gr. 16 m.	Bruges-Venice	B	(138) p.108
1396.04.06-25	33 gr. 18 m.	Bruges-Venice	B	(138) p.108
1396.05.25	33 gr. 20 m.	Bruges-Venice	B	(138) p.108
1396.06.27	33 gr. 18 m.	Bruges-Venice	B	(138) p.109
1396.07.24	32 gr. 16 m.	Bruges-Venice	B	(138) p.109
1396.08.22-25	33 gr.	Bruges-Venice	B	(138) p.109
1396.09.01	33 gr. 4 m.	Bruges-Venice	B	(138) p.109
1396.10.24	34 gr. 3 m.	Bruges-Venice	B	(138) p.109
1396.10.28-11.26	34 gr.	Bruges-Venice	B	(138) p.109
1396.12.07-08	34 gr. 18 m.	Bruges-Venice	B	(138) p.109
1396.12	35 gr.	Bruges-Venice	B	(138) p.53
1397.01.03	34 gr. 16 m.	Bruges-Venice	B	(138) p.109
1397.02.13	35 gr. 3 m.	Bruges-Venice	B	(138) p.109
1397.03.04	35 gr. 20 m.	Bruges-Venice	B	(138) p.109
1397.04.04	35 gr. 18 m.	Bruges-Venice	B	(138) p.110
1397.04.05-05.02	35 gr. 18 m.	Bruges-Venice	B	(138) p.110
1397.05.02-06	35 gr. 16 m.	Bruges-Venice	B	(138) p.110
1397.07.01	35 gr. 12 m.	Bruges-Venice	B	(138) p.110
1397.06.19	36 gr.	Bruges-Venice	B	(138) p.110
1397.08.01	34 gr. 18 m.	Bruges-Venice	B	(138) p.110
1397.09.07	34 gr. 6 m.	Bruges-Venice	B	(138) p.110
1397.10.26	35 gr. 22 m.	Bruges-Venice	B	(138) p.110
1397.11.21	35 gr. 16 m.	Bruges-Venice	B	(138) p.111
1397.12.01	36 gr.	Bruges-Venice	B	(138) p.111
1398.01.09	36 gr. 10 m.	Bruges-Venice	B	(138) p.111
1398.02.03	36 gr. 14 m.	Bruges-Venice	B	(138) p.111
1398.03.01-11	36 gr.	Bruges-Venice	B	(138) p.111
1398.04.02	35 gr. 1 m.	Bruges-Venice	B	(138) p.112
1398.05.09-11	34 gr. 16 m.	Bruges-Venice	B	(138) p.112
1398.06.10	35 gr. 3 m.	Bruges-Venice	B	(138) p.112
1398.07.05	34 gr. 20 m.	Bruges-Venice	B	(138) p.112
1398.08.08	34 gr. 20 m.	Bruges-Venice	B	(138) p.112
1398.09.06	34 gr. 9m.	Bruges-Venice	B	(138) p.113
1398.10.04	34 gr. 20 m.	Bruges-Venice	B	(138) p.113
1398.10.23-11.07	34 gr. 21 m.	Bruges-Venice	B	(138) p.113
1398.11.10	34 gr. 20 m.	Bruges-Venice	B	(138) p.113
1398.11.21-12.06	34 gr. 16 m.	Bruges-Venice	B	(138) p.113
1398.12.07	34 gr. 14 m.	Bruges-Venice	B	(138) p.113
1399.01.08	36 gr.	Bruges-Venice	B	(138) p.114
1399.01.29-02.10	35 gr. 16 m.	Bruges-Venice	B	(138) p.114
1399.03.08	35 gr. 20 m.	Bruges-Venice	B	(138) p.114
1399.04.03	36 gr. 4 m.	Bruges-Venice	B	(138) p.114
1399.04.12-18	36 gr. 3 m.	Bruges-Venice	B	(138) p.114
1399.05.02	36 gr. 2 m.	Bruges-Venice	B	(138) p.114
1399.06.07	36 gr. 8 m.	Bruges-Venice	B	(138) p.115
1399.07.04	36 gr. 12 m.	Bruges-Venice	B	(138) p.115
1399.07.30-08.02	35 gr. 16 m.	Bruges-Venice	B	(138) p.115
1399.08.06	35 gr. 12 m.	Bruges-Venice	B	(138) p.115
1399.09.09	35 gr. 8 m.	Bruges-Venice	B	(138) p.115
1399.10.02-04	35 gr.	Bruges-Venice	B	(138) p.116
1399.11.10-17	34 gr.	Bruges-Venice	B	(138) p.116
1399.12.07	34 gr. 16 m.	Bruges-Venice	B	(138) p.116
1400.01.03	34 gr. 8 m.	Bruges-Venice	B	(138) p.116
1400.02.05	34 gr. 22 m.	Bruges-Venice	B	(138) p.117
1400.02.06	36 gr.	Bruges	A	(295) Af.6, 21v
1400.02.09	34 gr. 18 m.	Bruges-Venice	B	(138) p.117
1400.02.28-03.05	35 gr. 4 m.	Bruges-Venice	B	(138) p.117
1400.03.13	35 gr. 2 m.	Bruges-Venice	B	(138) p.117
1400.04.07	35 gr. 10 m.	Bruges-Venice	B	(138) p.117
1400.05.05	34 gr.	Bruges-Venice	B	(138) p.117
1400.05.31-06.02	34 gr.	Bruges-Venice	B	(138) p.118
1400.06.05-07	34 gr. 2 m.	Bruges-Venice	B	(138) p.118
1400.07.01	33 gr. 20 m.	Bruges-Venice	B	(138) p.118

Date	Rate	Place	Type	Reference
1400.08.03-08	34 gr.	Bruges-Venice	B	(138) p.118
1400.09.02-03	34 gr. 2 m.	Bruges-Venice	B	(138) p.118
1400.10.03-04	33 gr. 16 m.	Bruges-Venice	B	(138) p.119
1400.10.27-11.03	33 gr. 12 m.	Bruges-Venice	B	(138) p.119
1400.11.13	33 gr. 8 m.	Bruges-Venice	B	(138) p.119
1400.11.30-12.01	32 gr. 21 m.	Bruges-Venice	B	(138) p.119
1400.12.04	32 gr. 12 m.	Bruges-Venice	B	(138) p.119
1400	62 gr.	Low Countries	C	(496)
1400	60 gr.	Low Countries	C	(496)
1401.01.06	33 gr. 12 m.	Bruges-Venice	B	(138) p.119
1401.02.16-23	34 gr. 12 m.	Bruges-Venice	B	(138) p.119
1401.03.05	34 gr. 16 m.	Bruges-Venice	B	(138) p.119
1401.04.09-14	34 gr. 6 m.	Bruges-Venice	B	(138) p.120
1401.05.13	34 gr. 14 m.	Bruges-Venice	B	(138) p.120
1401.05.30-06.08	34 gr. 16 m.	Bruges-Venice	B	(138) p.120
1401.06.08	34 gr. 8 m.	Bruges-Venice	B	(138) p.120
1401.07.02	34 gr. 10 m.	Bruges-Venice	B	(138) p.120
1401.07.13-08.11	34 gr. 3 m.	Bruges-Venice	B	(138) p.121
1401.08.15-16	34 gr.	Bruges-Venice	B	(138) p.121
1401.08.31-09.05	34 gr. 3 m.	Bruges-Venice	B	(138) p.121
1401.09.06-08	34 gr. 2 m.	Bruges-Venice	B	(138) p.121
1401.10.10	34 gr. 4 m.	Bruges-Venice	B	(138) p.121
1401.11.07	35 gr. 6 m.	Bruges-Venice	B	(138) p.121
1401.12.01	35 gr. 21 m.	Bruges-Venice	B	(138) p.121
1402.01.09	36 gr. 4 m.	Bruges-Venice	B	(138) p.121
1402.01.27-02.03	36 gr. 14 m.	Bruges-Venice	B	(138) p.121
1402.02.09	36 gr. 16 m.	Bruges-Venice	B	(138) p.121
1402.02.28-03.07	36 gr. 22 m.	Bruges-Venice	B	(138) p.121
1402.03.12-19	37 gr.	Bruges-Venice	B	(138) p.122
1402.04.06-08	37 gr.	Bruges-Venice	B	(138) p.122
1402.04.29	36 gr. 16 m.	Bruges-Venice	B	(138) p.122
1402.05.08	37 gr. 2 m.	Bruges-Venice	B	(138) p.122
1402.06.09	36 gr. 8 m.	Bruges-Venice	B	(138) p.122
1402.07.03	36 gr.	Bruges-Venice	B	(138) p.122
1402.08.16-21	37 gr.	Bruges-Venice	B	(138) p.122
1402.09.23	37 gr. 12 m.	Bruges-Venice	B	(138) p.123
1402.10.16	37 gr. 6 m.	Bruges-Venice	B	(138) p.123
1402.11.15	37 gr. 14 m.	Bruges-Venice	B	(138) p.123
1402.11.29-12.17	37 gr. 16 m.	Bruges-Venice	B	(138) p.123
1402.12.22-1403.01.03	37 gr. 18 m.	Bruges-Venice	B	(138) p.123
1403.01.09	37 gr. 20 m.	Bruges-Venice	B	(138) p.123
1403.02.07	38 gr. 4 m.	Bruges-Venice	B	(138) p.123
1403.03.12	38 gr. 20 m.	Bruges-Venice	B	(138) p.123
1403.04.11	38 gr. 4 m.	Bruges-Venice	B	(138) p.123
1403.04.26-05.02	38 gr. 14 m.	Bruges-Venice	B	(138) p.123
1403.05.06	38 gr. 18 m.	Bruges-Venice	B	(138) p.123
1403.06.22-25	39 gr.	Bruges-Venice	B	(138) p.124
1403.07.08	38 gr. 21 m.	Bruges-Venice	B	(138) p.124
1403.07.26-08.11	38 gr. 12 m.	Bruges-Venice	B	(138) p.124
1403.08.14	38 gr. 8 m.	Bruges-Venice	B	(138) p.124
1403.09.21-24	37 gr. 18 m.	Bruges-Venice	B	(138) p.124
1403.10.11	37 gr.	Bruges-Venice	B	(138) p.124
1403.11.03	35 gr. 18 m.	Bruges-Venice	B	(138) p.124
1403.12.10	37 gr. 20 m.	Bruges-Venice	B	(138) p.124
1403.12.22-31	37 gr. 12 m.	Bruges-Venice	B	(138) p.125
1404.01.06-14	37 gr. 6 m.	Bruges-Venice	B	(138) p.125
1404.02.01	37 gr. 12 m.	Bruges-Venice	B	(138) p.125
1404.03.04-06	37 gr. 20 m.	Bruges-Venice	B	(138) p.125
1404.04.08	37 gr. 18 m.	Bruges-Venice	B	(138) p.125
1404.05.07	36 gr. 16 m.	Bruges-Venice	B	(138) p.125
1404.06.11-12	36 gr. 4 m.	Bruges-Venice	B	(138) p.126
1404.06.28	37 gr. 12 m.	Bruges	A	(295) Af.1, 34v
1404.07.10	36 gr.	Bruges-Venice	B	(138) p.126
1404.08.01-02	36 gr. 6 m.	Bruges-Venice	B	(138) p.126
1404.09.02	35 gr. 21 m.	Bruges-Venice	B	(138) p.126
1404.10.05	36 gr. 4 m.	Bruges-Venice	B	(138) p.126
1404.10.31-11.10	36 gr. 18 m.	Bruges-Venice	B	(138) p.126
1404.11.17-12.04	36 gr. 22 m.	Bruges-Venice	B	(138) p.126
1404.12.10-11	37 gr.	Bruges-Venice	B	(138) p.126
1405.02.07	36 gr. 18 m.	Bruges-Venice	B	(138) p.127
1405.03.05	37 gr. 12 m.	Bruges-Venice	B	(138) p.127
1405.03.09	37 gr. 18 m.	Bruges-Venice	B	(138) p.127

Date	Rate	Place	Type	Reference
1405.04.06	37 gr. 14 m.	Bruges-Venice	B	(138) p.127
1405.05.12	36 gr. 12 m.	Bruges-Venice	B	(138) p.127
1405.06.05	36 gr. 8 m.	Bruges-Venice	B	(138) p.127
1405.07.01	35 gr. 22 m.	Bruges-Venice	B	(138) p.127
1405.08.03	36 gr.	Bruges-Venice	B	(138) p.127
1405.09.04	36 gr. 4 m.	Bruges-Venice	B	(138) p.127
1405.10.02-09	36 gr. 8 m.	Bruges-Venice	B	(138) p.127
1405.11.06	36 gr. 16 m.	Bruges-Venice	B	(138) p.128
1405.12.01-02	36 gr. 20 m.	Bruges-Venice	B	(138) p.128
1406.01.08	37 gr.	Bruges-Venice	B	(138) p.128
1406.01.30-02.10	37 gr. 2 m.	Bruges-Venice	B	(138) p.128
1406.02.12	37 gr. 3 m.	Bruges-Venice	B	(138) p.128
1406.03.11	36 gr. 21 m.	Bruges-Venice	B	(138) p.128
1406.04.10	36 gr. 20 m.	Bruges-Venice	B	(138) p.128
1406.05.01	36 gr. 14 m.	Bruges-Venice	B	(138) p.128
1406.05.29-06.09	36 gr. 8 m.	Bruges-Venice	B	(138) p.128
1406.06.15	35 gr. 18 m.	Bruges-Venice	B	(138) p.128
1406.07.05	35 gr. 20 m.	Bruges-Venice	B	(138) p.129
1406.08.16	34 gr. 22 m.	Bruges-Venice	B	(138) p.129
1406.09.13	35 gr.	Bruges-Venice	B	(138) p.129
1406.10.11	33 gr. 22 m.	Bruges-Venice	B	(138) p.129
1406.11.10	35 gr.	Bruges-Venice	B	(138) p.129
1406.12.04	35 gr. 14 m.	Bruges-Venice	B	(138) p.129
1407.01.03	35 gr. 20 m.	Bruges-Venice	B	(138) p.129
1407.01.10-02.06	36 gr.	Bruges-Venice	B	(138) p.129
1407.02.12	36 gr. 4 m.	Bruges-Venice	B	(138) p.129
1407.03.01	36 gr. 8 m.	Bruges-Venice	B	(138) p.129
1407.04.11	35 gr. 20 m.	Bruges-Venice	B	(138) p.130
1407.04.23-05.04	36 gr.	Bruges-Venice	B	(138) p.130
1407.06.08-09	35 gr. 8 m.	Bruges-Venice	B	(138) p.130
1407.07.06-08	34 gr. 12 m.	Bruges-Venice	B	(138) p.130
1407.08.27	35 gr. 8 m.	Bruges-Venice	B	(138) p.130
1407.09.14-21	35 gr. 12 m.	Bruges-Venice	B	(138) p.130
1407.09.28-11.13	36 gr.	Bruges-Venice	B	(138) p.130
1407.11.22	35 gr. 12 m.	Bruges-Venice	B	(138) p.130
1407.12.09-11	34 gr. 18 m.	Bruges-Venice	B	(138) p.131
1408.01.07	35 gr. 8 m.	Bruges-Venice	B	(138) p.131
1408.02.08	35 gr. 10 m.	Bruges-Venice	B	(138) p.131
1408.02.27-03.01	36 gr.	Bruges-Venice	B	(138) p.131
1408.03.07	36 gr. 6 m.	Bruges-Venice	B	(138) p.131
1408.05.09	35 gr. 4 m.	Venice	C	(370) p.101
1408.05.18	35 gr. 4 m.	Bruges-Venice	B	(138) p.131
1408.06.19-22	34 gr. 18 m.	Bruges-Venice	B	(138) p.131
1408.07.06	36 gr. 12 m.	Bruges	C	(370) p.142
1408.08.21	35 gr. 6 m.	Bruges-Venice	B	(138) p.131
1408.09.22	34 gr. 20 m.	Bruges-Venice	B	(138) p.131
1408.10.06-09	34 gr. 16 m.	Bruges-Venice	B	(138) p.131
1408.10.20	37 gr. 12 m.	Bruges	C	(370) p.142
1408.11.01	35 gr.	Low Countries	A	(472) Af.1, 34v
1408.11.05	34 gr. 8 m.	Bruges-Venice	B	(138) p.131
1408.12.03	34 gr.	Bruges-Venice	B	(138) p.131
1409.01.06	35 gr. 4 m.	Bruges-Venice	B	(138) p.132
1409.02.05	35 gr.	Bruges-Venice	B	(138) p.132
1409.02.06	36 gr. 12 m.	Bruges	C	(370) p.142
1409.03.09	35 gr.	Bruges-Venice	B	(138) p.132
1409.04.11-12	35 gr. 10 m.	Bruges-Venice	B	(138) p.132
1409.04.24	36 gr. 6 m.	Bruges	C	(370) p.142
1409.05.14	35 gr. 12 m.	Bruges-Venice	B	(138) p.132
1409.06.17	36 gr. 12 m.	Bruges-Venice	B	(138) p.132
1409.07.06	36 gr. 12 m.	Bruges-Venice	B	(138) p.132
1409.07.27-08.03	36 gr. 8 m.	Bruges-Venice	B	(138) p.132
1409.08.06	36 gr. 10 m.	Bruges-Venice	B	(138) p.132
1409.09.08	36 gr. 12 m.	Bruges-Venice	B	(138) p.132
1409.10.08-29	37 gr.	Bruges-Venice	B	(138) p.132
1409.11.04	37 gr. 6 m.	Bruges-Venice	B	(138) p.132
1409.12.12	39 gr.	Bruges-Venice	B	(138) p.132
1410.01.03-08	39 gr.	Bruges-Venice	B	(138) p.133
1410.02.05	39 gr. 20 m.	Bruges-Venice	B	(138) p.133
1410.02.11-04.09	40 gr.	Bruges-Venice	B	(138) p.133
1410.04.14	40 gr. 6 m.	Bruges-Venice	B	(138) p.133
1410.05.02-15	39 gr. 18 m.	Bruges-Venice	B	(138) p.133
1410.06.18	38 gr. 22 m.	Bruges-Venice	B	(138) p.133

THE VENETIAN DUCAT IN GROTEN AND MITEN OF FLANDERS

Date	Rate	Place	Type	Reference
1410.07.22-08.09	40 gr.	Bruges-Venice	B	(138) p.133
1410.08.18	40 gr. 2 m.	Bruges-Venice	B	(138) p.133
1410.09.12	39 gr. 20 m.	Bruges-Venice	B	(138) p.133
1410.10.16	40 gr. 4 m.	Bruges-Venice	B	(138) p.133
1410.10.25	40 gr.	Bruges	A	(295) Af.6, 73v
1410.10.25-11.07	40 gr.	Bruges	C	(370) p.142
1410.11.08	40 gr.	Bruges	A	(295) Af.6, 73v
Flemish currency was reformed 18.1.1411. For a short while rates were expressed in either new or old groten.				
1411.01.18	30 new gr. 16 m.	Bruges	B	(138) p.133
1411.01.30	30 new gr. 8 m.	Bruges	B	(138) p.133
1411.02.04	29 new gr. 16 m.	Bruges	B	(138) p.133
1411.02.22	41 old gr. 8 m.	Bruges	C	(370) p.142
1411.03.05	30 new gr. 15 m.	Venice	C	(469) p.88
1411.03.12-18	30 new gr. 4 m.	Venice	C	(469) p.88
1411.03.19-04.24	31 new gr. 1 m.	Venice	C	(469) p.88
1411.04.15	40 old gr. 12 m.	Bruges	C	(370) p.142
1411.04.17	41 old gr. 8 m.	Bruges	C	(370) p.142
1411.05.25-06.24	41 old gr. 16 m.	Bruges	C	(370) p.142
1411.06.08	29 new gr. 8 m.	Bruges	B	(138) p.134
1418.06	38 gr.	Flanders	O	(6) p.161
1423.09	46 gr.	Bruges	C	(470) p.382
1429	60 gr.	Flanders	C	(6) p.162
1433 Reformed Flemish coinage became common coinage of Burgundian Netherlands				
1436.04.16	69 gr. Brab. = 46 gr. Fl.	Brussels	O	(518) f.262r
1437.05.16	49 gr. 4 m.	Venice	B	(137) p.120
1437.08.26	47 gr.	Bruges	B	(137) p.120
1437.09.26	50 gr. 12 m.	Venice	B	(137) p.120
1438.09.15	46 gr. 20 m.	Bruges	B	(137) p.120
1438.09.18	49 gr. 18 m.	Venice	B	(137) p.118
1438.11.08	47 gr.	Bruges	B	(137) p.120
1438.11.16	49 gr. 6 m.	Venice	B	(137) p.120
1439.01.08	51 gr. 12 m.	Venice	B	(137) p.120
1439.07.07	48 gr.	Bruges	B	(137) p.120
1439.08.07	52 gr. 12 m.	Venice	B	(137) p.120
1439.10.24	50 gr. 18 m.	Bruges	B	(137) p.120
1439.12.24	54 gr.	Venice	B	(137) p.120
1441.05.27	51 gr. 12 m.	Bruges	B	(137) p.120
1441.07.27	55 gr.	Venice	B	(137) p.120
1442.03.08	46 gr.	Brussels	O	(518) f.270v
1443	49 gr. 12 m.	Flanders	L	(6) p.162
1443.03.14	52 gr.	Bruges	B	(137) p.120
1443.05.14	54 gr. 12 m.	Venice	B	(137) p.120
1443.06.27	49 gr.	Bruges	B	(137) p.120
1443.09.27	53 gr. 6 m.	Bruges	B	(137) p.120
1444.03.04	52 gr. 12 m.	Venice	B	(137) p.118
1444.07.04	52 gr. 12 m.	Bruges	B	(81) p.61
1444	48 gr.	Piedmont	A	(110) p.474
1455.07.30	52 gr.	Venice	B	(137) p.118
1455.08.30	50 gr. 12 m.	Bruges	B	(81) p.79
1455.11.17	52 gr. 12 m.	Venice	B	(137) p.118
1456.01.21	49 gr. 12 m.	Bruges	B	(81) p.79
1458.01.12	55 gr. 12 m.	Venice	B	(137) p.118
1458.01.12	55 gr. 8 m.	Venice	B	(137) p.118
1458.02.01	55 gr. 12 m.	Venice	B	(137) p.118
1458.04.08	42 gr.	Bruges	B	(81) p.86
1458.05.15	55 gr. 12 m.	Venice	B	(137) p.118
1458.06.07	55 gr. 12 m.	Venice	B	(137) p.118
1458.07.17	54 gr. 8 m.	Bruges	B	(81) p.87
1458.07.26	56 gr.	Venice	B	(137) p.118
1458.08.10	53 gr. 22 m.	Bruges	B	(81) p.87
1458.09.22	54 gr.	Bruges	B	(81) p.88
1458.10.04	54 gr.	Bruges	B	(81) p.88
1459.07.12	57 gr.	Venice	B	(137) p.118
1460.08.05	54 gr. 18 m.	Bruges	B	(81) p.93
1460.06.04	57 gr. 6 m.	Venice	B	(137) p.118
1460.08.13	58 gr. 6 m.	Venice	B	(137) p.118
1460.08.22	58 gr. 12 m.	Venice	B	(137) p.118

Date	Rate	Place	Type	Reference
1460.10.15	54 gr.	Bruges	B	(81) p.94
1460.10.23	53 gr. 12 m.	Bruges	B	(81) p.94
1460.11.24	57 gr. 6 m.	Venice	B	(137) p.118
1460.12.10	57 gr. 6 m.	Venice	B	(137) p.119
1461.01.26	53 gr. 18 m.	Bruges	B	(81) p.96
1461.01.30	54 gr. 6 m.	Bruges	B	(81) p.96
1461.01.16	57 gr. 12 m.	Venice	B	(137) p.119
1461.02.05	54 gr. 8 m.	Bruges	B	(81) p.96
1461.02.12	57 gr.	Venice	B	(137) p.119
1461.02.23	54 gr. 14 m.	Bruges	B	(81) p.97
1461.03.12	57 gr.	Bruges	B	(81) p.97
1461.03.17	54 gr. 8 m.	Bruges	B	(81) p.98
1461.03.30	54 gr. 12 m.	Bruges	B	(81) p.98
1461.05.23	56 gr. 12 m.	Venice	B	(137) p.119
1461.05.29	56 gr. 8 m.	Venice	B	(137) p.119
1461.07.24	56 gr. 12 m.	Bruges	B	(81) p.99
1461.07.31	54 gr. 16 m.	Bruges	B	(81) p.100
1462.01.28	56 gr. 12 m.	Venice	B	(137) p.119
1462.03.30	55 gr.	Bruges	B	(81) p.107
1462.09.16	56 gr. 18 m.	Venice	B	(137) p.119
1462.10.16	56 gr. 18 m.	Venice	B	(137) p.119
1462.11.19	56 gr. 12 m.	Venice	B	(137) p.119
1463.01.11	56 gr. 8 m.	Venice	B	(137) p.119
1463.01.21	56 gr. 6 m.	Venice	B	(137) p.119
1463.02.05	56 gr. 8 m.	Venice	B	(137) p.119
1463.03.12	54 gr.	Bruges	B	(81) p.113
1463.03.18	56 gr.	Venice	B	(137) p.119
1463.03.22	54 gr. 12 m.	Bruges	B	(81) p.114
1463.04.05	54 gr. 14 m.	Bruges	B	(81) p.115
1463.05.20	54 gr. 12 m.	Bruges	B	(81) p.115
1463.06.17	56 gr.	Venice	B	(137) p.119
1463.08.19	54 gr. 9 m.	Bruges	B	(81) p.116
1463.08.13	57 gr.	Venice	B	(137) p.119
1463.10.04	56 gr. 6 m.	Venice	B	(137) p.119
1463.12.19	56 gr. 18 m.	Venice	B	(137) p.119
1463.10.04	54 gr. 6 m.	Bruges	B	(81) p.117
1463.10.19	54 gr. 14 m.	Bruges	B	(81) p.119
1463.12.05	54 gr. 20 m.	Bruges	B	(81) p.120
1464.02.20	53 gr.	Bruges	B	(81) p.121
1465.03.03	55 gr.	Bruges	B	(137) p.120
1465.05.04	54 gr. 12 m.	Venice	B	(137) p.120
1474.10	60 gr.	Low Countries	C	(496)
1477.11.10	66 gr.	Flanders	O	(6) p.162
1477.11	66 gr.	Low Countries	C	(496)
1477.11.14	58 gr.	Brussels	O	(518) f.257v
1477.11.14-1478.10.24	58 gr.	Hague	O	(517) f.11r
1477	58 gr.	Low Countries	O	(173)
1478.07.01	68 gr. 8 m.	Bruges	C	(449) II p.249
1478.10.24	66 gr.	Hague	O	(517) f.12r
1478.10.24	66 gr.	Brussels	O	(518) f.258v
1479.06	66 gr.	Low Countries	C	(496)
1480.06-08	66 gr.	Low Countries	C	(496)
1480.07	70 gr.	Bruges	C	(449) II p.248
1482.03	68 gr.	Low Countries	C	(496)
1482.07	74 gr.	Low Countries	C	(496)
1482.07.28	74 gr.	Hague	O	(517) f.13r
1482.07.28	74 gr.	Brussels	O	(518) f.258v
1482	74 gr.	Low Countries	O	(173)
1483	114 gr. Brab. = 76 gr. Fl.	Brussels	O	(518) f.266r
1483	78 gr.	Utrecht	O	(522)
1485	74 gr.	Flanders	C	(6) p.162
1485.04.27	74 gr.	Hague	O	(517) f.13v
1485.04.27	84 gr.	Hague	O	(517) f.14r
1485.04.27	84 gr.	Brussels	O	(518) f.259r
1485.09	74 gr.	Low Countries	O	(173)
1485.12	74 gr.	Low Countries	C	(496)
1485.12	78 gr.	Utrecht	O	(522)
1485.12.12	74 gr.	Hague	O	(517) f.15r
1485.12.25	74 gr.	Brussels	O	(518) f.267r
1486.08	84 gr.	Utrecht	O	(522)
1486.08	80 gr.	Low Countries	O	(173)

THE VENETIAN DUCAT IN GROTEN AND MITEN OF FLANDERS

Date	Rate	Place	Type	Reference
1486.08.31	80 gr.	Hague	O	(517) f.16v
1486.09.03	80 gr.	Brussels	O	(518) f.259v
1487.06	84 gr.	Low Countries	O	(173)
1487.05-09	84 gr.	Low Countries	O	(496)
1487.06.01	84 gr.	Hague	O	(517) f.17v
1487.07.26	92 gr.	Brussels	O	(518) f.262v
1487.12.24	108 gr.	Brussels	O	(518) f.262v
1488.05.20	108 gr.	Brussels	O	(518) f.267v
1488.12	128 gr.	Utrecht	O	(522)
1488 Winter	132 gr.	Delft	O	(517) f.19r
expressed as 11s gr. Fl. and 3 rhguld 6 st.				
1489.07.26	168 gr.	Brussels	O	(518) f.263r
1489	50 gr.	Low Countries	O	(173)
1489.12.24	50 gr.	Hague	O	(517) f.20r
1491.04.18	62 gr.	Brussels	O	(518) f.260v
1491.05.26	60 gr.	Hague	O	(517) f.22v
1491	50 gr.	Utrecht	O	(522)
1492.04	60 gr.	Low Countries	O	(173)
1492.10	60 gr.	Utrecht	O	(522)
1492.12.10	74 gr.	Antwerp-Rome	B	(255) f.4
1493.01	70 gr.	Utrecht	O	(522)
1493.03.10	76 gr.	Middleburg	A	(255) f.12v
1493.03	73 gr.	Antwerp?-Rome	B	(255) f.13
1493.06.07	80 gr. 12 m.	Bruges-Rome	B	(255) f.13v
1493.10.10	82 gr.	Antwerp?-Rome	B	(255) f.13
1493.11	70 gr.	Brabant	O	(522)
1493	70 gr.	Low Countries	O	(173)
1493.11.09	70 gr.	Brussels	O	(518) f.261r
1493.11.12	70 gr.	Hague	O	(517) f.23r
1493.12	73 gr.	Antwerp?	A	(255) f.4
1495.05.06	82 gr.	Bruges-Rome	B	(255) f.14v
1495.05	84 gr.	Bruges-Rome	B	(255) f.14
1495.09	82 gr.	Antwerp?-Rome	B	(255) f.14v
1495.10.02	49 gr.	Antwerp?-Rome	B	(255) f.14v
1495.12	72 gr.	Antwerp?	?	(255) f.32v
1496.01	68 gr.	Low Countries	O	(173)
1496.03	82 gr.	Bruges	A	(255) f.14v
1496.04	80 gr.	Antwerp?	A	(255) f.129v
1496.05	68 gr.	Hague	O	(517) f.26r
1496.05.06	68 gr.	Bruges	A	(255) f.40
1496.11	68 gr.	Antwerp?	A	(255) f.14v
1496.12	72 gr.	Antwerp?	A	(255) f.75
1497.01.10	68 gr.	Antwerp?	A	(255) f.59
1497.03.01	72 gr.	Hague	O	(517) f.27v
1497.05.26	68 gr.	Antwerp?	A	(255) f.59
1497.06	80 gr.	Bruges-Rome	B	(255) f.151
1497.06	64 gr.	Antwerp?	A	(255) f.59
1497.12.16	68 gr.	Antwerp?	A	(255) f.59
1498.01	80 gr.	Antwerp?-Rome	B	(255) f.69
1498.02	84 gr.	Antwerp?	C	(255) f.159
1498.05	80 gr.	Bruges-Rome	B	(255) f.157
1498.06	68 gr.	Antwerp?-Rome	B	(255) f.130
1498.07.18	80 gr.	Antwerp?-Rome	B	(255) f.31
1498.11	79 gr.	Antwerp?-Rome	B	(255) f.131
1499.05.06	80 gr.	Bruges-Rome	B	(255) f.152
1499.08	66 gr.	Low Countries	O	(496)
1499.08	79 gr.	Antwerp?-Rome	B	(255) f.132v
1499.09	72 gr.	Low Countries	O	(173)
1499.09.14-12.24	72 gr.	Hague	O	(517) ff.29-30
1499.10.10	68 gr.	Antwerp?	A	(255) f.189
1499.12.15	75 gr.	Brussels	O	(518) f.261v
1499.12.24	75 gr.	Hague	O	(517) f.33r
1499.12	75 gr.	Low Countries	M	(522)
1500.01	79 gr.	Bruges-Rome	B	(255) f.247
1500.05.29	80 gr.	Tournai-Curia	B	(68) p.177
1500.06.06	80 gr.	Cambrai-Curia	B	(68) p.178
1500.08	79 gr.	Bruges	A	(255) f.249v
1500.12	75 gr.	Antwerp?	A	(255) f.246

The Hungarian ducat in groten of Flanders

A certain number of these quotations were expressed in stuivers. These have been reduced to groten at the rate of 2 groten to every stuiver.

Date	Rate	Place	Type	Reference
1365	27 gr.	Avignon	B	(439) p.62
1368	27 gr.	Rome	B	(439) p.62
1387-1388	41 gr.	Brabant	B	(439) p.62

1433 Reformed Flemish coinage became common coinage of Burgundian Netherlands

Date	Rate	Place	Type	Reference
1434	46 gr.	Holland	C	(76) pp.359-361
1453-1454	49 gr.	Holland	C	(522)
1459	50 gr.	Low Countries	C	(522)
1459	50 gr.	Low Countries	O	(522)
1474.10.27	60 gr.	Low Countries	C	(495) p.395
1474.10	60 gr.	Low Countries	C	(496)
1477.11	68 gr.	Low Countries	C	(496)
1478	68 gr.	Low Countries	C	(173)
1479-1482	68 gr.	Low Countries	C	(522)
1480.06-08	68 gr.	Low Countries	C	(496)
1482.07	76 gr.	Low Countries	C	(496)
1482	76 gr.	Low Countries	C	(173)
1483	80 gr.	Utrecht	C	(522)
1485.04.27	86 gr.	Brussels	O	(518) f.259r
1485.04	86 gr.	Low Countries	C	(173)
1485.09	76 gr.	Low Countries	C	(173)
1485.12.25	76 gr.	Brussels	O	(518) f.267r
1485.12	76 gr.	Low Countries	C	(496)
1485.12	80 gr.	Utrecht	C	(522)
1485	76 gr.	Low Countries	C	(495) p.402
1486.08	82 gr.	Low Countries	C	(173)
1486.08	88 gr.	Utrecht	C	(522)
1487.05-09	86 gr.	Low Countries	C	(496)
1487.06	86 gr.	Low Countries	C	(173)
1487.07	86 gr.	Brussels	O	(518) f.267v
1488.05.20	110 gr.	Brussels	O	(518) f.267v
1489.02.02	198 gr. Brab. = 132 gr. Fl.	Brussels	O	(518) f.268r
1489.12.24	52 gr.	Brussels	O	(518) f.260r
1489	52 gr.	Low Countries	C	(173)
1491	52 gr.	Low Countries	C	(522)
1492.10	62 gr.	Low Countries	C	(522)
1493	72 gr.	Low Countries	C	(522) and (173)
1493.11	72 gr.	Antwerp?	A	(255) f.32v
1494.06	72 gr.	Antwerp?	A	(255) f.42
1495.12	62 gr.	Antwerp?	A	(255) f.38
1496.06	70 gr.	Low Countries	C	(173)
1496.06	71 gr.	Low Countries	C	(173)
1499.08	66 gr.	Low Countries	C	(496)
1499.09	72 gr.	Low Countries	C	(173)
1499.12.15	78 gr.	Brussels	O	(518) f.261v
1499.12	78 gr.	Low Countries	M	(522)

Flemish money groot in other currencies of the Low Countries

The Flemish pond groot in livres, sous and deniers payement of Brabant

I wish to acknowledge my indebtedness to Professor John Munro for communicating these quotations to me.

Date	Rate	Place	Type	Reference
1368.04.09	76 li. 10 s. 9 d.	Malines	A	(363)
1370.04.14	74 li. 18 s. 7 d.	Malines	A	(363)
1370.12.25-1371.04.06	91 li. 5 s. 9 d.	Malines	A	(363)
1371.12.25-1373.04.17	109 li. 19 s. 10 d.	Malines	A	(363)
1373.12.25-1374.04.02	122 li. 14 s. 7 d.	Malines	A	(363)
1374.12.25-1375.04.22	86 li. 9 s. 10 d.	Malines	A	(363)

THE FLEMISH POUND GROOT IN LIVRES, SOUS AND DENIERS PAYEMENT OF BRABANT

Date	Rate	Place	Type	Reference
1375.12.25-1377.03.29	76 li. 11 s. 10 d.	Malines	A	(363)
1377.12.25-1378.04.18	124 li. 19 s. 4 d.	Malines	A	(363)
1378.12.25-1379.04.10	130 li. 12 s. 6 d.	Malines	A	(363)
1379.12.25-1380.03.25	134 li. 1 s. 5 d.	Malines	A	(363)
1380.12.25-1381.04.14	134 li. 7 s. 4 d.	Malines	A	(363)
1381.12.25-1383.03.22	139 li. 3 s. 4 d.	Malines	A	(363)
1383.12.25-1389.04.18	144 li.	Malines	A	(363)
1389.12.25-1390.04.03	219 li. 2 s. 9 d.	Malines	A	(363)
1390.12.25-1396.04.02	224 li.	Malines	A	(363)
1396.12.25-1398.04.07	256 li.	Malines	A	(363)
1398.12.25-1399.03.30	272 li.	Malines	A	(363)
1399.12.25-1410.03.23	288 li.	Malines	A	(363)
1411.04.12	302 li. 7 s. 4 d.	Malines	A	(363)
1412.04.03-1413.04.23	311 li. 17 s. 4 d.	Malines	A	(363)
1414.04.08	323 li. 2 s. 3 d.	Malines	A	(363)
1415.03.31	335 li. 19 s. 4 d.	Malines	A	(363)
1416.04.19	326 li. 14 s. 5 d.	Malines	A	(363)
1417.04.11	324 li.	Malines	A	(363)
1418.03.27	321 li. 3 s.	Malines	A	(363)
1419.04.16-1420.04.07	336 li.	Malines	A	(363)
1421.03.23	356 li. 10 s. 11 d.	Malines	A	(363)
1422.04.12-1428.10	360 li.	Malines	A	(363)
1428.10-1434.05	384 li.	Malines	A	(363)
1434.05	398 li. 17 s. 7 d.	Malines	A	(363)
1435	408 li.	Malines	A	(363)
1435 from 12	432 li.	Malines	A	(363)

The groot of Flanders in deniers payement of Brabant

Date	Rate	Place	Type	Reference
1338-1339	22 d.	Malines	A	(377) p.150
1340-1341	23 1/2 d.	Malines	A	(377) p.150
1341-1342	26 d.	Malines	A	(377) p.150
1342-1343	27 d.	Malines	A	(377) p.150
1345-1346	34 d.	Malines	A	(377) p.150
1346-1347	37 d.	Malines	A	(377) p.150
1347-1348	40 d.	Malines	A	(377) p.150
1348-1349	42 d.	Malines	A	(377) p.150
1349-1350	39 d.	Malines	A	(377) p.150
1350-1351	38 d.	Malines	A	(377) p.150
1351-1352	38 d.	Malines	A	(377) p.150
1352-1353	37 d.	Malines	A	(377) p.150
1353-1354	40 d.	Malines	A	(377) p.150
1354-1355	41 d.	Malines	A	(377) p.150
1355-1356	43 d.	Malines	A	(377) p.150
1356-1357	46 d.	Malines	A	(377) p.150
1357-1358	48 d.	Malines	A	(377) p.150
1358-1359	50 d.	Malines	A	(377) p.150
1359-1360	57 d.	Malines	A	(377) p.150
1360-1361	57 d.	Malines	A	(377) p.150
1361-1363	60 d.	Malines	A	(377) p.150
1363-1364	64 d.	Malines	A	(377) p.150
1364-1365	63 d.	Malines	A	(377) p.150
1365-1366	73 d.	Malines	A	(377) p.150
1366-1367	82 d.	Malines	A	(377) p.150
1367-1368	83 d.	Malines	A	(377) p.150
1368-1369	89 d.	Malines	A	(377) p.150
1369-1370	99 1/2 d.	Malines	A	(377) p.150
1370-1371	107 d.	Malines	A	(377) p.150
1371-1372	116 d.	Malines	A	(377) p.150
1372-1373	116 d.	Malines	A	(377) p.150
1373-1374	117 d.	Malines	A	(377) p.150
1374-1375	119 d.	Malines	A	(377) p.150
1375-1376	120 d.	Malines	A	(377) p.150
1376-1377	123 d.	Malines	A	(377) p.150
1377-1378	126 d.	Malines	A	(377) p.150
1378-1379	129 d.	Malines	A	(377) p.150
1379-1380	135 d.	Malines	A	(377) p.150
1380-1381	138 d.	Malines	A	(377) p.150
1381-1382	140 d.	Malines	A	(377) p.150

THE GROOT OF FLANDERS IN DENIERS PAYEMENT OF BRABANT

Date	Rate	Place	Type	Reference
1382-1383	142 d.	Malines	A	(377) p.150
1383-1384	140 d.	Malines	A	(377) p.150

The Flemish pond groot in schellingen and penningen groot of Brabant

The general tendency in any coinage was for it to be reduced in value as time passed. However, from time to time both the Flemish and the Brabançon groten were restored in value, instead of debased. For a short time after such changes there was always a certain amount of confusion and accounting was carried on both in 'old' money and 'new' money, in 'weak' money and 'strong' money. The following table always refers to 'strong' Flemish money groot. Some of the occasions when the coinages were radically improved are clearly visible in the table — for example in Flanders in 1389, and in Brabant in 1399.

Date	Rate	Place	Type	Reference
1368.04.09	31 s. 11 d.	Malines	A	(363)
1370.04.14	31 s. 3 d.	Malines	A	(363)
1370.12.25-1371.04.06	38 s. 1 d.	Malines	A	(363)
1371.12.25-1373.04.17	45 s. 10 d.	Malines	A	(363)
1373.12.25-1374.04.02	51 s. 2 d.	Malines	A	(363)
1374.12.25-1375.04.22	36 s. 1 d.	Malines	A	(363)
1375.12.25-1377.03.29	31 s. 11 d.	Malines	A	(363)
1377.12.25-1378.04.18	52 s. 1 d.	Malines	A	(363)
1378.12.25-1379.04.10	54 s. 5 d.	Malines	A	(363)
1379.12.25-1380.03.25	55 s. 10 d.	Malines	A	(363)
1380.12.25-1381.04.14	55 s.	Malines	A	(363)
1381.12.25-1383.03.22	58 s.	Malines	A	(363)
1383.12.25-1389.04.18	60 s.	Malines	A	(363)
1389.12.25-1390.04.03	91 s. 4 d.	Malines	A	(363)
1390.12.25-1396.04.02	93 s. 4 d.	Malines	A	(363)
1396.12.25-1398.04.07	106 s. 8 d.	Malines	A	(363)
1398.12.25-1399.03.30	113 s. 4 d.	Malines	A	(363)
1399.12.25	120 s.	Malines	A	(363)
1399.12.25-1410.03.23	20 s.	Malines	A	(363)
1411.04.12	21 s.	Malines	A	(363)
1412.04.03-1413.04.23	21 s. 4 d.	Malines	A	(363)
1414.04.08	22 s. 5 d.	Malines	A	(363)
1415.03.31	23 s. 4 d.	Malines	A	(363)
1416.04.19	22 s. 8 d.	Malines	A	(363)
1417.04.11	22 s. 6 d.	Malines	A	(363)
1418.03.27	22 s. 4 d.	Malines	A	(363)
1419.04.16-1420.04.07	23 s. 4 d.	Malines	A	(363)
1421.03.23	24 s. 9 d.	Malines	A	(363)
1422.04.12-1428.10	25 s.	Malines	A	(363)
1428.10-1434.05	26 s. 8 d.	Malines	A	(363)
1434.05	27 s. 8 d.	Malines	A	(363)
1435	28 s. 4 d.	Malines	A	(363)
1435 from 12	30 s.	Malines	A	(363)

Flemish money groot in currencies outside the general area of Tuscan exchanges after 1300

The Flemish pond groot in the money of Hamburg

Date	Rate	Place	Type	Reference
up to 1350	5 li.	Curia	B	(439) p.92

The Flemish pond groot in mark, schillinge, and pfennige of Lübeck
In Lübeck the mark was reckoned as 16 schillinge

Date	Rate	Place	Type	Reference
1341-1342	8 mk.	Lübeck	C	(259) p.220
1341	9 mk. 1 s.	Lübeck	C	(259) p.220
1342-1349	8 mk. 12 s.	Lübeck	C	(259) p.220

THE FLEMISH POUND GROOT IN MARK, SCHILLINGE, AND PFENNIGE OF LÜBECK

Date	Rate	Place	Type	Reference
1345-1350	7 mk. 8 s.	Lübeck	C	(259) p.220
1345-1350	7 mk. 11 s.	Lübeck	C	(259) p.220
1349	8 mk. 14 s.	Lübeck	C	(402) V p.XI
1349	8 mk. 13 s.	Lübeck	C	(402) V p.XI
1350	9 mk.	Lübeck	C	(402) V p.XI
1350	9 mk. 1 s.	Lübeck	C	(402) V p.XI
1353	7 mk. 12 s.	Lübeck	C	(259) p.220
1356	7 mk.	Lübeck	C	(259) p.220
1356	6 mk. 14 s.	Lübeck	C	(259) p.220
1357-1358	6 mk. 13 s.	Lübeck	C	(259) p.220
1357	7 mk. 2 s.	Lübeck	C	(259) p.220
1360-1364	6 mk.	Lübeck	C	(259) p.220
1363	6 mk.	Lübeck	C	(402) V p.XI
1368	5 mk.	Lübeck	C	(291) p.63
1368	6 mk.	Lübeck	C	(291) p.64
1368-1369	6 mk.	Lübeck	C	(402) V p.XI
1371	5 mk. 10 s.	Lübeck	C	(259) p.220
1373-1376	5 mk.	Lübeck	C	(402) V p.XI
1373-1374	5 mk. 2 s. 5 d.	Lübeck	C	(259) p.220
1373	5 mk. 1 s.	Lübeck	C	(259) p.220
1374	5 mk. 14 s.	Lübeck	C	(259) p.220
1375	5 mk. 3 s.	Lübeck	C	(259) p.220
1375	5 mk. 1 s.	Lübeck	C	(259) p.220
1376-1377	5 mk.	Lübeck	C	(259) p.220
1378	5 mk. 4 s. 7 d.	Lübeck	C	(259) p.220
1381	5 mk. 4 s.	Lübeck	C	(259) p.220
1385	4 mk. 12 s.	Lübeck	C	(402) V p.XI
1385	4 mk. 6 s.	Lübeck	C	(259) p.220
1387-1389	4 mk. 8 s.	Lübeck	C	(402) V p.XI
1393	4 mk. 2 s.	Lübeck	C	(259) p.220
1394	4 mk.	Lübeck	C	(402) V p.XI
1394	3 mk. 14 s. 7 d.	Lübeck	C	(259) p.220
1398	6 mk.	Lübeck	C	(259) p.220
1403-1404	5 mk. 6 s.	Lübeck	C	(259) p.220
1407	6 mk.	Lübeck	C	(259) p.220
1409	6 mk. 8 s.	Lübeck	C	(259) p.220
1410	6 mk. 5 s.	Lübeck	C	(259) p.220
1410	7 mk. 6 s.	Lübeck	C	(259) p.220
1411	6 mk. 4 s.	Lübeck	C	(259) p.220
1412	6 mk. 3 s.	Lübeck	C	(259) p.220
1412	6 mk. 12 s.	Lübeck	C	(259) p.220
1413	4 mk. 10 s.	Lübeck	C	(259) p.220
1413	4 mk. 14 s.	Lübeck	C	(259) p.220
1415	6 mk. 1 s.	Lübeck	C	(259) p.221
1415	6 mk. 7 s. 5 d.	Lübeck	C	(259) p.221
1416-1417	6 mk.	Lübeck	C	(259) p.221
1418	4 mk. 10 s.	Lübeck	C	(259) p.221
1419	6 mk. 15 s. 2 d.	Lübeck	C	(259) p.221
1419	6 mk. 13 s. 2 d.	Lübeck	C	(259) p.221
1420-1421	6 mk. 15 s. 2 d.	Lübeck	C	(259) p.221
1422	7 mk.	Lübeck	C	(259) p.221
1423	6 mk. 14 s.	Lübeck	C	(259) p.221
1423	6 mk. 14 s. 7 d.	Lübeck	C	(259) p.221
1429	6 mk. 15 s. 2 d.	Lübeck	C	(259) p.221
1431	9 mk.	Lübeck	C	(402) V p.XI
1431	8 mk. 12 s.	Lübeck	C	(402) V p.XI
1431	8 mk. 2 s.	Lübeck	C	(402) V p.XI
1431	8 mk.	Lübeck	C	(402) V p.XI
1434	6 mk. 15 s. 7 d.	Lübeck	C	(259) p.221
1436	6 mk. 10 s.	Lübeck	C	(259) p.221
1437	8 mk. 2 s.	Lübeck	C	(259) p.221
1445	8 mk.	Lübeck	C	(259) p.221
1446	8 mk. 4 s.	Lübeck	C	(259) p.221
1449-1474	8 mk.	Lübeck	C	(259) p.221

THE FLEMISH POND GROOT IN SCHILLINGE OF PRUSSIA

The Flemish pond groot in schillinge of Prussia

Date	Rate	Place	Type	Reference
1448	8 s.	Prussia	0	(506) II pp.74-75

For the florin of 12 gros in groten of Flanders see under AVIGNON p.128
For the rheingulden in Flemish groten and sterlings see under RHINELAND p.255
For the Sundisch mark in Flemish groten see under STRALSUND p.281

The gold royale

Pegolotti also noted that merchants who went to Bruges also reckoned in 'reale d'oro'. The 'reali d'oro' or royale was the French gold double florin, struck for Philip IV between 1296 and 1311, and known in France either as a 'roial', or more commonly, as a 'masse d'or'. No gold royales were minted in Flanders itself. Pegolotti went on to explain that these were worth 2 soldi di grossi tornesi, in the same way that the gold florin was worth 29 soldi a fiorino in Florence (177) p.239. This would, rather surprisingly, imply that the gros tournois was used as an accounting unit as one twenty-fourth part of the gold royale. It seems more probable, that it was the other way round, and that it was the royale that was used as an accounting unit to mean 24 silver groten. Pegolotti later inserted two ready reckoning tables which would support this later interpretation (177) pp.247-9. These give the equivalents for the royale, as a unit of 24 groten, in money a fiorino of Florence, and in grossi of Venice, for varying values of the Florentine gold florin in groten. When he was compiling his notebook reasonable values for the florin ranged from 12 groten to 16 groten. In 1313, the royale was rated at about forty-five sous of Genoa (154) III p.1085, as quoted by de Roover.

BURGUNDIAN NETHERLANDS AFTER 1433-5

After the unification of the coinages of the Burgundian Netherlands in 1433-5, the former moneys of the other principalities were tied in fixed relationships to the new Burgundian coinage, which was in effect a continuation of the money of Flanders. All exchange rates will therefore be found under FLANDERS above. Thereafter the pond groot of Flanders always equalled 1 li. 10s. groot of Brabant; 6 li. of Artois; 6 li. of Holland; 12 li. tournois of Hainault and 12 li. parisis of Flanders itself. In addition to the pond groot, and the livre parisis, there was a third Flemish accounting system, also based on the groot. This was the pond of forty groten. In the 1440s the electoral florins from the Rhineland were commercially current at forty Flemish groten, and in the 1450s they were officially current at that rate. They therefore became equated in men's minds with the pound of forty groten. The principal silver coin in circulation in the Low Countries, the Burgundian stuiver or patard, formed a natural shilling for it, being valued at two groten. Although by 1467 the gold rheingulden had officially become worth 42 Flemish groten and by 1488, 90 Flemish groten, gulden still remained in use, into the sixteenth century, as the name of the pound of forty groten.

BRABANT

In Brabant there were two parallel systems of accounting in use, as in Flanders. The one was based on the old deniers, monnaie de payement and the other on the newer gros or groot.

The relationship between the two varied. In 1337, for example, the gros was worth 2s. payement. About 1360 the relationship was fossilized at 1 gros = 4s. payement. When the coinage was reformed in July 1384 the new gros of that year = 3 old gros = 12s. payement. When it was again reformed in 1399 the new gros of that year = 6 old gros = 24s. payement.

The Florentine florin in livres, sous and deniers payement of Brabant

Date	Rate	Place	Type	Reference
1345.07.28	2 li. 5 s.	Louvain	A	(349)
1346.04.12	2 li. 8 s.	Louvain	A	(349)
1347.03.01	2 li. 9 s. 6 d.	Louvain	A	(349)
1347.11.19	2 li. 15 s. 4 d.	Louvain	A	(349)
1348.04.22	2 li. 19 s.	Louvain	A	(349)
1349.03.02	3 li.	Louvain	A	(349)
1350.01.17	3 li.	Louvain	A	(349)
1351.04.05	3 li.	Louvain	A	(349)
1352.02.19	3 li.	Louvain	A	(349)
1353.01	3 li.	Louvain	A	(349)
1353.05	3 li. 3 s.	Louvain	A	(349)
1353.09	3 li.	Louvain	A	(349)
1353.09	3 li. 3 s.	Louvain	A	(349)
1354.02	3 li. 3 s.	Louvain	A	(349)
1357	2 li. 19 s.	Brussels	A	(214) p.382
1358	4 li. 3 s.	Brussels	A	(214) p.382
1359	4 li. 5 s.	Brussels	A	(214) p.382
1360	4 li. 16 s.	Brussels	A	(214) p.382
1360	5 li.	Brussels	A	(214) p.382
1361	5 li. 10 s.	Brussels	A	(214) p.382
1362-1363	5 li. 16 s.	Brussels	A	(214) p.382
1364	6 li. 6 s.	Brussels	A	(214) p.382
1366	7 li. 4 s.	Brussels	A	(214) p.382
1367	8 li. 8 s.	Brussels	A	(214) p.382
1368	9 li.	Brussels	A	(214) p.382
1369	9 li. 8 s.	Brussels	A	(214) p.382
1370	11 li. 12 s.	Brussels	A	(214) p.382
1371	14 li.	Brussels	A	(214) p.382
1372	15 li.	Brussels	A	(214) p.382
1373	15 li. 4 s.	Brussels	A	(214) p.382
1375	16 li. 4 s.	Brussels	A	(214) p.382
1375	17 li.	Brussels	A	(214) p.382
1376-1377	16 li. 4 s.	Brussels	A	(214) p.382
1381	18 li. 12 s.	Brussels	A	(214) p.382
1382	19 li. 16 s.	Brussels	A	(214) p.382
1383	20 li.	Brussels	A	(214) p.382
1384	20 li. 8 s.	Brussels	A	(214) p.382
1385-1386	21 li. 12 s.	Brussels	A	(214) p.382
1387	22 li.	Brussels	A	(214) p.382
1387	22 li. 4 s.	Brussels	A	(214) p.382
1388	23 li. 8 s.	Brussels	A	(214) p.382
1389	24 li.	Brussels	A	(214) p.382
1390	26 li. 2 s.	Brussels	A	(214) p.382
1391-1392	27 li. 18 s.	Brussels	A	(214) p.382
1392	28 li.	Brussels	A	(214) p.382
1393-1394	28 li. 16 s.	Brussels	A	(214) p.382
1394	28 li.	Brussels	A	(214) p.382
1395	30 li.	Brussels	A	(214) p.382
1396	32 li. 8 s.	Brussels	A	(214) p.382
1396	33 li. 12 s.	Brussels	A	(214) p.382
1397	34 li. 4 s.	Brussels	A	(214) p.382
1397	35 li. 14 s.	Brussels	A	(214) p.382
1398	35 li. 14 s.	Brussels	A	(214) p.382
1400	37 li. 4 s.	Brussels	A	(214) p.382
1401-1403	37 li. 16 s.	Brussels	A	(214) p.382
1409	38 li. 14 s.	Brussels	A	(214) p.382
1417	39 li. 12 s.	Brussels	A	(214) p.382
1417-1420	43 li. 4 s.	Brussels	A	(214) p.382

The sou of Brabant in deniers of Artois

Date	Rate	Place	Type	Reference
1270-5	13 d.	Brabant	A	(74) p.XLI

The sou of Brabant in deniers of Liège

Date	Rate	Place	Type	Reference
mid 13th. century	8 d.	Brabant	A	(475) p.271

The sou of Brabant in deniers of Valenciennes

Date	Rate	Place	Type	Reference
mid 13th. century	16 d.	Brabant	A	(475) p.271

The Florentine florin in money groot of Brabant

These groten were sometimes confusingly known as 'Flemish' although struck in Brabant. Sometimes these quotations were given in terms of plaques or double groten. These have been reduced to groten. H = Hungarian ducat

Date	Rate	Place	Type	Reference
1339.04	16 gr.	Thérouanne	B	(28) p.120
1394-1395H	56 gr.	Brabant	C	(115) II

1399 currency 'restored'. For a short while rates were expressed in either new or old groten.

Date	Rate	Place	Type	Reference
1399.08.05-1400	61 old gr.	Brabant	C	(115) II
1401-1410	63 gr.	Brabant	A	(214) p.382
1403-1404	31 1/2 new gr.	Brabant	A	(214) p.382
1404.06-1405.06	36 new gr.	Brabant	A	(115) IV
1410-1417	66 gr.	Brabant	A	(214) p.382
1417-1421	36 new gr.	Brabant	A	(214) p.382
1418	72 gr.	Brabant	A	(214) p.382
1420	60 gr.	Brabant	A	(214) p.382
1420	78 gr.	Brabant	A	(214) p.382
1421-1450	66 gr.	Brabant	A	(214) p.382

From 1433 Brabant used the common coinage of the Burgundian Netherlands based on the coinage of Flanders. For accounting purposes 1 li. 10 s. groot of Brabant was reckoned as 1 li. groot of Flanders after 1433.

For the pound sterling in sous and deniers of Brabant see under ENGLAND p.210
For the Flemish pond groot in sous and deniers payement see under FLANDERS p.224
For the Flemish pond groot in schellingen and groten of Brabant see under FLANDERS p.226
For the livre of Liège in sous and deniers of Louvain see under LIÈGE p.232
For the mark of Cologne in sous of Louvain see under COLOGNE p.236
For the rheingulden in groten of Brabant see under RHINELAND p.255
For the pfund of heller in sous and deniers of Brabant see under HELLER p.265

HAINAULT

In Hainault, money tournois was used as the principal money of account, and diverged from French money tournois when the latter was so frequently altered by Philip IV in the years 1296 to 1306. I have tried to distinguish them, but some of the following rates may be royal, and some of the rates entered as French, above pp.172-80 may be of Hainault.

The Florentine florin in sous and deniers tournois of Hainault

Date	Rate	Place	Type	Reference
1308	14 s. 2 d.	Mons	A	(389) II p.145
1311-1326	22 s. 6 d.	Mons	A	(389) II p.146
1314-1315	14 s. 6 d.	Mons	A	(389) II p.145
1317-1318	12 s. 10 d.	Mons	A	(389) II p.145
1317-1318	13 s.	Mons	A	(389) II p.145
1321	13 s. 4 d.	Mons	A	(389) II p.145

THE FLORENTINE FLORIN IN SOUS AND DENIERS TOURNOIS OF HAINAULT

Date	Rate	Place	Type	Reference
1323	18 s.	Mons	A	(389) II p.145
1323	20 s. 8 d.	Mons	A	(389) II p.145
1324	19 s. 2 d.	Mons	A	(389) II p.146
1324	17 s. 6 d.	Mons	A	(389) II p.146
1325	19 s. 6 d.	Brussels	A	(455) I p.199
1325	19 s. 3 d.	Brussels	A	(455) I p.199
1326	19 s. 4 d.	Paris	A	(455) I p.178
1326	19 s. 3 d.	France	A	(455) I p.178
1326-1327	21 s. 2 d.	Mons	A	(389) II p.146
1327	17 s. 10 d.	Flanders	A	(455) I p.311
1327	24 s. 6 d.	Brussels	A	(455) I p.300
1328	25 s.	Holland	A	(455) I p.361
1328	27 s. 6 d.	Holland	A	(455) I p.362
1328	25 s.	Brussels	A	(455) I p.401
1328	26 s.	Paris	A	(455) I p.366
1328	27 s. 4 d.	France	A	(455) I p.408
1328-1329	21 s.	Mons	A	(389) II p.146
1330-1331	18 s.	Mons	A	(389) II p.146
1330-1331	13 s. 4 d.	Mons	A	(389) II p.146
1330-1331	13 s.	Holland	A	(455) I p.535
1332	16 s.	Mons	A	(389) II p.146
1332	13 s.	Brussels	A	(455) I p.641
1336-1337	14 s.	Mons	A	(389) p.146
1336-1337	13 s.	Mons	A	(389) p.146
1336-1340	17 s.	Mons	A	(389) p.146
1337.07	16 s.	Hainault	A	(207) p.153
1338	18 s. 6 d.	Mons	A	(389) II p.146
1338.07-12	19 s.	Mons	A	(207) p.153
1338.08.09	18 s. 6 d.	Mons	A	(207) p.153
1339	23 s.	Mons	A	(389) II p.146
1339.07-12	22 s. 6 d.	Mons	A	(207) p.153
1340-1341	23 s.	Mons	A	(389) II p.146
1340-1341	25 s.	Mons	A	(389) II p.146
1340.01.19	22 s. 6 d.	Mons	A	(207) p.153
1340.01.19	23 s.	Mons	A	(207) p.153
1340.01-06	23 s.	Mons	A	(207) p.153
1340.01-06	24 s.	Mons	A	(207) p.153
1341.01.01	25 s.	Mons	A	(207) p.153
1341.01-06	27 s.	Mons	A	(207) p.153
1341.03.01	30 s.	Hainault	A	(207) p.153
1341.05.17	32 s.	Mons	A	(207) p.153
1341.06.20	32 s.	Hainault	A	(207) p.153
1341.06.24	32 s.	Hainault	A	(207) p.153
1341.09.14	36 s.	Hainault	A	(207) p.153
1341.12.25	36 s.	Hainault	A	(207) p.153
1342	14 s.	Mons	A	(389) II p.146
1342	28 s. 6 d.	Mons	A	(389) II p.146
1342.01-06	37 s. 6 d.	Hainault	A	(207) p.153
1342.02.02	38 s.	Hainault	A	(207) p.153
1342.01-06	43 s.	Hainault	A	(207) p.153
1342.01-06	43 s. 6 d.	Hainault	A	(207) p.153
1342.07-12	47 s.	Mons	A	(207) p.153
1342.10.01	48 s.	Mons	A	(207) p.153
1343	12 s. 6 d.	Mons	A	(389) II p.146
1343	14 s.	Mons	A	(389) II p.146
1343.01-06	48 s.	Mons	A	(207) p.153
1343.01-06	52 s.	Mons	A	(207) p.153
1343.10.01	52 s.	Mons	A	(207) p.153
1344-1346	12 s. 6 d.	Mons	A	(389) II p.146
1344.01-06	12 s. 6 d.	Mons	A	(207) p.153
1344.07-12	12 s. 6 d.	Mons	A	(207) p.153
1345.01-06	12 s. 6 d.	Mons	A	(207) p.153
1345.07-12	12 s. 6 d.	Mons	A	(206) p.73
1346.01-06	12 s. 9 d.	Mons	A	(206) p.73
1346.07-12	13 s.	Mons	A	(206) p.73
1347-1348	13 s.	Mons	A	(389) II p.146
1347-1348	18 s. 6 d.	Mons	A	(389) II p.146
1347.01-06	13 s.	Mons	A	(206) p.73
1347.07-12	13 s.	Mons	A	(206) p.73
1348.01-06	13 s.	Mons	A	(206) p.73
1348.07-12	13 s. 8 d.	Mons	A	(206) p.70
1348.09.22	13 s. 8 d.	St Waudru	A	(206) p.73

THE FLORENTINE FLORIN IN SOUS AND DENIERS TOURNOIS OF HAINAULT

Date	Rate	Place	Type	Reference
1348.10	14 s. 6 d.	Hainault	O	(206) p.70
1349.01-06	14 s. 6 d.	Mons	A	(206) p.73
1350.01-06	14 s. 6 d.	Mons	A	(206) p.73
1350.07-12	14 s. 6 d.	Mons	A	(206) p.73
1351.11	15 s. 9 d.	St Waudru	A	(206) p.73
1352.01	15 s. 9 d.	Hainault	A	(206) p.73
1354.01.12	16 s. 6 d.	Hainault	A	(206) p.73
1355-1356	14 s.	Mons	A	(389) II p.146

From 1433 Hainault used the common coinage of the Burgundian Netherlands based on the coinage of Flanders. For accounting purposes 12 li. tournois of Hainault was reckoned as 1 li. groot of Flanders after 1433.

For the gros tournois in deniers tournois of Hainault see under FRANCE p.188
For the sou of Brabant in deniers of Valenciennes see under BRABANT p.230

NAMUR

In the fifteenth century accounting was done in florins of 45 heaumes. After 1433 Namur used the common coinage of the Burgundian Netherlands based on the coinage of Flanders. For accounting purpose the heaume of Namur was reckoned as equal to the groot of Flanders

LIÈGE

The livre of Liège in sous tournois of France

Date	Rate	Place	Type	Reference
1279	4 s.	Liège	A	(242) p.115

The livre of Liège in sous and deniers of Louvain

Date	Rate	Place	Type	Reference
1284	30 s. parvorum	Liège	A	(242) p.115

The livre of Liège in sous and deniers of St Trond

Date	Rate	Place	Type	Reference
1258	37 s. 6 d.	St Trond	A	(242) p.117

The livre of Liège in mark of Cologne

In 1250, 19 livres of Liège were reckoned at Liège as 18 mark of 12 s. of Cologne (242) p.115.

The florin in petits tournois del commun payement of Liège

At Liège, as in Hainault, and at Huy, money tournois was adopted instead of the original local money.

Date	Rate	Place	Type	Reference
1348	33 s.	Liège	A	(197) p.99

The livre of Liège in sous tournois of Huy

Date	Rate	Place	Type	Reference
1351	22 s.	Liège	A	(197) pp.97-98

The livre liégeois in livres tournois of Liège

When the local tournois had become too debased, a new money liégeois was adopted in its place.

Date	Rate	Place	Type	Reference
1358	4 li	Liège	A	(197) p.99

The ducat in florins and aidants of Liège

In the late fifteenth century the Liégois used their florin as their pound of account. The shilling in this system of account was the aidant. The florin of account was worth twenty aidants, which in the period 1477-86 were approximately the same as the stuivers or double gros in Flanders. The aidant itself was reckoned at this time as 24 of the older Liège deniers.

Date	Rate	Place	Type	Reference
1477.10.23	1 fl. 11 a.	Liège	A	(521)
1478.11.02	1 fl. 14 a.	Liège	A	(521)
1480.12.16	1 fl. 13 a.	Liège	A	(521)
1482.08.13	1 fl. 17 a.	Liège	A	(521)
1486.09.26	2 fl. 1 a.	Liège	A	(521)
1488.08.02	2 fl. 17 a.	Liège	A	(521)
1491.03.02	4 fl. 10 a.	Liège	A	(521)
1494.09.05	2 fl. 14 a.	Liège	A	(521)
1499.09.17 old ducats	2 fl. 14 a.	Liège	A	(521)

The Hungarian ducat in florins and aidants of Liège

Date	Rate	Place	Type	Reference
1478.11.02	1 fl. 14 a.	Liège	A	(521)
1480.12.16	1 fl. 14 a.	Liège	A	(521)
1482.08.13	1 fl. 18 a.	Liège	A	(521)
1486.09.26	2 fl. 2 a.	Liège	A	(521)
1488.08.02	2 fl. 18 a.	Liège	A	(521)
1491.03.02	4 fl. 12 a.	Liège	A	(521)
1494.09.05	2 fl. 15 a.	Liège	A	(521)
1499.09.17	2 fl. 15 a.	Liège	A	(521)

For the livre of Flanders in sous of Liège see under FLANDERS p.214
For the sou of Brabant in deniers of Liège see under BRABANT p.230

HOLLAND

The sou of Holland in deniers of Artois

Date	Rate	Place	Type	Reference
1265.12	16-16 1/2 d.	Douai	A	(475) p.271

From 1433 Holland used the common coinage of the Burgundian Netherlands based on the coinage of Flanders. For accounting purposes 8 d. Holland was reckoned as 1 groot of Flanders after 1433.

For the mark of Cologne in ponden of Holland see under COLOGNE p.237
For the rheingulden in groten of Holland see under RHINELAND p.256

UTRECHT

For the mark of Cologne in schellingen and penningen of Utrecht see under COLOGNE p.237
For the rheingulden in witten and stuivers of Utrecht see under RHINELAND p.256

GELDERLAND

For the rheingulden in stuivers and butkens of Gelderland see under RHINELAND p.257

DEVENTER

In 1179 the money of Deventer was equal to that of Utrecht in whose 'Oversticht' it lay (242) p.102. Accounting in the city accounts of Deventer used a succession of different units. From the beginning of the accounts in 1337 until 1346 a heavy pond of 20 groten was used; from 1347 to 1360 a light pond of 15 groten, or 60 d. Brabant. From 1361 to 1373 a light pond of 16 Flemish groten; from 1374 to 1390 a light pond of 10 plakken or 20 Flemish groten; from 1393 to 1433 a gulden of 24 plakken; from 1435 to 1447 a new gulden of 64 plakken; and from 1448 the heavy pond again, worth a variable number of plakken (132).

At the end of the fifteenth century Deventer belonged to the Overijssel monetary union with Kampen and Jülich-Berg. In 1448 8 plakken of Deventer = 1 stuiver of Overijssel.

The Venetian ducat in stuivers of Overijssel

Date	Rate	Place	Type	Reference
1488.10.27	25 st.	Deventer	0	(174) p.289

The Hungarian ducat in stuivers of Overijssel

Date	Rate	Place	Type	Reference
1488.10.27	26 st.	Deventer	0	(174) p.290

For the rheingulden in plakken, kromstaarten and stuivers see under RHINELAND p.258

GRONINGEN

For the pound sterling in schellingen and penningen of Groningen, see under ENGLAND p.210

SECTION IX
THE EMPIRE, apart from the NETHERLANDS, the ARELATE and NORTHERN ITALY

WESTPHALIA

The towns and princes of Westphalia frequently issued their coin under agreements with their neighbours. In the late fifteenth century Dortmund belonged to one such Westphalian monetary union of towns and princes.

The Venetian ducat in schillinge and pfennige of Dortmund

Date	Rate	Place	Type	Reference
1488.03.10	19 s.	Dortmund	O	(174) p.289
1489.05.06	12 s. 6 d.	Dortmund	O	(174) p.289

The Hungarian ducat in schillinge and pfennige of Dortmund

Date	Rate	Place	Type	Reference
1488.03.10	20 s.	Dortmund	O	(174) p.290
1489.05.06	13 s.	Dortmund	O	(174) p.290

Another league united the money of Osnabruck, Paderborn, Soest, Marsberg, and Brakel.

A third league united the money of Bielefeld, Herford and Lemgo. Höxter, Hameln, Hanover, and Minden generally maintained independent currencies.

For the rheingulden in schillinge and pfennige of Dortmund see under RHINELAND p.243
For the rheingulden in schillinge and pfennige pagyment of Westphalia (=Osnabruck, Paderborn, Soest, Marsberg and Brakel) see under RHINELAND p.245
For the rheingulden in schillinge and pfennige of Bielefeld, Herford and Lemgo see under RHINELAND p.245
For the rheingulden in schillinge and pfennige of Höxter, Hameln, Hanover and Minden see under RHINELAND p.246

RHINELAND

For the weisspfennige and rheingulden of the Rhineland Monetary Union see below pp.239 and 240

COLOGNE

The pfennige of Cologne provided much of the currency of the lower Rhineland in the central middle ages. Reckoning was carried out in mark of 12 schillinge and schillinge of 12 pfennige. All quotations have been reduced to schillinge and pfennige, although in the sources they may have appeared as 80 pfennige rather that 6 schillinge and 8 pfennige, or as 3 mark and 2 schillinge rather than 38 schillinge. See also WEISSPFENNIGE p.239, and RHEINGULDEN p.240

The Florentine florin in schillinge and pfennige pagament of Cologne
H = Hungarian ducat; B = Bohemian ducat

Date	Rate	Place	Type	Reference
1277-1286	2 s. 6 d.	Curia	B	(439) p.897
1298-1299	5 s. 1 d.	Curia	B	(439) p.898
1301	6 s. 8 d.	Curia	B	(439) p.898
1308	3 s. 4 d. new money	Curia	B	(439) p.899
1313	3 s. 4 d.	Curia	B	(439) p.900

THE FLORENTINE FLORIN IN SCHILLINGE AND PFENNIGE PAGAMENT OF COLOGNE

Date	Rate	Place	Type	Reference
1313	5 s.	Curia	B	(439) p.900
1318	15 s. 3 d.	Cologne	C	(267) p.LXXV
1319	16 s. 9 d.	Cologne & Trier	C	(267) p.LXXVI
1319	16 s. 10 d.	Worms	C	(267) p.LXXVI
1319	10 s. 2 d.	Curia	B	(439) p.900
1326-1327	12 s.	Cologne	B	(439) p.901
1342-1348	20 s.	Curia	B	(439) p.902
1344-1348	21 s.	Curia	B	(439) p.902
1346	20 s. 11 d.	Aachen	HC	(461) p.375
1349	22 s. 5 d.	Aachen	HC	(461) p.375
1357	22 s.	Aachen	C	(271) p.162
1358	24 s.	Aachen	C	(271) p.162
1359	25 s.	Aachen	C	(271) p.162
1360	25 s. 6 d.	Aachen	C	(271) p.162
1361.10.01	27 s.	Aachen	C	(271) p.162
1361	26 s. 6 d.	Aachen	C	(271) p.162
1362.10.01-1363	28 s.	Aachen	C	(271) p.162
1362	27 s. 4 d.	Aachen	C	(271) p.162
1364	30 s.	Aachen	C	(271) p.162
1365.07	30 s.	Aachen	C	(271) p.162
1365.11-1366	31 s.	Aachen	C	(271) p.162
1365	30 s. 6 d.	Aachen	C	(271) p.162
1366.04	32 s.	Aachen	C	(271) p.162
1366.10	30 s.	Aachen	C	(271) p.162
1367	32 s.	Aachen	C	(271) p.162
1368	33 s.	Aachen	C	(271) p.162
1370-1371	36 s.	Cologne	C	(272) p.27
1372-1380	37 s.	Cologne	C	(272) p.28
1372	40 s.	Aachen	C	(271) p.162
1375.09.19H	37 s. 6 d.	Cologne	C	(272) p.29
1376.01.23B	38 s. 5 d.	Cologne	C	(272) p.29
1376.11.28B	38 s.	Cologne	C	(272) p.29
1380-1390	40 s.	Cologne	C	(272) p.28
1383.07.01B	41 s.	Cologne	C	(272) p.29
1388.10.07-1421.10.22H	42 s.	Cologne	C	(272) p.29

The money of Cologne in other local currencies

In the twelfth century the Cologne pfennig was reckoned as equal to two pfennige of Andernach (242) p.172. In 1195 the Cologne pfennig was reckoned as equal to two pfennige of Coblenz (242) p.175. In 1203 the Cologne pfennig was reckoned as equal to two pfennige of the light money of Mainz (242) p.175, but between 1279 and 1290 it was reckoned as equal to the pfennig of Mainz (242) p.167. Between 1279 and 1290 the Cologne pfennig was also reckoned as equal to the pfennig of Aachen (242) p.167. In 1309 and 1316 the Cologne pfennig was reckoned as equal to two Wetterauer pfennige (242) p.191. At the end of the thirteenth century and in the early fourteenth century the Cologne pfennig was frequently, but not always, reckoned as equal to three heller in the Rhine-Main area (242) pp.161-208. For actual rates of the pfund of heller in schillinge and pfennige pagament of Cologne see under HELLER p.265.

The mark of Cologne (12s.) in schillinge of Marburg

Date	Rate	Place	Type	Reference
1313	18 s.	Marburg	A	(242) p.192

The mark of Cologne in currencies outside 'Germany'

The mark of Cologne (12s.) in sous of Louvain

Date	Rate	Place	Type	Reference
1247	30 s.	St Trond	A	(242) p.118

THE MARK OF COLOGNE IN PONDEN OF HOLLAND

The mark of Cologne (12s.) in ponden of Holland

In 1283 in Holland 10 mark of Cologne were reckoned as 13 pond (242) pp.103-7.

The mark of Cologne (12s.) in schellingen and penningen of Utrecht

Date	Rate	Place	Type	Reference
1265	27 s. 6 d.	Brabant	A	(242) pp.102-7

The mark of Cologne (12s.) in mark and schillinge of Denmark

In Denmark 1 mark = 16 schillinge

Date	Rate	Place	Type	Reference
1315.06.13	10 mk.	Denmark	C	(346) I n.218
1325.08.26	4 mk. 12 s.	Denmark	C	(346) I n.262
1343.11?	3 mk. 12 s.	Denmark	C	(346) II n.368
1358.10.23	6 mk.	Denmark	C	(346) II n.442

For the pound sterling in schillinge and pfennige of Cologne see under ENGLAND p.210
For the livre of Flanders in schillinge and pfennige of Cologne see under FLANDERS p.214
For the livre of Liège in mark of Cologne see under LIÈGE p.232
For the rheingulden in weisspfennige, and schillinge and pfennige pagament of Cologne see under RHEINGULDEN p.240
For the pfund of heller in schillinge and pfennige pagament of Cologne see under HELLER p.265
For the Hungarian denar and the pfennig of Cologne see under HUNGARY p.285

AACHEN

The Florentine florin in mark, schillinge and pfennige pagament of Aachen

As at Cologne, reckoning was carried out at Aachen in mark of 12 schillinge and schillinge of 12 pfennige.

Date	Rate	Place	Type	Reference
1334	1 mk. 7 d.	Aachen	A	(336) p.272
1338	1 mk. 4 s. 9 3/4 d.	Aachen	A	(336) p.272
1344	1 mk. 9 s.	Aachen	A	(336) p.272
1346	1 mk. 9 s.	Aachen	A	(336) p.272
1349	1 mk. 9 s.	Aachen	A	(336) p.272
1349	2 mk.	Aachen	A	(336) p.272
1353	1 mk. 9 s. 6 d.	Aachen	A	(336) p.272
1357	1 mk. 10 s.	Aachen	A	(336) p.272
1373	3 mk. 4 s.	Aachen	A	(336) p.272
1376	3 mk. 6 s.	Aachen	A	(336) p.272
1380	3 mk. 8 s.	Aachen	A	(336) p.272
1383	3 mk. 8 s.	Aachen	A	(336) p.272
1385	3 mk. 8 s.	Aachen	A	(336) p.272
1385	3 mk. 10 s.	Aachen	A	(336) p.272
1386	3 mk. 10 s.	Aachen	A	(336) p.272
1387	3 mk. 11 s.	Aachen	A	(336) p.272
1390	4 mk.	Aachen	A	(336) p.272
1391	4 mk.	Aachen	A	(336) p.272
1391	4 mk. 2 s.	Aachen	A	(336) p.272

For the rheingulden in mark, schillinge and pfennige pagament of Aachen see under RHEINGULDEN p.246
For the pfund of heller in schillinge and pfennige pagament of Aachen see under HELLER p.265
See also under COLOGNE p.236

ANDERNACH

See under COLOGNE p.236

COBLENZ

See under COLOGNE p.236

TRIER

Just as the archbishops of Cologne provided much of the currency for the Lower Rhineland, so the archbishop of Trier provided much of that for the Moselle valley.

The Florentine florin in schillinge and pfennige of Trier

Date	Rate	Place	Type	Reference
1374	47 s. 6 d.	Trier	HC	(461) p.384
1374	47 s. 9 d.	Trier	HC	(461) p.384
1375	47 s. 3 d.	Trier	HC	(461) p.384
1375	47 s. 7 d.	Trier	HC	(461) p.384
1377	51 s. 8 d.	Trier	HC	(461) p.384
1379-1380	70 s. 6 d.	Trier	HC	(461) p.385
1380	70 s. 10 d.	Trier	HC	(461) p.384
1382-1383	56 s. 1/4 d.	Trier	HC	(461) p.385

WETTERAU

See under COLOGNE p.236

MARBURG

See under COLOGNE p.236 and under HELLER p.265

MAINZ

See under COLOGNE p.236 and RHINELAND MONETARY UNION p.239

RHINELAND MONETARY UNION

From 1348 to 1638 a sequence of agreements were made between the principal rulers of the Rhineland to mint coins in common. The key participants in these agreements were four Rhineland electors: the archbishops of Cologne, Trier, Mainz and the Count Palatine. Small change for local use continued to be issued separately by each ruler; but both larger silver and gold were issued with common types.

WEISSPFENNIGE

The silver coins were known as albus (later raderalbus) or weisspfennige, 'white', pfennige as opposed to the small 'dark' pfennige of the individual rulers. Accounting might therefore be carried on in money current locally (pagament) or in weisspfennige. In the area of Cologne money (i.e. the Rhineland below Bingen), the weisspfennig was reckoned as two schillinge pagament. In 1464 in the Middle Rhineland, the Weisspfennig was reckoned at 8 pfennige of Mainz or the Palatinate.

Values were also fixed for heller in the Lower Rhineland (below Bingen) by the agreements of the Rhineland 'munzverein'. For heller, see below p.265

The weisspfennig in heller

Date	Rate	Place	Type	Reference
1399-1401	12 d.	Cologne	O	(172) p.907
1402-1403	12 1/2 d.	Cologne	O	(172) p.907
1404-1408	13 d.	Cologne	O	(172) p.907
1408-1411	13 1/2 d.	Cologne	O	(172) p.907
1412-1414	14 d.	Cologne	O	(172) p.907
1467-1475	12 d.	Cologne	O	(172) p.907
1476-1478	13 d.	Cologne	O	(172) p.907
1479-1485	14 d.	Cologne	O	(172) p.907
1486-1491	15 d.	Cologne	O	(172) p.907
1492-1493	16 d.	Cologne	O	(172) p.907
1494	17 d.	Cologne	O	(172) p.907
1495-1497	18 d.	Cologne	O	(172) p.907
1498-1499	19 d.	Cologne	O	(172) p.907
1500	20 d.	Cologne	O	(172) p.907

The Florentine florin in weisspfennige or albus

Date	Rate	Place	Type	Reference
1372	17 1/2 wpf.	Rhineland	C	(416) p.305
1374-1375	24 wpf.	Curia	B	(439) p.85
1386.06.08	20 wpf.	Trier	C	(371) p.356
1499-1500	circa 56 wpf.	Westphalia	HC	(461) p.384

The Venetian, Hungarian and Bohemian ducats in weisspfennige

Date	Rate	Place	Type	Reference
1372	18 3/4 wpf.	Rhineland	O	(416) p.305
1374	18 3/4 wpf.	Rhineland	O	(416) p.305
1374	18 3/4 wpf.	Rhineland	C	(416) p.305
1385	20 wpf.	Rhineland	O	(416) p.305
1385-1386	20 wpf.	Rhineland	C	(416) p.305
1386	20 wpf.	Rhineland	O	(416) p.305

The weisspfennig in money of Lübeck

Date	Rate	Place	Type	Reference
1389.04.21	4 bonos concavos	Denmark	C	(346) II no.534
1389.09.15	4 bonos concavos	Denmark	C	(346) II no.535
1393.03.25	4 bonos Lybicenses	Denmark	C	(346) II no.544
1394	4 bonos Lubicenses	Denmark	L	(346) II no.547
1397.01.06	4 Lybischer	Denmark	L	(346) II no.555

Date	Rate	Place	Type	Reference
1410.11.17	4 gode Lybeske.	Denmark	L	(346) II p.81

For the pound sterling in weisspfennige see under ENGLAND p.210

RHEINGULDEN, FLORIN OF THE RHINE

The gold coin issued in common by the great princes of the Rhineland under their sequence of agreements was a florin. Initially, in 1348 this was identical in weight and fineness with the Florentine florin. Between 1385 and 1419 its fineness was fairly rapidly reduced from nearly pure gold to 19 carat gold (79% gold), although its weight was maintained. Throughout the rest of the fifteenth century the fineness was not tampered with again, but the weight was gradually reduced.

The rheingulden was also known at the 'vertragsgulden' (treaty gulden), 'koerfurster gulden', 'florin des quatre eliseurs' (gulden of the electors, its principal issues), and in the 1420s and 1430s the 'oberländische gulden'. In the Rhineland itself it was also used for accounting, with weisspfennige, but this was often rather complex since the relation between the rheingulden and the weisspfennig was not constant. In the 1380s the rheingulden was exchanged for 20 weisspfennige or thereabouts (see below). Since each weisspfennig was reckoned as 2 schillinge pagament in Cologne, this temporarily gave the gulden a value of 40 schillinge pagament (3 mark 4 schillinge). Accounting in pagamento thereafter frequently used a pagament gulden or kaufmannsgulden as a 40 shillings unit of account, in the Cologne area, regardless of the current rate for the gold rheingulden itself. From the 1430s to the 1460s the rheingulden was exchanged for 24 weisspfennige or thereabout (see below). When the current rate for the gold rheingulden changed in 1467-8, a 24 weisspfennig unit of account survived. In the Cologne area, this was known as an oberländische gulden, and in the Trier area as a moselgulden.

The rheingulden became the common coin not only of the Rhineland, but also circulated widely in both north and south Germany and in the Netherlands, where it eventually became used in the fifteenth century as a pound of account, and as the prototype for the andriesgulden of the later dukes of Burgundy.

The long section of rates for rheingulden has been divided up in the following way. After the internal rates for the rheingulden in weisspfennige are the rates for rheingulden in other currencies within 'Germany' (p.243). These are arranged geographically in the same order as the main entries in the Handbook. They are followed by rates for rheingulden in currencies outside 'Germany' (p.250). These are also arranged geographically in the same order as the main entries in the Handbook.

The rheingulden in weisspfennige, and schillinge and pfennige pagament of Cologne
2 schillinge pagament = 1 weisspfennig

Date	Rate	Place	Type	Reference
1357	11 wpf.	Lower Rhine	O	????
1370	18 wpf.	Cologne	A	(272) I p.XXVII
1371	18 wpf.	Cologne	A	(272) I p.XXVII
1371.01.08 levis	17 wpf.	Cologne	A	(272) I p.XXVII
1371.06.25 levis	17 wpf.	Cologne	A	(272) I p.XXVII
1371.11.19 levis	17 wpf.	Cologne	A	(272) I p.XXVII
1372	18 wpf. 1 s.	Rhineland	O	(416) pp.304-305
1372.04.28	18 wpf. 1 s.	Cologne	A	(272) I p.XXVII
1372.07.07	19 wpf. 1 s.	Cologne	A	(272) I p.XXVII
1372.10.27	18 wpf.	Cologne	A	(272) I p.XXVII
1373	18 wpf. 1 s.	Cologne	A	(272) I p.XXVII
1373.02.02	18 wpf. 1 s. 6 d.	Cologne	A	(272) I p.XXVII
1373.06.22	17 wpf. 1 s.	Cologne	A	(272) I p.XXVII
1374	18 wpf. 1 s.	Rhineland	O	(416) p.305
1374.11.29 gravis	21 wpf. 1 s.	Cologne	A	(272) I p.XXVII
1375-1380	18 wpf. 1 s.	Cologne	A	(272) I p.XXVII
1375.06.20	18 wpf. 1 s. 3 d.	Cologne	A	(272) I p.XXVII
1375.11.28	18 wpf. 1 s. 8 d.	Cologne	A	(272) I p.XXVII
1375.12.26	19 wpf.	Cologne	A	(272) I p.XXVII
1376.01.16	19 wpf.	Cologne	A	(272) I p.XXVIII
1376.01.23	19 wpf.	Cologne	A	(272) I p.XXVIII
1376.02.06	19 wpf.	Cologne	A	(272) I p.XXVIII
1376.04.02	19 wpf.	Cologne	A	(272) I p.XXVIII
1376.04.16	19 wpf.	Cologne	A	(272) I p.XXVIII

Date	Rate	Place	Type	Reference
1376.04.23	19 wpf.	Cologne	A	(272) I p.XXVIII
1377.09.30	19 wpf. 4 d.	Cologne	A	(272) I p.XXVIII
1378.03.10	19 wpf.	Cologne	A	(272) I p.XXVIII
1378.04.21	19 wpf. 1 s.	Cologne	A	(272) I p.XXVIII
1378.06.20	19 wpf. 1 s.	Cologne	A	(272) I p.XXVIII
1378.09.22	19 wpf. 1 s.	Cologne	A	(272) I p.XXVIII
1378.11.24	20 wpf.	Cologne	A	(272) I p.XXVIII
1378.12.15	19 wpf. 1 s.	Cologne	A	(272) I p.XXVIII
1378.12.29	20 wpf.	Cologne	A	(272) I p.XXVIII
1379.02.23	20 wpf.	Cologne	A	(272) I p.XXVIII
1379.04.06	20 wpf.	Cologne	A	(272) I p.XXVIII
1379.07.20	20 wpf.	Cologne	A	(272) I p.XXVIII
1379.08.17	20 wpf.	Cologne	A	(272) I p.XXVIII
1380.01.11	30 wpf. 6 d.	Cologne	A	(272) I p.XXVIII
1380.02.01	20 wpf.	Cologne	A	(272) I p.XXVIII
1380.02.22	20 wpf.	Cologne	A	(272) I p.XXVIII
1380.03.21-1390	20 wpf.	Cologne	A	(272) I p.XXVIII
1380.08.08	20 wpf. 6 d.	Cologne	A	(272) I p.XXVII
1380.09.12	20 wpf. 6 d.	Cologne	A	(272) I p.XXVIII
1380.09.12	18 wpf. 1 s.	Cologne	A	(272) I p.XXVIII
1380.10.03	20 wpf. 6 d.	Cologne	A	(272) I p.XXVIII
1380.11.28	20 wpf. 6 d.	Cologne	A	(272) I p.XXVIII
1381.02.06	21 wpf. 1 s.	Cologne	A	(272) I p.XXVIII
1381.03.06	20 wpf. 1 s.	Cologne	A	(272) I p.XXVIII
1381.08.20	18 wpf. 1 s.	Cologne	A	(272) I p.XXVIII
1381.08.21	20 wpf. 1 s.	Cologne	A	(272) I p.XXVIII
1381.08.21	18 wpf. 1 s.	Cologne	A	(272) I p.XXVIII
1381.11.20	20 wpf. 1 s.	Cologne	A	(272) I p.XXVIII
1383.04.15	20 wpf. 6 d.	Cologne	A	(272) I p.XXVIII
1383.05.27	20 wpf. 6 d.	Cologne	A	(272) I p.XXVIII
1383.06.15 new gulden	20 wpf. 6 d.	Cologne	A	(272) I p.XXVIII

1385.11.26 Rheingulden reduced to 23 carat gold

Date	Rate	Place	Type	Reference
1385	19 wpf.	Rhineland	O	(416) p.304
1385 new gulden	20 wpf.	Rhineland	O	(416) pp.304-305
1386	19 wpf.	Rhineland	O	(416) p.304
1386 new gulden	20 wpf.	Rhineland	O	(416) pp.304-305
1386.02.14	20 wpf. 6 d.	Cologne	A	(272) I p.XXVIII
1386.06	20 wpf.	Cologne	H	(166) Tab.1
1386.06.27	20 wpf. 6 d.	Cologne	A	(272) I p.XXVIII
1390.10.05-1396 ponderosus	18 wpf.	Cologne	A	(272) I p.XXVIII
1399	21 wpf.	Cologne	O	(172) P.907

1399.09.19 Rheingulden reduced to 22 1/2 carat gold

Date	Rate	Place	Type	Reference
1399.09	20 wpf. 1 s.	Cologne	H	(166) Tab.1
1399.09.19-1420.03.20	20 wpf. 1 s.	Trier	C	(371) p.356
1400.03	20 wpf. 1 s.	Cologne	H	(166) Tab.1
1400	21 wpf. 6 d.	Cologne	O	(172) p.907
1401	22 wpf.	Cologne	O	(172) p.907
1402	22 wpf. 6 d.	Cologne	O	(172) p.907
1403	22 wpf. 6 d.	Cologne	O	(172) p.907
1404	32 wpf.	Cologne	O	(172) p.907
1405	23 wpf. 6 d.	Cologne	O	(172) p.907
1406	23 wpf. 6 d.	Cologne	O	(172) p.907
1407	24 wpf.	Cologne	O	(172) p.907
1408	24 wpf. 6 d.	Cologne	O	(172) p.907
1409	25 wpf.	Cologne	O	(172) p.907

1409.08.15 Rheingulden reduced to 22 carat gold

Date	Rate	Place	Type	Reference
1409.08	20 wpf. 1 s.	Cologne	H	(166) Tab.1
1410	25 wpf.	Cologne	O	(172) p.907
1411	25 wpf. 6 d.	Cologne	O	(172) p.907
1412	26 wpf.	Cologne	O	(172) p.907
1413	26 wpf. 6 d.	Cologne	O	(172) p.907
1414	27 wpf.	Cologne	O	(172) p.907
1414-1419	18 wpf.	Cologne	A	(272) I p.XXVIII

1417.03.08 Rheingulden reduced to 20 carat gold

Date	Rate	Place	Type	Reference
1417	20 wpf.	Curia	B	(439) p.86
1419.03.20 Rheingulden reduced to 19 carat gold				
1419.05	20 wpf. 1 s.	Cologne	H	(166) Tab.1
1420.03	20 wpf. 1 s.	Cologne	H	(166) Tab.1
1420.09.23	21 wpf.	Cologne	A	(123) p.XXVIII
1422.09.23	21 wpf. 1 s.	Cologne	A	(272) I p.XXVIII
1423	21 wpf.	Cologne	C	(439) p.86
1424.01.05	22 wpf.	Cologne	A	(272) I p.XXVIII
1424.01.12	21 wpf. 1 s. 6 d.	Cologne	A	(272) I p.XXVIII
1427.02.05	22 wpf.	Cologne	A	(272) I p.XXVIII
1427.06.11	23 wpf.	Cologne	A	(272) I p.XXVIII
1428.02.04	23 wpf. 1 s.	Cologne	A	(272) I p.XXVIII
1431.12.05	23 wpf. 1 s.	Cologne	A	(272) I p.XXVIII
1432.02.06	23 wpf.	Cologne	A	(272) I p.XXVIII
1432.10.04	24 wpf.	Cologne	A	(272) I p.XXVIII
1433 seldom	23 wpf. 1 s.	Cologne	A	(272) I p.XXVIII
1435	22 wpf.	Cologne	A	(272) I p.XXVIII
1437.09.17-1477.06.29	24 wpf.	Trier	C	(371) p.356
1437.09	24 wpf.	Cologne	H	(166) Tab. 1
1454.10	24 wpf.	Cologne	H	(166) Tab. 1
1458	24 wpf.	Cologne	M	(508) 1857, p.1
1464.10	24 wpf.	Cologne	H	(166) Tab. 1
1467	24 wpf. 6 d.	Cologne	O	(172) p.907
1468	25 wpf.	Cologne	H	(166) Tab. 1
1468	25 wpf.	Cologne	O	(172) p.907
1469	25 wpf.	Cologne	O	(172) p.907
1470	25 wpf.	Cologne	O	(172) p.907
1471	25 wpf.	Cologne	O	(172) p.907
1470	25 wpf. 1 s.	Cologne	H	(166) Tab. 1
1472	26 wpf.	Cologne	O	(172) p.907
1473	26 wpf.	Cologne	O	(172) p.907
1474	26 wpf.	Cologne	O	(172) p.907
1475	27 wpf.	Cologne	O	(172) p.907
1476	28 wpf.	Cologne	O	(172) p.907
1477	29 wpf.	Cologne	O	(172) p.907
1477	27 wpf.	Cologne	A	(272) I p.XXIX
1478	29 wpf.	Cologne	O	(172) p.907
1479	30 wpf.	Cologne	O	(172) p.907
1480	30 wpf.	Cologne	O	(172) p.907
1481	27 wpf.	Cologne	H	(166) Tab. 1
1481	30 wpf.	Cologne	A	(272) I p.XXIX
1481	31 wpf.	Cologne	O	(172) p.907
1481	27 wpf.	Rhineland	O	(371) p.356
1482	31 wpf.	Cologne	O	(172) p.908
1483	30 wpf.	Cologne	O	(172) p.908
1484	30 wpf.	Cologne	O	(172) p.908
1486	32 wpf.	Cologne	O	(172) p.908
1487	32 wpf.	Cologne	O	(172) p.908
1487.02.10	31 wpf.	Cologne	A	(272) I p.XXIX
1488	32 wpf.	Cologne	O	(172) p.908
1488.04.04	32 wpf.	Cologne	A	(272) I p.XXIX
1489	32 wpf.	Cologne	O	(172) p.908
1490	33 wpf.	Cologne	O	(172) p.908
1490-1491	36 1/2 wpf.	Siegen	HC	(461) p.384
1491	33 wpf.	Cologne	O	(172) p.908
1491	34 wpf.	Cologne	O	(172) p.908
1491.04.23	33 wpf.	Cologne	A	(272) I p.XXIX
1491.12.17	34 wpf.	Cologne	A	(272) I p.XXIX
1492	35 wpf.	Cologne	O	(172) p.908
1492	36 wpf.	Cologne	O	(172) p.908
1492.01.06	36 wpf.	Cologne	A	(272) I p.XXIX
1493	36 wpf.	Cologne	O	(172) p.908
1493.03	24 wpf.	Cologne	H	(166) Tab. 1
1494	37 wpf. 1 s.	Cologne	H	(166) Tab. 1
1494	37 wpf.	Cologne	O	(172) p.908
1494	38 wpf.	Cologne	O	(172) p.908
1494.12	24 wpf.	Cologne	H	(166) Tab. 1
1495	31 wpf.	Cologne	O	(172) p.908
1495	39 wpf.	Cologne	O	(172) p.908
1496	40 wpf.	Cologne	O	(172) p.908

Date	Rate	Place	Type	Reference
1496.03.19	39 wpf.	Cologne	A	(272) I p.XXIX
1496.03.19	33 wpf.	Cologne	A	(272) I p.XXIX
1496.03.19	38 wpf.	Cologne	A	(272) I p.XXIX
1497	41 wpf.	Cologne	O	(172) p.908
1498	42 wpf.	Cologne	O	(172) p.908
1499	35 1/4 wpf.	Siegen	HC	(461) p.384
1499	42 wpf.	Cologne	O	(172) p.908
1500	43 wpf.	Cologne	O	(172) p.908

100 Venetian ducats in rheingulden

Date	Rate	Place	Type	Reference
1401	110 fl.	Florence-Frankfurt or Nuremberg	B	(472) I p.214
1402.01.07	115 fl.	Venice-Frankfurt	B	(472) I p.211
1402.01.23	110 fl.	Venice-Trento	B	(472) I p.211
1425-1427	130 fl.	Nuremberg	L	(472) II p.346
1426.12.25	129 1/2 fl.	Nuremberg	C	(472) II p.364
1427.07.25	129 fl.	Nuremberg	C	(472) II p.364
1431	125 fl.	Nuremberg-Venice	L	(472) II p.346

The rheingulden in other currencies within 'Germany'

The rheingulden in schillinge and pfennige of Dortmund

Date	Rate	Place	Type	Reference
1355-1384	3 s. 4 d.	Dortmund	A	(196) p.218
1370	4 s.	Dortmund	A	(196) p.221
1375	4 s.	Dortmund	A	(196) p.222
1384	3 s. 4 d.	Dortmund	A	(196) p.247
1394	5 s.	Dortmund	A	(196) p.288
1418	6 s. 1 d.	Dortmund	A	(196) p.298
1419	6 s. 1 d.	Dortmund	A	(196) p.298
1422	7 s. 6 d.	Dortmund	A	(196) p.300
1423	7 s. 6 d.	Dortmund	A	(196) p.302
1424	9 s.	Dortmund	A	(196) p.302
1425	8 s.	Dortmund	A	(196) p.303
1425	9 s.	Dortmund	A	(196) p.303
1426	7 s. 6 d.	Dortmund	A	(196) p.304
1426	9 s.	Dortmund	A	(196) p.304
1427	8 s.	Dortmund	A	(196) p.304
1428	8 s.	Dortmund	A	(196) p.305
1428	9 s.	Dortmund	A	(196) p.305
1429	8 s.	Dortmund	A	(196) p.305
1429	9 s.	Dortmund	A	(196) p.305
1430	8 s.	Dortmund	A	(196) p.306
1430	10 s. 3 d.	Dortmund	A	(196) p.306
1431	9 s.	Dortmund	A	(196) p.307
1431	10 s. 6 d.	Dortmund	A	(196) p.307
1433	9 s.	Dortmund	A	(196) p.308
1433	11 s.	Dortmund	A	(196) p.308
1434	9 s.	Dortmund	A	(196) p.308
1434	10 s. 6 d.	Dortmund	A	(196) p.408
1435	10 s. 2 d.	Dortmund	A	(196) p.309
1436	11 s. 9 d.	Dortmund	A	(196) p.310
1438	9 s.	Dortmund	A	(196) p.312
1438	12 s.	Dortmund	A	(196) p.312
1439	10 s.	Dortmund	A	(196) p.313
1439	12 s. 3 d.	Dortmund	A	(196) p.313
1440	10 s.	Dortmund	A	(196) p.314
1440	12 s. 6 d.	Dortmund	A	(196) p.314
1441	10 s.	Dortmund	A	(196) p.315
1441	13 s. 3 d.	Dortmund	A	(196) p.315
1442	10 s.	Dortmund	A	(196) p.315
1442	13 s. 3 d.	Dortmund	A	(196) p.315
1443	10 s.	Dortmund	A	(196) p.316
1444	11 s. 3 d.	Dortmund	A	(196) p.317

THE RHEINGULDEN IN SCHILLINGE AND PFENNIGE OF DORTMUND

Date	Rate	Place	Type	Reference
1445	13 s. 3 d.	Dortmund	A	(196) p.319
1446	10 s.	Dortmund	A	(196) p.320
1446	13 s. 3 d.	Dortmund	A	(196) p.320
1447	14 s.	Dortmund	A	(196) p.321
1448	14 s.	Dortmund	A	(196) p.322
1449	10 s.	Dortmund	A	(196) p.322
1449	12 s.	Dortmund	A	(196) p.322
1450	13 s. 3 d.	Dortmund	A	(196) p.322
1451	10 s.	Dortmund	A	(196) p.323
1451	13 s. 3 d.	Dortmund	A	(196) p.323
1452	10 s.	Dortmund	A	(196) p.323
1452	13 s. 4 d.	Dortmund	A	(196) p.323
1453	10 s.	Dortmund	A	(196) p.323
1453	14 s.	Dortmund	A	(196) p.323
1454	10 s.	Dortmund	A	(196) p.324
1454	14 s.	Dortmund	A	(196) p.324
1455	10 s.	Dortmund	A	(196) p.324
1455	14 s. 4 d.	Dortmund	A	(328) p.324
1457	10 s.	Dortmund	A	(196) p.325
1458	10 s.	Dortmund	A	(196) p.325
1458	9 s. 6 d.	Dortmund	A	(196) p.325
1459	10 s.	Dortmund	A	(196) p.326
1459	15 s.	Dortmund	A	(196) p.326
1460	10 s.	Dortmund	A	(196) p.326
1460	15 s.	Dortmund	A	(196) p.326
1461	10 s.	Dortmund	A	(196) p.327
1462	10 s.	Dortmund	A	(196) p.327
1462	15 s.	Dortmund	A	(196) p.327
1463	10 s. 2 d.	Dortmund	A	(196) p.328
1463	15 s.	Dortmund	A	(196) p.328
1464	10 s. 2 d.	Dortmund	A	(196) p.328
1464	15 s. 3 d.	Dortmund	A	(196) p.328
1465	10 s.	Dortmund	A	(196) p.330
1465	15 s. 6 d.	Dortmund	A	(196) p.330
1466	10 s. 4 d.	Dortmund	A	(196) p.331
1466	15 s. 6 d.	Dortmund	A	(196) p.331
1467	10 s. 4 d.	Dortmund	A	(196) p.334
1467	15 s. 6 d.	Dortmund	A	(196) p.334
1468	10 s. 6 d.	Dortmund	A	(196) p.335
1468	15 s. 2 d.	Dortmund	A	(196) p.335
1469	10 s. 6 d.	Dortmund	A	(196) p.336
1470	10 s. 6 d.	Dortmund	A	(196) p.336
1470	15 s. 9 d.	Dortmund	A	(196) p.336
1471	11 s. 2 d.	Dortmund	A	(196) p.336
1471	16 s.	Dortmund	A	(196) p.336
1472	10 s. 6 d.	Dortmund	A	(196) p.338
1472	16 s. 3 d.	Dortmund	A	(196) p.338
1473	10 s. 10 d.	Dortmund	A	(196) p.338
1473	16 s. 4 d.	Dortmund	A	(196) p.338
1474	11 s.	Dortmund	A	(196) p.338
1475	11 s. 6 d.	Dortmund	A	(196) p.339
1475	16 s. 3 d.	Dortmund	A	(196) p.339
1476	11 s. 8 d.	Dortmund	A	(196) p.341
1476	17 s. 6 d.	Dortmund	A	(196) p.341
1477	12 s.	Dortmund	A	(196) p.341
1477	18 s.	Dortmund	A	(196) p.341
1478	13 s.	Dortmund	A	(196) p.342
1478	20 s.	Dortmund	A	(196) p.342
1479	13 s. 4 d.	Dortmund	A	(196) p.342
1480	13 s. 6 d.	Dortmund	A	(196) p.343
1481	14 s.	Dortmund	A	(196) p.344
1482	15 s.	Dortmund	A	(196) p.346
1483	16 s.	Dortmund	A	(196) p.347
1484	16 s. 6 d.	Dortmund	A	(196) p.348
1485	16 s. 6 d.	Dortmund	A	(196) p.348
1487	17 s. 6 d.	Dortmund	A	(196) p.351
1487	18 s.	Dortmund	A	(196) p.351
1487	18 s. 6 d.	Dortmund	A	(196) p.351
1487	20 s.	Dortmund	A	(196) p.351
1487	15 s.	Dortmund	O	(196) p.351
1488	20 s.	Dortmund	A	(196) p.352
1488.03.10	15 s.	Dortmund	O	(196) p.352

THE RHEINGULDEN IN SCHILLINGE AND PFENNIGE OF DORTMUND

Date	Rate	Place	Type	Reference
1488.09.29	16 s.	Dortmund	A	(196) p.351
1489	16 s. 6 d.	Dortmund	A	(196) p.352
1489.05.06	10 s.	Dortmund	O	(196) p.362
1490	10 s. 6 d.	Dortmund	A	(196) p.352
1491	11 s.	Dortmund	A	(196) p.355
1491	11 s. 6 d.	Dortmund	A	(196) p.355
1492	11 s. 6 d.	Dortmund	A	(196) p.357
1492	12 s.	Dortmund	A	(196) p.357
1492	13 s.	Dortmund	A	(196) p.357
1493	12 s.	Dortmund	A	(196) p.358
1493	12 s. 5 d.	Dortmund	A	(196) p.358
1493	13 s.	Dortmund	A	(196) p.358
1494	13 s. 6 d.	Dortmund	A	(196) p.359
1495	14 s.	Dortmund	A	(196) p.360
1496	14 s.	Dortmund	A	(196) p.362
1496	14 s. 6 d.	Dortmund	A	(196) p.362
1496	15 s.	Dortmund	A	(196) p.362
1496.06.24	12 s.	Dortmund	O	(196) p.362
1496.06.25	13 s.	Dortmund	A	(196) p.362
1496.06.26	12 s.	Dortmund	O	(196) p.362
1497	12 s.	Dortmund	A	(196) p.364
1497	15 s.	Dortmund	A	(196) p.364
1498.11.13	13 s.	Dortmund	O	(196) p.368
1499	13 s.	Dortmund	A	(196) p.369
1499	13 s. 6 d.	Dortmund	A	(196) p.369
1499	14 s.	Dortmund	A	(196) p.369
1500	14 s.	Dortmund	A	(196) p.370

The rheingulden in schillinge and pfennige pagyment of Westphalia

A Westphalian league united the money of Osnabruck, Paderborn, Soest, Marsberg and Brakel.

Date	Rate	Place	Type	Reference
1370.12.24	6 s. Paderborn & Soest	Everstein	A	(27)
1385.09.15	6 s. Osnabruck	Herford	A	(27)
1390.04.10	7 s. 9 d. Paderborn & Soest	Büren	A	(27)
1418.03.21	8 s. 4 d. Paderborn & Soest	Paderborn	A	(27)
1473.03.04	10 s. Brakel	Brakel	A	(25) p.52
1475.10.05	10 s. Paderborn & Soest	Paderborn	A	(25) p.55
1479.11.13	10 s. Brakel	Brakel	A	(27)
1481.05.13	10 s. Osnabruck	Rietberg	A	(25) p.55
1483.02.05	10 s. Brakel	Brakel	A	(27)
1483.02.14 Kopmansgulden	10 s. Paderborn & Soest	Paderborn	A	(27)
1483.02.17	10 s. pagyment	Lippe	A	(25) p.55
1484.09.28	10 s. Brakel	Asseburg	A	(27)
1495.06.24	10 s. Marsberg	Marsberg	A	(27)
1500.12.21	10 s. Brakel	Brakel	A	(27)

The rheingulden in schillinge and pfennige of Bielefeld, Herford and Lemgo

12 schillinge = 1 mark

Date	Rate	Place	Type	Reference
1381.09.08	8 s.	Minden	A	(25) p.48
1386.06.03	8 s. 6 d.	Bielefeld	A	(27)
1386.06.03	8 s. 6 d.	Detmold	A	(27)
1387.01.17	8 s. 4 d.	Detmold	A	(27)
1388.03.28	9 s.	Lippe	A	(27)
1388.07.16	9 s.	Minden	A	(27)
1389.07.21	9 s. 4 d.	Detmold	A	(27)
1389.11.11	9 s.	Lemgo	A	(27)
1390.04.25	9 s. 6 d.	Detmold	A	(27)
1393.03.06	10 s. 3 d.	Herford	A	(27)

THE RHEINGULDEN IN SCHILLINGE AND PFENNIGE OF BIELEFELD, HERFORD AND LEMGO

Date	Rate	Place	Type	Reference
1393.03.16	10 s.	Obernkirchen im Schaumburg	A	(27)
1403.01.22	12.	Herford	A	(27)
1426.07.10	12 s.	Westphalia	A	(27)
1428.12.29	12 s. 6 d.	Lemgo	A	(27)
1463.07.22	20 s. 6 d.	Westphalia	A	(27)
1465.03.10	20 s.	Detmold	A	(27)
1485.01.06	20 s.	Detmold	A	(27)
1487.04.04	34 s.	Herford	A	(27)
1487.09.29	34 s.	Bielefeld	A	(27)
1500.09.29	48 s.	Herford	A	(27)

The rheingulden (Kopmansgulden) in money of Höxter

Date	Rate	Place	Type	Reference
1490	30 s.	Corvey	A	(27)

The rheingulden in schillinge of Hameln

Date	Rate	Place	Type	Reference
1483.11.23	32 s.	Hameln	A	(27)

The rheingulden in schillinge of Hanover

Date	Rate	Place	Type	Reference
1494.06.15	34 s.	Obernkirchen im Schaumburg	A	(27)

The rheingulden in schillinge and pfennige of Minden
12 schillinge = 1 mark

Date	Rate	Place	Type	Reference
1381.09.08	6 s. gravium	Minden	A	(25) p.48
1387.10.14	9 s. levium	Minden	A	(27)
1400.03.28	6 s. 10 d.	Minden	A	(27)
1410.04.14	6 s. 10 d.	Minden	A	(27)

The rheingulden in mark, schillinge and pfennige pagament of Aachen

At Aachen reckoning was carried out in mark of 12 schillinge, and schillinge of 12 pfennige.

Date	Rate	Place	Type	Reference
1346-1356	1 mk. 9 s.	Aachen	H	(336) p.272
1357	1 mk.	Aachen	H	(336) p.272
1359	2 mk. 1 s.	Aachen	H	(336) p.272
1360	2 mk. 1 s. 6 d.	Aachen	H	(336) p.272
1361 until 01.13	2 mk. 2 s. 6 d.	Aachen	H	(336) p.272
1361.01.13	2 mk. 3 s.	Aachen	H	(336) p.272
1362 until 01.13	2 mk. 3 s. 4 d.	Aachen	H	(336) p.272
1362.01.13	2 mk. 4 s.	Aachen	H	(336) p.272
1364	2 mk. 6 s.	Aachen	H	(336) p.272
1365	2 mk. 6 s. 6 d.	Aachen	H	(336) p.272
1365.11	2 mk. 7 s.	Aachen	H	(336) p.272
1366.04	2 mk. 8 s.	Aachen	H	(336) p.272
1368	2 mk. 9 s.	Aachen	H	(336) p.272
1372-1420	3 mk. 4 s.	Aachen	H	(336) p.272
1421	4 mk. 10 s.	Aachen	H	(336) p.272
1422	4 mk. 11 s.	Aachen	H	(336) p.272
1423-1441	5 mk.	Aachen	H	(336) p.272
1442-1475	6 mk.	Aachen	H	(336) p.272
1476	7 mk. 4 s.	Aachen	H	(336) p.272
1477	7 mk. 10 s.	Aachen	H	(336) p.272
1479	8 mk.	Aachen	H	(336) p.272
1483	8 mk. 2 s.	Aachen	H	(336) p.272

THE RHEINGULDEN IN MARK, SCHILLINGE AND PFENNIGE PAGAMENT OF AACHEN

Date	Rate	Place	Type	Reference
1484	8 mk. 2 s. 6 d.	Aachen	H	(336) p.272
1485	8 mk. 3 s.	Aachen	H	(336) p.272
1486	8 mk. 4 s.	Aachen	H	(336) p.273
1487	8 mk. 9 s.	Aachen	H	(336) p.273
1488	9 mk.	Aachen	H	(336) p.273
1490.06.24	11 mk.	Aachen	H	(336) p.273
1490.12.25	11 mk. 6 s.	Aachen	H	(336) p.273
1491.06.24	9 mk. 3 s.	Aachen	H	(336) p.273
1491.12.25	9 mk. 9 s.	Aachen	H	(336) p.273
1492	10 mk.	Aachen	H	(336) p.273
1493	10 mk. 3 s.	Aachen	H	(336) p.273
1494	10 mk. 6 s.	Aachen	H	(336) p.273
1496	10 mk.	Aachen	H	(336) p.273
1497	10 mk. 3 s.	Aachen	H	(336) p.273
1498	10 mk. 6 s.	Aachen	H	(336) p.273
1500	11 mk.	Aachen	H	(336) p.273

The rheingulden in schillinge and pfennige of Strassburg

Date	Rate	Place	Type	Reference
1391-1417	10 s.	Strassburg	C	(75) p.154
1425-1477	10 s. 6 d.	Strassburg	C	(75) p.154
1490	11 s.	Strassburg	C	(75) p.154

The rheingulden in schillinge and pfennige of Basle

Date	Rate	Place	Type	Reference
1433.08.21	23 s.	Basle	OM	(482) p.7
1433.08.21	23 s. 2 d.	Basle	OM	(482) p.7

The lower rate was the minimum for which money changers should accept rheingulden; the higher rate was the maximum that they should charge for rheingulden. These official rates were established jointly by the city and the church council then sitting at Basle.

The rheingulden in schillinge and pfennige (haller) of Bern

Date	Rate	Place	Type	Reference
1416.06.13	27 s. 4 d.	Bern	O	(322) p.326
1477.09.05	28 plapparts = 37 s. 4 d.	Bern	O	(322) p.327
1487.09.01	2 li 16 fünfers = 46 s. 8 d.	Bern	O	(322) p.327

See BERN below p.261

The rheingulden in schillinge of Constance

Date	Rate	Place	Type	Reference
1423-1433	13 s.	Constance	O	(266) p.170
1435 until 08.13	16 s.	Constance	O	(266) p.170
1435.08.13	14 s.	Constance	O	(266) p.170
1436	14 s.	Constance	O	(266) p.70
1439-43	14 s.	Constance	A	(266) p.45

The rheingulden in pfennige of Franconia

Date	Rate	Place	Type	Reference
1428-1430	132 konventions pf.	Nuremberg	O	(167) p.13
1432	150 pf.	Wurzburg	O	(167) p.149
1457	174 new pf.	Nurnberg	M	(167) p.149
1457-1462	174 - 220 pf.	Franconia	H	(167) p.225
1463	220 pf.	Franconia	H	(167) p.40
1467.03	150 pf.	Wurzburg	O	(167) p.150
1469	252 old Frankish pf.	Franconia	M	(167) p.150
1469	168 new Frankish pf.	Franconia	M	(167) p.150
1469	168 3/4 pf.	Wurzburg	H	(167) p.150

THE RHEINGULDEN IN PFENNIGE OF FRANCONIA

Date	Rate	Place	Type	Reference
1470	248 pf.	Bamberg	O	(167) p.150
1472	252 pf.	Bamberg	O	(167) p.150
1482	169 3/4 pf.	Wurzburg	M	(167) p.150
1482	252 old Frankish pf.	Bamberg	O	(167) p.150
1484	252 pf.	Franconia	H	(167) p.40
1492	252 pf.	Franconia	O	(167) p.301
1500	252 pf.	Franconia	H	(167) p.40

The rheingulden in heller

Date	Rate	Place	Type	Reference
1366	20 s. new heller	Lower Rhine	O	(271) p.184
1399	30 s.	Germany	C	(416) p.237
1444	28 s.	Constance	C	(266) p.70

The rheingulden in pfennige of Augsburg

Date	Rate	Place	Type	Reference
1437	168 pf.	Germany	C	(169) I p.119
1445	160 pf.	Germany	C	(169) I p.119
1462	208 pf.	Germany	C	(169) I p.119
1466	214 pf.	Germany	C	(169) I p.119
1467-1468	208 pf.	Germany	C	(169) I p.119
1473-1476	210 pf.	Germany	C	(169) I p.119
1479-1480	213 pf.	Germany	C	(169) I p.119
1479	210 pf.	Germany	C	(169) I p.119
1480	211 pf.	Germany	C	(169) I p.119
1490	212 pf.	Germany	C	(169) I p.119

The rheingulden in Prague groschen

Date	Rate	Place	Type	Reference
1386	18 gr.	Rothenburg	H	(97) App.I b
1398	19 gr.	Eger	H	(97) App.I b
1400	18 gr.	Eger	H	(97) App.I b
1403	18 gr.	Eger	H	(97) App.I b
1406	21 gr.	Eger	H	(97) App.I b
1407	21 gr.	Eger	H	(97) App.I b
1415.03.30	20 gr.	Treboň	H	(97) App.I b
1417	19 gr.	Eger	H	(97) App.I b
1421	19 gr.	Brüx	H	(97) App.I b
1432	20 gr.	Brüx	H	(97) App.I b
1434	20 gr.	Karlstein	H	(97) App.I b
1434.03.10	21 1/2 gr.	Würzburg	H	(97) App.I b
1439.07.05	22 gr.	Freiberg	H	(97) App.I b
1447	24 gr.	Bohemia	H	(97) App.I b
1457.08.10	26 gr.	Krumau	H	(97) App.I a
1459	30 gr.	Bohemia	H	(97) App.I b
1460.12.20	24 gr.	Louny	H	(97) App.I b
1461.10.16	26 gr.	Krumau	H	(97) App.I b
1461.10.18	24 gr.	Krumau	H	(97) App.I b
1462.04.30	32 gr.	Bohemia	H	(97) App.I b
1463.07.02	38 gr.	Louny	H	(97) App.I b
1463.08.20	38 gr.	Louny	H	(97) App.I b
1463.10.16	35 gr.	Krumau	H	(97) App.I b
1464.04.23	35 gr.	Krumau	H	(97) App.I b
1469.06.05	18 gr.	Bohemia	OH	(97) App.I b
1469.03.06	51 gr.	Louny	H	(97) App.I b
1469.07.15	60 gr.	Louny	H	(97) App.I b
1469.10.16	55 gr.	Krumau	H	(97) App.I b
1469	18 gr.	Prague	A	(239)
1470	38 gr.	Prague	A	(239)
1470.03.24	38 gr.	Louny	H	(97) App.I b
1470.09.15	45 gr.	Louny	H	(97) App.I b
1471.01.19	45 gr.	Louny	H	(97) App.I b
1471.04.27	45 gr.	Louny	H	(97) App.I b
1471.09.14	45 gr.	Louny	H	(97) App.I b

THE RHEINGULDEN IN PRAGUE GROSCHEN

Date	Rate	Place	Type	Reference
1471	21 gr.	Empire	H	(97) App.I b
1471	24 4/5 gr.	Prague	A	(239)
1472	18 gr.	Prague	A	(239)
1474	23 1/2 gr.	Prague	A	(239)
1477	22 4/5 gr.	Prague	A	(239)
1477.08	22 gr.	Kutna Hora	H	(97) App.I b
1477.10	22 gr.	Kutna Hora	H	(97) App.I b
1478	23 gr.	Prague	A	(239)
1478.05.14	22 gr.	Krumau	H	(97) App.I b
1478.05.23	21 1/2 gr.	Krumau	H	(97) App.I b
1478.08.14	23 gr.	Krumau	H	(97) App.I b
1485.10.11-13	21 1/2 gr.	Bohemia	OH	(97) App.I b
1485.03.12-20	20 gr.	Kutna Hora	H	(97) App.I b
1485	20 gr.	Prague	O	(239)
1485	21 1/2 gr.	Prague	O	(239)
1486	22 gr.	Prague	A	(239)
1486	22 gr.	Prague	O	(239)
1494	22 gr.	Prague	O	(239)
1495	24 gr.	Meissen	H	(97) App.I b
1500	22 gr.	Prague	O	(239)

The rheingulden in groschen of Meissen

Date	Rate	Place	Type	Reference
1478.08.14	46 gr.	Krumau	H	(97) App.I b
1478.05.14	44 gr.	Krumau	H	(97) App.I b
1478.05.23	43 gr.	Krumau	H	(97) App.I b

The rheingulden in pfennige of Saxony

Date	Rate	Place	Type	Reference
1444	180 pf.	Saxony	H	(167) p.40
1457	180 pf.	Saxony	H	(167) p.40
1465	180 pf.	Saxony	H	(167) p.40
1474-1475	180 pf.	Saxony	H	(167) p.40
1482	240 pf.	Saxony	H	(167) p.40
1490	252 pf.	Saxony	H	(167) p.40
1492-1493	252 pf.	Saxony	H	(167) p.40

The rheingulden in grote of Bremem

Date	Rate	Place	Type	Reference
1405-1406	16 gr.	Bremen	?	(462) p.194
1416	19 gr.	Bremen	?	(462) p.194
1436	29 gr.	Bremen	?	(462) p.194
1439	32 gr.	Bremen	?	(462) p.194
1464	34 gr.	Bremen	?	(462) p.194
1466	33-37 gr.	Bremen	?	(462) p.194

The rheingulden in schillinge and pfennige of Lübeck

Date	Rate	Place	Type	Reference
1371	10 s.	Lübeck	C	(402) V p.XI
1371	10 s.	Lübeck	C	(469) p.75
1387	11 s.	Lübeck	C	(402) V p.XI
1389	12 s.	Lübeck	C	(402) V p.XI
1389	12 s.	Lübeck	C	(469) p.75
1403	13 s.	Lübeck	O	(259) p.214
1403	13 s.	Lübeck	C	(469) p.75
1406	14 s. 4 d.	Lübeck	O	(259) p.214
1410	13 s. 6 d.	Lübeck	O	(259) p.214
1410-1418	14 s.	Lübeck	C	(469) p.75
1423-1424	16 s.	Lübeck	C	(469) p.75
1424	16 s.	Lübeck	C	(259) p.216
1432-1433	20 s.	Lübeck	C	(259) p.216
1435	20 s.	Lübeck	B	(376) II p.135

THE RHEINGULDEN IN SCHILLINGE AND PFENNIGE OF LÜBECK

Date	Rate	Place	Type	Reference
1441	20 s. 9 d.	Lübeck	O	(259) p.216
1441-1450	21 s.	Lübeck	C	(469) p.75
1448.05.19	24 s.	Denmark	L	(346) III no.754
1450	21 s.	Lübeck	C	(259) p.216
1451-1500	23 s.	Lübeck	C	(259) p.216
1451-1500	24 s.	Lübeck	C	(259) p.218
1460-1470	20 s.	Denmark	A	(346) III p.42
1462	22 s.	Lübeck	C	(259) p.216
1463-1468	21 s.	Lübeck	C	(259) p.216
1468	22 s.	Lübeck	C	(259) p.218
1470-1478	24 s.	Lübeck	O	(259) p.218
1479-1492	22 s.	Lübeck	C	(259) p.218

The rheingulden in schillinge of Denmark

Date	Rate	Place	Type	Reference
1443.09.30	22 s.	Borglum	C	(346) III no.729
1447	22 s.	Denmark	A	(346) III no.749
1455.02.18	28 s.	Stockholm	C	(346) III p.39
1474.02.13	23 s.	Hanse	C	(346) III p.52

The rheingulden in mark and schillinge of Stralsund
At Stralsund 16 schillinge = 1 mark

Date	Rate	Place	Type	Reference
1428	2 m. 4 s.	Stralsund	C	(462) p.201
1443	3 m.	Stralsund	C	(462) p.201
1448	2 m. 12 s.	Stralsund	C	(462) p.201
1455	3 m.	Stralsund	C	(462) p.201
1489	3 m.	Stralsund	C	(462) p.201
1491	3 m.	Stralsund	C	(462) p.201

The rheingulden in mark, schillinge and pfennige of Riga
At Riga 36 schillinge = 1 mark

Date	Rate	Place	Type	Reference
1343	9 s. 9 pf.	Riga	A	(462) p.198
1348-1361	9 s. 6 pf.	Riga	A	(462) p.198
1412-1415	22 s. 6 pf.	Riga	A	(462) p.198
1416-1417	24 s.	Riga	A	(462) p.198
1420	27 s.	Riga	A	(462) p.198
1420	27 s. 6 pf.	Riga	A	(462) p.198
1422	1 m. 3 s.	Riga	A	(462) p.198
1425	1 m. 9 s. 6 pf.	Riga	A	(462) p.198
1432	1 m. 18 s.	Riga	A	(462) p.198
1434	1 m. 18 s.	Reval	A	(503) p.13
1434	1 m. 20 s.	Riga	A	(462) p.198
1448	1 m. 21 s.	Reval	A	(503) p.13
1454-1458	1 m. 24 s.	Riga	A	(462) p.198
1457	1 m. 24 s.	Reval	A	(503) p.13
1461	1 m. 24 s.	Reval	A	(503) p.13
1471	1 m. 24 s.	Riga	A	(462) p.198

The rheingulden in currencies outside 'Germany'

The rheingulden in sous and deniers of Avignon

Date	Rate	Place	Type	Reference
1376.10.15	27 s. 6 d.	Pisa	B	(268) p.202
1376	27 s.	Avignon	B	(343) p.154

The rheingulden in Savoy gros of Geneva

Date	Rate	Place	Type	Reference
1439-1440	17 gr.	Geneva	A	(354) p.239
1452.10.28-1453.01.06	18 gr.	Geneva	A	(354) p.238
1453.08.01-10.27	18 gr.	Geneva	A	(354) p.238
1453.10.28-1454.01.05	19 1/2 gr.	Geneva	A	(354) p.238
1454.01.06	20 gr.	Geneva	A	(354) p.238
1480	17 gr.	Geneva	A	(354) p.239

The rheingulden in sols and deniers lausannois petits

Date	Rate	Place	Type	Reference
1402	18 s.	Fribourg	A	(354) p.253
1411.01-06	17 s. 6 d.	Fribourg	A	(352) p.138
1411.01-06	18 s.	Fribourg	A	(352) p.138
1411.07-12	17 s. 6 d.	Fribourg	A	(352) p.138
1412	17 s. 6 d.	Fribourg	A	(354) p.253
1413.07-12	17 s. 6 d.	Fribourg	A	(352) p.138
1414.07.12	17 s. 8 d.	Fribourg	A	(352) p.138
1415.01-06	17 s. 9 d.	Fribourg	A	(352) p.138
1415.07-12	17 s. 9 d.	Fribourg	A	(352) p.138
1416.01-1419.06	17 s. 9 d.	Fribourg	A	(352) p.138
1419.01-06	18 s.	Fribourg	A	(352) p.138
1419.07-12	17 s. 9 d.	Fribourg	A	(354) p.253
1419.01-12	18 s. 11 d.	Fribourg	A	(352) p.138

The rheingulden in sols and deniers lausannois petits of Fribourg

Date	Rate	Place	Type	Reference
1420.01-12	24 s.	Fribourg	A	(354) p.283
1420.07-12	25 s. 6 d.	Fribourg	A	(352) p.138
1420.12.10	23 s.	Fribourg	A	(354) p.283
1421.01-06	23 s.	Fribourg	A	(354) p.283
1421.01-06	24 s.	Fribourg	A	(354) p.283
1421.07-12	24 s.	Fribourg	A	(354) p.283
1422.01-06	25 s.	Fribourg	A	(354) p.283
1422.07-12	25 s.	Fribourg	A	(354) p.283
1422.07-12	25 s. 3 d.	Fribourg	A	(354) p.283
1422.07-12	25 s. 6 d.	Fribourg	A	(354) p.283
1423.01-06	25 s.	Fribourg	A	(354) p.283
1423.01-06	25 s. 6 d.	Fribourg	A	(354) p.283
1423.01-06	26 s. 6 d.	Fribourg	A	(354) p.283
1423.01-06	26 s. 8 d.	Fribourg	A	(354) p.283
1423.07-12	27 s. 3 d.	Fribourg	A	(354) p.283
1423.09.29	27 s.	Fribourg	A	(354) p.283
1423.07-12	27 s.	Fribourg	A	(354) p.283
1424.01-06	27 s.	Fribourg	A	(354) p.283
1424.01-06	27 s. 3 d.	Fribourg	A	(354) p.283
1424.03.8	27 s. 6 d.	Fribourg	A	(354) p.283
1424.01-06	30 s.	Fribourg	A	(354) p.283
1424.07-12	31 s. 3 d.	Fribourg	A	(354) p.283
1424.07-12	31 s.	Fribourg	A	(354) p.283
1424.07-12	30 s.	Fribourg	A	(354) p.283
1425.01-06	29 s. 6 d.	Fribourg	A	(354) p.283
1425.01-06	30 s.	Fribourg	A	(354) p.283
1425.01-06	30 s.	Fribourg	A	(354) p.283
1425.01.06	30 s.	Fribourg	A	(354) p.283
1426.01-06	30 s.	Fribourg	A	(354) p.283
1426.07-12	30 s.	Fribourg	A	(354) p.283
1427.04.11	30 s.	Fribourg	A	(354) p.283
1427.06.10	30 s. 6 d.	Fribourg	M	(354) p.283
1427.07-12	30 s.	Fribourg	A	(354) p.283
1428.01-06	30 s.	Fribourg	A	(354) p.283
1428.07-12	30 s.	Fribourg	A	(354) p.283
1429.08.04	30 s.	Fribourg	A	(354) p.283
1429.01.15	30 s.	Fribourg	A	(354) p.283
1429.01-06	29 s.	Fribourg	A	(354) p.283
1429.04.22	28 s.	Fribourg	A	(354) p.283
1429.07-12	28 s.	Fribourg	A	(354) p.283

THE RHEINGULDEN IN SOLS AND DENIERS LAUSANNOIS PETITS OF FRIBOURG

Date	Rate	Place	Type	Reference
1429.07.17	27 s. 6 d.	Fribourg	O	(354) p.283
1430.01.31	27 s. 6 d.	Fribourg	A	(354) p.283
1430.04.15	28 s.	Fribourg	A	(354) p.283
1430.08.07	27 s. 6 d.	Fribourg	O	(354) p.283
1430.07-12	28 s.	Fribourg	A	(354) p.283
1431.01-06	27 s. 6 d.	Fribourg	A	(354) p.283
1431.07-12	27 s. 6 d.	Fribourg	A	(354) p.283
1432.01-06	27 s. 6 d.	Fribourg	A	(354) p.283
1432.01-06	27 s. 2 1/2 d.	Fribourg	A	(354) p.283
1432.07-12	27 s. 6 d.	Fribourg	A	(354) p.283
1433.01-06	27 s. 6 d.	Fribourg	A	(354) p.283
1433.07-12	27 s. 6 d.	Fribourg	A	(354) p.283
1434.01.26	27 s. 6 d.	Fribourg	A	(354) p.283
1434.04.21 & 24	28 s.	Fribourg	A	(354) p.283
1434.06.05-07	28 s. 6 d.	Fribourg	A	(354) p.283
1434.06	28 s. 9 d.	Fribourg	A	(354) p.283
1434.08.09	28 s. 6 d.	Fribourg	A	(354) p.283
1434.09.12	28 s. 6 d.	Fribourg	A	(354) p.283
1434.11.26	28 s.	Fribourg	A	(354) p.283
1435.01-06	28 s.	Fribourg	A	(354) p.284
1435.01-06	28 s. 3 d.	Fribourg	A	(354) p.284
1435.01-06	28 s. 6 d.	Fribourg	A	(354) p.284
1435.11.01	28 s. 3 d.	Fribourg	A	(354) p.284
1435.12.08 & 31	28 s. 3 d.	Fribourg	A	(354) p.284
1436.01-06	28 s. 3 d.	Fribourg	A	(354) p.284
1436.07-12	28 s. 3 d.	Fribourg	A	(354) p.284
1437.01-06	28 s. 6 d.	Fribourg	A	(354) p.284
1437.01-06	28 s. 9 d.	Fribourg	A	(354) p.284
1437.07-12	28 s. 6 d.	Fribourg	A	(354) p.284
1437.07-12	28 s. 9 d.	Fribourg	A	(354) p.284
1437.09.17	29 s.	Fribourg	A	(354) p.284
1437.09.17	29 s. 9 d.	Fribourg	A	(354) p.284
1438.04.01	28 s. 6 d.	Fribourg	A	(354) p.284
1438.01-06	29 s.	Fribourg	A	(354) p.284
1438.07-12	29 s.	Fribourg	A	(354) p.284
1439.01-06	29 s.	Fribourg	A	(354) p.284
1439.07-12	29 s.	Fribourg	A	(354) p.284
1439-1440	29 s.	Fribourg	A	(354) p.239
1440.01-06	29 s.	Fribourg	A	(354) p.284
1440.01-06	29 s.	Fribourg	A	(354) p.284
1440.07-12	29 s.	Fribourg	A	(354) p.284
1441.01-06	29 s.	Fribourg	A	(354) p.284
1441.07-12	29 s.	Fribourg	A	(354) p.284
1442.01-06	29 s.	Fribourg	A	(354) p.284
1442.07-12	29 s.	Fribourg	A	(354) p.284
1443.01-06	29 s.	Fribourg	A	(354) p.284
1443.07-12	29 s.	Fribourg	A	(354) p.284
1444.01-06	29 s.	Fribourg	A	(354) p.284
1444.06-12	29 s.	Fribourg	A	(354) p.284
1445.01-06	29 s.	Fribourg	A	(354) p.284
1445.07-12	29 s.	Fribourg	A	(354) p.284
1446.03.26	28 s.	Fribourg	O	(354) p.284
1446.01-06	29 s.	Fribourg	A	(354) p.284
1446.07-12	28 s.	Fribourg	A	(354) p.284
1447.01-06	29 s.	Fribourg	A	(354) p.284
1447.07-12	29 s.	Fribourg	A	(354) p.284
1448.01-06	29 s.	Fribourg	A	(354) p.284
1448.07.14	29 s.	Fribourg	A	(354) p.284
1448.08.01	29 s. 6 d.	Fribourg	M	(354) p.284
1448.11.01	29 s. 6 d.	Fribourg	A	(354) p.284
1449.01-06	29 s. 6 d.	Fribourg	A	(354) p.284
1449.01-06	29 s. 9 d.	Fribourg	A	(354) p.284
1449.06.30	29 s. 9 d.	Fribourg	A	(354) p.284
1449.07.17	29 s. 9 d.	Fribourg	A	(354) p.284
1449.08.28	30 s.	Fribourg	A	(354) p.284
1449.11.29	30 s.	Fribourg	A	(354) p.284
1450.01-06	30 s.	Fribourg	A	(354) p.284
1450.07-12	30 s.	Fribourg	A	(354) p.284
1451.01-06	30 s.	Fribourg	A	(354) p.284
1451.07-12	30 s.	Fribourg	A	(354) p.284
1452.01-06	30 s.	Fribourg	A	(354) p.284
1452.10.28-1453.01.06	30 s.	Fribourg	A	(354) p.238

THE RHEINGULDEN IN SOLS AND DENIERS LAUSANNOIS PETITS OF FRIBOURG

Date	Rate	Place	Type	Reference
1452.07-12	30 s.	Fribourg	A	(354) p.284
1453.01-06	30 s.	Fribourg	A	(354) p.284
1453.08.01-10.27	30 s.	Fribourg	A	(354) p.238
1453.07-12	30 s.	Fribourg	A	(354) p.284
1453.07-12	31 s. 8 d.	Fribourg	A	(354) p.285
1453.10.28-1454.01.05	32 s. 6 d.	Fribourg	A	(354) p.238
1454.01-06	31 s. 8 d.	Fribourg	A	(354) p.285
1454.01-06	32 s. 6 d.	Fribourg	A	(354) p.285
1454.01.06	33 s. 4 d.	Fribourg	A	(354) p.238
1454.03	33 s. 4 d.	Fribourg	A	(354) p.285
1454.07-12	32 s. 2 1/2 d.	Fribourg	A	(354) p.285
1454.07-12	32 s. 4 d.	Fribourg	A	(354) p.285
1454.01-06	32 s. 6 d.	Fribourg	A	(354) p.285
1454.01-06	33 s. 6 d.	Fribourg	A	(354) p.285
1455.01-06	33 s. 4 d.	Fribourg	A	(354) p.285
1455.07-12	33 s. 4 d.	Fribourg	A	(354) p.285
1456.01-06	33 s. 4 d.	Fribourg	A	(354) p.285
1456.01-06	34 s. 2 1/2 d.	Fribourg	A	(354) p.285
1456.07-12	33 s. 4 d.	Fribourg	A	(354) p.285
1457.07-12	33 s. 4 d.	Fribourg	A	(354) p.285
1457.11	33 s. 4 d.	Fribourg	A	(354) p.285
1457.07-12	33 s. 10 d.	Fribourg	A	(354) p.285
1457.07-12	35 s.	Basle, Strassburg, Cologne	A	(354) p.285
1458.01	35 s.	Fribourg	A	(354) p.285
1458.01-06	33 s. 8 d.	Fribourg	A	(354) p.285
1458.01-06	34 s. 2 d.	Fribourg	A	(354) p.285
1458.07-12	34 s.	Fribourg	A	(354) p.285
1458.07-12	35 s.	Fribourg	A	(354) p.285
1459.01-06	35 s.	Fribourg	A	(354) p.285
1459.07-12	35 s.	Fribourg	A	(354) p.285
1460.01-06	35 s.	Fribourg	A	(354) p.285
1460.07-12	35 s.	Fribourg	A	(354) p.285
1461.01-06	35 s.	Fribourg	A	(354) p.285
1461.07-12	35 s.	Fribourg	A	(354) p.285
1462.01-06	35 s.	Fribourg	A	(354) p.285
1462.07-12	35 s.	Fribourg	A	(354) p.285
1463.01-06	35 s.	Fribourg	A	(354) p.285
1463.07-12	35 s.	Fribourg	A	(354) p.285
1464.01-06	35 s.	Fribourg	A	(354) p.285
1464.07-12	35 s.	Fribourg	A	(354) p.285
1465.01-06	35 s.	Fribourg	A	(354) p.285
1465.07-12	35 s.	Fribourg	A	(354) p.285
1466.01-06	35 s.	Fribourg	A	(354) p.285
1466.07-12	35 s.	Fribourg	A	(354) p.285
1467.01-06	35 s.	Fribourg	A	(354) p.285
1467.07-12	35 s.	Fribourg	A	(354) p.285
1468.01-06	35 s.	Fribourg	A	(354) p.285
1468.07-12	35 s.	Fribourg	A	(354) p.285
1469.01-06	35 s.	Fribourg	A	(354) p.285
1469.07-12	35 s.	Fribourg	A	(354) p.285
1470.01-06	35 s.	Fribourg	A	(354) p.286
1470.01-06	35 s. 10 d.	Fribourg	A	(354) p.286
1470.07-12	35 s.	Fribourg	A	(354) p.286
1470.07-12	35 s. 5 d.	Fribourg	A	(354) p.286
1470.07-12	35 s. 10 d.	Fribourg	A	(354) p.286
1471.01-06	35 s. 10 d.	Fribourg	A	(354) p.286
1471.02 & 04 & 08	35 s.	Fribourg	A	(354) p.286
1471.12	35 s. 10 d.	Fribourg	A	(354) p.286
1471.07-12	35 s.	Fribourg	A	(354) p.286
1472.01-06	35 s.	Fribourg	A	(354) p.286
1472.07-12	35 s.	Fribourg	A	(354) p.286
1472.07-12	34 s. 6 d.	Fribourg	A	(354) p.286
1473.01-06	35 s.	Fribourg	A	(354) p.286
1473.01-06	35 s. 5 d.	Fribourg	A	(354) p.286
1473.07-12	35 s.	Fribourg	A	(354) p.286
1473.08	35 s. 10 d.	Fribourg	A	(354) p.286
1473.09	36 s. 1 d.	Fribourg	A	(354) p.286
1474.02.03	36 s. 8 d.	Fribourg	A	(354) p.286
1474.07-12	37 s. 6 d.	Fribourg	A	(354) p.286
1475.01	38 s. 6 d.	Fribourg	A	(354) p.286
1475.02	37 s. 6 d.	Fribourg	A	(354) p.286

THE RHEINGULDEN IN SOLS AND DENIERS LAUSANNOIS PETITS OF FRIBOURG

Date	Rate	Place	Type	Reference
1475.07-12	39 s. 2 d.	Fribourg	A	(354) p.286
1475.07-12	40 s.	Fribourg	A	(354) p.286
1475.07-12	41 s. 7 d.	Fribourg	A	(354) p.286
1476.01-06	40 s.	Fribourg	A	(354) p.286
1476.07-12	40 s.	Fribourg	A	(354) p.286
1477.01-06	40 s.	Fribourg	A	(354) p.286
1477.07-12	40 s.	Fribourg	A	(354) p.286
1478.01-06	40 s.	Fribourg	A	(354) p.286
1478.05.26	41 s. 8 d.	Fribourg	A	(354) p.286
1478.07-12	41 s. 8 d.	Fribourg	A	(354) p.286
1479.01-06	41 s. 8 d.	Fribourg	A	(354) p.286
1479.07	41 s. 8 d.	Fribourg	A	(354) p.286
1479.08	42 s. 1 d.	Fribourg	A	(354) p.286
1480.01-06	41 s. 8 d.	Fribourg	A	(354) p.286
1480	29 s.	Fribourg	A	(354) p.239
1480.07-12	41 s. 8 d.	Fribourg	A	(354) p.286
1480.07-12	40 s.	Fribourg	A	(354) p.286
1481.01-06	41 s. 8 d.	Fribourg	A	(354) p.286
1481.04	40 s.	Fribourg	A	(354) p.286
1481.07-12	41 s. 8 d.	Fribourg	A	(354) p.286
1482.01-06	40 s.	Fribourg	A	(352) p.138
1482.07-12	35 s.	Fribourg	A	(352) p.138
1482.07-12	40 s.	Fribourg	A	(352) p.138
1482.07-12	41 s. 8 d.	Fribourg	A	(352) p.138
1483.01-12	41 s. 8 d.	Fribourg	A	(352) p.138
1483.07-12	35 s.	Fribourg	A	(352) p.138
1484.01-06	41 s. 8 d.	Fribourg	A	(352) p.138
1484.01-06	41 s. 10 d.	Fribourg	A	(352) p.138
1484.07-12	43 s. 4 d.	Fribourg	A	(352) p.138
1485.01-06	43 s. 4 d.	Fribourg	A	(352) p.138
1485.07-12	45 s.	Fribourg	A	(352) p.138
1486.07-12	46 s. 8 d.	Fribourg	A	(352) p.138
1487.07-12	46 s. 8 d.	Fribourg	A	(352) p.138
1488.01-06	46 s. 8 d.	Fribourg	A	(352) p.138
1488.07-12	40 s.	Fribourg	A	(352) p.138
1488.07-12	47 s. 6 d.	Fribourg	A	(352) p.138
1489.01-06	47 s. 6 d.	Fribourg	A	(352) p.138
1489.07-12	47 s. 6 d.	Fribourg	A	(352) p.138
1490.01-06	43 s. 4 d.	Fribourg	A	(352) p.138
1490.01-06	47 s. 6 d.	Fribourg	A	(352) p.138
1490.07-12	43 s. 4 d.	Fribourg	A	(352) p.138
1491.01-06	47 s. 6 d.	Fribourg	A	(352) p.138
1491.01-06	48 s. 4 d.	Fribourg	A	(352) p.138
1491.07-12	47 s. 6 d.	Fribourg	A	(352) p.138
1491.07-12	48 s. 4 d.	Fribourg	A	(352) p.138
1492.07-12	48 s. 4 d.	Fribourg	A	(352) p.138
1493.01-06	58 s. 8 d.	Fribourg	A	(352) p.138
1493.07-12	48 s. 8 d.	Fribourg	A	(352) p.138
1494.01-12	48 s. 4 d.	Fribourg	A	(352) p.138
1495.01-06	47 s. 7 d.	Fribourg	A	(352) p.138
1495.01-06	48 s. 4 d.	Fribourg	A	(352) p.138
1495.07-12	48 s. 4 d.	Fribourg	A	(352) p.138
1495.07-12	48 s. 10 d.	Fribourg	A	(352) p.138
1496.01-06	48 s. 4 d.	Fribourg	A	(352) p.138
1497.01-06	48 s. 4 d.	Fribourg	A	(352) p.138
1497.01-06	49 s.	Fribourg	A	(352) p.138
1497.07-12	48 s. 4 d.	Fribourg	A	(352) p.138
1498.01-06	51 s. 1 d.	Fribourg	A	(352) p.138
1498.07-12	48 s. 4 d.	Fribourg	A	(352) p.138
1499.01-06	48 s. 4 d.	Fribourg	A	(352) p.138
1499.07-12	48 s. 4 d.	Fribourg	A	(352) p.138
1500.01-12	48 s. 4 d.	Fribourg	A	(352) p.138

The rheingulden in sueldos and dineros of Barcelona

Date	Rate	Place	Type	Reference
1472-1473	12 s. 6 d.	Barcelona	C	(450) II p.248
1474	18 s. 8 d.	Barcelona	C	(450) II p.248
1477	16 s.	Barcelona	C	(450) II p.248
1478	18 s.	Barcelona	C	(450) II p.248

THE RHEINGULDEN IN SUELDOS AND DINEROS OF BARCELONA

Date	Rate	Place	Type	Reference
1479	12 s. 6 d.	Barcelona	C	(450) II p.248
1480	11 s. 7 d.	Barcelona	C	(450) II p.248
1480	12 s. 9 d.	Barcelona	C	(450) II p.248

The rheingulden in shillings and pence sterling of England

Date	Rate	Place	Type	Reference
1500	3 s. 4 d.	England	H	(399) p.163

The rheingulden in Flemish groten and sterlings

3 sterlings = 1 groot

Date	Rate	Place	Type	Reference
1400	33 gr.	Bruges	A	(295) Af.I, 55r
1404 end 09	33 gr.	Bruges	A	(295) Af.I, 41v
1409.05.12-09.06	31 gr.	Bruges	A	(295) Af.6, 33r
1409.07.03	33 gr.	Bruges	C	(370) p.138
1409.10	32 gr.	Bruges	C	(370) p.138
1410.04.25	33 gr.	Bruges	A	(295) Af.6, 54v
1410	32 gr. 2 st.	Bruges	C	(370) p.138
1410.04-05	33 gr.	Bruges	C	(370) p.138
1410.06.05	33 gr.	Bruges	C	(370) p.138
1410.08	32 1/2 gr.	Bruges	C	(370) p.138
1410.08.14-1411	33 gr.	Bruges	C	(370) p.138
1410.08.14	32 1/2 gr.	Cologne	C	(370) p.101
1410.10.27	33 gr.	Cologne	C	(370) p.101
1410	34 gr.	Bruges	C	(370) p.138
1411.03.04	33 gr. 1 st.	Bruges	C	(370) p.138
1411.03.07	33 gr.	Bruges	A	(295) Af.6, 76r
1411.05.24	33 gr.	Bruges	C	(370) p.138
1411.06.19	32 gr.	Bruges	C	(370) p.138
1417.02.20	36 gr.	Bruges	C	(370) p.138
1417.12.22	35 gr. 1 st.	Bruges	C	(370) p.138
1419	32 gr.	Burgundy	O	(349) IV p.503
1420.03.02	33 gr.	Bruges	C	(370) p.138
1420.06.16	32 gr.	Bruges	C	(370) p.138
1420.06.24	31 gr. 2 st.	Bruges	C	(370) p.138
1420.06.24	32 gr. 1 st.	Bruges	C	(370) p.138
1420.08.23	33 gr. 1 st.	Bruges	C	(370) p.138
1420.11.18	33 gr.	Bruges	C	(370) p.138
1466.09	41 gr.	Liège	O	(58) p.607
1467.10	44 gr.	Low Countries	A	(7)
1467.12	43 gr.	Low Countries	A	(7)
1467.12	42 gr.	Low Countries	A	(7)
1474.10.27	46 gr.	Low Countries	O	(495) p.395
1479.06	52 gr.	Low Countries	C	(496)
1480.06-08	52 gr.	Low Countries	C	(496)
1481.06-07	52 gr.	Low Countries	C	(496)
1482.03	54 gr.	Low Countries	C	(496)
1482.04	54 gr.	Low Countries	C	(496)
1482.10	58 gr.	Low Countries	C	(496)
1485.12	56 gr.	Low Countries	C	(496)
1493.11	54 gr.	Antwerp?	A	(255) f.32v
1494.06	54 gr.	Antwerp?	A	(255) f.42
1495	56 gr.	Antwerp?	C	(255) f.75
1495.11	54 gr.	Antwerp?	C	(255) f.42v
1497	54 gr.	Middleburg	A	(255) f.66
1500	48 gr.	England?	H	(399) p.163

The rheingulden in groten of Brabant

Date	Rate	Place	Type	Reference
1448.Easter	57 gr.	Malines	A	(238) p.45

The rheingulden in groten of Holland

Date	Rate	Place	Type	Reference
1393	32 gr.	Holland	A	(175)
1398	36 gr.	Holland	A	(175)
1399	38 gr.	Holland	A	(175)
1403	39 gr.	Holland	A	(175)
1404	44 gr.	Holland	A	(175)
1407	33 gr.	Holland	A	(175)
1408-1409	32 gr.	Holland	A	(175)
1410-1412	33 gr.	Holland	A	(175)
1418	41 gr.	Holland	A	(175)
1418	50 gr.	Holland	A	(175)
1419	52 gr.	Holland	A	(175)
1420	52 gr.	Holland	A	(175)
1420	55 gr.	Holland	A	(175)
1420	56 gr.	Holland	A	(175)
1421	58 gr.	Holland	A	(175)
1422	64 gr.	Holland	A	(175)
1423	66 gr.	Holland	A	(175)
1425	81 gr.	Holland	A	(175)
1433	48 gr.	Holland	A	(175)
1433	49 gr.	Holland	A	(175)

The rheingulden in witten (albi) of Utrecht
30 witten = 1 gulden of account

Date	Rate	Place	Type	Reference
1395-1397	52 witten	Utrecht	A	(477) p.570
1400-1402	51 witten	Utrecht	A	(477) p.570
1403-1404	54 witten	Utrecht	A	(477) p.570
1404-1405	55 witten	Utrecht	A	(477) p.570
1406-1408	55 witten	Utrecht	A	(477) p.570
1413-1414	56 witten	Utrecht	A	(477) p.570
1418-1419	65 witten	Utrecht	A	(477) p.570
1419-1423	66 witten	Utrecht	A	(477) pp.570-571
1424	74 witten	Utrecht	A	(396) p.25
1424-1425	81 witten	Utrecht	A	(477) p.571
1426	84 witten	Utrecht	A	(396) p.25
1426-1427	88 witten	Utrecht	A	(477) p.571
1428	94 witten	Utrecht	A	(396) p.25
1429	120 witten	Utrecht	A	(396) p.25
1430-1432	135 witten	Utrecht	A	(396) p.25
1434-1435	156 witten	Utrecht	A	(477) p.571
1435-1437	171 witten	Utrecht	A	(477) p.571
1438	168 witten	Utrecht	A	(396) p.25
1439	174 witten	Utrecht	A	(396) p.25
1440	177 witten	Utrecht	A	(396) p.25
1441-1443	186 witten	Utrecht	A	(477) p.571
1443-1444	189 witten	Utrecht	A	(477) p.571
1443-1448	192 witten	Utrecht	A	(477) p.571
1449	198 witten	Utrecht	A	(396) p.26
1450-1451	201 witten	Utrecht	A	(477) p.571
1455-1458	220 witten	Utrecht	A	(396) p.26
1459	225 witten	Utrecht	A	(396) p.26
1460-1461	225 witten	Utrecht	A	(477) p.600
1461-1463	230 witten	Utrecht	A	(477) p.600
1463-1464	234 witten	Utrecht	A	(477) p.600

The rheingulden in stuivers of Utrecht
12 witten = 1 stuiver; 20 stuivers = 1 gulden of account

Date	Rate	Place	Type	Reference
1464-1468	20 1/2 st. = 246 witten	Utrecht	A	(477) p.600
1468-1471	21 st.	Utrecht	A	(477) p.600
1471-1472	21 st.	Utrecht	A	(477) p.600
1471-1472	21 1/2 st.	Utrecht	A	(477) p.600
1472-1473	21 1/2 st.	Utrecht	A	(477) p.600
1473-1475	22 st.	Utrecht	A	(477) p.600

THE RHEINGULDEN IN STUIVERS OF UTRECHT

Date	Rate	Place	Type	Reference
1475-1477	23 st.	Utrecht	A	(477) p.600
1477-1478	24 st.	Utrecht	A	(477) p.600
1479-1480	26 st.	Utrecht	A	(477) p.600
1480-1481	26 st.	Utrecht	A	(257)
1482	27 st.	Utrecht	A	(257)
1483	29 st.	Utrecht	A	(257)
1484	31 st.	Utrecht	A	(257)
1485	32 1/2 st.	Utrecht	A	(257)
1485	30 st.	Utrecht	A	(257)
1486	30 st.	Utrecht	A	(257)
1486	32 st.	Utrecht	A	(257)
1486	32 1/2 st.	Utrecht	A	(257)
1486	33 st.	Utrecht	A	(257)
1487	33 st.	Utrecht	A	(257)
1487	33 1/2 st.	Utrecht	A	(257)
1487	34 st.	Utrecht	A	(257)
1487	35 st.	Utrecht	A	(257)
1487	36 st.	Utrecht	A	(257)
1487	37 st.	Utrecht	A	(257)
1488	40 st.	Utrecht	A	(257)
1488	42 st.	Utrecht	A	(257)
1489	45 st.	Utrecht	A	(257)
1490	19 st. moneta gravis	Utrecht	A	(257)
1490	20 st. moneta gravis	Utrecht	A	(257)
1491	20 st. moneta gravis	Utrecht	A	(257)
1492	24 st. moneta gravis	Utrecht	A	(257)
1493	27 st. moneta gravis	Utrecht	A	(257)
1493	26 st. moneta gravis	Utrecht	A	(257)
1493	28 st. moneta gravis	Utrecht	A	(257)
1494-1495	28 st. moneta gravis	Utrecht	A	(257)
1496	28 st. moneta gravis	Utrecht	A	(257)
1496	30 st. moneta gravis	Utrecht	A	(257)
1497-1500	30 st. moneta gravis	Utrecht	A	(257)

The rheingulden in stuivers of Gelderland

Date	Rate	Place	Type	Reference
1470	20 1/2 st.	Zutphen	A	(442) p.253
1471	21 st.	Zutphen	A	(442) p.253
1472	21 1/2 st.	Zutphen	A	(442) p.253
1473	21 1/2 st.	Zutphen	A	(442) p.253
1473	22 st.	Zutphen	A	(442) p.253
1474	22 st.	Zutphen	A	(442) p.253
1475	23 st.	Zutphen	A	(442) p.253
1476	23 st.	Zutphen	A	(442) p.253
1477	23 st.	Zutphen	A	(442) p.253
1478	24 st.	Zutphen	A	(442) p.253
1478	26 st.	Zutphen	A	(442) p.253
1478	28 st.	Zutphen	A	(442) p.253
1479	26 st.	Zutphen	A	(442) p.253
1480	26 st.	Zutphen	A	(442) p.253
1480	28 st.	Zutphen	A	(442) p.253
1481	27 st.	Zutphen	A	(442) p.253
1482	27 st.	Zutphen	A	(442) p.253
1482	29 st.	Zutphen	A	(442) p.253
1482	30 st.	Zutphen	A	(442) p.253
1483	32 st.	Zutphen	A	(442) p.253
1484	32 st.	Zutphen	A	(442) p.253
1485	33 st.	Zutphen	A	(442) p.253
1486	33 st.	Zutphen	A	(442) p.253
1487	34 st.	Zutphen	A	(442) p.253
1487	36 st.	Zutphen	A	(442) p.253
1488	36 st.	Zutphen	A	(442) p.253
1488	37 st.	Zutphen	A	(442) p.253
1488	38 st.	Zutphen	A	(442) p.254
1488	39 st.	Zutphen	A	(442) p.254
1488	40 st.	Zutphen	A	(442) p.254
1488	41 st.	Zutphen	A	(442) p.254
1488	42 st.	Zutphen	A	(442) p.254
1488	43 st.	Zutphen	A	(442) p.254

THE RHEINGULDEN IN STUIVERS OF GELDERLAND

Date	Rate	Place	Type	Reference
1489	44 st.	Zutphen	A	(442) p.254

The rheingulden in butkens of Gelderland

Date	Rate	Place	Type	Reference
1489	40 butkens	Zutphen	A	(442) p.254
1490	40 butkens	Zutphen	A	(442) p.254
1490	41 butkens	Zutphen	A	(442) p.254
1490	42 butkens	Zutphen	A	(442) p.254
1490	43 butkens	Zutphen	A	(442) p.254
1491	40 butkens	Zutphen	A	(442) p.254
1491	43 butkens	Zutphen	A	(442) p.254
1491	44 butkens	Zutphen	A	(442) p.254
1492	44 butkens	Zutphen	A	(442) p.254
1492	45 butkens	Zutphen	A	(442) p.254
1492	46 butkens	Zutphen	A	(442) p.254
1492	47 butkens	Zutphen	A	(442) p.254
1492	48 butkens	Zutphen	A	(442) p.254
1493	48 butkens	Zutphen	A	(442) p.254
1493	49 butkens	Zutphen	A	(442) p.254
1493	50 butkens	Zutphen	A	(442) p.254
1493	52 butkens	Zutphen	A	(442) p.254
1493	54 butkens	Zutphen	A	(442) p.254
1493	55 butkens	Zutphen	A	(442) p.254
1493	56 butkens	Zutphen	A	(442) p.254
1493	57 butkens	Zutphen	A	(442) p.254
1493	58 butkens	Zutphen	A	(442) p.254
1494	58 butkens	Zutphen	A	(442) p.254
1494	60 butkens	Zutphen	A	(442) p.254
1495	60 butkens	Zutphen	A	(442) p.254
1496-1500	62 butkens	Zutphen	A	(442) p.254

The rheingulden in plakken of Deventer

Date	Rate	Place	Type	Reference
1386	28 pl. 1 d. brab.	Deventer	A	(132) p.XXI
1391	30 pl.	Deventer	A	(132) p.XXI
1391	30 3/4 pl.	Deventer	A	(132) p.XXI
1391	31 1/2 pl.	Deventer	A	(132) p.XXI
1397	39 3/4 pl.	Deventer	A	(132) p.XXI
1400	41 1/2 pl.	Deventer	A	(132) p.XXI
1402	43 pl.	Deventer	A	(132) p.XXI
1408	44 pl.	Deventer	A	(132) p.XXI
1411	44 pl.	Deventer	A	(132) p.XXII
1412	45 pl.	Deventer	A	(132) p.XXII
1413	47 pl.	Deventer	A	(132) p.XXII
1414	50-51 pl.	Deventer	A	(132) p.XXII
1415	51 pl.	Deventer	A	(132) p.XXII
1416	52 pl.	Deventer	A	(132) p.XXII
1417	51-54 pl.	Deventer	A	(132) p.XXII
1418	54-56 pl.	Deventer	A	(132) p.XXII
1419	57-59 pl.	Deventer	A	(132) p.XXII
1420	60 pl.	Deventer	A	(132) p.XXII
1421	63 pl.	Deventer	A	(132) p.XXII
1422	64 pl.	Deventer	A	(132) p.XXII
1423	68 pl.	Deventer	A	(132) p.XXII
1424	72 pl.	Deventer	A	(132) p.XXII
1421	63 pl.	Deventer	A	(132) p.XXII
1422	64 pl.	Deventer	A	(132) p.XXII
1423	68 pl.	Deventer	A	(132) p.XXII
1424	72 pl.	Deventer	A	(132) p.XXII
1425	75 pl.	Deventer	A	(132) p.XXII
1428	90 pl.	Deventer	A	(132) p.XXII
1429	90 pl.	Deventer	A	(132) p.XXII
1429	93 pl.	Deventer	A	(132) p.XXII
1429	96 pl.	Deventer	A	(132) p.XXII
1432	114 pl.	Deventer	A	(132) p.XXII
1323	108 pl.	Deventer	A	(132) p.XXII
1333	110 3/4 pl.	Deventer	A	(132) p.XXII

THE RHEINGULDEN IN PLAKKEN OF DEVENTER

Date	Rate	Place	Type	Reference
1433	117 pl.	Deventer	A	(132) p.XXII
1434	122 pl.	Deventer	A	(132) p.XXII
1435	120 pl.	Deventer	A	(132) p.XXII
1436	120 pl.	Deventer	A	(132) p.XXII
1440	125-126 pl.	Deventer	A	(132) p.XXII
1441	121-124 pl.	Deventer	A	(132) p.XXII

The rheingulden in kromstaarten of Deventer

Date	Rate	Place	Type	Reference
1437	29 kromstaarts	Deventer	A	(132) p.XXIII
1438	29 kromstaarts	Deventer	A	(132) p.XXIII
1439	29 1/2 kromstaarts	Deventer	A	(132) p.XXIII
1440	28 1/2 kromstaarts	Deventer	A	(132) p.XXIII
1441	28 1/2 kromstaarts	Deventer	A	(132) p.XXIII
1442	31 kromstaarts	Deventer	A	(132) p.XXIII
1443-1447	32 kromstaarts	Deventer	A	(132) p.XXIII
1448	33 kromstaarts	Deventer	A	(132) p.XXIII
1451	34 kromstaarts	Deventer	A	(132) p.XXIII
1452	35 kromstaarts	Deventer	A	(132) p.XXIII
1453	35 kromstaarts	Deventer	A	(132) p.XXIII
1454	37 1/2 kromstaarts	Deventer	A	(132) p.XXIII
1455-1459	36 kromstaarts	Deventer	A	(132) p.XXIII
1466-1467	36 1/2 kromstaarts	Deventer	A	(176)
1468-1469	37 kromstaarts	Deventer	A	(176)
1470-1473	38 kromstaarts	Deventer	A	(176)
1474-1475	40 kromstaarts	Deventer	A	(176)

The rheingulden in stuivers of Deventer

Date	Rate	Place	Type	Reference
1476-1477	23 st.	Deventer	A	(176)
1478	25 st.	Deventer	A	(176)
1479-1481	26 st.	Deventer	A	(176)
1482	29 st.	Deventer	A	(176)
1483-1484	30 st.	Deventer	A	(176)
1485-1486	32 st.	Deventer	A	(176)
1487	36 st.	Deventer	A	(176)

The rheingulden in stichtse stuivers (of Overijssel)
8 plakken of Deventer = 1 stuiver of Overijssel

Date	Rate	Place	Type	Reference
1488.10.27	20 st.	Deventer	O	(174) p.288
1488-9	20 st.	Deventer	A	(176)

For 100 cameral florins in rheingulden see under AVIGNON p.128

UPPER RHINELAND

STRASSBURG

For many centuries Strassburg provided much of the currency for the upper Rhineland. There had been a mint there since the Carolingian period. It was operated for the city of Strassburg from 1296 onwards.

The Florentine florin in schillinge and pfennige of Strassburg

Date	Rate	Place	Type	Reference
1318	16 s. 3 d.	Strassburg	C	(267) p.LXXVI
1393	10 s. 4 d.	Alsace	C	(236) p.238
1407	12 s.	Rome	B	(439) p.118
1414	9 s. 10 1/4 d.	Strassburg	HC	(461) p.382
1416	10 s. 4 d.	Strassburg	HC	(461) p.382
1417	10 s.	Strassburg	HC	(461) p.382
1424	12 s. 10 1/2 d.	Strassburg	HC	(461) p.382
1425	14 s. 2 d.	Strassburg	HC	(461) p.382
1426	14 s. 1/2 d.	Strassburg	HC	(461) p.382
1426	13 s. 8 d.	Strassburg	HC	(461) p.384
1475	14 s. 1 d.	Strassburg	HC	(461) p.385
1492	14 s. 1 d.	Strassburg	HC	(461) p.383
1498	14 s. 7 d.	Strassburg	HC	(461) p.383

For the rheingulden in schillinge and pfennige of Strassburg see under RHINELAND p.247

BASLE AND THE RAPPENMÜNZBUND

As early as 1311 the city of Basle, which had acquired the right of minting from its bishop in 1273, joined the duke of Austria, as ruler of Upper Alsace, the Breisgau and the Sundgau to produce a common coinage. Over the next two and a half centuries various other south-west German cities joined this 'münzbund'. The principal cities were Freiburg, Colmar and Breisach. The coinage of the 'münzbund' was based on the pfennige of Basle, which were known as stäbler from the crozier (stab) which formed the type of the coin. It was not until the fifteenth century that rappen (2 stäbler) and plapparts or blapharts (schillinge) were also issued. Basle did not join the Swiss Confederation until 1501.

The Florentine florin in money current in Basle

Date	Rate	Place	Type	Reference
1309	12 s.	Piedmont	A	(110) p.490
1318.07.11	15 s. 7 d.	Frickgau	B	(309) II p.346
1319.09.12	16 s. 1 d.	Frickgau	B	(309) II p.346
1319.10.21	16 s.	Frickgau	B	(309) II p.346
1328	30 s. 7 d.	Veltin	HC	(461) p.375
1328	31 s. 2 d.	Veltin	HC	(461) p.375
1425	37 s.	Alsace	C	(236) I p.244
1455.10.01	23 s. 4 d.	Basle	C	(449) I p.497
1499	32 s. 9 d.	Basle	HC	(461) p.380

For the rheingulden in schillinge and pfennige of Basle see under RHINELAND p.247

SWISS CONFEDERATION

The original three cantons who joined together in 1291 did not contain any mints, but several of the later cantons did so. In 1425 all eight cantons, except Bern, formed a monetary league. In 1483 these seven cantons attempted but failed, to bring Bern, and the two new cantons of Fribourg and Solothurn into a new monetary league. The money of Zürich was the key currency of these leagues.

ZÜRICH

The city of Zürich, which had acquired the right of minting from the abbey, joined in the agreements of the Rappenmünzbund in 1377 and 1387, but later again minted an independent coinage of its own, which became the key coinage of the Swiss monetary league after 1425.

The Florentine florin in schillinge and pfennige of Zürich

Date	Rate	Place	Type	Reference
1388	20 s.	Zürich	HC	(461) p.378
1401	25 s.	Zürich	HC	(461) p.378
1401	25 s. 3 d.	Zürich	HC	(461) p.378
1404-1405	30 s. 2 d.	Zürich	HC	(461) p.378
1416-1417	27 s. 2 d.	Zürich	HC	(461) p.378
1426	40 s. 6 d.	Zürich	HC	(461) p.379
1498-1499	53 s.	Zürich	HC	(461) p.380

For the pfund of pfennige of Constance in schillinge and heller of Zürich see under CONSTANCE p.262

BERN

Bern was founded in 1191 by the duke of Zähringen and joined the Swiss Confederation in 1353. Minting of bernerpfennige began there shortly after its foundation, and the mint was taken over by the city in 1370. Bern, like Zürich, joined the agreements of the Rappenmünzbund in 1377 and 1387. In 1416 it joined a monetary league with Zürich and Solothurn, but in 1425 and again in 1483 it remained outside the monetary leagues formed by the other cantons. In the fifteenth century accounting was not only carried on in pfund, schillinge, and pfennige (haller), but also in a variety of actual coins fünfers (5d.), creuzer, plapparts, and, at the end of the century, batz. Of these the plappart was the most important. It was a coin comparable to the French blanc. It was first minted in 1388 as a schilling. In 1416 it was worth 14d. In 1421 it was worth 15d. In 1424 it was worth 16d. It was still worth 16d. in 1483. The creuzer was valued as a half-plappart, and the batz, when introduced, as a double-plappart (32d). A few relationships between the currency of Bern and that of the other cantons are published in (322).

In 1390 12d. of Bern = 10d. of Fribourg
In 1498 5d. of Bern = 6d. of Basle
In 1488 4d. of Bern = 6d. of Zürich
= 5d. of Lucerne
= 5d. of Solothurn

The Florentine florin in schillinge and pfennige of Bern

Date	Rate	Place	Type	Reference
1385.04.30	21 s. stäbler current in Bern	Fribourg	B	(4) I p.33
1416.06.13	31 s. 2 haller	Bern	0	(322) p.326

The Venetian ducat in schillinge and pfennige (haller) of Bern

Date	Rate	Place	Type	Reference
1416.06.13	32 s. 2 d.	Bern	0	(322) p.326
1477.09.05	36 plapparts = 48 s.	Bern	0	(322) p.327
1487.09.01	3 li. 8 fünfers = 63 s. 4 d.	Bern	0	(322) p.327

In 1479 the city received a papal grant of the right to strike its own florins of the same weight and fineness as florins of the Rhine (Rheingulden). For rates for rheingulden in schillinge and pfennige (haller) of Bern see above p.247

The florin (?of Bern) in schillinge and pfennige (haller) of Bern

Date	Rate	Place	Type	Reference
1483 before 07.08	40 s.	Bern	O	(322) p.327

Other cantons

Lucerne acquired the right to mint in 1418, from the emperor.

See above pp.134-7 for the currencies of Geneva, Lausanne and Fribourg. Fribourg joined the confederation in 1481. Geneva and Lausanne were not associated with it until the sixteenth century.

CONSTANCE

In 1423 by the Riedlinger monetary convention the issues of coin in Swabia bound themselves to mint common coin for Swabia based on that of Constance. The monetary convention was renewed in 1436. The pfund of pfennige was taken as 2 pfund of heller.

The Florentine florin in schillinge and pfennige of Constance

Date	Rate	Place	Type	Reference
1423	14 s.	Constance	C	(416) p.243
1443	18 s. 6 d.	Constance	HC	(461) p.380

The pfund of pfennige of Constance in schillinge and pfennige (heller) of Zürich

Date	Rate	Place	Type	Reference
1458	circa 51 s. 6 d.	Constance	A	(266) p.103

For the rheingulden in schillinge and pfennige of Constance see under RHINELAND p.247

HELLER

The heller was originally the pfennig of Swäbisch Hall, where it had been minted since the twelfth century. It circulated widely throughout south Germany and the Rhineland, and a very large number of cities and principalities issued their own heller. Other coins of a similar size, such as the Stäbler of Basle and the Rappenmünzbund, were also sometimes known as heller. In 1356 the Emperor Charles IV stipulated that Nuremberg heller should be the standard for other heller and that the gulden should equal the pfund of heller.

It is not clear from the sources which heller are intended in the following quotations — but they seem to be mainly south German heller rather than Lower Rhineland heller, apart from the rates between heller and the money of Cologne. Only a few are specifically called Nuremberg heller.

The Florentine florin in schillinge and heller

Date	Rate	Place	Type	Reference
1265-1311	10 s.	Curia	B	(439) p.899
1308	12 s.	Curia	B	(439) p.899
1313	circa 14 s.	Curia	B	(439) p.900
1315-1319	circa 15 s.	Curia	B	(439) p.900
1317-1320	15 s. 3 d.	Cologne	C	(268) p.39
1317.07	16 s. 2 d.	Trier	B	(309) I p.239
1318	15 s. 6 d.	Regensburg	C	(20) I p.672

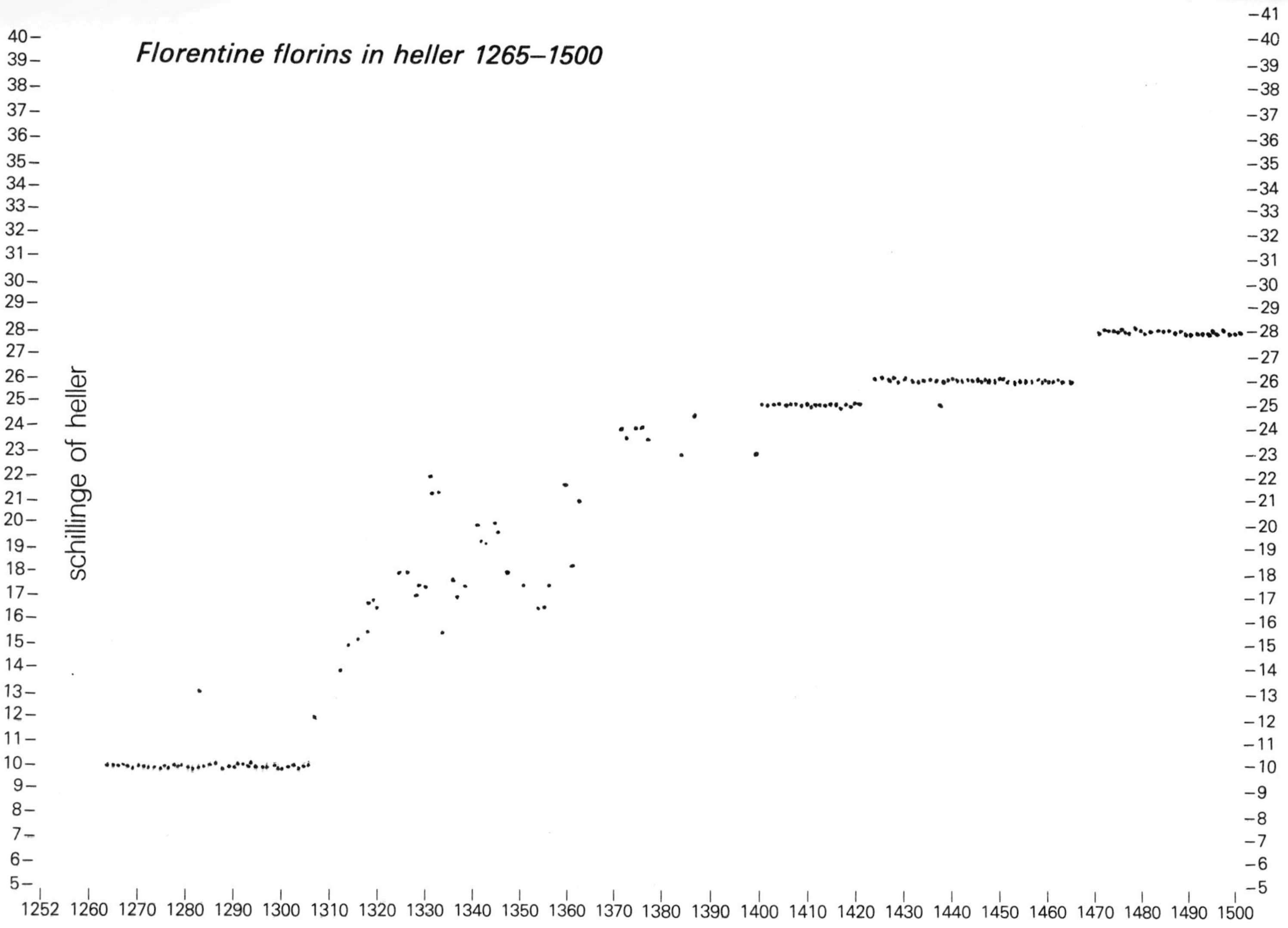

Florentine florins in heller 1265–1500

THE FLORENTINE FLORIN IN SCHILLINGE AND HELLER

Date	Rate	Place	Type	Reference
1319	16 s. 10 d.	Regensburg	C	(20) I p.672
1319	16 s. 3 d.	Curia	B	(439) p.900
1320	16 s. 10 d.	Curia	B	(439) p.900
1321	16 s. 8 d.	Regensburg	C	(20) I p.672
1325-1326	18 s.	Regensburg	C	(20) I p.672
1326.02	17 s. 8 d.	Regensburg	C	(20) I p.672
1329.07-1330.05	17 s. 6 d.	Regensburg	C	(20) I p.672
1330.09	19 s.	Regensburg	C	(20) I p.672
1331.04-05	22 s.	Regensburg	C	(20) I p.672
1332.06-1333.07	21 s. 6 d.	Regensburg	C	(20) I p.673
1334.10	15 s. 6 d.	Regensburg	C	(20) I p.673
1335.02.05	16 s. 6 d.	Regensburg	C	(20) I p.673
1337-1355	20 s.	Curia	B	(439) p.902
1337	17 s. 10 d.	Regensburg	C	(20) I p.673
1338	17 s.	Regensburg	C	(20) I p.673
1339.05.30	17 s. 6 d.	Regensburg	C	(20) I p.673
1341	20 s.	Regensburg	C	(20) I p.673
1343.03-1344.07	19 s. 2 d.	Regensburg	C	(20) I p.673
1344.07-1345.05	20 s.	Regensburg	C	(20) I p.673
1346	19 s. 4 d.	Regensburg	C	(20) I p.673
1347	18 s.	Regensburg	C	(20) I p.673
1351	17 s. 6 d.	Regensburg	C	(20) I p.674
1354.07-1355	16 s. 8 d.	Regensburg	C	(20) I p.674
1355-1336.08	17 s. 3 d.	Regensburg	C	(20) I p.675
1358	20 s.	Regensburg	C	(20) I p.674
1359	21 s. 8 d.	Regensburg	C	(20) I p.674
1361	18 s. 4 d.	Regensburg	C	(20) I p.674
1362	21 s.	Regensburg	C	(20) I p.674
1371	24 s. 1/2 d.	Augsburg	HC	(461) p.380
1373	23 s. 11 d.	Augsburg	HC	(461) p.380
1374-1375	24 s.	Curia	B	(439) p.85
1376	23 s. 11 d.	Augsburg	HC	(461) p.380
1384	23 s.	Bavaria	C	(20) I p.688
1386	24 s. 6 d.	Bavaria	C	(20) I p.668
1399	23 s.	Germany	C	(169) I p.122
1400-1420	25 s.	Germany	C	(169) I p.122
1400	25 s.	Nuremberg	C	(403) X p.13
1424-1464	26 s.	Germany	C	(169) I p.122
1437	25 s.	Germany	C	(169) I p.135
1469-1509	28 s.	Germany	C	(169) I p.122

The Bohemian ducat in Nuremberg heller

Date	Rate	Place	Type	Reference
1366	240 d.	Bohemia	H	(97) p.25
1373	240 d.	Bohemia	H	(97) p.25
1376	240 d.	Bohemia	H	(97) p.25
1377	243 d.	Bohemia	H	(97) p.25
1378	246 d.	Bohemia	H	(97) p.25
1381	252 d.	Bohemia	H	(97) p.25
1382	252 d.	Bohemia	H	(97) p.25
1384	264 d.	Bohemia	H	(97) p.25
1385	264 d.	Bohemia	H	(97) p.25
1386	267 d.	Bohemia	H	(97) p.25
1387	273 d.	Bohemia	H	(97) p.25
1388	271 d.	Bohemia	H	(97) p.25
1389	282 d.	Bohemia	H	(97) p.25
1390	299 d.	Bohemia	H	(97) p.25
1391	318 d.	Bohemia	H	(97) p.25
1392	318 d.	Bohemia	H	(97) p.25
1394	354 d.	Bohemia	H	(97) p.25
1395	490 d.	Bohemia	H	(97) p.25
1396	720 d.	Bohemia	H	(97) p.25
1397	285 d.	Bohemia	H	(97) p.25

The pfund of heller in schillinge and pfennige pagament of Cologne

Date	Rate	Place	Type	Reference
1293	6 s. 8 d.	Nassau	A	(242) p.161
1295	6 s. 8 d.	Nassau	A	(242) p.161
1296	6 s. 8 d.	Cologne	C	(271) p.115
1296	9 s. 3 d.	Cologne	A	(271) p.186
1297	6 s. 8 d.	Frankfurt am Main	A	(242) p.183
1298	6 s. 8 d.	Nassau	A	(242) p.161
1298	6 s. 8 d.	Siegen in Siegerland	A	(242) p.208
1300	6 s. 8 d.	Nassau	A	(242) p.161
1301	6 s. 8 d.	Ehrbach im Rheingau	A	(242) p.165
1302	6 s. 8 d.	Ehrbach im Rheingau	A	(242) p.165
1302	6 s. 8 d.	Mainz	A	(242) p.167
1303	6 s. 8 d.	Siegen	A	(242) p.208
1304	6 s. 8 d.	Ehrbach im Rheingau	A	(242) p.165
1304	6 s. 8 d.	Siegen	A	(242) p.208
1305	6 s. 8 d.	Ehrbach im Rheingau	A	(242) p.165
1305	6 s. 8 d.	Mainz	A	(242) p.167
1306	6 s. 8 d.	Mainz	A	(242) p.167
1306	6 s. 8 d.	Hessen	A	(242) p.191
1307	13 s. 4 d.	Cologne	A	(271) p.186
1309	6 s. 8 d.	Wetterau	A	(242) p.191
1311	6 s. 8 d.	Mainz	A	(242) p.167
1313	6 s. 8 d.	Mainz	A	(242) p.167
1317	6 s. 8 d.	Mainz	A	(242) p.167
1317	13 s. 4 d.	Cologne	C	(267) p.LXXV
1317-1319	13 s. 4 d.	Cologne	C	(267) p.LXXV
1319	6 s. 8 d.	Mainz	A	(242) p.167
1322	6 s. 8 d.	Mainz	A	(242) p.167
1325	6 s. 8 d.	Mainz	A	(242) p.167
1325.08.03	13 s. 4 d.	Dansweiler	M	(271) p.185
1347	13 s. 4 d.	Cologne	O	(271) p.186
1347	26 s. 8 d.	Cologne	M	(271) p.186

The pfund of heller in schillinge and pfennige pagament of Aachen

Date	Rate	Place	Type	Reference
1334	13 s. 4 d.	Aachen	A	(271) p.185
1338	6 s.	Aachen	A	(271) p.185
1344	24 s.	Aachen	A	(271) p.185
1346	26 s. 8 d.	Aachen	A	(271) p.185
1349	30 s.	Aachen	A	(271) p.185

The pfund of heller in schillinge and pfennige of Marburg

Date	Rate	Place	Type	Reference
1336.07.22	10 s.	Marburg?	H	(249) p.77

The pfund of heller in sous and deniers of Brabant

Date	Rate	Place	Type	Reference
1329.12.06	6 s. 8 d.	Jüchen	M	(271) p.185
1333.08.04	6 s. 8 d.	Jüchen	M	(271) p.185

For the weisspfennig and the rheingulden in heller see under RHINELAND pp.239 and 248
For the Regensburger pfennig in heller see under REGENSBURG p.269
For the Prague groschen in heller see under BOHEMIA p.278

FRANCONIA

In the fifteenth century the issuers of coin in Franconia (Franken), principally the bishops of Bamberg and Würzburg and the electors of Brandenburg for their Franconian lands (the former burggraviate of Nuremberg) leagued together to issue common coin. For value of rheingulden in Franconian currency see above p.247

AUGSBURG

The Florentine florin in schillinge and pfennige of Augsburg

Date	Rate	Place	Type	Reference
1318	15 s. 6 d.	Augsburg	C	(267) p.LXXVI
1321	8 s. 4 d.	Regensburg	C	(20) I p.672
1326.02	8 s. 10 d.	Regensburg	C	(20) I p.672
1330.09	9 s. 6 d.	Regensburg	C	(20) I p.672
1331.04-05	11 s.	Regensburg	C	(20) I p.672
1370	18 s.	Bavaria	C	(20) I p.663
1371	17 s. 8 d.	Bavaria	C	(20) I p.663
Mid 1372	18 s. 6 d.	Bavaria	C	(20) I p.663
Summer 1372	17 s. 8 d.	Bavaria	C	(20) I p.663
End 1372	18 s.	Bavaria	C	(20) I p.663
Summer 1373	20 s. 8 d.	Bavaria	C	(20) I p.663
1374.02	23 s. 4 d.	Bavaria	C	(20) I p.664
1375.06	22 s. 2 d.	Bavaria	C	(20) I p.663
1375.07	22 s. 4 d.	Bavaria	C	(20) I p.663
1375.09	23 s. 4 d.	Bavaria	C	(20) I p.663
Mid 1376	24 s.	Bavaria	C	(20) I p.664
1376.09	24 s. 8 d.	Bavaria	C	(20) I p.664
1377.03	26 s. 4 d.	Bavaria	C	(20) I p.664
1377.04	26 s.	Bavaria	C	(20) I p.664
1377.05	26 s. 8 d.	Bavaria	C	(20) I p.664
1378.05	27 s. 8 d.	Bavaria	C	(20) I p.664

For the rheingulden in pfennige of Augsburg see under RHINELAND p.248

BAVARIA

REGENSBURG

Regensburger pfennige were struck according to a series of conventions between the bishops of Regensburg and the dukes of Bavaria, not only in Regensburg, but also in Amberg, Neumarkt, Sulzbach and Erlangen. However, Regensburger and Amberger pfennige were not always the same. In 1390 5 d. Amberger were worth 3 d. Regensburger. The region of south German currency dominated by Regensburger pfennige lay to the south and east of that dominated by the Nuremburg heller, and to the north of the area dominated by the money of Verona and its alpine derivatives. At the beginning of the thirteenth century the Regensburger pfennig was worth 8 1/3 d. Veronenses, but at the beginning of the fourteenth century, 10 d. — 11 d. Veronenses (447) p.72. In Bavaria a 'long' schilling of 30 pfennige was frequently used, together with a pfund of 8 'long' schillinge. The values for the florin, and both the Venetian and Hungarian ducats have been given in pfennige to avoid confusion.

The Florentine florin in pfennige of Regensburg

Date	Rate	Place	Type	Reference
1317	61 d.	Regensburg	C	(20) I p.672
1318	62 d.	Regensburg	C	(20) I p.672
1319	67 1/3 d.	Regensburg	C	(20) I p.672
1321	66 2/3 d.	Regensburg	C	(20) I p.672
1325.07-1326.07	72 d.	Regensburg	C	(20) I p.672
1325.11	75 1/3 d.	Regensburg	C	(20) I p.672
1326.02	70 2/3 d.	Regensburg	C	(20) I p.672
1329.07-1330.05	70 d.	Regensburg	C	(20) I p.672
1330.09	91 d.	Regensburg	C	(20) I p.672
1331.08	75 d.	Regensburg	C	(20) I p.672
1331.08-1332.05	69 d.	Regensburg	C	(20) I p.673
1332.06-1333.07	54 d.	Regensburg	C	(20) I p.673
1334.10	56 d.	Regensburg	C	(20) I p.673
Autumn 1335	60 d.	Regensburg	C	(20) I p.673
1337	62 d.	Regensburg	C	(20) I p.673
1338	57 d.	Regensburg	C	(20) I p.673
1339.03.30	59 d.	Regensburg	C	(20) I p.673
1341	64 d.	Regensburg	C	(20) I p.673
1343.03-1344.07	61 d.	Regensburg	C	(20) I p.673
1344.07-1345.05	60 d.	Regensburg	C	(20) I p.673
1346	58 d.	Regensburg	C	(20) I p.673
1346	57 1/2 d.	Regensburg	C	(20) I p.673
1347	54 d.	Regensburg	C	(20) I p.674
1350	circa 55 d.	Regensburg	C	(20) I p.674
1351	52 1/2 d.	Regensburg	C	(20) I p.674
1354.07-1355	50 d.	Regensburg	C	(20) I p.674
1355-1356.08	48 d.	Regensburg	C	(20) I p.674
Summer 1359	60 d.	Regensburg	C	(20) I p.674
1361	51 d.	Regensburg	C	(20) I p.674
1362-1363.06	57 d.	Regensburg	C	(20) I p.674
1370	60 d.	Regensburg	HC	(461) p.380
Summer 1373	62 d.	Regensburg	C	(20) I p.736
1374.06.10	66 1/2 d.	Regensburg	C	(20) I p.736
1374.07.04	67 d.	Regensburg	C	(20) I p.736
1376.02.17	70 d.	Regensburg	C	(20) I p.736
1376.09.19	74 d.	Regensburg	C	(20) I p.736
1377.05.03	80 d.	Regensburg	C	(20) I p.736
1378.05	83 d.	Regensburg	C	(20) I p.736
Autumn 1378	82 d.	Regensburg	C	(20) I p.736
1378.10.25	83 d.	Regensburg	C	(20) I p.736
1379	84 d.	Regensburg	C	(20) I p.736
1379	86 d.	Regensburg	C	(20) I p.736
1381.09.29	85 d.	Regensburg	C	(20) I p.736
1382-1382.07.25	84 1/2 d.	Regensburg	C	(20) I p.736
1382-1832.07.25	86 d.	Regensburg	C	(20) I p.736
1387.12.19	102 d.	Regensburg	C	(20) I p.738
1389.03.26	100 d.	Regensburg	C	(20) I p.738
Early 1390	104 d.	Regensburg	C	(20) I p.738
Early 1390	102 d.	Regensburg	C	(20) I p.738
1391	110 d.	Regensburg	C	(20) I p.738
1397.12	180 d.	Regensburg	C	(20) I p.811
1398.05	182 1/2 d.	Regensburg	C	(20) I p.811
1398.09	181 d.	Regensburg	C	(20) I p.811
1398.11	178 3/4 d.	Regensburg	C	(20) I p.811
1399.03	186 1/4 d.	Regensburg	C	(20) I p.811
1399.05	181 1/4 d.	Regensburg	C	(20) I p.811
1408-1409	72 d.	Regensburg	C	(20) I p.816
1410-1413	70 d.	Regensburg	C	(20) I p.816
1414	70 d.	Regensburg	C	(20) I p.816
1414	72 d.	Regensburg	C	(20) I p.816
1415-1423	72 d.	Regensburg	C	(20) I p.816
1424	72 1/2 d.	Regensburg	C	(20) I p.816
1424	73 d.	Regensburg	C	(20) I p.816
1425-1426	73 1/2 d.	Regensburg	C	(20) I p.816

The Venetian ducat in pfennige of Regensburg

Date	Rate	Place	Type	Reference
1396.11.16	63 d.	Regensburg	C	(20) I p.820
1397.02.08	62 d.	Regensburg	C	(20) I p.820
1397.04.08	66 1/2 d.	Regensburg	C	(20) I p.820
1397.05.04	66 d.	Regensburg	C	(20) I p.820
1398.04.01	70 1/2 d.	Regensburg	C	(20) I p.820
1398.04.20-05.24	71 d.	Regensburg	C	(20) I p.822
1398.07.06-08.06	73 d.	Regensburg	C	(20) I p.822
1398.09.18	72 1/2 d.	Regensburg	C	(20) I p.822
1398.11.11-12.23	72 d.	Regensburg	C	(20) I p.822
1399.03.03	72 1/2 d.	Regensburg	C	(20) I p.822
1399.03.04-08.01	73 d.	Regensburg	C	(20) I p.822
1399.10.30	73 1/2 d.	Regensburg	C	(20) I p.822
1399.12.03	73 d.	Regensburg	C	(20) I p.822
1399.12.29	74 d.	Regensburg	C	(20) I p.824
1400.03.17-04.04	74 1/2 d.	Regensburg	C	(20) I p.824
1400.09.16	73 d.	Regensburg	C	(20) I p.824
1400.12.16	74 d.	Regensburg	C	(20) I p.824
1401.03.11	circa 74 1/2 d.	Regensburg	C	(20) I p.824
1401.06.17	74 d.	Regensburg	C	(20) I p.824
1401.10.20	74 1/2 d.	Regensburg	C	(20) I p.826
1402.01.07	154 d.	Regensburg	C	(20) I p.826
1402.01.12-10.27	75 d.	Regensburg	C	(20) I p.826
1403.01.17	75 1/2 d.	Regensburg	C	(20) I p.826
1403.06.30	153 d.	Regensburg	C	(20) I p.828
1404.04.30	154 d.	Regensburg	C	(20) I p.828
1404.06.15	155 d.	Regensburg	C	(20) I p.828
1404.11.27	154 d.	Regensburg	C	(20) I p.828
1405.09.05	158 d.	Regensburg	C	(20) I p.828
1406.02.25	161 d.	Regensburg	C	(20) I p.830

The Hungarian ducat in pfennige of Regensburg

Date	Rate	Place	Type	Reference
1396.02.04-08	64 d.	Regensburg	C	(20) I p.820
1396.04.13	57 1/2 d.	Regensburg	C	(20) I p.820
1396.06.06-09.19	60 d.	Regensburg	C	(20) I p.820
1396.10.06-25	60 d.	Regensburg	C	(20) I p.820
1396.10.06-25	61 d.	Regensburg	C	(20) I p.820
1396.11.16	61 1/2 d.	Regensburg	C	(20) I p.820
1397.02.12	62 d.	Regensburg	C	(20) I p.820
1397.04.02	66 d.	Regensburg	C	(20) I p.820
1397.04.08	65 d.	Regensburg	C	(20) I p.820
1397.06.12	66 d.	Regensburg	C	(20) I p.820
1397.06.12	67 d.	Regensburg	C	(20) I p.820
1397.06.12	66 1/2 d.	Regensburg	C	(20) I p.820
1397.07.04-09.01	68 d.	Regensburg	C	(20) I p.820
1397.10.23	68 1/5 d.	Regensburg	C	(20) I p.820
1397.10.27	68 d.	Regensburg	C	(20) I p.820
1397.11.22	68 17/19 d.	Regensburg	C	(20) I p.820
1397.11.26-12.29	69 d.	Regensburg	C	(20) I p.820
1398.02.20-04.01	70 d.	Regensburg	C	(20) I p.820
1398.05.04	70 1/2 d.	Regensburg	C	(20) I p.822
1398.05.24	71 d.	Regensburg	C	(20) I p.822
1398.07.06	72 d.	Regensburg	C	(20) I p.822
1398.07.28-08.06	72 1/2 d.	Regensburg	C	(20) I p.822
1398.09.12	72 d.	Regensburg	C	(20) I p.822
1398.11.11-12.03	71 1/2 d.	Regensburg	C	(20) I p.822
1399.01.07	72 d.	Regensburg	C	(20) I p.822
1399.03.04	72 1/2 d.	Regensburg	C	(20) I p.822
1399.04.14-05.12	73 d.	Regensburg	C	(20) I p.822
1399.05.12	72 1/2 d.	Regensburg	C	(20) I p.822
1399.10.27	73 d.	Regensburg	C	(20) I p.822
1399.10.30-12.03	72 d.	Regensburg	C	(20) I p.822
1399.12.06-19	73 d.	Regensburg	C	(20) I p.824
1400.02.03-03.17	74 d.	Regensburg	C	(20) I p.824
1400.05.01	72 1/2 d.	Regensburg	C	(20) I p.824
1400.06.25	150 d.	Regensburg	C	(20) I p.824
1400.09.16	72 1/2 d.	Regensburg	C	(20) I p.824

THE HUNGARIAN DUCAT IN PFENNIGE OF REGENSBURG

Date	Rate	Place	Type	Reference
1400.12.16-1401.02.01	73 d.	Regensburg	C	(20) I p.824
1401.02.11	74 d.	Regensburg	C	(20) I p.824
1401.03.11-06.17	73 1/2 d.	Regensburg	C	(20) I p.824
1401.06.28-07.02	73 1/2 d.	Regensburg	C	(20) I p.826
1401.10.20-1402.01.07	74 d.	Regensburg	C	(20) I p.826
1401.11.15	74 1/2 d.	Regensburg	C	(20) I p.826
1401.11.15	152 d.	Regensburg	C	(20) I p.826
1401.11.15	154 d.	Regensburg	C	(20) I p.826
1402.01.12	155 d.	Regensburg	C	(20) I p.826
1402.03.10	75 d.	Regensburg	C	(20) I p.826
1402.04.08	74 3/4 d.	Regensburg	C	(20) I p.826
1402.04.08	75 d.	Regensburg	C	(20) I p.826
1402.04.08	74 1/2 d.	Regensburg	C	(20) I p.826
1402.05.20	75 d.	Regensburg	C	(20) I p.826
1402.05.20	153 d.	Regensburg	C	(20) I p.826
1402.05.24-31	75 d.	Regensburg	C	(20) I p.826
1402.06.23-09.01	152 d.	Regensburg	C	(20) I p.826
1402.06.23-09.01	75 d.	Regensburg	C	(20) I p.826
1402.10.27	74 1/2 d.	Regensburg	C	(20) I p.826
1403.01.17	75 d.	Regensburg	C	(20) I p.826
1403.06.26	76 d.	Regensburg	C	(20) I p.826
1403.06.30-1404.02	152 d.	Regensburg	C	(20) I p.828
1403.10.25	151 1/2 d.	Regensburg	C	(20) I p.828
1404.04.21	75 d.	Regensburg	C	(20) I p.828
1404.04.30	153 d.	Regensburg	C	(20) I p.828
1404.06.15-08.22	154 d.	Regensburg	C	(20) I p.828
1404.10.09	155 d.	Regensburg	C	(20) I p.828
1404.11.27	153 d.	Regensburg	C	(20) I p.828
1405.03.29	76 d.	Regensburg	C	(20) I p.828
1405.06.09	159 d.	Regensburg	C	(20) I p.828
1405.07.25	158 d.	Regensburg	C	(20) I p.828
1405.09.05	157 d.	Regensburg	C	(20) I p.828
1405 Mid 10	154 d.	Regensburg	C	(20) I p.830
1405.12.06	156 d.	Regensburg	C	(20) I p.830
1406.04.14	154 d.	Regensburg	C	(20) I p.830
1406.08.06	66 2/3 d.	Regensburg	C	(20) I p.830
1406.11.03	64 d.	Regensburg	C	(20) I p.830
1406.11.19	158 d.	Regensburg	C	(20) I p.830

The pfennig of Regensburg in heller

Date	Rate	Place	Type	Reference
1291-1294	2 1/4 heller	Bavaria	C	(20) I p.650
1300	2 1/3 heller	Bavaria	C	(20) I p.650
1302	3 heller	Bavaria	C	(20) I p.651
1345-1346	4 1/5 heller	Bavaria	C	(20) I p.650
1345-1346	4 2/5 heller	Bavaria	C	(20) I p.650
1345	3 1/3 heller	Bavaria	C	(20) I p.651
1352	4 heller	Bavaria	C	(20) I p.650
1354	3 2/3 heller	Bavaria	C	(20) I p.650
1354	4 heller	Regensburg	O	(447) p.555
1359	3 1/2 heller	Bavaria	C	(20) I p.650
1363	4 4/9 heller	Bavaria	C	(20) I p.651
1364-1365	5 heller	Bavaria	C	(20) I p.651

For the Hungarian denar and the pfennig of Regensburg see under HUNGARY p.285

AMBERG

The Florentine florin in pfennige of Amberg

Date	Rate	Place	Type	Reference
1385.10.15	96 d.	Regensburg	C	(20) I p.738
1386.09.24-10.30	102 d.	Regensburg	C	(20) I p.738
1387.04.25-11.26	103 d.	Regensburg	C	(20) I p.738
1388.07.18	100 d.	Regensburg	C	(20) I p.738

THE FLORENTINE FLORIN IN PFENNIGE OF AMBERG

Date	Rate	Place	Type	Reference
1389.07.20	102 d.	Regensburg	C	(20) I p.738
1389.11.11	103 1/2 d.	Regensburg	C	(20) I p.738
1391.02.16	128 d.	Regensburg	C	(20) I p.738

MUNICH

The Florentine florin in pfennige of Munich

Date	Rate	Place	Type	Reference
1317	110 d.	Regensburg	C	(20) I p.672
1318	112 d.	Regensburg	C	(20) I p.672
1319	121 d.	Regensburg	C	(20) I p.672
1321	120 d.	Regensburg	C	(20) I p.672
1325-1326	123 d.	Regensburg	C	(20) I p.672
Autumn 1326	127 d.	Regensburg	C	(20) I p.672
1329.07-1330.05	126 d.	Regensburg	C	(20) I p.672
1330.09	137 d.	Regensburg	C	(20) I p.672
1332.04	150 d.	Regensburg	C	(20) I p.673
1332.06-1333.07	90 d.	Regensburg	C	(20) I p.673
1334.10	93 d.	Regensburg	C	(20) I p.673
1335.02.05	99 d.	Regensburg	C	(20) I p.673
1337	107 d.	Regensburg	C	(20) I p.673
1338	102 d.	Regensburg	C	(20) I p.673
1339.05.30	105 d.	Regensburg	C	(20) I p.673
1341	120 d.	Regensburg	C	(20) I p.673
1343.03-1344.07	115 d.	Regensburg	C	(20) I p.673
1344.07-1345.05	120 d.	Regensburg	C	(20) I p.673
1346	116 d.	Regensburg	C	(20) I p.673
1347	108 d.	Regensburg	C	(20) I p.674
1351	105 d.	Regensburg	C	(20) I p.674
1354.07-1355	100 d.	Regensburg	C	(20) I p.674
1355-1356.08	103 1/2 d	Regensburg	C	(20) I p.674
1358	120 d.	Regensburg	C	(20) I p.674
1359	130 d.	Regensburg	C	(20) I p.674
1361	110 d.	Regensburg	C	(20) I p.674
1362	126 d.	Regensburg	C	(20) I p.674
1394-1395	150 d.	Regensburg	C	(20) I p.781
1394	145 d.	Regensburg	C	(20) I p.781
1396.09.13	122 1/8 d.	Regensburg	C	(20) I p.792
1396	148 d.	Regensburg	C	(20) I p.781
1397.02.04H	120 d.	Munich	C	(34) XXIX p.37
1397.03.06	132 d.	Regensburg	C	(20) I p.792
1397.04.04	140 d.	Regensburg	C	(20) I p.792
1397.07.04	150 d.	Regensburg	C	(20) I p.792
1397.07.12	155 d.	Regensburg	C	(20) I p.792
1407	180 d.	Regensburg	C	(20) I p.816
1408	178 d.	Regensburg	C	(20) I p.816
1409	180 d.	Regensburg	C	(20) I p.816
1410-1411	176 d.	Regensburg	C	(20) I p.816
1410	182 d.	Regensburg	C	(20) I p.816
1412	177 d.	Regensburg	C	(20) I p.816
1413	174 d.	Regensburg	C	(20) I p.816
1414-1415	176 d.	Regensburg	C	(20) I p.816
1414-1415	176 1/2 d.	Regensburg	C	(20) I p.816
1416-1417	177 d.	Regensburg	C	(20) I p.816
1418-1419	180 d.	Regensburg	C	(20) I p.816
1420	181 d.	Regensburg	C	(20) I p.816
1421-1422	180 d.	Regensburg	C	(20) I p.816
1423	183 d.	Regensburg	C	(20) I p.816
1424	181 d.	Regensburg	C	(20) I p.816
1425	180 d.	Regensburg	C	(20) I p.816
1426	182 d.	Regensburg	C	(20) I p.816

AUSTRIA

In Austria the 'long' Bavarian schilling of 30 pfennige was also in use. The following rates have therefore also been given in pfennige.

The Florentine florin in pfennige of Vienna

Date	Rate	Place	Type	Reference
1262	60 d.	Curia	B	(439) p.130
1298	66 2/3 d.	Curia	B	(439) p.130
1336	90 d.	Regensburg	C	(20) I p.720
1341	96 d.	Regensburg	C	(20) I p.720
1346	90 d.	Regensburg	C	(20) I p.720
1354	94 d.	Regensburg	C	(20) I p.720
1360	96 d.	Regensburg	C	(20) I p.720
1364	98 2/3 d.	Regensburg	C	(20) I p.720
1371-1373	100 d.	Regensburg	C	(20) I p.720
1375	96 d.	Regensburg	C	(20) I p.720
1376	108 d.	Regensburg	C	(20) I p.720
1378	114 d.	Curia	B	(439) p.130
1389	120 d.	Curia	B	(439) p.130
1407-1415	160 d.	Austria	C	(20) I p.816
1415-1416	160 1/2 d.	Vienna	HC	(461) p.381
1416	165 d.	Regensburg	C	(20) I p.816
1420-1436	180 d.	Regensburg	C	(20) I p.816

The Hungarian ducat in pfennige of Vienna

Date	Rate	Place	Type	Reference
1355-1359	95 d.	Austria	C	(398) p.72
1361-1363	97 d.	Austria	C	(398) p.72
1376	110 d.	Austria	C	(398) p.72
1377-1378	115 d.	Austria	C	(398) p.72
1390	126 d.	Austria	C	(398) p.72
1391	132 d.	Austria	C	(398) p.72
1392	138 d.	Austria	C	(398) p.72
1393	144 d.	Austria	C	(398) p.72
1394-1401	150 d.	Austria	C	(398) p.72
1402-1406	155 d.	Austria	C	(398) p.72
1417	170 d.	Austria	C	(398) p.72
1418	176 d.	Austria	C	(398) p.73
1419	178 d.	Austria	C	(398) p.73
1437	190 d.	Austria	C	(398) p.73
1438	200 d.	Austria	C	(398) p.73
1439-1440	205 d.	Austria	C	(398) p.73
1440	200 d.	Vienna	C	(329) p.170
1441-1447	210 d.	Austria	C	(398) p.73
1448	216 d.	Austria	C	(398) p.73
1449-1450	222 d.	Austria	C	(398) p.73
1451-1454	225 d.	Austria	C	(398) p.73
1455	230 d.	Vienna	C	(329) p.170
1455-1461	240 d.	Austria	C	(398) p.73
1457	244 d.	Vienna	C	(329) p.170
1458	250 d.	Vienna	C	(329) p.170
1459	420 d.(sic)	Vienna	C	(329) p.170
1460	210 d.	Vienna	C	(329) p.170
1460-1462	270 d.	Austria	C	(398) p.73
1462-1463	280 d.	Vienna	C	(329) p.170
1464	285 d.	Austria	C	(398) p.73
1465	290 d.	Austria	C	(398) p.73
1466-1470	300 d.	Austria	C	(398) p.73
1471	310 d.	Austria	C	(398) p.73
1472	320 d.	Austria	C	(398) p.73
1473-1474	330 d.	Austria	C	(398) p.73
1475-1488	310 d.	Austria	C	(398) p.73
1489	317 d.	Austria	C	(398) p.73
1489-1498	320 d.	Vienna	C	(398) p.170
1489-1498	330 d.	Vienna	C	(398) p.170

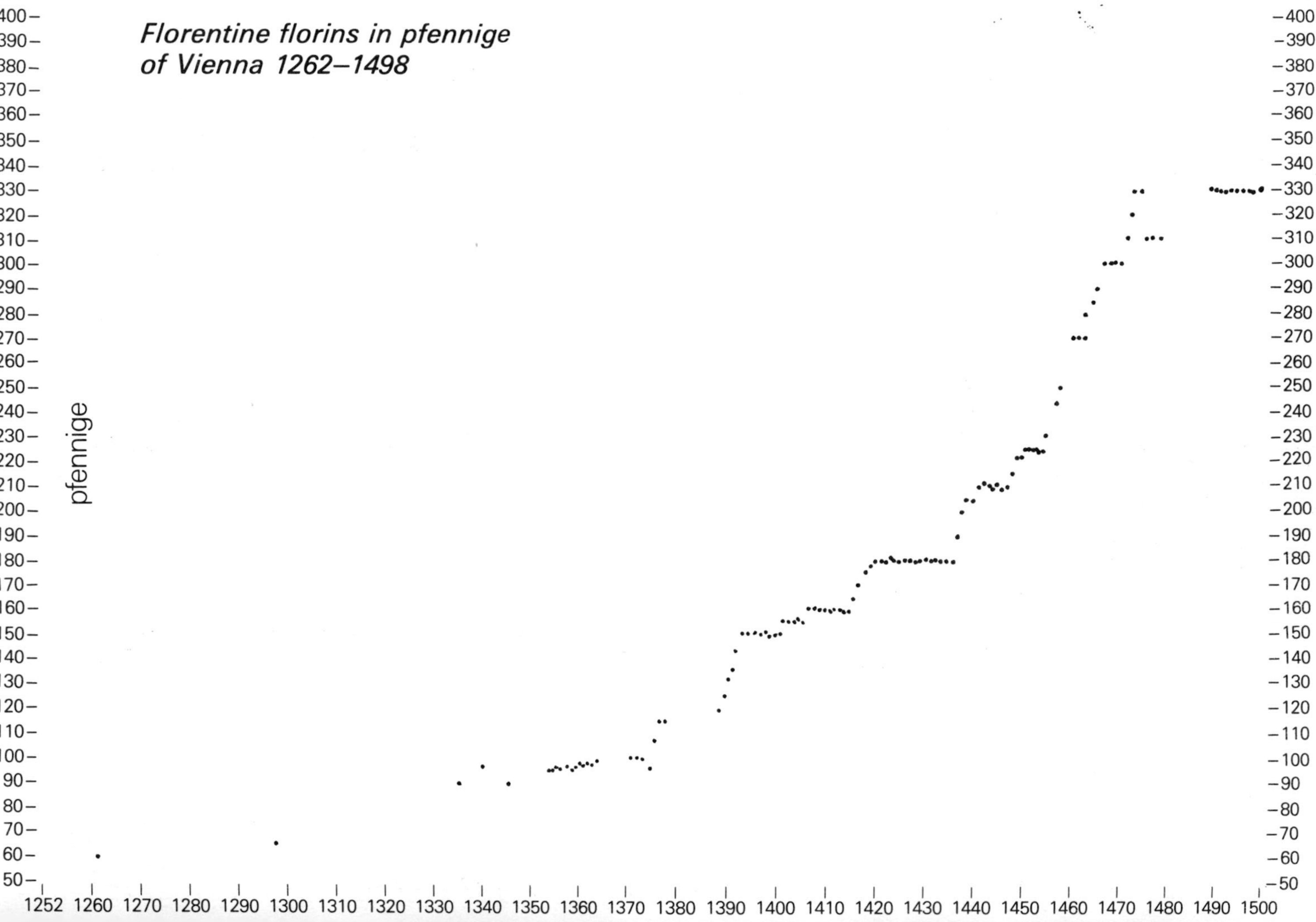
Florentine florins in pfennige
of Vienna 1262–1498
pfennige
410
400
390
380
370
360
350
340
330
320
310
300
290
280
270
260
250
240
230
220
210
200
190
180
170
160
150
140
130
120
110
100
90
80
70
60
50
1252
1260
1270
1280
1290
1300
1310
1320
1330
1340
1350
1360
1370
1380
1390
1400
1410
1420
1430
1440
1450
1460
1470
1480
1490
1500

FRIESACH

See HUNGARY p.285

BOHEMIA

After the discovery of rich new silver mines at Kutna Hora (Küttenberg), the kings of Bohemia from 1300 onwards began to mint the 'grossus pragensis' there. It was initially worth 12 of the pre-existing Bohemian pfennige. It was struck in very large quantities and circulated widely in Germany, and north Italy as well as in central Europe. The groschen both of Bohemia and neighbouring Meissen were frequently reckoned in schocks of 60 groschen.

The florin and Hungarian, Venetian and Bohemian ducats in Prague groschen and heller

In the fifteenth century 1 groschen = 7 pfennige or 14 heller.
For the late fourteenth century see below p.000 The Bohemian ducat was introduced by king John of Luxembourg in 1328 and was destined for foreign trade and payments. It was exclusively minted in Prague, its model being the Florentine florin. It was taken as identical in value to the Hungarian ducat. For the Hungarian ducat see below, under HUNGARY p.000.

F = Florentine florin H = Hungarian and Bohemian ducats

Date	Rate	Place	Type	Reference
1300F	12-13 gr.	Avignon	H	(97) App.I a
1300F	12 gr.	Poland	H	(97) App.I a
1309F	16 gr.	Poland	H	(97) App.I a
1316F	12 gr.	Curia	B	(439) p.900
1316F	13 gr.	Curia	B	(439) p.900
1317F	12 gr.	Avignon	H	(97) App.I a
1317F	13 gr.	Avignon	H	(97) App.I a
1317F	17 gr.	Avignon	H	(97) App.I a
1317-1320F	16 gr.	Hungary	B	(404) I p.27
1317F	17 gr.	Salzburg	C	(258) p.260
1317-1320F	16 gr.	Avignon	H	(97) App.I a
1321-1326F	12 gr.	Curia	B	(439) p.900
1321-1326F	13 gr.	Curia	B	(439) p.900
1328-1330F	16 gr.	Curia	B	(439) p.901
1329	16 gr.	Avignon	H	(97) App.I a
1329	16 gr.	Poland	H	(97) App.I a
1330	16 gr.	Avignon	H	(97) App.I a
1331F	16 gr.	Poland?	H	(263) p.147
1338-1342F	15 1/2 gr.	Curia	B	(439) p.902
1341	15 1/2 gr.	Avignon	H	(97) App.I a
1341F	17 gr.	Curia	B	(439) p.902
1343.06.12F	13 gr.	Curia	B	(347) p.486
1343	13 gr.	Poland	H	(97) App.I a
1345	12 1/2 gr.	Brünn	H	(97) App.I a
1345	13 gr.	Brünn	H	(97) App.I a
1345	16 gr. 3 heller	Vienna	H	(97) App.I a
1345	16 gr. 9 heller	Vienna	H	(97) App.I a
1346	12 3/10 gr.	Poland	H	(97) App.I a
1347	12 gr.	Brünn	H	(97) App.I a
1348	11 1/10-8/10 gr.	Brünn	H	(97) App.I a
1348	12 gr.	Brünn	H	(97) App.I a
1350	12 4/5 gr.	Brünn	H	(97) App.I a
1350	13 gr.	Brünn	H	(97) App.I a
1352	12 gr. 6 heller	Brünn	H	(97) App.I a
1352	13 gr.	Brünn	H	(97) App.I a
1353	12 gr.	Brünn	H	(97) App.I a
1353	13 gr.	Empire	H	(97) App.I a
1355	13 gr.	Brünn	H	(97) App.I a
1356	13 gr.	Empire	H	(97) App.I a
1356F	13 gr.	Poland?	H	(263) p.147
1357	15 gr. 1 heller	Brünn	H	(97) App.I a
1358F	13 gr.	Poland?	H	(263) p.147

Date	Rate	Place	Type	Reference
1358F	13 1/2 gr.	Poland?	H	(263) p.147
1359.08.12F	13 1/2 gr.	Curia	B	(251) p.275
1359-1363F	13 gr.	Poland?	H	(263) p.147
1360	13 gr.	Empire	H	(97) App.I a
1360F	14 gr.	Poland?	H	(263) p.147
1360F	16 2/12 gr.	Poland?	H	(263) p.147
1361F	14 gr.	Poland?	H	(263) p.147
1362F	14 gr.	Poland?	H	(263) p.147
1363F	13 1/2 gr.	Poland?	H	(263) p.147
1363F	14 gr.	Poland?	H	(263) p.147
1365	14 1/2 gr.	Brünn	H	(97) App.I a
1365	15 gr.	Brünn	H	(97) App.I a
1365	15 1/2 gr.	Brünn	H	(97) App.I a
1367	14 gr. 6 heller	Prague	H	(97) App.I a
1368	15 gr.	Prague	H	(97) App.I a
1368F	14 gr.	Poland?	H	(263) p.147
1368F	16 gr.	Poland?	H	(263) p.147
1370	14 1/2 gr.	Prague	H	(97) App.I a
1370F	15 gr.	Poland?	H	(263) p.147
1372F	16 gr.	Poland?	H	(263) p.147
1373	13 gr. minus 3 heller	Bohemia	H	(97) App.I a
1373	15-16 gr.	Brünn	H	(97) App.I a
1374-1375	16 gr. 3 heller	Brünn	H	(97) App.I a
1375	17 gr.	Brünn	H	(97) App.I a
1375-1377	17 gr. 9 heller	Brünn	H	(97) App.I a
1377	16 4/5 gr.	Bohemia	H	(97) App.I a
1377	17 gr. 14 heller	Brünn	H	(97) App.I a
1378	16 gr. 8 heller -17 gr.	Brünn	H	(97) App.I a
1378	16 gr. 8 heller	Silesia	H	(97) App.I a
1378F	16 1/3 gr.	Poland	B	(198) p.66
1378	17 gr.	Empire	H	(97) App.I a
1379	17 gr.	Prague	H	(97) App.I a
1380	18 gr.	Prague	H	(97) App.I a
1380	18 gr.	Frankfurt am Main	H	(97) App.I a
1382	18 gr.	Prague	H	(97) App.I a
1383	18-18 1/2 gr.	Regensburg	H	(97) App.I a
1383	18 gr. 6 heller	Regensburg	H	(97) App.I a
1383.09.23F	18 1/3 gr.	Regensburg	C	(20) I p.617
1383.07.09H	18 1/2 gr.	Regensburg	C	(20) I p.617
1383.10.11-12H	18 gr.	Regensburg	C	(20) I p.617
1383.11.09H	18 1/5 gr.	Regensburg	C	(20) I p.617
1383.12.02H	18 1/4 gr.	Regensburg	C	(20) I p.617
1383.12.24-1384.9.6H	18 gr.	Regensburg	C	(20) I p.617
1384	18 gr.	Prague	H	(97) App.I a
1384	18 gr.	Regensburg	H	(97) App.I a
1384.11.28-1385.2.21H	18 3/4 gr.	Regensburg	C	(20) I p.617
1385	18 gr. 9 heller	Prague	H	(97) App.I a
1385	18 gr.	Regensburg	H	(97) App.I a
1385.04.20H	18 3/4 gr.	Regensburg	C	(20) I p.617
1385.04.24-05.19H	18 2/3 gr.	Regensburg	C	(20) I p.617
1385.07.09-20H	18 3/4 gr.	Regensburg	C	(20) I p.617
1385.08.19H	18 2/3 gr.	Regensburg	C	(20) I p.617
1385.10.18-21H	18 1/2 gr.	Regensburg	C	(20) I p.617
1385.12.13-1386.01H	18 1/4 gr.	Regensburg	C	(20) I p.617
1386	18 gr. 4 heller	Regensburg	H	(97) App.I a
1386	19-20 gr.	Regensburg	H	(97) App.I a
1386.05.04H	18 1/3 gr.	Regensburg	C	(20) I p.617
1387	19 gr.	Bohemia	H	(97) App.I a
1387	18 gr. 8 heller	Regensburg	H	(97) App.I a
1387	19 gr.	Regensburg	H	(97) App.I a
1387.03.11H	18 2/3 gr.	Regensburg	C	(20) I p.617
1388	18 gr. 9 heller	Danzig	H	(97) App.I a
1390	22 gr.	Olmütz	H	(97) App.I a
1390	20 gr.	Poland	H	(97) App.I a
1392-1396	20 gr.	Prague	H	(97) App.I a
1396	20 1/2 gr.	Prague	H	(97) App.I a
1396	20 gr.	Eger	H	(97) App.I a
1397	20 1/2 gr.	Prague	H	(97) App.I a
1400	20 gr.	Eger	H	(97) App.I a
1400	22 gr.	Poland	H	(97) App.I a

THE FLORIN AND DUCAT IN PRAGUE GROSCHEN

Date	Rate	Place	Type	Reference
1401	21 gr. 3 heller	Prague	H	(97) App.I a
1401-1402	20 1/5 gr.	Eger	H	(97) App.I a
1402	21 gr.	Prague	H	(97) App.I a
1402.07.25H	20 gr.	Marienburg	C	(506) p.23
1404	22 gr.	Prague	H	(97) App.I a
1409	20 gr.	Prague	H	(97) App.I a
1409	23 gr.	Prague	H	(97) App.I a
1412	23 gr.	Olmütz	H	(97) App.I a
1415	23 gr.	Brünn	H	(97) App.I a
1421	24 gr.	Brüx	H	(97) App.I a
1423	24 gr.	Bohemia	H	(97) App.I a
1424	24 gr.	Prague	H	(97) App.I a
1424	24 gr.	Poland	H	(97) App.I a
1425	24 gr.	Brüx	H	(97) App.I a
1428	24 gr.	Karlstein	H	(97) App.I a
1429-1431	25 gr.	Karlstein	H	(97) App.I a
1430-1432H	24 gr.	Poland	C	(198) p.67
1430	24 gr.	Silesia	H	(97) App.I a
1432	26 gr.	Silesia	H	(97) App.I a
1434	26 gr.	Karlstein	H	(97) App.I a
1434	28 gr.	Eger	H	(97) App.I a
1434	28 gr.	Silesia	H	(97) App.I a
1434	28 1/2 gr.	Würzburg	OH	(97) App.I a
1434H	28 gr.	Poland	C	(198) p.67
1437	31 gr.	Poland	H	(97) App.I a
1440	28 gr.	Polná	H	(97) App.I a
1441	30 gr.	Znaim	H	(97) App.I a
1442	28 gr.	Eger	H	(97) App.I a
1446	30 gr.	Gorlitz	H	(97) App.I a
1447	32 gr.	Eger	H	(97) App.I a
1449	31 gr.	Krumau	H	(97) App.I a
1450	31 gr.	Krumau	H	(97) App.I a
1451	32 gr.	Louny	H	(97) App.I a
1451	36 gr.	Poland	H	(97) App.I a
1452	33 gr.	Louny	H	(97) App.I a
1452	34 gr.	Zittau	H	(97) App.I a
1453	31 1/2 gr.	Bohemia	H	(97) App.I a
1453	33 gr.	Silesia	H	(97) App.I a
1454	32 gr.	Bohemia	H	(97) App.I a
1454.06.15	33 gr.	Louny	H	(97) App.I a
1454.10.12	36 gr.	Louny	H	(97) App.I a
1454.11.09	32 gr.	Louny	H	(97) App.I a
1454	28 gr.	Glatz	OH	(97) App.I a
1456.08.16H	26 gr.	Torun	C	(506) II p.201
1457.04.23	32-35 gr.	Krumau	H	(97) App.I a
1457.04.25	30 gr.	Krumau	H	(97) App.I a
1457.04.25	33 gr.	Krumau	H	(97) App.I a
1457.07.27	35 gr.	Krumau	H	(97) App.I a
1457.09.28	35 gr.	Krumau	H	(97) App.I a
1457.10.15	33 gr.	Krumau	H	(97) App.I a
1457.10.15	35 gr.	Krumau	H	(97) App.I a
1457.10.16	33 gr.	Krumau	H	(97) App.I a
1457.10.16	35 gr.	Krumau	H	(97) App.I a
1457.10.16	30 gr.	Krumau	H	(97) App.I a
1457.10.17	35 gr.	Krumau	H	(97) App.I a
1457.10.17	34 gr.	Krumau	H	(97) App.I a
1457.10.17	30 gr.	Krumau	H	(97) App.I a
1457.10.18	35 gr.	Krumau	H	(97) App.I a
1457.10.18	34 gr.	Krumau	H	(97) App.I a
1457.10.18	33 gr.	Krumau	H	(97) App.I a
1457.10.19-29	35 gr.	Krumau	H	(97) App.I a
1457.11.11	36 gr.	Krumau	H	(97) App.I a
1458.02.07-05.04	35 gr.	Krumau	H	(97) App.I a
1458.08.24	37 gr.	Krumau	H	(97) App.I a
1458.10.01	37 gr.	Krumau	H	(97) App.I a
1458.10.16	40 gr.	Krumau	H	(97) App.I a
1458.10.16	37 gr.	Krumau	H	(97) App.I a
1458.10.16	36 gr.	Krumau	H	(97) App.I a
1459	40-42 gr.	Bohemia	H	(97) App.I a
1459.04.23	36 gr.	Krumau	H	(97) App.I a
1459.04.23	33 gr.	Krumau	H	(97) App.I a
1459.04.23	32 gr.	Krumau	H	(97) App.I a

Date	Rate	Place	Type	Reference
1459.04.23	40 gr.	Krumau	H	(97) App.I a
1459.04.23	34 gr.	Krumau	H	(97) App.I a
1459.01.16	40 gr.	Krumau	H	(97) App.I a
1459	29-30 gr.	Eger	H	(97) App.I a
1460	30 gr.	Bohemia	H	(97) App.I a
1460	32 gr.	Bohemia	H	(97) App.I a
1460	34 gr.	Bohemia	H	(97) App.I a
1460	42 gr.	Bohemia	H	(97) App.I a
1460	47 1/2 gr.	Bohemia	H	(97) App.I a
1460.03.02	40 gr.	Bohemia	H	(97) App.I a
1460.07.05	40 gr.	Louny	H	(97) App.I a
1460.04.23	30 gr.	Krumau	H	(97) App.I a
1460.04.23	36 gr.	Krumau	H	(97) App.I a
1460.10.16	34 gr.	Krumau	H	(97) App.I a
1460.10.16	33 gr.	Krumau	H	(97) App.I a
1460.10.16	37 gr.	Krumau	H	(97) App.I a
1460	32 gr.	Brüx	H	(97) App.I a
1460	30 gr. 2 1/3 heller	Eger	H	(97) App.I a
1461	32 gr.	Bohemia	H	(97) App.I a
1461	34 gr.	Bohemia	H	(97) App.I a
1461	42 gr.	Bohemia	H	(97) App.I a
1461.04.23	34 gr.	Krumau	H	(97) App.I a
1461.07.07	34 gr.	Krumau	H	(97) App.I a
1461.10.15	33 gr.	Krumau	H	(97) App.I a
1461.10.16	34 gr.	Krumau	H	(97) App.I a
1461.10.16	33 gr.	Krumau	H	(97) App.I a
1461.10.17	37 gr.	Krumau	H	(97) App.I a
1461.10.20	34 gr.	Krumau	H	(97) App.I a
1461	34 gr.	Poland	H	(97) App.I a
1462	42 gr.	Bohemia	H	(97) App.I a
1462.05.29	44 gr.	Louny	H	(97) App.I a
1462.02.06	40 gr.	Louny	H	(97) App.I a
1462.02.11	40 gr.	Louny	H	(97) App.I a
1462.03.19	34 gr.	Louny	H	(97) App.I a
1462.04.23	43 gr.	Louny	H	(97) App.I a
1462.04.23	37 gr.	Louny	H	(97) App.I a
1462.04.24	37 gr.	Louny	H	(97) App.I a
1462.10.16	31 gr.	Louny	H	(97) App.I a
1462.10.16	33 gr.	Louny	H	(97) App.I a
1462.12.20	37 gr.	Louny	H	(97) App.I a
1462.12.20	34 gr.	Louny	H	(97) App.I a
1463	48 gr.	Bohemia	H	(97) App.I a
1463.03.19	45 gr.	Louny	H	(97) App.I a
1463.04.23	33 gr.	Krumau	H	(97) App.I a
1463.04.23	32 gr.	Krumau	H	(97) App.I a
1463.04.23	40 gr.	Krumau	H	(97) App.I a
1463.04.23	34 gr.	Krumau	H	(97) App.I a
1463.10.16	46 gr.	Krumau	H	(97) App.I a
1463.10.16	45 gr.	Krumau	H	(97) App.I a
1464	48 gr.	Bohemia	H	(97) App.I a
1464.02.18	37 gr.	Krumau	H	(97) App.I a
1464.04.23	45 gr.	Krumau	H	(97) App.I a
1464.04.23	40 gr.	Krumau	H	(97) App.I a
1464.04.23	32 1/2 gr.	Krumau	H	(97) App.I a
1465	40 gr.	Bohemia	H	(97) App.I a
1465	46 1/2 gr.	Bohemia	H	(97) App.I a
1465.04.29	40 gr.	Krumau	H	(97) App.I a
1465.10.16	40 gr.	Krumau	H	(97) App.I a
1466.10.16	50 gr.	Krumau	H	(97) App.I a
1466.10.16	35 gr.	Krumau	H	(97) App.I a
1467.02.27	25 gr.	Bohemia	OH	(97) App.I a
1467.07.19	50 gr.	Bohemia	H	(97) App.I a
1467.09.24	25 gr.	Bohemia	OH	(97) App.I a
1468.05.06	24 gr.	Bohemia	OH	(97) App.I a
1468.10.17	32 gr.	Krumau	H	(97) App.I a
1469H	24 gr.	Prague	O	(239)
1469H	34 gr.	Prague	A	(239)
1469H	28 gr.	Prague	A	(239)
1469	26 gr.	Bohemia	H	(97) App.I a
1469.03.13	34 gr.	Krumau	H	(97) App.I a
1469.06.03	70 gr.	Louny	H	(97) App.I a
1469.12.08	28 gr.	Prague	H	(97) App.I a

Date	Rate	Place	Type	Reference
1470H	30 gr.	Prague	A	(239)
1470H	37 gr.	Prague	A	(239)
1470.01.27	70 gr.	Louny	H	(97) App.I a
1470.02.17	70 gr.	Louny	H	(97) App.I a
1470.05.05	60 gr.	Louny	H	(97) App.I a
1470.08	62 gr.	Slaný	H	(97) App.I a
1470.04.25	60 gr.	Krumau	H	(97) App.I a
1470.04.25	40 gr.	Krumau	H	(97) App.I a
1470.10.16	37 gr.	Krumau	H	(97) App.I a
1470	32 1/2 gr.	Poland	H	(97) App.I a
1471H	24 gr.	Prague	O	(239)
1471H	24-27 gr.	Prague	A	(239)
1471	28 gr.	Bohemia	H	(97) App.I a
1471	24 gr.	Kutna Hora	H	(97) App.I a
1471.01.19	55 gr.	Louny	H	(97) App.I a
1472H	26-30 gr.	Prague	A	(239)
1472	24 gr.	Kutna Hora	H	(97) App.I a
1472	26 gr.	Kutna Hora	H	(97) App.I a
1472	50 gr.	Zvikov	H	(97) App.I a
1473H	26 gr.	Prague	A	(239)
1473H	30 gr.	Prague	A	(239)
1473	30 gr.	Kutna Hora	H	(97) App.I a
1474H	28 gr.	Prague	A	(239)
1474.09.05	28 gr.	Bohemia	H	(97) App.I a
1475H	24 gr.	Prague	A	(239)
1475H	30 gr.	Prague	A	(239)
1475.03.06	70 gr.	Slaný	H	(97) App.I a
1476H	36 gr.	Prague	A	(239)
1476H	27 gr.	Prague	A	(239)
1476.07.20	27 gr.	Brünn	H	(97) App.I a
1476.07.20	30 gr.	Brünn	H	(97) App.I a
1477H	29 gr.	Prague	A	(239)
1477H	30 gr.	Prague	A	(239)
1477	29 gr.	Rakovnik	H	(97) App.I a
1477	30 gr.	Hostinné	H	(97) App.I a
1478H	28 gr.	Prague	A	(239)
1478H	31 gr.	Prague	A	(239)
1478H	29 gr.	Prague	A	(239)
1478H	28 1/2 gr.	Prague	A	(239)
1478H	29 gr.	Prague	A	(239)
1478	28 gr.	Kutna Hora	H	(97) App.I a
1478	36 gr. 10 heller	Bohemia	H	(97) App.I a
1481.05.14	58 gr.	Krumau	H	(97) App.I a
1481.05.23	58 gr.	Krumau	H	(97) App.I a
1482	30 gr.	Bohemia	H	(97) App.I a
1482H	25 gr.	Prague	A	(239)
1482H	28 4/5 gr.	Prague	A	(239)
1482H	30 gr.	Prague	A	(239)
1482.04	58 gr.	Kutna Hora	H	(97) App.I a
1482	25 gr.	Znaim	H	(97) App.I a
1484H	30 gr.	Prague	A	(239)
1484H	40 gr.	Prague	A	(239)
1484	30 gr.	Kutna Hora	H	(97) App.I a
1485H	27 gr.	Prague	O	(239)
1485H	29 gr.	Prague	O	(239)
1485H	30 gr.	Prague	A	(239)
1486	35 gr.	Bohemia	H	(97) App.I a
1487H	29 gr.	Prague	O	(239)
1487H	30 gr.	Prague	A	(239)
1487	37 gr.	Kutna Hora	H	(97) App.I a
1488H	30 gr.	Prague	A	(239)
1490H	32 gr.	Prague	A	(239)
1490H	30 gr.	Prague	O	(239)
1490H	30 1/2 gr.	Prague	A	(239)
1491H	31 gr.	Prague	A	(239)
1491H	30 7/10 gr.	Prague	A	(239)
1491	31 gr.	Bohemia	H	(97) App.I a
1491.10	30 gr. 10 heller	Kutna Hora	H	(97) App.I a
1492	28 gr.	Bohemia	H	(97) App.I a
1492H	28 gr.	Prague	A	(239)
1492H	32 gr.	Prague	A	(239)
1493H	32 gr.	Prague	A	(239)

Date	Rate	Place	Type	Reference
1493	30 gr.	Poland	H	(97) App.I a
1494H	30 gr.	Prague	O	(239)
1495H	33 gr.	Prague	A	(239)
1495	33 gr.	Kutna Hora	H	(97) App.I a
1497H	33 gr.	Prague	A	(239)
1498H	30 gr.	Prague	A	(239)
1498	30 gr.	Bohemia	H	(97) App.I a
1499	28 gr.	Kutna Hora	H	(97) App.I a
1499H	28 gr.	Prague	A	(239)
1500H	30 gr.	Prague	O	(239)
1500H	30 gr.	Prague	A	(239)
1500	30 gr.	Bohemia	H	(97) App.I a

The Prague groschen in Nuremberg heller

Date	Rate	Place	Type	Reference
1373	15 d.	Bohemia	H	(97) p.25
1377	14.2 d.	Bohemia	H	(97) p.25
1378	14.3 d.	Bohemia	H	(97) p.25
1381	14 d.	Bohemia	H	(97) p.25
1382	14 d.	Bohemia	H	(97) p.25
1384	14.1 d.	Bohemia	H	(97) p.25
1385	14.1 d.	Bohemia	H	(97) p.25
1386	14.1 d.	Bohemia	H	(97) p.25
1387	14.4 d.	Bohemia	H	(97) p.25
1397	13.9 d.	Bohemia	H	(97) p.25

In the fifteenth century the groschen was reckoned as 14 heller in Bohemia (368).

For the Bohemian ducat in weisspfennige see under RHINELAND p.239
For the Bohemian ducat in Nuremberg heller see under HELLER p.264
For the rheingulden in Prague groschen see under RHINELAND p.248

MEISSEN

The Florentine florin in groschen of Meissen

Date	Rate	Place	Type	Reference
1453	33 gr.	Poland	C	(198) p.67
1492	45 gr.	Brünn	C	(97) App.I a
1498	66 gr.	Bohemia	C	(97) App.I a

For the rheingulden in groschen of Meissen see under RHINELAND p.249

SAXONY

See under RHINELAND p.249

SECTION X
NORTHERN AND EASTERN EUROPE

NORTH GERMANY

BREMEN

See under LÜBECK below and under RHINELAND p.249

HAMBURG

The Florentine florin in schillinge and pfennige of Hamburg
V = Venetian ducat; H = Hungarian ducat

Date	Rate	Place	Type	Reference
1317-1320	12 s.	Curia	B	(439) p.92
1353	8 s. 1 d.	Hamburg	C	(446) p.19
1354	8 s. 6 d.	Curia	B	(439) p.92
1355	8 s. 11 d.	Curia	B	(439) p.92
1400	12 s. 6 d.	South Germany	C	(416) p.247
1400H	13 s.	South Germany	C	(416) p.247
1400V	13 s. 9 d.	South Germany	C	(416) p.247

For the Flemish pond groot in money of Hamburg see under FLANDERS p.226

LÜBECK — THE WENDISH MONETARY UNION

The six principal cities of the Hanseatic League joined together in a series of agreements from 1379 onwards to mint a common coinage. The coinage of Lübeck was taken as the basis for this coinage. For a description of Wendish coinage see Jesse (259), and for the whole accounting and payment system in the Baltic see Sprandel (462). Lübeck was becoming an Italian exchange place in the fifteenth century (137) p.63. The common coinage itself consisted of pfennige, witten (4pf.), sechslinger (6pf.) and, from 1432, schillinge. For accounting purposes the Lübeck mark of 16 schillinge or 192 pfennige was used.

The Florentine florin and the Hungarian ducat in schillinge and pfennige of Lübeck
H = Hungarian ducat

Date	Rate	Place	Type	Reference
1288-1289	8 s.	Lübeck	HC	(462) p.197
1317-1320	12 s. 1 d.	Lübeck	C	(267) p.LXXV
1317-1320	12 s.	Curia	B	(270) p.92
1345	8 s.	Lübeck	C	(259) p.56
1410	16 s.	Danzig	A	(429) p.54
1460H	28 s.	Lübeck	C	(65) p.227
1470H	31 s.	Lübeck	C	(65) p.227

The mark of pfennige of Lübeck (16 s.) in grote of Bremen

Date	Rate	Place	Type	Reference
1405-1406	19.2 grote	Bremen	H	(462) p.194
From 1406	24 grote	Bremen	H	(462) p.194

The mark of pfennige (16s.) of Lübeck in mark, schillinge and pfennige of Riga

At Riga 36 schillinge=1 mark

Date	Rate	Place	Type	Reference
1319	1 m. 9 s.	Riga	A	(462) p.199
1406	1 m. 8 s. 3 pf.	Riga	A	(462) p.199
1432-1433	1 m. 9 s.	Riga	A	(462) p.199
1456	1 m. 6 s.	Reval	A	(503) p.13
1457	1 m. 6 s.	Riga	A	(462) p.199
1457	1 m. 9 s.	Reval	A	(503) p.13
1461	1 m. 5 s.	Riga	A	(462) p.199

See also the mark of pfennige of Riga in schillinge and pfennige of Lübeck under RIGA p.283

For the gros tournois in schillinge and pfennige of Lübeck see under FRANCE p.189
For the pound sterling in schillinge and pfennige of Lübeck see under ENGLAND p.210
For the Flemish pond groot in mark, schillinge and pfennige of Lübeck see under FLANDERS p.226
For the weisspfennig and the rheingulden in schillinge and pfennige of Lübeck see under RHINELAND p.239 and p.249
For the mark of Rostock in schillinge and pfennige of Lübeck see under ROSTOCK p.281
For the mark of pfennige of Stralsund in schillinge and pfennige of Lübeck see under STRALSUND p.281
For the Danish mark in schillinge of Lübeck see under DENMARK p.283

The Lübeck gulden

Unlike the Rhenish monetary league, that of the Wendish towns did not extend to gold, and Lübeck was for long the only city in northern Europe to mint gold coins. It began to mint florins or gulden in 1340 of nominally pure gold and very slightly heavier than their Florentine prototypes. Lübeck continued to mint its own florins until 1801.

The Lübeck gulden in schillinge and pfennige of Lübeck

Date	Rate	Place	Type	Reference
1343-1347	8 s.	Lübeck	C	(259) p.214
1347-1352	8 s. 6 d.	Lübeck	C	(259) p.214
1354	9 s.	Lübeck	C	(259) p.214
1355-1371	9 s. 5 d.	Lübeck	C	(259) p.214
1355-1371	10 s.	Lübeck	C	(259) p.214
1368-1374	10 s.	Lübeck	C	(402) X p.65
1374	11 s. 6 d.	Lübeck	C	(259) p.214
1375-1382	12 s.	Lübeck	C	(259) p.214
1375	11 s. 6 d.	Lübeck	C	(259) p.214
1375	11 s.	Lübeck	C	(259) p.214
1391	13 s. 4 d.	Lübeck	C	(259) p.214
1402	15 s. 6 d.	Lübeck	C	(259) p.214
1411-1415	16 s.	Lübeck	C	(259) p.214
1411	17 s.	Lübeck	C	(259) p.214
1415	15 s.	Lübeck	C	(259) p.214
1418	18 s.	Lübeck	C	(259) p.214
1418	20 s.	Lübeck	C	(259) p.214
1422-1423	20 s.	Lübeck	C	(259) p.216
1424	21 s. 6 d.	Lübeck	C	(259) p.216
1432-1439	26 s. 4 d.	Lübeck	C	(259) p.216
1441	27 s.	Lübeck	C	(259) p.216
1449	32 s.	Lübeck	C	(259) p.216
1456	33 s. 7 d.	Lübeck	C	(259) p.216
1457-1458	34 s.	Lübeck	C	(259) p.216
1462	29 s.	Lübeck	C	(259) p.216
1467	28 s.	Lübeck	C	(259) p.216
1467	30 s.	Lübeck	C	(259) p.216
1468-1472	32 s.	Lübeck	C	(259) p.218
1472	34 s. 6 d.	Lübeck	C	(259) p.218
1476	34 s.	Lübeck	C	(259) p.218
1482-1483	32 s.	Lübeck	C	(259) p.218

The Lübeck gulden in schillinge and pfennige of Denmark

1 schilling = 18 pfennige

Date	Rate	Place	Type	Reference
1443.09.30	26 s. 6 d.	Borglum	C	(346) III no.729
1447	27 s.	Denmark	A	(346) III no.750

MECKLENBURG

Accounting in Mecklenburg in the thirteenth and early fourteenth century was carried out in Wendish mark. At Rostock the following equivalents were used (240) p.6.

Date	Rate
End 13th century	5 Wendish mark = 4 Lübeck mark
1300	4 Wendish mark = 3 Lübeck mark
1324	3 Wendish mark = 2 Lübeck mark
1329	2 Wendish mark = 1 Lübeck mark

ROSTOCK

The mark of Rostock in schillinge and pfennige of Lübeck

Up to 1325 the mark of Rostock was the same as the Wendish mark of Mecklenburg. After 1325 it was the same as the mark of pfennige of Stralsund (240) p.6.

Date	Rate	Place	Type	Reference
From 1325	10 s. 8 d.	Rostock	A	(240) p.6
1387	10 s. 8 d.	Rostock	A	(240) p.6

STRALSUND

From around 1325 seven mints in Mecklenburg and Pomerania between Schwerin and Stettin, including Rostock and Stralsund, issued coin based on that of Stralsund. Accounting was in mark of 192 Stralsund pfennige (16 schillinge), or in sundisch or strale mark of 24 schillinge (288 Stralsund pfennige).

The Sundisch mark (24 s.) in Flemish groten

Date	Rate	Place	Type	Reference
1368	28 s.	Lübeck	C	(291) p.65

The mark of pfennige of Stralsund (16 s.) in schillinge and pfennige of Lübeck

Date	Rate	Place	Type	Reference
1331	10 s. 8 d.	Doberan	A	(462) p.201
1335	10 s.	Schwerin	A	(462) p.201
1336	10 s. 8 d.	Schwerin	A	(462) p.201
1345	10 s. 8 d.	Rostock	A	(462) p.201
1349	10 s. 8 d.	Schwerin	A	(462) p.201
1354	10 s. 8 d.	Schwerin	A	(462) p.201

THE MARK OF STRALSUND IN SCHILLINGE AND PFENNIGE OF LÜBECK

Date	Rate	Place	Type	Reference
1363	10 s. 8 d.	Rostock	A	(240) p.6
1373	10 s. 8 d.	Stralsund	A	(462) p.201
1400R	8 s.	Rostock	A	(240) p.6
1403	10 s. 8 d.	Stralsund	A	(462) p.201
1410	12 s.	Stralsund	A	(462) p.201
1425	10 s. 8 d.	Stralsund	A	(462) p.201
1489	12 s.	Stralsund	A	(462) p.201
1491	12 s.	Stralsund	A	(462) p.201

See also the mark of Rostock above p.281

For the rheingulden in mark and schillinge of Stralsund see under RHINELAND p.250

DENMARK

The Danish economy was closely associated with the Hanse towns and its money was linked to Hanse currencies, especially the mark of Lübeck. A royal tax return of 1334 explained the Danish currency system along the following lines

8 Scania pfennige = 1 örtug
10 Danish pfennige = 1 örtug
3 örtugs = 1 ore
8 ore = 1 mark

The Danish mark was thus a unit of 240 Danish pfennige or 192 Scania pfennige. After 1400 reckoning carried out in schillinge of 18 pfennige, of which 16 made one mark.

The economic preponderance of the Hanse towns put the Danish currency at a disadvantage and in 1356 a new copper money 'peior meliori' was introduced by the king, which was apparently known as a sterling.

In 1432 a further attempt to redress the balance of payments was made by the Danish king who imposed a new copper coinage on his subjects. The Hanse demanded and obtained the return of 'bonam monetam cum civitatibus maritimis equivalentem' within the year (346) III p.20. Generally, payment of large sums appears to have been made in foreign currency, for example 'in prompta pecunia videlicet turonensibus sterlingis et lybicensibus intergraliter persolvendis' in a diploma dated 1342.01.04 (346) II, no.358.

The mark of Danish pfennige in sous and deniers tournois

Date	Rate	Place	Type	Reference
1282 of Dacia	9 s. 6 d.	Denmark	A	(346) I no.96
1282 of Rua and Dacia	13 s. 6 d.	Denmark	A	(346) I no.96

The mark of Danish pfennige in gros tournois

Date	Rate	Place	Type	Reference
1334.08.30	12 gros	Denmark	O	(346) I no.311
1338.01.15	72 gros	Denmark	C	(346) I no.333
1351.03.12	12 gros	Denmark	L	(346) II no.408
1354.05.01	12 gros	Denmark	O	(346) II no.423
1355.04.16	12 gros	Denmark	C	(346) II no.27
1390	13.1/3 gros	Lund	A	(346) II no.722
1442.01.29	12 gros	Kalundborg	C	(346) III no.722

The mark of Danish pfennige in shillings and pence sterling of England

Date	Rate	Place	Type	Reference
1263.04.12	3 s. new sterling	Denmark	M	(346) I no.69
266.09.04 Ribe mark	3 s.	Denmark	C	(346) I no.74
1330.10.18 mark of copper pence	2 s.	Denmark	M	(346) I no.286
1334.08.30	3 s.	Denmark	O	(346) I no.311
1357.11.22	3 s. 4 d.	Denmark	C	(346) II no.439

THE MARK OF DANISH PFENNIGE IN STERLING

Date	Rate	Place	Type	Reference
1386.04.04	3 s. 4 d. old sterling	Lund	A	(346) II no.525

See also the pound sterling in mark, öre and pfennige of Denmark under ENGLAND p.210

The Danish mark in schillinge of Lübeck

Date	Rate	Place	Type	Reference
1357.11.22	10 s. antiq.	Denmark	L	(346) II no.439
1386.04.04	10 s.	Lund	A	(346) II no.525
1406.03.31	12 s.	Hanse	O	(346) II no.582

For the mark of Cologne in mark and schillinge of Denmark see under COLOGNE p.237
For the rheingulden in schillinge of Denmark see under RHINELAND p.250
For the Lübeck gulden in schillinge and pfennige of Denmark see under LÜBECK p.281

TEUTONIC KNIGHTS

Prussia

In Prussia (as also in Poland and Silesia) pfennige were reckoned in Sköter. Each scot or skot was a unit of 30 pfennige. The Prussian mark was a unit of account reckoned as 24 skot or 720 pfennige.

The Florentine florin in sköter of Prussia

Date	Rate	Place	Type	Reference
1317-1320	13 sköter	Prussia	C	(267) p.100
1415	36 sköter	Prussia	C	(462) p.198
1415	40 sköter	Prussia	C	(462) p.198

For the Flemish pond groot in schillinge of Prussia see under FLANDERS p.228
For the mark of pfennige of Riga in sköter of Prussia see under RIGA below

RIGA

Accounting was carried out in mark of 432 Riga pfennige. The mark was thus a unit of 36 schillinge. The mark was sometimes divided into 48 öre, each öre being 3 artiger or 9 pfennige

The mark of pfennige of Riga in schillinge and pfennige of Lübeck

Date	Rate	Place	Type	Reference
1368	36 s.	Lübeck	C	(291) p.64
1346	10 s.	Reval	A	(503) p.13
1456	13 s. 4 d.	Riga	A	(462) p.199

The mark of pfennige of Riga in sköter of Prussia

Date	Rate	Place	Type	Reference
Before 1415	29 sköter	Prussia	A	(462) p.198
1436	20 sköter	Prussia	A	(462) p.198
1439	16 sköter	Prussia	A	(462) p.198
1442	16 sköter	Prussia	A	(462) p.198
1447	16 sköter	Prussia	A	(462) p.198

For the rheingulden in mark, schillinge and pfennige of Riga see under RHINELAND p.250

RIGA

For the mark of pfennige of Lübeck in mark, schillinge and pfennige of Riga see under LÜBECK p.280

POLAND

Prague groschen circulated extensively in Poland in the fourteenth century, when they were known as grosz. A large number of the quotations for florins and ducats in prague groschen (pp.273-8) are derived from Polish sources. The grosz was incorporated into the Polish system of reckoning, although no actual Polish groszy were minted except briefly under Casimir the Great (d. 1370). Half groszy were however commonly minted in fourteenth and fifteenth century Poland, and these were the effective coins represented by reckoning in groszy. Although it began at the same value as the Prague groschen, the Polish grosz gradually diverged from it. In Poland the grzywna, or mark of account, was 48 groszy.

The florin or ducat in grosz

It may be presumed that most, if not all, of these quotations are for Hungarian ducats in the money of Krakow. In most cases this is not specified. H and K have been added to the specific cases.

Date	Rate	Place	Type	Reference
1369	14 gr.	Krakow	A	(378) p.2
1381-90	22 gr.	Poland	A	(510) p.51
1391	25 gr.	Krakow	A	(378) p.2
1392-1393F	24 1/2 gr.	Krakow	H	(461) p.381
1393	24 gr.	Krakow	A	(275) pp.194-195
1397	28 1/2 gr.	Krakow	A	(378) p.2
1398	24 gr.	Poland	A	(275) pp.194-5
1399	24 gr.	Krakow	A	(275) pp.194-195
1400	24 gr.	Krakow	A	(275) pp.194-195
1401	24 gr.	Poland	A	(275) pp.194-195
1404	24 gr. k.	Krakow	A	(275) pp.194-195
1405F	29 1/4 gr.	Krakow	H	(461) p.381
1406	24 gr. k.	Lwów	A	(275) pp.194-195
1407	26 1/4 gr. k.	Krakow	A	(275) pp.194-195
1417	34 gr. k.	Krakow	A	(275) pp.194-195
1422	37 1/2 gr. k.	Lwów	A	(275) pp.194-195
1425	28 gr. k.	Lwów	A	(275) pp.194-195
1432H	32 gr. k.	Płock (Mazovia)	L	(275) pp.194-195
1437H	36 gr. k.	Sanok (Little Poland)	C	(230) p.232
1438H	48 gr. k.	Piotrków	L	(275) pp.194-195
1441H	48 gr. k.	Krakow	C	(275) pp.194-195
1442F	45 1/2 gr.	Krakow	H	(461) p.382
1444H	41 gr. k.	Krakow	A	(275) pp.194-195
1445	34 gr.	Poland	A	(378) p.2
1448	35 gr.	Poland	A	(378) p.2
1451	36 gr.	Poland	A	(230) p.233
1452	34 gr.	Poland	A	(388) p.243
1453	30 gr.	Krakow	A	(378) p.2
1455H	30 gr. k.	Poland	A	(388) p.243
1456	31 gr.	Poland	A	(388) p.244
1457	32 gr. k.	Poland	A	(388) p.244
1458	32 gr.	Krakow	A	(378) p.2
1459	32 gr.	Krakow	A	(378) p.2
1460	34 gr.	Poland	A	(388) p.244
1461	36 gr.	Krakow	A	(378) p.2
1462	36 gr.	Krakow	A	(378) p.3
1465	32 gr.	Krakow	A	(378) p.3
1466	32 gr.	Krakow	A	(378) p.3
1467	30 gr.	Krakow	A	(378) p.3
1468H	32 gr.	Poland	A	(388) p.244
1469	32 gr.	Krakow	A	(378) p.3
1470	32 1/2 gr.	Poland	A	(230) p.233
1471	32 1/2 gr.	Krakow	A	(378) p.3
1472	32 gr.	Krakow	A	(378) p.3
1473	32 gr.	Krakow	A	(378) p.3
1474	32 gr.	Krakow	A	(378) p.3
1475	32 gr.	Krakow	A	(378) p.3

THE FLORIN OR DUCAT IN GROSZ

Date	Rate	Place	Type	Reference
1475	36 gr.	Poland	A	(230) p.233
1476	33 gr.	Krakow	A	(378) p.3
1478	32 gr.	Poland	A	(388) p.245
1480	36 1/2 gr.	Poland	A	(230) p.233
1480	30 gr.	Krakow	A	(378) p.3
1483	32 gr.	Krakow	A	(378) p.3
1485	28 gr.	Krakow	A	(378) p.3
1487	28 gr.	Krakow	A	(378) p.3
1488	28 gr.	Krakow	A	(378) p.3
1488	29 gr.	Krakow	A	(378) p.3
1489	29 gr.	Krakow	A	(378) p.3
1489	28 gr.	Krakow	A	(378) p.3
1493	30 gr.	Poland	A	(230) p.233
1496	30 gr.	Poland	A	(388) p.245
1499	30 gr.	Poland	A	(378) p.3
1500	30 gr.	Poland	A	(378) p.3

HUNGARY

The Hungarian denar was encountered on the First Crusade by German crusaders.

The Hungarian denar to the pfennig of Cologne

Date	Rate	Place	Type	Reference
From 1189	2.1/2d. = 1 pf.	Hungary	M	(437) p.20

The Hungarian denar to the pfennig of Regensburg

Date	Rate	Place	Type	Reference
From 1189	1d. = 1 pf.	Hungary	M	(437) p.20

The Hungarian denar to the pfennig of Friesach

Date	Rate	Place	Type	Reference
From 1189	2d. = 1 pf.	Hungary	M	(437) p.20

The Hungarian ducat

The gold mines of the kingdom of Hungary, principally those at Kremnica (Kremnitz) in Slovakia, were the principal source of gold in the fourteenth and fifteenth century for Europe and therefore circulated widely in many parts of Europe. The florins or ducats minted from 1328 from this gold were intended to be identical in weight and fineness with the ducats of Venice. They have therefore frequently been included in this Handbook with or immediately after those of Venice.

For the curial florin in Hungarian ducats see under AVIGNON p.128
For the Hungarian ducat in sols and deniers lausannois of Fribourg see under FRIBOURG p.137
For the Hungarian ducat in sueldos and dineros carlines see under NAVARRE p.163
For the Hungarian ducat in Flemish groten see under FLANDERS p.224
For the Hungarian ducat in florins and aidants of Liège see under LIÈGE p.233
For the Hungarian ducat in stuivers of Overijssel see under DEVENTER p.234
For the Hungarian ducat in weisspfennige see under RHINELAND p.239
For the Hungarian ducat in pfennige of Regensburg see under REGENSBURG p.268
For the Hungarian ducat in pfennige of Vienna see under AUSTRIA p.271
For the Hungarian ducat in Prague groschen see under BOHEMIA p.273
For the Hungarian ducat in schillinge and pfennige of Dortmund see under WESTPHALIA p.235
For the Hungarian ducat in schillinge and pfennige of Lübeck see under LÜBECK p.279
For the Hungarian ducat in grosz see under POLAND p.284

SECTION XI
BYZANTIUM AND THE LEVANT

BYZANTIUM

In late medieval Byzantium the principal monetary unit was the hyperpyron, the direct successor to Constantine's gold solidus. The original solidus had weighed 24 carats. The late medieval hyperpyron was also divided into 24 carats, but these were by then unit of accounts rather than units of weight. Gold hyperpyra were still being struck at the end of the thirteenth century, but in the mid-fourteenth century, after they had become very debased, their issue ceased altogether. Even after it ceased to be struck the hyperpyron survived as a unit of account, still divided into 24 carats, but payments had to made in a variety of silver coins. Both the gold hyperpyron and, later, the silver-based accounting hyperpyron were known to west Europeans as perpers. Exchange with west european currencies was limited to those of the two principal Italian trading cities, Venice and Genoa. Exchange was quoted in a variety of ways. When Byzantium was rich and powerful and its currency the most stable in the Mediterranean, rates were naturally quoted in terms of hyperpyra in variable amounts of western currencies. However, by the mid-fourteenth century, Byzantine currency was much weaker than that of Venice, so that from then onwards rates were also quoted in terms of ducats in variable sums of hyperpyra and carats.

The hyperpyron in soldi and denari of Verona

The Venetians were at this time still extensively using Veronese currency.

Date	Rate	Place	Type	Reference
1147.08	17 s. 3 d.	Venice-Constantinople	B	(32) p.32
1152	20 s.	Venice	M	(412) p.92
1155.12	18 s.	Constantinople	C	(32) p.32
1157.08	16 s. 9 1/2 d.	Constantinople	L	(32) p.33
1160.05	12 s.	Venice	L	(32) p.33
1161.01	20 s.	Torcello	L	(32) p.33
1164.08	12 s.	Venice	L	(32) p.33
1184.02	22 s. 10 1/4 d.	Venice-Alexandria	B	(32) p.33
1184	26 s. 7 d.	Venice-Romania or Alexandria	B?	(412) p.93
1184	29 s. 5 d.	Venice-Constantinople	B	(412) p.93
1184.08	29 s. 5 d.	Alexandria	B	(32) p.33

The hyperpyron in soldi and denari of Venice

Date	Rate	Place	Type	Reference
1144.01	50 s.	Constantinople-Venice	B	(32) p.32
1152.09	40 s.	Venice	L	(32) p.32
1196.03	40 s.	Abydos (Dardanelles)	L	(32) p.33
1200.10	39 s.	Constantinople-Venice	B	(32) p.33
1205.04	25 s.	Venice	B	(32) p.35
1207.04	30 s.	Venice-Constantinople	B	(32) p.35
1207.04	28 s.	Venice-Constantinople	L	(32) p.35
1207.06	42 s.	Constantinople	M	(32) p.35
1210.02	40 s.	Constantinople-Venice	B	(32) p.35
1210.03	45 s.	Constantinople-Crete or Venice	B	(32) p.36
1211.04	37 s.	Constantinople-Venice	C	(32) p.36
1212	37 s.	Constantinople-Venice	B	(412) p.93
1213.11	20 s. 6 d.	Venice-Coron	B	(412) p.93
1217	39 s.	Constantinople-Venice	B	(412) p.93
1217	36 s.	Constantinople-Tyre -Venice	B	(412) p.93
1217.04	36 s.	Constantinople-Venice	B	(32) p.36
1224.02	40 s.	Venice	O	(32) p.36
1224	37 s. 4 d.	Venice	M	(32) p.37
1225	40 s.	Venice	M	(412) p.92
1225	40 s.	Venice-Crete	M	(412) p.92
1225	40 s. 6 d.	Venice	M	(412) p.92
1226	35 s. 4 d.	Venice-Crete	M	(412) p.92

THE HYPERPYRON IN SOLDI AND DENARI OF VENICE

Date	Rate	Place	Type	Reference
1227	35 s.	Venice	M	(412) p.92
1228	38 s.	Modon-Venice	M	(412) p.92
1284.08.12	20 s.	Venice	O	(101) no.35
1315.08	32 s.	Venice	O	(32) p.40
1344.05.20	30 s.	Venice	O	(32) p.44
1344.06.04	30 s.	Venice	O	(32) p.44
1346.09.05	30 s.	Venice	O	(32) p.44
1347.06.23	30 s.	Venice	O	(32) p.44

The hyperpyron in Venetian grossi and denari

Note that there were a variable number of denari to the grosso - see p.85

Date	Rate	Place	Type	Reference
1241.05	9 gr.	Negroponte	M	(32) p.37
1315.08	12 gr. 12 d.	Venice	O	(32) p.40
1316.11	12 gr.	Venice	O	(32) p.40
1318.10.05	10 1/2 gr.	Constantinople	O	(32) p.40
1321	14 gr.	Venice	MO	(32) p.42
1323.08.17	10 1/2 gr.	Constantinople	C	(32) p.42
1324.06.28	12 gr.	Venice	A	(298) I p.257
1324.06.28	12 gr. 15 d.	Venice	A	(298) I p.257
1324.06.28	12 gr. 13 d.	Venice	MO	(32) p.42
1333.03.13	13 1/2 gr.	Venice	M	(32) p.43
1336.07.16	12 1/2 gr.	Venice	O	(32) p.43
1340.10	12 gr.	Pera	M	(32) p.43
1341.03.08	12 gr.	Venice	O	(32) p.43
1344.05.20	11 gr. 8 d.	Venice	O	(32) p.44
1349-1350	12 gr.	Venice	O	(32) p.45
1350.04.08	11 gr.	Venice	O	(32) p.45
1352.09	14 gr.	Constantinople	O	(32) p.45
1357.07.29-1376.06.05	12 gr.	Venice	O	(32) pp.45-47
1369.05.07	12 gr.	Venice	M	(32) p.46
1382.05.12	11 gr.	Venice	O	(32) p.48
1382.07.10	12 gr.	Venice	O	(32) p.48
1383.06.01	11 gr.	Venice	O	(32) p.48
1384.06.02	11 gr.	Venice	O	(32) p.48
1385.05.07	11 gr.	Venice	O	(32) p.48
1386.05.24	9 2/3 gr.	Venice	O	(32) p.48
1391.08-09	10 1/3 gr.	Pera	M	(32) p.49
1392.06.01	9 2/3 gr.	Venice	O	(32) p.49
1393.05.29	9 gr.	Venice	O	(32) p.50
1394.06.04	9 gr.	Venice	O	(32) p.50
1395.05.27	8 gr.	Venice	O	(32) p.50
1397.05.14-1412.02.22	7 1/4 gr.	Venice	O	(32) pp.50-51
1413.06.10-1420.06.01	6 1/4 gr.	Venice	O	(32) p.51
1422.09.02	9 gr.	Venice	O	(32) p.52
1432-3	8 gr.	Constantinople	M	(32) p.53
1433.06.22	7 1/2 gr.	Pera	M	(32) p.53
1436.09.03	8 gr.	Constantinople	A	(32) p.53
1438	8 gr.	Constantinople	M	(32) p.53
1440-4	8 gr.	Constantinople	M	(32) p.53
1443	8 gr.	Venice-Constantinople	C	(32) pp.56-57
1444.05.06	7 1/4 gr.	Venice	O	(32) p.57
1446	8 gr.	Venice-Constantinople	C	(32) pp.56-57
1447-1448	8 gr.	Constantinople	M	(32) p.53
1449	8 gr.	Venice-Constantinople	C	(32) pp.56-57

The Venetian ducat in hyperpyra and carats

24 carats = 1 hyperpyron

Date	Rate	Place	Type	Reference
1366.06.12-1368.01.22	2 hyp.	Pera/Constantinople	C?	(49) p.277
1387.06.01-1391.06.03	2 hyp. 12 carats	Venice	O	(32) pp.48-49
1396.06.03	3 hyp.	Venice	O	(32) p.50
1400.09.03	3 hyp. 8 1/2 carats	Pera	B	(225) p.153
1400.09.16	3 hyp. 9 carats	Pera	B	(225) p.153
1400.09.16	3 hyp. 10 carats	Pera	B	(225) p.153
1400.09.16	3 hyp. 6 carats	Pera	B	(225) p.153
1400.10.08	3 hyp. 7 carats	Pera	B	(225) p.153

Date	Rate	Place	Type	Reference
1412.02.22	3 hyp. 8 carats	Venice	O	(32) p.51
1440	3 hyp.	Florence	?	(32) p.56
1448.08	3 hyp. 6 carats	Venice	O	(32) p.57
1449.05	3 hyp. 8 carats	Venice	O	(32) p.57
1450.05	3 hyp. 7 carats	Venice	O	(32) p.57
1450.05	3 hyp. 6 carats	Venice	O	(32) p.57
1450.07	3 hyp. 2 carats	Venice	O	(32) p.57
1450.08	3 hyp. 5 carats	Venice	O	(32) p.57
1451.02	3 hyp. 9 carats	Venice	O	(32) p.57
1451.05	3 hyp. 5 carats	Venice	O	(32) p.57
1451.07	3 hyp. 6 carats	Venice	O	(32) p.57
1451.10	3 hyp. 8 carats	Venice	O	(32) p.57
1452.05	3 hyp. 8 carats	Venice	O	(32) p.57
1452.08	3 hyp. 8 carats	Venice	O	(32) p.57

The hyperpyron in soldi and denari of Genoa

At Constantinople the Genoese were principally based in the suburb of Pera

Date	Rate	Place	Type	Reference
1156.06.08	5 s. 2 d.	Genoa-Constantinople	L	(105) no.84
1157.07.19	6 s. 8 d.	Genoa-Constantinople	L	(105) no.219
1157.07.11	3 s. 9 d.	Genoa-Palermo	L	(105) no.292
1158.11.12	4 s. 2 d.	Genoa	C	(105) no.519
1160	5 s. 4 d.	Genoa	B	(187A) f.1072
1160.03.09	5 s. 4 d.	Genoa-Constantinople	L	(105) no.615
1160.05.26	5 s. 4 d.	Genoa-Constantinople	L	(105) no.666
1160.06.08	5 s. 4 d.	Genoa-Constantinople	L	(105) no.676
1161.06.18	7 s. 3 d.	Genoa-Romania	C	(105) no.840
1186	5 s.	Genoa	C?	(344) p.228
1191.09.25	6 s. 8 d.	Constantinople	L	(233) no.1134
1206	7 s. 3 d.	Genoa	B	(187A) f.1073
1206.03.18	5 s.	Salonica	C	(234) no.1683
1251	7 s. 3 d.	Genoa	C?	(344) p.228
1261	10 s.	Pera-Genoa	B	(16) p.652
1262	8 s. 10 1/2 d.	Constantinople-Genoa	B	(187A) f.1073
1263	10 s.	Genoa	B	(187A) f.1073
1264	9 s.	Pera-Genoa	B	(16) p.652
1268	9 s. 6 d.	Pera-Genoa	B	(16) p.652
1274	10 s. 1 d.	Pera-Genoa	B	(16) p.652
1275	10 s. 2 d.	Pera-Genoa	B	(16) p.652
1278-1279	10 s. 2 d.	Pera-Genoa	B	(16) p.652
1282	11 s.	Pera-Genoa	B	(464) p.652
1284	10 s.	Constantinople	B	(187A) f.1073
1287	10 s. 6 d.	Pera-Genoa	B	(16) p.652
1291	11 s.	Pera-Genoa	B	(16) p.652
1292	11 s.	Pera-Genoa	B	(16) p.652
1292	9 s. 5 d.	Constantinople	B	(187A) f.1073
1294	10 s. 6 d.	Pera-Genoa	B	(16) p.652
1296	11 s.	Pera-Genoa	B	(16) p.652
1296	10 s.	Pera	B	(187A) f.1073
1300	11 s.	Pera-Genoa	B	(16) p.653
1301	11 s.	Pera-Genoa	B	(16) p.653
1302	10 s.	Constantinople	A	(187B) f.776
1302	11 s. 9 d.	Pera-Genoa	B	(16) p.653
1305	12 s. 2 d.	Pera-Genoa	B	(16) p.653
1309	11 s. 6 d.	Pera-Genoa	B	(16) p.653
1310	10 s.	Romania	B	(187A) f.1073
1311	10 s. 5 d.	Genoa-Syria	B	(187B) f.775
1311	13 s.	Genoa	B	(187B) f.775
1311	11 s.	Genoa-Foggia	B	(187B) f.775
1311	11 s. 9 d.	Genoa-Scio	B	(187B) f.775
1311	12 s.	Genoa-Syria	B	(187B) f.775
1311	13 s. 4 d.	Pera-Genoa	B	(16) p.653
1312	13 s. 4 d.	Pera-Genoa	B	(16) p.653
1313-1314	13 s. 9 d.	Pera-Genoa	B	(16) p.653
1316	11 s. 6 d.	Genoa	B	(187B) f.775
1323	12 s. 2 d.	Pera	C	(16) p.653
1330	16 s.	Pera-Genoa	B	(16) p.653
1334-1335	15 s.	Pera-Genoa	B	(16) p.653
1336	14 s. 11 d.	Pera-Genoa	B	(16) p.653

THE HYPERPYRON IN SOLDI AND DENARI OF GENOA

Date	Rate	Place	Type	Reference
1338	15 s.	Pera-Genoa	B	(16) p.653
1339	15 s. 3 d.	Pera-Genoa	B	(16) p.653
1343	18 s.	Genoa-Syria	B	(187B) f.775
1343-1344	14 s.	Pera-Genoa	B	(16) p.653
1346	14 s.	Pera-Genoa	B	(16) p.653
1346	15 s.	Genoa-Syria	B	(187B) f.775
1347	15 s.	Genoa-Syria	B	(187B) f.776
1348	16 s.	Genoa-Syria	B	(187B) f.776
1348	15 s. 6 d.	Pera-Genoa	B	(16) p.653
1349	15 s.	Pera-Genoa	B	(16) P.654
1350	14 s. 5 d.	Pera-Genoa	B	(16) p.654
1351	14 s.	Pera-Genoa	B	(16) p.654
1352	14 s.	Genoa	B	(187B) f.776
1353	15 s.	Pera-Genoa	B	(16) p.654
1357-1358	13 s.	Pera-Genoa	B	(16) p.654
1361	14 s. 3 d.	Pera-Genoa	B	(16) p.654
1364	13 s.	Pera-Genoa	B	(16) p.654
1367	12 s. 6 d.	Pera	C	(16) p.654
1369	13 s. 9 d.	Pera-Genoa	B	(16) p.654
1370	14 s. 1 d.	Pera-Genoa	B	(16) p.654
1374	14 s. 6 d.	Pera-Genoa	B	(16) p.654
1376	16 s.	Genoa-Pera	B	(16) p.654
1377	16 s.	Genoa-Pera	B	(16) p.654
1378	16 s.	Genoa-Pera	B	(16) p.654
1383	14 s. 3 d. average	Pera-Genoa	B	(16) p.654
1384	13 s. 8 d. average	Pera-Genoa	B	(16) p.654
1385	13 s. 5 d. average	Pera-Genoa	B	(16) p.655
1388	16 s.	Genoa-Pera	B	(16) p.655
1388	12 s.	Pera-Genoa	B	(16) p.655
1388	12 s.	Pera	O	(16) p.655
1389	10 s. 11 d. average	Pera-Genoa	B	(16) p.655
1390	11 s. 3 d. average	Pera-Genoa	B	(16) p.655
1391	10 s. 9 d. average	Pera-Genoa	B	(16) p.655
1393	13 s.	Genoa-Pera	B	(16) p.655
1395	10 s. 11 d.	Pera-Genoa	B	(16) p.655
1396	10 s.	Pera-Genoa	B	(16) p.655
1398	9 s. 6 d.	Pera-Genoa	B	(16) p.655
1401	9 s. 6 d.	Pera-Genoa	B	(16) p.655
1402	9 s. 8 d.	Pera-Genoa	B	(16) p.655
1404	8 s. 8 d.	Pera	C	(16) p.655

The hyperpyron in Turkish aspers and torneselli

Date	Rate	Place	Type	Reference
1440.09.07?	11 aspers 4 tornes.	Brusa	C	(225) p.154
1440.09.07?	9 aspers	Adrianople	C	(225) p.154
1440.09.07	11 aspers 6 tornes.	Saliet	C	(225) p.154

For the sommo of Caffa in hyperpyra and carats see under BLACK SEA p.290

BLACK SEA

The standard unit of account in and around the Black Sea was the sommo, which was subdivided into 45 saggi. The sommo as a unit of account derived from the sommo weight, just as west European pounds and marks as units of account derived from west European pound and mark weights. In the later middle ages 'virge sommorum argenti', sommo bars of silver, were still used as the principal means of making large payments around the Black Sea and in the steppe region, just as mark bars had been used in western Europe up to the fourteenth century. The principal coins in use in the area were silver aspers, of which there were a large number of different issuers from the late thirteenth century onwards. In the early fourteenth century Pegolotti reported that at Tana, on the sea of Azov, 202 aspers were worth one sommo. In the late fifteenth century at Caffa, in the Crimea, 190 aspers were worth one sommo. (178)

The sommo of Caffa in lire, soldi and denari of Genoa

Date	Rate	Place	Type	Reference
1343-1344	7 li. 10 s.	Caffa-Genoa	B	(16) p.663
1351	8 li. 7 s.	Caffa-Genoa	B	(16) p.663
1361	9 li.	Caffa-Genoa	B	(16) p.663
1374-1375	7 li. 15 s.	Caffa-Genoa	B	(16) p.663
1377	7 li. 15 s.	Caffa-Genoa	B	(16) p.663
1381-1382	7 li. 2 s. 6 d.	Caffa-Genoa	B	(16) p.663
1385-1386	7 li. 10 s.	Caffa-Genoa	B	(16) p.663
1388	7 li. 13 s.	Caffa-Genoa	B	(16) p.663
1391	7 li. 15 s.	Caffa-Genoa	B	(16) p.663
1393	7 li. 10 s.	Caffa-Genoa	B	(16) p.663
1395	7 li. 7 s.	Caffa-Genoa	B	(16) p.663
1399-1400	7 li. 5 s.	Caffa-Genoa	B	(16) p.663
1401	7 li. 9 s.	Caffa-Genoa	B	(16) p.663
1409-1410	7 li. 5 s.	Caffa-Genoa	B	(16) p.663

The sommo of Caffa in hyperpyra and carats
24 carats = 1 hyperpyron

Date	Rate	Place	Type	Reference
1343-1344	8 hyp. 6 carats	Caffa-Pera	B	(16) p.663
1358	10 hyp.	Caffa-Pera	B	(16) p.663
1374-1375	11 hyp. 12 carats	Caffa-Pera	B	(16) p.663
1381-1382	12 hyp. 12 carats	Caffa-Pera	B	(16) p.663
1385-1386	12 hyp.	Caffa-Pera	B	(16) p.663
1391	12 hyp. 12 carats	Caffa-Pera	B	(16) p.663
1401	14 hyp.	Caffa-Pera	B	(16) p.663

The Venetian ducat in silver aspers

Date	Rate	Place	Type	Reference
1366.06.12-1368.01.22	32 a.	Venice?	M?	(49) p.277
Late 14th century	34 to 40 a.	Caffa	C	(178) MS.9 fo.6v
1432	50 a. of Konya	Levant	H	(11) App.C
1436	35 a.	Pera?	H	(225) p.154
1482/886.9.30-887.5.21	47 a.	Ottoman empire	O	(11) p.324
1489	47 a.	Bosnia	M	(261) p.156
1509	52 a.	Pera?	H	(225) p.154

The genovino in silver aspers

Date	Rate	Place	Type	Reference
circa 1442 (Uzzano)	30 a.	Caffa	C	(373)

For the lira of Genoa in aspers see under GENOA p.109
For the hyperpyron in aspers and torneselli see under BYZANTIUM p.289
For the dirham in aspers see under EGYPT p.306

The Florentine florin in silver ducats 'monete Burgarie'

Date	Rate	Place	Type	Reference
1366.06.12-1368.01.22	18	Venice?	C?	(49) p.278

The Florentine florin in silver ducats 'monete Mesembrie'

Date	Rate	Place	Type	Reference
1366.06.12-1368.01.22	18	Venice?	C?	(49) p.278

The gold hyperpyron of Mesembrie in Florentine florins

Date	Rate	Place	Type	Reference
1366.06.12-1368.01.22	2 1/8 florins	Venice?	C?	(49) p.278

EPIROS

In the despotate of Epiros, an independent state from 1267 to 1479, the hyperpyron was the principal unit of account.

The Venetian ducat in hyperpyra of Epiros

Date	Rate	Place	Type	Reference
1319	1 1/2 hyp.	Epiros	?	(366) p.224
1324	2 hyp.	Arta	?	(366) p.224
1396	4 hyp.	Epiros	?	(366) p.224

RAGUSA (DUBROVNIK)

In the fourteenth and fifteenth century Ragusa the hyperpyron, the principal unit of account, was a multiple of twelve silver dinari. The dinar of Ragusa was sometimes called a grosso, and derived ultimately from the Venetian grosso.

The Venetian ducat in hyperpyra and dinari of Ragusa

Date	Rate	Place	Type	Reference
1356.06-09.29	2 hyp. 2 d.	Ragusa	O	(339) p.197
1357.01-04.09	2 hyp. 1 d.	Ragusa	O	(339) p.197
1395	2 hyp. 6 d.	Ragusa	O	(339) p.197
1444.01.28	3 hyp.	Ragusa	M	(273) p.77
1445-1459	3 hyp. to 3 hyp. 4 d.	Ragusa	A	(273) p.77

VENETIAN COLONIES

From the Latin conquest of 1204 onwards the currency of Frankish Greece was made up of the surviving Byzantine coins, particularly hyperpyra (perpers) and newly imported western coins. In the thirteenth century the principal western imports were English sterlings (mainly introduced before 1247), French deniers tournois (mainly introduced circa 1230-65) and Venetian grossi. From the 1260s to 1340s imitative denier tournois were struck by various princes in Frankish Greece itself, so that although fresh deniers tournois were not brought from the west, tournois continued as the principal currency. Imitative sterlings were not struck in the same way, so that actual sterlings ceased to circulate. They survived however as an accounting unit of 4 deniers tournois. When Pegolotti noted down the currency of Chiarenza and the Morea he reported that that the perper was worth 20 sterlings of 4 tournois and the Venetian grosso 3 sterlings of 4 tournois. From the mid-fourteenth century, when other Greek issues of deniers tournois were coming to an end, the Venetians began to mint them for their Greek colonies; Negroponte (Euboea), Crete, and various places in the Peloponnese. These deniers passed under the name of torneselli. At around the time that the first torneselli were struck, considerable quantities of soldo coins, soldini, were being sent out from Venice itself. The soldino took over from the sterling as the four denier unit, and even when soldini were not available, reckoning continued to be carried out in soldi of 4 torneselli. At the beginning of the fifteenth century, the Venetian senate established an official rate of 96 soldi per ducat for calculating the pay of Venetian employees in Greece. Although the actual effective rate was much higher, the official rate was maintained throughout the century (467). For the expression of torneselli in hyperpyra of Crete, Corfu, Negroponte and the Greek mainland (Modon, Coron, Chiarenza and Patras) see Stahl (467).

The Venetian ducat in soldi of 4 torneselli

Date	Rate	Place	Type	Reference
1352.09	64 s.	Crete;Modon	H	(467)
1359.10.03	66 s.	Negroponte	A	(467)
1359.10.16	56 s.	Negroponte	C	(298) III p.304
1361.01	73-74 s.	Vostitsa	A	(467)
1375.05.21	73 s.	Crete	M	(467)
1379.11	75 s.	Achaia	A	(467)
1382.10.22	75 s.	Zante	M	(467)
1390.10.15	83 s.	Crete	A	(467)
1394.08.26	86 s.	Crete	A	(467)
1395	107 s.	Crete	M	(467)
1403.09.07	102 s.	Crete	M	(467)
1403.10.02	100 s.	Coron;Modon	A	(467)
1408.05.31	111 s.	Corfu	A	(467)
1410.01.23	100 s.	Crete	A	(467)
1410.07.24	120 s.	Negroponte	A	(467)
1410.08.27	109 s.	Crete	A	(467)
1410.09.05	105 s.	Crete	A	(467)
1411.01.14	120 s.	Corfu	A	(467)
1411.08.22	116 s.	Crete	A	(467)
1417.05.21	116 s.	Crete	A	(467)
1420.07.20	140 s.	Negroponte	A	(467)
1420.07.26	128 s.	Crete	A	(467)
1424.12.04	130 s.	Crete;Modon	A	(467)
1425.02.07	140 s.	Crete	M	(467)
1429.03.10	140 s.	Negroponte	A	(467)
circa 1434	154 s.	Venice	A	(467)
1438.05.13	152 s.	Modon	A	(467)
1438.05.13	153 s.	Modon	A	(467)
1441.10.04	154 s.	Crete	A	(467)
1441.10.17	160 s.	Negroponte	A	(467)
1442.02.11	154 s.	Crete	A	(467)
1442.12.17	152 s.	Crete	A	(467)
1450.03.11	174 s.	Crete	A	(467)
1450.09.22	152 s.	Crete	A	(467)
1457.02.15	175 s. 6 d.	Nauplia	A	(467)
1458	152 s.	Crete	H	(467)
1464.09.26	156 s.	Crete	A	(467)
1466.03.02	198 s.	Corfu	A	(467)

The florin of Genoa in soldi of 4 torneselli

Date	Rate	Place	Type	Reference
1382.04.14	80 s.	Corfu	M	(121) p.654
1382.04.22	80 s.	Modon	M	(121) p.654
1382.04.24	80 s.	Castelli	M	(121) p.654
1382.04.26	80 s.	Paximadhia?	M	(121) p.654
1382.10.22	75 s.	Zante	M	(121) p.654
1382.10.25-27	80 s.	Corfu	M	(121) p.654
1382.10.25-27	78 s.	Corfu	M	(121) p.654

For the uncia of Sicily in soldi of Chiarenza see under SICILY p.62

CHIOS

Chios became a Genoese colony in 1346, and was granted an island mint in 1347. The current coinage of Chios included perpers (hyperpyra) of 20 carats and zigliati, silver grossi struck by the Mahonesi. By 1479 Chios was striking zigliati of base alloy, and they were abolished. Following this, a new Chian ducat, the ducato largo, was introduced.

The Chian florin of account in lire and soldi of Genoa

Date	Rate	Place	Type	Reference
14th century	1 li. 5 s.	Genoa	H	(5) p.410
1403	1 li. 5 s.	Chios	H	(5) p.401

The Chian ducat in zigliati

Date	Rate	Place	Type	Reference
1473.07	10 gr.	Chios	H	(5) p.614

The Chian ducat in lire and soldi of Genoa

Date	Rate	Place	Type	Reference
1444	2 li. 2 s.	Genoa	O	(5) p.603
1450.09	2 li.	Chios?	C	(5) p.603

The Chian ducat in perpers and carats

Date	Rate	Place	Type	Reference
1479.09.15	2 hyp. 8 carats	Chios	O	(5) p.245

The ducato largo in zigliati

Date	Rate	Place	Type	Reference
1479.09.15	11 gr.	Chios	O	(5) p.254

The ducato largo in perpers and carats

Date	Rate	Place	Type	Reference
1498.07.07	6 hyp. 10 carats	Chios	O	(5) p.267

For the lira of Genoa in good zigliati see under GENOA p.109

RHODES

The ducat of Rhodes was one of the more successful imitations of the Venetian ducat, especially the issues made under Grand Master Antonio de Fluviano. (1421-37). The money market in Barcelona gave different rates for the Rhodes ducat in Barcelona and in Rhodes.

The ducat of Rhodes in sueldos and dineros of Barcelona

Date	Rate	Place	Type	Reference
1450.10.26	12 s.	Barcelona	C	(129) p.81
1450.10.26	18 s.	Rhodes	C	(129) p.81
1451.03.23	13 s.	Barcelona	C	(129) p.81
1451.05.12	16 s. 6 d.	Rhodes	C	(129) p.81
1451.09.18	17 s. 6 d.	Rhodes	C	(129) p.81
1451.11.30	16 s.	Rhodes	C	(129) p.81
1452.01.28	17 s.	Rhodes	C	(129) p.81

THE DUCAT OF RHODES IN SUELDOS AND DINEROS OF BARCELONA

Date	Rate	Place	Type	Reference
1452.01.31	12 s. 6 d.	Barcelona	C	(129) p.81
1452.02.04	12 s. 6 d.	Barcelona	C	(129) p.81
1452.11	16 s. 6 d.	Rhodes	C	(129) p.81
1455.10.01	11 s. 6 d.	Barcelona	C	(129) p.81
1461.09.09	18 s.	Rhodes	C	(129) p.81
1462.07.01	12 s.	Barcelona	C	(129) p.81

THE BESANT

In the later middle ages west Europeans used the term besant not only for the gold dinar, but also for various units of account, which ultimately derived from the gold dinar. Besants were therefore extensively used as units of account by Europeans in the Levant and the Maghreb. The type of besant was normally specified, and specific besant entries occur below under Lesser Armenia, Syria, Acre, Cyprus, Egypt and Tunis. However a number of rates involving besants without any qualification have been found and are grouped here.

The besant (unspecified) in soldi and denari provisini of Rome

Date	Rate	Place	Type	Reference
1291.09.27	16 s.	Orvieto	A	(179) III p.87

The besant (unspecified) in soldi and denari of Ravenna

Date	Rate	Place	Type	Reference
1291.03.23	17 s.	Pesaro	A	(179) III p.89

The besant (unspecified) in soldi and denari of Venice

Date	Rate	Place	Type	Reference
1227.01.11	70 s.	Venice	M	(101) no.6
1284.08.12 old besant	40 s.	Venice	O	(101) no.35
1288.04.04	33 s.	Venice	O	(101) no.49

The besant (unspecified) in soldi and denari of Pavia

Date	Rate	Place	Type	Reference
1154 ?gold morabetino	3s. 4d.	Barcelona	C	(93) pp.105-111

The besant (unspecified) in soldi and denari of Genoa

Date	Rate	Place	Type	Reference
1239	5 s. 3 d.	Genoa	A	(187A) f.1043
1249	9 s.	Genoa	A	(187A) f.1044
1266	5 s.	Genoa	A	(187A) f.1045

See also the lira of Genoa in besants under GENOA p.109

The besant (unspecified) in sueldos and dineros of Barcelona

Date	Rate	Place	Type	Reference
1302	2 s.	Barcelona	A	(163) p.529

The besant (unspecified) in sous and deniers tournois

Date	Rate	Place	Type	Reference
1292.07.15	8 s.	Boulogne	A	(179) III p.18

The besant (unspecified) in gros tournois

Date	Rate	Place	Type	Reference
1337.11.25	9 gr.	Curia	A	(216) p.24
1343.06.27	10 gr.	Curia	A	(347) p.7
1348.05.02	9 gr.	Curia	A	(347) p.29
1350.04.13	9 gr.	Curia	A	(347) p.36
1355.03.18	8 2/3 gr.	Curia	A	(252) p.83
1357.05.24	8 2/3 gr.	Curia	A	(252) p.167

The besant (unspecified) in shillings and pence sterling

Date	Rate	Place	Type	Reference
1162	2 s.	England	A	(292) p.88
1213	1 s. 9 d.	London	A	(392) p.20

LESSER ARMENIA

At Alaya in Little Armenia the besant qualified by Pegolotti as besant of Romania was used. It was divided into 24 carats and in Pegolotti's time was worth 10 silver tacorinos.

The Genoese florin in besants and carats at Alaya

Date	Rate	Place	Type	Reference
1382.06.14	4 besants 4 cts.	Alaya	M	(121) p.654

The besant of Armenia in Venetian soldi a grossi

Date	Rate	Place	Type	Reference
circa 1380	23s.	Venice	C	(178) MS.2

Around 1380 twelve Armenian besants were reckoned as equivalent to 32 white besants or 10 saracen besants in Cyprus (178) MS.2

SYRIA

The Syrian besant in soldi and denari of Genoa

Date	Rate	Place	Type	Reference
1156.04.21	6 s. 8 d.	Genoa	LB	(105) no.62
1157.06.18	10 s.	Genoa	B	(105) no. 197
1158.08.23	5 s.	Outremer	C	(105) no.458
1160.08.27	6 s. 2 d.	Alexandria	C	(105) no.726
1190	6 s. 6 d.	Genoa?	C?	(344) p.200
1191.06.20	5 s. 8 d.	Outremer	LB	(233) no.755
1191.11.09	7 s.	Genoa-Constantinople	LB	(233) no.924
1191.09.07	6 s. 8 d.	Outremer	LB	(233) no.950
1191.09.24	6 s. 11 d.	Outremer	LB	(233) no.1100
1191.09.25	6 s. 8 d.	Outremer	LB	(233) no.1134
1203.09.11	6 s. 8 d.	Outremer	B	(234) no.572

THE SYRIAN BESANT IN SOLDI AND DENARI OF GENOA

Date	Rate	Place	Type	Reference
1203.09.17	6 s. 8 d.	Outremer	B	(234) no.574
1203.09.19	6 s. 11 d.	Outremer	C	(234) no.628
1203.09.23	6 s. 11 d.	Outremer	LB	(234) no.816
1203.09.23	6 s. 11 d.	Outremer	C	(234) no.836
1205.05.13	6 s. 8 d.	Sicily-Outremer	B	(234) no.1166
1205.05.16	6 s. 8 d.	Acre-Sicily	LB	(234) no.1190
1205.05.04	6 s. 8 d.	Outremer	C	(234) no.1238
1205.05.25	6 s. 8 d.	Outremer	LB	(234) no.1253
1205.05.27	6 s. 8 d.	Outremer	LB	(234) no.1298
1205.05.28	6 s. 8 d.	Outremer	LB	(234) no.1306
1205.05.31	6 s. 8 d.	Outremer	C	(234) no.1356
1210	4 s. 10 d.	Genoa?	C?	(344) p.200
1210	6 s. 8 d.	Genoa?	C?	(344) p.200
1210	6 s. 5 d.	Genoa	C?	(344) p.200
1211	6 s. 11 d.	Genoa	C?	(344) p.200
1213	6 s. 8 d.	Genoa	C?	(344) p.200
1213	8 s. 11 d.	Genoa	C?	(344) p.200
1214	6 s. 8 d.	Genoa	C?	(344) p.201
1214	7 s. 3 d.	Genoa	C?	(344) p.201
1214	6 s. 11 d.	Genoa	C?	(344) p.201
1216	10 s.	Genoa	A	(187A) f.1042
1214	9 s. 1 d.	Genoa	C?	(344) p.201
1216	6 s. 8 d.	Genoa	C?	(344) p.201
1216	8 s.	Genoa	C?	(344) p.201
1216	7 s. 8 d.	Genoa	C?	(344) p.201
1217	10 s.	Genoa	C?	(344) p.201
1224	8 s.	Genoa	C?	(344) p.201
1224	5 s. 4 d.	Genoa	C?	(344) p.201
1226	8 s.	Genoa	C?	(344) p.201
1226	6 s. 11 d.	Genoa	C?	(344) p.201
1227	8 s.	Genoa	A	(187A) f.1042
1227	9 s. 6 d.	Genoa	C?	(344) p.201
1227	10 s.	Genoa	C?	(344) p.201
1236	7 s. 1/2 d.	Genoa	C?	(344) p.201
1236	9 s. 6 d.	Genoa	C?	(344) p.201
1239	7 s. 8 d.	Genoa	C?	(344) p.201
1240	6 s. 8 d.	Genoa	C?	(344) p.201
1240	6 s. 5 d.	Genoa	C?	(344) p.201
1248	5 s. 8 1/2 d.	Genoa	A	(187A) f.1043
1248	6 s. 2 d.	Genoa	M	(187A) f.1043
1248	6 s. 2 d.	Genoa	A	(187A) f.1043
1248	13 s. 4 d.	Genoa	C?	(344) p.201
1248	6 s. 11 d.	Genoa	C?	(344) p.201
1248	6 s. 1/2 d.	Genoa	C?	(344) p.201
1248	8 s.	Genoa	C?	(344) p.201
1248	7 s. 3 1/2 d.	Genoa	C?	(344) p.201
1248	5 s. 8 d.	Genoa	C?	(344) p.201
1248	6 s. 2 d.	Genoa	C?	(344) p.201
1248	5 s. 8 d.	Genoa	C?	(344) p.201
1248	8 s.	Genoa	C?	(344) p.202
1248	6 s. 8 d.	Genoa	C?	(344) p.202
1248	5 s. 8 d.	Genoa	C?	(344) p.202
1248	11 s. 9 d.	Genoa	C?	(344) p.202
1248	6 s. 8 d.	Genoa	C?	(344) p.202
1248	5 s. 4 d.	Genoa	C?	(344) p.202
1248	6 s. 8 d.	Genoa	C?	(344) p.202
1248	6 s. 1/2 d.	Genoa	C?	(344) p.202
1248	6 s. 2 d.	Genoa	C?	(344) p.202
1248	6 s.	Genoa	C?	(344) p.202
1248	5 s. 8 d.	Genoa	C?	(344) p.202
1248	6 s.	Genoa	C?	(344) p.202
1248	5 s. 8 d.	Genoa	C?	(344) p.202
1250	14 s. 3 d.	Genoa	C?	(344) p.202
1251	5 s. 4 d.	Genoa	A	(187A) f.1043
1251	7 s. 3 d.	Genoa	C?	(344) p.202
1251	10 s. 6 d.	Genoa	C?	(344) p.202
1251	9 s. 1 d.	Genoa	C?	(344) p.202
1251	7 s. 3 d.	Genoa	C?	(344) p.202
1251	7 s. 8 d.	Genoa	C?	(344) p.202
1251	8 s.	Genoa	C?	(344) p.202
1253	7 s. 3 d.	Genoa	C?	(344) p.202
1253	7 s. 8 d.	Genoa	C?	(344) p.202

THE SYRIAN BESANT IN SOLDI AND DENARI OF GENOA

Date	Rate	Place	Type	Reference
1253	8 s. 4 d.	Genoa	C?	(344) p.202
1253	6 s. 8 d.	Genoa	C?	(344) p.202
1253	7 s. 7 d.	Genoa	C?	(344) p.202
1253	6 s. 11 d.	Genoa	C?	(344) p.202
1253	7 s. 6 d.	Genoa	C?	(344) p.202
1253	6 s. 8 d.	Genoa	C?	(344) p.202
1253	7 s. 3 d.	Genoa	C?	(344) p.202
1253	6 s. 8 d.	Genoa	C?	(344) p.202
1253	7 s. 4 1/2 d.	Genoa	C?	(344) p.202
1253	6 s. 8 d.	Genoa	C?	(344) p.203
1253	5 s.	Genoa	C?	(344) p.203
1253	8 s. 11 d.	Genoa	C?	(344) p.203
1253	9 s. 1 d.	Genoa	C?	(344) p.203
1253	7 s. 10 d.	Genoa	C?	(344) p.203
1253	11 s. 11 d.	Genoa	C?	(344) p.203
1253	8 s.	Genoa	C?	(344) p.203
1253	7 s. 4 d.	Genoa	C?	(344) p.203
1253	7 s. 6 d.	Genoa	C?	(344) p.203
1257	8 s.	Acre	B	(187A) f.1044

ACRE

In the twelfth and thirteenth centuries the crusaders struck imitations of gold islamic dinars in Antioch, Tyre, Tripoli and Acre, which were known to west Europeans as saracen besants, besants of 'outremer' or besants of Acre, since Acre was not only the principal trading port of 'outremer' but also the principal, and eventually the only, mint at which they were struck. The saracen besant, bisante saracinato, was also the principal unit of account in the crusader states. It was divided into 24 carats. After the fall of Acre in 1291 the saracen besant was also used as a unit of account in Cyprus alongside the white besant of Cyprus.

The besant of Acre in soldi and denari of Venice

Date	Rate	Place	Type	Reference
1284.08.12	20 s.	Venice	M	(101) no.35
1289.02.12	33 s.	Venice	O	(101) no.53

The 'outremer' or Acre besant in soldi and denari of Genoa

Date	Rate	Place	Type	Reference
1210	6 s. 8 d.	Genoa	A	(187A) f.1042
1214	6 s. 8 d.	Genoa	M	(187A) f.1042
1214 Acre besant	7 s. 7 d.	Outremer	A	(187A) f.1042
1291 Acre besant	12 s.	Genoa	A	(187A) f.1044

The besant of Acre in sous and deniers royaux coronats of Provence

Date	Rate	Place	Type	Reference
1210.03.22	6 s.	Marseille	C	(45) no.3
1242.08.16	5 s.	Marseille	C	(45) no.153
1244.04.15	5 s. 5 d.	Marseille	C	(45) no.98
1244.08.27	5 s. 2 d.	Marseille	C	(45) no.101
1248.03.30	5 s. 5 d.	Marseille	C	(45) no.328
1248.03.30	8 s.	Marseille	C	(45) no.332
1248.03.30	7 s. 10 d.	Marseille	C	(45) no.281
1248.03.30	7 s. 10 d.	Marseille	C	(45) no.305
1248.03.30	8 s. 3 d.	Marseille	C	(45) no.279
1248.03.30	7 s. 10 d.	Marseille	C	(45) no.277
1248.03.30	9 s.	Marseille	C	(45) no.269

The besant of Acre in sous and deniers of the mixed money of Marseille

Date	Rate	Place	Type	Reference
1229.08.09	6 s. 7 d.	Marseille	C	(45) no.22
1240.02.23	6 s. 7 d.	Marseille	C	(45) no.87
1248.03.18	4 s. 7 d.	Marseille	C	(45) no.89
1248.03.23	8 s.	Marseille	C	(45) no.111
1248.03.23	7 s. 2 1/2 d.	Marseille	C	(45) no.127
1248.03.23	7 s. 10 d.	Marseille	C	(45) no.146
1248.03.23	7 s. 7 d.	Marseille	C	(45) no.154
1248.03.23	7 s. 10 d.	Marseille	C	(45) no.166
1248.03.27	6 s. 2 d.	Marseille	C	(45) no.183
1248.03.27	8 s.	Marseille	C	(45) no.185
1248.03.27	7 s. 10 d.	Marseille	C	(45) no.200
1248.03.27	10 s.	Marseille	C	(45) no.210
1248.03.27	7 s. 11 d.	Marseille	C	(45) no.211
1248.03.30	8 s. 5 d.	Marseille	C	(45) no.238
1248.04.09	7 s.	Marseille	C	(45) no.426
1248.04.15	16 s. 2 d.	Marseille	C	(45) no.522
1248.04.15	5 s. 1 d.	Marseille	C	(45) no.541
1248.04.18	6 s. 5 d.	Marseille	C	(45) no.565
1248.05.02	7 s. 3 d.	Marseille	C	(45) no.644
1248.05.13	6 s. 9 d.	Marseille	C	(45) no.718
1248.07.15	5 s. 4 d.	Syria	C	(45) no.977

The besant of Acre in sous and deniers melgorians

Date	Rate	Place	Type	Reference
1248.03.18	4 s. 8 d.	Marseille	C	(45) no.90

The saracen besant of Acre in sous and deniers tournois

Date	Rate	Place	Type	Reference
1248.02.20	7 s.	Acre	M	(328) p.195

CYPRUS

Accounting in fourteenth century Cyprus was primarily carried out in white besants and carats. The last gold besants of Cyprus, issued at the beginning of the reign of Henry II (1285-1324) had been of such poor gold, 4 carats fine or less, that they were known as white besants, since they were predominantly silver coins. The white besant, bisante bianco, was used as the principal unit of account for two centuries after it had ceased to be struck as a coin. As a unit of account it was divided into 24 carats like the Byzantine hyperpyron. The coinage of fourteenth century Cyprus consisted of silver grossi and billon denari cipresi and it was from these coins that the white besant was valued. The bisante bianco was taken as equivalent to two grossi or 4 soldi of cipresi. The saracen besant, bisante saracinato, formerly used in Acre (see above p.297), was also used as a unit of account in fourteenth century Cyprus. It was taken as equivalent to 3 1/2 white besants or 14 soldi of cipresi in the 1320s, Pegolotti (177) p.97; in 1372 (308) p.280; and around 1380 (178) MS 2. In the early years of the fourteenth century the anonymous author of the Venetian Tarifa noted that copper, iron, tin, lead, cotton, canvas and oil, when sold in bulk, were priced in saracen besants, and that all other commodities were priced in white besants (476) pp.23-4, 52-5. Pegolotti's observations were more or less the same in the 1320s when he was branch manager for the Bardi in Famagusta (177) p.77. The ranges of exchange values that Pegolotti put down in the form of a handy ready reckoner, and which I have quoted below, presumably include the most extreme values that could possibly be met with. I would therefore expect normal values in the 1320s to be in the middle of his range.

The Florentine florin in white besants and carats
24 carats = 1 besant

Date	Rate	Place	Type	Reference
1320s (Pegolotti)	4 b. to 5 b. 1 ct.	Cyprus	C	(177) pp.96-97
1369.05	4 besants 6 cts.	Cyprus	A	(312)
1478	5 old besants 6 cts.	Cyprus	C	(178) MS.46

The white besant in soldi and denari affiorino of Florence

Date	Rate	Place	Type	Reference
1320s (Pegolotti)	5 s. 9 d. to 7 s. 3 d.	Cyprus	C	(177) pp.96-97
1335.03	6 s. 3 d.	Florence	A	(425) pp.7 & 191
1339.05.21	6 s. 9 d.	Florence	A	(425) p.131
1340.07.13	6 s. 9 d.	Florence	A	(425) p.78
1340.08.30	7 s.	Florence	A	(425) p.152

The Venetian ducat in white besants and carats

Date	Rate	Place	Type	Reference
1320s (Pegolotti)	4 to 5 besants	Cyprus	C	(177) p.98
1372	5 besants	Cyprus	C	(308) p.280
1464	7 besants	Cyprus	C	(308) p.280

The saracen besant in Venetian soldi and denari a grossi

Date	Rate	Place	Type	Reference
(Tarifa)	40 s.	Cyprus	C	(476) p.52
1320s (Pegolotti)	36 s. 4 d. to 45 s. 6 d.	Cyprus	C	(177) p.98

The Genoese florin in white besants and carats

Date	Rate	Place	Type	Reference
1320s (Pegolotti)	4 b. 4 cts. to 5 b.	Cyprus	C	(177) pp.98-99
1382.05.18-20	4 besants 12 cts.	Famagusta	M	(121) p.654
1382.05.18-20	4 besants 22 cts.	Famagusta	M	(121) p.654
1382.05.18-20	4 besants 6 cts.	Famagusta	M	(121) p.654
1382.06.1-10	4 besants 18 cts.	Famagusta	M	(121) p.654
1382.06.20-07.03	4 besants 18 cts.	Famagusta	M	(121) p.654
1382.07.07-08.01	4 besants 18 cts.	Famagusta	M	(121) p.654
1458 (Chiarini)	5 besants	Cyprus	C	(57)

The white besant in soldi and denari of Genoa

Date	Rate	Place	Type	Reference
1307	6 s. 6 d.	Genoa	A	(187A) f.1045
1311	4 s.	Genoa	A	(187B) f.798
1311	4 s.	Famagusta	A	(187B) f.798
1315	4 s.	Genoa	A	(187B) f.798
1316	4 s. 3 d.	Genoa	A	(187B) f.798
1320s (Pegolotti)	5 s. to 6 s.	Cyprus	C	(177) pp.98-99
1331	4 s.	Genoa	A	(187B) f.798
1363	6 s. 8 d.	Genoa	A	(187B) f.798
1363	7 s.	Genoa	A	(187B) f.798

The currency of Egypt consisted of gold dinars, silver dirhams and copper fulus.

Dinars or besants

The Egyptian dinar was known to west Europeans as the besant, or besant of Alexandria, since western merchants trading with the Sultanate were more or less confined to Alexandria. The dinar or besant was divided into 24 carats. Until the mid-twelfth century gold dinars were made with great accuracy. However, at the end of the Fatimid period, the third quarter of the twelfth century, individual dinars ceased to be minted to a uniform weight, although still conforming to a fixed fineness. Dinars of variable weight continued to be minted throughout the thirteenth and fourteenth centuries. As a consequence Egyptians differentiated between the actual dinar coin, of variable weight, and the mithqāl of gold, which was the weight of gold (4.25 grams) that had been contained in earlier dinars. Italians in Egypt sometimes similarly distinguished between the two, using the name besant for the actual dinar, and peso di bisante for the mithqāl. Unfortunately they were not consistent in their terminology, and besant was frequently used for mithqāl.

By A.H. 801/1399 A.D. the Venetian ducat, introduced in enormous quantities by way of trade, had become the dominant coin in the internal economy of Mamluk Egypt and remained so for thirty years. The Mamluk sultans reacted by again coining dinars of a fixed weight. However they kept changing their minds as to what that weight should be. in A.H. 800 Faraj decided to mint dinars that weighed a mithqāl, in A.H. 810 he decided to mint dinars that weighed the same as the ducat, in A.H. 821 Shaykh reverted to the mithqāl, and finally in A.H. 827/1425 A.D. al-Ashraf Barsbai returned again to the ducat weight. Within a few years the gold dinar of 1425, known as the ashrafī, replaced the ducat as the principal gold currency of the Mamluk sultanate, and remained so until the Ottoman conquest of 922/1517. With a uniform weight of dinar the term peso di besante was no longer needed. No certainty can be attached to what sort of dinar or besant is involved in the following rates.

Dirhams

Under the Ayyubids, starting with Saladin (1171-93), the minting of silver dirhams became much more common. As a result accounting was also carried out in Egypt in terms of dirhams, which were known to west Europeans as miglioresi or millarenses. The silver dirham of the Sultanate was encountered by European merchants in Tripoli, Beirut and Alexandria, where it was regularly quoted at 18 dirhams to the florin. About 1384 Frescobaldi tells us it was exactly equal to the Venetian grosso (121) p.633. When newly minted dirhams were also allowed to vary in weight, accounting continued to be carried out in terms of standard dirhams, called by the Italian merchants pesi di miglioresi. No certainty can be attached to what sort of dirham is involved in the following rates.

The dinar in dirhams

Date	Rate	Place	Type	Reference
1323	6 dirhams	Cairo	0	(276) p.267
1339	20 dirhams	Cairo	0	(276) p.267
1339	25 dirhams	Cairo	0	(276) p.267
1340	20 dirhams	Cairo	0	(276) p.267
1342	11 dirhams	Cairo	0	(276) p.267
1342-1390s	20-30 dirhams	Cairo	0	(276) p.267
1344-1382	20 dirhams	Greater Syria	H	(13) p.35
1385.02.12-1386.02.01/787	20 dirhams	Cairo	0	(11) p.327
1386.06/788.04	23 1/3 dirhams	Cairo	0	(11) p.327
1387.01/788.11	23 1/4 dirhams	Cairo	0	(11) p.327
1387.01.22-1388/789	20 dirhams	Cairo	0	(11) p.327
1388.01.11-1388.12.31	25 dirhams	Cairo	0	(11) p.327
1388.10/790.09.24	30 dirhams	Cairo	0	(11) p.327
1389-1396/790s	20 - 17 dirhams	Cairo	0	(11) p.327
1389.12.20-1390.12.09/792	24 dirhams	Cairo	0	(11) p.327
1390.02/792.02.20	20 dirhams	Cairo	0	(11) p.327
1391.11.29-1396.11.17/794	20 dirhams	Cairo	0	(11) p.327

THE DINAR IN DIRHAMS

Date	Rate	Place	Type	Reference
1394/796.04.09	26 1/2 dirhams	Cairo	O	(11) p.327
1394/797.11.27	26 2/3 dirhams	Cairo	O	(11) p.327
1398.09.13/801.01.01	31 dirhams	Cairo	O	(11) p.327
1399/801.09.01	32 dirhams	Cairo	O	(11) p.327
1399/801 from 10.15	32 dirhams	Cairo	O	(11) p.327
1399/801 from 10.15	25 dirhams	Cairo	O	(11) p.327
1399/801 from 10.15	31 dirhams	Cairo	O	(11) p.327
1399/801.10.21	30 dirhams	Cairo	O	(11) p.327
1399/801.11.08	30 dirhams	Cairo	O	(11) p.327
1399.09.03/802.01.01	30 dirhams	Cairo	O	(11) p.327
1400/803.01.01	30 dirhams	Cairo	O	(11) p.327
1401/803.06.02	39 dirhams	Cairo	O	(11) p.328
1401/803.06.07	25 dirhams	Cairo	O	(11) p.328
1401/803.09	38 dirhams	Cairo	O	(11) p.328
1401.08.11/804.01.01	36 dirhams	Cairo	O	(11) p.328
1402.08.01/805.01.01	50 dirhams	Cairo	O	(11) p.328
1403/805.06	65 dirhams	Cairo	O	(11) p.328
1403/805.06	67 dirhams	Cairo	O	(11) p.328
1403/805.10	70 dirhams	Cairo	O	(11) p.328
1403/805.10	60 dirhams	Cairo	O	(11) p.328
1403.06.18/806.01	60 dirhams	Cairo	O	(11) p.328
1403/806.02.16	64 dirhams	Cairo	O	(11) p.328
1403/806.02.22	83 dirhams	Cairo	O	(11) p.328
1403/806.02.29	80 dirhams	Cairo	O	(11) p.328
1420/824.04	20 dirhams	Cairo	O	(11) p.334
1423/826.05	12 dirhams	Cairo	O	(11) p.335

The florin of Genoa in dirhams

Date	Rate	Place	Type	Reference
1382.05.23-28	18 dirhams	Tripoli	M	(121) p.654
1382.06.05	18 dirhams	Beirut	M	(121) p.654

The Genoese florin in millares

Date	Rate	Place	Type	Reference
1382.08.10-09.22	35 millares	Alexandria	M	(121) p.654

The ducat in dirhams

Date	Rate	Place	Type	Reference
1344-1382	18 dirhams	Greater Syria	O	(13) p.95
1389-1396/790s	17 dirhams	Cairo	O	(11) p.327
circa 1390	20 dirhams	Cairo	A	(11) App.C
1395-1399/797-802	25 dirhams	Damascus	H	(11) p.324
1396	18 dirhams	Alexandria	A	(11) p.323
1396	18 1/4 dirhams	Alexandria	A	(11) p.323
1398.09.13/801.10.11	30 dirhams	Cairo	O	(11) p.327
1399/801 from 10.15	25 dirhams	Cairo	O	(11) p.327
1399/801 from 10.15	20 dirhams	Cairo	O	(11) p.327
1399/801.10.25	24 dirhams	Cairo	O	(11) p.327
1399/801.10.25	30 dirhams	Cairo	O	(11) p.327
1399/801.11.08	28 dirhams	Cairo	O	(11) p.327
1399/802.01.01	25 dirhams	Cairo	O	(11) p.327
1400.09.03/803.01.01	29 dirhams	Cairo	O	(11) p.327
1401/803.06.02	38 dirhams	Cairo	O	(11) p.327
1401/803.09	38 dirhams	Cairo	O	(11) p.327
1401/803.09	39 dirhams	Cairo	O	(11) p.327
1401/803.09	35 dirhams	Cairo	O	(11) p.327
1401.08.11/804.01.01	34 dirhams	Cairo	O	(11) p.327
1402.08.01/805.01.01	47 dirhams	Cairo	O	(11) p.327
1403/805.06	60 dirhams	Cairo	O	(11) p.327
1403/805.10	60 dirhams	Cairo	O	(11) p.327
1403/805.10	45 dirhams	Cairo	O	(11) p.327
1403/805.11	30 dirhams	Damascus	O	(11) p.353
1403/805.11	35 dirhams	Damascus	M	(11) p.353
1403/806.07	40 dirhams	Damascus	O	(11) p.353

Date	Rate	Place	Type	Reference
1405/808.02	25 dirhams	Damascus	O	(11) p.354
1413/815.12	65 mašudi dirhams	Mecca	H	(11) p.355
1413/816	60 mašudi dirhams	Mecca	H	(11) p.355
1416/819	15 mašudi dirhams	Mecca	H	(11) p.355
1432	24 dirhams	Levant	H	(11) App.C
1442	18 1/4 dirhams	Alexandria	A	(11) p.323
1450	18-20 dirhams	Alexandria	A	(11) p.232

The dirham in Florentine soldi

Date	Rate	Place	Type	Reference
1384.10.09	4 s. 6 d.	Jerusalem	A	(11) App.C

The dirham in Venetian grossi

Date	Rate	Place	Type	Reference
1384.10.5-9	1 gr.	Cairo	A	(11) App.C
1384.11.25	1 gr.	Jerusalem	A	(11) App.C

Fulus

The dinar in fulus

Date	Rate	Place	Type	Reference
1232	45 fulus	Egypt	H	(276) p.267
1248	90 fulus	Egypt	H	(276) p.267
1248	100 fulus	Egypt	H	(276) p.267
1248	120 fulus	Egypt	H	(276) p.267
1412	230 fulus	Cairo	O	(276) p.427
1415	230 fulus	Cairo	O	(276) p.427
Barsbai(1422-37)	250 fulus	Cairo	O	(276) p.428
Barsbai(1422-37)	270 fulus	Cairo	O	(276) p.428
1430	230 fulus	Egypt	O	(276) p.429
1430(1 month later)	280-285 fulus	Cairo	O	(276) p.429
1430(after plague)	285 fulus	Cairo	O	(276) p.429
1443 ashrafi	285 fulus	Cairo	O	(276) p.432
1443 ashrafi	290 fulus	Cairo	M	(276) p.432
1458	450-460 fulus	Cairo	O	(276) p.433
1458	300 fulus	Cairo	O	(276) p.433
Late 15th century	450-460 fulus	Cairo	H	(276) p.427

The dirham in fulus

Date	Rate	Place	Type	Reference
1423 ashrafi	24 fulus	Cairo	O	(276) p.430
1429 ashrafi	20 fulus	Cairo	O	(276) p.430
1440 ashrafi	20 fulus	Cairo	O	(276) p.430
1440 ahiri	24 fulus	Cairo	O	(276) p.430

The ducat in fulus

Date	Rate	Place	Type	Reference
circa 1408	150 fulus	Cairo	H	(276) p.274
circa 1408	300 fulus	Alexandria	H	(276) p.274
1412	210 fulus	Cairo	O	(276) p.427
1415	220 fulus	Cairo	O	(276) p.427
1422	220 fulus	Cairo	O	(276) p.428
Barsbai (1422-37)	225 fulus	Cairo	O	(276) p.428
Barsbai (1422-37)	220 fulus	Cairo	O	(276) p.428
1430	230 fulus	Cairo	O	(276) p.429
1430(1 month later)	270 fulus	Cairo	O	(276) p.429
1430(after plague)	280 fulus	Cairo	O	(276) p,429

Date	Rate	Place	Type	Reference
1442	275 fulus	Cairo	M	(276) p.432

Copper or trade dirhams

The costs of defence against Timur's invasions, combined with the decline in the supply of silver from the west, brought political and financial chaos to Egypt and economic impoverishment at the same time. Amongst other consequences the system of calculation in silver dirhams also collapsed. In 1403, the silver coin ceased to be the monetary unit in which transactions were calculated, although the word 'dirham' was maintained as a technical term, all calculations for the value of money, goods and services were made in 'dirhams of copper', dirhams of fulūs. Dinars, dirhams and fulus were worth so many copper or 'trade' dirhams.

The following rates for dinars and ducats in dirhams are taken from Arabic chroniclers, many of them compiled in J.Bacharach's comprehensive thesis (11). The Arab historian's source of most of the information containing exchange rates was the Mamlūk government itself. The exchange rates for gold, silver and copper coins were established by official decree. The announcement of a rate of exchange was a newsworthy event and therefore recordable. A few incidents occur when chroniclers listed both an official transaction rate and also one for cash. Many of the following rates have been designated 'O' on the strength of the above.

The dinar in trade dirhams

Date	Rate	Place	Type	Reference
1403/806.03.01	70 dirhams	Cairo	O	(11) p.328
1403/806.04	72 dirhams	Cairo	O	(11) p.328
1403/806.05	73 dirhams	Cairo	O	(11) p.328
1404/806.08	60 dirhams	Cairo	O	(11) p.328
1404/806.09.01	90 dirhams	Cairo	O	(11) p.328
1404/806.10.04	100 dirhams	Cairo	O	(11) p.328
1404.07.10/807.01	90 dirhams	Cairo	O	(11) p.328
1404/807.02.02	100 dirhams	Cairo	O	(11) p.328
1404/807.02.21	100 dirhams	Cairo	O	(11) p.329
1404/807.02	110 dirhams	Cairo	O	(11) p.329
1404/807.04	120 dirhams	Cairo	O	(11) p.329
1404/807.05	100 dirhams	Cairo	O	(11) p.329
1404/807.10.10	130 dirhams	Cairo	O	(11) p.329
1404/807.10.10	80 dirhams	Cairo	O	(11) p.329
1404/807.10.12	130 dirhams	Cairo	O	(11) p.329
1404/807.10.12	100 dirhams	Cairo	O	(11) p.329
1404/807.10.15	130 dirhams	Cairo	O	(11) p.329
1404/807.11.02	100 dirhams	Cairo	O	(11) p.329
1405.06-1406.06/808	250 dirhams	Cairo	O	(11) p.329
1405.06.29/808 circa 01.01	150 dirhams	Cairo	O	(11) p.329
1405/808 circa 01.01	140 dirhams	Cairo	O	(11) p.329
1405/808.01.01	140 dirhams	Cairo	O	(11) p.329
1405/808.03.07	150 dirhams	Cairo	O	(11) p.329
1405/808.03.07	140 dirhams	Cairo	O	(11) p.329
1405/808.04.18	150 dirhams	Cairo	O	(11) p.329
1406/808.12	130 dirhams	Cairo	O	(11) p.329
1406.01.01	135 dirhams	Cairo	O	(11) p.330
1406.06.18/809.01.01	135 dirhams	Cairo	O	(11) p.330
1406/809.01.28	130 dirhams	Cairo	O	(11) p.330
1406/809.01.28	150 dirhams	Cairo	O	(11) p.330
1408/811.01.01	140 dirhams	Cairo	O	(11) p.330
1409/811.09.06	170 dirhams	Cairo	O	(11) p.330
1409/811.09.21	120 dirhams	Cairo	O	(11) p.330
1409/811.10	100 dirhams	Cairo	O	(11) p.330
1409/812.01	160 dirhams	Cairo	O	(11) p.330
1409/812.06.02	200 dirhams	Cairo	O	(11) p.330
1410.05.06/813.01	180 dirhams	Cairo	O	(11) p.330
1410/813.02.23	200 dirhams	Cairo	O	(11) p.330
1410/813.03.09	200 dirhams	Cairo	O	(11) p.330
1411/813.11	220 dirhams	Cairo	O	(11) p.330
1411/813 end 12	220 dirhams	Cairo	O	(11) p.330
1411/813 end 12	200 dirhams	Cairo	O	(11) p.330
1411.04.25/814.01.01	215 dirhams	Cairo	O	(11) p.330
1411/814.01.01	210 dirhams	Cairo	O	(11) p.330

THE DINAR IN TRADE DIRHAMS

Date	Rate	Place	Type	Reference
1411/814.03.06	210 dirhams	Cairo	0	(11) p.330
1411/814.03.06	220 dirhams	Cairo	0	(11) p.330
1411/814.07	225 dirhams	Cairo	0	(11) p.330
1412/814.10	230 dirhams	Cairo	0	(11) p.331
1412.04.25/815.01.01	240 dirhams	Cairo	0	(11) p.331
1412/815.02	240 dirhams	Cairo	0	(11) p.331
1412/815 from 05.01	205 dirhams	Cairo	0	(11) p.331
1413.04.03/816.01.01	250 dirhams	Cairo	0	(11) p.331
1413/816.02.01	250 dirhams	Cairo	0	(11) p.331
1413/816.08	250 dirhams	Cairo	0	(11) p.331
1414.03.23/817.01	250 dirhams	Cairo	0	(11) p.331
1414/817.02	250 dirhams	Cairo	0	(11) p.331
1414/817.02.01	250 dirhams	Cairo	0	(11) p.331
1415.05/818.02.24	250 dirhams	Cairo	0	(11) p.331
1415/818.08	260 dirhams	Cairo	0	(11) p.331
1415/818.09.24	270 dirhams	Cairo	0	(11) p.331
1416/818.11.30	280 dirhams	Cairo	0	(11) p.331
1416/818.12.25	250 dirhams	Cairo	0	(11) p.331
1416/818.12.25	280 dirhams	Cairo	0	(11) p.331
1416/818 from 12.25	250 dirhams	Cairo	0	(11) p.331
1416.04/819.02.26	290 dirhams	Cairo	0	(11) p.331
1416/819 from 02.26	270 dirhams	Cairo	0	(11) p.333
1416/819.02.28	270 dirhams	Cairo	0	(11) p.333
1416/819.03	280 dirhams	Cairo	0	(11) p.333
1416/819 from 03	230 dirhams	Cairo	0	(11) p.333
1416/819.04.13	280 dirhams	Cairo	0	(11) p.333
1416/819.04.21	250 dirhams	Cairo	0	(11) p.333
1416.06.18	250 dirhams	Cairo	0	(13) p.82
1416/819.06.16	270 dirhams	Cairo	0	(11) p.333
1416/819.07.18	250 dirhams	Cairo	0	(11) p.333
1417/819.12.25	260 dirhams	Cairo	0	(11) p.333
1417/819 from 12.25	250 dirhams	Cairo	0	(11) p.333
1417.02.23/820.01.05	250 dirhams	Cairo	0	(11) p.333
1417/820.01.06	208 1/3 dirhams	Cairo	0	(11) p.333
1417/820.01.19	250 dirhams	Cairo	0	(11) p.333
1417/820.02.04	280 dirhams	Cairo	0	(11) p.333
1417/820.04.20	280 dirhams	Cairo	0	(11) p.334
1417/820.05.09	250 dirhams	Cairo	0	(11) p.334
1418/820.11.30	280 dirhams	Cairo	0	(11) p.334
1418/820.12.03	260 dirhams	Cairo	0	(11) p.334
1418.03.12/821.02.10	280 dirhams	Cairo	0	(11) p.334
1418/821.02.10	260 dirhams	Cairo	0	(11) p.334
1418/821.02.16	230 dirhams	Cairo	0	(11) p.334
1418/821.03.15	270 dirhams	Cairo	0	(11) p.334
1420.01.17-1421.01.06/823	230 dirhams	Cairo	0	(11) p.334
1421.01.06/824.01.01	230 dirhams	Cairo	0	(11) p.334
1421/824.01.02	200 dirhams	Cairo	0	(11) p.334
1422.02.12/825.02.18	140 dirhams	Cairo	0	(11) p.335
1423/826.04.20	240 dirhams	Cairo	0	(11) p.335
1423/826.05	240 dirhams	Cairo	0	(11) p.335
1423.12.05 /827 from 12.05	250 dirhams	Cairo	0	(11) p.335
1425/828.11.27	270 dirhams	Cairo	0	(11) p.335
1427 ashrafi	214 dirhams	Cairo	0	(13) p.88
1429 ashrafi	214 dirhams	Cairo	0	(13) p88

The ducat in trade dirhams

Date	Rate	Place	Type	Reference
1403.06.18/806.01	45 dirhams	Cairo	0	(11) p.328
1403/806.02.16	more than 50 dirhams	Cairo	0	(11) p.328
1403/806.02.22	63 dirhams	Cairo	0	(11) p.328
1403/806.02.29	60 dirhams	Cairo	0	(11) p.328
1403/806.03.01	60 dirhams	Cairo	0	(11) p.328
1403/806.05	57 dirhams	Cairo	0	(11) p.328
1404/806.08	40 dirhams	Cairo	0	(11) p.328
1404/806.09.01	70 dirhams	Cairo	0	(11) p.328
1404/806.10.04	75 dirhams	Cairo	0	(11) p.328
1404/807.01	70 dirhams	Cairo	0	(11) p.328

THE DUCAT IN TRADE DIRHAMS

Date	Rate	Place	Type	Reference
1404/807.02	90 dirhams	Cairo	O	(11) p.329
1404/807.04	100 dirhams	Cairo	O	(11) p.329
1404/807.05	80 dirhams	Cairo	O	(11) p.329
1404/807.06.29	250 dirhams	Alexandria	O	(11) p.352
1405/807.10.12	80 dirhams	Cairo	O	(11) p.329
1405/807.10.10	60 dirhams	Cairo	O	(11) p.329
1405.06.29/808.01.01	120 dirhams	Cairo	O	(11) p.329
1405/808.03.07	130 dirhams	Cairo	O	(11) p.329
1405/808.03.07	120 dirhams	Cairo	O	(11) p.329
1406.06.18/809.01.01	115 dirhams	Cairo	O	(11) p.330
1407.06.08/810.01	140 dirhams	Cairo	O	(11) p.330
1409/811.09.21	100 dirhams	Cairo	O	(11) p.330
1409/812.06.07	185 dirhams	Cairo	O	(11) p.330
1410.05.06/813.01	160 dirhams	Cairo	O	(11) p.330
1410/813.02.23	180 dirhams	Cairo	O	(11) p.330
1410/813.03.09	180 dirhams	Cairo	O	(11) p.330
1411/813.11	200 dirhams	Cairo	O	(11) p.330
1411/813.12end	200 dirhams	Cairo	O	(11) p.330
1411/813.12end	180 dirhams	Cairo	O	(11) p.330
1411.04.25/814.01.01	195 dirhams	Cairo	O	(11) p.330
1411/814.01.01	190 dirhams	Cairo	M	(11) p.330
1411/814.03.06	200 dirhams	Cairo	O	(11) p.331
1411/814.07	205 dirhams	Cairo	O	(11) p.331
1412/814.10	210 dirhams	Cairo	O	(11) p.331
1412/815 from 05.01	220 dirhams	Cairo	O	(11) p.331
1413.04.03/816.01.01	230 dirhams	Cairo	O	(11) p.331
1413/816.08	230 dirhams	Cairo	O	(11) p.331
1414.03.23/817.01	230 dirhams	Cairo	O	(11) p.331
1414/817.02	230 dirhams	Cairo	O	(11) p.331
1414/817.02.01	230 dirhams	Cairo	O	(11) p.331
1415.05/818.02.24	230 dirhams	Cairo	O	(11) p.331
1415/818.08.18	250 dirhams	Cairo	O	(11) p.331
1415/818.08	240 dirhams	Cairo	O	(11) p.331
1415/818.09.24	250 dirhams	Cairo	O	(11) p.331
1416/818.11.30	260 dirhams	Cairo	O	(11) p.331
1416/818.12.25	230 dirhams	Cairo	O	(11) p.331
1416/818.12.25	260 dirhams	Cairo	O	(11) p.331
1416/818 from 12.25	230 dirhams	Cairo	O	(11) p.331
1416.03.05/819.01.05	240 dirhams	Cairo	C	(11) p.331
1416/819.01.05	250 dirhams	Cairo	C	(11) p.331
1416/819.01.05	230 dirhams	Cairo	C	(11) p.331
1416/819.02.26	290 dirhams	Cairo	C	(11) p.331
1416/819 from 02.26	250 dirhams	Cairo	O	(11) p.333
1416/819.02.28	250 dirhams	Cairo	O	(11) p.333
1416/819.03	250 dirhams	Cairo	O	(11) p.333
1416/819 from 03	210 dirhams	Cairo	O	(11) p.333
1416/819.04.13	260 dirhams	Cairo	O	(11) p.333
1416/819.04.21	230 dirhams	Cairo	O	(11) p.333
1416.06.14	230 dirhams	Cairo	O	(13) p.82
1416/819.06.16	252 dirhams	Cairo	O	(11) p.333
1416/819 from 06.16	260 dirhams	Cairo	O	(11) p.333
1416/819.07.18	230 dirhams	Cairo	O	(11) p.333
1416/819.09.09	230 dirhams	Cairo	O	(11) p.333
1417/819.12.25	230 dirhams	Cairo	O	(11) p.333
1417/819 from 12.25	230 dirhams	Cairo	O	(11) p.333
1417.02.23/820.01.05	230 dirhams	Cairo	O	(11) p.333
1417/820.02.04	260 dirhams	Cairo	O	(11) p.333
1417/820.04.20	260 dirhams	Cairo	O	(11) p.334
1417/820.05.09	230 dirhams	Cairo	O	(11) p.334
1418/820.11.30	260 dirhams	Cairo	O	(11) p.334
1418/821.02.10	260 dirhams	Cairo	O	(11) p.334
1418.03.12/821.02.10	230 dirhams	Cairo	O	(11) p.334
1418/821.02.16	210 dirhams	Cairo	O	(11) p.334
1418/821.03.15	210 dirhams	Cairo	O	(11) p.334
1418/821.08.09	210 dirhams	Cairo	O	(11) p.334
1420.01.17- 1421.01.06/823	210 dirhams	Cairo	O	(11) p.334
1421.01.06/824.01.01	210 dirhams	Cairo	O	(11) p.334
1422.02.12//825.02.18	220 dirhams	Cairo	O	(11) p.335
1423/826.12.21	220 dirhams	Cairo	O	(11) p.335
1423/826.12.21	230 dirhams	Cairo	O	(11) p.335
1423/826 from 12.21	220 dirhams	Cairo	O	(11) p.335

Date	Rate	Place	Type	Reference
1423.12.05/827	220 dirhams	Cairo	O	(11) p.335
1424.11.23/828.01.01	225 dirhams	Cairo	O	(11) p.335
1425/828.11.27	225 dirhams	Cairo	O	(11) p.335
1425.11.24/829.01.11	225 dirhams	Cairo	O	(11) p.335
1425/829.03.01	220 dirhams	Cairo	O	(11) p.335
1426.02	220 dirhams	Cairo	O	(13) p.88
1427	220 dirhams	Cairo	O	(13) p.88
1429	199-210 dirhams	Cairo	O	(13) p.88
1429.11/833.02.14	260 dirhams	Cairo	O	(11) p.336
1430/833.08	260 dirhams	Cairo	O	(11) p.336
1430.11/834.02.29	230 dirhams	Cairo	O	(11) p.336
1430/834.03.04	270 dirhams	Cairo	O	(11) p.336
1430/834.03.07	225 dirhams	Cairo	O	(11) p.336
1432.08.28/836.01.01	250 dirhams	Cairo	O	(11) p.336
1453.06.02/857.05.21	290 dirhams	Cairo	O	(11) p.336
1453.12/857.11.01	300 dirhams	Cairo	O	(11) p.336
1457.02/861.03.30	420 dirhams	Cairo	O	(11) p.336

The dirham in aspers

Date	Rate	Place	Type	Reference
1470-1471	2.85 aspers	Constantinople/Anatolia	H	(261) p.68
1470-1471	2.83 aspers	Serres	H	(261) p.68
1470-1471	2.81 aspers	Novo Brodo	H	(261) p.68
1488	3 aspers	Serbia	O	(261) p.56

The dinar or besant in other currencies

The besant in florins

Date	Rate	Place	Type	Reference
1382.04.03-08	1 1/4 florins	Alexandria	H	(11) p.324
1384.10.5-9	1 1/4 florins	Cairo	A	(11) App.C

The besant in Venetian ducats

Date	Rate	Place	Type	Reference
1384.10.5-9	1-1 1/2 ducats	Cairo	A	(11) App.C
1396	1 1/6 ducats	Alexandria	H	(11) p.324
1442	1 1/4 ducats	Alexandria	A	(11) p.322
1442	1 1/8, 1 1/3 ducats	Alexandria	A	(11) p.322

The gold dinar in tari and grani of Sicily

Date	Rate	Place	Type	Reference
1294	7 t. 10 g.	Sicily?	H	(163) p.528

The besant of Alexandria in soldi of Venice

Date	Rate	Place	Type	Reference
1290.07.25	60 s.	Venice	O	(338) no.55

The besant of Alexandria in soldi and denari of Genoa

Date	Rate	Place	Type	Reference
1156.08.17	13 s. 4 d.	Genoa-Alexandria	L	(105) no.238
1156.08.19	8 s.	Genoa-Alexandria	L	(105) no.243
1156.08.19	6 s. 5 d.	Genoa	C	(105) no.111
1156.08.20	7 s. 3 d.	Genoa-Alexandria	L	(105) no.117
1160.05.16	8 s.	Genoa-Alexandria	L	(105) no.661
1160.05.25	7 s. 8 d.	Genoa-Alexandria	L	(105) no.665

THE BESANT OF ALEXANDRIA IN SOLDI AND DENARI OF GENOA

Date	Rate	Place	Type	Reference
1160.08.17	13 s. 4 d.	Genoa-Alexandria	L	(105) no.718
1210	11 s. 5 d.	Genoa	C?	(344) p.227
1210	8 s. 7 d.	Genoa	C?	(344) p.227
1210	10 s.	Genoa	C?	(344) p.227
1210.07.19	10 s. 6 d.	Genoa-Alexandria	B	(274) no.641
1214	8 s. 10 1/2 d.	Genoa	C?	(344) p.227
1268	20 s.	Genoa	A	(187A) f.1044

The gold besant of Alexandria in sous and deniers royaux coronats of Provence

Date	Rate	Place	Type	Reference
1235.04.06	10 s.	Marseille	C	(45) no.59

The gold dinar in sueldos and dineros of Barcelona

Date	Rate	Place	Type	Reference
1285	15 s.	Barcelona	O	(163) pp.528-529
1286	15 s.	Barcelona	M	(163) pp.528-529
1292-1293 dobla	17 s. 1 d.	Barcelona	O?	(163) pp.528-529
1294	15 s.	W.Mediterranean	A	(163) p.528
1295	17 s.	Aragon	O?	(163) p.528
1304	20 s.	Barcelona?	C	(163) p.529
1307	21 s. 6 d.	Barcelona	A	(163) p.529
1308	20-21s.	Barcelona	C	(163) p.529
1309	20 s.	Barcelona	O	(163) p.529
1315-1316	20 s.	Barcelona	A	(163) p.529
1316,1317	19 s. 6 d.	Barcelona	A	(163) p.529
1318 al-Rachid	18 s. 9 d.	Barcelona	A	(163) p.529
1319	20 s.	Barcelona	A	(163) pp.528-529
1320-1321	20 s.	Barcelona	A	(163) p.529
1326-1327	20 s.	Barcelona	A	(163) p.530

The old gold besant of Alexandria in sueldos and denaros 'de terno' of Barcelona

Date	Rate	Place	Type	Reference
1299.09.03	13 s. 4 d.	Barcelona	C	(315) no.67

The gold dinar in sueldos and dineros of Valencia

Date	Rate	Place	Type	Reference
1288	14 s.	Valencia?	C	(163) p.528
1288	15 s.	Valencia?	C	(163) p.528
1302	16 s.	Sarria	C	(163) p.529

The gold dinar in sueldos and dineros of Majorca

Date	Rate	Place	Type	Reference
1310	32 s.	Majorca?	A	(163) p.530
1310	24 s.	Majorca?	A	(163) p.530
1326	21 s. 7 d.	Majorca?	A	(163) p.531
1326 al-Rachid	21 s.	Majorca?	A	(163) p.531

The gold dinar in maravedis

Date	Rate	Place	Type	Reference
1309	24 m.	Morocco	A	(163) p.529

The gold dinar in besants of Tunis

Date	Rate	Place	Type	Reference
1285	5 besants	Tunis	O	(163) p.528
1286	8 besants	Tlemcen	O	(163) p.528
1287	5 besants	Tunis	O	(163) p.528
1290	5 besants	Tunis	O	(163) p.528
1308	6 besants	Barcelona	C	(163) p.529

For the dobla in carats of Alexandria see under CASTILE p.161

SECTION XII
BARBARY (THE MAGHREB)

The besant of millarenses

In the course of the twelfth century, under the Mazmuda or Almohads, the weight of the gold dinar was so greatly reduced that in the thirteenth century the double dinar (dobra, dobla or massamutino to Europeans) became the standard gold coin of north Africa and Muslim Spain, so much so that the dinar, when encountered, came to be thought as an obol or half massamutino. At the same time as the dinar ceased to be the standard gold coin, the dinar of account became attached to the silver coin, the dirham, as a unit of ten dirhams. Europeans described this dinar of dirhams as a besant of millarenses or as a besant of silver.

After the break up of the Almohad state in the thirteenth century the successor states each had slightly different values to their moneys of account. In Pegolotti's notebook the dobla was worth 6.1/2 besants in Tripoli, 6 besants in Jerba, 12 besants at Ceuta and 6 besants and 2 to 5 millarenses at Safi (177). In Granada in 1443 the dobla was worth 12 to 12.1/2 besants (178). In all these states from Tripoli (in modern Libya) to Safi (in modern Morocco), Granada (in modern Spain) and Majorca the besant of account was always a unit of ten millarenses. Cf. Castile, where the maravedi, originally a Christian gold dinar, became a unit of account of ten silver dineros in the thirteenth century. See above p.157

TUNIS

The dobla in besants of millarenses

Date	Rate	Place	Type	Reference
1285.06.13	5 besants	Barcelona	C	(82) II p.59
Pegolotti	6 1/2 besants	Tunis	C	(177)
1348	6 besants	Tunis	C	(187B) f.761
1465	18 besants	Tunis	C	(178)

The besant of millarenses in soldi and denari of Genoa

Date	Rate	Place	Type	Reference
1191.04	4 s. 3 d.	Ceuta	B	(233) no.491
1191.09.06	5 s. 1 1/2 d.	Genoa	L	(4239 no.945
1192.03.21	4 s. 3 d.	Bougie	L	(233) no.1776
1192.09.01-05	5 s.	Bougie	C	(168) no.1
1198.11.01	4 s.	Bougie	B	(168) no.58
1198.10.13	4 s. 9 d.	Bougie	B	(168) no.125
1201.05.30	4 s. 8 d.	Genoa	L	(234) no.136
1203.09.22	5 s.	Genoa	L	(234) no.711
1203.04.28	5 s.	Ceuta	C	(234) no.895
1203.10.11	5 s.	Bougie/Ceuta	L	(234) no.913
1203.11.13	5 s. 1 1/2 d.	Bougie	B	(234) no.1017
1203.04.17	4 s. 8 1/2 d.	Ceuta	B	(274) no.233
1203.04.25	5 s.	Ceuta	B	(274) no.263
1203.05.09	4 s. 8 d.	Ceuta	B	(274) no.297
1203.05.31	5 s.	Ceuta	B	(274) no.324
1203.06.13	5 s.	Ceuta	B	(274) no.365
1203.06.25	5 s.	Bougie	B	(274) no.432
1205.05.09	4 s. 10 d.	Bougie	L	(234) no.1091
1205.05.09	5 s.	Bougie	L	(234) no.1098
1203	16 s. 8 d.	Genoa	A	(187A) f.1042
1206.03.09	4 s. 7 d.	Bougie	L	(234) no.1583
1206.03.09	4 s. 3 d.	Tunis	L	(234) no.1583
1206.03.10	4 s. 9 d.	Barbary	L	(234) no.1587
1206.03.15	5 s.	Syria	C	(234) no.1647
1206.03.21	5 s.	Ceuta	L	(4199 no.1704
1206.03.22	4 s. 10 d.	Bougie	L	(234) no.1713
1206.03.23	4 s. 10 d.	Bougie	C	(234) no.1747

THE BESANT OF MILLARENSES IN SOLDI AND DENARI OF GENOA

Date	Rate	Place	Type	Reference
1206.03.27	5 s.	Bougie	L	(234) no.1780
1206.03.29	4 s. 8 d.	Bougie	L	(4199 no.1787
1206.04.01	5 s.	Ceuta	L	(234) no.1801
1206.04.05	5 s.	Ceuta	L	(234) no.1840
1207	5 s.	Genoa	C?	(344) p.206
1210	4 s. 11 1/2 d.	Genoa	C?	(344) p.207
1210	5 s.	Genoa	C?	(344) p.207
1210	4 s. 8 d.	Genoa	C?	(344) p.207
1213	5 s.	Genoa	C?	(344) p.207
1214	4 s. 8 d.	Genoa	C?	(344) p.207
1214	5 s. 3 d.	Genoa	C?	(344) p.207
1214	8 s.	Genoa	C?	(344) p.207
1214	4 s. 3 d.	Genoa	C?	(344) p.207
1214	4 s.	Genoa	C?	(344) p.207
1214	7 s.	Genoa	C?	(344) p.207
1215	5 s.	Genoa	C?	(344) p.207
1220	4 s. 2 1/2 d.	Genoa	C?	(344) p.207
120	5 s. 4 d.	Genoa	C?	(344) p.207
1222	5 s. 3 d.	Genoa	C?	(344) p.207
1222	5 s. 1 1/2 d.	Genoa	C?	(344) p.207
1224	2 s. 6 d.	Genoa	C?	(344) p.207
1224	5 s.	Genoa	C?	(344) p.207
1224	6 s. 3 d.	Genoa	C?	(344) p.207
1224	2 s. 7 d.	Genoa	C?	(344) p.207
1224	4 s. 7 d.	Genoa	C?	(344) p.207
1226	5 s.	Genoa	C?	(344) p.208
1227	5 s.	Genoa	A	(187A) f.1042
1233	3 s. 9 d.	Genoa	C?	(344) p.208
1233	5 s.	Genoa	C?	(344) p.208
1233	4 s. 5 d.	Genoa	C?	(344) p.208
1233	4 s. 6 1/2 d.	Genoa	C?	(344) p.208
1234	4 s. 4 d.	Genoa	C?	(344) p.208
1236	4 s.	Genoa	C?	(344) p.208
1236	5 s. 6 d.	Genoa	C?	(344) p.208
1236	6 s. 11 d.	Genoa	C?	(344) p.208
1236	4 s. 3 d.	Genoa	C?	(344) p.208
1236	4 s. 8 d.	Genoa	C?	(344) p.208
1236	6 s. 8 d.	Genoa	C?	(344) p.208
1236	4 s. 4 d.	Genoa	C?	(344) p.208
1236	4 s. 8 d.	Genoa	C?	(344) p.208
1237	5 s. 6 d.	Genoa	C?	(344) p.208
1237	4 s.	Genoa	C?	(344) p.208
1237	8 s.	Genoa	C?	(344) p.208
1237	15 s. 5 d.	Genoa	C?	(344) p.208
1237	16 s. 8 d.	Genoa	C?	(344) p.208
1237	5 s. 6 d.	Genoa	C?	(344) p.208
1238	3 s. 10 d.	Genoa	C?	(344) p.208
1243	5 s. 5 d.	Genoa	C?	(344) p.208
1243	4 s. 6 1/2 d.	Genoa	C?	(344) p.208
1244	5 s.	Genoa	C?	(344) p.208
1245	6 s. 3 d.	Genoa	C?	(344) p.209
1245	4 s. 5 d.	Genoa	C?	(344) p.209
1248	4 s. 5 d.	Genoa	C?	(344) p.209
1248	3 s. 7 1/2 d.	Genoa	C?	(344) p.209
1248	6 s. 1/2 d.	Genoa	C?	(344) p.209
1248	5 s.	Genoa	C?	(344) p.209
1248	5 s. 3 d.	Genoa	C?	(344) p.209
1248	4 s. 8 d.	Genoa	C?	(344) p.209
1248	4 s.	Genoa	C?	(344) p.209
1248	4 s. 11 d.	Genoa	A	(187A) f.1043
1248	5 s. 6 d.	Genoa	A	(187A) f.1043
1248	4 s. 4 1/2 d.	Genoa	A	(187A) f.1043
1248	4 s. 8 1/2 d.	Genoa	A	(187A) f.1043
1248	5 s. 1 1/2 d.	Genoa	C?	(344) p.209
1250	4 s. 8 d.	Genoa	A	(187A) f.1043
1250	5 s.	Genoa	C?	(344) p.209
1251	4 s. 8 d.	Genoa	C?	(344) p.209
1251	4 s. 7 d.	Genoa	C?	(344) p.209
1251	2 s. 5 d.	Genoa	C?	(344) p.209
1251	4 s. 4 d.	Genoa	C?	(344) p.209
1251	4 s. 2 d.	Genoa	C?	(344) p.209
1251	6 s. 8 d.	Genoa	C?	(344) p.209

THE BESANT OF MILLARENSES IN SOLDI AND DENARI OF GENOA

Date	Rate	Place	Type	Reference
1252	3 s. 7 d.	Genoa	C?	(344) p.209
1252	5 s.	Genoa	C?	(344) p.209
1252	5 s.	Genoa	A	(187A) f.1042
1253.11.15	4 s. 7 1/2 d.	Genoa	H	(93) p.215
1253.11.22	4 s. 8 d.	Genoa	H	(93) p.215
1253	5 s. 8 1/2 d.	Genoa	C?	(344) p.209
1253	4 s. 9 d.	Genoa	C?	(344) p.209
1253	4 s. 5 d.	Genoa	C?	(344) p.209
1253	4 s. 8 d.	Genoa	C?	(344) p.209
1253	4 s. 10 1/2 d.	Genoa	C?	(344) p.209
1253	3 s. 8 d.	Genoa	C?	(344) p.209
1253	4 s. 8 d.	Genoa	C?	(344) p.209
1253	5 s.	Genoa	C?	(344) p.209
1253	4 s.	Genoa	C?	(344) p.209
1257 ad pondus maiorica	4 s. 5 d.	Genoa	A	(187A) f.1044
1264	4 s. 5 d.	Tunis	B	(187A) f.1044
1275	3 s. 10 1/2 d.	Genoa	A	(187A) f.1044
1348	6 s. 8 d.	Genoa	B	(187B) f.761

The besant of millarenses in sous and deniers royaux coronats of Provence

Date	Rate	Place	Type	Reference
1210.09.06	4 s. 5 d.	Marseille	C	(45) no.4
1211.04.02	3 s. 6 d.	Marseille	C	(45) no.5
1212.08.17	4 s. 4 d.	Marseille	C	(45) no.6
1226.02.20	4 s. 11 d.	Marseille	C	(45) no.12
1226.03.28	4 s. 7 d.	Marseille	C	(45) no.13
1227.12.24	4 s. 5 d.	Marseille	C	(45) no.17
1228.11.04	4 s.	Marseille	C	(45) no.18
1229.03.01	4 s.	Marseille	C	(45) no.19
1229.04.11	4 s.	Marseille	C	(45) no.21
1232.02.28	4 s.	Marseille	C	(45) no.28
1233.05.10	4 s.	Marseille	C	(45) no.33
1234.10.23	4 s. 2 d.	Marseille	C	(45) no.54
1235.07.31	3 s. 4 d.	Marseille	C	(45) no.67
1236.03.11	3 s. 10 d.	Marseille	C	(45) no.72
1237.05.13	3 s. 2 d.	Marseille	C	(45) no.75
1240.04.07	3 s. 9 d.	Marseille	C	(45) no.88
1242.04.08	3 s. 4 d.	Marseille	C	(45) no.93
1247.02.21	3 s. 10 d.	Marseille	C	(45) no.105

The besant of millarenses in the mixed money of Marseille

Date	Rate	Place	Type	Reference
1248.04.23	6 s.	Marseille	C	(45) no.577
1248.04.23	6 s.	Marseille	C	(45) no.592
1248.04.27	6 s.	Marseille	C	(45) no.607
1248.04.29	6 s. 1/2 d.	Marseille	C	(45) no.623
1248.05.08	5 s. 5 d.	Marseille	C	(45) no.657
1248	6 s.	Marseille	C	(45) no.862

See also the livre of mixed money of Marseille in besants and millarenses under MARSEILLE p.120

The besant of millarenses in sous and deniers tournois

Date	Rate	Place	Type	Reference
1248.05.19	16.8	Marseille	M	(45) no.737

The dinar (obol massamutino) of Tunis in soldi and denari of Genoa

Date	Rate	Place	Type	Reference
1158.10.13	4 s.	Genoa-Bougie	C	(105) no.511
1162.04.23	4 s.	Genoa-Bougie	L	(105) no.1041
1182	4 s. 5 d.	Sicily	H	(93) p.179
1182	4 s. 8 1/2 d.	Sicily	H	(93) p.179

THE DINAR OF TUNIS IN SOLDI AND DENARI OF GENOA

Date	Rate	Place	Type	Reference
1182	5 s.	Genoa	C?	(344) p.228
1182	4 s. 7 d.	Genoa	C?	(344) p.228
1182	5 s. 6 d.	Genoa	C?	(344) p.228
1184	11 s. 2 d.	Genoa	C?	(344) p.228
1191	3 s. 4 d.	Genoa	C?	(344) p.228
1191.04.11	4 s. 10 d.	Bougie	C	(233) no.604
1191.97.28	6 s.	Tunisia	L	(233) no.1836
1191-1192	4 s. 5 d.	Sicily	H	(93) p.179
1191-1192	4 s. 8 1/2 d.	Sicily	H	(93) p.179
1198	6 s. 2 d.	Genoa	A	(187A) f.1042
1216	6 s. 3 d.	Genoa	A	(187A) f.1061
1216	6 s. 4 d.	Genoa	C?	(344) p.228

The double dinar (dobla) in soldi and denari of Genoa

Date	Rate	Place	Type	Reference
1213 auri duplex	12 s. 2 1/2 d.	Genoa	A	(187A) f.1042
1313	30 s.	Genoa	B	(187B) f.761
1348	40 s.	Genoa	A	(187B) f.758
1348	31 s.	Bougie	A	(187B) f.761
1350	30 s.	Genoa	A	(187B) f.761
1410	30 s.	Genoa	A	(187B) f.761
1416	29 s.	Genoa	A	(187B) f.761

The double gold 'massamutino' in sueldos 'de terno' of Barcelona

Date	Rate	Place	Type	Reference
1268.05.22	10 s.	Barcelona	C	(315) no.24
1268.06.07	10 s.	Barcelona	C	(315) no.25

For the dinar in besants of Tunis see under EGYPT p.308

GRANADA

An entry for Granada has been included in the section on the Iberian Peninsula p.162

PAIOLA GOLD

Paiola gold featured in Mediterranean and international commerce of the thirteenth century and later. It was native gold dust from the Wangara country around the upper Niger and Senegal in Africa. Paiola gold reached Europe through Morocco and Tunis, where it circulated in sealed leather packets and was commonly weighed by the ounce (uncia). For the ounce as a weight of gold, and later as a unit of account in Sicily see above pp.59-66. For the circulation of coined gold sealed in leather packets see (500) III pp.275-6, and above pp.25-6.

The uncia of paiola gold (21 carat) in soldi and denari of Genoa

Date	Rate	Place	Type	Reference
1213	53 s.	Genoa	H	(93) p.186
1213	54 s.	Genoa	H	(93) p.186
1213	53 s.	Genoa	A	(187A) f.1028
1214	54 s. 3 d.	Genoa	H	(93) p.186
1214	55 s.	Genoa	H	(93) p.186
1244	55 s.	Genoa	A	(187A) f.1028

THE UNCIA OF PAIOLA GOLD IN SOLDI AND DENARI OF GENOA

The uncia of paiola gold (20 1/2 carat) in soldi and denari of Genoa

Date	Rate	Place	Type	Reference
1190	50 s.	Genoa	A	(187A) f.1027
1213	50 s.	Genoa	A	(187A) f.1028
1213	50 s.	Genoa	H	(93) p.186
1214	48 s. 7 d.	Genoa	A	(187A) f.1026
1214	49 s. 4 1/2 d.	Genoa	H	(93) p.186
1229	62 s.	Diano	M	(93) p.187
1237	59 s. 6 d.	Diano	M	(93) p.188
1239	50 s.	Genoa	H	(93) p.189

The uncia of paiola gold (fineness unspecified) in soldi and denari of Genoa

Date	Rate	Place	Type	Reference
1229	60 s.	Genoa	A	(187A) f.1029
1239	60 s.	Genoa	A	(187A) f.1029
1244	50 s.	Genoa	A	(187A) f.1028
1254	70 s. 3 d.	Genoa	A	(187A) f.1029

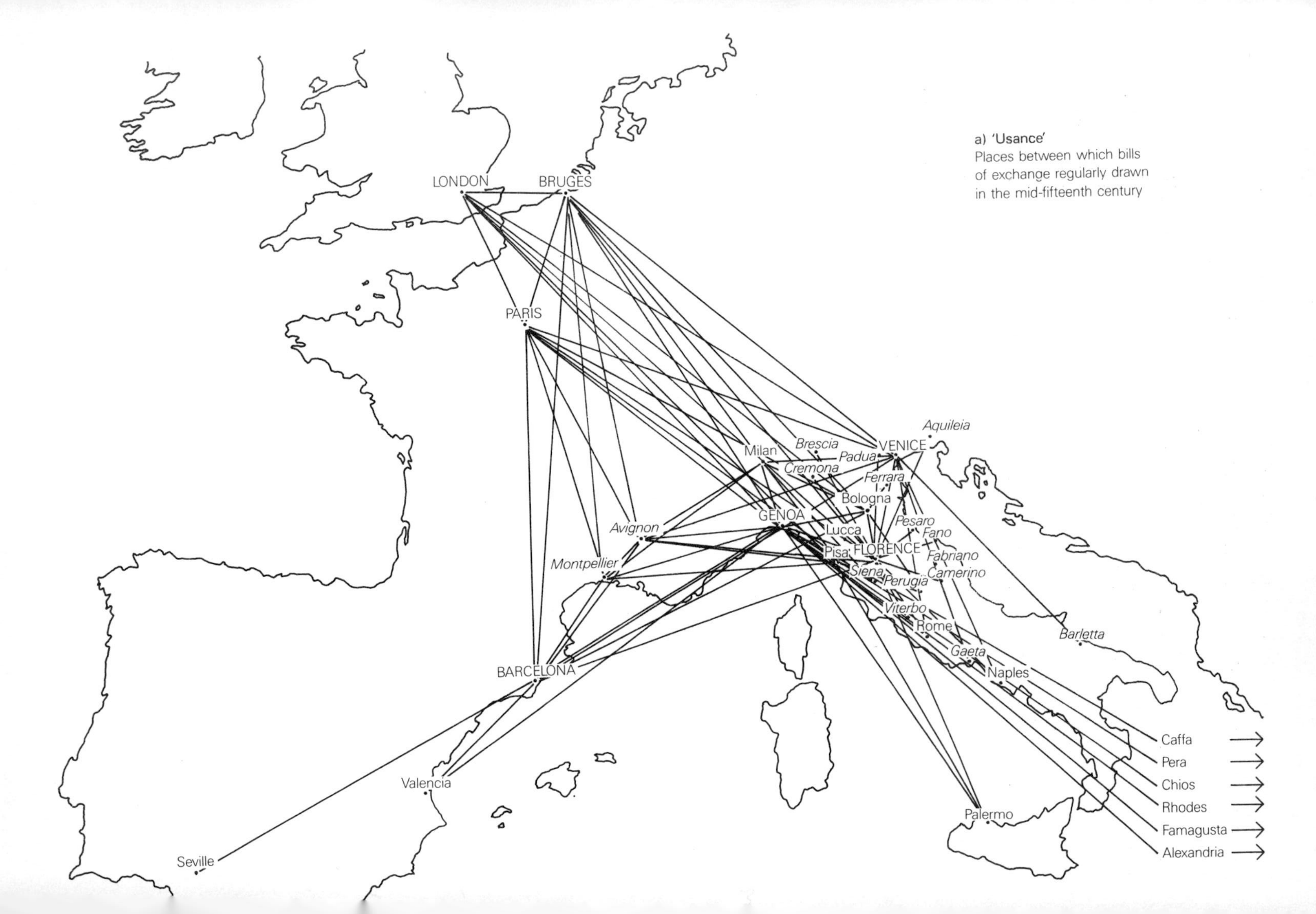

a) 'Usance'
Places between which bills of exchange regularly drawn in the mid-fifteenth century

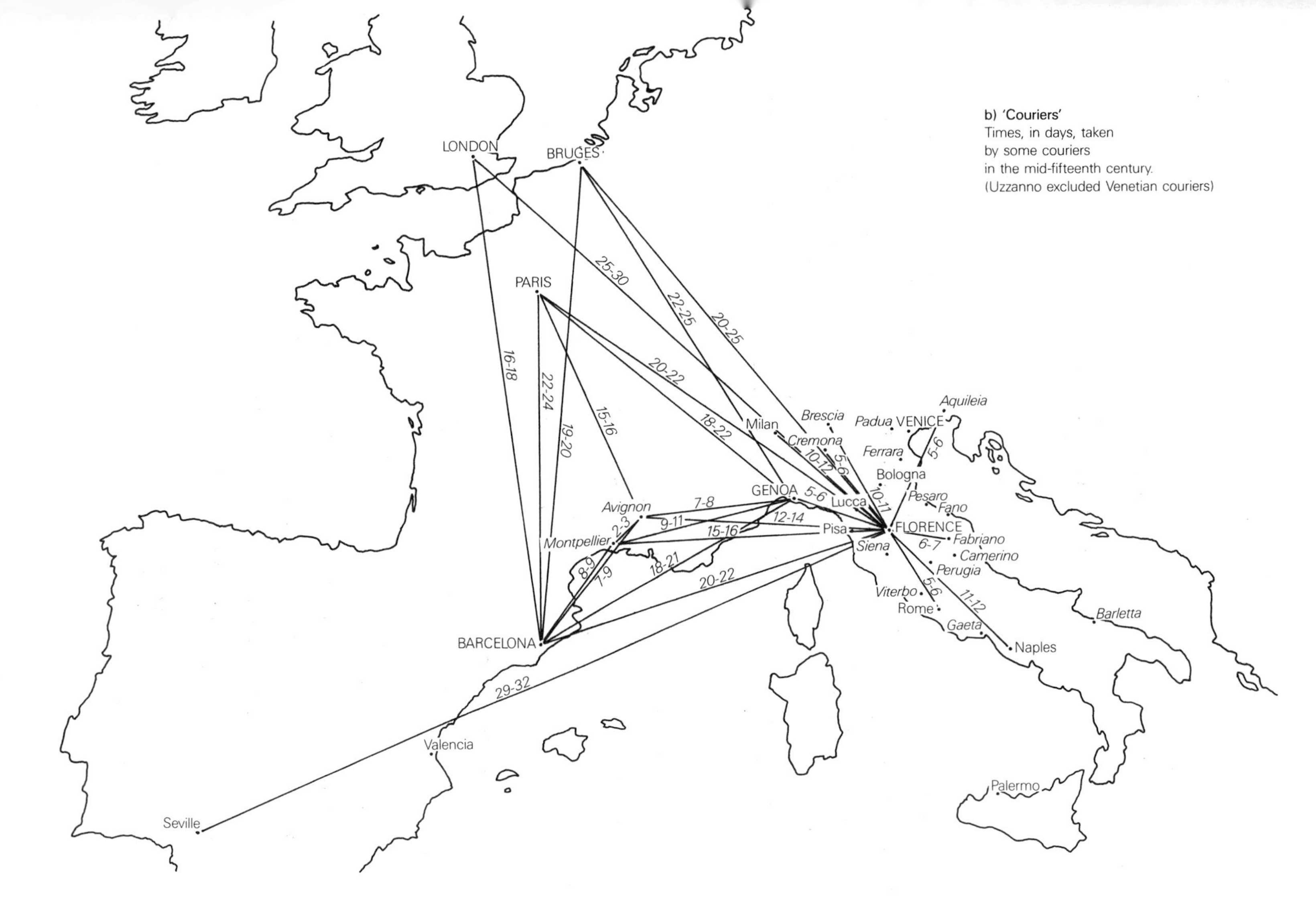

b) 'Couriers'
Times, in days, taken
by some couriers
in the mid-fifteenth century.
(Uzzano excluded Venetian couriers)

APPENDIX

USANCE AND COURIERS

Usance

Usance was the customary term at which letters of exchange from one place to another became due for payment. The terms most commonly specified were of two sorts, either, alla fata, from the original date when the bill of exchange was drawn up, or vista la lettera, from the date when the payer had sight of the bill presented to him by the payee for acceptance. The following table of terms is based on chapters 8 and 9 of the notebook compiled up to 1442 by Giovanni da Uzzano (373). Uzzano also took the trouble to note down the length of time normally taken by couriers between various places (below pp.320-1) as this gives some idea of the length of time between the drawing of a bill and its presentation.

Florence

To Pisa, 3 days from sight, and the same from Pisa.

To Genoa, 8 days from sight, and the same from Genoa.

To Avignon, 30 days from drawing, but from Avignon, 45 days from drawing.

To Montpellier, 44 days from drawing, but from Montpellier, 45 days from drawing.

To Barcelona, 2 months from drawing, and the same from Barcelona.

To Paris and Bruges, 2 months from drawing, and the same from Paris and Bruges.

To London, three months from drawing, from London, it depends on what arrangement is made (secondo i patti).

To Siena, 2 days from sight, and the same from Siena.

To Perugia, 5 days from sight, and the same from Perugia.

To Rome, 10 days from sight, and the same from Rome.

To Naples and Gaeta, 20 days from drawing, and the same from Naples and Gaeta.

To Venice, 5 days from drawing (sic), but from Venice, 20 days from drawing. (However note that under Venice, the term to and from Florence is 5 days from sight)

USANCE

To Bologna, 3 days from sight, and the same from Bologna.

To Milan, 10 days from sight, and the same from Milan.

To Palermo, 15 days from signt, but from Palermo, 30 days from drawing.

To Padua, 5 days from sight, but from Padua, 10 days from sight.

To Ferrara, 5 days from sight, and the same from Ferrara.

To Camerino, 8 days from sight, and the same from Camerino.

To Aquileia and Cremona, 10 days from sight and the same from Aquileia and Cremona.

To Fano and Pesaro, 5 days from sight, and the same from Fano and Pesaro.

To Viterbo, 10 days from sight, and the same from Viterbo.

To Lucca, (blank)

Pisa

To Genoa, 5 days from sight, and the same from Genoa.

To Avignon, 30 days from drawing, and the same from Avignon.

To Barcelona, 30 days from sight, and the same from Barcelona.

To Montpellier, 40 days from drawing, and the same from Montpellier.

To Paris and Bruges, 2 months from drawing, and the same from Paris and Bruges.

To Siena, 3 days from sight, and the same from Siena.

To Perugia, 8 days from sight, and the same from Perugia.

To Rome, 10 days from sight, and the same from Rome.

To Naples and Gaeta, 10 days from sight, and the same from Naples and Gaeta.

To Palermo, 15 days from sight, and the same from Palermo.

To Bologna, 5 days from sight, and the same from Bologna.

To Venice, 20 days from drawing, and the same from Venice.

To Milan, 10 days from sight, and the same from Milan.

To London, 3 months from drawing, and the same from London.

To Lucca, one day after sight, and the same from Lucca.

To Alexandria, 30 days from sight, and the same from Alexandria.

USANCE

Montpellier

To Barcelona, 13 days from sight, and the same from Barcelona.

To Paris, 30 days from drawing, and the same from Paris.

To Bruges, 40 days from drawing, and the same from Bruges.

Paris

To Bruges, 10 days from sight, and the same from Bruges.

To London, 1 month from drawing, and the same from London.

To Barcelona, (blank, but note, under Barcelona, term to and from Paris is 30 days from sight).

Genoa

To Venice, 10 days from sight, and the same from Venice.

To Avignon, 10 days from sight, and the same from Avignon.

To Barcelona, 20 days from sight, and the same from Barcelona.

To Valencia, 30 das from sight, and the same from Valencia.

To London, 3 months from drawing, and the same from London.

To Bologna, 15 days from sight, and the same from Bologna.

To Milan, 5 days from sight, and the same from Milan.

To Rome, 10 days from sight, and the same from Rome.

To Pisa, 5 days from sight, and the same from Pisa.

To Naples and Gaeta, 10 days from sight, and the same from Naples and Gaeta.

To Palermo, 15 days from sight, but from Palermo, 15 to 20 days from sight.

To Montpellier, 10 days from sight, but from Montpellier, 30 days from drawing.

To Paris and Bruges, 10 days from sight, but from Paris and Bruges, 2 months from drawing.

To Seville, 20 days from sight, but from Seville, 30 days from sight.

To Caffa, Famagusta and Pera, 30 days from sight, and the same from Caffa, Famagusta and Pera.

To Rhodes and Chios, 30 days from sight, and the same from Rhodes and Chios.

Milan

To Avignon, 10 days from sight, and the same from Avignon.

To Paris and Bruges, 2 months from drawing, and the same from Paris and Bruges.

To Rome, Montpellier, Bologna, Siena, and Perugia, 10 days from drawing, and the same from Rome, Montpellier, Bologna, Siena, and Perugia.

Venice

To Milan, 20 days from sight, and the same from Milan.

To Florence, 5 days from sight, and the same from Florence (but see under Florence).

To Barcelona, Paris, and Bruges, 2 months from drawing, and the same from Barcelona, Paris and Bruges.

To Naples, Barletta and Gaeta, 10 days from sight and the same from Naples, Barleta and Gaeta.

To Rome, 10 days from sight, and the same from Rome.

To London, 3 months from drawing, and the same from London.

To Pisa, 20 days from drawing, and the same from Pisa.

To Perugia, 10 days from sight, and the same from Perugia.

To Bologna, 15 days from drawing, but from Bologna, 5 days from sight. (but seen under Bologna)

To Paris and Avignon, 2 months from drawing, and the same from Paris and Avignon.

Bologna

To Venice, 15 days from sight, and the same from Venice. (but see under Venice).

To Milan, 10 days from sight, and the same from Milan.

To Barcelona, Paris and Bruges, 2 months from drawing, and the same from Barcelona, Paris and Bruges.

To Siena, 5 days from sight, and the same from Siena.

To Perugia, 8 days from sight, and the same from Perugia.

To Rome, 10 days from sight, and the same from Rome.

To Ferrara, 3 days from sight, and the same from Ferrara.

To Lucca, 5 days from sight, and the same from Lucca.

To London, 2 months from drawing, and the same from London.

Barcelona

To Paris and Bruges, 30 days from sight, and the same from Paris and Bruges.

To Valencia, 8 days from sight, and the same from Valencia.

Avignon

To Montpellier, 3 days from sight, and the same from Montpellier.

To Barcelona, 10 days from sight, and the same from Barcelona.

To Bruges and Paris, a month from drawing, and the same from Bruges and Paris.

Bruges

To London, a month from drawing.

To Barcelona, 30 days from sight, and the same from Barcelona.

Couriers

The expected length of time taken by couriers to travel from one place to another, from da Uzzano's notebook, chapter 10.

Genoa to Avignon, 7 — 8 days.

Genoa to Montpellier, 9 — 11 days.

Genoa to Barcelona, 18 — 21 days.

Genoa to Bruges, 22 — 25 days.

Genoa to Paris, 18 — 22 days.

COURIERS

Avignon to Barcelona, 7 — 9 days.

Avignon to Montpellier, 2 — 3 days.

Avignon to Paris, 15 — 16 days.

Avignon to Florence, 12 — 14 days.

Barcelona to Bruges, 19 — 20 days.

Barcelona to Paris, 22 — 24 days.

Barcelona to Montpellier, 8 — 9 days.

Barcelona to London, 16 — 18 days.

(Note that these times from Barcelona are mutually inconsistent)

Florence to London, 25 — 30 days.

Florence to Bruges, 20 — 25 days.

Florence to Milan, 10 — 12 days.

Florence to Rome, 5 — 6 days.

Florence to Brescia, 10 — 11 days.

Florence to Naples, 11 — 12 days.

Florence to Seville, 29 — 32 days.

Florence to Paris, 20 — 22 days.

Florence to Barcelona, 20 — 22 days.

Florence to Montpellier, 15 — 16 days.

Florence to Avignon, 12 — 14 days.

Florence to Genoa, 5 — 6 days.

Florence to Fabriano, 6 — 7 days.

Florence to Aquileia, 5 — 6 days.

Florence to Cremona, 5 — 6 days.

SOURCES AND BIBLIOGRAPHY

The two principal guides to sources used in preparing this Handbook have been:

POTTHAST, A. et al., Eds., Repertorium Fontium Historiae Medii Aevi, I Ser. Collectionum. Istituto Storico Italiano per il Medio Evo, Rome, 1962, supplement 1977.

and

GRIERSON, P., Bibliographie Numismatique, 2nd. ed. Cercle d'Études Numismatiques, Travaux IX. Brussels, 1979.

The identifying number of each item in this list of sources is that used, in brackets, for reference purposes throughout the Introduction and the Listings of Exchange Rates.

1 ABED AL-HUSSEIN, F.H., 'Trade and Business Community in Old Castile, Medina del Campo 1500-1575', (Ph.D. thesis) University of East Anglia, 1982.

2 ABULAFIA, D., The two Italies. Cambridge, 1977.

3 AERTS, E., 'Prof. R. de Roover and Medieval Banking History', Revue de la Banque. Brussels, 1980.

4 AMMAN, H., Ed., Mittelalterliche Wirtschaft im Alltag. Quellen zur Geschichte von Gewerbe, Industrie und Handel des 14. und 15. Jahrhunderts, aus den Notariatsregistern von Freiburg im Üchtland, 3 vols. Aarau, 1942-54.

5 ARGENTI, P., The occupation of Chios by the Genoese 1346-1566, I, 1958.

6 ARNOULD, M.A., Une estimation des revenus et des dépenses de Philippe le Bon en 1445. Brussels, 1974.

7 ARNOULD, M.A. Privately communicated by Professor Arnould from his research in the Archives départementales du Nord at Lille.

8 ASHTOR, E., Les Métaux précieux et la Balance des Payements du Proche-Orient à la basse époque. Paris, 1971.

9 ASHTOR, E., 'Banking Instruments between the Muslim East and the Christian West', Journal of European Economic History, I, 1972 pp. 553-73.

10 ASTUTI, G., Il libro dell'entrata e dell'uscita di una compagnia mercantile senese del secolo XIII, 1277-82. Documenti e Studi per la storia del commercio e del diritto commerciale italiano. V, Patetta, F. and Chiaudano, M., Eds. Turin, 1934.

11 BACHARACH, J.L., 'A study for the correlation between textual sources and numismatic evidence for Mamluk Egypt and Syria', (Ph.D Thesis) University of Michigan, 1967.

12 BACHARACH, J.L., 'Circassian monetary policy: Silver', Numismatic Chronicle, 7th Ser. XI, 1971 pp. 267-81.

13 BACHARACH, J.L., 'The Dinar versus the Ducat', International Journal of Middle Eastern Studies, IV, 1973 pp. 77-96.

14 BAETHGEN, F., 'Quellen und Untersuchungen zur Geschichte der Päpstlichen Hof- und Finanzverwaltung unter Bonifaz VIII', Quellen und Forschungen aus italienischen Archiven und Bibliotheken, XIX. Deutsche Historische Institut, Rome-Tübingen, 1928-9 pp. 114-237.

15 BAIX, Fr. and UYTTERBROUCK, A., La chambre apostolique et les 'Libri Annatarum' de Martin V. 1417-31, 3 vols. Analecta Vaticana Belgica. XIV. Institut historique Belge de Rome. Brussels-Rome, 1947-60.

16 BALARD, M., La Romanie genoise (XIIe — début du XVe siècle), 2 vols. Bibliothèque des Écoles Françaises d'Athénes et de Rome. Rome, 1978.

17 BARATIER, E. and REYNAUD, F., Histoire du commerce de Marseille II 1291-1480. Rambert, G., Ed. Paris, 1951.

18 BARATIER, E., Ed., État des droits et revenus du comte Charles Ier en Provence (1252 et 1278). Collection de Documents inédits sur l'histoire de France, 4° Ser. Bibliothèque nationale, Paris.,

19 BARTHÉLÉMY, A. DE, 'Recherches sur les origines de la monnaie tournois et de la monnaie parisis', Revue Numismatique, 4th Ser. I, 1897 pp. 153-73.

20 BASTIAN, F., Das Runtingerbuch 1383-1407 und verwandtes Material zum Regensburger-süddeutschen Handel und Münzwesen. Deutsche Handelsakten des Mittelalters und der Neuzeit, VI-VIII. Historische Kommission bei der Bayerischen Akademie der, Wissenschaften. Regensburg 1935-44.

21 BAUTIER, R-H., 'Marchands Siennois et "Draps d'Outremonts" aux foires de Champagne (1294)', Annuaire Bulletin de la société de l'Histoire de France, LXXXI, 1945 pp. 87-107.

22 BEAUREPAIRE, C. de, Ed., 'Ancien Compte de Voyage, 1285', Bulletin de la Société de l'Histoire de Normandie, III, 1884, for 1880-3, pp. 232-5.

23 BELGRANO, L.T., 'L'interesse del denaro e le cambiarli appi i Genovesi dal secoli XII al XV', Archivo storico italiano, 3rd Ser. III, pt. I, 1866 pp. 102-22.

24 BENSA, E., Francesco di Marco da Prato. Notizie e documenti sulla mercatura italiana del secolo XIV. Milan, 1928.

25 BERGHAUS, P., Währungsgrenzen des Westfälischen oberwesergebietes im Spätmittelalter. Numismatische Studien, I, Hävernick, W., Ed. Museum für Hamburgischer Geschichte, Hamburg, 1951.

26 BERGHAUS, P., 'Die Münzpolitik der deutschen Städte im Mittelalter', Finances et Comptabilité Urbaines du XIIIe au XIVe siècle. Collection Histoire, Pro Civitate, 8° Ser. VII. 1964.

27 BERGHAUS, P. I am much indebted to Professor Berghaus of Münster for permission to abstract these rates from notes that he has taken over many years in various Westphalian archives.

28 BERLIÈRE, U., Ed., Les collectoires pontificales dans les anciens diocèses de Cambrai, Thérouanne et Tournai au XIVe siècle. Analecta Vaticana Belgica. X. Institut Historique Belge de Rome. Rome Paris Bruges, 1929.

29 BERLOW, R. Privately communicated by Prof. R. Berlow from MSS in the Archives départementales of the Côte d'Or, Dijon.

30 BERNAYS, E., Histoire numismatique du comté de Namur

31 BERNOCCHI, M., Le monete della republica Fiorentina, III and IV. Documentazione arte e archeologia, Studi e Documenti 7. Florence, 1976 and 1978.

32 BERTELÉ, T., 'Moneta veneziana e moneta bizantina', Venezia e il Levante fino al secolo XV, II. Florence, 1973 pp. 1-144.

33 BIANCHINI, L., Della storia delle finanze del regno di Napoli. Palermo, 1839.

34 BIERLEIN, F.P., 'Die Bayerischen Münzen des Hauses Wittelsbach', Oberbayerisches Archiv für Vaterländische Geschichte, XXXIX. Munich, 1869-70 pp. 1-64.

35 BIGWOOD, G. and GRUNZWEIG, A., Eds., Les livres des comptes des Gallerani, 2 vols. Commission Royale d'Histoire. Académie Royale de Belgique. Brussels, 1961-2.

36 BIROCCHI, E., Zecche e monete della Sardegna nei periodi di dominazione aragonese e spagnuola. Cagliari, 1952.

37 BISCARO, G., 'Contributo alla storia del diritto cambiaro', Rivista Italiana per le Scienze Guiridiche, XXIX. Rome, 1900 pp. 189-99.

38 BISCARO, G., 'Il banco Borromei e compagno di Londra 1436-1439', Archivio storico Lombardo, 4th Ser. XIX, 1913 pp. 37-126.

39 BISSON, T. N., Conservation of Coinage. Oxford, 1979.

40 BIZZARRI, D., Ed., Liber imbreviaturarum Appulliesis notarii comunis Senarum 1221-23. Imbreviature Notarili, 2 vols. Documenti e Studi per la storia del commercio e del diritto commerciale italiano. IV, Patetta, F. and Chiaudano, M., Eds. Turin, 1933.

41 BIZZARI, D. and CHIAUDANO, M., Eds., Liber Imbreviaturum Ildibrandini notarii 1227-29. Imbreviature Notarili, 2 vols. Documenti e studi per la storia del commercio e del diritto commerciale italiano. IX, Patetta, F. and Chiaudano, M., Eds. Turin, 1938.

42 BLANC, A., Le livre de comptes de Jacme Oliver, marchand narbonnais du XIVe siècle, II. Paris, 1899.

43 BLANCARD, L., Essai sur les monnaies de Charles Ier, comte de Provence. Paris, 1868-79.

44 BLANCARD, L., 'Note sur la lettre de change à Marseille', Bibliothèque de l'école des Chartes, XXXIX, 1878 pp. 110-128.

45 BLANCARD, L., Documents inédits sur le commerce de Marseille au Moyen Âge édités intégralement ou analysés, I & II. Amalric register. Marseille, 1884-5.

46 BLANCHET, A. and DIEUDONNÉ, A., Manuel de Numismatique Française, II Monnaies Royales, IV Monnaies Féodales, 1916 and 1936.

47 BLOMQVIST, T., 'Lucchese exchange rates in the 13th and 14th centuries. Paper presented to the XVIIIth International Conference on Medieval Studies', Michigan, 1983.

48 BLOMQVIST, T. Privately communicated from the LL series in the capitular archive of Lucca.

49 BOLLATI DI SAINT PIERRE, F., Illustrazioni della spedizione in Oriente di Amadeo VI. Il conte verde. Biblioteca Storica Italiana, V. 1900.

50 BOMPAIRE, M., 'L'Atelier monétaire royal de Montpellier et la circulation monétaire en Bas Languedoc jusqu'au milieu du XVe siècle', (Thesis) École Nationale des Chartes, Paris, 1980.

51 BOMPAIRE, M., 'La Monnaie de Pont-de-Sorgues dans la première moitié du XIVe siècle', Revue Numismatique, 6th Ser. XXV, 1983 pp. 139-76.

52 BOMPAIRE, M., 'La Monnaie comtale de Blois au début du XIVe siècle', Bulletin de la Société Française de Numismatique, XXXIX, 1984 pp. 460-4.

53 BOMPAIRE, M. Privately communicated by M. Marc Bompaire of the Cabinet des Médailles in Paris.

54 BOREL, F., Les foires de Genève au XVe siècle. Geneva, 1892.

55 BORLANDI, A., Ed., Il Manuale di Mercatura di Saminiato de' Ricci, Istituto di Storia Medievale e Moderno, University of Genoa, Fonti et Studi IV. Genoa, 1963.

56 BORLANDI, A., 'Moneta e congiuntura a Bologna 1360-1364', Bullettino dell'Istituto Storico Italiano per il medio evo e Archivio Muratoriano, LXXXII, 1970 pp. 391-478.

57 BORLANDI, F., Ed., Il libro de mercatantie et usanze de' paesi. Documenti e Studi per la Storia del Commercio e del Diritto Commerciale Italiano. VII, Patetta, F. and Chiaudano, M., Eds. Turin, 1936.

58 BORMANS, S., Recueil des Ordonnances de la Principauté de Liège. Première série. Brussels, 1878.

59 BOSCOLO, A., Documenti inediti sui traffici commerciali tra la Liguria e la Sardegna nel secolo XIII. 1957.

60 BOSCOLO, A., Documenti inediti relativi ai rapporti economici tra la Sardegna e Pisa nel Medioevo, 2 vols, 1961-2.

61 BOSSJAT, A., 'Une enquête sur la monnaie de Clermont à la fin du XIIIe siècle', Bulletin philologique et historique. Comité des travaux historiques et scientifiques. 1942 pp. 1-21.

62 BOUGARD, P. and WYFFELS, C., Les finances de Calais au XIIIe siècle. Collection Histoire, Pro Civitate, 8° Ser. VIII. Brussels, 1966.

63 Bourgeois of Paris trans. J. Shirley, A Parisian Journal 1405-49. Oxford, 1968.

64 BOWSKY, W.M., A medieval Italian commune — Siena under the Nine 1287-1355. London, 1981.

65 BRANDT, A. VON, 'Die gesellschaftliche Struktur des spätmittelalterlichen Lübeck', Vorträge und Forschungen. Konstanzer Arbeitskreis für Mittelalterliche Geschichte, XI, 1963-4 pp. 215-39.

66 BRIDGE, J.S.C., A history of France. Oxford, 1921.

67 BROM, G., Archivalia in Italië. 's Rijks Geschiedkundige Publicatien. Small Ser., II pt. I. 1908-14.

68 BROUETTE, E., Ed., "Libri Annatarum" pour les pontificats d'Eugène IV à Alexandre VI, IV, 1484-1503. Analecta Vaticana Belgica 1st Ser. XXIV. Institut Historique Belge de Rome. Brussels Rome, 1963.

69 BROWN, E. Privately communicated by Professor Elisabeth Brown of the City University of New York, from Manuscripts in the Bibliothèque nationale in Paris, the Bibliothèque municipale in Rouen, the Archives nationales in Paris, the Archives départementales of

Aveyron and Lot and the Archives communales of Martel, Millau and Perigueux.

70 BROWN, R.P., 'Social Development and Economic Dependence: Northern Sardinia, C. 1100-1330', (Ph.D. Thesis) University of Cambridge, 1985.

71 BRUCKER, G., Ed., Two Memoirs of Renaissance Florence. New York, 1967.

72 BRULEZ, W., De Firma della Faille en de internationale handel van vlaamse firmas in de 16e eeuw. Brussels, 1959.

73 BRUTAILS, J-A., Documents des Archives de la Chambre des comptes de Navarre 1196-1394. Paris, 1890.

74 BUNTINX, J., Het Memorial van Jehan Makiel. Brussels, 1944.

75 CAHN, J., Münz-und Geldgeschichte der Stadt Strasburg im Mittelalter. Strasburg, 1895.

76 CALAND, F., 'Bouwstoffen voor eene Geschiedenis van het Nederlandsche Geld en Muntwezen', Tijdschrift van het Koniklijk Nederlandsch Genootschap voor Munt- en Penningkunde, IX, 1901 pp. 355-66.

77 Calendar of State Papers Milanese. I. Public Record Office. London, 1912.

78 Calendar of State Papers Venetian. Public Record Office. London, 1864-1947.

79 Calendar of the Close Rolls 1313-81. Public Record Office. London, 1893-1914.

80 Calendar of the Patent Rolls. Public Record Office. London.,

81 CAMERANI MARRI, G., I documenti commerciali del Fondo Diplomatico Mediceo nell'archivio di Stato di Firenze (1230-1492). Florence, 1951.

82 CAPMANY Y DE MONPALAU, A. DE, Memorias historicas, sobre la Marina, Comercio, y Artes de la Antiqua Ciudad de Barcelona, 4 vols. Madrid, 1779-92.

83 CAPOBIANCHI, V., 'Il denaro pavese e il suo corso in Italia nel XII secolo', Rivista Italiana di Numismatica, IX, 1896 pp. 21-60.

84 CAPRA, P.J., 'Recherches sur la valeur des monnaies dans le Bordelais au temps de la lieutenance du Prince Noir 1354-7', Bulletin philologique et historique. Comité des travaux historiques et scientifiques. 1957 pp. 417-563.

85 CAPRA, P.J., 'Le Léopard et le Guyennois d'or, monnaie d'Aquitaine.', Annales du Midi LXXII, 1960.

86 CAPRA, P.J., 'L'histoire monétaire de l'Aquitaine anglo-gasconne aux temps du Prince Noir 1354-1372', Bulletin et Mémoires de la Société d'Archéologie de Bordeaux, LXIV, 1968.

87 CAPRA, P.J., 'Pour une histoire de la monnaie Anglo-Gasconne', Annales du Midi, LXXXVII, 1975 pp. 405-30.

88 CAPRA, P.J., 'Les espèces, les ateliers, les frappes et les émissions monétaires en Guyenne anglo-gasconne aux XIVe et XVe siècles', Numismatic Chronicle, 7th Ser. XIX, 1979 pp. 139-53.

89 CARABELLESE, F., 'Un nuovo libro di mercanti alle fiere di Sciampagna', Archivio storico italiano. 1894.

90 CARPENTIER, E., Une ville devant la peste; Orvieto et la peste noire de 1348. Paris, 1962.

91 CARRÈRE, C., Barcelone, centre économique à l'époque des difficultés 1380-1460, 2 vols. Civilisations, Sociétés V. École Pratique des Hautes Études, VIe section. Paris, 1967.

92 CASALINI, E.M., Condizioni economiche a Firenze negli anni 1286-9. Studi Storici dell'Ordine dei Servi di Maria IX, 1959. Rome, 1960.

93 CASARETTO, P.F., La moneta genovese in confronto con le altre valute mediterranee nei secoli XII e XIII. Atti della Società ligure di Storia Patria, LV. 1928.

94 CASINI, B., 'Il corso dei cambi tra il fiorino e la moneta di piccioli a Pisa dal 1252 al 1500.', Studi sugli strumenti di scanbio a Pisa nel medioevo. Garzella, P., Ed. Pisa, 1979.

95 CASSANDRO, G., 'Vicende storiche della lettera di cambio', Bolletino dell'Archivio storico del Banco di Napoli, IX-XII. Naples, 1955-6 pp. 1-91.

96 CASTELLANI, A., Nuovi Testi Fiorentini del Dugento, 2 vols. Florence, 1952.

97 CASTELLIN, K., Grossus Pragensis. Der Präger Groschen und seine Teilstücke. 1300-1547, 2nd ed. Brunswick, 1973.

98 CASTER, G., Le commerce du pastel et de l'épicerie à Toulouse de 1450 environs à 1561. Mémoires et Documents publiés par la Société de l'École de Chartes. 1962.

99 CAUWENBERGHE, E. VAN and IRSIGLER, F., Minting, Monetary Circulation and Exchange Rates. Trierer Historische Forschungen, VII. Trier, 1984.

CAUWENBERGHE see also VAN CAUWENBERGHE

100 CAZELLES, R. privately communicated by Dr Raymond Cazelles from MSS Paris, Archives nationales, KK7 Finance des Lombards dans le duché de Bourgogne.

101 CESSI, R., Problemi monetari veneziani fino a tutto il secolo XIV. Documenti finanziari della Repubblica di Venezia. 4th Ser. I. Accademia Nazionale dei Lincei. Padua, 1937.

102 CHAUVIN, M., Les comptes de la châtellenie de Lamballe (1387-1482). Paris, 1977.

103 CHIAUDANO, M., 'I Rothschild del Duecento. La Gran Tavola di Orlando Bonsignori', Bulletino senese di Storia Patria, New Ser. VI, 1935 pp. 103-42.

104 CHIAUDANO, M., 'La moneta di Genova nel secolo XII', Studi in Onore di Armando Sapori, I. Milan, 1957 pp. 189-214.

105 CHIAUDANO, M. and MORESCO, M., Ed., Il cartolare di Giovanni Scriba. 1154-64, 2 vols. Documenti e studi per la storia del commercio e del diritto commerciale italiano. I, II, Patetta, F. and Chiaudano, M., Eds. Turin, 1935, also in Regesta Chartarum Italie, Istituto Storico Italiano per il medio evo, Rome.

106 CHIAUDANO, M. and MOROZZO DELLA ROCCA, R., Ed., Oberto Scriba de Mercato, 1190, 1186, 2 vols. Notai liguri del secolo XII., I, IV. Turin, 1938-40.

107 CHMEL, J., Ed., Der Österreichische Geschichtsforschen, 2 vols. Vienna, 1838-41.

108 CIAMPI, I., Chronache e statuti della città di Viterbo. Documenti di Storia Italiana. V. Florence, 1872.

109 CIANO, C., Ed., 'La Pratica di Mercatura' Datiniana. Biblioteca della Rivista 'Economia e Storia', IX. Milan, 1964.

110 CIBRARIO, L., Della economia politica del medio evo. Turin, 1842.

111 CIPOLLA, C.M., Studi di storia della moneta I: I movimenti dei cambi in Italia dal secolo XIII al XV. Pubblicazioni della Università di Pavia, 101. Studi nelle Scienze guiridiche e sociale. Pavia, 1948.

112 CIPOLLA, C.M., Le avventure della lira. Milan, 1958.

113 COLLIN, H., 'Le compte de la construction de la maison forte du duc de Bar a Pont-a-Mousson de 1395 à 1398', Bulletin philologique et historique. Comité des travaux historiques et scientifiques. 1966 pp. 366-409.

114 Constructions civiles d'intérêt publique dans les villes, d'Europe au Moyen Âge et sous l'Ancien Régime et leur financement. Colloque International, Actes. Collection Histoire, Pro Civitate, 8° Ser., XXVI. Brussels, 1971.

115 CUMONT, G., 'Les monnaies dans les chartes du Brabant', Annales de la Société royale d'archéologique de Bruxelles, XV, 1901 pp. 5-14.

116 CUMONT, G., 'Étude sur les cours des monnaies en Brabant.', Annales de la Société royale d'archéologie de Bruxelles, XVI, 1902 pp. 93-159.

117 D'ARIENZO, L., Documenti sui Visconti di Narbona e la Sardegna. Padua, 1977.

118 DAVIDSOHN, R., Forschungen zur älteren Geschichte von Florenz, 4 vols. Berlin, 1896-1908.

119 DAVISO DI CHARVENSOD, M.C., I Pedaggi delle Alpi Occidentali nel Medio Evo. Miscellanea di storia italiana 4th. Ser. V. Deputazione Subalpina di Storia Patria, Turin, 1961.

120 DAY, J., 'I conti privati della famiglia Adorno 1402-8', Miscellanea di Storia Ligure. Fonti e Studi I. Istituto di Storia Medievale e Moderno. University of, Genoa 1958.

121 DAY, J., 'Prix agricoles en Méditerranée à la fin du XIVe siècle 1382', Annales Économies Sociétés Civilisations, XVI, 1961 pp. 629-56.

122 DAY, J., Les douanes de Gênes, 1376-7. Paris, 1963.

123 DAY, J., 'The decline of a money economy; Sardinia in the late Middle Ages', Studi in memoria di F. Melis, III. Naples, 1978 pp. 155-76.

124 DAY, J., Ed., Études d'Histoire Monétaire. Lille, 1984 includes relevant essays by R. Mueller, pp. 195-219; P. Roqué, pp. 221-47; J. Munro, pp. 263-94; N. Morard, pp. 295-334; and P. Spufford, pp. 355-95.

125 DAY, J. Privately communicated by Dr John Day from a variety of Genoese documents.

126 DE BOÜARD, M., 'Problèmes de Subsistances dans un état médiéval: Le marché et les prix des céréales au royaume angevin de Sicile (1266-82)', Annales d'Histoire, Économique et Sociale, X, 1938 pp. 483-

501.

127 DELISLE, L., Actes normands de la chambre des comptes sous Philippe de Valois. Société de l'Histoire de Normandie. 1871.

128 DELISLE, L., Mémoire sur les opérations financières des templiers. Mémoires de L'Institut National de France. CCCXXXIII, pt. 2. Académie des Inscriptions et Belles Lettres. Paris, 1888.

129 DEL TREPPO, M., I mercanti Catalani e l'espansione della corona de Aragona nel secolo XV. Documentos de Cultura X. Barcelona, 1976.

130 DE MADDALENA, A. Privately communicated by Professor Aldo De Maddalena of the Bocconi University of Milan from Archivio Saminiato, Guasconi, Pazzi. MS.1. Istituto di Storia Economica, Università Luigi Bocconi, Milan.

131 DE MARCHÉVILLE, M., 'Le Denier d'or à la reine', Revue Numismatique, 1889 pp. 567-95.

132 DEMEYER, G.M., 'Introduction', De stadrekeningen van Deventer, V, 1979.

133 DE ROOVER, R., Money, Banking and Credit in Medieval Bruges. Cambridge, Mass., 1948.

134 DE ROOVER, R., L'évolution de la lettre de change (XIVe — XVIIIe siècles). Paris, 1953.

135 DE ROOVER, R., 'New Interpretations of the History of Banking', Journal of World History, II. 1954, reprinted in his selected studies Business, Banking, and Economic Thought in Late Medieval and Early Modern Europe, Chicago, 1974

136 DE ROOVER, R., 'The Development of Accounting prior to Luca Pacioli', Studies in the History of Accounting. Littleton, A.C. and Yamey, B.S., Eds. London, 1956.

137 DE ROOVER, R., The Rise and Decline of the Medici Bank, 1397-1494. Cambridge, Mass., 1963.

138 DE ROOVER, R., The Bruges Money Market around 1400. Verhandelingen van de Koninklijk Vlaamse Academie van Wettenschapen, Letteren en Schone Kunsten von Belgie. Klasse de Letteren LXIII. Brussels, 1968.

139 DE ROOVER, R., 'Le Marché monétaire à Paris du règne de Philippe le Bel au début du XVe siècle', Académie des Inscriptions et Belles Lettres, Comptes Rendus. 1968.

140 DE ROOVER, R., 'Le marché monétaire au moyen âge et au début des temps modernes', Revue Historique, CCXLIV, 1970 pp. 5-40.

141 DE ROOVER, R., 'Renseignements complémentaires sur le marché monétaire à Bruges au XIVe et au XVe siècle', Handelingen van het Genootschap "Société d'Emulation" te Brugge, CIX, 1972.

142 DE ROOVER, R. Abstract made by Raymond de Roover, now in the Library of the American Numismatic Society from Medici Account Books in the Harvard Business School Library.

143 DESIMONI, C. and BELGRANO, L.T., Documenti riguardanti le relazione di Genova col Brabante, la Fiandra e la Borgogna. Atti della Società ligure di Storia Patria. V, fasc. 3. Genoa, 1871.

144 DESIMONI, C., Ed. G. Pesce, 'Schede numismatiche de Cornelio Desimoni', Atti della Società ligure di Storia Patria, New Ser. XII, 1972 pp. 155-85 and 517-47.

145 DES MAREZ, G., La lettre de foire à Ypres au XIIIe. siècle. Contribution à l'étude des papiers de credit. Académie Royale de Belgique. Mémoire LX. Brussels, 1901.

146 DES MAREZ, G. and DE SAGHER, E., Comptes de la ville de Ypres 1267-1329, I. Brussels, 1909.

147 DEVAILLY, G., Le Berry du Xe siècle au milieu du XIIIe. Paris, 1973.

148 DE VIENNE, M., 'La livre de Parisis et la livre de Tournois; origine et établissement d'une proportion permanente entre ces deux unités', Annuaire de la Societé Française de Numismatique, XX, 1896 pp. 425-464.

149 DE VIENNE, M., 'Éclaircissements sur les monnaies d'Alphonse X de Castille', Revue Numismatique, 4th Ser. III, 1899.

150 DHONDT, J., Finances et Comptabilité Urbaines du XIIIe au XVIe siècle. Collection Histoire, Pro Civitate, 8° series, VII. Brussels, 1964.

151 DIEUDONNÉ, A., 'Les variations monétaires sous Philippe le Bel', Le Moyen Âge. 1905 pp. 217-57.

152 DIEUDONNÉ, A., 'Le Livre de Raison de Guillaume d'Ercuis', Revue Numismatique, 4th Ser. X, 1906 pp. 62-75.

153 DOEHAERD, R., 'Les galères génoises dans la Manche et la mer du Nord à la fin du XIIIe et au début du XIVe siècles', Bulletin du l'Institut historique Belge de Rome, XIX, 1938 pp. 5-76.

154 DOEHAERD, R., Relations commerciales entre Gênes, la Belgique et l'Outremont d'après les archives notariales génoises. Études d'histoire économique et sociale. II-V. Institut historique belge de Rome. Brussels Rome, 1941-52.

155 DOEHAERD, R., 'Chiffres d'assurance à Gênes en 1427-28', Revue Belge de Philologie et d'Histoire, XXVII, 1949 pp. 736-53.

156 DOLLEY, M., 'Anglo-Irish Monetary Policies, 1172-1637', Historical Studies. Papers read before the Irish Conference of Historians, VII. London, 1969 pp. 45-64.

157 DORINI, V. and BERTELÉ, T., Ed., Il libro dei conti di Giacomo Badoer 1436-40. Libreria dello Stato. Rome, 1956.

158 DOUCET, R., 'Livres tournois et livres sterling pendant l'occupation anglaise sous Charles VI et Charles VII', Revue Numismatique, 4th Ser. XXIX, 1926 pp. 102-5.

159 DOUËT D'ARCQ, L., Ed., Comptes de l'argenterie des rois de France au XIVe siècle. Société de l'Histoire de France. 1851.

160 DOUËT D'ARCQ, L., Ed., Comptes de l'Hotel des Rois de France aux XIVe et XVe siècles. Société de l'Histoire de France. 1865.

161 DOUËT D'ARCQ, L., Ed., Nouveau recueil de comptes de l'argenterie des rois de France. Société de l'Histoire de France. 1874.

162 DU CANGE, C., Glossarium Mediae et Infimae Latinitatis, 10 vols. Fèvre, L., Ed. Niort, 1883-7.

163 DUFOURCQ, Ch. E., L'Espagne catalane et le Maghrib aux 13e et 14e siècles. Bibliothèque de l'école des hautes études hispaniques, XXXVII. 1966.

164 DUMAS, F., 'Les Monnaies Normandes (X^{e}-XIIe siècles)', Revue Numismatique, 6th Ser. XXI, 1979 pp. 84-103.

165 DUMAS, F. and BARRANDON, J.-N., 'Le titre et le poids de fin des monnaies sous le règne de Philippe Auguste (1180-1223)', Cahiers Ernest-Babelon, I, 1982.

166 EBELING, D. and IRSIGLER, I., Getreideumsatz, Getreide- und Brotpreise in Köln 1368 - 1797. Mitteilungen an den Stadtarchiv von Köln LXV. Cologne, 1976.

167 EICHHORN, H., Der Strukturwandel im Geldumlauf Frankens zw. 1437 u. 1610. Vierteljahrschrift für Sozial- und Wirtschaftsgeschichte, Beiheft LVIII. 1973.

168 EIERMAN, J.E., KRUEGER, H.G., REYNOLDS, R.L., Ed., Bonvillano 1198. Notai liguri del secolo XII., III. Turin, 1939.

169 ELSAS, J., Umriss einer Geschichte der Preise und Löhne in Deutschland, 3 vols. Leiden, 1939-49.

170 ENDEMAN, W., Studien in der romanisch-kanonistischen Wirtschafts- und Rechtslehre bis gegen Ende des XVII. Jahrhunderts. Berlin, 1874.

171 ENGEL, A. and SERRURE, R., Traité de numismatique du Moyen Âge, 3 vols. Paris, 1891-1905 reprinted Bologna 1964.

172 ENNEN. L., Die Geschichte der Stadt Köln. Cologne and Rienz, 1863-5.

173 ENNO VAN GELDER, H., 'Les plus anciens tarifs monétaires illustrés des Pays-Bas', Centennial publication of the American Numismatic Society. Ingholt, H., Ed. New York, 1958 pp 239-72.

174 ENNO VAN GELDER, H., 'Münzvalvation in Deventer und Dortmund 1488/89', Dona Numismatica Walter Hävernick. Berghaus, P. and Hatz, G., Eds. Hamburg, 1965 pp.281-300.

175 ENNO VAN GELDER, H. Privately communicated by Professor Enno van Gelder from the unpublished accounts of the Treasurer of Holland. The Hague, Algemeen Rijks Archief, MSS Rekenkamer 54-133.

176 ENNO VAN GELDER, H. Privately communicated by Professor Enno van Gelder from the unpublished municipal accounts of Deventer.

177 EVANS, A., Ed., Francesco Balducci Pegolotti La Pratica Della Mercatura. Medieval Academy of America XXIV. Cambridge, Mass., 1936.

178 EVANS, A. Notes on medieval merchants' notebooks, with transcripts of 55 texts, in the library of the American Numismatic Society, New York. I am grateful to the American Numismatic Society for permission to draw freely on this material, and to Dr Alan Stahl for making it so agreeable to work on it.

179 FABRE, M.P., Ed., Liber Censum, 3 vols. Bibliothèque des Écoles françaises d'Athènes et de Rome. 2nd Ser. VI. Paris, 1905-52.

180 FARAGLIA, N.F., Storia dei prezzi in Napoli dal 1131 al 1860. Naples, 1878.

181 FAVIER, J., 'Les monnaies des pays avignonnais du grand schisme', Bulletin de la Société nationale des Antiquaires de France. Paris, 1962.

182 FAVIER, J., Les finances pontificales à l'époque du Grand Schisme d'Occident 1378-1409. Bibliothèque des Écoles françaises d'Athènes et de Rome. CCXI. 1966.

183 FAVIER, J., Finance et Fiscalité au bas moyen âge. Paris, 1971.

184 FAWTIER, R. and LANGLOIS, Ch-V., Eds., Comptes du Trésor 1296, 1316, 1384, 1477. Documents Financiers II. Recueil des historiens de la

France. Académie des Inscriptions et Belles Lettres. Paris, 1930.

185 FAWTIER, R. and MAILLARD, F., Eds., Comptes Royaux 1285-1314. Documents Financiers III. Recueil des historiens de la France. Académie des Inscriptions et Belles Lettres. Paris, 1953-4.

186 FELLONI, G. Privately communicated by Professor Giuseppe Felloni of the University of Genoa.

187 FELLONI, G. Richerio MSS, 18th. century selections from early notarial deeds of Genoa. Kindly procured by Prof. G. Felloni from the Archivio di Stato di Genova. MSS nos. 534 and 539. MS 534 = (187A). MS 539 = (187B).

188 FILANGIERI, R., Testi e Documenti di Storia Napoletana; I Registri della cancelleria Angioina XVIII 1272-73. 1957.

189 FINOT, J., Relations commerciales entre la France et la Flandre au moyen âge. Paris, 1894.

190 FLYNN, V.J., 'Englishmen in Rome during the Renaissance', Modern Philology, XXXVI, 1938 pp. 121-38.

191 FORESTIÉ, E., 'Les livres des comptes des frères Bonis, marchands Montalbanais du XIVe siècle', Archives historiques de la Gascoyne, 1st Ser. XX, XXIII, XXVI, 1890, 1893, 1894.

192 FOURNIAL, E., 'L'indexation des créances et des rentes au XIVe siècle', Le Moyen Âge, 4th Ser. XVIII, 1963 pp. 538-96.

193 FOURNIAL, E., Les villes et l'économie d'échange en Forez aux XIIIe et XIVe siècles. Paris, 1967.

194 FOURNIAL, E., Histoire Monétaire de l'Occident Médiéval. Paris, 1970.

195 FOURNIER, P.F. and GUÉBRIN, P., Enquêtes administratives d'Alfonse de Poitiers. Arrêts de son parlement tenu à Toulouse. 1249-1271. Paris, 1959.

196 FRANCK, J., Ed., 'Die Chronik des Dietrich Westhoff von 750-1550', Die Chroniken der Westfälischen und Niederrheinischen Städte, I. Chroniken der deutschen Städte XX. Leipzig, 1887.

197 FRÈRE, H., 'Numismatique Liégeoise. Notes sur la monnaie de compte dans la Principauté de Liège', Bulletin de l'Institut Archéologique Liégeois, LXXX, 1967 pp. 91-112.

198 FRIEDENSBURG, F., Schlesiens Münzgeschichte im Mittelalter. Codex diplomaticus Silesiae, XII, XIII. Breslau, 1887-8.

199 GARNIER, J. and CHAMPEAUX, E., Chartes de communes et d'affranchissement en Bourgogne Dijon, 1867.

200 GAUTHIER, L., Les Lombards dans les deux-Bourgognes. Bibliothèque de l'école des hautes études CLVI. 1907.

201 GAUTIER DALCHÉ, J., 'Remarques sur les premières mutations monétaires d'Alfonse de Castille', Mélanges en l'honneur d'Etienne Fournial. Université St Etienne,

GELDER, H.E. van, see ENNO VAN GELDER, H.

202 GENTIL DA SILVA, J., Banque et Crédit en Italie au XVIIe siècle, 2 vols. Paris, 1969.

203 GERMAIN, A., Histoire du commerce de Montpellier, 2 vols. Montpellier, 1891.

204 GHYSSENS, J., 'Essai de classement de monnaies au début du XIVe siècle à partir de la convention monétaire Brabant-Hainaut de 1323', Bulletin du Cercle d'Études Numismatiques, VII n° 4, 1970.

205 GHYSSENS, J., Les Petits Deniers de Flandre des XIIe et XIIIe siécles. Cercle d'Études Numismatiques. Travaux V. Brussels, 1971.

206 GHYSSENS, J., 'Un coup d'œil sur le monnayage de Marguerite d'Avesnes', Bulletin du Cercle d'Études Numismatiques, VIII n° 4, 1971.

207 GHYSSENS, J., 'Le monnayage d'argent en Flandre, Hainaut et Brabant au début de la guerre de Cent Ans (1337-45)', Revue Belge de Numismatique, CXX, 1974 pp. 109-91.

208 GHYSSENS, J., 'La monnaie de Hainaut sous Guillaume le Bon', Bulletin du Cercle d'Études Numismatiques, XI n° 1, 1974.

209 GHYSSENS, J., 'Monnaies de Brabant d'après les comptes de la ville de Louvain de 1345 à 1354', Revue Belge de Numismatique, CXXIII, 1977 pp. 149-57.

210 GHYSSENS, J. Privately communicated by J. Ghyssens from the accounts of the town of Louvain.

211 GIL FARRES, O., Historia de la moneda española, 2nd ed. Madrid, 1976.

212 GILLIODTS VON SEVEREN, L., Inventaire des archives de la ville de Bruges. 1871-8.

213 GLENISSON, J. and DAY, J., Textes et documents d'histoire du Moyen Age XIVe — XVe siècles, I. Paris, 1970.

214 GODDING, P., Le droit foncier à Bruxelles au moyen âge. Études d'histoire et d'éthnologie juridiques. Brussels, 1960.

215 GÖLLER, E., Ed., Die Einnahmen der Apostolischen Kammer unter Johann XII. Vatikanische Quellen zur Geschichte der päpstlichen Hof- und Finanzverwaltung, 1316-78, Historisches Institut in Rom. I. Görresgesellschaft. Paderborn, 1910.

216 GÖLLER, E., Ed., Die Einnahmen der Apostolischen Kammer unter Benedikt XII. Vatikanische Quellen zur Geschichte der päpstlichen Hof- und Finanzverwaltung, 1316-78, Historisches Institut in Rom. IV. Görresgesellschaft. Paderborn, 1920.

217 GOÑI GAZTAMBIDE, J., 'El fiscalismo pontificio en España en el tiempo de Juan XXII', Anthologica Annua, XIV, 1966 pp. 65-99.

218 GORIS, J.A., Études sur les colonies marchandes méridionales à Anvers de 1488 à 1567. 1925.

219 GORRINI, G., Ed., Documenti sulle relazioni fra Voghera e Genova 960-1325. Biblioteca della Società storica subalpina. XLVIII. 1908.

220 GRAUS, F., Dejiny venkovskeho lidu v Čechách v době předhusitské, II. Prague, 1957.

221 GRICE-HUTCHINSON, M.E.H., The School of Salamanca: readings in Spanish monetary theory 1544-1605. Oxford, 1952.

222 GRIERSON, P., Monnaies du Moyen Age. Fribourg, 1976.

223 GRIERSON, P., 'The weight of the Gold Florin in the Fifteenth Century', Quaderni ticinesi di Numismatica e antichità classiche, X. Lugano, 1981 pp. 421-31.

224 GRUNZWEIG, A., 'Le fonds de la mercanzia aux Archives d'État de Florence', Bulletin de l'Institut Historique Belge de Rome, XIII,

1933 pp. 5-184.

225 GUADAN, A.M., 'Las equivalencias monetarias del Mediterraneo oriental en el periodo 1436-1440', Acta Numismatica, III, 1973.

226 GUIDI, P., SELLA, P. et al., Eds., Rationes decimarum Italiae nei secoli XIII e XIV, 12 vols. Studi e Testi LVIII, LX, LXIX, LXXXIV, XCVI-XCVIII, CXII, CXIII, CXXVIII, CXLVIII, CLXI, CLXII. Vatican City, 1932-52.

227 GUILHERMOZ, P., 'Avis sur la question monétaire donnés aux rois Philippe le Hardi, Philippe le Bel, Louis X et Charles IV le Bel', Revue Numismatique, 4th Ser. XXV, XXVII, XXVIII, XXIX, 1922, 1924, 1925, 1926.

228 GUILHERMOZ, P. and DIEUDONNÉ, A., 'Chronologie des documents monétaires de la numismatique royale des origines à 1330 et 1337,', Revue Numismatique, 4th Ser. XXXIII, 1930 pp. 85-118, 233-54.

229 GUILLEMAIN, B., Les recettes et les dépenses de la chambre apostolique pour la 4e. année du pontificat de Clement V 1308-1309. Rome-Paris, 1978.

230 GUMOWSKI, M., 'Moneta Złota w Polsce średniowiecznej', Rozprawy Akademii Umiejętności Wydział Historyczno-Filozoficzny, 2nd Ser. XXX (55). Krakow, 1912 pp. 130-234.

231 HAENENS, A., D', 'Le Budget de St Martin de Tournai de 1331 à 1348', Revue Belge de Philologie et d'Histoire, XXXVII, 1959 pp. 317-42.

232 HAENENS, A., D', Comptes et documents de l'abbaye de Saint-Martin de Tournai sous l'administration des gardiens royaux 1312-1355. Brussels, 1962.

233 HALL, M.W., KRUEGER, H.G., REYNOLDS, R.L., Eds., Guglielmo Cassinese 1190-92, 2 vols. Notai liguri del secolo XII, II. Genoa, 1938.

234 HALL-COLE, M.W., KRUEGER, H.G., REINERT, R.G., REYNOLDS, R.L., Eds. Giovanni di Guiberto 1200-1211, 2 vols. Notai liguri del secolo XII, V. Genoa and Turin, 1939-40.

235 HAMILTON, E.J., Money, Prices and Wages in Valencia, Aragon and Navarre, 1351-1500. Cambridge, Mass., 1936.

236 HANAUER, C.A., Études économiques sur l'Alsace ancienne et moderne, 2 vols. Paris, 1878.

237 HANHAM, A., Ed., The Cely Letters 1482-88. Early English Text Society, CCLXXIII. London, 1975.

238 HARTE, N.B. and PONTING, K.G., Cloth and Clothing in Medieval Europe. Essays in memory of Professor E.M. Carus-Wilson. London, 1983.

239 HASKOVA, J., Die Währungs und Münzentwicklung unter den Jagellonen in Böhmen und Mähren. Acta Musei Nationalis Pragae. Ser. A XXII. 1969.

240 HAUSCHILD, U., Studien zu Löhnen und Preisen in Rostock in Spätmittelalter. Quellen und Darstellungen zur Hansische Geschichte, New Ser., XIX. Cologne-Vienna, 1973.

241 HAVERKAMP, A., Herrschaftsformen der Frühstäufer in Reichsitalien. Stuttgart, 1970-1.

242 HÄVERNICK, W., Der kölner Pfennig im 12. und 13. Jahrhundert. Vierteljahrschrift für Sozial und Wirtschaftsgeschichte, Beiheft XVIII. Stuttgart, 1930.

243 HEERS, J., 'Il commercio nel Mediterraneo alla fine del secolo XIV e nei primi anni del XV', Archivio storico italiano, CIII, 1955 pp. 157-209.

244 HEERS, J., 'Le commerce des Basques en Méditerranée au XIVe siècle', Bulletin Hispanique, LVII, Bordeaux, 1955 pp. 292-324.

245 HEERS, J., 'L'expansion maritime portugaise à la fin du moyen âge: la Mediterranée', Revista de Facultà de Letras, 2nd Ser. II. Lisbon., 1956 pp. 84-103.

246 HEERS, J., Le livre des comptes de Giovanni Piccamiglio, homme d'affaires génois, 1456-9. Affaires et gens d'affaires, XII. École pratique des Hautes Études, VIe section. Centre, de recherches historiques. Paris 1959.

247 HEERS, J., Gênes au XVe siècle. Activité économique et problèmes sociaux. Paris, 1961.

248 HERLIHY, D., Pisa in the Early Renaissance. Yale, 1958.

249 HESS, W., 'Der Marburger Pfennig', Hessisches Jahrbuch für Landesgeschichte, VIII, 1958 pp. 71-105.

250 HESS, W., 'Der Rheinische Münzwesen im 14. Jahrhundert und die Entstehung des Kurrheinischen Münzvereins', Vorträge und Forschungen, XIII. Sigmaringen, 1970 pp. 257-323.

251 HOBERG, H., Ed., Die Einnahmen der Apostolischen Kammer unter Innocenz VI. 1352-62. Pt. I. Die Einnahmenregesten des päpstlichen Thesaurus. Vatikanische Quellen zur Geschichte der päpstlichen Hof- und Finanzverwaltung 1316-78 Historisches Institut in Rom. VII. Görresgesellschaft. Paderborn, 1955.

252 HOBERG, H., Ed., Die Einnahmen der Apostolischen Kammer unter Innocenz VI. 1352-62. Pt. II Die Servitenquittungen des päpstlichen Kammers. Vatikanische Quellen zur Geschichte der päpstlichen Hof- und Finanzverwaltung 1316-78 Historisches Institut in Rom. VIII. Görresgesellschaft. Paderborn, 1972.

253 HUICI MIRANDA, A. and CABANES PECOURT, M.D., Eds., Documents de Jaime I de Aragon, I, 1216-1236. Textos Medievales, XLIX. Valencia, 1976.

254 ILIESCU, O., 'Nouvelle éditions d'actes notariés instrumentés au XIVe siècle dans les colonies genoises des bouches du Danube. Actes du Kilia et de Licostomo', Revue des études sud-est Européennes, XV, 1977 pp. 113-29.

255 INNES, C., The Ledger of Andrew Halyburton 1492-1503. Edinburgh, 1867.

256 IZQUIERDO BENITO, R., Precios y Salarios en Toledo durante el siglo XV. (1400-75). Caja de Ahorros de Toledo. Toledo, 1983.

257 JAPPE ALBERTS, W., Ed., Bronnen tot der bouwgeschiednis van den Dom te Utrecht, II part 2. The Hague, 1969.

258 JESSE, W., Quellenbuch zur Münz-und Geldgeschichte des Mittelalters. Halle-Saale, 1924 reprinted 1968.

259 JESSE, W., Die Wendische Münzverein. Quellen und Darstellungen zur Hansischen Geschichte. New Ser. VI. Lübeck, 1928.

260 JONES, M. Privately communicated by Dr Michael Jones of the University of Nottingham.

261 KELLENBENZ, H., Precious metals in the age of expansion. Stuttgart, 1981.

262 KESSEDJIAN, M., 'Une seigneurie rurale des marches de Bretagne au XVe siècle. St Brice en Coglès sous la famille des Scepeaux (Étude des comptes)', Mémoire de Maitrise. University of Rennes, 1972 from Archives départementales Ille-et-Vilaine, 2Eg, Fonds Gurrin, fos 16r-40r. I am indebted to Dr Michael Jones of the University of Nottingham for this reference.

263 KIERSNOWSKI, R., 'Złoto na rynku polskim w XIII — XIV w.', Wiadomósci Numizmatyczne, XVI. Warsaw, 1972-3.

264 KING, P., 'Cistercian Financial Organisation 1335-1392', Journal of Ecclesiastical History, XXIV, 1973.

265 KING, P., The Finances of the Cistercian Order in the Fourteenth Century. Kalamazoo, Michigan, Forthcoming. I am indebted to Dr Peter King for sending me an extract from this volume in advance.

266 KIRCHGÄSSNER, B., Das Steuerwesen der Reichsstadt Konstanz 1418-1460. Konstanzer Geschichts- und Rechtsquellen, New Ser. X. Constance, 1960.

267 KIRSCH, J.P., Ed., Die päpstlichen Kollektorien in Deutschland während des XIV. Jahrhunderts. Quellen und Forschungen aus dem Gebiete der Geschichte. III. Historisches Institut in Rom. Görresgessellschaft. Paderborn, 1894.

268 KIRSCH, J.P., Ed., Die Rückkehr der Päpste Urban V und Gregor XI von Avignon nach Rom. Auzüge aus dem Kameralregistern des Vatikanischen Archivs. Quellen und Forschungen aus dem Gebiete der Geschichte. VI. Historiches Institut in Rom. Görresgesellschaft. Paderborn, 1900.

269 KIRSCH, J.P., Ed., Die päpstlichen Annaten in Deutschland während des XIV. Jahrhunderts von Johann XII bis Innocenz VI. Quellen und Forschungen aus dem Gebiete der Geschichte. IX. Historisches Institut in Rom. Görresgesellschaft. Paderborn, 1903.

270 KIRSCH, J.P., 'La fiscalité pontificale dans les diocèses de Lausanne, Genève et Sion à la fin du XIIIe et XIVe siècles', Zeitschrift für Schweizerische Kirchengeschichte, II, 1908.

271 KLÜSSENDORF, N., Studien zu Währung und Wirtschaft am Niederrhein vom Ausgang der Periode des regionalen Pfennigs bis zum Münzvertrag von 1357. Rheinisches Archiv. XCIII. 1974.

272 KNIPPING, R., Die Kölner Stadtrechnungen des Mittelalters. Publikationen der Gesellschaft für Rheinische Geschichtskunde, XV. Bonn., 1897-8.

273 KREKIC, B., Dubrovnik (Ragusa) et le Levant au Moyen Âge. Paris, 1961.

274 KRUEGER, H.G., REYNOLDS, R.L., Ed., Lanfranco 1202-26, 3 vols. Notai liguri del secolo XII. VI. Genoa and Turin, 1951-3.

275 KUBIAK, S., Monety pierwszych Jagellonów (1386-1444). Wroclaw Warsaw Kraków, 1970.

276 LABIB, S.Y., Handelsgeschichte Ägyptens im spät Mittelalter 1171-1517. Vierteljahrschrift für Sozial- und Wirtschaftsgeschichte, Beiheft XLVI. Wiesbaden, 1965.

277 LACAVE, M., 'Crédit et la Consommation et conjoncture économique: L'Isle-en-Venaissin (1460-1560)', Annales, Économies Sociétés

Civilisations, XXXII, 1977 pp. 1128-53.

278 LADERCHI, C., Ed., Statuti di Ferrara dell'anno 1288. Dei monumenti istorici pertinenti alle provincie della Romagna 1st Ser. A. Deputazione di Storia Patria per le Provincie di Romagna,, Bologna 1864.

279 LADERO QUESADA, M.A., 'Les Finances royales de Castille à la veille des temps modernes', Annales Économies Sociétés Civilisations, XXV, 1970 pp. 775-88.

280 LADERO QUESADA, M.A., 'Moneda y tasa de precios en 1462', Moneda y Credito: Revista de Economia, CXXIX. Madrid, 1974 pp. 91-115.

281 LAGRÈZE-FOSSAT, M.A., 'De la valeur de quelques monnaies en usage à Moissac dans la seconde moitié du XVe siècle', Mémoires de la Société Impériale des Antiquaires de France, 4th Ser. XXXI pp. 132-46.

282 LANDUCCI, Luca, Ed. I. del Badia,, A Florentine Diary from 1450 to 1516. 1882, English translation, London, 1927.

283 LANE, F.C., 'Venetian Bankers 1496-1533', Journal of Political Economy, XLV, 1937 pp. 187-206, reprinted in Venice and History, Baltimore, 1966

284 LANE, F.C. and MUELLER, R.C., Money and Banking in Medieval and Renaissance Venice, I. Baltimore, 1985; vol. II forthcoming. I am much indebted to Professors Lane and Mueller for allowing me to use material from their forthcoming work.

285 LAPEYRE, H., 'Une lettre de change endossée en 1430', Annales, Économies Sociétés Civilisations, XIII, 1958 pp. 260-4.

286 LAPEYRE, H., 'Alphonse V et ses banquiers', Le Moyen Age, LXVII, 1961 pp. 93-136.

287 LAPEYRE, H., 'Contribution à l'histoire de la lettre de change en Espagne du XIVe au XVIIIe siècle', Anuario de Historia Economica y Social, I. Madrid, 1968 pp. 107-25.

288 LA RONCIÈRE, C.M. DE, Un changeur florentin du trecento: Lippo di Fede del Sega (vers 1285 — vers 1363). Paris, 1973.

289 LA RONCIÈRE, C.M. DE, Florence, centre économique régional au 14e. siècle, 5 vols. Aix-en-Provence, 1976

290 LATHAM, R.E., Ed., Dictionary of Medieval Latin from British Sources. Oxford, 1981.

291 LECHNER, G., Ed., Die Hansischen Pfundzollisten des Jahres 1368. Quellen und Dastellungen zur Hansische Geschichte, New Ser., X. Lubeck, 1935.

292 LEES, B.A., Ed., Records of the Templars in the XIIth century. Records of Social and Economic History. IX. British Academy, London, 1935.

293 LEONE, A., 'Note sul movimento cambiario nella seconda metà del secolo XV. Barcellona-Avignone-Napoli', Medioevo, Saggi e Rassegne, VI. Cagliari, 1981.

294 LEQUIN, C. and MARIOTTE, J.Y., La Savoie au moyen âge. Chambéry, 1970

295 LESNIKOV, M.P., Die Handelsbücher des hansischen Kaufmanns Veckinchusen, XIX. Forschungen zur Mittelalterlichen Geschichte. Berlin, 1973.

296 LEVEROTTI, F., 'Scritture finanziarie dell'età sforzesca', Squarci d'archivio sforzesco. Mostra storica documentaria. Como, 1981 pp. 123-42.

297 LIAGRE-DE STURLER, L., Les relations commerciales entre Gênes la Belgique et l'Outremont, 1320-1400. Études d'histoire économique et sociale VII, VIII. Institut Historique Belge de Rome. Brussels Rome, 1969.

298 Libri Commemoriali della Republica di Venezia Monumenti storici publicati della R. Deputazione Veneta di Storia patria Ist. Ser. Venice, 1876-

299 LIÈVRE, L., 'La monnaie et le change en Bourgogne sous les ducs valois', (Thesis) University of Dijon, 1927.

300 LODDO-CANEPA, F., 'Stato economico e demographico di Cagliari alle spirari del dominio aragonese in rapporto all'attivita commerciale mediterraneo', Studi Sardi, XV. Cagliari, 1957 pp. 162-79.

301 LOEB, I., 'Deux livres de commerce du commencement du XIVe siècle', Revue des Études Juives, VIII, pp. 161-96; IX, pp. 21-187. 1884.

302 LOGNON, A. et al., Eds., Pouillés, 9 vols. Recueil des historiens de la France. Académie des Inscriptions et Belles Lettres. Paris, 1903-52.

303 LONCHAY, H., 'Recherches sur l'origine et la valeur des ducats et des écus espagnols', Bulletin de la Classe des lettres de l'Académie Royale de Belgique. 1906. pp. 517-614.

304 LOPÈZ DE MENESES, A., 'Documentos culturales de Pedro el ceremonioso', Estudios de Edad Media de la Corona de Aragón, V, 1952 pp. 667-771.

305 LOPEZ, R.S., 'Back to Gold, 1252', Economic History Review, 2nd Ser. IX, 1956 pp. 219-40.

306 LOPEZ, R.S., 'Une histoire à trois niveaux: la circulation monétaire', Mélanges en l'honneur de Fernand Braudel, II, 1973 pp. 335-41.

307 LOT, F. and FAWTIER, R., Le premier budget de la monarchie française. Bibliothèque de l'École des Hautes Études, CCLIX. Paris, 1932.

308 LUNARDI, G., Le monete delle colonie Genovesi. Atti della Socièta Ligure di Storia Patria New Ser. XX. Genoa, 1980.

309 LUNT, W.E., Papal revenues in the Middle Ages, 2 vols. New York, 1934.

310 LUNT, W.E., Financial relations of the Papacy with England to 1327, 2 vols. Cambridge, Mass., 1939.

311 LUNT, W.E., Ed., Accounts rendered by Papal Collectors in England 1317-78. Philadelphia, 1968.

312 LUTTRELL, A. Privately communicated from the Accounts of the Hospitallers in Rhodes.

313 LUZZATTO, G., 'L'oro e l'argento nella politica monetaria veneziana dei secoli XIII-XIV', Rivista Storica Italiana. 1937.

314 MACKAY, A., Money, Prices and Politics in 15th. c. Castile. Studies in History Ser., XXVIII. Royal Historical Society, London, 1981.

315 MADURELL MARIMON, J. and GARCIÁ SANZ, A., Comandas comerciales Barcelonesas de la baja edad media. Anejos del 'Anuario de Estudios

medievales' IV. Barcelona, 1973.

316 MAILLARD, F. and FAWTIER, R., Eds., Comptes Royaux, 1314-28. Documents Financiers IV. Recueil des historiens de la France. Académie des Inscriptions et Belles Lettres. Paris, 1961.

317 MALATESTA, S., Statuti delle gabelle di Roma. Biblioteca dell'Accademia Storico-guiridica. V. Rome, 1885.

318 MANCA, C., Aspetti dell'espansione economica Catalano-Aragonese nel Mediterraneo occidentale. Il commercio internazionale del sale. Biblioteca della Rivista 'Economia e Storia', XVI. Milan, 1966.

319 MANCA, C., Ed., Il libro di conti di Miquel Ca-Rovira. Pubblicazione dell'Istituto di storia medioevale e moderna dell'Università degli studi di Cagliari. XI, XII. Padua, 1969.

320 MANTELS, W., Aus dem Memorial- oder Geheimbüche des Lübecker Kramers Heinrich Dunkelgud. Beiträge zur Lübisch-Hansischen Geschichte. Jena, 1881-6.

321 MARIÑION, J.M.M., 'Contabilidad de una compañia mercantil trecentista barcelonesa, 1334-42', Anuario de historia del derecho espanol, XXXV p.42, XXXVI p.457. Madrid,

322 MARTIN, C., Essai sur la politique monétaire de Berne 1400-1798. Lausanne, 1978.

323 MARTIN, P.E., Mélanges offerts à Paul-Edmond Martin. Genèva, 1961.

324 MARTIN-CHABOT, E., Ed., Les archives de la Cour des comptes, aides et finances de Montpellier, avec un essai de restitution des premiers registres de Sénéchausée. Bibliothèque de la Faculté de lettres de Paris. XXII. 1907.

325 MASSAGLI, O., Della Zecca e delle monete di Lucca. Memorie e Documenti per servire alla Storia di Lucca 1970.

326 MATEU Y LLOPIS, F., 'La politica monetaria de Alfonso IV de Aragón y su repercusión en Cerdeña', Anuario de Estudios Medievales, VII, 1970-1 pp. 337-49.

327 MAXE-WERLY, L., 'Histoire Numismatique du Barrois', Revue Belge de Numismatique, LI, 1895 pp. 326-60.

328 MAYER, H.E., Marseilles Levantehandel und eine akkonensisches Fälscheratelier des 13. Jahrhunderts. Bibliothek des deutschen historischen Instituts in Rom XXXVIII. Tübingen, 1972.

329 MAYER, T., Der auswärtige Handel des Herzogtums Österreich im Mittelalter. Innsbruck, 1909.

330 MCCUSKER, J.J., Money and Exchange in Europe and America 1600-1775. New York, 1978.

331 MELIS, F., Note di storia della banca pisana nel Trecento. Pisa, 1955.

332 MELIS, F., 'Malaga sul Sentiero Economico del XIV e XV Secolo', Economia e Storia, III, 1956 pp. 19-59, 139-63.

333 MELIS, F., 'Una girata cambiaria del 1410 nell'archivio datini di Prato', Economica e Storia. 1958 pp. 412-21.

334 MELIS, F., Documenti per la storia economica dei secoli XIII-XVI. Florence, 1972.

335 MELTZING, O., Das Bankhaus der Medici und seine Vorläufer. Jena, 1906.

336 MENADIER, J., 'Münzprägung und Münzumlauf Aachens in ihrer geschichtlichen Entwicklung.; and Urkunden und Akten zur Aachener Münzgeschichte', Zeitschrift für Numismatik, XXXI, 1914 pp. 216-73 and 274-459.

337 MENJOT, D. privately communicated by D. Menjot, Assistant en Histoire, University of Nice, from official rates fixed by the royal receiver, Actas Capitulares, Año 1409-10. Archivio Municipal, Murcia.

338 MERONI, U., Ed., Declarationes valoris monetarum per officiales monetarum civitatis Januae sedentes in Cecha per tribunali ad bancum iuris. Registi Officii, 3 vols. Fonti per la storia della moneta in Italia negli evi medio e moderno. Zecca di Genova III. Mantua, 1953.

339 METCALF, D.M., Coinage in South-Eastern Europe 820-1396. Royal Numismatic Society, Special Publication XI. London, 1979.

340 METCALF, D.M., Ed., Coinage in Medieval Scotland (1100-1600). British Archaeological Reports British Ser. XLV. 1977.

341 MEYER, P., 'Le livre-journal de Maître Ugo Teralh, notaire et drapier à Forcalquier 1330-2', Notices et extraits des manuscripts de la Bibliothèque Nationale, XXXVI. pp. 129-71.

342 MIKA, A., 'Nástin cen zemědělského zboží w Čechách 1427-1547', Českosloveský Časopis Historický, VII, 1959 pp. 545-570.

343 MIROT, L., La politique pontificale et le retour du St Siége à Rome en 1376. Paris, 1899.

344 MISBACH, H.L., 'Genoese trade and the flow of gold 1154-1253', (Ph.D. Thesis) University of Wisconsin, 1968.

345 MISKIMIN, H.A., HERLIHY, D. and UDOVITCH, D., Eds., The Medieval City. Yale, 1977.

346 MØRKHOLM, O., 'Kilder til Danmarks Møntvaesen i Middelalderen I, II, III', Nordisk Numismatisk Årsskrift. 1955, 1960, 1961.

347 MOHLER, L., Die Einnahmen der Apostolischen Kammer unter Klemens VI. Vatikanische Quellen zur Geschichte der päpstlichen Hof- und Finanzverwaltung 1316-78. Historisches Institut in Rom. V. Görresgesellschaft. Paderborn, 1931.

348 MOLLAT, M., Le commerce maritime normand à la fin du Moyen Âge. Paris, 1952.

349 MOLLAT, M. and FAVREAU, R., Comptes généraux de l'état bourguignon entre 1416 et 1420, 4 vols. Documents Financiers. V. Recueil des historiens de la France. Académie des Inscriptions et Belles Lettres. Paris, 1965-76.

350 MONACO, M., Il De officio Collectoris in Anglia 1469-1516. Rome, 1973

351 MONTALVO, J.H., Ed., Cuentas de la Industria Naval (1406, 1415). Textos Medievales, XXXV. Valencia, 1973.

352 MORARD, N., Les monnaies de Fribourg. Fribourg, 1969.

353 MORARD, N., 'Contribution à l'histoire monétaire du Pays de Vaud et la "mauvaise" monnaie de Guillaume de Challant', Revue Historique Vaudoise. 1975.

354 MORARD, N., 'Florins, ducats et marc d'argent à Fribourg et à Genève au XVe siècle; cours des espèces et valeur de la monnaie de compte 1420-1481', Revue Suisse de Numismatique, LVIII, 1979 pp. 223-86.

355 MOREL-FATIO, A., Histoire monétaire du diocèse de Lausanne, 1273-1354, 1476-1588. 1882.

356 MOROZZO DELLA ROCCA, R. and LOMBARDO, A., Ed., Documenti del commercio veneziano nei secoli XI-XIII, 2 vols. Documenti e Studi per la storia del commercio e del diritto commerciale italiano. XIX, XX, Patetta, F. and Chiaudano, M., Eds. Turin, 1940.

357 MUELLER, R.C., 'The Procurati di San Marco and the Venetian Credit Market', (Ph.D. Thesis) Johns Hopkins University, 1969, printed Arno Press, New York, 1977.

358 MUELLER, R.C., 'The Role of Bank Money in Venice 1300-1500', Studi Veneziani, New Ser. III, 1979.

359 MUELLER. R.C., 'L'imperialismo monetario veneziano nel Quattrocento', Società e Storia, VIII, 1980.

360 MÜLLER, K.O., Welthandelsbräuche, 1480-1540. Deutsche Handelsakten des Mittelalters und der Neuzeit V. Historische Kommission bei der Bayerischen Akademie der Wissenschaften. Stuttgart, 1934 reprinted Wiesbaden, 1962.

361 MUNRO, J.H.A., Wool, Cloth and Gold; the struggle for bullion in Anglo-Burgundian trade 1340-1478. Brussels Toronto, 1973.

362 MUNRO, J.H.A., 'Money and coinage of the Age of Erasmus', The Collected Works of Erasmus, I. Toronto, 1974 pp. 311-47.

363 MUNRO, J.H.A. Privately communicated by Professor John Munro of Toronto University from Stadsarchief van Mechelen, Stadsrekeningen 1368-1435.

364 MÛNZ, E., 'L'argent et le luxe à la cour pontificale d'Avignon', Revue des Questions Historiques, New Ser. XXII, 1899 pp. 5-44.

365 NAGL, A., 'Die Goldwährung und die handelsmässige Geldrechnung im Mittelalter', Numismatische Zeitschrift, XXVI, 1894 pp. 41-258.

366 NICOL, D.M., The Despotate of Epiros 1267-1479. Cambridge, 1984.

367 NICOLINI, U. and MAJARELLI, S., Eds., Il Monte Dei Poveri di Perugia 1462-74. Perugia, 1962.

368 NOHEJLOVÁ-PRÁTOVÁ, E., Česckého Mincovnictuí a tabulky cen a mezd. Prague, 1964.

369 NOONAN, J.T., The Scholastic Analysis of Usury. Cambridge, Mass., 1957.

370 NORDMANN, C., 'Die Veckinchusen Handelsblâtter. Zur Frage ihrer Edition', Hansische Geschichtsblâtter, LXIV. Weimar, 1940 pp. 74-144.

371 NOSS, A., Die Münzen von Trier. Publikationen der Gesellschaft für Rheinische Geschichtskunde, XXX. Bonn, 1916.

372 ORIGO, I., The World of San Bernardino. London, 1963.

373 PAGNINI DELLA VENTURA, G.F., Ed., 'La Pratica della mercatura scritta de Giovanni di Antonio da Uzzanno', Della Decima e delle altre gravezze, IV. Lisbon Lucca, 1766.

374 PAOLI, C. and PICCOLOMINI, E., Eds., Lettere volgari del secolo XIII scritte de Senese. Siena, 1871, reprinted Bologna 1968.

375 PARKS, G.B., The English Traveller to Italy, I. Rome, 1954.

376 PAULI, K.W., 'Über die frühere Bedeutung Lübecks als Wechselplatz des Nordens', Lübeckische Zustände im Mittelalter, II, 1872 pp. 98-171.

377 PEETERS, J.P., De rekenmunt in de Mechelse Stadsrekeningen. Handelingen van de koninklijk kring voor oudeheidkunde letteren en kunst van Mechelen. LXXXIV. 1980.

378 PELC, J., Ceny w Krakowie w latach 1369-1600. Lwow, 1935.

379 PEREZ-EMBID, F., 'Navigation et commerce dans le port de Seville au bas moyen âge', Le Moyen Âge, 4th Ser. XXIV, 1969 pp. 263-89.

380 PERROY, E. and FOURNIAL, E., 'Réalités Monétaires et Réalités Économiques', Annales Économies Sociétés Civilisations, XIII, 1958 pp. 533-40.

381 PESCE, G. and FELLONI, G., Le monete Genovesi. Genoa, 1975.

382 PETIT, E., Histoire des ducs de Bourgogne. Paris, 1885-1905.

383 PETIT, E., 'Le poète Jean Regnier', Bulletin de la société des sciences historiques et naturelles de l'Yonne. 1903.

384 PETOT, P., Ed., Registre des Parlements de Beaune et de St Laurent-les-Chalon. 1357-80. Paris, 1927.

385 PFAFF, V., 'Die Einnahmen der römanischen Kurie am Ende des XII. Jahrhunderts', Vierteljahrschrift für Sozial- und Wirtschaftsgeschichte, XL, 1953 pp. 97-118.

386 PFAFF, V., 'Aufgaben und Probleme der päpstlichen Finanzverwaltung am Ende des XII. Jahrhunderts', Mitteillungen des Instituts für Österreichische Geschichtsforschung, LXIV, 1956 pp. 1-24.

387 PFEIFFER, G., et al., Eds., Beiträge zur Wirtschaftsgeschichte Nürnbergs; Stadtarchiv Nürnberg, 2 vols. Beiträge Zur Geschichte und Kultur der Stadt Nürnberg XI. Nuremberg, 1967.

388 PIEKOSIŃSKI, F., 'O monecie i stopie menniczej w Polsce w XIV i XV w', Rozprawy i Sprawozdania z Posiedzeń Wydziału Historyczno-Filozoficznego Akademii Umiejętności, IX. Krakow, 1878.

389 PIÉRAND, C., Les plus anciens comptes de la ville de Mons, 1279-1356, 2 vols. Commission Royale d'Histoire II, Académie Royale de Belgique. 1973.

390 PIEROTTI, R., 'La circulazione monetaria nel territorio perugino nei secoli XII-XIV', Bolletino della Deputazione di Storia Patria per l'Umbria, LXXVIII. Perugia, 1981 pp. 81-151.

391 Pipe Roll 5 John. Publications of the Pipe Roll Society New Ser. XVI. 1938.

392 Pipe Roll 17 John. Publications of the Pipe Roll Society New Ser. XXXVII. 1964

393 PITON, C., Les Lombards en France et à Paris, 2 vols. Paris, 1892-3.

394 PLANCHER, U., Histoire générale et particulière de Bourgogne avec des notes des dissertations et les preuves justificatives, 4 vols. Paris, 1736-81.

395 POCQUET DU HAUT-JUSSÉ, B.A., La France gouvernée par Jean sans Peur. Paris, 1959.

396 POSTHUMUS, N.W. and KETNER, F., Inquiry into the History of Prices in Holland, II. Leiden, 1964.

397 PRESTWICH, M. Privately communicated by Dr Michael Prestwich, mostly later printed in 'Early Fourteenth Century Exchange Rates', Economic History Review, 2nd Ser. XXXII, 1979 pp. 470-82.

398 PRIBRAM, A.F., Materialien zur Geschichte der Preise und Löhne in Österreich. 1938.

399 PRIOR, W.H., 'Notes on the weights and measures of medieval England', Bulletin du Cange, I, 1924 pp. 79-97 and 141-70, reprinted separately as Notes on the Weights and Measures of Medieval England, Paris, 1924.

400 PROU, M., 'Recueil de documents relatifs à l'histoire monétaire', Revue Numismatique, 4th Ser. I, 1897 pp. 174-92.

401 PROU, M., 'Compte de la maison de l'aumône de Saint-Pierre de Rome', Le Moyen Âge, 2nd Ser. XIX, 1915 pp. 301-46.

402 Quellen und Darstellungen zur Hansischen Geschichte. New Ser. Lübeck,

403 Quellen zur Wirtschaftgeschichte Frankens, Veröffentlichungen der Gesellschaft für Fränkische Geschichte. 10th Ser. Erlangen Würzburg,

404 Rationes Collectorum Pontificiorum. 1281-1375. Monumenta Vaticana historiam regni Hungariae illustrantia. 1st Ser. Budapest, 1885-91.

405 RAVEAU, P., 'Le pouvoir d'achat de l'argent et de la livre tournois en Poitou du règne de Louis XI à celui de Louis XIII', Bulletin de la Société des Antiquaires de l'Ouest, 3rd Ser. VI, 1922.

406 RECHENBACH, M.C., 'The Gascon money of Edward III — a study in monetary history', (Ph.D Thesis) University of Maryland, 1955.

407 RENOUARD, Y., Les relations des papes d'Avignon et des compagnies commerciales et bancaires de 1316 à 1378. Bibliothèque des Écoles Françaises d'Athènes et de Rome, CLI. 1941.

408 REY, M., 'La monnaie estevenante', Mémoires de la société d'Émulation du Doubs, New Ser., 1958 pp. 35-66

409 RICHARDS, J.F., Ed., Precious Metals in the Later Medieval and Early Modern Worlds. Durham, North Carolina, 1983.

410 RICHEBÉ, C., Les monnaies féodales d'Artois du Xe au début du XIVe siècle. Paris, 1963.

411 RICHET, D., 'Le cours officiel des monnaies étrangères circulant en France au 16e siècle', Revue Historique, CCXXV, 1961 pp. 359-96.

412 ROBBERT, L.B., 'The Venetian Money Market 1150-1229', Studi Veneziani, XIII, 1971 pp. 3-14.

413 ROGERS, J.E.T., A History of agriculture and prices in England. Oxford, 1866.

414 ROLLAND, H., Monnaies des comtes de Provence aux XIIe — XVe siècles. Paris, 1956.

415 ROMESTAN, G., 'Les marchands languedociens dans le royaume de Valence pendant la première moitié du XIVe siècle', Bulletin philologique et historique. Comité des travaux historiques et scientifiques. 1969 pp. 115-92.

416 RÖSENER, W., Reichsabtei Salem; Verfassungs- und Wirtschaftsgeschichte des Zisterzienserklosters von der Gründung bis zur Mitte des 14. Jahrhunderts. Vorträge und Forschungen. Konstanzer Arbeitskreis für Mittelalterliche Geschichte Sonderband XIII. 1974.

417 ROSSI-SABATINI, G., Pisa ai tempi dei Donoratico. Florence, 1938.

418 ROSSO, G., Documenti sulle relazioni commerciali fra Asti e Genova 1182-1310. Biblioteca della Societa Storica Subalpina LXXII. 1913.

419 RUIS SERRA, J., Raciones decimarum Hispaniae, 2 vols. Textos. Consejo Superior de Investigaciones Ciétificas. Escuela de Estudios Medievales IV, VIII. Barcelona Madrid, 1947, 1949.

420 RYMER, T., Foedera, Conventiones, Literae, et cujuscunque generis acta publica, inter Reges Angliae et alios quosvis Imperatores, Reges, Pontifices et Principes, revised ed. 7 vols. London, 1816-69.

421 SAEZ, L., Demostración histórica del verdadero valor de todas las monedas, que corrian en Castilla durante el Reynado del Senor Don Enrique III, 2 vols. Madrid, 1796, 1805.

422 SANCHÉZ MARTINÉZ, M., 'Les Peruzzi e les Acciaiuoli en la Corona de Aragón', Anuario de estudios medievales. 1970 p.299.

423 SANTIARD, M.Th., 'La glandée dans les forêts ducales au XIVe siècle', Annales de Bourgogne, XLVI, 1974.

424 SAPORI, A., Una compagnia dei Calimala ai primi del Trecento. Florence, 1932.

425 SAPORI, A., I libri di commercio dei Peruzzi, Gianfigliazzi, Alberti del Giudice. Studi Medievali. I-III. Milan, 1934-52.

426 SAPORI, A., La compagnia dei Frescobaldi in Inghilterra. Biblioteca Storica Toscana IX. 1947.

427 SAPORI, A., Studi di Storia Economica. Secoli XIII, XIV, XV, I. Florence, 1955.

428 SAPORI, A., 'Gli Italiani in Polonia fino a tutto il quattrocento', Studi di Storia Economica, III. Florence, 1967 pp. 149-76.

429 SATTLER, C., Handelsrechnungen des Deutschen Ordens. Leipzig, 1887.

430 SAULCY, F. DE, Recueil de documents relatifs à l'histoire des monnaies frappées par les rois de France depuis Philippe II jusqu'à François Ier, 4 vols. Collection de documents inédits sur l'histoire de France. Sec. 3. Paris, 1879-92.

431 SAUVE, F., 'Un régistre de notaire artésien du XIVe siècle.', Bulletin philologique et historique Comité des travaux historiques et scientifiques. 1913 pp. 12-36.

432 SAYOUS, A., 'Les Mandats de St Louis sur son trésor et le mouvement international des capitaux pendant la septième croisade 1248-54', Revue Historique, CLXXVII, 1931 pp. 254-304.

433 SAYOUS, A., 'Les méthodes commerciales de Barcelone au XIIIe siècle, d'après des documents inédits des Archives de la Cathédrale', Estudis Universitaris Catalans, XVI. Barcelona, 1933.

434 SAYOUS, A., 'Les méthodes commerciales de Barcelone au XIVe siècle, surtout d'après des protocoles inédits de ses archives notariales', Estudis Universitaris Catalans, XVIII, 1933 pp. 209-35.

435 SAYOUS, A., 'L'Origine de la lettre de change', Revue historique de droit français et étranger, 4th Ser. XII, 1933.

436 SAYOUS, A., 'Les transferts des risques, les associations commerciales et la lettre de change à Marseille pendant le XIVe siècle', Revue historique de droit français et étranger, 4th Ser. XIV, 1935.

437 SCAMOTA, I., Régí utazások. Alte Reisen. Budapest, 1891.

438 SCHÄFER, K.H., Deutsche Ritter und Edelknechte in Italien. Quellen und Forschungen aus dem Gebiete der Geschichte XXV. Görresgesellschaft. Paderborn, 1940.

439 SCHÄFER, K.H., Ed., Die Ausgaben der apostolischen Kammer unter Johann XII, nebst den Jahresbilanzen von 1316-35. Vatikanische Quellen zur Geschichte der päpastlichen Hof- und Finanzverwaltung 1316-78, Historisches Institut in Rom. II. Görresgesellschaft. Paderborn, 1911.

440 SCHÄFER, K.H., Ed., Ausgaben der apostolichen Kammer unter Benedict XII, Klement VI, Innocent VI. 1335-62. Vatikanische Quellen zur Geschichte der päpstlichen Hof- und Finanzverwaltung 1316-78, Historisches Institut in Rom. III. Görresgesellschaft. Paderborn, 1914.

441 SCHÄFER, K.H., Ed., Ausgaben der apostolischen Kammer unter Urban V und Gregor VI. 1362-72. Vatikanische Quellen zur Geschichte der päpstlichen Hof- und Finanzverwaltung 1316-78. VI. Historisches Institut in Rom. Görresgesellschaft. Paderborn, 1937.

442 SCHAÏK, R. VAN, 'Prijs- en levensmiddelenpolitiek in de Nordelijke Nederlanden van der 14e tot der 17e eeuw', Tijdschrift voor Geschiedenis, XCI, 1978 pp. 214-255.

443 SCHAUBE, A., 'Ein Kursbericht von den Champagnermessen', Zeitschrift für Sozial- und Wirtschaftsgeschichte, V, 1897.

444 SCHIAFFINI, A., Testi Fiorentini del Dugento e dei primi del Trecento. Florence, 1926.

445 SCHNEIDER, J., La Ville de Metz aux XIIIe et XIVe siècles. Nancy, 1950.

446 SCHRADER, T., Rechnungsbücher der Hamburgischen Gesandten in Avignon 1338-55. Hamburg and Leipzig, 1907.

447 SCHRÖTTER, F. VON, Wörterbuch der Münzkunde. Berlin-Leipzig, 1930.

448 SCHUBERT, H., Die Geschichte der Nassauischen Eisenindustrie. Veröffentlichungen der Historischen Kommission für Nassau IX. Wiesbaden, 1937.

449 SCHULTE, A., Geschichte des mittelalterlichen Handels und Verkhers zwischen Westdeutschland und Italien mit Ausschluss von Venedig, 2 vols. Leipzig, 1900.

450 SCHULTE, A., Geschichte der Grossen Ravensburger Handelsgesellschaft 1380-1530, 3 vols. Deutsche Handelsakten des Mittelalters und der Neuzeit I, II, III. Stuttgart Berlin, 1923.

451 SCOTT, W.W., 'Sterling and Usual Money of Scotland 1370-1415', Scottish Economic and Social History. 1985. I am indebted to Mr Scott for permission to use this article before publication.

452 SIVÉRY, G., 'L'évolution du prix du blé à Valenciennes aux XIVe et XVe siècles', Revue du Nord, XLVII, 1965 pp. 177-94.

453 SIVÉRY, G., 'L'entrée du Hainaut dans la principauté bourguignonne.', Revue du Nord, LVI, 1974 pp. 323 ff.

454 SIVÉRY, G., 'Mouvements de capitaux et taux d'interét en Occident au XIIIe siècle', Annales Economies Sociétés Civilisations, XXXVIII, 1983.

455 SMIT, H.J., Ed., De Rekeningen der Graven en Gravinnen uit het Henegouwsche Huis, 3 vols. Amsterdam, 1924-39.

456 SOBREQUÉS CALLICÓ, J., 'Aspectos economicos de la vida en Barcelona durante la guerra civil catalana de 1462-72', Cuadernos de Historia economica de Catulunya, III, pp. 215-86.

457 SOLDI RONDININI, G., 'Politica e teoria monetarie dell'etàviscontea', Nuova Rivista Storica, LIX. Milan, 1975 pp. 288-330.

458 SOLDI RONDININI, G., 'Politica e teoria monetarie dell'eta Viscontea', La Moneta nell'Economia Europea, Secoli XIII-XVIII. Settimana di Studio VII 1975. Istituto Internazionale di Storia Economica 'Francesco, Datini' Prato 1983.

459 SOSSON, J-P., 'Un compte inédit de construction de galères à Narbonne (1318-20)', Bulletin de l'Institut Historique Belge de Rome, XXXIV, 1962 pp. 57-318.

460 SPALLANZANI, M., 'A Note on Florentine Banking in the Renaissance: Orders of Payment and Cheques', Journal of European Economic History, VII, 1978 pp. 145-65.

461 SPRANDEL, R., Das Eisengewerbe in Mittelalter. Stuttgart, 1968.

462 SPRANDEL, R., Der Mittelalterliche Zahlungssystem. Monographien zur Geschichte des Mittelalters. X. Stuttgart, 1975.

463 SPRANDEL, R. Privately communicated by Professor Rolf Sprandel of the University of Würzburg from unpublished 14th and 15th century Würzburg accounts.

464 SPUFFORD, P., 'Coinage and Currency', Cambridge Economic History of Europe, III, Economic organization and policies in the Middle Ages. Cambridge, 1963 pp. 576-602.

465 SPUFFORD, P., Money and its use in Medieval Europe. Cambridge, 1986.

466 SPUFFORD, P. and WILKINSON, W., Interim Listing of the Exchange Rates of Medieval Europe. Keele, 1977.

467 STAHL, A.M., The Venetian Tornesello. A Medieval Colonial Coinage. American Numismatic Society; Numismatic Notes and Monographs CLXIII. New York, 1985.

468 STEFKE, G, ''Goldwährung' und 'lübisches' Silbergeld in Lübeck um die Mitte des 14. Jahrhunderts', Zeitschrift des Vereins für Lübeckische Geschichte und Altertumskunde, LXIII, 1983 pp. 25-81.

469 STIEDA, W., Hansisch-Venetianische Handelsbeziehungen im XV. Jahrhundert. Rostock, 1894.

470 STIEDA, W., Hildebrand Veckinchusen; Briefwechsel eines deutschen Kaufmanns im 15. Jahrhundert. Leipzig, 1921.

471 STOLZ, O., Zollwesens und Landesverkehrs in Tirol und Vorarlberg. Wiesbaden, 1955.

472 STROMER VON REICHENBACH, W., Oberdeutsche Hochfinanz 1350-1450. II. Vierteljahrschrift für Sozial- un Wirtschaftsgeschichte, Beihefte LV-LVII. 1970.

473 STROMER VON REICHENBACH, W., Die Gründung der Baumwollindustrie in Mitteleuropa. Monographien zur Geschichte des Mittelalters XVII. Stuttgart, 1978.

474 STUSSI, A., Ed., Zibaldone da Canal, Manoscritto Mercantile del Secolo XIV. Fonti per la Storia di Venezia. Venice, 1967.

475 TAILLIAR, E., Recueil d'Actes des XIIe et XIIIe siècles en langue romane wallonne du Nord de la France. Douai, 1849

476 TARIFA zoè noticia dy pexi e mexure di luogi e tere, che s'adovra marcadantia per el mondo (Ed. V. Orlandini, introduction by R. Cessi). Venice, 1925.

477 TENHAEFF, N.B., Ed., Bronnen tot der bouwgeschiedenis van den Dom de Utrecht, II part 1. The Hague, 1948. Professor H. Enno van Gelder has supplied me with corrections from the accounts themselves.

478 THEINER, A., Vetera monumenta historica Hungariam sacram illustrantia. 1216-1526, 2 vols Rome Paris Vienna, 1859-60.

479 THEINER, A., Ed., Codex diplomaticus dominii temporalis S. Sedis, I and II. Rome, 1861-2.

480 THIELEMANS, M-R., Bourgogne et Angleterre 1435-67. Brussels, 1966.

481 THOMAS, A., 'Nouveaux documents sur les états provinciaux de la Haute Marche 1418-1446', Annales du Midi, XXV, 1913 pp. 429-52.

482 THOMMEN, R., 'Ein Münzvertrag aus dem XV Jahrundert', Revue Suisse de Numismatique, V, 1895 pp. 5-8.

483 TORRE, A. de la, Ed., Documentos sobre relaciones internacionales de los reyes católicos, I. 1479-1483. Biblioteca Reyes Catolicos, Documentos y Textos. Barcelona, 1949.

484 TORRES FONTES, J., 'La vida en la ciudad de Murcia en 1442-1444', Anuario de Historia Economica y Social, I. Madrid, 1968 pp. 691-714.

485 TOUT, T.F., Chapters in the Administrative History of Medieval England 7 vols. Manchester, 1920-37.

486 TOUT, T.F., The Place of Edward II in English History 3rd ed. Manchester, 1936.

487 TRAMOYERES BLASCO, L., 'Letras De Cambio Valencianas', Revista de Archivos. Madrid, 1900 pp. 489-96

488 TRASELLI, C., Note per la storia dei banchi in Sicilia del sec. XI, I. Zecche e monete. Palermo, 1959.

489 TRASELLI, C., 'Aree monetarie in Mediterraneo centro-occidentale', La Moneta nell'Economia Europa: Secoli XIII-XVIII. Settimana di Studio VII 1975. Istituto Internazionale di Storia Economica 'Francesco, Datini', Prato 1983.

490 UBIERTO ARTETA, A., 'Monedas que circulaban en Navarra en el siglo XIV y sus valores', Numisma, XVII, 1967 pp. 59-66.

491 USHER, A.P., The Early History of Deposit Banking in Mediterranean Europe. Cambridge, Mass., 1934

492 VALDÉON, J., 'Las réformas monetarias de Enrique II de Castilla', Homenaje al Excmo Sr Dr D. Emilio García Alarco, II. Università de Valladolid, 1957 pp. 337-49.

493 VALE, M. Privately communicated by Dr Malcolm Vale, of St John's College Oxford.

494 VAN CAUWENBERGHE, E., Het Vorstelijk Domein en de Overheidsfinancien in de Nederlanden (15de en 16de eeuw). Collection Histoire, Pro Civitate, 8° Ser., LXI. Brussels, 1982.

VAN CAUWENBERGHE see also CAUWENBERGHE

495 VAN DER CHIJS, P.O., De munten der Nederlanden van de vroegste tijden tot aan de Pacificatie van Gend. 1576, 9 vols. Haarlem, 1851-66.

496 VAN RIJ, H., Ed., Miscellanea Mediaevalia in memoriam de J.F. Niermeyer. Groningen, 1967.

497 VERACHTER, F., Inventaire des anciens chartes et privilèges et autres documents conservés aux archives de la ville d'Anvers, 1193-1856. Antwerp, 1860.

498 VERHULST, A. and GYSSELING, M., Le Compte Général de 1187, et les institutions financières du Comté de Flandre au XIIe siècle. 1962.

499 VERLINDEN, Ch., 'L'esclavage dans le royaume de Naples à la fin du Moyen Âge et la participation des marchands espagnols à la traite', Anuario de Historia Economica y Social, I. Madrid, 1968 pp. 345-401

500 VERMIGLIOLI, G.B., Della zecca e delle monete perugine, memorie e documenti inediti, raccolti e pubblicati. Perugia, 1816.

501 VIDAL, A., Comptes consulaires d'Albi 1359-1360. Bibliothèque méridionale 1st Ser., V. Toulouse, 1900.

502 VILLAIN-GANDOSSI, C., Comptes du Sel de Francesco di Marco Datini pour sa compagnie d'Avignon 1376-9. Collection de documents inédits sur l'histoire de France. VII. Paris, 1969.

503 VOGELSANG, R., Ed., Kämmereibuch der Stadt Reval 1432-63. Quellen und Darstellungen zur Hansische Geschichte, New Ser., XXII. Cologne Vienna, 1976.

504 WAILLY, N. de, 'Mémoire sur les variations de la livre tournois', Mémoires de l'Institut: Académie des Inscriptions et Belles Lettres, XXI. pt. 2. Paris,

505 WATSON, A.M., 'Back to Gold — and Silver', Economic History Review, 2nd Ser. XX, 1967 pp. 1-34.

506 WEISE, E., Ed., Staatsverträge des Deutschen Ordens in Preussen, I and II. Königsberg Marburg, 1939-55.

507 WHITWELL, R.J., 'Italian bankers and the English Crown', Transactions of the Royal Historical Society, New Ser. XVII, 1903 pp. 175-233.

508 WILLIAMSON, G., Ed., The Itineraries of William Way, 2 vols. Roxburghe Club. London, 1857 and 1867.

509 WOLFF, P., Commerces et Marchands de Toulouse (c.1350 — c.1450). Paris, 1954.

510 ŻABIŃSKI, Z., Systemy Pieniężne na Ziemiach Polskich. Polska Akademia Nauk. Oddział w Krakowie. Prace Komisji Archeologicznej, XX. Warsaw, 1981.

511 ZANETTI, G.A., Nuova Raccolta delle Monete e Zecche d'Italia, 2 vols. Bologna, 1775 and 1779

512 ZENO, R., Documenti per la storia del diritto marittimo nei secoli XIII e XIV. Documenti e Studi per la storia del commercio e del diritto commerciale italiano. VI, Patetta, F. and Chiaudano, M., Eds. Turin, 1936.

513 ZERBI, T., Le origine della partita doppia. Milan, 1952.

514 ZERBI, T., Moneta effectiva e moneta di conto nelle fonti contabili di storia economica. Milan, 1953.

515 ZINGERLE, J.V., Aus den Reiserechnungen des Bischofs Wolfger von Passau. 1877.

516 MSS Brussels. Archives Générales du Royaume. Divers 385B.

517 MSS Brussels. Archives Générales du Royaume. Divers 883ter.

518 MSS Brussels. City Archives. XI Swerdtboek.

519 MSS Florence, Archivio di Stato, Carte Strozziane, 5th Ser., Filza 1760.

520 MSS Florence, Archivio di Stato, Miscellanea Republica, Box 33.

521 MSS Liège, Archives d'État, Chambres des Comptes, 183. Évaluation des Monnaies 1477-1618.

522 MSS Lille, Archives du Nord, B 644/15, 975.

523 MSS Prato, Archivio Datini.

524 MSS Palma di Majorca, Archivio Historico, Escribania Cartas Reales I am indebeted to Mrs Sarah Tolley for this reference.

INDEX OF CURRENCIES

CURRENCIES OF LATE MEDIEVAL EUROPE

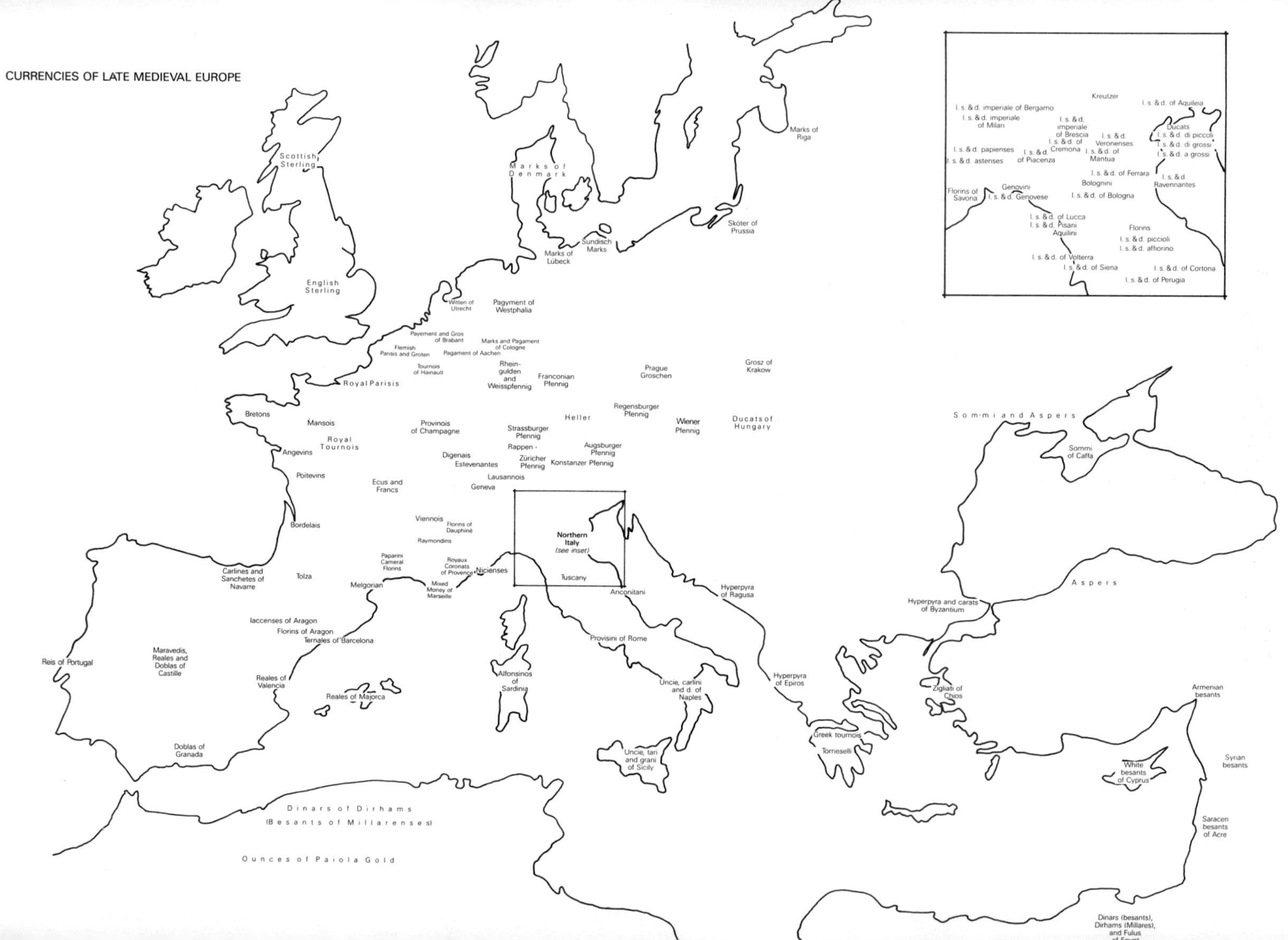

INDEX OF CURRENCIES

In this index references to the pounds, shillings and pence (or their equivalents) of a particular place have been indexed under that place as 'Money of ...'. No entries therefore appear for libra, lira, livre, pfund, pond, pound or for schelling, schilling, shilling, sol, soldo, sou, sueldo or for denar, denaro, denier, diner, dinero, dinheiro, penning, penny, pfennig or for obol, obole (1/2 d.). When the name of its currency is very similar to that of the place of issue, as with amberger or anconitano, no separate entry has been provided. On the other hand when the name of the currency is very different from the name of place, as arnaldensis and chapotensis, or is separated from it in the alphabet, as tirolino from the Tyrol, entries have been provided both under the currency and under the place. Separate entries have also been made for large silver coins and currencies based on them. These are largely, but not entirely, gathered under the heading 'Groat' which covers all gros, groschen, grossi, grosz and groten. Similarly grouped entries appear for gold coins and currencies based on them, under 'besant', 'ducat', 'florin' and so forth.

INDEX OF CURRENCIES

INDEX OF CURRENCIES

INDEX OF PLACES

INDEX OF PLACES

INDEX OF PLACES

PLACES MENTIONED IN THE HANDBOOK

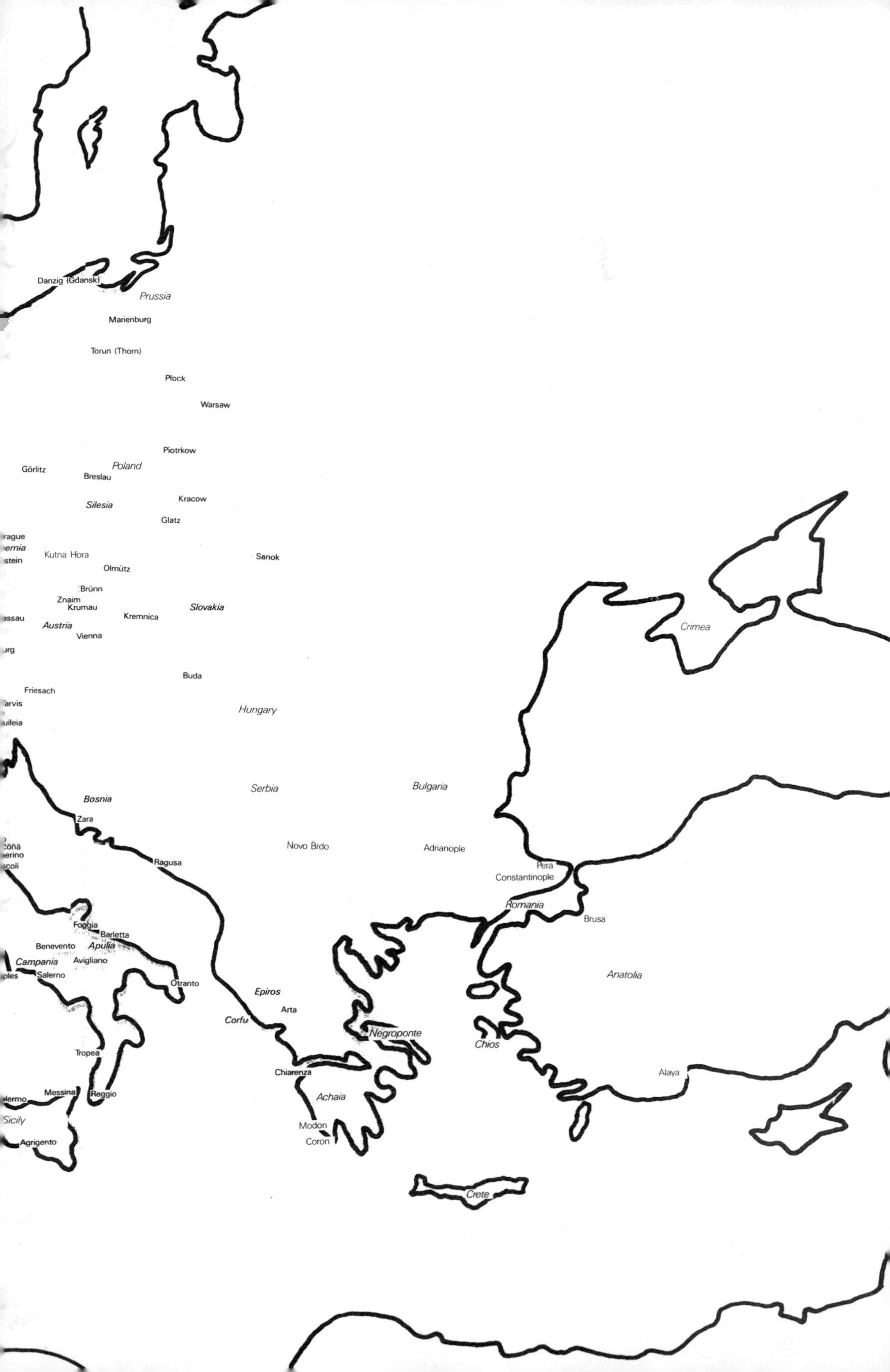

Danzig (Gdansk)
Prussia
Marienburg
Torun (Thorn)
Płock
Warsaw
Piotrkow
Görlitz
Poland
Breslau
Silesia
Kracow
Glatz
Kutna Hora
Sanok
Olmütz
Brünn
Znaim
Krumau
Slovakia
Kremnica
Austria
Vienna
Crimea
Buda
Friesach
Hungary
Serbia
Bulgaria
Bosnia
Zara
Novo Brdo
Adrianople
Ragusa
Pera
Constantinople
Romania
Brusa
Foggia
Barletta
Benevento
Apulia
Campania
Avigliano
Salerno
Otranto
Epiros
Anatolia
Arta
Corfu
Negroponte
Chios
Tropea
Chiarenza
Alaya
Messina
Reggio
Achaia
Sicily
Modon
Coron
Agrigento
Crete